Pro Office 365 Development

Mark J Collins
Michael Mayberry

Pro Office 365 Development

ISBN-13 (pbk): 978-1-4302-4074-7

ISBN-13 (electronic): 978-1-4302-4075-4

Trademarked names, logos, an d images may app ear in this book. Rather than us e a trademark s ymbol with every occurrence of a trademarked name, logo, or image we use the names, logos, and images only in an editorial fashion and to the benefit of the trademark owner, with no intention of infringement of the trademark.

The use in this publication of trade names, tr ademarks, service marks, and similar terms, ev en if th ey are not identified as such, is not to be ta ken as an expression of opinion as to whether or not they are subject to proprietary rights.

While the advice and information in this book are believed to be true and accurate at the date of publication, neither the authors nor the editors nor the publisher can accept any legal responsibility for any errors or o missions that may be made. The publisher makes no warranty, express or implied, with respect to the material contained herein.

President and Publisher: Paul Manning
Lead Editor: Matthew Moodie
Technical Reviewer: Martina Grom
Editorial Board: Steve Anglin, Ewan Buckingham, Gary Cornell, Louise Corrigan, Morgan Ertel, Jonathan Gennick, Jonathan Hassell, Robert Hutchinson, Michelle Lowman, James Markham, Matthew Moodie, Jeff Olson, Jeffrey Pepper, Douglas Pundick, Ben Renow-Clarke, Dominic Shakeshaft, Gwenan Spearing, Matt Wade, Tom Welsh
Coordinating Editor: Corbin Collins
Copy Editor: Mary Behr
Compositor: Bytheway Publishing Services
Indexer: SPI Global
Artist: SPI Global
Cover Designer: Anna Ishchenko

Distributed to the book trade worldwide by Springer Scie nce+Business Media New York, 233 Spring Street, 6th Floor, New York, NY 10013. Phone 1-800-SPRINGER, fax (201) 348-4505, e-mail orders-ny@springer-sbm.com, or v isit www.springeronline.com.

For information on translations, please e-mail rights@apress.com, or visit www.apress.com.

Apress and friends of ED book s may be purchased in bulk f or academic, corporate, or promo tional use. eBoo k versions and licenses are also available for most titles. For more information, reference our Special Bulk Sales–eBook Licensing web page at www.apress.com/bulk-sales.

Any source code or other supplementary materials referenced by the author i n this text is av ailable to re aders at www.apress.com. For detailed in formation about how to locate y our book's source code, go to www.apress.com/source-code/.

To my beautiful wife, Donna: You're the sparkle in my eye and the joy in my heart.

–Mark Collins

To my wife, Camille: I always want to do big things. You believe that I can. And to Jack, Ian, Ava, and Evan: You make the world a better place. You make every day fun and exciting. I love being your dad.

–Michael Mayberry

Contents at a Glance

iv

Contents

About the Authors

■ **Mark Collins** has been developing software solutions for over 30 years. Some of the key technology areas of his career include COM, .NET, and SQL Server. He currently supports a large non-profit organization, serving as data architect and back office automation and integration specialist. You can see more info on his web site, www.TheCreativePeople.com. For questions and comments, contact Mark at markc@thecreativepeople.com.

■ **Michael Mayberry** began writing software professionally over 12 years ago. The vast majority of that time has been spent using Microsoft technologies. He currently serves as a software architect for a large nonprofit organization, utilizing his skills to build CRM and BI solutions. As an enterprise-centered architect, he focuses on the integration of new technologies with existing systems. He aims to build solutions that unify the different areas within an organization in order to better accomplish the common goal. For questions and comments, contact Michael at michaelmayberry@hotmail.com.

About the Technical Reviewer

Martina Grom works as an IT consultant and is co-founder and CEO of atwork information technology. atwork, founded in 1999 and located in Austria/Europe, specializes in development of online solutions.

Martina has worked in IT since 1995. She is recognized as an expert in Microsoft Office Online Services solutions and was one of the first eight MVPs awarded in 2011 for her expertise in Office 365. She writes numerous articles and blogs. Her passions are online and social media, cloud computing, and Office 365.

Martina consults companies on their way to the cloud. Her expertise is related to online technologies, especially Microsoft Online Services and Office 365.

Martina has a Master's degree in International Business Administration from University of Vienna, Austria. You can follow her on Twitter (@magrom), Facebook (www.facebook.com/martina.grom) or Linkedin (www.linkedin.com/in/martinagrom) or read her blogs at http://blog.atwork.at or http://cloudusergroup.at. atwork's web site is www.atwork.at.

Acknowledgments

First and foremost, I acknowledge my Lord and Savior, Jesus Christ. The divine and eternal perspective on life, which can only be found in Him, is an anchor, steadfast and sure. I humbly conclude that His hand has guided me, often carrying me, through every endeavor, great and small.

I want to say a very big thank you to my beautiful wife, Donna. I can honestly say that I would not be who I am if it were not for what you have sown into my life. I am truly blessed to be able to share my life with you. Thank you for your loving support and for making life fun!

Also, I want to thank Michael Mayberry for his tremendous help on this project. As with every project that we have done together, I believe the result is always greater than the sum of our efforts.

Next, I'd like to thank all the people at Apress who made this book possible and for all the hard work that turned it into the finished product you see now. Everyone at Apress has made writing this book a pleasure.

—Mark Collins

I first bow my head in thanks to Jesus Christ for giving meaning to life and providing the way for us to see the love God has for us all. Thank you for the blessings that make a project like this even possible.

I humbly thank my wife, Camille. Our house of four kids is busy enough without this type of project going on, but you helped to somehow add it to the mix. You did not even flinch at the idea. Thank you for your patience and support.

Thank you, Mark, for inviting me into this project. It has been challenging and intriguing, even frustrating at times. Thanks for pushing me and helping me along the way. It was great to work on this book with you.

Finally, thank you to everyone at Apress who worked so hard on this book. Thank you especially to Corbin Collins, Matthew Moodie, Martina Grom, and Jonathan Hassell.

—Michael Mayberry

Introduction

Office 365 takes productivity to the cloud. It offers all of the tools a business office needs without the hassle of supporting the necessary infrastructure. But what if you need customization? What can developers do to extend the tools of Office 365?

Office 365 brings together a fully integrated suite of office automation tools, including the key server components: SharePoint, Exchange, and Lync. Volumes have been written on each of these products. In addition, there is an impressive list of client applications that can be leveraged, including

- Access
- Excel
- Visio
- InfoPath
- SharePoint Designer
- Visual Studio

There is so much that you can do with this platform that it's not possible to cover every aspect in a single book. However, we have tried to pack in as much as possible and to demonstrate the features that are the most useful. The topics span a broad range, including web databases, declarative workflows, custom Lync and Exchange applications, and public-facing web sites.

Intended Audience

Because of the variety of ways the Office 365 platform can be customized, the techniques described will appeal to a range of audiences. About half of the book demonstrates non-code solutions. If you're an end user or power user, this book provides many useful tips that you can use to get the most out of Office 365. The second half of the book focuses on developing against the various technologies within Office 365. For developers, this book shows you how to build applications using Visual Studio to create custom solutions.

Book Structure

The first two sections of this book provide an overview of Office 365, instructions for configuring your account, and a host of non-code solutions. The next two sections demonstrate coded solutions using the Office 365 server components (SharePoint, Exchange, and Lync). The final section serves as a review by pulling together some key concepts presented earlier to build a fully integrated solution.

Each chapter invites you to work through the exercise yourself with step-by-step instructions. You can simply read the chapter and learn a great deal. But following along will be even more beneficial. During this process we explain some of the hows and whys.

Prerequisites

To work through the exercises in this book you need an Office 365 account. A few of the solutions require one of the Enterprise plans, but most can be implemented on any plan. Some of the chapters require additional Office products such as Access or Excel. These are included with some of the Office 365 plans and can be added to others for a monthly fee.

Tip You can get a free 30-day trial subscription for either the Small Business or Enterprise plan. If you need more time, you can generally get a 30-day extension. Also, the Small Business plan is a monthly subscription, and you can cancel it at any time.

You also need Visual Studio 2010 to work through the coded solutions. To develop coded SharePoint solutions, you must have a local (on-premise) installation of SharePoint server. Some of the exercises require other free products and these are explained in the appropriate chapters.

PART 1

Introducing Office 365

This section is a high-level overview of the Office 365 platform, which provides a great deal of functionality out of the box. This is intended for readers who are relatively new to Office 365. Before building custom applications it's a good idea to understand the initial feature set so you can envision how the new solutions fit into the big picture.

Many of the Office 365 features are exposed to custom applications through custom controls, web services, or managed APIs. These building blocks simplify the building of some great custom applications. The functionality of each of the server components (SharePoint, Exchange, and Lync) is impressive on its own. But combining them in a fully integrated environment makes these tools even more fun to develop with.

Chapter 1 provides a high-level walkthrough of a basic Office 365 platform. This will give you a good idea of how each of the components contributes to the overall platform. Chapter 2 demonstrates some of the advanced configuration options, such as using a custom domain name. Chapter 3 explains how each server component works in terms, primarily, of how it can be used by a developer. I'll begin to show how the existing functionality can be leveraged in custom applications.

CHAPTER 1

Getting Started with Office 365

Throughout this book I will be showing you how to create custom applications that take advantage of the features provided in Office 365 platform. In this chapter I want to first give you a quick, high-level overview of the capabilities of Office 365 right out of the box. Before you begin developing, it's helpful to know what you're starting with so you can better envision how your custom applications will fit into the overall solution.

If you've used the Office platform in an on-premise solution, Office 365 won't be too surprising; it's essentially the same feature set as a traditional on-premise solution. The same basic capabilities of Exchange, SharePoint, and Lync (the successor of Office Communications Server (OCS) 2007), are packaged into a cloud-based solution. What is revolutionary about Office 365 is that a fully integrated Office solution is now available to anyone in a matter of minutes.

Office 365 comes in two varieties, Small Business and Enterprise, which are the same basic offering but packaged differently in terms of licensing and configurability. The Small Business solution is targeted toward small teams with little or no IT staff, while the Enterprise plans provide more advanced features for integrating into the existing on-premise network solution. In this chapter I will set up a Small Business account and show you the basic features that are provided with both plans. I'll explain some of the more advanced features in the next chapter, most of which are unique to the Enterprise plans.

▓ **Note** The Small Business and Enterprise solutions are often referred to as P plans and E plans, respectively. These letter designations are used when purchasing Office 365 subscriptions. There are several E plans and each user can be licensed for a different E plan based on their needs. There are also K plans, which are kiosk plans that have limited ability at a much reduced cost. Throughout this book, I will use the terms *Small Business* and *Enterprise* to differentiate between the two basic offerings. For a concise comparison of these solutions, see the article at `http://blogs.technet.com/b/lystavlen/archive/2011/09/23/office-365-comparing-p-and-e-plans.aspx`.

Administering an Office 365 Account

Once you have created an Office 365 account, you are taken to the main portal page, shown in Figure 1-1.

Figure 1-1. The initial Office 365 portal page

The initial user created when the account was set up is configured as an administrator. This gives them the ability to set up and manage additional user accounts as well as general account configuration. Notice that there is an Admin link as the top of the portal page. You use this link to go to the Admin page shown in Figure 1-2.

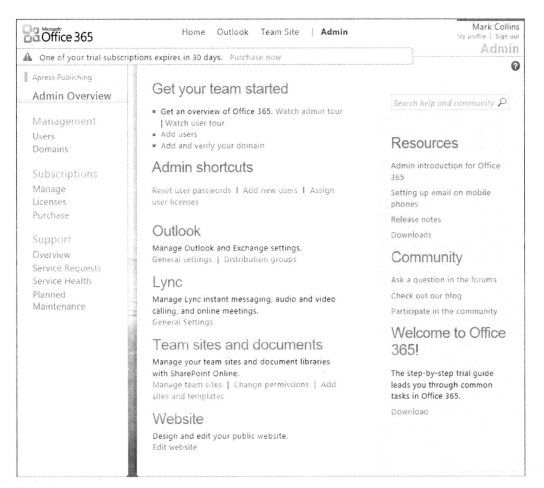

Figure 1-2. The Office 365 Admin page

The Admin page provides links for managing licenses and general system configuration. You can check on planned maintenance, enter a service request, and verify billing information.

Adding a User

The first thing you'll want to do is set up the additional users. You add a user by filling in a series of forms. In the first form, shown in Figure 1-3, you'll enter the basic information such as the first name, last name, and user name that is used for their login.

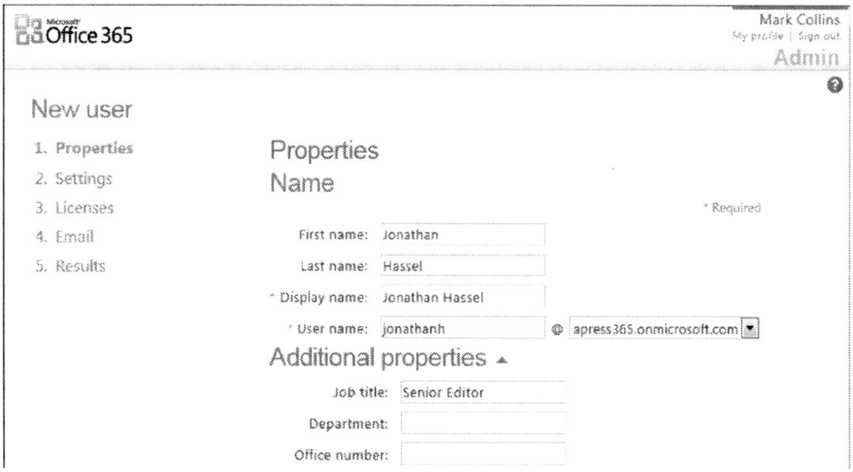

Figure 1-3. Step 1 of creating a new user

When setting up an Office 365 account, you specify a domain name, which is actually a subdomain under onmicrosoft.com. For my account I chose apress365. This means that all of the logins (and e-mail addresses) will be *someone*@apress365.onmicrosoft.com.

■ **Tip** If you already have a domain name, you can configure Office 365 to use it instead. I will explain how to do this in the next chapter. This is available for both Small Business and Enterprise accounts.

Figure 1-4 shows the next form where you'll specify whether this account is an administrator or not. You should have at least two administrators so there is a backup in case one isn't available. Administrators can create accounts, reset passwords, and set general configuration settings.

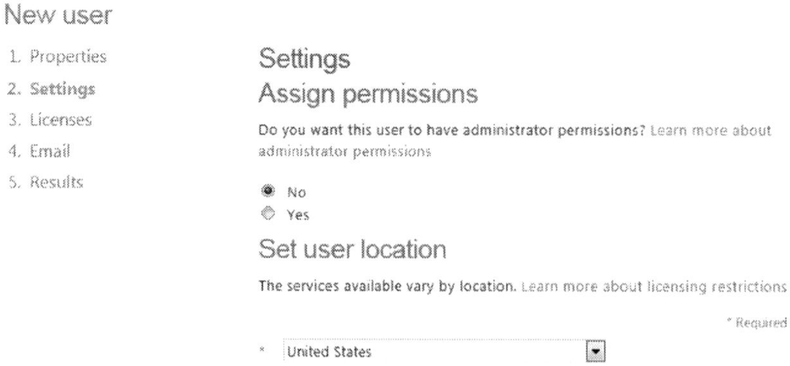

Figure 1-4. Step 2 of creating a new user

> ▓ **Note** At this level, a user account is either an administrator or not. However, you can create user groups in SharePoint to configure role-based security. I will demonstrate this briefly in Chapter 2.

In the third form you assign licenses for each of the server products. With the Small Business plan, the pricing is a flat per-person rate and everyone is licensed for all products, as shown in Figure 1-5.

New user

1. Properties
2. Settings
3. **Licenses**
4. Email
5. Results

Assign licenses

☑ Microsoft Office 365 Plan P1   9 of 10 licenses available
  ☑   Lync Online (P1)
  ☑   SharePoint Online (P1)
  ☑   Exchange Online (P1)

Figure 1-5. Step 3 of creating a new user

In the final form, shown in Figure 1-6, you specify if you want the user details such as login and password to be e-mailed and the address to which they should be sent.

New user

1. Properties
2. Settings
3. Licenses
4. **Email**
5. Results

Send results in email

The results (user names and temporary passwords for users who have them) will be displayed on the next page. You can also send the results in email to yourself or someone else; enter the email addresses of up to five recipients separated by semicolons.

☑ Send email

markc@apress365.onmicrosoft.com
Note: Passwords are sent in clear text through email.

Figure 1-6. Step 4 of creating a new user

When the final form is submitted, the login and password of the new user is displayed in the Results page, as shown in Figure 1-7.

New user

1. Properties
2. Settings
3. Licenses
4. Email
5. **Results**

Results

Review your results.

User name	Temporary password
jonathanh@apress365.onmicrosoft.com	Comu4030

Figure 1-7. New user results

Repeat this process to set up all user accounts.

Using the Bulk Add Feature

If you have a lot of users to create, setting them up one at a time can be tedious. Office 365 provides a feature for loading them all at once. To do that, you'll use the Bulk Add page shown in Figure 1-8.

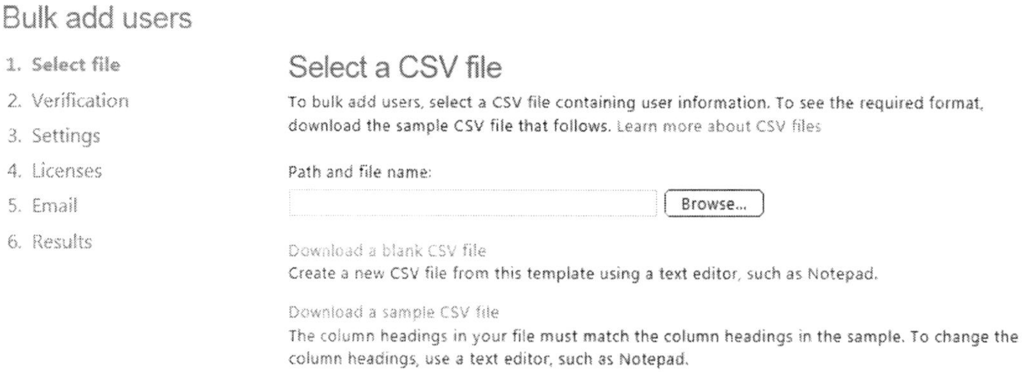

Bulk add users

1. **Select file**

2. Verification

3. Settings

4. Licenses

5. Email

6. Results

Select a CSV file

To bulk add users, select a CSV file containing user information. To see the required format, download the sample CSV file that follows. Learn more about CSV files

Path and file name:

| | Browse... |

Download a blank CSV file
Create a new CSV file from this template using a text editor, such as Notepad.

Download a sample CSV file
The column headings in your file must match the column headings in the sample. To change the column headings, use a text editor, such as Notepad.

Figure 1-8. Using the Bulk Add feature

The user details are provided in a comma-separated values (CSV) file. For this to work, you'll need to make sure the file is formatted with the correct column names. This page contains a link to download a blank file. After downloading the file, add your user details to it and then upload the file from the Bulk Add page. The columns that need to be included (in this order) are:

- User name
- First name
- Last name
- Display name
- Job title
- Department
- Office number
- Office phone
- Mobile phone
- Fax
- Address
- City
- State or province
- ZIP or postal code
- Country or region

The only columns that you must supply data for are the User name, which is the actual login and includes the @domain designation, and the Display name, which is how this user's name will be displayed. The other fields are useful but not required.

Managing Users

Once you have created your initial set of user accounts, you can use the Users link to view the user accounts. This will display the Users page, shown in Figure 1-9.

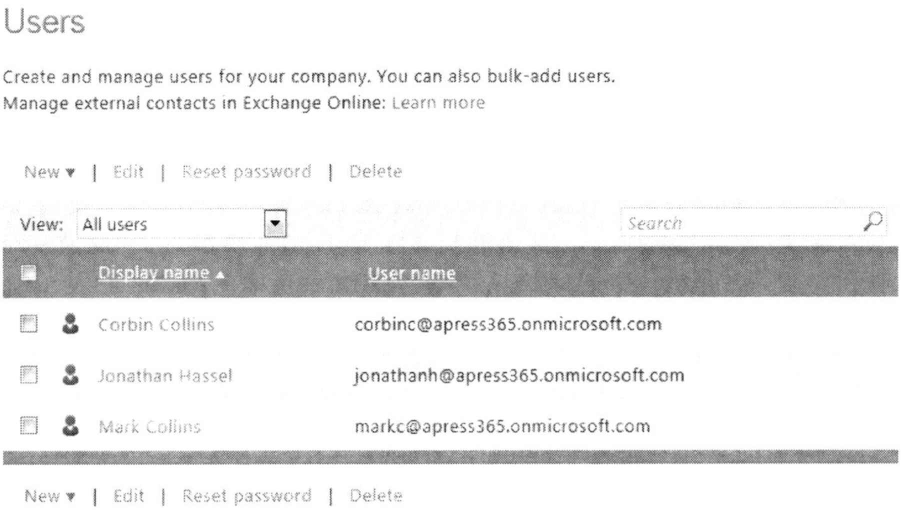

Users

Create and manage users for your company. You can also bulk-add users.
Manage external contacts in Exchange Online: Learn more

New ▾ | Edit | Reset password | Delete

View:	All users ▾		Search 🔍
☐	**Display name** ▲	**User name**	
☐ 👤	Corbin Collins	corbinc@apress365.onmicrosoft.com	
☐ 👤	Jonathan Hassel	jonathanh@apress365.onmicrosoft.com	
☐ 👤	Mark Collins	markc@apress365.onmicrosoft.com	

New ▾ | Edit | Reset password | Delete

Figure 1-9. Managing the existing users

If a user forgets their password, you'll use this page to reset it for them. Only administrators can reset passwords, which is another important reason to have at least two administrators. If your only administrator forgets their password, you'll need to call customer support. The reset function will generate a new temporary password, which you'll send to the user. The user will need to change their password when they log in.

You can also use this page to edit the user's attributes, such as phone, title, or department, and set them up as an administrator. You can also block a user from accessing the system. This is used when you need to temporarily block a user without permanently removing their account.

Logging In for the First Time

After you have created a user account, you'll need to provide each user with their login and temporary password. To access the system, all users (including administrators) must go to the login page, which is https://portal.microsoftonline.com. The login page is shown in Figure 1-10.

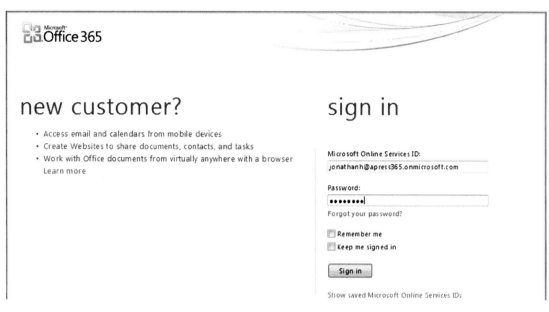

Figure 1-10. *User login page*

The "Remember me" check box will store the user name that you used in a cookie so it will be pre-filled when you want to log in again. Selecting the "Keep me signed in" check box will keep you signed in even after closing the browser. You will be able to go directly to your home page without reentering your credentials. This is a nice feature if you're using a dedicated desktop. You should not use the "Keep me signed in" option if you're sharing a workstation, however.

The first time you log in, the Change Password page will be displayed (see Figure 1-11).

Change password

	* Required	
Microsoft Online Services ID:	jonathanh@apress365.onmicrosoft.com	
* Old password:	●●●●●●●●	
* Create new password:		
	8-character minimum; case sensitive.	
	Password strength	
* Confirm new password:		

Strong password required. Enter 8-16 characters. Do not include common words or names. Combine uppercase letters, lowercase letters, numbers, and symbols. ✕

Submit   Cancel

Figure 1-11. *Changing the initial password*

You will need to enter the temporary password you were given and then specify a new password. Notice the help text that displays the password requirements.

Using Outlook Web App

Once signed in, the first thing you'll probably want to do is read your e-mail. From the Home page, click the Inbox link to start the Outlook Web App.

Configuring Outlook Web App

The first time you use the Outlook Web App you'll need to set up some configuration options using the dialog box shown in Figure 1-12.

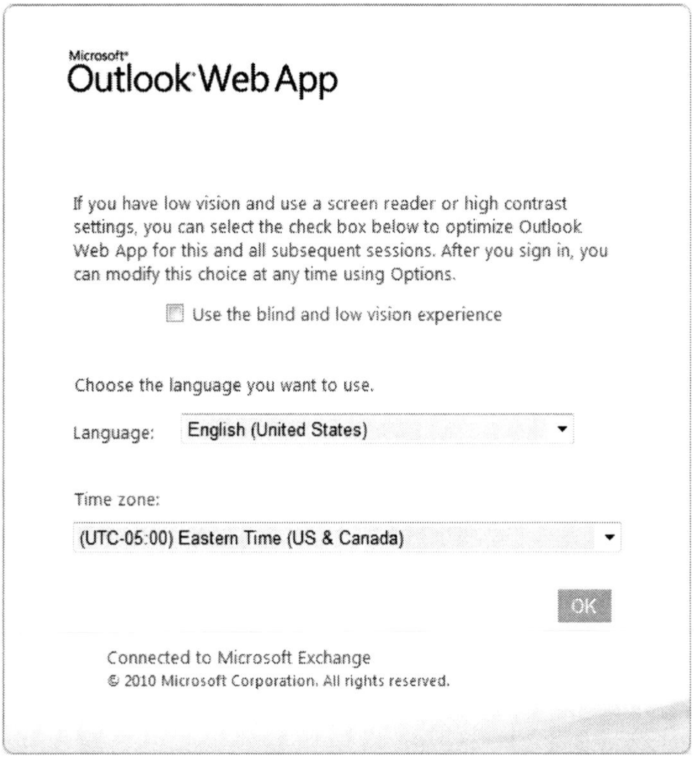

Figure 1-12. Configuring Outlook Web App

The time zone is needed to properly display meeting times. All times in Exchange are stored using the Coordinated Universal Time (UCT). They are displayed to each user based on their time zone. If you schedule a meeting with people in multiple time zones, each user will see the start time in their local time.

Sending E-mail

When I created the user accounts, I specified my e-mail address as the one to receive user account details. From my inbox, I selected this e-mail and clicked the Forward link. I then added my instructions and forwarded the login information to the user so they could access their account. This is demonstrated in Figure 1-13.

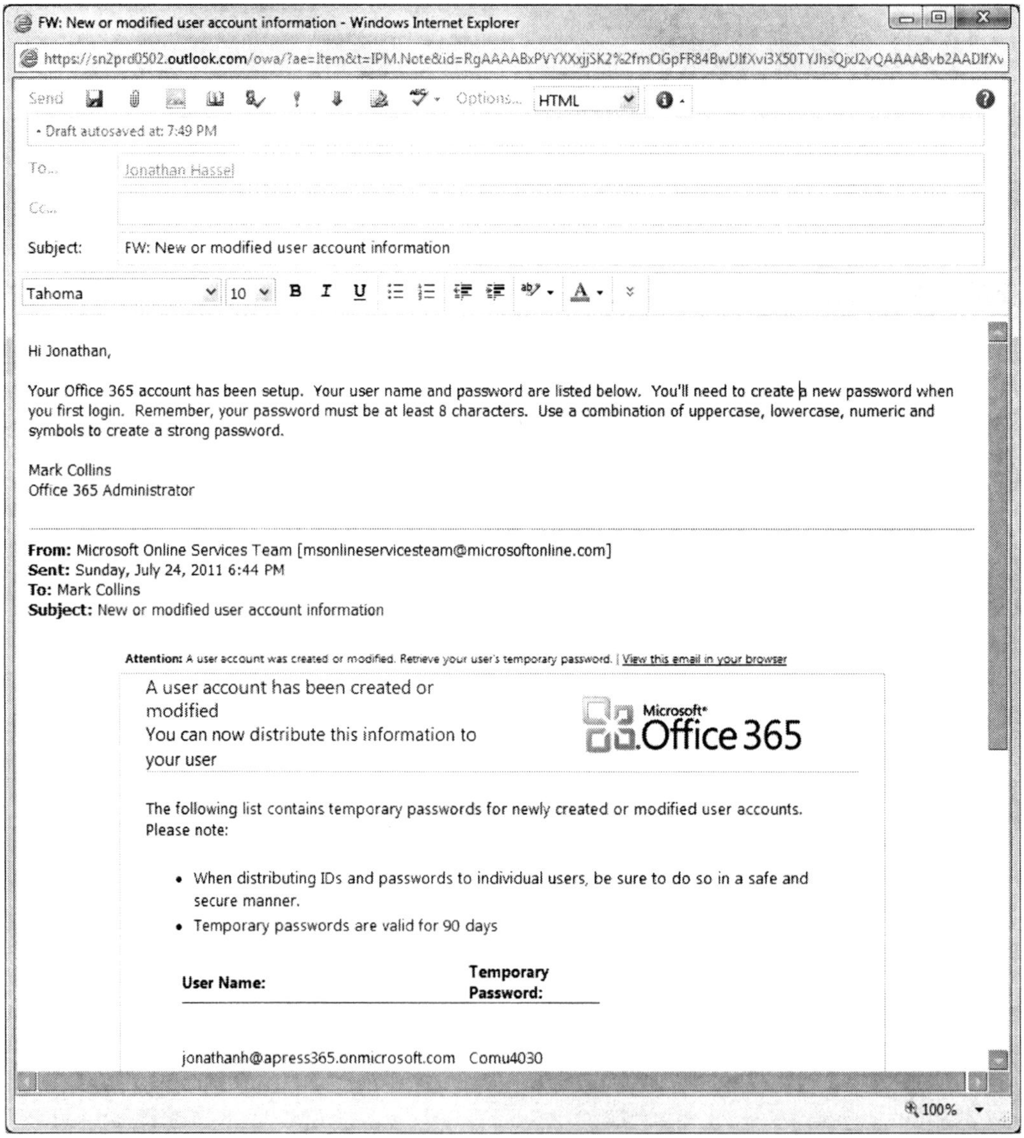

Figure 1-13. Forwarding user account information

■ **Note** I sent this to Jonathan's new Office 365 e-mail address. He won't be able to read it until he has logged in to Office 365. In a live scenario, I would need to send this message to an alternative e-mail address (not in Office 365).

Using the Calendar

Use the Calendar link on the Home page to view your calendar and schedule meetings. In the appointment shown in Figure 1-14, Jonathan has scheduled a meeting with Corbin and me. Just like an on-premise Exchange solution, the Scheduling Assistant shows when each attendee is available.

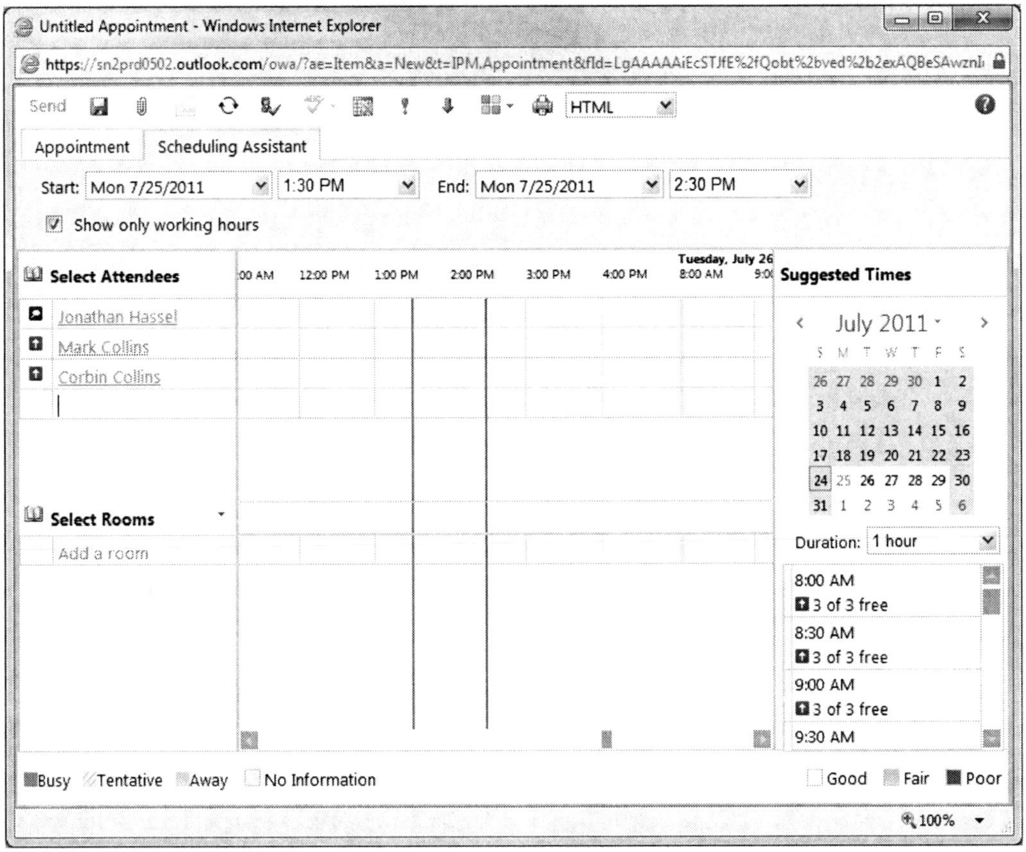

Figure 1-14. Scheduling a meeting

Meeting reminders will let you know when a meeting is about to start. You can see from the reminder shown in Figure 1-15 that I'm already 15 minutes late.

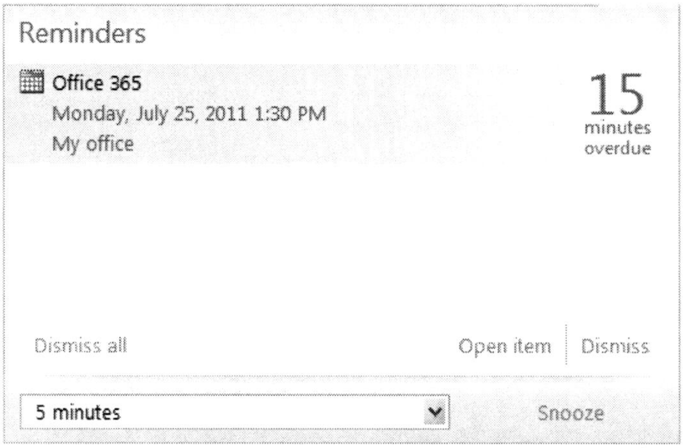

Figure 1-15. Displaying a meeting reminder

Using the SharePoint Sites

The initial Office 365 Small Business account is set up with two SharePoint sites. The Team Site is an internal site used for sharing documents within a team. Only logged-in users have access to this site. There is also an external, public-facing web site called Website that is available to all users, even those that are not logged in.

Using the Team Site

The initial Team Site is shown in Figure 1-16.

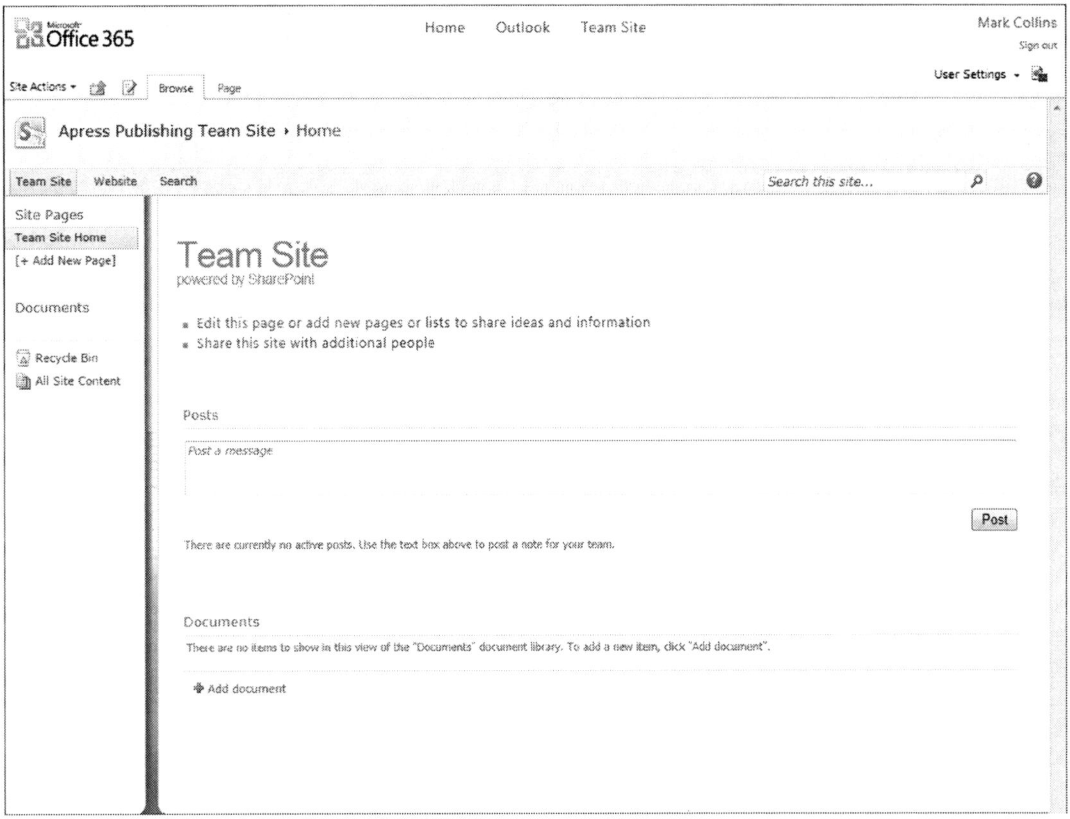

Figure 1-16. The initial Team Site

As you can see, this is a pretty basic site with a place for posting messages and a document library. In Chapter 4 I'll show you how to use SharePoint to build more useful sites. You will probably need additional libraries to organize your documents. It's pretty easy to add a new library from the Site Actions menu; just click the New Document Library link. In the Create dialog box, shown in Figure 1-17, you can configure the new library.

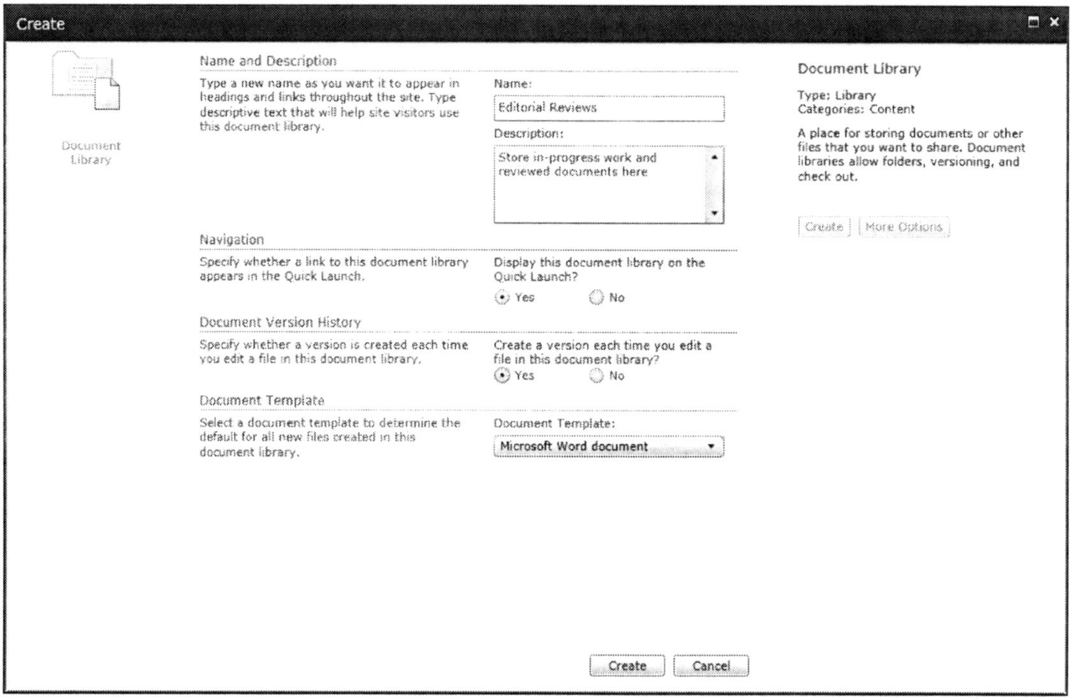

Figure 1-17. Creating a new document library

Using Shared Documents

To add a document to the library you can either upload a file from your local PC or you can create a new document using the Office Web Apps. The initial document library has links on the page for creating a new document, as shown in Figure 1-18.

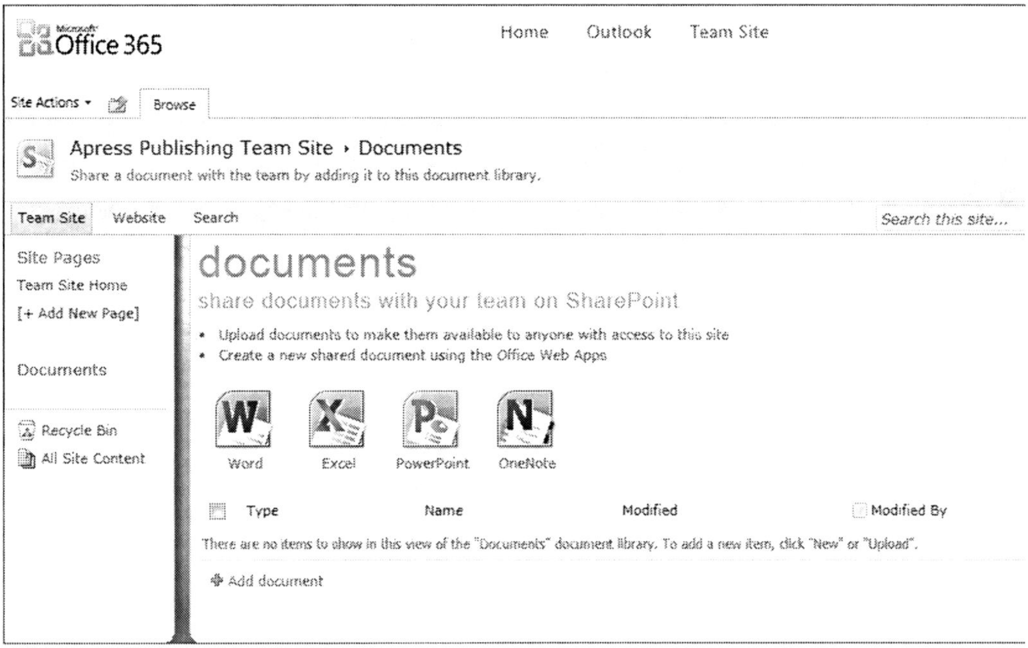

Figure 1-18. The initial document library

■ **Caution** If you have client versions of these Office applications installed locally, these links will probably not work correctly. When opening an Office document in Office 365, the client applications will be used if available. The links specify a template file that is likely not available to the client applications so the application will fail. Instead, create a new document using the client apps but save it to the document library. I will explain this further in Chapter 2.

Modifying the Public-Facing Web Site

The second SharePoint site that is set up is made available to non-authenticated users. Use this site as your online presence. This site is intended to provide information about your company. The default public web site is shown in Figure 1-19.

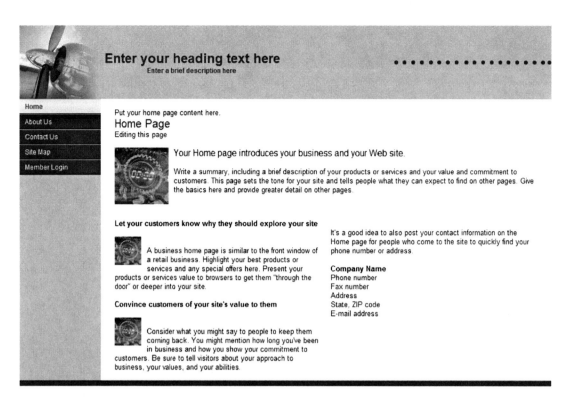

Figure 1-19. The default public-facing web site

If you select the Website link in the navigation bar of the Team Site, you'll see the list of web pages included in this site. The default set of pages is shown in Figure 1-20.

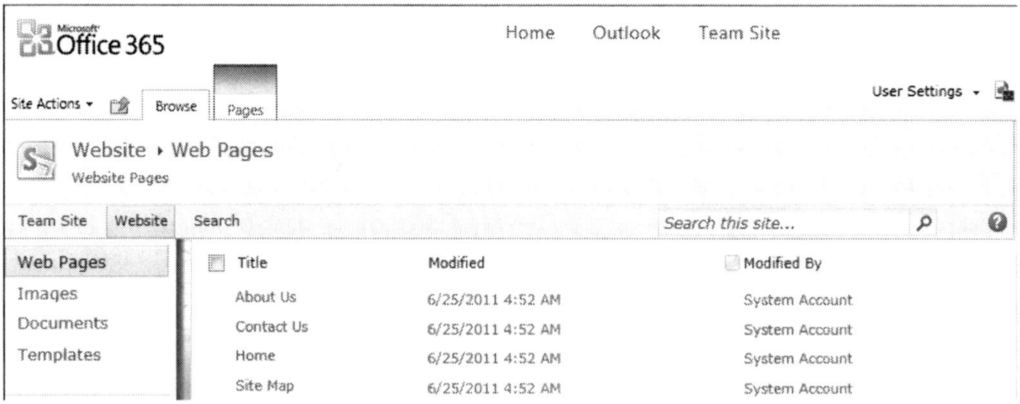

Figure 1-20. Editing the web site

You can use the SharePoint design features to edit these pages and create additional pages. For example, selecting the Home page will allow you to edit the page using the features provided in the Design tab of the ribbon (see Figure 1-21). I will explain these features in Chapter 4.

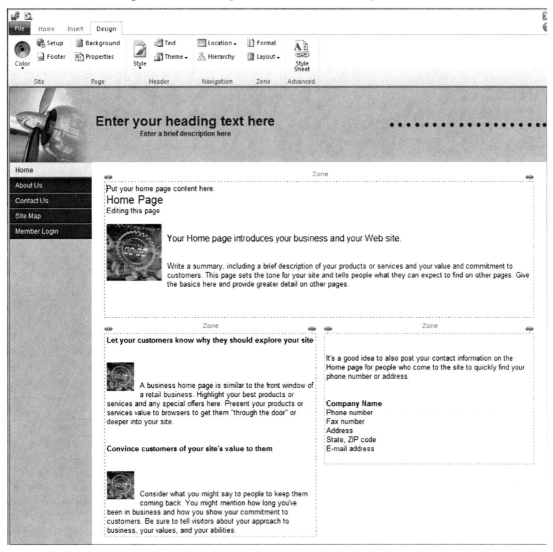

Figure 1-21. Updating the Home page

Using Lync

Microsoft Lync Server 2010 is the successor of Office Communications Server 2007. It provides peer-to-peer instant messaging, audio and video conversations, screen sharing, and more. The Office 365 version of this server is called Lync Online and, just like the other Online servers, provides essentially the same feature set in a cloud-based solution.

Launching Lync from Outlook Web App

In a browser-only environment from the Office 365 platform you can use a limited subset of these features, namely presence indicators and instant message. With the Outlook Web App, for example, you can see the presence indicators, as illustrated in Figure 1-22.

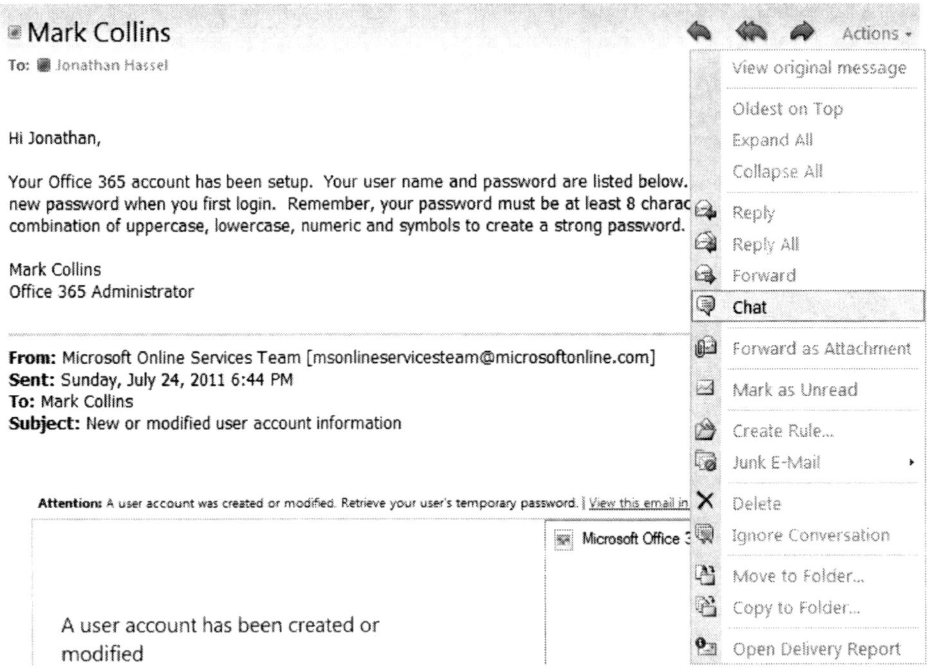

Figure 1-22. Starting an instant message conversation from Outlook Web App

You can see from this e-mail that Jonathan is in a meeting and I am available. Since I am available, he selects the Chat link from the Actions drop-down list in the Office Web App, which opens a Lync conversation between Jonathan and myself, as shown in Figure 1-23.

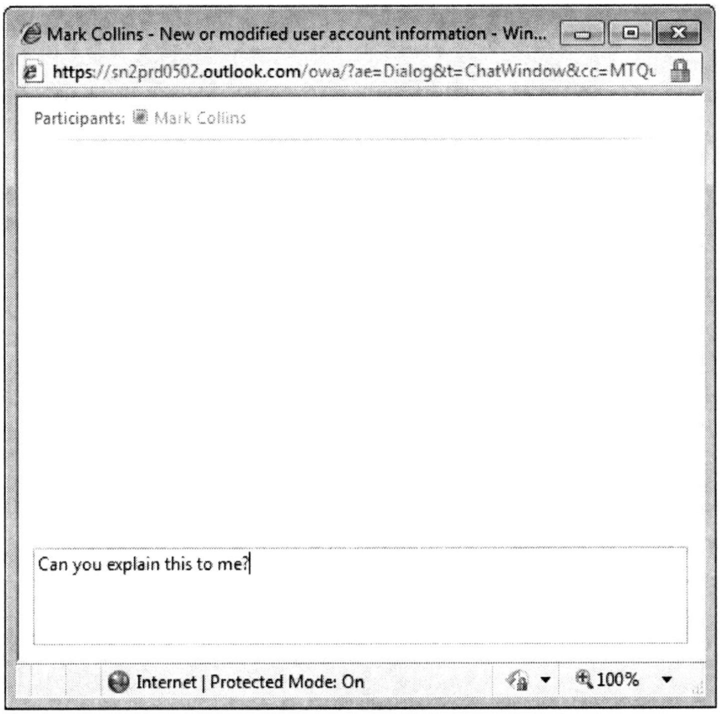

Figure 1-23. A web-based Lync conversation

Outlook knows to initiate the conversation with me because I was the one who sent the e-mail.

Downloading the Lync Client

To utilize the full feature set, you will need to install the Lync 2010 client application. From the Home page on Office 365, you can use Downloads link in the Resources section. This will display the Downloads page shown in Figure 1-24.

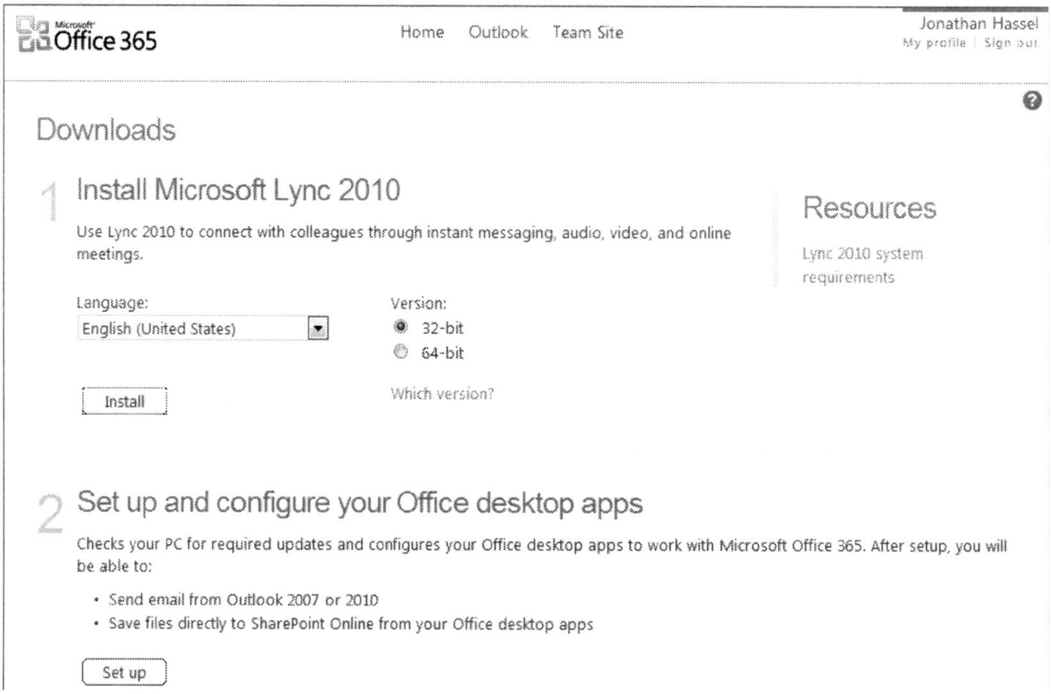

Figure 1-24. *Instaling the Lync 2010 client application*

Select the appropriate language, choose either the 32-bit or 64-bit version, and click the Install button to download and install the Lync 2010 client.

Installing the Sign-In Assistant

The Lync 2010 client application uses the Microsoft Online Services Sign-In Assistant. When the application is started but this is not already installed, you will be prompted to install it, as shown in Figure 1-25.

Figure 1-25. *Installing the Online Service Sign-In Assistant*

Click the "Download and install now?" link. After this is installed, the Lync 2010 client will prompt you for your credentials. Enter your Office 365 login for both the Sign-In address and User name fields, as shown in Figure 1-26. If you're using a dedicated workstation, you can select the "Save my password" check box so you won't have to enter your password each time you start Lync.

Figure 1-26. Logging into Lync

Using the Lync Client

The Lync client application is exactly the same one that you would use with an on-premise installation of Lync Server 2010. In Office 365, the server is hosted in the cloud and the client application connects to it just as if it were on-premise.

Using the Presence Indicators

The Lync client allows you to see the current status of your contacts. The contact's picture is also displayed if one has been configured (see Figure 1-27).

Figure 1-27. Viewing frequent contacts

Tip You can load a photo or other image that others will see from their Lync client. Upload an image file from your profile page on Office 365 or from the Lync client.

You can change your status using the Lync client, as shown in Figure 1-28.

Figure 1-28. Changing your current status

If you hover the mouse over one of the contacts, contact details will be displayed, as shown in Figure 1-29.

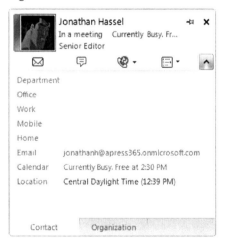

Figure 1-29. Displaying a contact's information

Using Lync Conversations

Lync allows you to communicate in real time between two or more individuals. This communication is referred to generically as a *conversation*. Instant messaging, video conferencing, and screen sharing are all types of conversations. When you initiate (or accept) a conversation, the Lync client launches a new window to manage the conversation. An instant message conversation is shown in Figure 1-30.

***Figure 1-30.** An instance message conversation*

Notice that the background behind Jonathan's picture is red and the text reads "In a meeting." Lync is integrated with the calendar in Exchange and updates the user's status based on the calendar events.

Using Screen and Application Sharing

Lync 2010 allows you to share your desktop with one or more individuals. There have been many times that I was talking (or chatting) with someone and thought if I could just let them see what was on my screen, it would simplify the whole conversation. With Lync 2010 this is easy.

Lync allows several options for screen sharing. You can share

- A single application window
- Your main monitor
- Your secondary monitor
- All monitors

When you initiate a sharing conversation, you will see the pop-up dialog box shown in Figure 1-31.

Figure 1-31. Starting a screen-sharing conversation

■ **Caution** This is warning you that the conversation participants will be able to see everything currently on your screen. You can turn this warning off but it is a good reminder to double check what is currently being displayed.

Each participant will then receive a sharing request that they can either accept or decline, as shown in Figure 1-32.

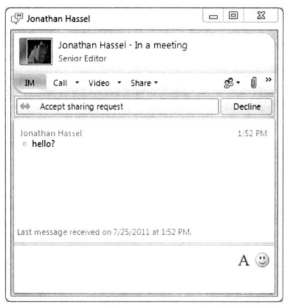

Figure 1-32. An invitation for screen sharing

Once the request has been accepted, the conversation window is expanded to show the area being shared, as demonstrated in Figure 1-33.

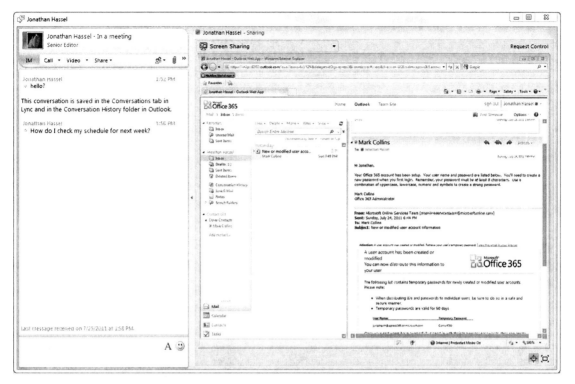

Figure 1-33. A screen-sharing conversation

You can click the Request Control link in the top-right corner to request permission from the screen's owner to take control of the application being displayed. You can then use your keyboard and mouse to control the application that is running on the other user's desktop. When you're done, click the link again to return control to the screen's owner.

Using a Whiteboard

You can also share a whiteboard in a Lync conversation. A whiteboard is a blank screen that you can draw on just as you would a real whiteboard. All the participants can write on the board, which is visible in real-time to all participants. You can also point to an area on the board and everyone will see a color-coded dot indicating who is pointing, as demonstrated in Figure 1-34.

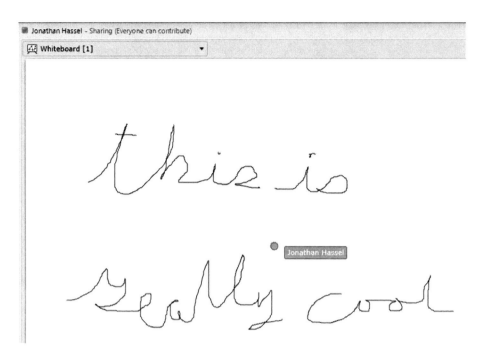

Figure 1-34. *A whiteboard conversation*

Configuring the Outlook Client

If you have Office client applications such as Outlook and Word installed on your client, you can use these instead of the web apps. This will work the same way as if you had an on-premise Exchange or Lync server. You can use both as well. For example, you can use the client apps when you're in the office and use the web apps from home or when you're travelling.

Adding an Outlook Account

Configuring Outlook to use the Exchange Online server is pretty simple. Add a new account and then enter your Office 365 e-mail address and password, as shown in Figure 1-35.

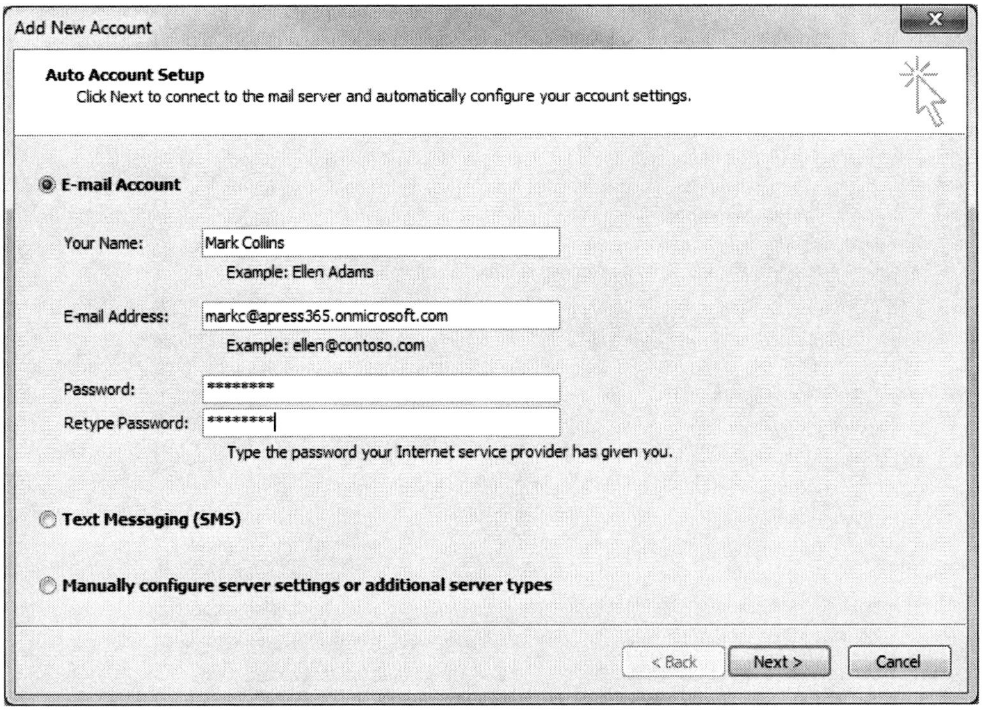

Figure 1-35. Creating an Outlook account with Exchange Online 2010

Outlook will find the appropriate Exchange Online server, authenticate your account, and configure the client to access the Exchange server (see Figure 1-36).

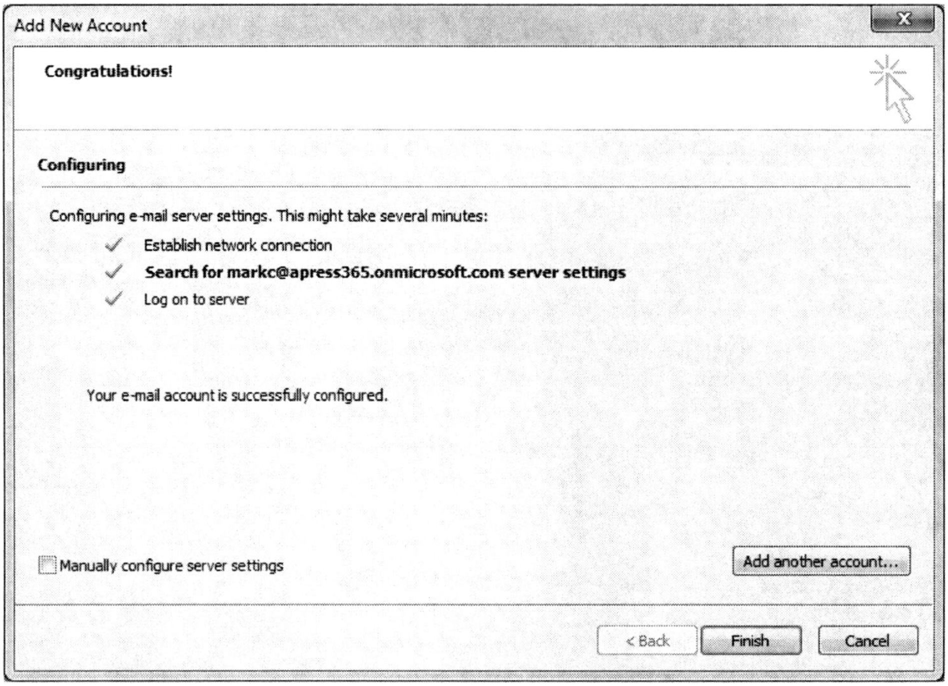

Figure 1-36. New account setup

This usually requires you to close Outlook and restart it for this change to take effect. When you restart Outlook, it will prompt you for your Office 365 credentials, as shown in Figure 1-37.

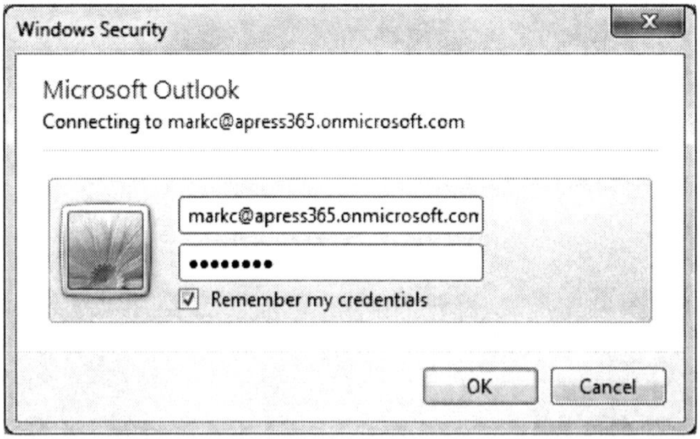

Figure 1-37. Entering Exchange credentials

If this is a dedicated workstation, you can select the "Remember my credentials" check box so you won't need to reenter them each time you start Outlook.

Configuring Outlook 2007

You can access the Office 365 Exchange Online server from Outlook 2007 as well as the 2010 version. However, Outlook 2003 and previous versions are not supported.

If you are using Outlook 2007 you will probably get an error like the one shown in Figure 1-38.

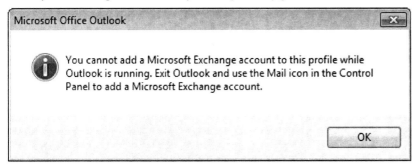

Figure 1-38. Error adding account with Outlook 2007 running

If this happens, you must close Outlook and configure the new e-mail account when Outlook is not running. To do that, click the Mail icon in the control panel. This will display the window shown in Figure 1-39.

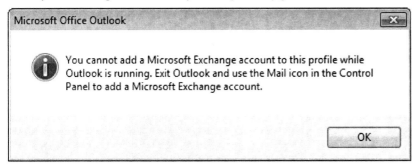

Figure 1-39. Using the Mail Setup application

Click the E-mail Accounts button, which will display the same dialog box shown in Figure 1-35. Configure the new e-mail account the same way as described earlier. When you're finished, you may see the warning shown in Figure 1-40. Just click the OK button.

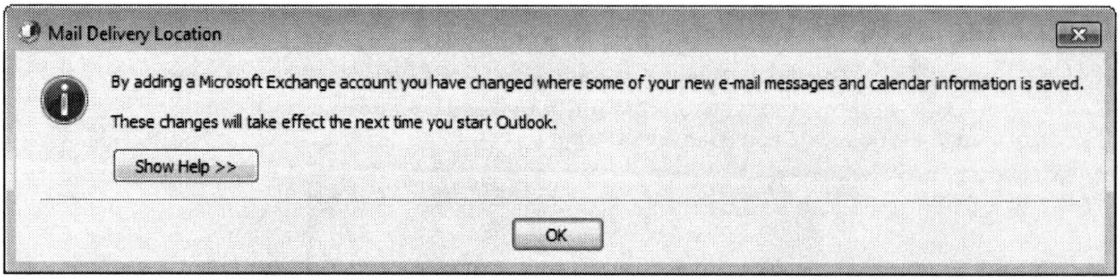

Figure 1-40. Warning about mail changes

Using the Outlook Client

When using the Outlook client application, the data still resides on the Exchange Online server just like it did with the Outlook Web App. Changes made in either application are immediately available in the other. The meeting request that was created earlier, for example, is displayed in Figure 1-41 using the Outlook client application.

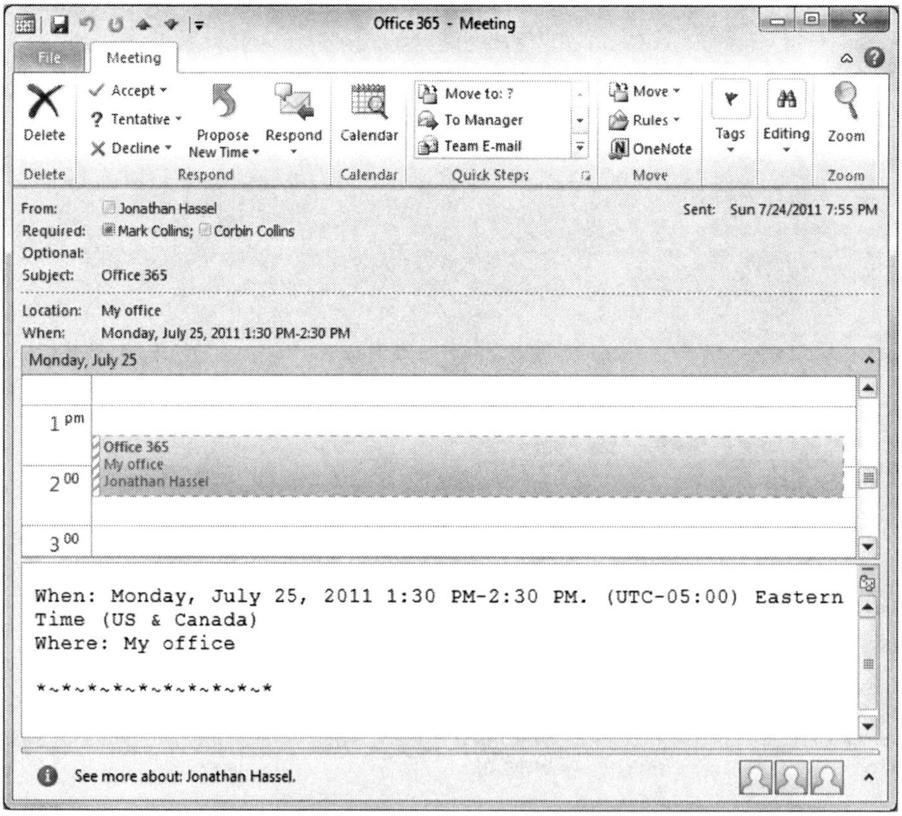

Figure 1-41. Viewing a meeting with the Outlook client

You can also reply to an e-mail using an instant message. To do that, use the Reply with IM link shown in Figure 1-42.

Figure 1-42. Using the Reply with IM feature

■ **Tip** The following article provides help with configuring a mobile phone to use Office 365:

`http://onlinehelp.microsoft.com/en-us/office365-smallbusinesses/ff637559.aspx`.

Summary

I presented a quick overview of the standard features of Office 365. It is by no means an exhaustive list of features but it should give you a sense of what you can do right out of the box. One of the nice benefits of Office 365 is that the components are fully integrated. For example, there are presence indicators in Outlook and SharePoint, which rely on Lync. By default, the Office Web Apps read and write files from/to the shared document libraries in SharePoint.

In the next chapter I will show you how Office 365 can be used to replace an on-premise Office implementation. This allows the same rich user experience but moves the servers to a cloud environment. I will also cover some of the advanced features of Office 365.

CHAPTER 2

Using Advanced Features

As I demonstrated in the previous chapter, using a Small Business account on the Office 365 platform, you can quickly set up a fully integrated Office environment. The setup is simplified, requiring no IT staff to get up and running. This works well for small teams that don't have much office automation already in place. Office 365 also provides an Enterprise solution that is geared towards larger and more established organizations. These will likely already have an on-premise solution and want to move to a cloud-based solution.

In this chapter I will explain how to configure some of the more advanced features of Office 365, including:

- Adding a custom domain name.

- Using single sign-on.

- Configuring the advanced Exchange Online features.

- Managing the SharePoint permissions.

- Installing Office Professional Plus.

Changing the Domain Name

One of the major drawbacks of the solution I described in Chapter 1 is the long domain name. The domain name used for login, e-mail addresses, and web sites was apress365.onmicrosoft.com. It would be much better to just use apress365.com. This is especially true if you already have e-mail accounts and don't want to change everyone's e-mail address.

To use a vanity address such as apress365.com, you'll need to own that domain name and have access to configure its DNS settings. You can purchase a new domain name if you don't already have one. Both the Small Business and Enterprise solutions allow you to change the domain name but the process for implementing this is different in each. I will show you how to configure this on both platforms.

Using a Small Business Account

Log in to your Office 365 account and go to the Admin page. On the left side, click the Domains link, which will display the Domain Manager page. Initially there will be a single domain that was established when the account was created.

■ **Note** For this example I will be using a different Office 365 account than I used in the previous chapter.

Adding a Domain

Click the Add a domain link, which will display the page shown in Figure 2-1.

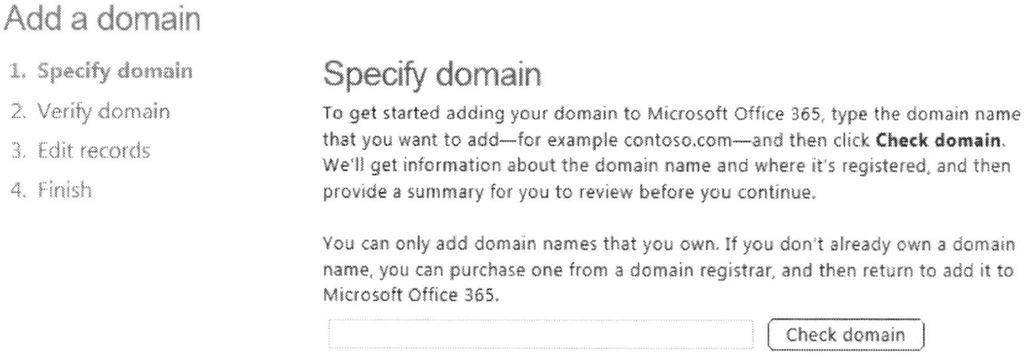

Add a domain

1. Specify domain
2. Verify domain
3. Edit records
4. Finish

Specify domain

To get started adding your domain to Microsoft Office 365, type the domain name that you want to add—for example contoso.com—and then click **Check domain**. We'll get information about the domain name and where it's registered, and then provide a summary for you to review before you continue.

You can only add domain names that you own. If you don't already own a domain name, you can purchase one from a domain registrar, and then return to add it to Microsoft Office 365.

[Check domain]

Figure 2-1. Adding a domain

Enter the domain name that you wish to use and click the Check domain button. This will look up this domain and the registrar details will be displayed as shown in Figure 2-2.

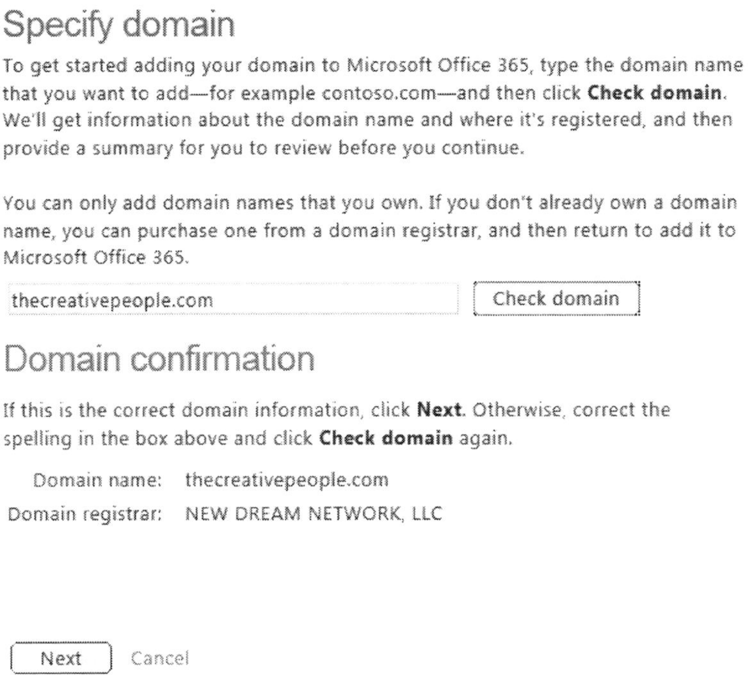

Specify domain

To get started adding your domain to Microsoft Office 365, type the domain name that you want to add—for example contoso.com—and then click **Check domain**. We'll get information about the domain name and where it's registered, and then provide a summary for you to review before you continue.

You can only add domain names that you own. If you don't already own a domain name, you can purchase one from a domain registrar, and then return to add it to Microsoft Office 365.

thecreativepeople.com		Check domain

Domain confirmation

If this is the correct domain information, click **Next**. Otherwise, correct the spelling in the box above and click **Check domain** again.

Domain name: thecreativepeople.com

Domain registrar: NEW DREAM NETWORK, LLC

Next	Cancel

Figure 2-2. *Confirming the domain details*

Office 365 uses a verification process to ensure that you can configure the DNS. You will be asked to add a TXT record to DNS. This will have no effect on how the existing DNS works. Office 365 will then query your DNS to see if that record is there.

When you click the Next button to continue, the Verify page, shown in Figure 2-3, is displayed.

Verify domain

Before we can add your domain name to Microsoft Office 365, we must verify that you are the owner of the domain. To begin the verification process, you add a specific record to the DNS records at your domain registrar. We then look for the record to verify ownership.

Each DNS provider supports different features, so we provide two ways that you can verify ownership: by creating a TXT record or an MX record.

Note: The new DNS record does not affect how your domain works. Learn more

Select a verification method: Add TXT record (preferred method) ▼

Use the table and instructions below to create a TXT record for a domain that is registered at your domain registrar. For general instructions about verifying a domain, see Verify a domain at any domain name registrar.

Create a TXT record at your domain registrar

Note: Your domain registrar's website may differ from that described in these instructions.

Alias or Host Name	Destination or *Points to* Address	TTL
thecreativepeople.com	v=verifydomain MS=ms13983370	1 Hour

1. Sign in to your domain registrar's website, and then select the domain that you're verifying.
2. In the DNS management area for your account, choose the option to add a TXT record for your domain.
3. In the **TXT** box for the domain, type or paste thecreativepeople.com.
4. In the **Fully qualified domain name (FQDN)** or **Points to** box, type or paste v=verifydomain MS=ms13983370.
5. Where it asks for **TTL** information, type or paste 1 Hour.
6. Save your changes, and then sign out of your domain registrar's website. Wait at least 15 minutes for this change to take effect.
7. Return to Office 365 and click the **Verify** button below.

Note:
Typically it takes about 15 minutes for your changes to take effect. However, it can take up to 72 hours for the record that you created to propagate through the DNS system.

 Cancel

Figure 2-3. *Verify access to the domain*

Add the TXT record to your DNS using the exact text provided. In my case this was **v=verifydomain MS=ms13983370** but yours will be different.

■ **Tip** Each registrar usually provides a facility for configuring DNS but they all work differently. Office 365 tries to provide specific instructions based on where your domain is being managed, so the text you see may be different from what is shown here. Use this text as a guide but your particular registrar may require some adjustments to these instructions.

For my registrar, the TXT record was added using the page shown in Figure 2-4 but yours will likely be different.

Add a custom DNS record to thecreativepeople.com:

Name: (leave blank for just 'thecreativepeople.com')	[ ] .thecreativepeople.com
Type: (Want MX? Go here!)	TXT ▾
Value:	v=verifydomain MS=ms1:
Comment: (optional)	[ ]
	Add Record Now!

Figure 2-4. Adding a TXT record to DNS

Allow a few minutes for this record to be added. The instructions say to wait at least 15 minutes but I have found it to usually take less time than that. If you click the Verify button and it was not able to find this record, wait a little longer and click the Verify button again.

Moving the Name Servers

Once the verification process has completed, you're ready to make the actual adjustments. You will update the registrar's database to reference name servers provided by Office 365. This means that all requests for this domain will be sent to DNS servers on Office 365. Any DNS configuration will then be handled within Office 365.

■ **Note** This will work differently with an Enterprise account, as I will explain later in this chapter.

When the domain has been verified, you will be presented with instructions similar to those in Figure 2-5 for updating your name servers at your registrar's database.

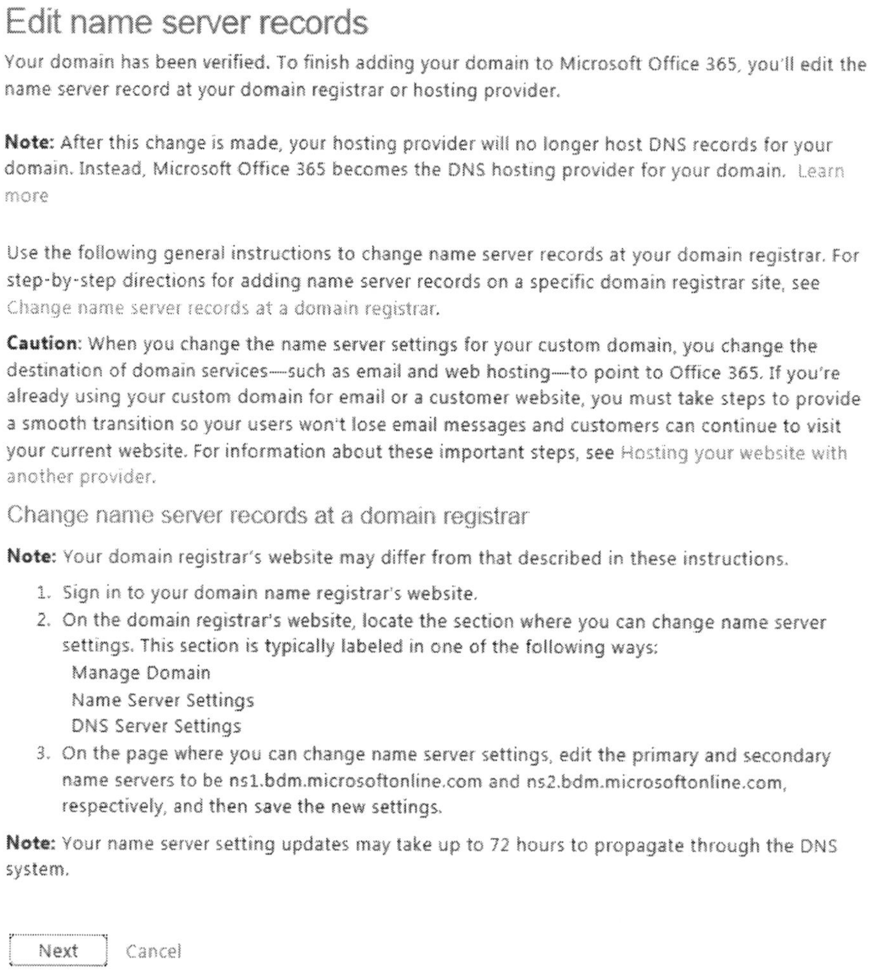

Edit name server records

Your domain has been verified. To finish adding your domain to Microsoft Office 365, you'll edit the name server record at your domain registrar or hosting provider.

Note: After this change is made, your hosting provider will no longer host DNS records for your domain. Instead, Microsoft Office 365 becomes the DNS hosting provider for your domain. Learn more

Use the following general instructions to change name server records at your domain registrar. For step-by-step directions for adding name server records on a specific domain registrar site, see Change name server records at a domain registrar.

Caution: When you change the name server settings for your custom domain, you change the destination of domain services—such as email and web hosting—to point to Office 365. If you're already using your custom domain for email or a customer website, you must take steps to provide a smooth transition so your users won't lose email messages and customers can continue to visit your current website. For information about these important steps, see Hosting your website with another provider.

Change name server records at a domain registrar

Note: Your domain registrar's website may differ from that described in these instructions.

1. Sign in to your domain name registrar's website.
2. On the domain registrar's website, locate the section where you can change name server settings. This section is typically labeled in one of the following ways:
   Manage Domain
   Name Server Settings
   DNS Server Settings
3. On the page where you can change name server settings, edit the primary and secondary name servers to be ns1.bdm.microsoftonline.com and ns2.bdm.microsoftonline.com, respectively, and then save the new settings.

Note: Your name server setting updates may take up to 72 hours to propagate through the DNS system.

[Next] Cancel

Figure 2-5. Instructions for configuring DNS

Go back to the registrar's web site and change the name servers to point to the addresses provided. For my registrar the configuration page looks like Figure 2-6. Again, yours will likely be different.

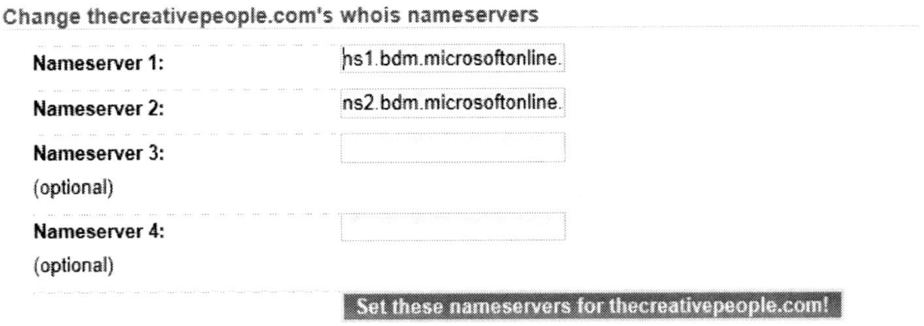

Change thecreativepeople.com's whois nameservers

Nameserver 1:	hs1.bdm.microsoftonline.
Nameserver 2:	ns2.bdm.microsoftonline.
Nameserver 3: (optional)	
Nameserver 4: (optional)	

Set these nameservers for thecreativepeople.com!

Figure 2-6. Moving the name servers

After these changes have been made, click the Next button on the Office 365 admin page. This should add this domain to your account.

■ **Tip** Be patient. The TXT records that are used for verification are usually available in a few minutes. However, while the other DNS changes can be made in minutes, it often takes hours or even days before the changes are fully propagated. You might find that it's working…sort of. During this transition some things will work, while others won't. Just be patient and give it plenty of time for everything to work smoothly.

Viewing the Domain in Office 365

Your Domain Manager page should now show both the initial domain provided by Office 365 as well as your custom domain, as shown in Figure 2-7.

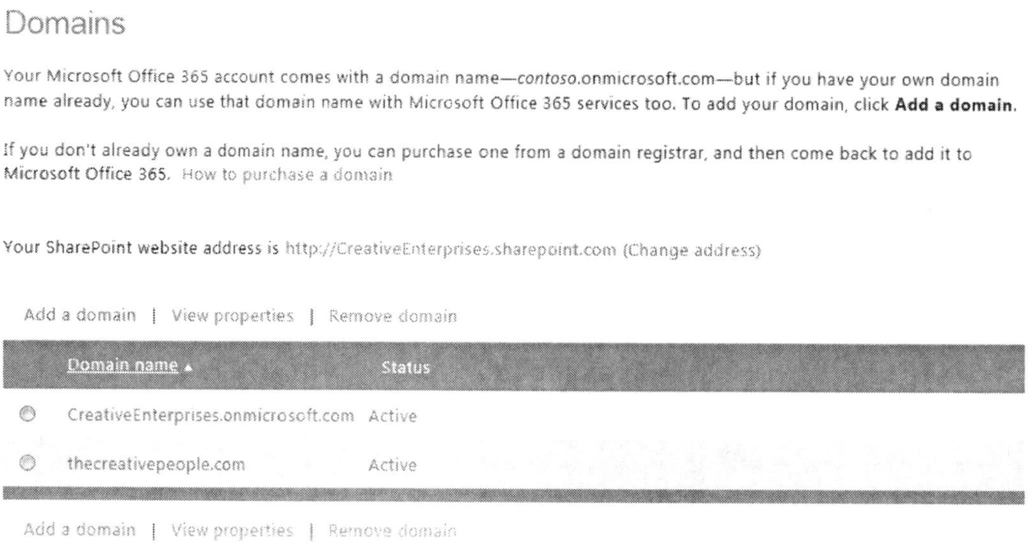

Domains

Your Microsoft Office 365 account comes with a domain name—*contoso*.onmicrosoft.com—but if you have your own domain name already, you can use that domain name with Microsoft Office 365 services too. To add your domain, click **Add a domain**.

If you don't already own a domain name, you can purchase one from a domain registrar, and then come back to add it to Microsoft Office 365. How to purchase a domain

Your SharePoint website address is http://CreativeEnterprises.sharepoint.com (Change address)

Add a domain | View properties | Remove domain

Domain name ▲	Status
◎ CreativeEnterprises.onmicrosoft.com	Active
◎ thecreativepeople.com	Active

Add a domain | View properties | Remove domain

Figure 2-7. *Listing the existing domains*

If you select the new domain and click the View properties link, you can see the DNS entries that were created for you in the Office 365 DNS server. These are the DNS settings that will allow your client applications such as Outlook and Lync to communicate with the cloud-based servers on Office 365. The settings should be similar those in Figure 2-8.

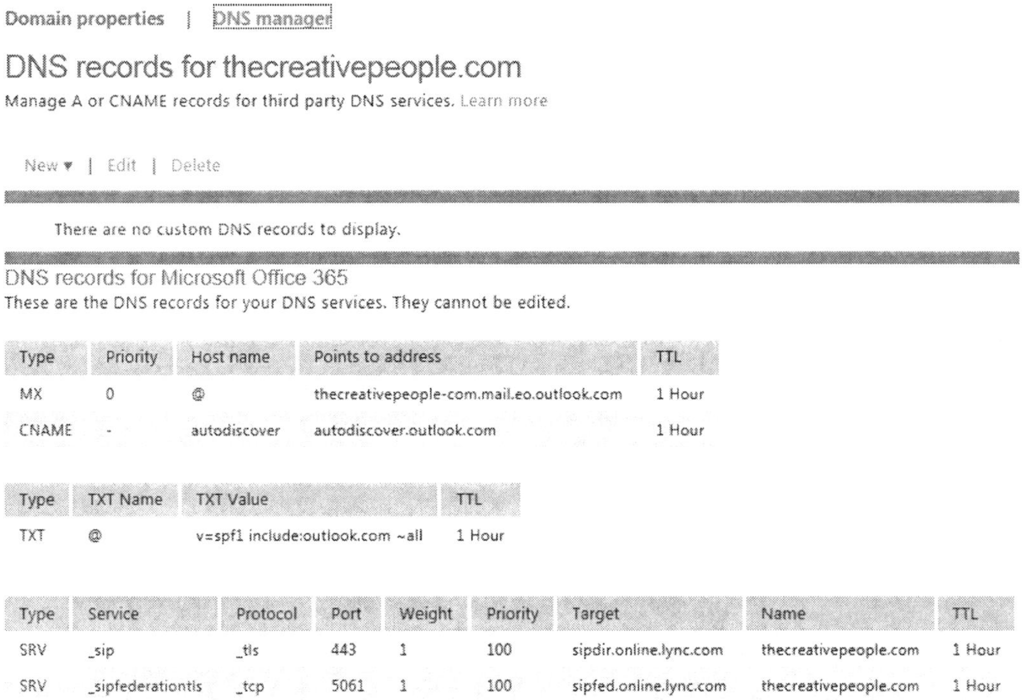

Domain properties | DNS manager

DNS records for thecreativepeople.com
Manage A or CNAME records for third party DNS services. Learn more

New ▼ | Edit | Delete

There are no custom DNS records to display.

DNS records for Microsoft Office 365
These are the DNS records for your DNS services. They cannot be edited.

Type	Priority	Host name	Points to address	TTL
MX	0	@	thecreativepeople-com.mail.eo.outlook.com	1 Hour
CNAME	-	autodiscover	autodiscover.outlook.com	1 Hour

Type	TXT Name	TXT Value	TTL
TXT	@	v=spf1 include:outlook.com ~all	1 Hour

Type	Service	Protocol	Port	Weight	Priority	Target	Name	TTL
SRV	_sip	_tls	443	1	100	sipdir.online.lync.com	thecreativepeople.com	1 Hour
SRV	_sipfederationtls	_tcp	5061	1	100	sipfed.online.lync.com	thecreativepeople.com	1 Hour

Figure 2-8. The DNS records in the new nameserver

Changing the SharePoint Address

To move the URL of your SharePoint sites you'll need to make an additional change. You now have two domains (the original domain and the new custom domain). If you want your public web site to use the new domain, you must configure SharePoint Online to use it.

From the Domain Manager page (shown in Figure 2-7), click the Change address link, which will display the page shown in Figure 2-9. Just select the new domain in the drop-down list and click the OK button.

Figure 2-9. Changing the web site address

▪ **Caution** This will move both the public site as well as the Team Site to this address. The URL for the Team Site will use your custom domain in the /teamsite folder. For example, my Team Site will be at www.thecreativepeople.com/teamsite. These are both public addresses; however, the Team Site is only available to authenticated users. If anyone tries to access this site, they will be forwarded to the Office 365 login page.

Again, like other DNS changes, this can take some time to propagate. The message shown in Figure 2-10 is letting you know that the change can take up to 24 hours to complete.

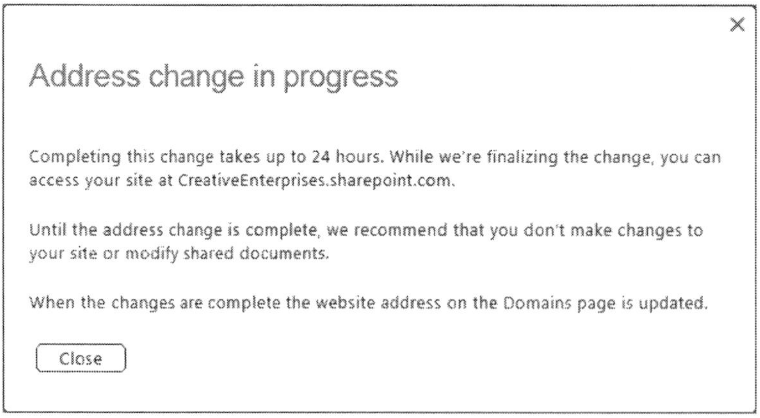

Figure 2-10. Warning about the address change

Adding Users to the New Domain

The last step in this process is to move existing users to the new domain. All existing users will still be on the initial domain (that includes `.onmicrosoft`). To move their logins and e-mail addresses to the new domain, you just need to change the domain in the User setup (see Figure 2-11).

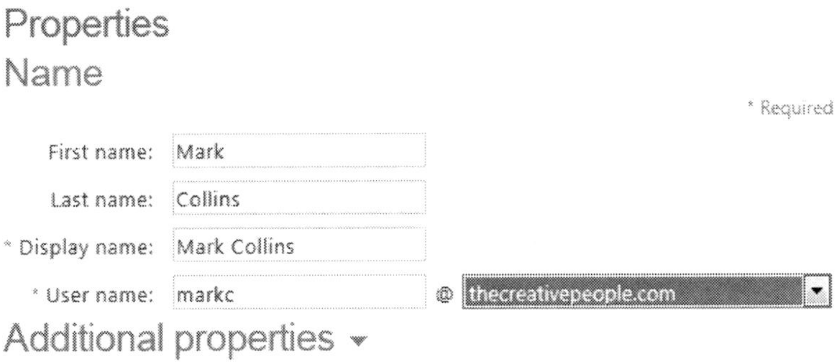

Properties
Name

* Required

First name: Mark

Last name: Collins

* Display name: Mark Collins

* User name: markc   @ thecreativepeople.com

Additional properties ▼

Figure 2-11. Moving a user to the new domain

Using an Enterprise Account

If you have an Enterprise account, you can also use your own domain name but the process is different. The primary difference is that you will leave the DNS at its current location but configure it to point to the appropriate Office 365 servers. This gives you more flexibility. For example, you could use one domain for e-mail and a different one for Lync.

Adding a Domain

This first step is adding a domain to your Office 365 account. From the Admin page, click the Domain link; you should see the initial domain listed, as shown in Figure 2-12.

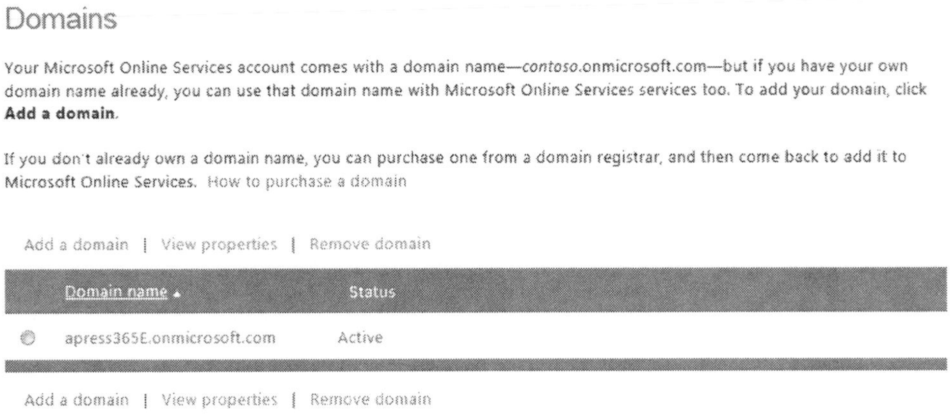

Domains

Your Microsoft Online Services account comes with a domain name—*contoso*.onmicrosoft.com—but if you have your own domain name already, you can use that domain name with Microsoft Online Services services too. To add your domain, click **Add a domain**.

If you don't already own a domain name, you can purchase one from a domain registrar, and then come back to add it to Microsoft Online Services. How to purchase a domain

Add a domain | View properties | Remove domain

Domain name ▲	Status
apress365E.onmicrosoft.com	Active

Add a domain | View properties | Remove domain

Figure 2-12. The initial domain

▪ **Note** For this example I am using a different Office 365 account. This one, `apress365E`, was setup as an Enterprise account.

Enter the new domain name just like with a Small Business account. In this case, I purchased a new domain name from Network Solutions so I'll be using their web site to configure this domain. The registrar details are shown in Figure 2-13.

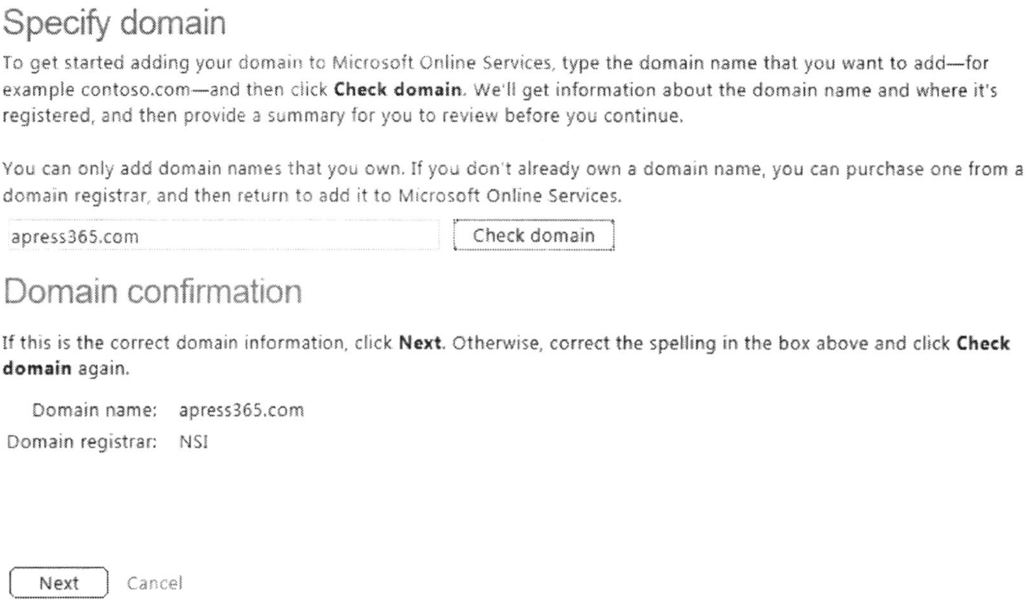

Specify domain

To get started adding your domain to Microsoft Online Services, type the domain name that you want to add—for example contoso.com—and then click **Check domain**. We'll get information about the domain name and where it's registered, and then provide a summary for you to review before you continue.

You can only add domain names that you own. If you don't already own a domain name, you can purchase one from a domain registrar, and then return to add it to Microsoft Online Services.

apress365.com	Check domain

Domain confirmation

If this is the correct domain information, click **Next**. Otherwise, correct the spelling in the box above and click **Check domain** again.

    Domain name: apress365.com
Domain registrar: NSI

[Next]   Cancel

Figure 2-13. Adding a new domain

The verification instructions are different from the last exercise because they are specific for the NSI registrar, as illustrated in Figure 2-14.

Verify domain

Before we can add your domain name to Microsoft Online Services, we must verify that you are the owner of the domain. To begin the verification process, you add a specific record to the DNS records at your domain registrar. We then look for the record to verify ownership.

Each DNS provider supports different features, so we provide two ways that you can verify ownership: by creating a TXT record or an MX record.

Note: The new DNS record does not affect how your domain works. Learn more

Select a verification method: Add TXT record (preferred method) ▾

Use the table and instructions below to create a TXT record for a domain that is registered at Network Solutions. For general instructions about verifying a domain, see Verify a domain at any domain name registrar.

Create a TXT record at Network Solutions

Note: Your domain registrar's website may differ from that described in these instructions.

Alias or Host Name	Destination or *Points to* Address	TTL
apress365.com	v=verifydomain MS=ms77557165	1 Hour

1. Go to your account at Network Solutions.
2. Click **Login** and type your user ID and password.
3. In the drop-down list, select **Manage My Domain Names**, and then click **Login**.
4. Select the domain name that you're verifying, and then go to the **Domain Names** page.
5. On the **Domain Names** page, click **Edit Advanced DNS Records.**
6. On the **Update Advanced DNS page**, under **Text (TXT Records)**, click **Edit TXT Records.**
7. In the first empty row, in the **Host** box, type or paste apress365.com.
8. In the **TTL** box, type or paste 1 Hour.
9. In the **Text** box, type or paste v=verifydomain MS=ms77557165.
10. Click **Continue.**
11. In the **Confirm Your Request** dialog box, review the DNS record that you created, and then click **Save Changes.**
12. Sign out of the Network Solutions website. Wait at least 15 minutes for the changes to take effect.
13. Return to Office 365 and click the **Verify** button below.

Note:
Typically it takes about 15 minutes for your changes to take effect. However, it can take up to 72 hours for the record that you created to propagate through the DNS system.

Verify | Cancel

Figure 2-14. *Verifying the new domain*

I entered the TXT record but didn't wait long enough, so I received the error shown in Figure 2-15.

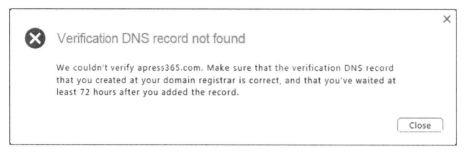

Figure 2-15. Verification failure message

■ **Tip** If the verification process takes a while, you can log off the Office 365 web site and come back to it later. From the Domain Manager page, the new domain with be listed as "Pending Verification." If you click the Troubleshoot domain button, the Verify page will be displayed and you can continue the process.

Configuring the New Domain

Once the verification process is complete, you'll then need to specify the domain intent using the page shown in Figure 2-16. The term *domain intent* simply means the Office 365 services that are intended for that domain.

Specify domain services

Specify the services you'll use with your domain. Learn more

☑ Exchange Online
☑ Lync Online
☐ SharePoint Online

Figure 2-16. Using Exchange and Lync with the new domain

You can't host both SharePoint Online and either Exchange Online or Lync Online on the same domain. You'll host Exchange Online and Lync Online on this domain. I will then show you how to create another domain to host SharePoint Online. After selecting the Exchange Online and Lync Online services, the page shown in Figure 2-17 will be displayed.

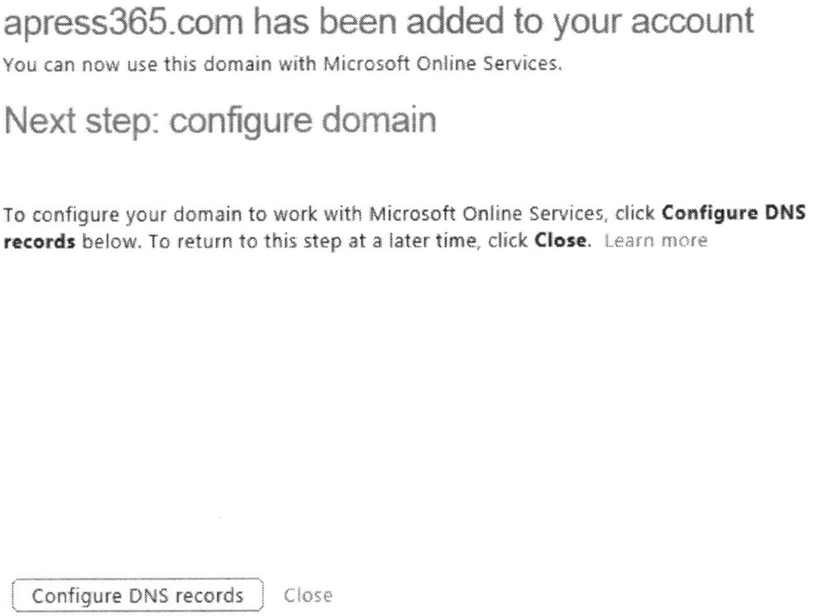

apress365.com has been added to your account

You can now use this domain with Microsoft Online Services.

Next step: configure domain

To configure your domain to work with Microsoft Online Services, click **Configure DNS records** below. To return to this step at a later time, click **Close**. Learn more

[Configure DNS records]   Close

Figure 2-17. The new domain has been added

Updating the DNS Records

Click the Configure DNS records button and then click the Next button to display the necessary DNS records, which will be similar those in Figure 2-18.

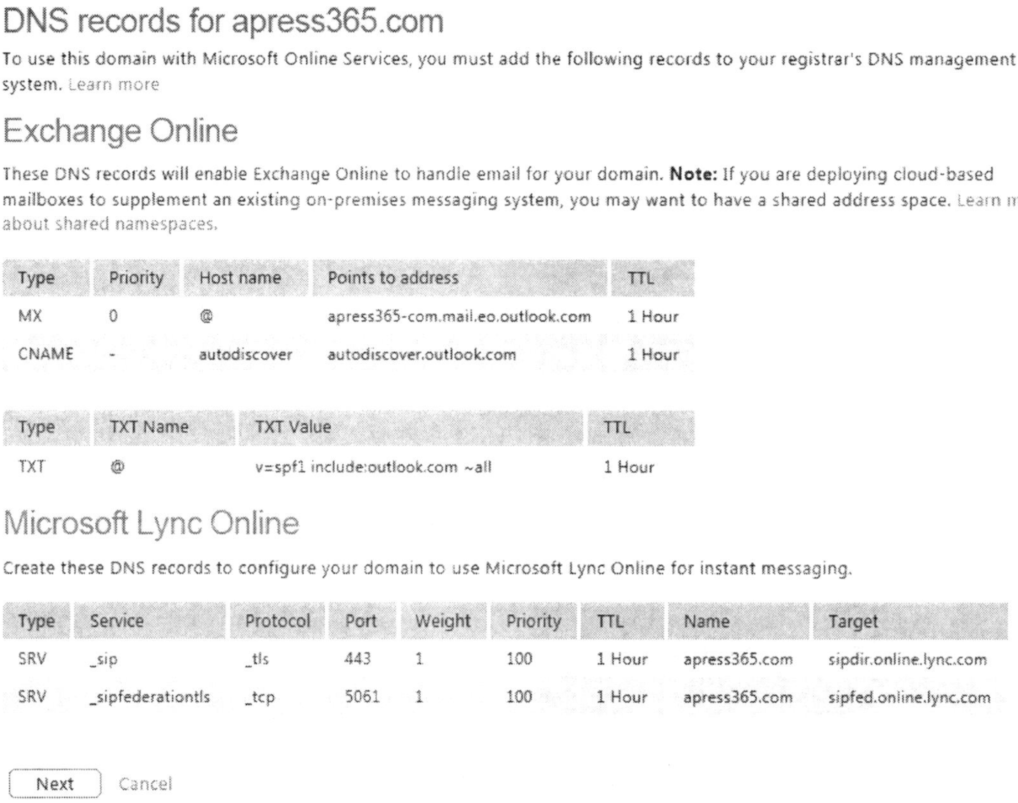

DNS records for apress365.com

To use this domain with Microsoft Online Services, you must add the following records to your registrar's DNS management system. Learn more

Exchange Online

These DNS records will enable Exchange Online to handle email for your domain. **Note:** If you are deploying cloud-based mailboxes to supplement an existing on-premises messaging system, you may want to have a shared address space. Learn more about shared namespaces.

Type	Priority	Host name	Points to address	TTL
MX	0	@	apress365-com.mail.eo.outlook.com	1 Hour
CNAME	-	autodiscover	autodiscover.outlook.com	1 Hour

Type	TXT Name	TXT Value	TTL
TXT	@	v=spf1 include:outlook.com ~all	1 Hour

Microsoft Lync Online

Create these DNS records to configure your domain to use Microsoft Lync Online for instant messaging.

Type	Service	Protocol	Port	Weight	Priority	TTL	Name	Target
SRV	_sip	_tls	443	1	100	1 Hour	apress365.com	sipdir.online.lync.com
SRV	_sipfederationtls	_tcp	5061	1	100	1 Hour	apress365.com	sipfed.online.lync.com

[Next] Cancel

Figure 2-18. *The DNS record details*

You will then go to your existing DNS server and enter the records that are listed. When you're done, click the Next button (in Office 365) and you should see the Finish page shown in Figure 2-19.

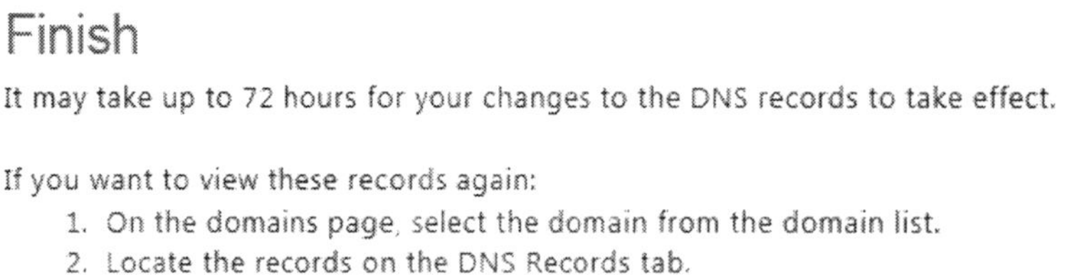

Finish

It may take up to 72 hours for your changes to the DNS records to take effect.

If you want to view these records again:
1. On the domains page, select the domain from the domain list.
2. Locate the records on the DNS Records tab.

Figure 2-19. *The domain setup is complete*

Your Outlook and Lync clients can now use the new domain as soon as the DNS changes have propagated.

Adding a Third-Level Domain

To move the public web site on SharePoint Online to the custom URL you'll need to add another domain. You'll add a third-level domain, www.apress365.com in my case. (To clarify, .com is the first level, apress365 is the second level, and www is the third level.) Just prefix the first custom domain name with www. Add a new domain in your Office 365 account using this name, as shown in Figure 2-20.

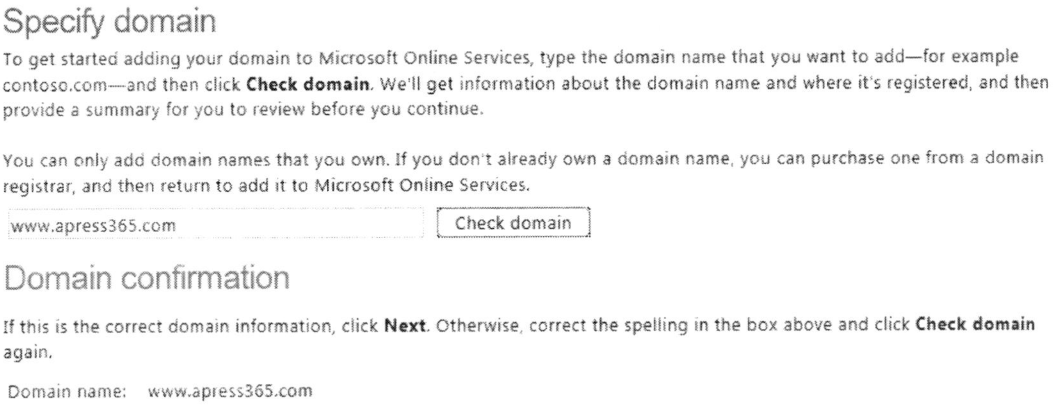

Specify domain

To get started adding your domain to Microsoft Online Services, type the domain name that you want to add—for example contoso.com—and then click **Check domain**. We'll get information about the domain name and where it's registered, and then provide a summary for you to review before you continue.

You can only add domain names that you own. If you don't already own a domain name, you can purchase one from a domain registrar, and then return to add it to Microsoft Online Services.

| www.apress365.com | Check domain |

Domain confirmation

If this is the correct domain information, click **Next**. Otherwise, correct the spelling in the box above and click **Check domain** again.

Domain name: www.apress365.com

Figure 2-20. Creating a third-level domain

Since this is a sub-domain under the one you just added, there is no need to repeat the verification process. Specify the SharePoint Online service only, as shown in Figure 2-21.

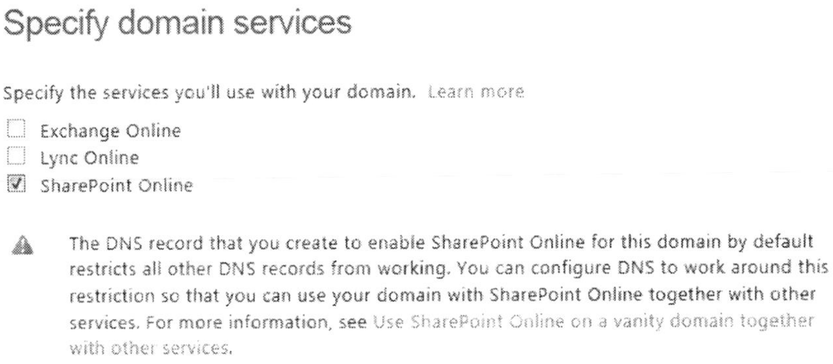

Specify domain services

Specify the services you'll use with your domain. Learn more

- ☐ Exchange Online
- ☐ Lync Online
- ☑ SharePoint Online

⚠ The DNS record that you create to enable SharePoint Online for this domain by default restricts all other DNS records from working. You can configure DNS to work around this restriction so that you can use your domain with SharePoint Online together with other services. For more information, see Use SharePoint Online on a vanity domain together with other services.

Figure 2-21. Using this domain for SharePoint only

Now you'll have a third domain added to your account. You will need to create a public web site and configure it to use this domain (see Figure 2-22).

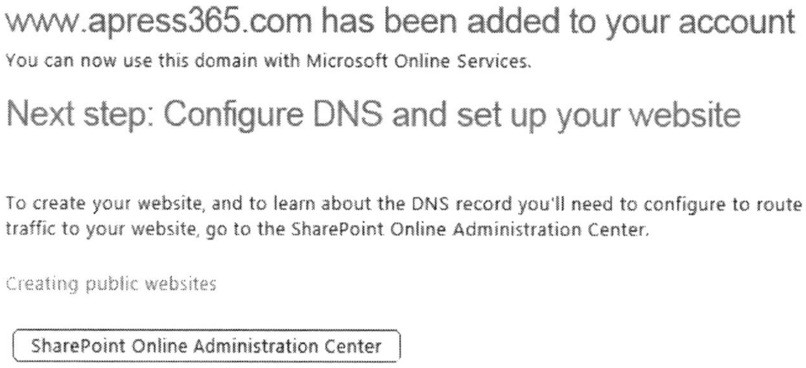

www.apress365.com has been added to your account

You can now use this domain with Microsoft Online Services.

Next step: Configure DNS and set up your website

To create your website, and to learn about the DNS record you'll need to configure to route traffic to your website, go to the SharePoint Online Administration Center.

Creating public websites

SharePoint Online Administration Center

Figure 2-22. The domain has been added

Configuring the Public SharePoint Site

In the Small Business account, explained in Chapter 1, both a Team Site and a public-facing web site were created for you. With the Enterprise account, only the Team Site is set up by default. You will now create the public-facing web site in the Enterprise account and then configure it to use the custom domain name that you just added. This is more complicated with the Enterprise plans because of the increased flexibility. You will need to first create user accounts that will be set up as the site owner and administrator. You will also need to create a new site collection. I will explain these steps now.

Creating a Global Administrator

Before you create the web site, you'll need to set up one or more accounts. In an Enterprise account, each site collection in SharePoint must be assigned an owner. You can also define one or more site administrators.

The only users that are currently set up will be on the old domain. You can either create new accounts or move your existing account to the new domain (use the first custom domain, not the one starting with www). When you configure a user in an Enterprise account, if you choose to make them an administrator, you will then need to choose a type of administrator. For now, just set your account as a global administrator, as shown in Figure 2-23.

Settings
Assign role

Do you want this user to have administrator **permissions?** Learn more about administrator roles

○ No
◉ Yes

| Global administrator ▼ |

Email address
This email address is used for important notifications and self service password reset. Learn more about lost password recovery

| markc@apress365.com |

Set user location

The services available vary by location. Learn more about licensing restrictions

* Required

| * | United States ▼ |

| Back | | Next | Cancel

***Figure 2-23.** Creating a global administrator on the new domain*

Creating a New Site Collection

With a Small Business account, you have a single site collection that contains both the public web site and the internal Team Site. With an Enterprise account, you will create separate site collections. Each site collection can be configured differently in terms of owners and administrators, installed features, and resource quotas. (I will explain quotas in more detail in the next chapter.)

From the Admin page, click the Manage link under the SharePoint Online section. Then click the "Manage site collections" link, which will display the page shown in Figure 2-24.

| Site Collections |

| New | Delete | Properties | Owners | Storage Quota | Resource Usage Quota | Settings | Website Domains | DNS Information |
| Contribute | | | | Manage | | | Website | |

| Search by URL... 🔍 | 5000 resources available ▭ |
| | 21500 MB available ▭ |

☐ URL	Total Storage Quota (MB)	Total Resource Usage Quota
Site Collections		
https://apress365e.sharepoint.com ⊡ NEW	1000	300

***Figure 2-24.** Viewing the current site collection*

As you can see, a single internal site collection was created for you. If you click on the URL field, you'll see the properties of that site collection (see Figure 2-25).

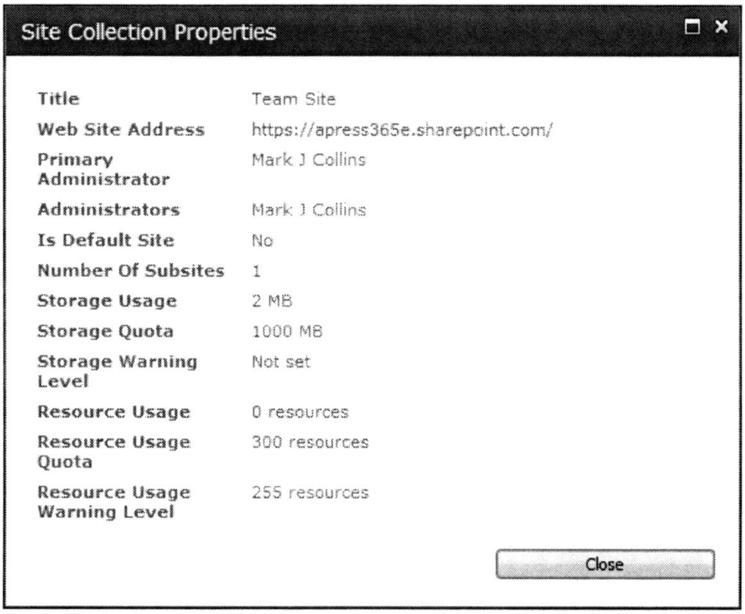

Figure 2-25. The site collection properties

Close that dialog box, click the New button in the ribbon, and click the Public Website link, as shown in Figure 2-26.

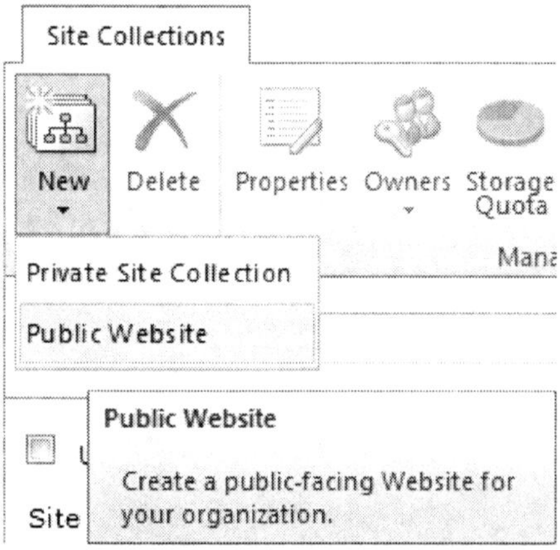

Figure 2-26. Adding a public web site

In the Create Your Website dialog box, make sure you select the domain that includes the www, as shown in Figure 2-27. You'll need to enter your user account as the site administrator.

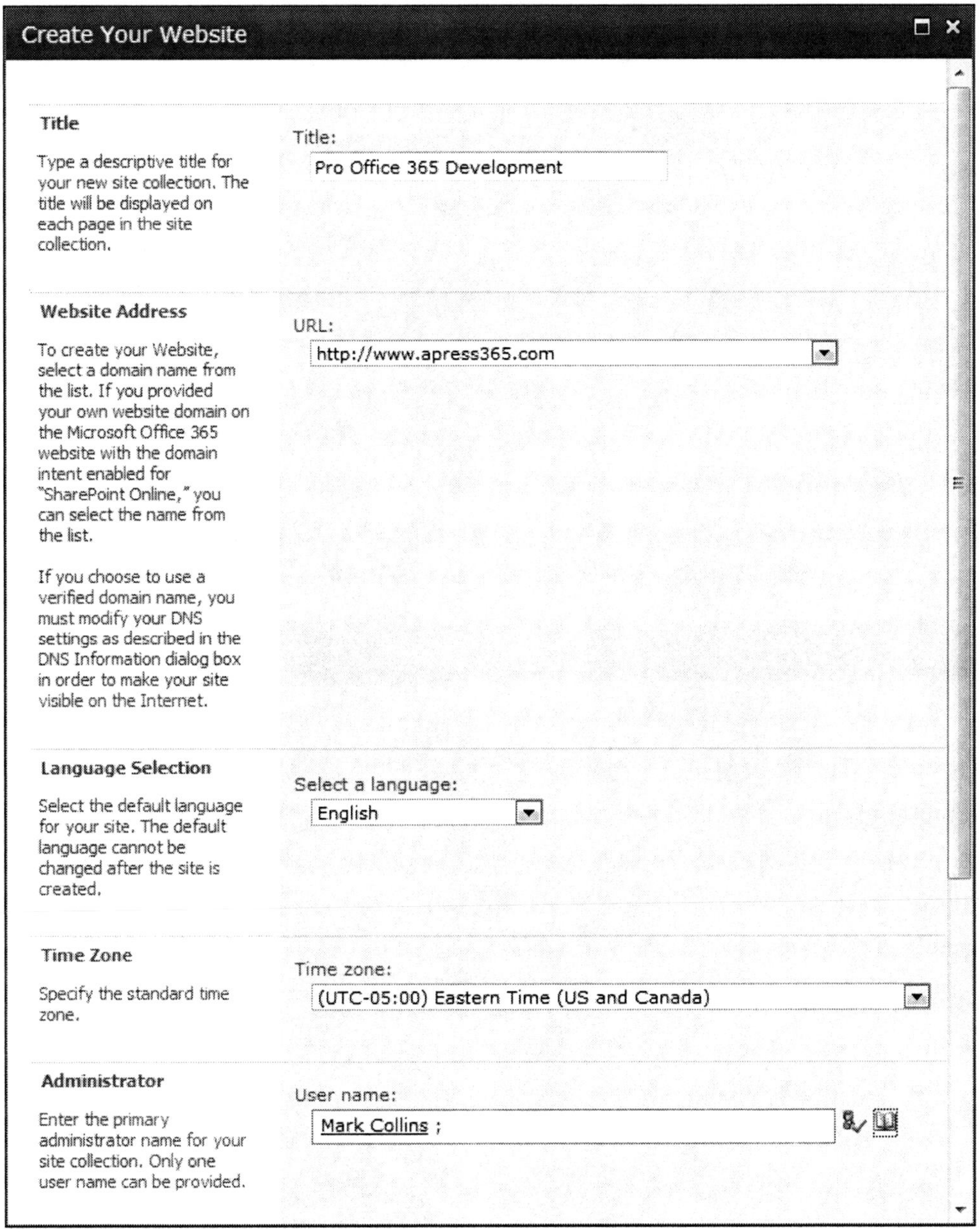

Create Your Website ▫ ✕

Title

Type a descriptive title for your new site collection. The title will be displayed on each page in the site collection.

Title:

Pro Office 365 Development

Website Address

To create your Website, select a domain name from the list. If you provided your own website domain on the Microsoft Office 365 website with the domain intent enabled for "SharePoint Online," you can select the name from the list.

If you choose to use a verified domain name, you must modify your DNS settings as described in the DNS Information dialog box in order to make your site visible on the Internet.

URL:

http://www.apress365.com

Language Selection

Select the default language for your site. The default language cannot be changed after the site is created.

Select a language:

English

Time Zone

Specify the standard time zone.

Time zone:

(UTC-05:00) Eastern Time (US and Canada)

Administrator

Enter the primary administrator name for your site collection. Only one user name can be provided.

User name:

Mark Collins ;

Figure 2-27. Configuring the public web site

The list of site collections should now include the public web site, as shown in Figure 2-28.

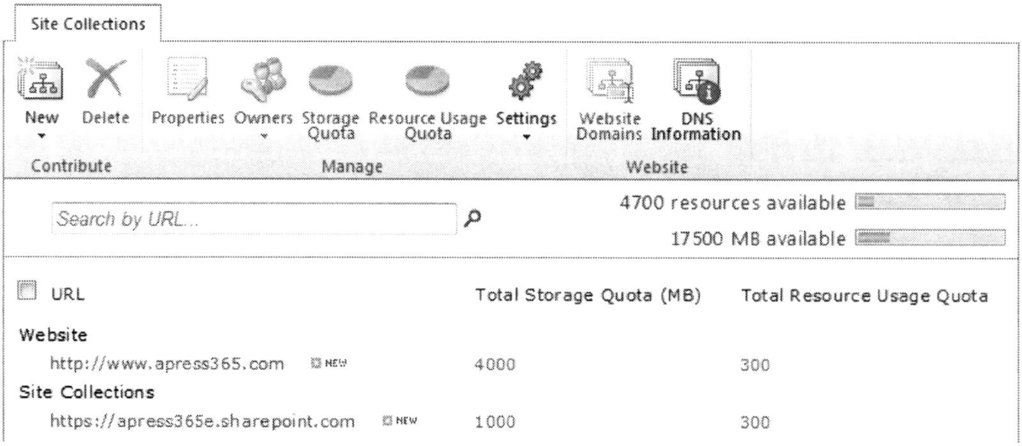

Figure 2-28. Viewing the list of site collections

The last step is to update your DNS server to point to this web site. In the site collection list, select the new web site and then click the DNS Information button in the ribbon. This will display the dialog box shown in Figure 2-29.

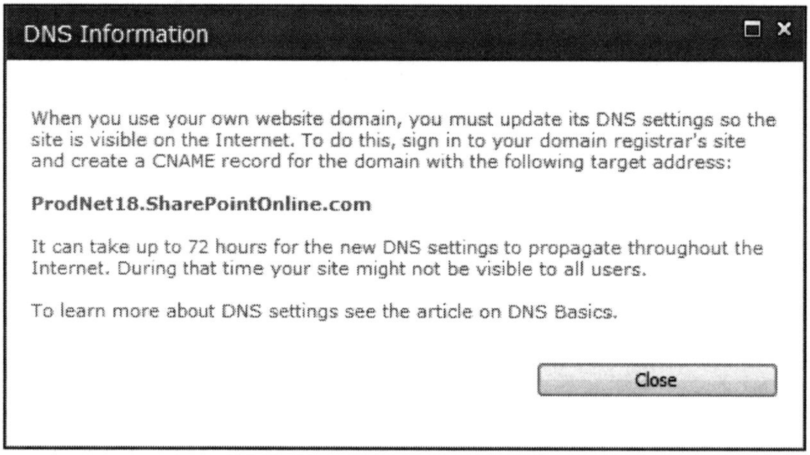

Figure 2-29. Viewing the CNAME details for DNS

This tells you the actual address of this web site. In my case, this was ProdNet18.SharePointOnline.com. You will need to create a CNAME record in your DNS server that maps this to your new domain (the one starting with www). The final CNAME records for my DNS server are shown in Figure 2-30.

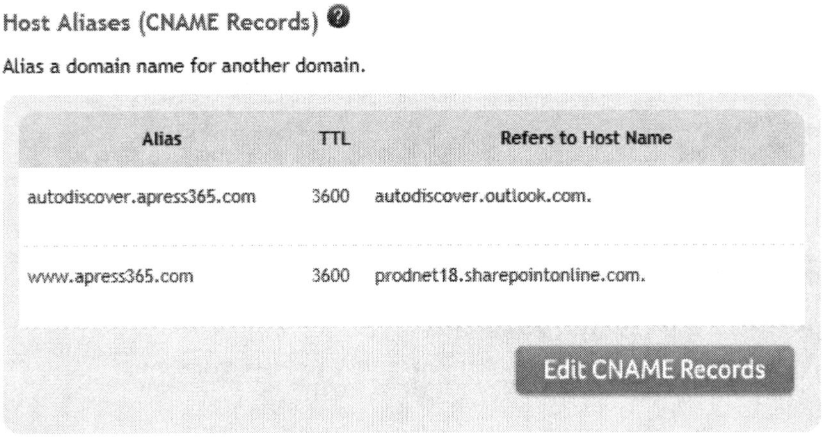

Host Aliases (CNAME Records) ❓

Alias a domain name for another domain.

Alias	TTL	Refers to Host Name
autodiscover.apress365.com	3600	autodiscover.outlook.com.
www.apress365.com	3600	prodnet18.sharepointonline.com.

Edit CNAME Records

Figure 2-30. The CNAME records in DNS

Designing the Public Web Site

When the DNS changes have been propagated, which can take several hours or more, you'll be able to view your Office 365-hosted public web site by entering your custom domain. For my site this is www.apress365.com, as demonstrated in Figure 2-31.

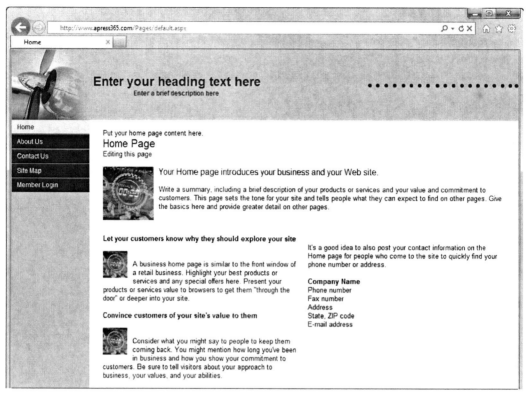

Figure 2-31. The pubic web site's home page

To edit this site, click the Member Login link in the navigation pane. If you are not already logged in, you will be taken to the Office 365 login page. Then your web site will be opened using SharePoint Online, as shown in Figure 2-32.

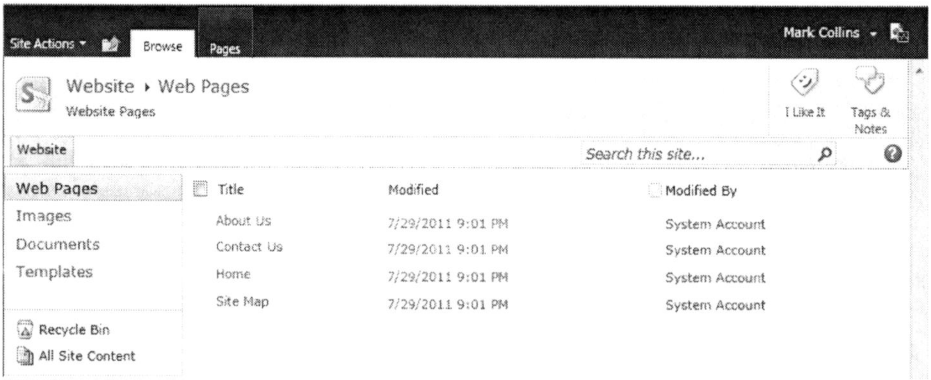

Figure 2-32. Viewing the site pages

Click on one of the pages and it will be opened for editing, as shown in Figure 2-33.

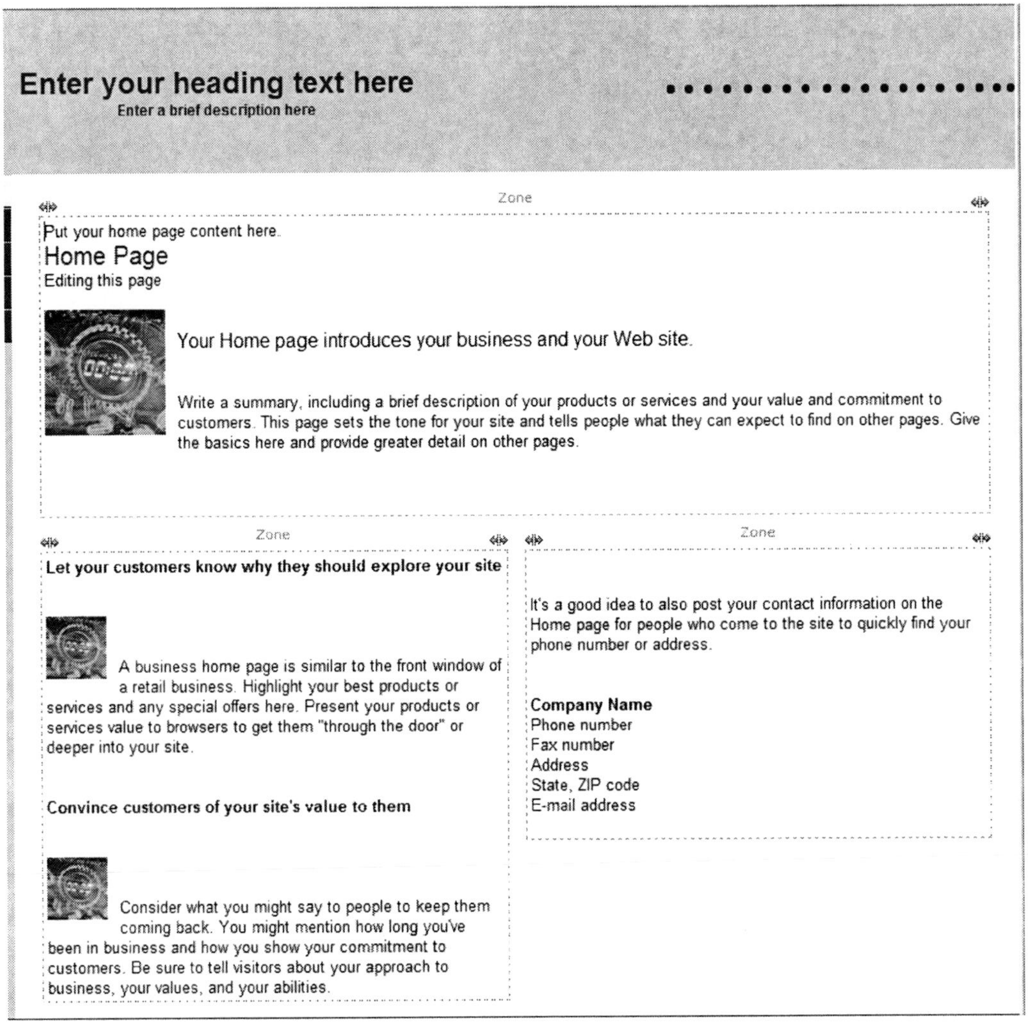

Enter your heading text here
Enter a brief description here

Zone

Put your home page content here.
Home Page
Editing this page

Your Home page introduces your business and your Web site.

Write a summary, including a brief description of your products or services and your value and commitment to customers. This page sets the tone for your site and tells people what they can expect to find on other pages. Give the basics here and provide greater detail on other pages.

Zone   Zone

Let your customers know why they should explore your site

It's a good idea to also post your contact information on the Home page for people who come to the site to quickly find your phone number or address.

A business home page is similar to the front window of a retail business. Highlight your best products or services and any special offers here. Present your products or services value to browsers to get them "through the door" or deeper into your site.

Company Name
Phone number
Fax number
Address
State, ZIP code
E-mail address

Convince customers of your site's value to them

Consider what you might say to people to keep them coming back. You might mention how long you've been in business and how you show your commitment to customers. Be sure to tell visitors about your approach to business, your values, and your abilities.

Figure 2-33. Editing the Home page

Now that you have added the custom domain and have configured the public-facing web site, you're ready to set up the Exchange and Lync applications.

Using Single Sign-On

Another key feature of Office 365 for supporting an on-premise client solution is the ability for a single sign-on. With single sign-on, once you have logged in to your corporate domain and have been authenticated, you can access the Office 365 services without requiring any additional authentication. This will provide a user experience that is nearly identical to an on-premise Office solution.

Single sign-on is accomplished by synchronizing the users in the on-premise Active Directory with your Office 365 account. This is a fairly complicated process to set up and is beyond the scope of this book. If you want to implement single sign-on, I suggest you start with this article: http://onlinehelp.microsoft.com/en-us/office365-enterprises/hh125004.aspx. It provides a good overview with links for more information.

Configuring Exchange Online

The Enterprise solution includes advanced options for configuring Exchange Online, including distribution groups and external contacts. I will briefly demonstrate some of the more common features.

From the Admin page, click the Manage link under the Exchange Online section, which will display the page shown in Figure 2-34.

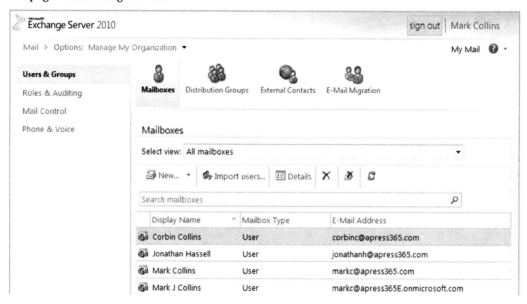

Figure 2-34. Displaying the Exchange mailboxes

Creating Additional E-mail Addresses

When you add a user to Office 365, a mailbox is created in Exchange Online and the primary e-mail address is the same as the user name. This address is determined by the domain to which that user is assigned. You can see from Figure 2-34 that my Office 365 account has my user with the initial domain (apress365.onmicrosoft.com). There are also three other users assigned to the new custom domain (apress365.com).

You can also create additional e-mail addresses that will be assigned to a mailbox. This is useful if you want to expose multiple e-mail addresses to the public and route them to an individual or shared inbox. Figure 2-35 shows that my mailbox also includes two additional e-mail addresses, markc1371@apress365.onmicrosoft.com and support@apress365.com.

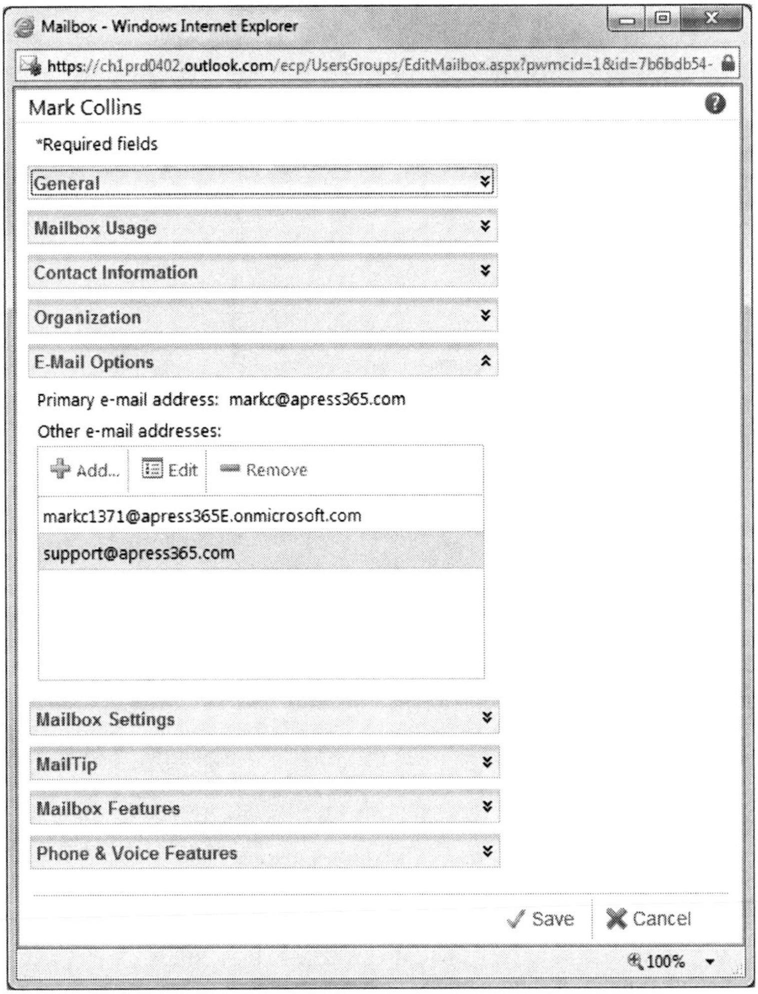

Figure 2-35. Displaying the mailbox properties

To assign an additional e-mail address, click the Add link, which will display the dialog box shown in Figure 2-36.

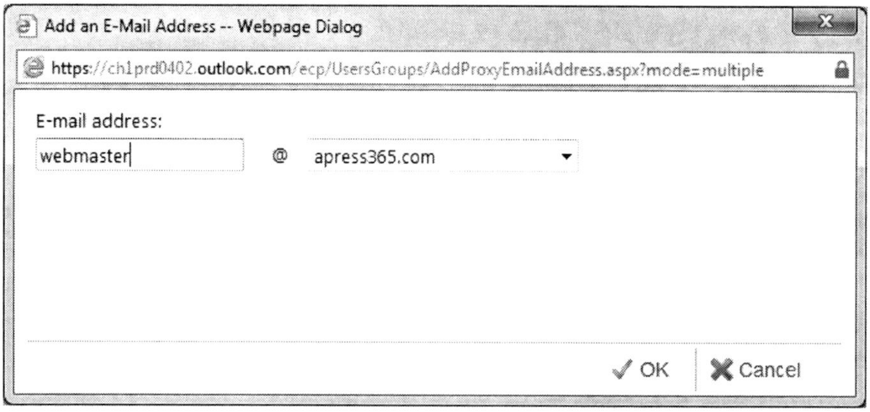

Figure 2-36. Adding an e-mail address

Enter an e-mail address and select the appropriate domain. In Figure 2-36, I'm adding webmaster@apress365.com. Any e-mails sent to the webmaster address will go to my inbox.

Adding a Room Mailbox

You can also create a special type of mailbox called a room. You use these for scheduling resources like a meeting room or shared equipment such as a projector. These mailboxes will have a calendar associated with them so you can see when they are available. When scheduling a meeting you can include these as attendees and check for availability just like other attendees.

The difference with these mailboxes is that you don't sign in to an inbox. Consequently, you can add these to Exchange without the need for an additional user license. However, this means there is no inbox to send the meeting invitation to, so there are two options for accepting the meeting invitation.

- *Automatically accept or reject based on availability.* If the room or resource is available during the time period requested, the invitation is automatically accepted. Otherwise, the invitation is declined.

- *Assign one or more delegates to this resource.* The invitation will go to their inbox and they can accept or decline the invitation on behalf of the resource.

To add a room mailbox, click the New link and click the Room Mailbox link. Then fill in the New Room dialog box shown in Figure 2-37.

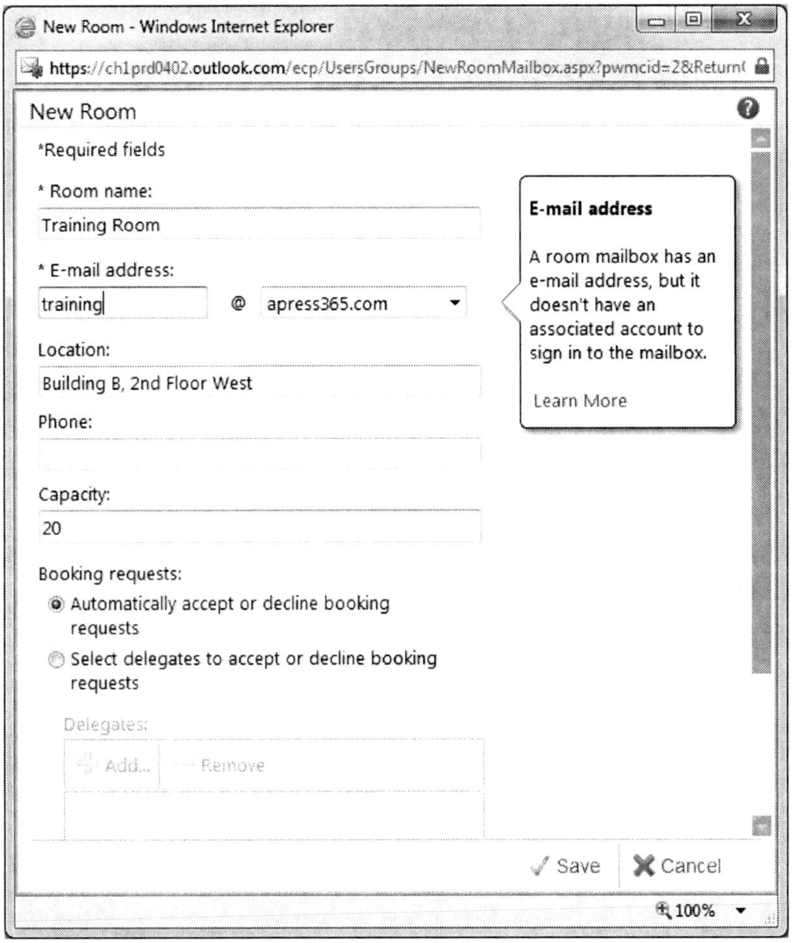

Figure 2-37. Adding a room mailbox

Creating a Distribution Group

You can also set up distribution groups, which allow you to send an e-mail to a single address and have that e-mail sent to everyone in the group. Click the Distribution Groups button to see the groups that have already been set up. To add a new one, click the New link, which will display the New Group dialog box shown in Figure 2-38.

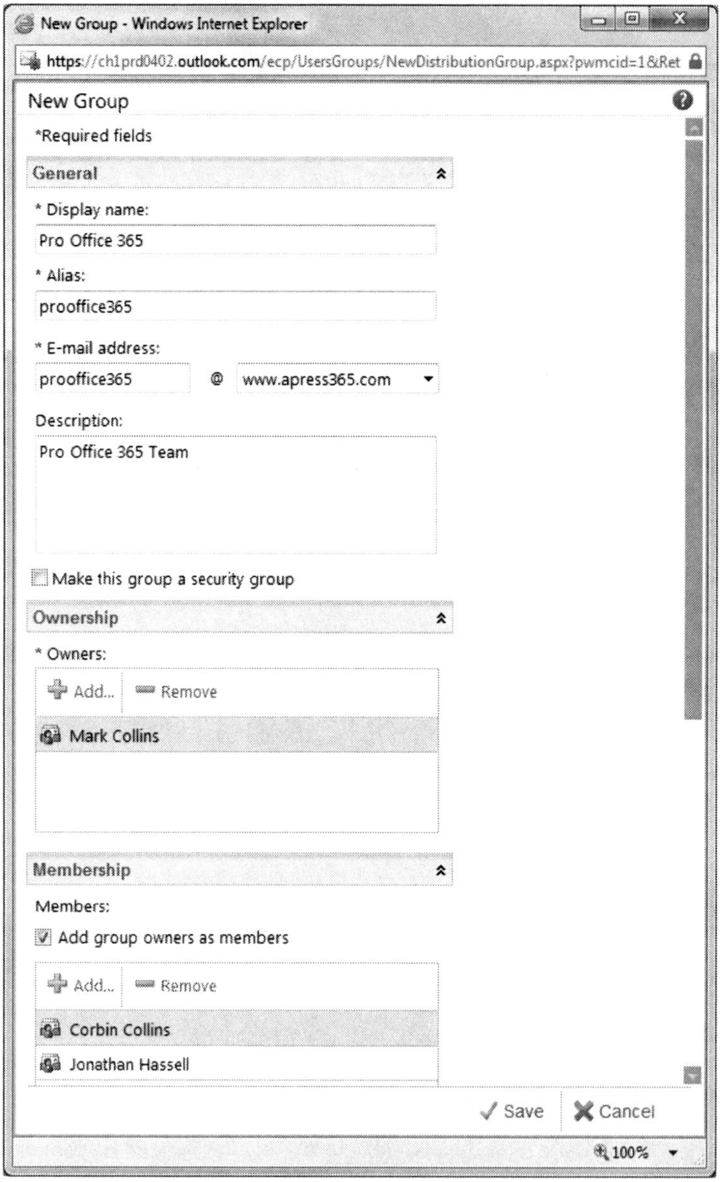

Figure 2-38. Adding a new distribution group

For each group you'll specify the name that is displayed as well as a unique e-mail address. You'll also need to assign one or more owners. The user that is creating the groups is set up as an owner by default but you can remove this and add others. You can control whether anyone can join or leave the group or if only owners can add or remove members.

■ **Tip** There is no inbox associated with a distribution group; when an e-mail is sent to the group, it is merely copied to each member of the group. Consequently, you don't need a user license when creating a distribution group.

Adding External Contacts

You can add *external contacts* in Exchange, which are e-mail addresses that are not part of your organization. This will include them in the address book, but no mailbox is set up for these addresses nor can they login in Office 365. They are included simply for convenience when sending an e-mail.

To add an external contact, click the External Contact button and then click the New link. This will display the External Contact dialog box shown in Figure 3-39.

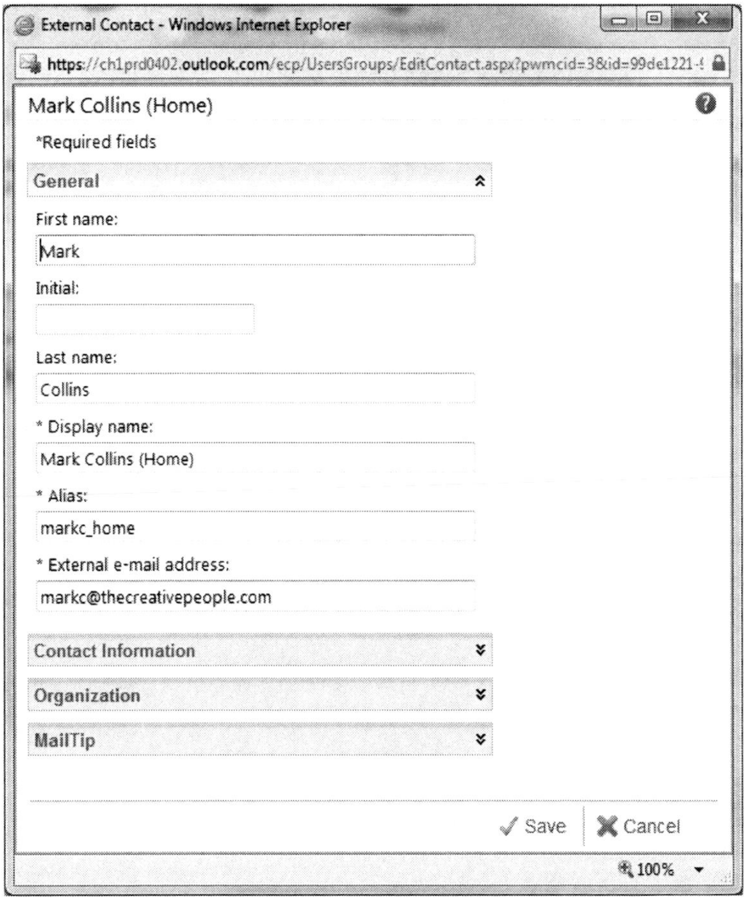

Figure 2-39. Adding an external contact

Creating a Migration Plan

I have demonstrated the basics for configuring a new Exchange Online server with Office 365. However, if you have an existing e-mail system you will need to create a migration plan. This plan will describe the process you'll use for moving your users from the existing e-mail system to Office 365. There are several options available and the right one for you will depend on the system you are migrating from and the number of users that will be moved. This is beyond the scope of this book; however, I suggest you review the article at `http://help.outlook.com/en-US/140/ms.exch.ecp.EmailMigrationStatusLearnMore.aspx` as a good starting point.

Configuring Role-Based Security in SharePoint

Now you'll configure the existing SharePoint sites to define the users and their access levels. As you create new SharePoint sites, you will want to restrict access to the appropriate users. For a small team, it may be sufficient to give everyone access to everything. For larger organization, you will likely want to limit someone's access. For example, each department may set up their own Team Site with a `Tasks` list, `Calendar`, and `Shared Documents` library. Typically, this would be restricted to only members of that department. Creating and managing user groups in SharePoint Online is done just like a standard on-premise SharePoint Server installation. I will provide a very brief introduction here.

If you go to your Team Site, from the Site Actions menu you can click the Site Settings link. This will display the Site Settings page shown in Figure 2-40.

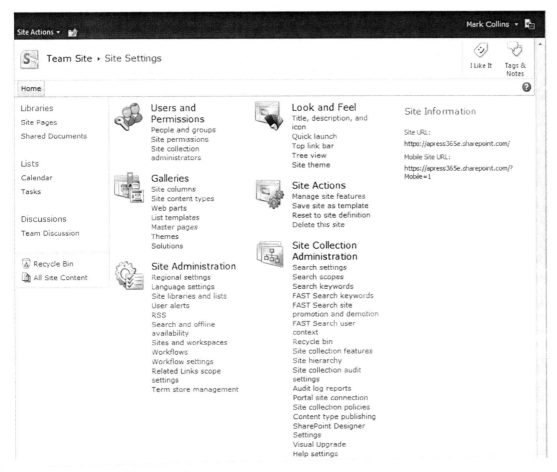

Figure 2-40. Viewing the site settings

Click the "People and groups" link to display the People and Groups page. Select a group in the navigation pane and the members of that group will be listed. Notice that the Team Site Members group, for example, doesn't have anyone in the group yet.

■ **Tip** By default, none of the SharePoint groups have any members; you'll need to add the appropriate people to the groups. You have access to the site because you are a global administrator. However, non-administrators won't be able to see the Team Site until you add them to the group.

To add users, click the New link and then click the Add Users link, as shown in Figure 2-41.

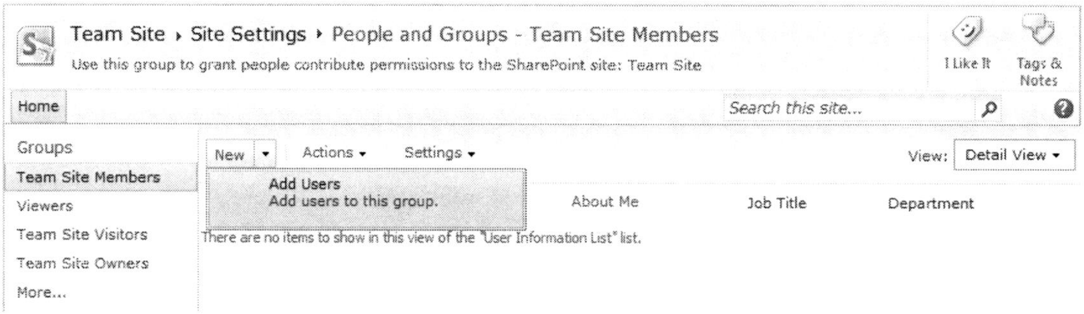

Figure 2-41. Displaying the Team Site members

In the Grant Permissions dialog box, add the appropriate users to this group, as shown in Figure 2-42.

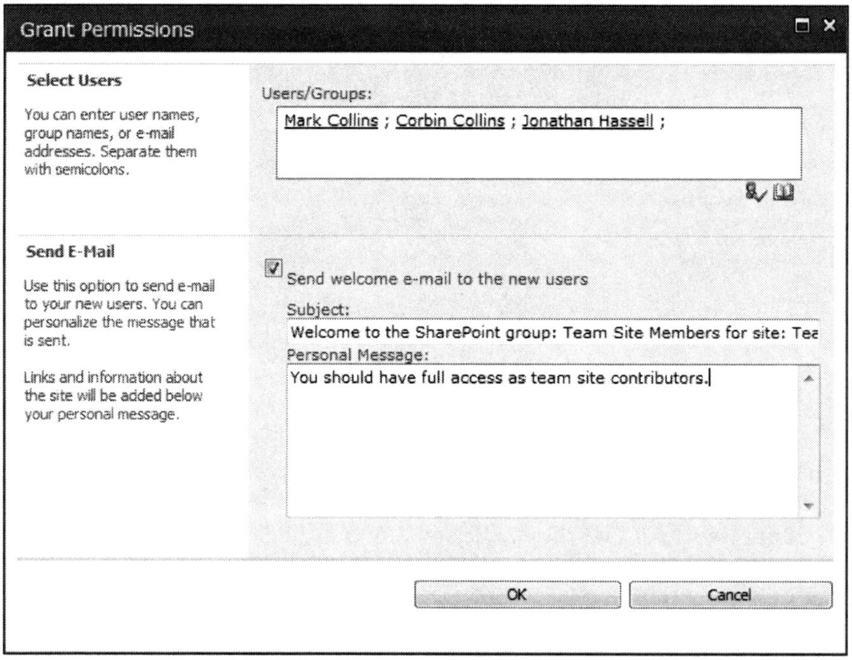

Figure 2-42. Adding users to the Team Site Member group

Using this same procedure you can add users to the Owners and Visitors groups as well. These groups are set up with standard privileges that work for most situations. You can also create custom groups if necessary.

Using Office Professional Plus

Some of the Office 365 subscription plans include Office Professional Plus. This can also be added to the existing plan for an additional monthly amount. Office Professional Plus is a package of client applications including Outlook, Word, Excel, PowerPoint, One Note, Access, Publisher, and InfoPath. These client applications provide a richer and more familiar user experience than the web-based counterparts that are included with Office 365.

You can simply purchase these applications and install them on your client. Provisioning them through Office 365 allows you purchase them through an annual or monthly subscription, which minimizes your up-front costs. It also simplifies licensing and installation. The Office Professional Plus plan includes a full suite of Office products including Visio (you'll use this in Chapter 5), Access (you'll need this for Chapters 6 and 14), Publisher, and others. SharePoint Workspace is another useful application that allows you to keep local lists and libraries synchronized with the SharePoint server.

Installing from Office 365

From the Admin page on Office 365 you can check the licenses that have been assigned to a particular user. Figure 2-43, for example, shows the licenses assigned to my user account, which includes Office Professional Plus.

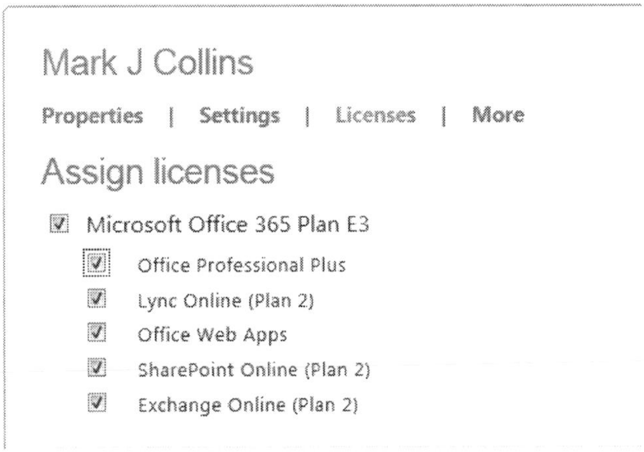

Figure 2-43. Viewing the assigned licenses

If your user account includes a license for Office Professional Plus, the Downloads page will include the option to install this product, as shown in Figure 2-44. Just select the 32-bit or 64-bit version and click the Install button.

Downloads

1 Install Microsoft Office Professional Plus

⚠ Upgrading to Office Professional Plus

Installing this product will upgrade the current version of Office on your computer to Office 2010 Professional Plus. If you're not quite ready to upgrade all your programs, choose **Customize** during installation and select which of your programs you want to upgrade and which you want to keep without upgrading. Click **Install** to get started.

Get more information about installing and upgrading Office.

Microsoft Office Professional Plus is a complete suite of Office desktop apps that you install on your PC.

Language:

English (United States) ▼

Version:
◉ 32-bit (recommended)
○ 64-bit

[Install]

Which version?

2 Install Microsoft Lync 2010

Use Lync 2010 to connect with colleagues through instant messaging, audio, video, and online meetings.

Figure 2-44. *Installing Office Professional Plus*

Saving Documents to the Team Site

When using the client applications you can still save the files directly to the SharePoint site. There are several benefits to doing this.

- The documents are stored in a shared location, making them available to other team members (subject to the site permissions).

- You can access them with the Office Web Apps when not at your workstation.

- The files are backed up automatically.

From the File tab of the ribbon (the backstage view), click the Save & Send tab and then click the Save to SharePoint button, as demonstrated in Figure 2-45.

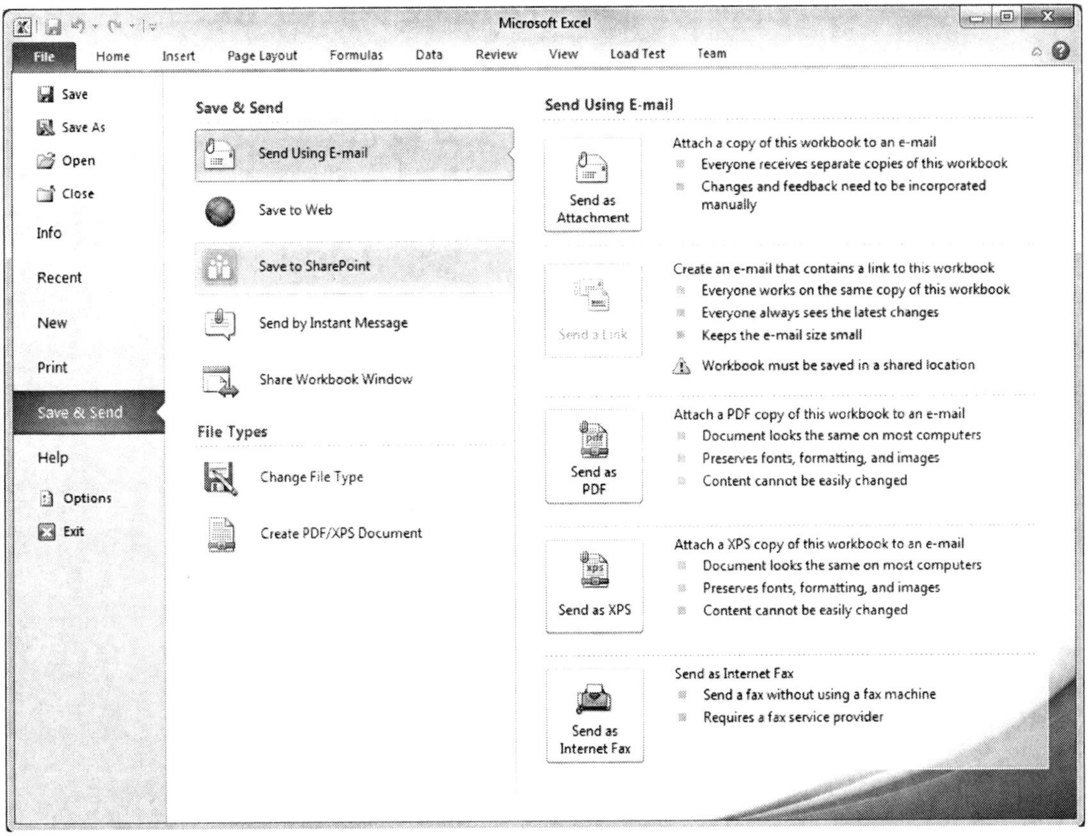

Figure 2-45. Clicking the Save to SharePoint button

This will display the Save to SharePoint window that is shown in Figure 2-46.

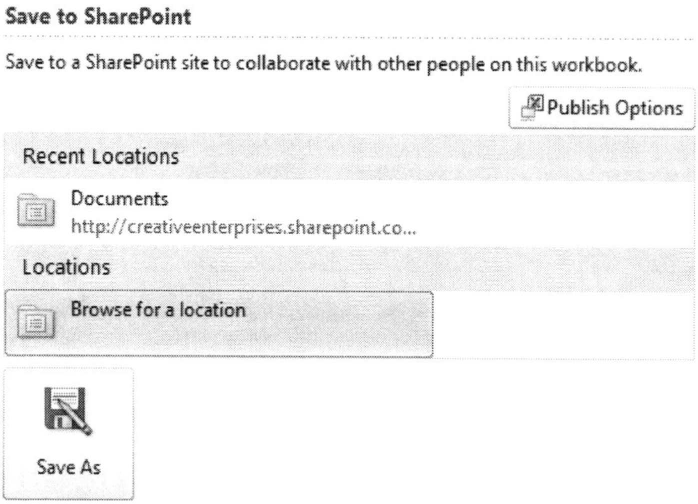

Save to SharePoint

Save to a SharePoint site to collaborate with other people on this workbook.

🗐 Publish Options

Recent Locations

📠 Documents
http://creativeenterprises.sharepoint.co...

Locations

📠 Browse for a location

💾 Save As

Figure 2-46. The Save to SharePoint window

▪ **Note** In Chapter 7 I will demonstrate some of the advanced features of publishing an Excel document to SharePoint using the Publish Options button.

Select "Browse for a location" and click the Save As button. This will launch the File dialog box. Enter the address of the SharePoint site that you want to use. In this scenario, I want to save it to the Small Business site I set up at the beginning of the chapter so I entered `http://www.thecreativepeople.com/teamsite`. If you're not already logged in to this site (and don't have single sign-on configured), you'll see a login page similar to Figure 2-47.

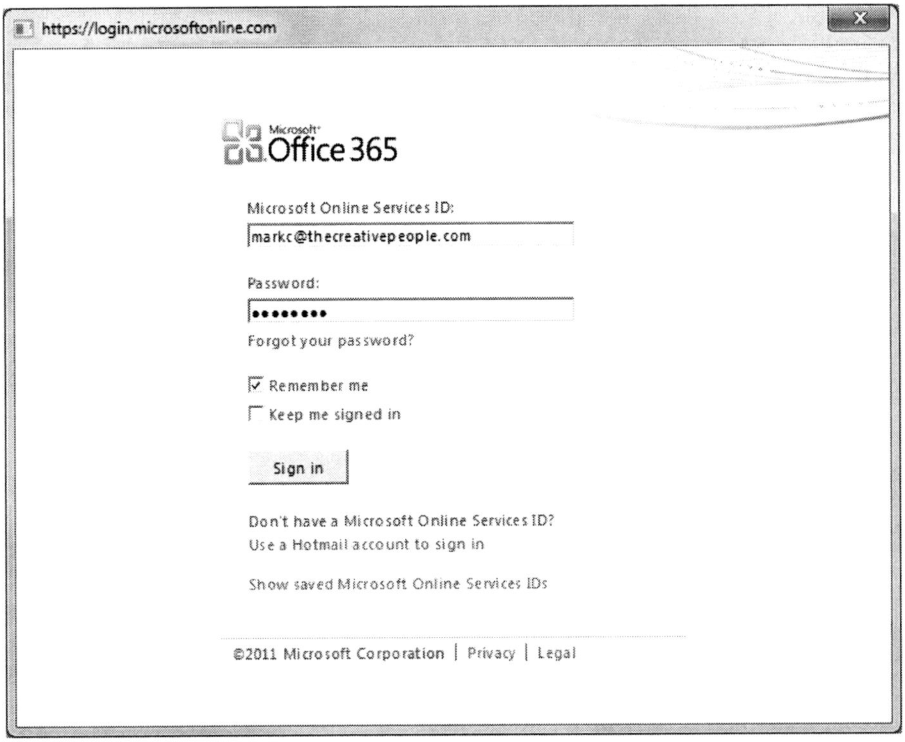

Figure 2-47. *Entering your Office 365 credentials*

Once logged in, the dialog box should display the existing lists and libraries on this site. Select the appropriate library and click the Save button. You'll be prompted to select a content type. Select the appropriate one depending on the type of document you're saving, as demonstrated in Figure 2-48.

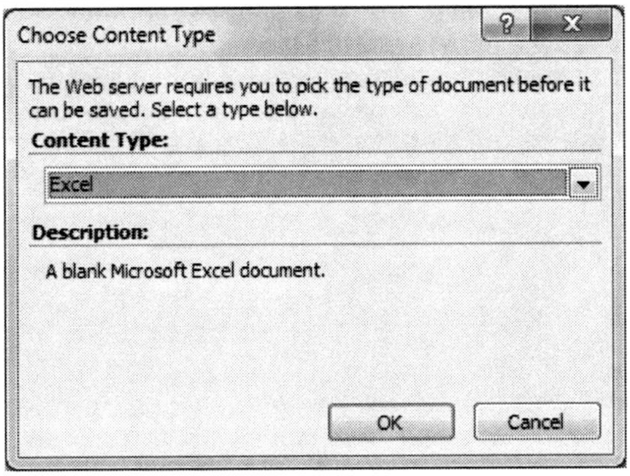

Figure 2-48. *Selecting the content type*

If you go to the Team Site, you'll see the new document included in the selected document library. This is available to anyone who has access to this library.

Office will remember this location. If you save another Office document such as Word or Excel, you should see this library listed in the Recent Locations (see Figure 2-49).

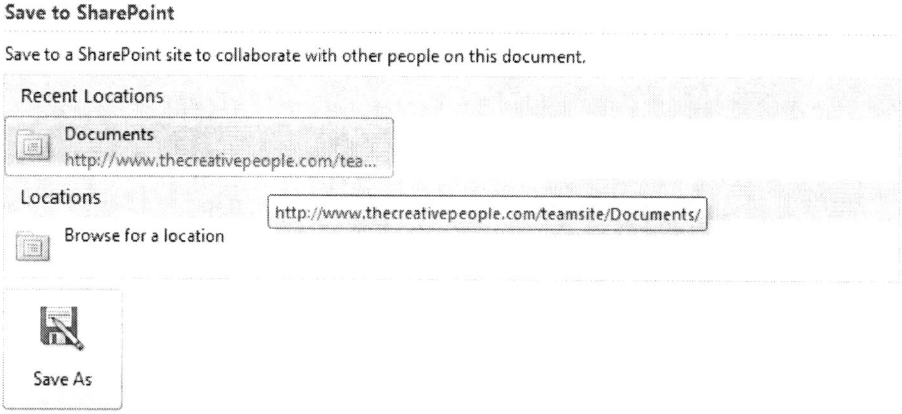

Save to SharePoint

Save to a SharePoint site to collaborate with other people on this document.

Recent Locations

Documents
http://www.thecreativepeople.com/tea...

Locations   http://www.thecreativepeople.com/teamsite/Documents/

Browse for a location

Save As

Figure 2-49. The libray saved as a Recent Location

Whenever you create a new document you can easily save it to the same document library by selecting this location and clicking the Save As button.

Summary

In this chapter I explained some of the advanced configuration options like setting up a custom domain for your account. These features in Office 365 allow you to use it to replace an existing on-premise Office solution. The Enterprise account requires more work to set up but it provides more flexibility in configuring your system.

The Small Business account provides a simple platform that is easy to set up and provides a fully integrated collaboration solution that meets the needs of most small teams. The Enterprise account provides greater flexibility in supporting the more demanding requirements of a larger and more established organization. Fortunately, from a developer's perspective, once configured, both platforms are essentially the same. Your custom applications should generally work well in both configurations. I will explain the few differences throughout this book as you encounter them.

CHAPTER 3

Office 365 Overview

Before you dive into developing some nifty applications on Office 365, I want to first explain what Office 365 is and how it works. If you've made any Office customizations previously, you will likely find that Office 365 works pretty much the same way. I will point out the differences as we go along.

Office 365 Architecture

Office 365 is an interesting collection of both server and client applications that allows you to experience a fully integrated Office solution. This is provided as a hosted solution, which requires little or no IT infrastructure.

Traditional Office Server Environment

To fully explain Office 365, I need to start by describing the traditional on-premise Office server environment. If you had an unlimited budget and installed all of the Office server products, your network might look something like Figure 3-1.

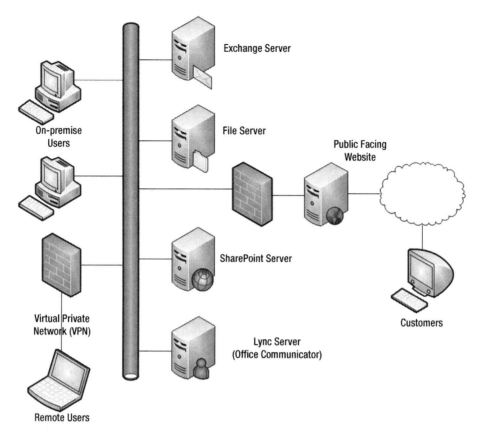

Figure 3-1. The traditional Office server environment

You would have

- An Exchange server to handle incoming and outgoing e-mails.

- One or more file servers for storing documents.

- A SharePoint server for collaboration features such as shared documents and task lists.

- A Lync server to support instant messaging and online meetings.

For larger organizations you would likely cluster these servers to provide redundancy as well as increased capacity. So instead of a single Exchange server, for example, you might have two or more. You can see that the number of servers you would need could become extensive.

You would also have a public-facing web site for your online presence. This would provide basic content for your customers such as details provided on the Contact Us page; your company's mission statement, core values, products or services offered; company history; and so on.

On each of the client workstations you would install the Office client applications such as Outlook, Word, Excel, and One Note. To support remote users, you would need to provide a virtual private network (VPN), which would allow them to connect into your network and work just like the local users.

The Office 365 Environment

All of the functionality described in Figure 3-1 can be easily provisioned on Office 365. The same feature set implemented on Office 365 would look like Figure 3-2.

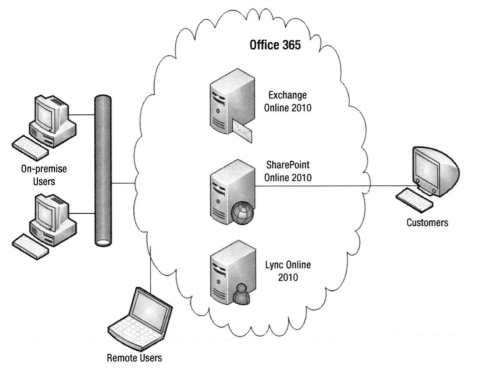

Figure 3-2. The Office 365 solution

The most obvious change in this environment is that the servers have been moved to a hosted environment. Instead of an on-site server running Exchange Server 2010, for example, you'll use Exchange Online 2010, which is hosted on a remote server farm. These online versions of the Office server products are implemented with the same code base as their on-site counterparts. When you set up an Outlook client, you must specify the location of the Exchange server. In an Office 365 environment, you provide the URL that was specified when your Office 365 account was created. The fact that the server is now hosted off-site is essentially transparent. You can send and receive e-mails, check the calendars of team members, and schedule meetings just like you would in a traditional on-site Exchange solution.

The file servers are removed from this diagram because the SharePoint server is used for this purpose. As you'll see throughout this book, the document libraries in SharePoint are a great place to store most of your files for both on-premise and browser-based users.

■ **Note** There are some limitations regarding the size of files you can store on Office 365. For example, the largest file you can upload is 250MB. For more details, see the article at http://office.microsoft.com/en-us/sharepoint-online-enterprise-help/sharepoint-online-software-boundaries-and-limits-HA102694293.aspx.

There are a couple of really nice benefits that are inherent in a cloud-based solution: support for remote users and role-based access. Notice that there is no VPN support in Figure 3-2 because it is not needed. Clients access the Office 365 servers (Exchange Online 2010, SharePoint Online 2010, and Lync Online 2010) through an Internet connection. Office 365 doesn't care whether you are connecting from work, your home, the public library, or your favorite coffee shop.

■ **Note** You will need to be authenticated in order to access these servers, which is typically done through a login and password. If you are on an Active Directory domain, you can synchronize your AD users with Office 365, which will enable a single sign-on to your domain. Once authenticated in AD, you can access Office 365 without supplying your credentials. I explained this further in Chapter 2.

Providing access to remote users in Office 365 is really easy. There's no need for VPN software or firewalls. Best of all, there's no threat of a remote user infecting your network with viruses or malware because they are not connected to your network.

The other inherent benefit is a little more subtle. In the network described in Figure 3-1, a public-facing web site was implemented using a dedicated web server that is separated from your internal network with a firewall. This is a standard practice that provides protection from someone hacking into the web server and accessing the internal network. In Office 365, the public-facing web site is implemented as a SharePoint site hosted on the same SharePoint Online server that is hosting your internal sites.

In a hosted environment, a SharePoint farm will contain potentially hundreds of sites. This is referred to as a *multi-tenant* environment. So how does someone@companyA.com have access to their site while someone@companyB.com does not? Providing separation of customer data is a core competency of hosting services. It is accomplished through advanced technology, including Active Directory, state-of-the-art anti-virus solutions, and continual monitoring and auditing.

As a result, you can create a public-facing SharePoint site that non-authenticated users can access while your internal sites are kept safely hidden. You can create multiple sites and configure each user's access using role-based security.

Office 365 Client Applications

In addition to hosting the server components you can also use the web-based Office applications. Your e-mails, for example, are stored in the Exchange Online server and you can access them either through the Outlook client application or the Outlook Web App that is available in the Office 365 environment. You can configure this differently for each user. You can also use both. A typical configuration would use the Outlook application from an on-site PC while using the web app from a remote laptop or mobile device, as demonstrated in Figure 3-3.

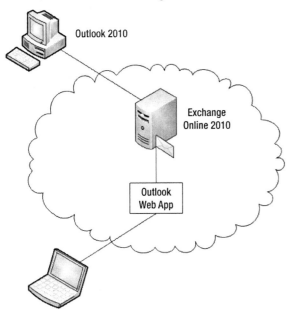

Figure 3-3. Accessing Exchange Online

The key point to remember here is that the data is stored in the cloud. Whichever application you use, it is accessing the same data.

■ **Tip** In Chapter 12, I will show you how to build your own custom e-mail client. While the user experience will be different, the data resides on the server and can still be accessed through the other e-mail client applications.

Office 365 also provides a lightweight web-based version of Word, Excel, OneNote, and PowerPoint. These have a limited feature set compared to their client-based counterparts but read and write files in the same format. This allows you to create, view, and edit a file using the web app and then open it with the client application to perform advanced editing capabilities. Other users can then view the modified documents.

Storing Documents in SharePoint

Office 365 is designed to support browser-only clients. In this configuration there are no local applications; the client is simply a web browser. I demonstrated this in Chapter 1. The benefit of this approach from an IT perspective is that there is no software to install or maintain and no data that needs to be backed up. From an application perspective, this means that all your documents must be stored in the cloud.

Office uses SharePoint Online as the document repository. When you create documents using the web apps, Office 365 automatically stores them in a document library on the SharePoint site. You can set up multiple document libraries configuring different levels of access to each. Libraries can also contain a hierarchy of subfolders so you can keep your documents organized. You can use this structure to control what documents are shared and with whom. Document libraries on SharePoint also provide advanced collaboration features such as checking out files and version tracking.

Storing documents on SharePoint is pretty much a necessity when using the web apps. It is also the recommended approach with full-featured client applications. As I demonstrated in Chapter 2, these applications can be configured to access the document libraries directly, much like the web apps. This provides file sharing, data backup, and a consistent experience across both client and web applications.

Office 365 and Windows Azure

Both Office 365 and Azure are cloud-based offerings from Microsoft, and you might be wondering how they relate to each other. Can they be used together? Well, they were designed to solve two different needs. The US Department of Defense (DoD) makes a similar distinction with the unfortunate terms of *mission critical* and *data processing*. From a military perspective, software that navigates an aircraft or controls a radar system is considered mission critical. Software used to maintain personnel records and process the payroll is called data processing.

In business terms, mission-critical software is used to generate income while data processing is used to run your business. If you sell products online, your shopping cart would be considered mission critical. If you're a plumber you won't have any mission-critical software. In both cases, however, you would use data processing software to manage expenses, pay employees, and file taxes. I say the terms are unfortunate because some might considered getting paid to be mission critical.

The distinction, however, is an important one. The DoD may spend $20 million to develop mission-critical software, but it will expect you to purchase data processing software off the shelf. The reason is obvious; data processing needs are fairly generic. A decent payroll system should work for just about anyone, including the plumber and the e-commerce business. In the mission-critical arena, you'll find many custom applications and companies are usually willing to spend big dollars to get a competitive edge. Data processing software is typically viewed as a commodity. As long as the solution meets their minimum requirements, the lowest cost provider is usually chosen.

I mention this to illustrate the difference between Azure and Office 365. Azure is a platform that is primarily targeted towards mission-critical solutions. It provides an operating system, relational databases, and file storage. You must supply the application(s) that use these resources. In contrast, Office 365 provides a full-featured application suite that offers the features needed by most organizations. You can implement your own customizations, as I will demonstrate throughout this book. If you want to develop a shopping cart, however, you should be using Azure.

Happily, the two platforms can be used together with each one serving the needs it was designed to address. A fully cloud-based infrastructure might look like Figure 3-4.

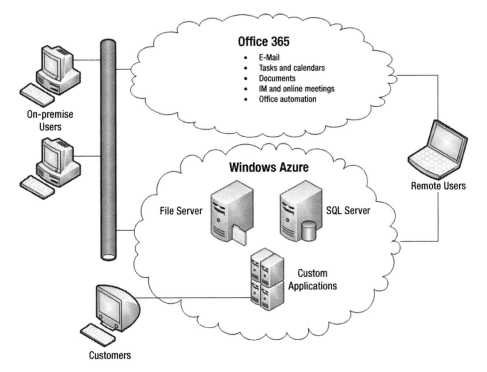

Figure 3-4. Using Office 365 and Azure

The Office 365 platform provides the office automation and team collaboration tools that you'll use to manage your business. Your mission-critical applications, including custom solutions, can be deployed on the Windows Azure platform. Users can then connect to both to perform their daily tasks. In Chapter 8, I'll show you how you can also access data in Azure from within Office 365 using Business Connectivity Services (BCS).

Office 365 Online Servers

The server products (Exchange Online 2010, Lync Online 2010, and SharePoint Online 2010) form the core of the Office 365 platform. As a developer, you will be using and extending the features provided by the servers to implement custom applications. As mentioned, these products are very similar to their on-premise counterparts. The differences stem primarily from the fact that they are running in a multi-tenant environment. It's a little bit like living in a large apartment building; having close neighbors places some restrictions on what you're allowed to do.

I will get into this in much more detail in the rest of this book but I wanted to give you an overview of these products. This will help you see what you're up against as you begin developing on the Office 365 platform.

SharePoint Online 2010

SharePoint is the workhorse of an Office-based collaborative solution. It's a great place to store and share documents, but it's also an effective platform for gathering and analyzing data. Workflows in SharePoint can automate processes and keep data flowing through your organization.

Sandboxed Solutions

There are some significant enhancements in SharePoint 2010, and one of the most significant to the Office 365 platform is the support of sandboxed solutions. Essentially, a sandboxed solution is one that can be deployed to the server by an end user without requiring administrative access. While that may not sound like a big deal, consider the other side of that coin. The SharePoint administrators who are responsible for keeping the system running smoothly have just opened up a door for rogue users to do whatever they want. To make this work, these administrators need some assurances, primarily that these end-user–deployed solutions can't negatively affect the system or other solutions running on it.

To protect the rest of the system from badly behaved applications, sandboxed solutions have certain limitations, including:

- Scoped access to the SharePoint object model.

- Limited access to external (non-SharePoint) resources such as the file system based on Code Access Security (CAS) policies.

- No code-based workflows, which use Workflow Foundation in .NET 3.5.

These restrictions provide isolation of each solution so one solution is not negatively affected by another.

░ **Note** These restrictions apply to code that runs on the server, which is where most SharePoint applications are executed. As I will demonstrate later in this book, you can write client-side code using Java or Silverlight, which is not subject to these limitations.

I will now explain the details of sandboxed solutions as this has a profound effect on how these solutions are developed and deployed. You will create sandboxed solutions starting with Chapter 9.

Scoped Access to the SharePoint Object Model

Code in a sandboxed solution runs with only partial trust, which restricts access to farm or web app features. In contrast, a farm solution has full access to the entire SharePoint object model. This object model provides the ability to access and manipulate all of the SharePoint objects. These objects are arranged in a hierarchical fashion, as illustrated in Figure 3-5.

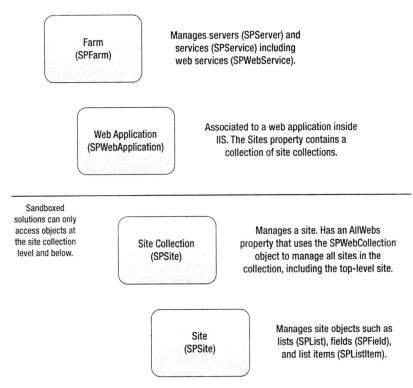

Manages servers (SPServer) and services (SPService) including web services (SPWebService).

Associated to a web application inside IIS. The Sites property contains a collection of site collections.

Sandboxed solutions can only access objects at the site collection level and below.

Manages a site. Has an AllWebs property that uses the SPWebCollection object to manage all sites in the collection, including the top-level site.

Manages site objects such as lists (SPList), fields (SPField), and list items (SPListItem).

Figure 3-5. SharePoint Object Model hierarchy

In Office 365, the SharePoint farm and web application are already set up so you don't need to configure or maintain any of the features defined at these levels of the hierarchy. You will, however, create sites as well as all the items below this, such as lists and list items. Sandboxed solutions can access the object model at the site collection level and below. Access to the farm or web application is blocked since this would affect other solutions hosted on the same SharePoint farm.

Executing in a Sandboxed Environment

In a farm solution, requests run under the IIS worker process just like most web applications. They can run with elevated privileges and access the entire object model. With a sandboxed solution, however, this is locked down. To enforce this, requests go through a few extra layers, as shown in Figure 3-6.

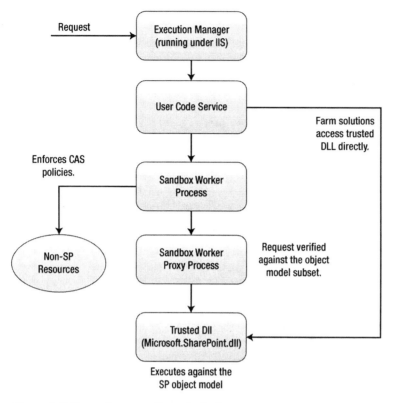

Figure 3-6. Executing a sandboxed solution

When a request is executed in the SharePoint server, it is passed to the User Code Service (SPUCHostService.exe). In a farm solution, this calls the SharePoint DLL (Microsoft.SharePoint.dll) directly. In a sandboxed solution, however, this is passed to the Sandbox Worker Process (SPUCWorkerProcess.exe). This provides two important functions. First, requests for any non-SharePoint resources such as the file system are filtered through the CAS policy. The request is rejected if the needed access is not allowed. Secondly, it verifies that the SharePoint objects being used are within the scope allowed for sandboxed solutions. Calls that manipulate the SPFarm object, for example, will be blocked.

■ **Note** There is a good article at http://msdn.microsoft.com/en-us/library/gg552610.aspx#BKMK_ExecutionModel that explains some of the under-the-cover details of SharePoint Server 2010.

An important point to remember here is that these restrictions are enforced at runtime. Applications that don't conform to the limitations of sandboxed solutions will generate runtime errors.

Resource Restrictions

Remember those assurances I mentioned? Well, in addition to behaving properly (following the rules), administrators need to ensure that a poorly written solution doesn't consume too many system resources. A third function of this execution model is to monitor the resource utilization and to block requests from a solution that exceeds the specified thresholds.

Resource usage is defined by a complex model that consists of three sets of rules based on what is being penalized (the request, the process, or the site collection). The first is rather simple: any request that takes too long to complete is penalized by being terminated.

For the other two types (process and site collection), there are 15 system resources that are monitored including CPU execution time, thread count, query time, and unhandled exception count. For each of these, there is a maximum amount allowed. If a request exceeds any one of these limits, the process is terminated. This affects all solutions running on that process.

For the final rule, resources points are accumulated for each site collection. Each of the 15 resource metrics defines a minimum amount that will trigger the allocation of a resource point. They also define the number of points assigned for each unit of resource usage. For example, a point is added for every 200 seconds of CPU execution time. If a site collection exceeds its allowed points, the site collection is terminated for the remainder of the day. The accumulators are reset daily.

■ **Note** For more information on resource limits, see the article at `http://msdn.microsoft.com/en-us/library/gg615462.aspx`.

Deploying SharePoint Solutions

Now that I've explained the limitations of sandboxed solutions and how they are implemented, let me show you the benefit of this approach. A SharePoint solution is packaged as a file with a `.wsp` extension. These solution packages can be simply uploaded to your SharePoint site just like you would a shared document.

From the top-level site in your site collection, you can display the Solution Gallery shown in Figure 3-7.

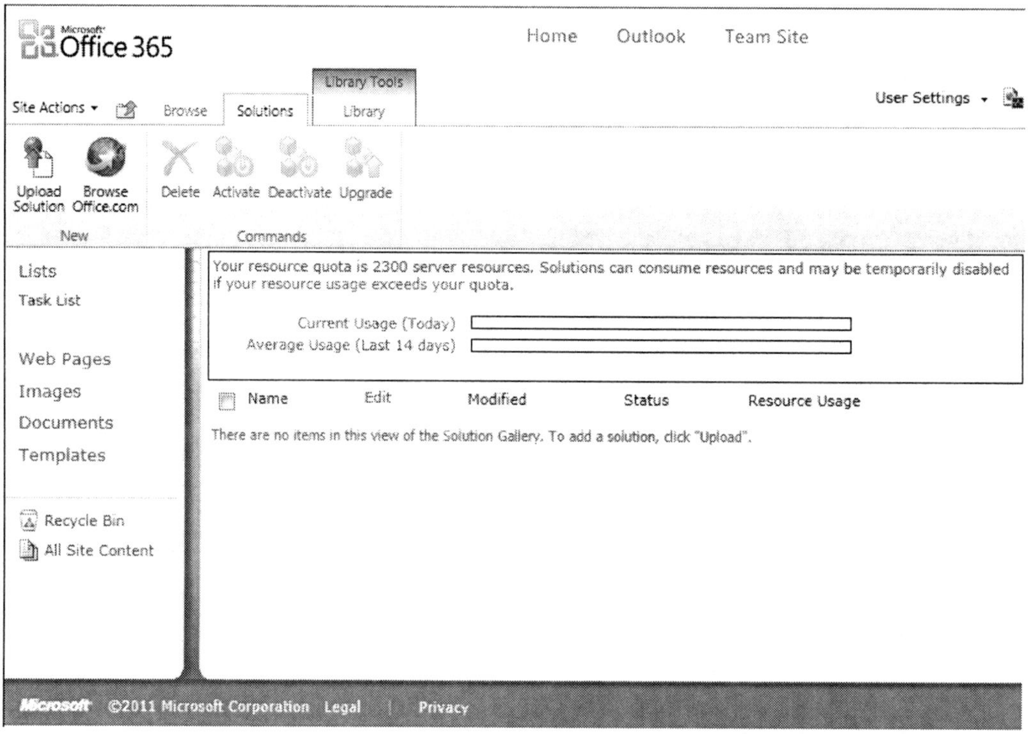

Figure 3-7. The Solution Gallery

In this case, the gallery is empty because there are no user solutions installed. To upload a new solution, click the Upload Solution button in the ribbon, which will display the Upload Solution dialog box shown in Figure 3-8.

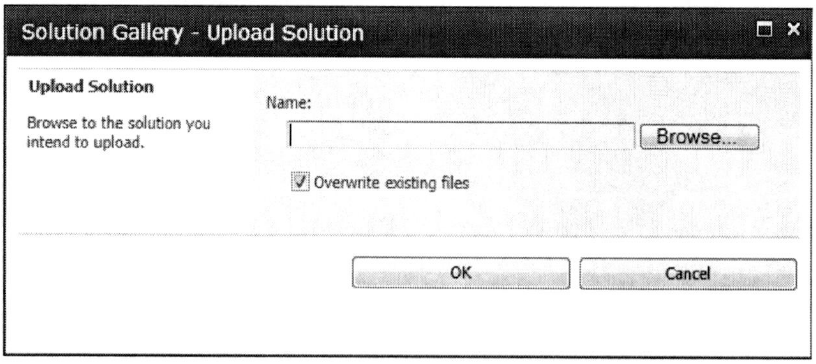

Figure 3-8. The Upload Solution dialog box

Throughout this book, you will be developing solution packages and loading them to your SharePoint Online server. You can also download solutions from Office.com by clicking the "Browse Office.com" button in the ribbon. For this demonstration, I will download a solution from Office.com. I have selected the Classroom and Study Group solution, as shown in Figure 3-9.

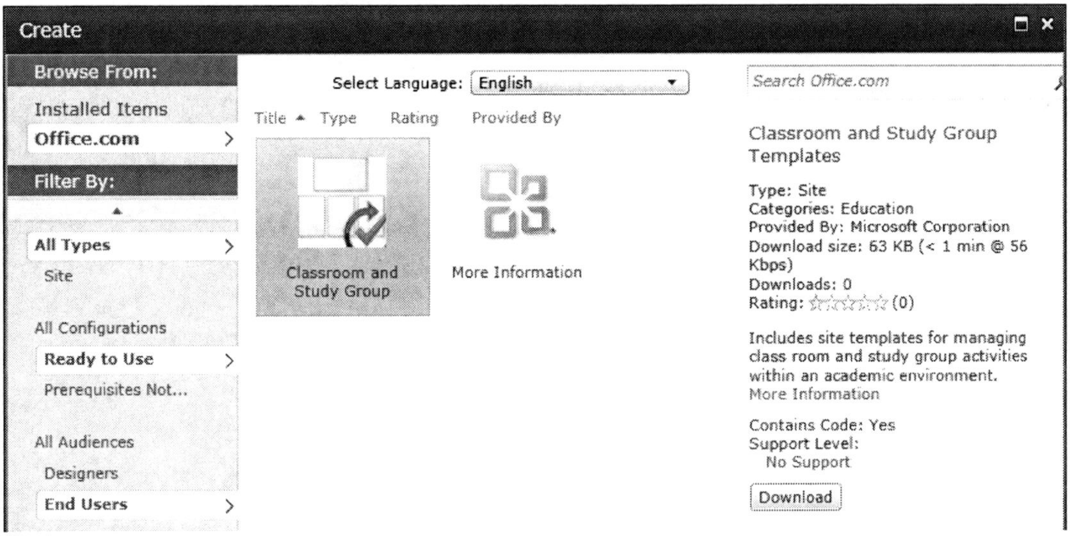

Figure 3-9. Selecting the Classroom and Study Group solution

After clicking the Download button, the solution will be uploaded to your site and activated. In this case, the solution contains site templates so the SharePoint site was not affected. However, if you create a new site in your site collection, you will now have two additional templates to choose from, as shown in Figure 3-10.

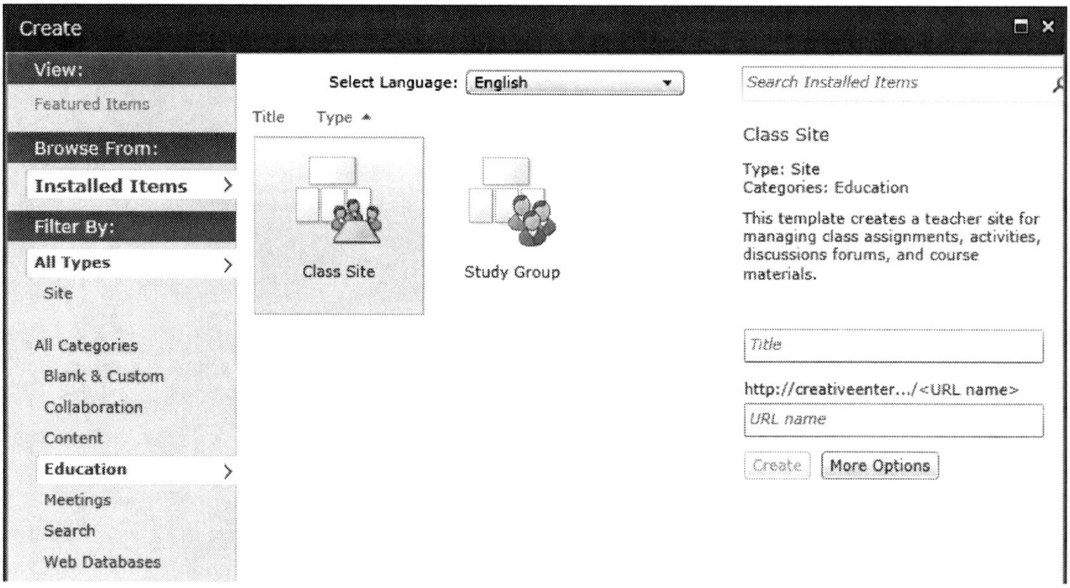

Figure 3-10. Two additional site templates

If you create a new site using the Class Site template, you will have a new site that looks like Figure 3-11.

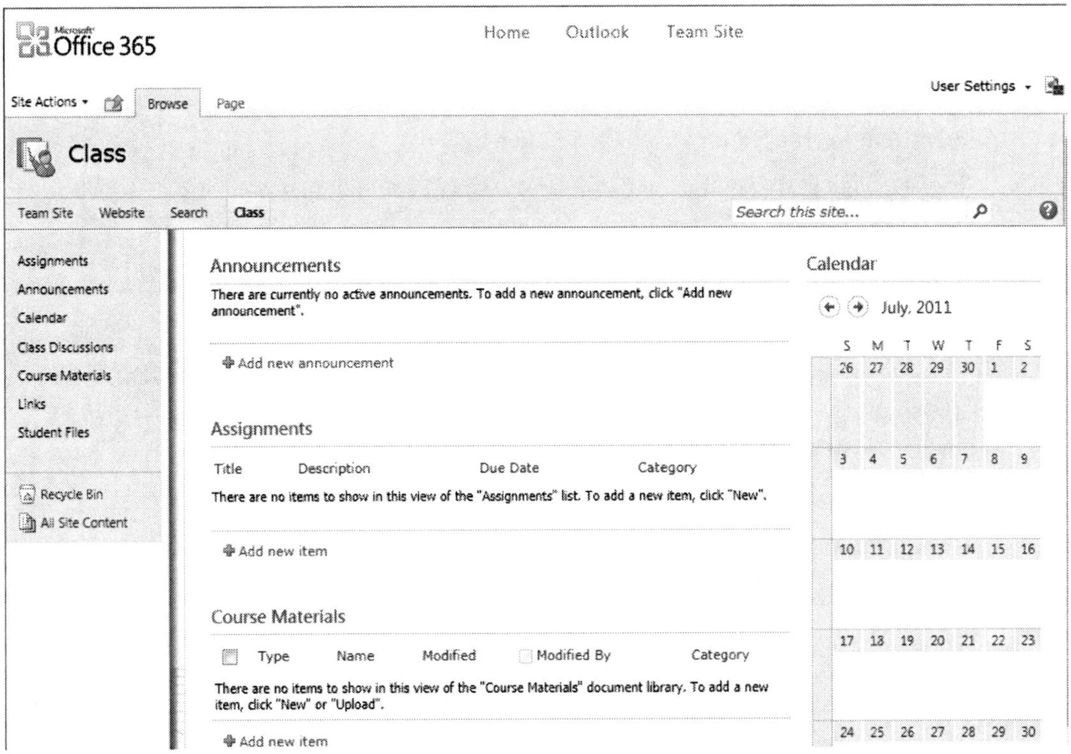

Figure 3-11. The new Class site

You can see how easy it is to load and use a custom solution without requiring administrative access. If you go back to the Solution Gallery, you can see the new solution and how many resource units have been expended so far (see Figure 3-12).

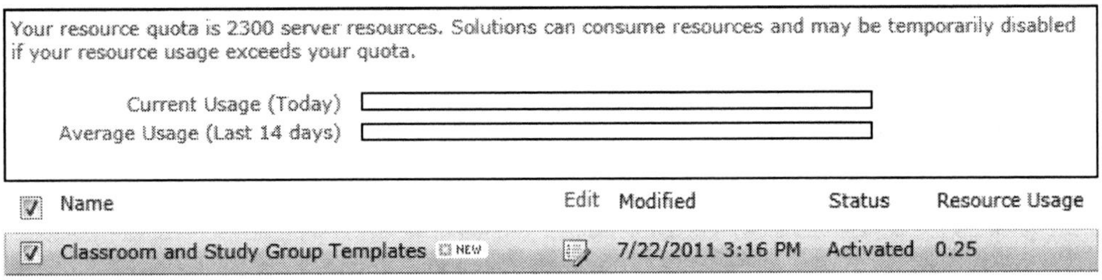

Figure 3-12. The updated Solution Gallery

Deploying a solution package to SharePoint requires both uploading and activating. The following terms are used to describe the steps of this process:

- **Upload** adds the solution to the Solution Gallery. This requires the user to have admin privileges to the site collection.

- **Activation** Deploys files and registers event receivers. Site collection features are also activated; Site features, however, must be individually activated on each site.

- **Deactivation** disables the features.

- **Delete** removes the features from the Solution Gallery.

- **Upgrade** deploys the solution with the same ID but a different name, and new features will be activated.

Developing Solutions in Visual Studio 2010

Visual Studio 2010 includes some significant enhancements to facilitate SharePoint development. I will demonstrate these features in later chapters. Here is a short list of some of the most important ones:

- **IntelliSense**: If you specify a sandboxed solution when creating a new project, IntelliSense will automatically limit your access to SharePoint objects to only those that are compatible with sandboxed solutions (at the site collection level and below).

- **Solution Packaging**: Creates solution package (.wsp) files that are ready for easy upload and activation.

- **F5 Debugging**: After developing your solution, just press F5 to build, deploy, and debug your code. This requires a local SharePoint instance for debugging.

■ **Tip** You should also download the Power Tools, which are available from at
`http://visualstudiogallery.msdn.microsoft.com/8e602a8c-6714-4549-9e95-f3700344b0d9`. This provides an additional item template for creating a Visual Web Part that is compatible with sandboxed solutions. This also provides compile-time errors when object model members are accessed that are not compatible with sandboxed solutions.

Your development environment must include a local instance of SharePoint Server 2010. This will provide a convenient way to develop and debug your solutions before deploying them to the cloud. This will require a 64-bit OS but can run on Windows 7 or even Vista. As long as your development workstation has a 64-bit OS, you can install SharePoint server on your workstation. A server-based SharePoint site is fine as long as it is on-premise (not cloud-based). The recommended development and deployment approach is shown in Figure 3-13.

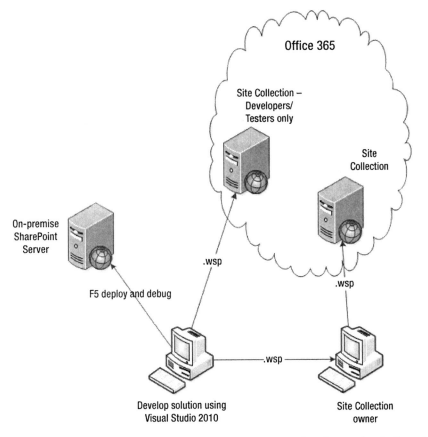

Figure 3-13. Recommended development environment for SharePoint Online 2010

You use Visual Studio to build the solution and automatically deploy and debug it from within the IDE. When you have finished unit testing, you then upload the solution to a special site collection on Office 365 that is used for development and testing. The test team then accesses the solution there and performs end user testing. Once it has been tested, the site collection owner can deploy the solution to the live SharePoint site.

Customization Scenarios

SharePoint Online provides a variety of ways develop custom solutions. I will explain each of these in detail throughout this book with practical examples that you can follow. If you have experience developing in SharePoint, you'll find that SharePoint Online 2010 is very familiar. The techniques I'll cover include:

- **Native development**: You can create custom lists and document libraries using the UI provided within SharePoint online.

- **SharePoint Designer**: This is a power tool for editing SharePoint sites. SharePoint Designer allows you to create and edit SharePoint objects such as lists, fields, and content types.

- **Declarative Workflows**: I mentioned earlier that you can't create code-based workflows (using WF in .NET 3.5). However, you can create declarative workflows using SharePoint Designer. You can also design a workflow using Visio, import it into your SharePoint site, and then use SharePoint Designer to implement it. You can create custom actions and also use InfoPath 2010 to create custom workflow forms.

- **Access Web Databases**: You can create a web database in Access 2010, including tables, forms, queries, and reports, and then export the database to SharePoint Online. This is a great way to quickly implement a sophisticated web application.

- **Excel Services**: SharePoint Online allows you to expose an Excel spreadsheet or a subset of one on your SharePoint site.

- **Visual Studio**: You can also develop solutions using Visual Studio 2010. This allows you to access the SharePoint object model using familiar C# syntax. You can also use Linq to SharePoint to retrieve and manipulate your lists and list items. Visual Studio 2010 provides project items for creating content types, lists, and Web Parts. These can be verified using standard F5 debugging. Your project can be packaged into a solution package (.wsp) for easy deployment.

- **Client Application**: You can also create a rich user experience by writing client-side code using technology such as Silverlight or Java.

Exchange Online 2010

Exchange Online 2010 exposes its features to client applications through a set of web services known as Exchange Web Services (EWS). You can use these web services by adding a service reference to the EWS. Visual Studio will then generate a set of proxy classes that you'll use to communicate with the web service. However, Exchange Online also provides a managed API that provides an easier and more intuitive way to use EWS. So your application can either call the web service directly or use the managed API, as shown in Figure 3-14.

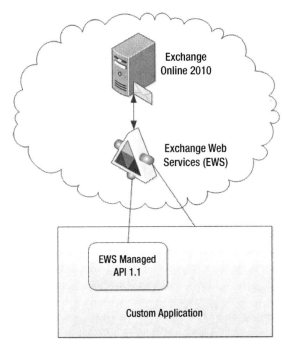

Figure 3-14. Using the Exchange Web Services (EWS)

Customization Scenarios

Exchange Online 2010 exposes many features through EWS to client applications such as Outlook and Outlook Web App. Your custom application can use these as well. Some of the more common ways you can integrate Exchange functionality in your application include:

- Accessing the mailbox items stored in Exchange. Think of Exchange as a specialized database containing objects such as e-mails, appointments, tasks, and contacts, which are organized in a hierarchy of folders. You can view, modify, and create these objects programmatically through EWS or the managed API.

- Availability is another Exchange feature that allows you to see when someone (or a group of people) will be available based on their calendars. You can also use this feature to suggest windows when the specified group of people and resources will be available.

- Exchange provides notifications when certain events occur, such as the arrival of a new message. Your custom application can receive these notifications and take appropriate actions.

Using Autodiscover

To optimize availability and capacity, especially in a cloud-based solution, the specific URL of the appropriate EWS can be dynamic. For this reason you should never hard-code this URL. Instead, when connecting to Exchange, you'll use a process called *autodiscover*. In this process, the managed API performs some handshaking with the Exchange Online servers to determine the optimum path to associated server, as illustrated in Figure 3-15.

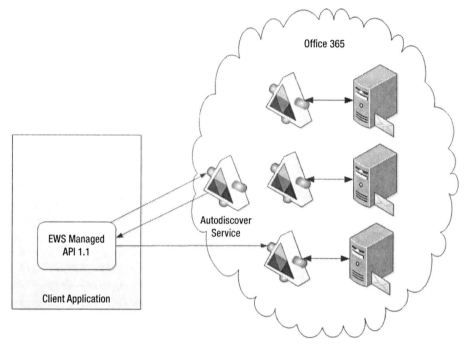

Figure 3-15. The autodiscover process

The managed API makes a request to the autodiscover service on Office 365. Through a series of callbacks, the URL to the appropriate web service is returned. The API then connects to the specified web server.

Lync Online 2010

Lync provides the ability for various types of *conversations* between two or more individuals. A conversation can include one or more of the following types (referred to as *modality*):

- Instant Message

- Audio

- Video

- Online meeting

- Desktop sharing
- File transfer

Lync Architecture

Lync Online 2010 provides the server component and is hosted by the Office 365 platform. The Lync 2010 Client must be installed on each device that will participate in a conversation. The overall architecture is shown in Figure 3-16.

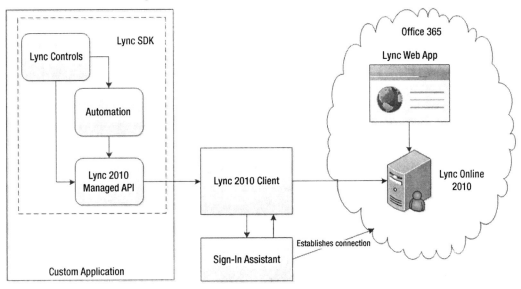

Figure 3-16. Lync architecture

The Lync 2010 client application controls the connection to the Lync Online 2010 server. It uses the Online Services Sign-In Assistant to provide the credentials to the server and establish the connection. In many cases, the Sign-In Assistant will use the current user's login credentials if this has been configured or cached credentials if enabled. In this case, this application performs its role in the background. If credentials are needed, it will display a window and prompt the user for a login and password.

Office 365 also provides a Lync Web App, which allows users to participate in an online meeting without needing to install the Lync Online client application. This does not include the full set of features that are provided by the Lync 2010 client application. This is a solution specific to online meetings.

⁣ **Note** For more information about how Lync Online 2010 can be used without the Lync 2010 client application, check out the article at http://blogs.technet.com/b/jenstr/archive/2010/11/30/launching-lync-web-app.aspx. It explains the process used by the web page to find a suitable client application.

Lync SDK

The Lync SDK provides some really useful tools for developing custom applications that use Lync. The SDK consists of three components.

- **Lync 2010 Managed API**: A powerful yet easy-to-use API that allows your custom application to use the features provided by the Lync 2010 client application.

- **Automation library**: Provides the ability to launch and manage a conversation. This is explained in more detail later in this chapter.

- **Lync controls**: A set of controls that can be dropped directly on your application, much like you would a TextBox or ComboBox control. The available controls include:

  - Presence indicator

  - Contact search results

  - Contact list

  - Custom contact list

  - Contact information

  - Start IM or Audio Call controls

The Lync controls also support contextual conversations, as I will explain later. This allows data from your applications to be passed into the conversation.

Automation

The Automation library, which is part of the Lync SDK, provides an easy way to embed Lync functionality in your custom application. You use the API to instruct the Lync 2010 client application to start a particular type of conversation. This will launch a new window that displays and manages that conversation. This is depicted in Figure 3-17.

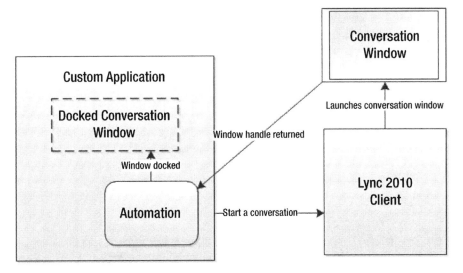

Figure 3-17. Using Lync automation

A handle to the new window is returned to your custom application so you can control the conversation in your code. You can also dock the new window inside your application's window so the UI will be completely contained by your application.

Contextual Conversations

Lync allows you to embed information into a conversation to help the participants better understand the context of your question. For example, if you wanted to ask a colleague about a particular product, the initial message can contain details of that product. There are two ways to do this.

- Launch Link allows you to include a link to launch an application from the conversation window. In this example, the link could load an inventory application and pre-load the specific product.

- Context Window Extensibility (CWE) allows you to host Silverlight application code inside the conversation window. In this case, this application could display details of the product in question.

You can use both of these techniques in the same conversation. You can include the details directly in the conversation window with a link to launch the application. The recipient can then view the details already provided but also have the option to use the application to browse for more information.

This requires that both the Silverlight application and the launched applications be configured with Lync using the Windows Registry. This is needed to prevent executing untrusted applications.

Unsupported Features

There are a couple of features in Lync Server 2010 that are not currently available in Lync Online 2010. These include:

- UCMA (Unified Communications Managed API)
- PSTN calls to an external number

These are server-side features that are locked down primarily due to the multi-tenancy of the Lync Online platform.

Summary

The Office 365 platform is a fully integrated Office solution that provides an enormous amount of functionality right out of the box. It provides the following cloud-based services:

- SharePoint Online
- Exchange Online
- Lync Online

Each of these services was designed to expose its feature to custom applications. By utilizing this functionality, you can quickly implement some very useful custom applications. Throughout the remainder of this book I will be demonstrating ways to create custom Office 365 solutions.

PART 2

Creating SharePoint Online Solutions

In this section, you'll learn several techniques for customizing a SharePoint solution that do not require coding. Using an impressive collection of applications such as SharePoint Designer, Visio, Access, Excel, and InfoPath you will see just how easy it is to create non-code customizations.

In Chapter 4, you will explore the capabilities within the native SharePoint UI for creating and modifying SharePoint sites. I will also provide a brief introduction to SharePoint Designer and then demonstrate the features of the Website Design Tool for building great looking public-facing web sites.

In Chapter 5, you will create a complete workflow solution using Visio to design the overall process, SharePoint Designer to implement the declarative workflow, and InfoPath to create custom forms.

Chapter 6 demonstrates how to create a web database using Access. I will show you how to download a template and publish the Access database to your SharePoint site.

Then, in Chapter 7, you will implement several useful techniques using Excel. These techniques including publishing spreadsheets and using the Excel REST services.

In Chapter 8, you will use the Business Connectivity Services (BCS) to access external data using web services. You will host a simple web service on Azure and then map that service to an external list in SharePoint. The external data can then be used just as if it were a native list in SharePoint.

CHAPTER 4

Customizing SharePoint

There are several ways to create and modify a SharePoint site. This chapter demonstrates the authoring tools that are available for code-less implementations.

- The SharePoint UI allows power users to create their own sites and modify existing sites.

- SharePoint Designer provides a more developer-oriented design experience and can implement more advanced features such as workflow (explained further in Chapter 5).

- Web Site Design Tool (only available for public-facing web sites) provides an easy-to-use design experience for content-based web sites.

You can quickly create a powerful SharePoint solution using these tools.

Note In this chapter you will be using the Small Business account (P1 plan) that you set up in Chapter 1. If you're using an Enterprise account, this navigation may vary slightly from the examples presented here.

Creating a Site with the SharePoint UI

SharePoint provides a facility for creating and customizing a site using the normal SharePoint user interface. This allows end users (or at least power users) to implement their site without requiring a developer or IT support. I will show you how to use this to create a new site based on an existing site template. You will also create a custom list and several custom views.

Creating a New Site

A SharePoint site has a collection of lists and document libraries, which contain the data that is stored and manipulated on the site. A site can include one or more web pages that can contain static text, Web Parts, or forms. When creating a SharePoint site you will need to design these elements that make up the content of the web site.

Using a Site Template

Using an existing site template is the easiest way to create a new site. The template defines the lists, document libraries, and other assets that should be included in the site. SharePoint Online 2010 provides a variety of templates. The default Team Site that was set up for you was created using one of these templates. You can also download templates from the web or create your own template.

1. Go to the default Team Site that was created when the Office 365 account was set up. From the Site Actions menu, click the New Site link, which will display the Create dialog shown in Figure 4-1.

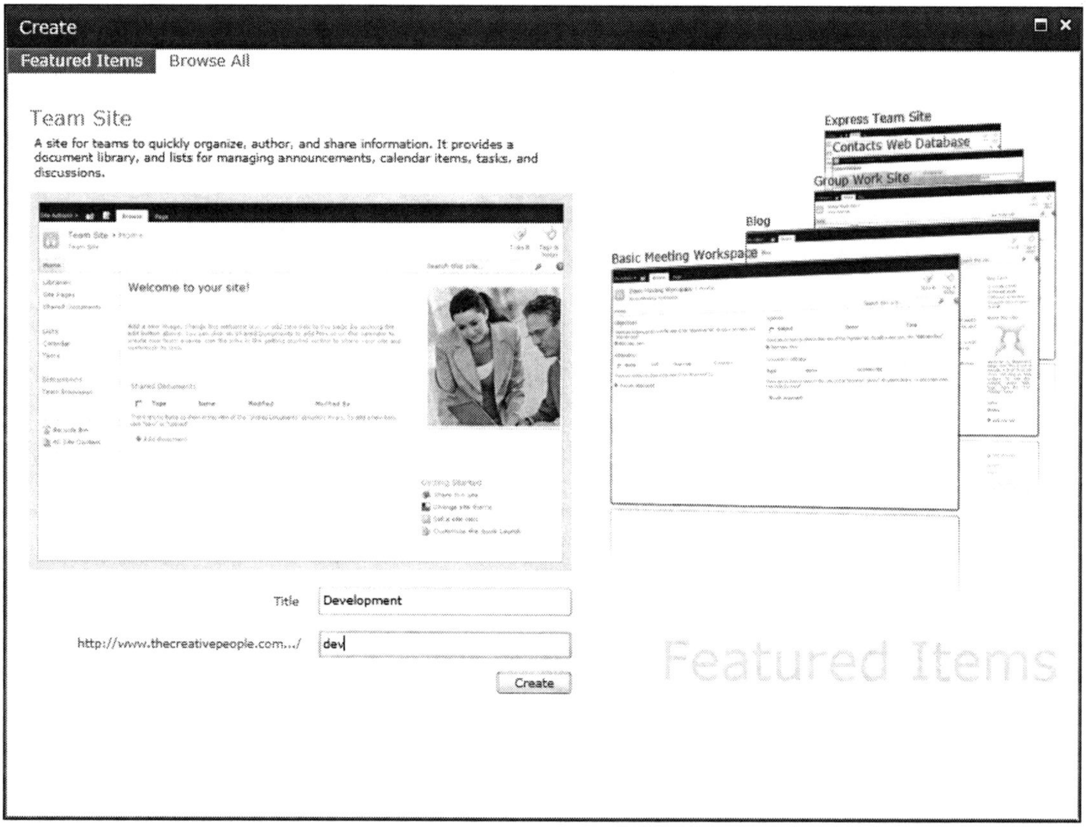

Figure 4-1. Creating a new site using a featured template

2. The Create dialog box shows the Featured Items tab that contains the most popular site templates. You can select one of the images on the right-hand side and it will be displayed on the left-hand side. This allows you to see a simple preview of each template. If you want to use one of these templates with its default options, you can select it, enter a title and URL, and click the Create button.

3. If you want to choose a different template or specify the template options, select the Browse All tab. Select this now to display the standard Create dialog box, which offers many more templates. Select the Team Site template and enter a title and URL, as shown in Figure 4-2.

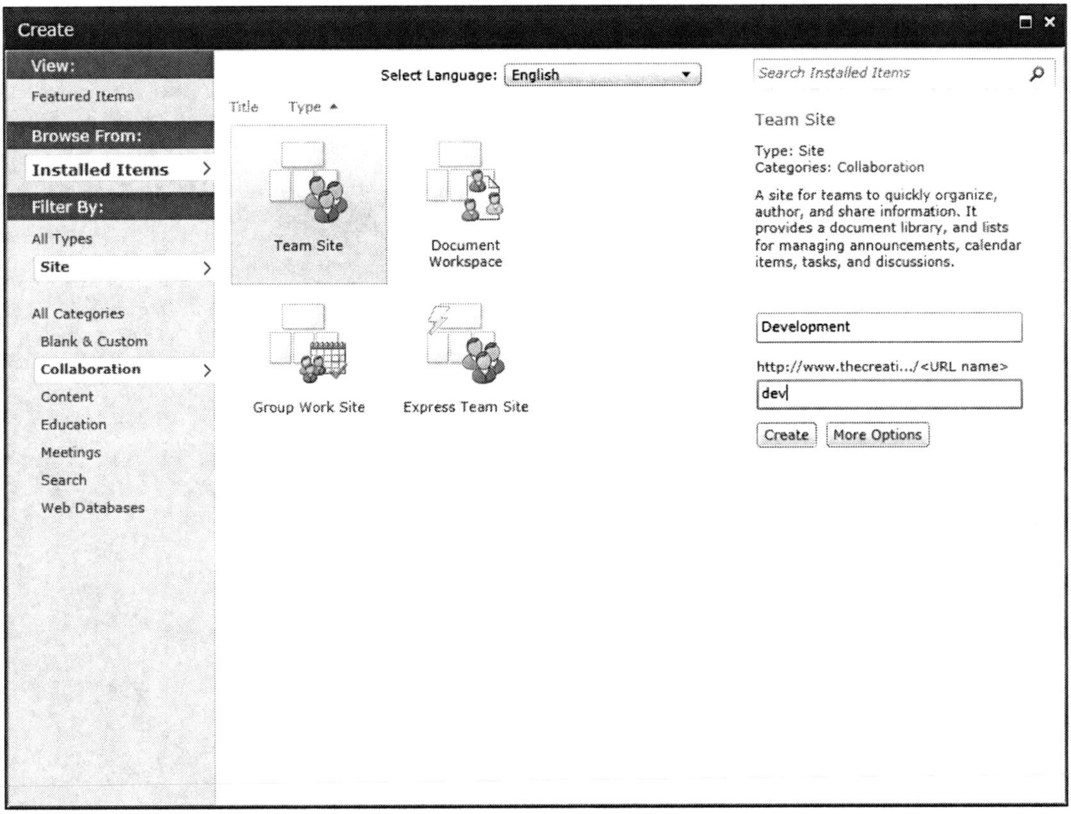

Figure 4-2. Using the standard Create dialog box

4. Click the More Options button, which will display a dialog box that allows you to configure some advanced options. A portion of this form is shown in Figure 4-3.

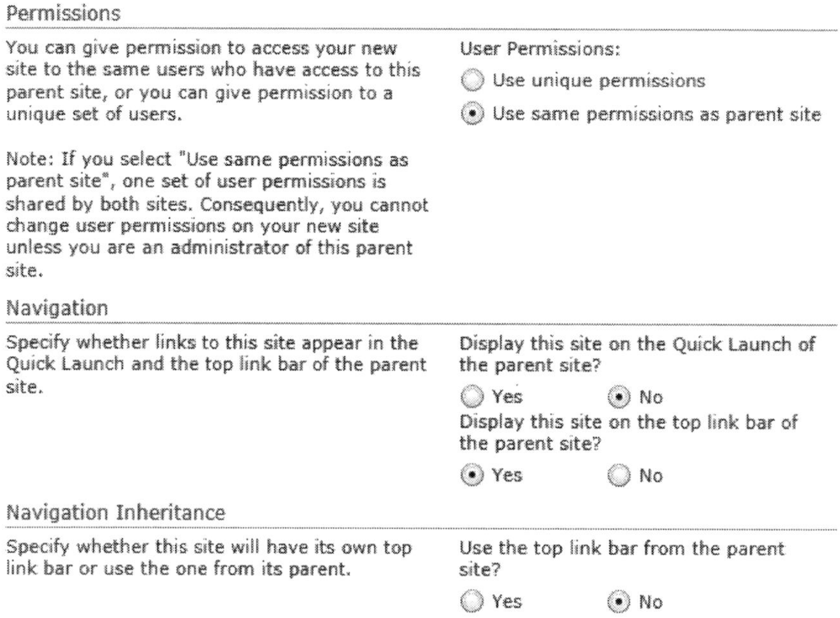

Permissions

You can give permission to access your new site to the same users who have access to this parent site, or you can give permission to a unique set of users.

Note: If you select "Use same permissions as parent site", one set of user permissions is shared by both sites. Consequently, you cannot change user permissions on your new site unless you are an administrator of this parent site.

User Permissions:

○ Use unique permissions
● Use same permissions as parent site

Navigation

Specify whether links to this site appear in the Quick Launch and the top link bar of the parent site.

Display this site on the Quick Launch of the parent site?

○ Yes   ● No

Display this site on the top link bar of the parent site?

● Yes   ○ No

Navigation Inheritance

Specify whether this site will have its own top link bar or use the one from its parent.

Use the top link bar from the parent site?

○ Yes   ● No

Figure 4-3. Specifying advanced options

All of the default values are fine for this site but I wanted you to see the available options. Since you started on the Team Site, the new site will be created as a child (or sub) site of the Team Site. You can control whether permissions are inherited and what links are available for navigating to it.

Exploring the New Site

After creating the new site, its default page should be displayed. Click the Lists link to see the lists that were created as defined by the site template (see Figure 4-4).

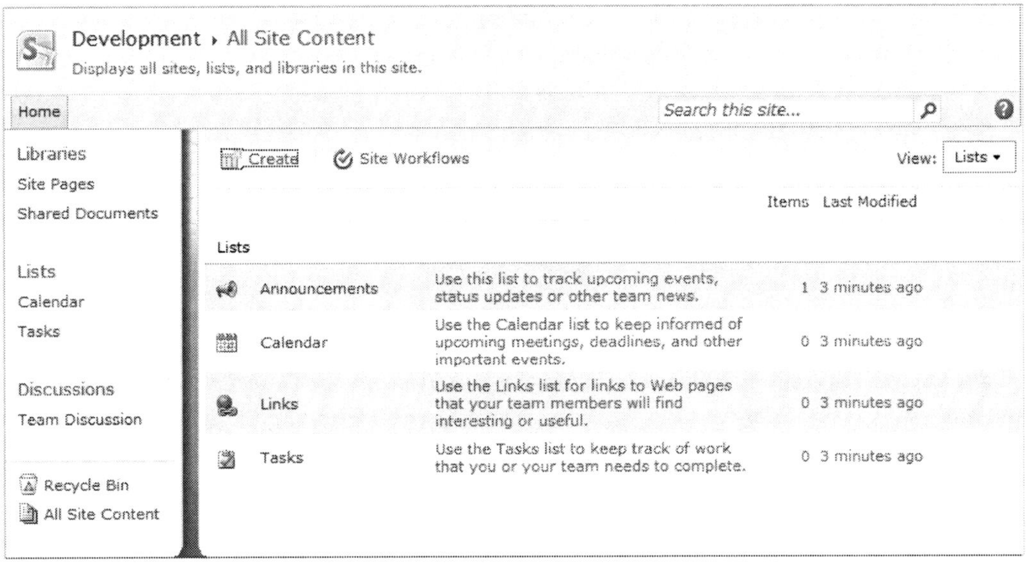

Figure 4-4. *The lists created by the Team Site template*

The Team Site template created four lists.

- **Announcements:** This is a fairly simple list where each item includes a title and a body where you can specify the text of the announcement. Each item has an expiration date so old items are automatically hidden.

- **Calendar:** This is a shared calendar for your team. You can enter meetings, milestones, and other events. You can also use this to track when people are unavailable, such as during a vacation.

- **Links:** As the title suggests, use this list to store useful links to internal or external web sites. You can use other types as links, such as mailto or file.

- **Tasks:** This list contains user tasks that are tracked, assigned, and worked on by your team. This is a key component of SharePoint workflows, which I will explain in Chapter 5.

The Team Site template also created several document libraries.

- **Shared Documents:** Use this to store documents that should be available to your team; this can include both documents created by your team or reference documents that your team may use.

- **Site Assets:** This contains images or other types of media used by other pages in your SharePoint site.

- **Site Pages:** This contains the web pages included in your SharePoint site. The Team Site template generates two initial pages: "Home" and "How To Use This Library."

The Team Site template also created a Team Discussion list. Use this to store comments and track the conversation history.

Creating a Custom List

Now you'll create a new list that will be used to record requests that are sent to your team. This list will record details of each request, such as the current status, who it is assigned to, and when it was completed.

A list contains a collection of fields that define the data elements supported for each item in the list. You can also define other list attributes such as views, workflows, and forms.

■ **Note** The terms *field* and *column* are often used interchangeably. The SharePoint object model that you will use in later chapters has an SPField class that represents a column definition. Technically, a field is a column definition; when that field has been included in a list, that instance is referred to as a column. However, even SharePoint doesn't follow this terminology consistently. In the SharePoint UI, fields and columns are both called columns.

Using a List Template

Just like with sites, you'll use a template to create a list. The template defines the columns and other attributes of the list.

1. From the All Site Content page shown in Figure 4-4, click the Create link. This will display the Create dialog box.

2. Filter the items to only show List templates. You can also filter the items by category to further narrow down the templates that are displayed.

■ **Tip** You'll notice that the lists that were created by the Team Site template, such as Announcements and Calendar, are listed here as well. You could have created a blank site and then added each of these lists separately. Also, using these lists templates, you can add these same lists to an existing site.

---

3. Select the Custom List template and enter **Requests** for the name, as shown in Figure 4-5, and click the Create button. This template creates a blank list; you can then specify the fields that you want included in your list.

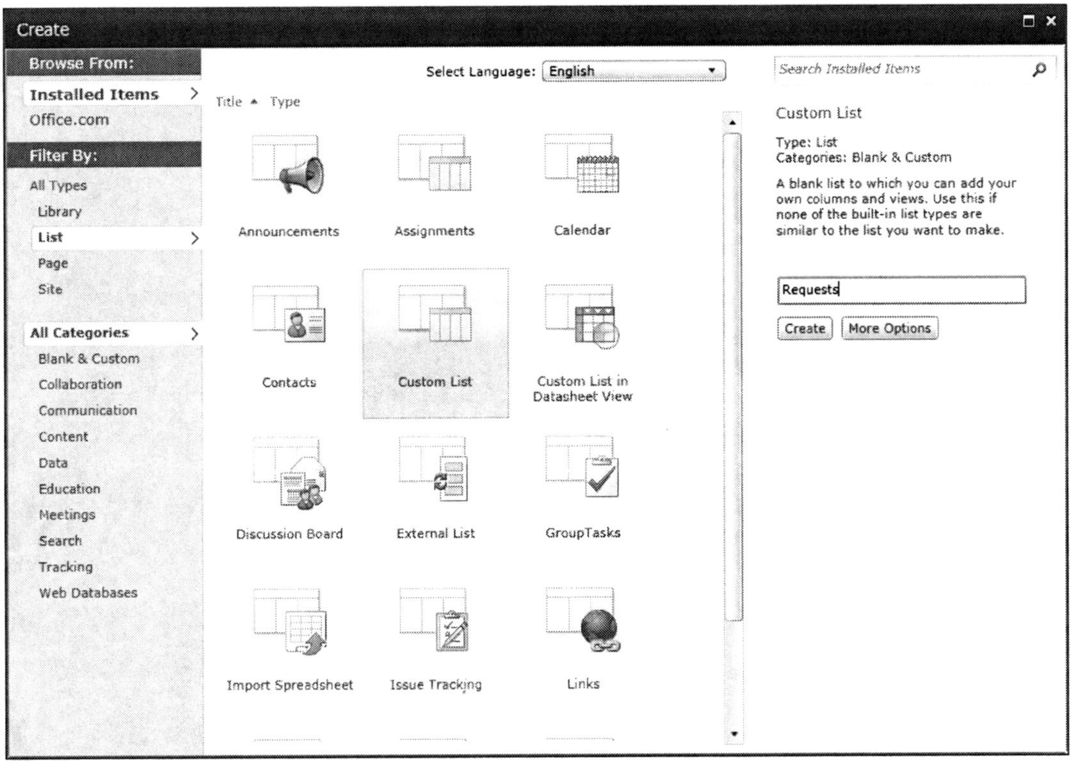

Figure 4-5. Adding a custom list

■ **Note** By convention, the name of a list describes the content of the list. This means that the name is usually plural because the Requests list, for example, will usually contain more than one request. The Calendar list is singular because the list contains a single calendar, which is a collection of calendar events. You don't have to follow this convention and you can rename the lists to use whatever convention you choose. However, most sites that you'll see will likely follow this convention.

4. Once the Requests list has been created, the empty list will be displayed. To modify the list definition, go to the Lists tab of the ribbon and click the List Settings button, as shown in Figure 4-6.

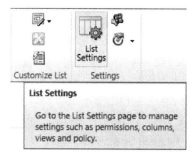

Figure 4-6. Modifying the lists settings

The Lists Settings page, shown in Figure 4-7, allows you to modify the list properties including columns, views, and workflow settings.

List Information

Name: Requests
Web Address: http://www.thecreativepeople.com/TeamSite/dev/Lists/Requests/AllItems.aspx
Description:

General Settings	Permissions and Management	Communications
Title, description and navigation	Delete this list	RSS settings
Versioning settings	Save list as template	
Advanced settings	Permissions for this list	
Validation settings	Workflow Settings	
Audience targeting settings		

Columns

A column stores information about each item in the list. The following columns are currently available in this list:

Column (click to edit)	Type	Required
Title	Single line of text	✔
Created By	Person or Group	
Modified By	Person or Group	

Create column
Add from existing site columns
Column ordering
Indexed columns

Views

A view of a list allows you to see a particular selection of items or to see the items sorted in a particular order. Views currently configured

View (click to edit)	Default View	Mobile View	Default Mobile View
All Items	✔	✔	✔

Create view

Figure 4-7. The initial list definition

The "blank" list actually contains three columns.

- Title
- Created By
- Modified By

Adding Existing Site Columns

A SharePoint site includes a collection of site columns. A site column provides a standard definition of a column including the data type (such as text, number, or date), if the column requires data, if it has a default value, and how the data should be displayed. You should use an existing site column if an appropriate one is available. This helps with consistency across lists and sites. If one is not available, you should create a new site column, especially if you think it may be reused on a different list.

■ **Tip** Site columns are normally defined by the parent site and inherited by each subsite. If you create a new site column on a sub-site, it will be inherited by all of its subsites but will not be available to the parent site.

To add existing site columns to your list, click the "Add from existing site columns" link on the List Settings page. This will display all of the existing site columns so you can select the column(s) that you want to add. Select the following columns and click the Add button (as shown in Figure 4-8):

- Date Created
- Due Date
- Comments
- Assigned To
- % Complete
- Date Completed

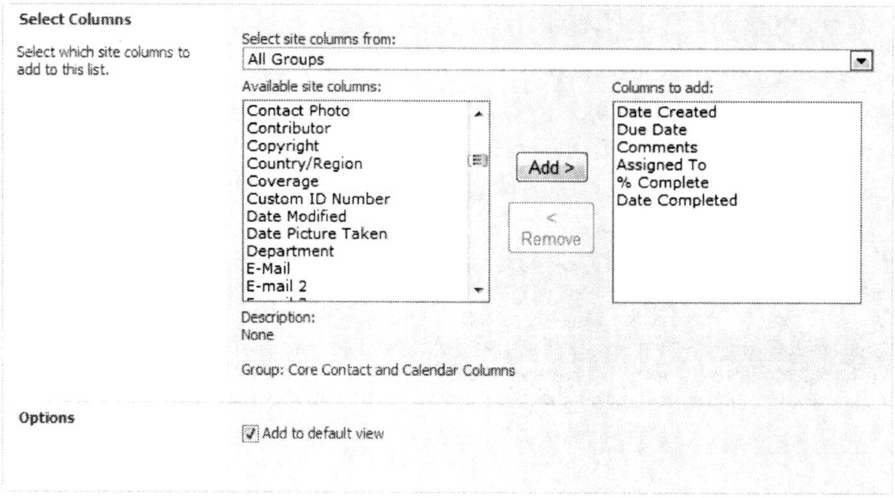

Figure 4-8. Adding existing site columns

Click the OK button when you have selected all of the desired columns.

Creating a New Column

You can also add a column to a list without using the site columns. You will need to define the various column attributes manually. To add a new column, click the Create Column link from the List Settings page. In the Create Column page, enter **Request Status** for the column name, select the Choice data type, and enter the following values:

- **Pending**

- **Assigned**

- **InProgress**

- **Cancelled**

- **Completed**

Also, make this a required column and set the default value as **Pending**, as shown in Figure 4-9.

Name and Type

Type a name for this column, and select the type of information you want to store in the column.

Column name:

Request Status

The type of information in this column is:

○ Single line of text
○ Multiple lines of text
● Choice (menu to choose from)
○ Number (1, 1.0, 100)
○ Currency ($, ¥, €)
○ Date and Time
○ Lookup (information already on this site)
○ Yes/No (check box)
○ Person or Group
○ Hyperlink or Picture
○ Calculated (calculation based on other columns)
○ External Data
○ Managed Metadata

Additional Column Settings

Specify detailed options for the type of information you selected.

Description:

Require that this column contains information:
● Yes ○ No

Enforce unique values:
○ Yes ● No

Type each choice on a separate line:

Assigned
InProgress
Cancelled
Completed

Display choices using:
● Drop-Down Menu
○ Radio Buttons
○ Checkboxes (allow multiple selections)

Allow 'Fill-in' choices:
○ Yes ● No

Default value:
● Choice ○ Calculated Value

Pending

☑ Add to default view

Figure 4-9. Defining the Request Status column

113

Modifying an Existing Column

You can also modify a column that is already included in your list. This will update the attributes in this list without affecting the other places where the column is used.

From the List Settings page, click the Date Created link in the Columns section. This will display the existing attributes for this column. Make this a required field and select Today's Date as the default value, as shown in Figure 4-10.

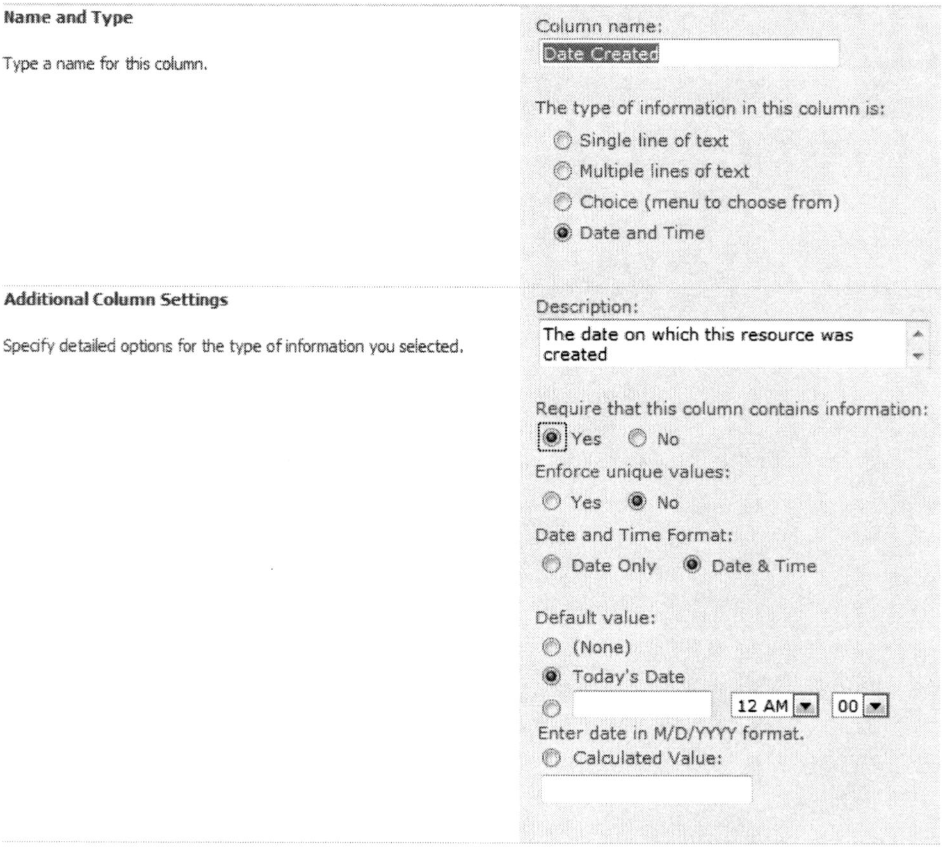

Name and Type

Type a name for this column.

Column name:

Date Created

The type of information in this column is:

○ Single line of text

○ Multiple lines of text

○ Choice (menu to choose from)

● Date and Time

Additional Column Settings

Specify detailed options for the type of information you selected.

Description:

The date on which this resource was created

Require that this column contains information:

● Yes   ○ No

Enforce unique values:

○ Yes   ● No

Date and Time Format:

○ Date Only   ● Date & Time

Default value:

○ (None)

● Today's Date

○ _____   12 AM ▼ 00 ▼

Enter date in M/D/YYYY format.

○ Calculated Value:

Figure 4-10. Modifying the Date Created column

▪ **Tip** If you want to change the column definition globally, edit the site column directly and SharePoint will update every place where it is used. To edit a site column, go to the Site Settings page using the Site Actions menu. Then click the Site columns link. This page will list all of the existing site columns. When you select one, a dialog box similar to Figure 4-10 is presented for you to modify the site column.

Defining List Views

Views are a handy way to manage a list, especially larger lists. A view defines a subset of items by specifying the filter criteria. Views also define a subset of columns that are included, the order of the columns, and the way the items are sorted. You can specify groups and subtotals for more advances views.

When you create a list, its default view, called All Items, is automatically created. As you add columns, you can choose to add these to the default view. The All Items view does not specify a filter, so it will display all of the items in the list. Now you'll create two additional views.

- **Pending Requests:** Requests that have not yet been assigned.

- **My Requests:** Requests not completed and assigned to the current user.

■ **Tip** You can add a filter to the All Items view. In this case it would not actually display all items so the name would be misleading. There may be scenarios where there are certain items that you would never want to display. In general, however, you should create a new view with an appropriate name and make it the default view, if desired.

Creating the Pending Requests View

To create a new view, click the Create View link on the List Settings page. The first step is to specify the type of view to create. The options are shown in Figure 4-11. You can also start with an existing view; this will make a copy of the selected view. This will save you some time if the new view is similar to an existing view.

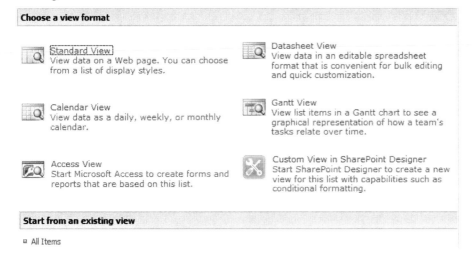

Choose a view format

Standard View
View data on a Web page. You can choose from a list of display styles.

Datasheet View
View data in an editable spreadsheet format that is convenient for bulk editing and quick customization.

Calendar View
View data as a daily, weekly, or monthly calendar.

Gantt View
View list items in a Gantt chart to see a graphical representation of how a team's tasks relate over time.

Access View
Start Microsoft Access to create forms and reports that are based on this list.

Custom View in SharePoint Designer
Start SharePoint Designer to create a new view for this list with capabilities such as conditional formatting.

Start from an existing view

▫ All Items

Figure 4-11. Choosing a view format

Click the Standard View link. Enter the name **Pending Requests** and select the following columns as shown in Figure 4-12:

- Attachments
- Title
- Date Created
- Due Date
- Comments
- Request Status

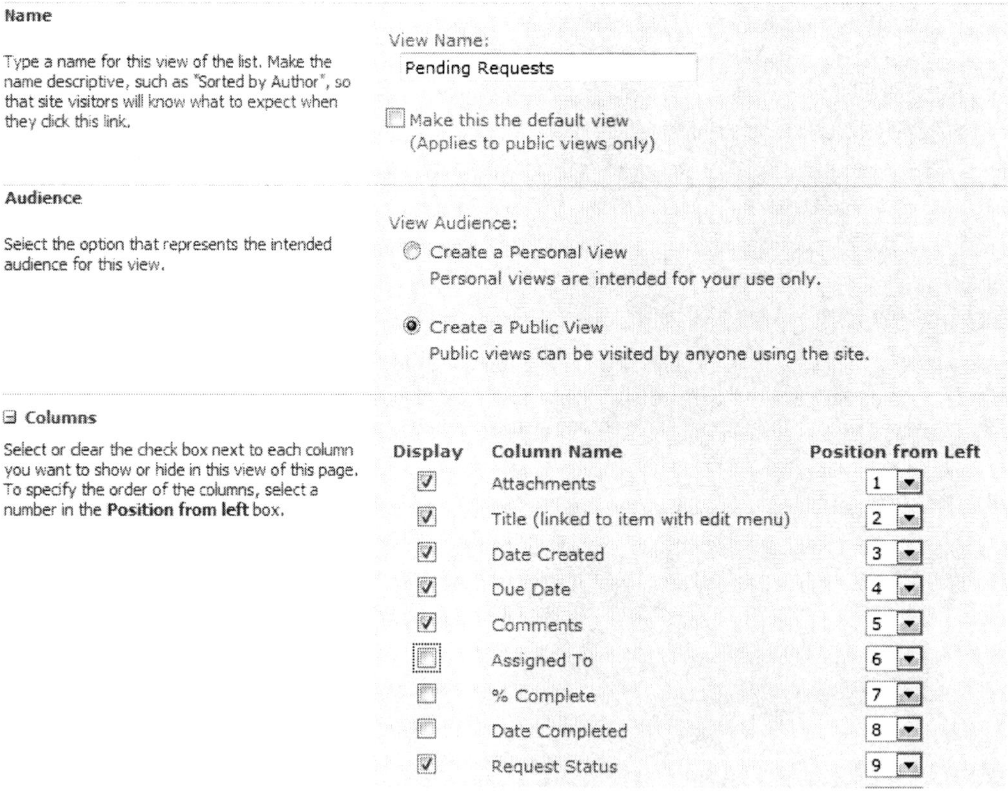

Name

Type a name for this view of the list. Make the name descriptive, such as "Sorted by Author", so that site visitors will know what to expect when they click this link.

View Name:

Pending Requests

☐ Make this the default view
(Applies to public views only)

Audience

Select the option that represents the intended audience for this view.

View Audience:

○ Create a Personal View
Personal views are intended for your use only.

◉ Create a Public View
Public views can be visited by anyone using the site.

⊟ Columns

Select or clear the check box next to each column you want to show or hide in this view of this page. To specify the order of the columns, select a number in the **Position from left** box.

Display	Column Name	Position from Left
☑	Attachments	1
☑	Title (linked to item with edit menu)	2
☑	Date Created	3
☑	Due Date	4
☑	Comments	5
☐	Assigned To	6
☐	% Complete	7
☐	Date Completed	8
☑	Request Status	9

Figure 4-12. Selecting the view columns

■ **Tip** You can change the order of the columns by specifying the Position. For example, if you wanted the Request Status column to be first, select 1 in the Position from Left drop-down list.

Specify the Sort and Filter sections as shown in Figure 4-13. This will display the oldest first and only include requests that have not yet been assigned. Click the OK button when you're finished.

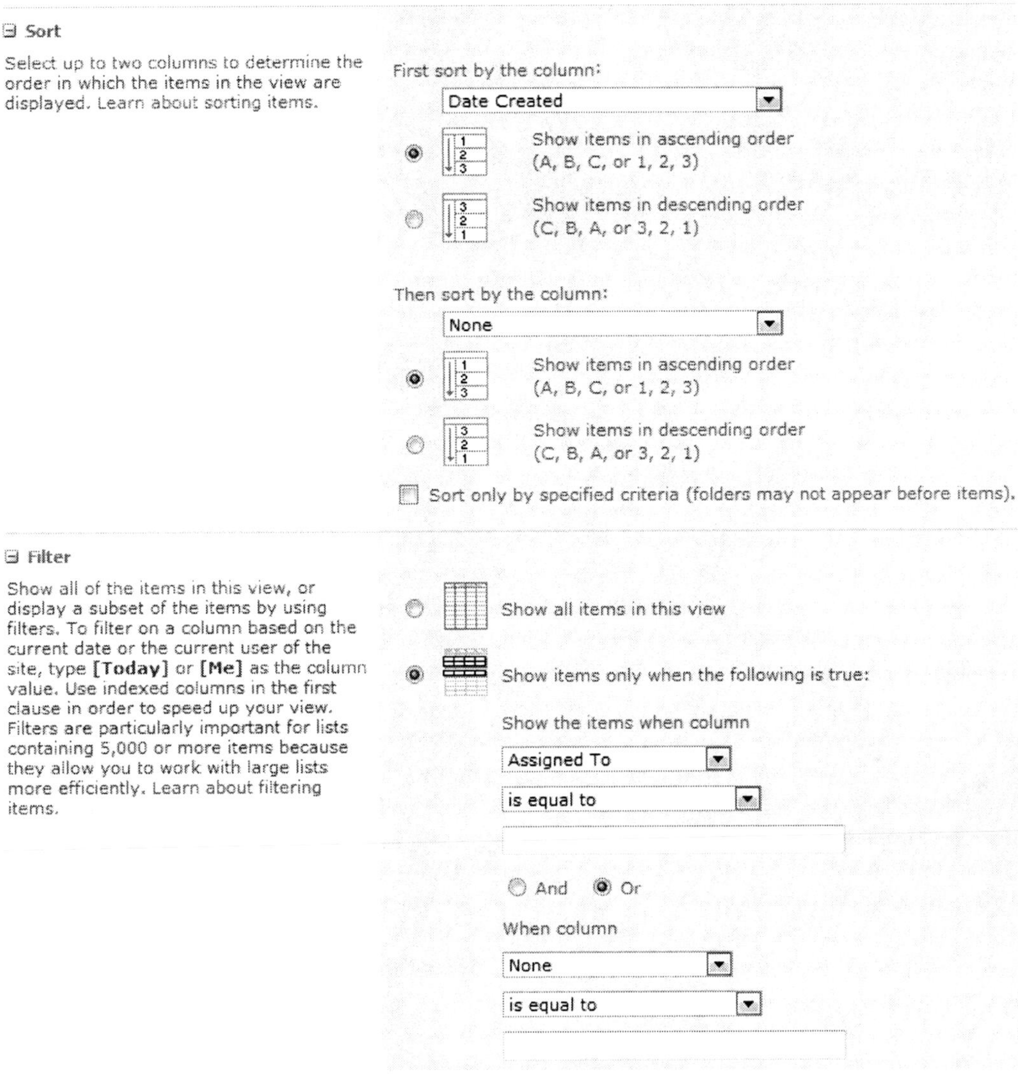

Figure 4-13. Specifying the Sort and Filter criteria

Creating the My Requests View

You'll now create a second view to list the requests that have been assigned to the current user. Create this view just like the Pending Requests view except set the filter criteria as shown in Figure 4-14.

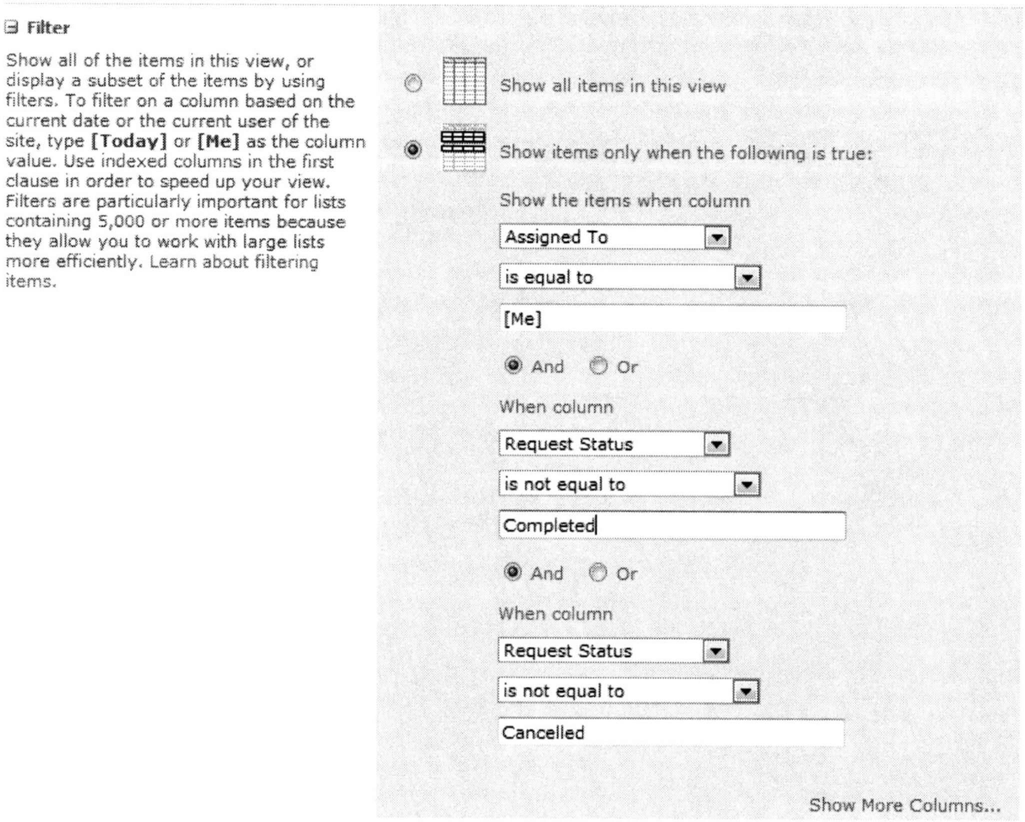

Figure 4-14. Setting the filter criteria for the My Requests view

This will only show records assigned to the current user. This is done by using the [Me] value, which SharePoint converts to the current user when evaluating the filter. The filter also ignores requests that have been completed or cancelled.

■ **Tip** The Filter section initially only supports two criteria. Use the Show More Columns link to include additional criteria.

Testing the New Site

With these changes done, you're ready to test the new site, including the custom Requests list. You'll need to first add some users to the new site so you'll have the users to assign requests to. Then you'll create some requests, assign them, and verify that the views are working as expected.

Adding Users to the Site

The new site should inherit the users and permissions from the parent site (if you selected that option when creating the site). However, if you didn't add any users to the default Team Site, there won't be any in the new subsite either.

To add users, from the Site Actions menu, select the Site Settings link. Then click the People and groups link. In the Navigation pane, select the Members group. To add new users to this group, click the New link. Enter one or more users, separated by a semicolon as shown in Figure 4-15. Click the OK button when you're done.

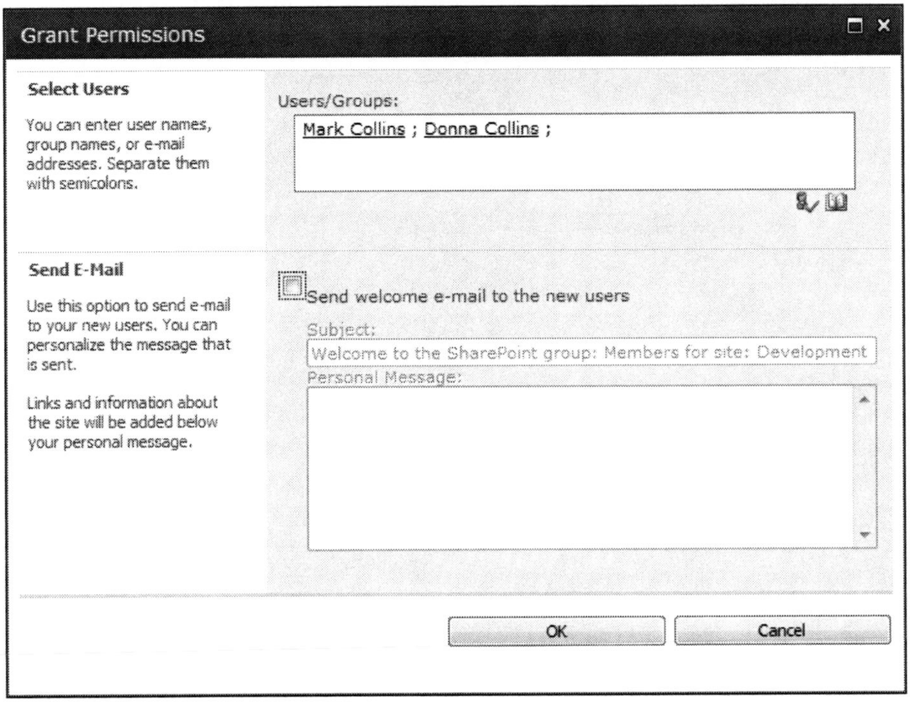

Figure 4-15. Adding users to the Members group

■ **Note** The users you enter must be set up in your Office 365 account. After entering the names, use the Check Names button to verify that these users exist.

Adding Requests

Now you'll add some requests to this list and test the custom views. Go to the Requests list and click the Add new item link. This will display the Requests – New Item form. Enter information into the Title, Due Date, and Comments fields. The Request Status field should default as Pending; leave this as it is. Leave the

Assigned To, % Complete, and Date Completed fields blank, as shown in Figure 4-16. Click the Save button to create the request.

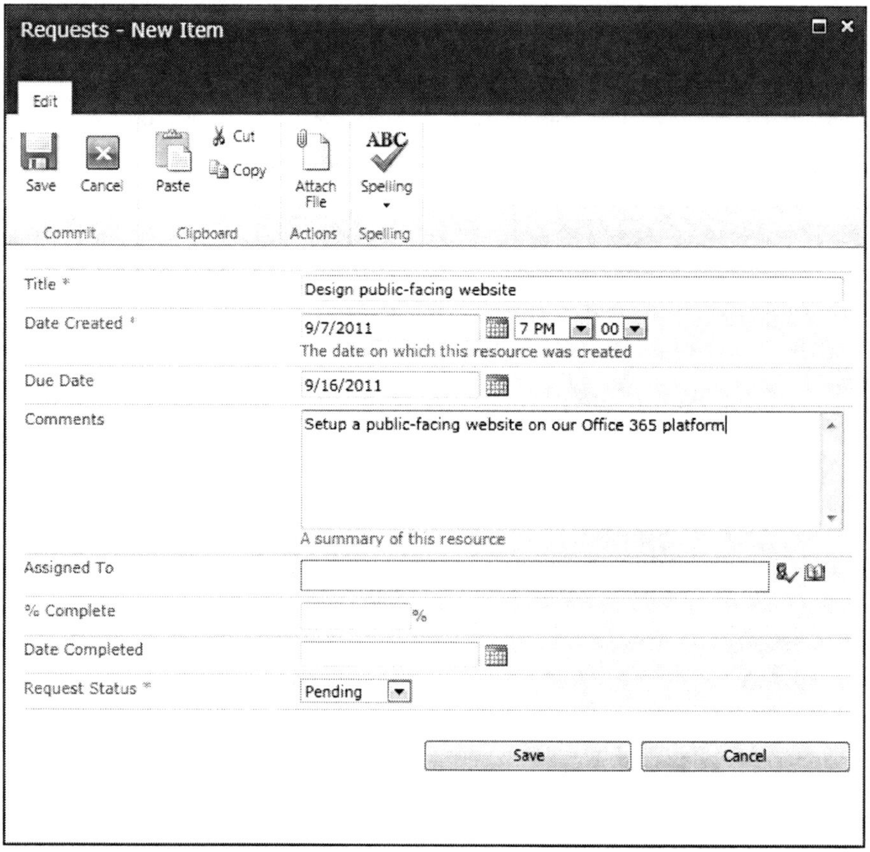

Figure 4-16. Creating a new request

Add at least one more request.

Testing the Views

From the List tab of the ribbon, select the Pending Requests view shown in Figure 4-17.

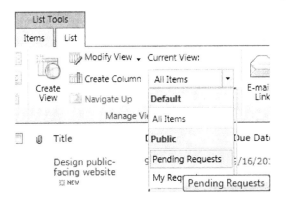

Figure 4-17. Selecting the Pending Requests view

Since none of the requests have been assigned yet, they will be included in the Pending Requests view. However, there should be fewer columns displayed, as demonstrated in Figure 4-18.

	Title	Date Created	Due Date	Comments	Request Status
	Design public-facing website ⬜ NEW	9/7/2011 7:00 PM	9/16/2011	Setup a public-facing website on our Office 365 platform	Pending
	New Document Library ⬜ NEW	9/7/2011 7:00 PM	9/14/2011	Setup a new document library for our design documents.	Pending

⊕ Add new item

Figure 4-18. Displaying the Pending Requests view

Select one of these requests and assign it to yourself by setting the Assigned To field. After saving the changes, it should no longer be included in the Pending Requests view. Select the My Requests view and it should be included in this view (see Figure 4-19).

			Development ▸ Requests ▸ My Requests ▾			

Home				Search this site...	🔍	❓

Libraries		Title	Date Created	Due Date	Comments	Request Status
Site Pages		New Document Library	9/7/2011 7:00 PM	9/14/2011	Setup a new document library for our design documents.	Pending
Shared Documents						

Figure 4-19. Displaying the My Requests view

Viewing a Site with SharePoint Designer

SharePoint Designer is a free utility from Microsoft that you can use to create and modify SharePoint sites. It is a desktop application that connects to a local or on-premise SharePoint 2010 server. It works equally well connected to a SharePoint Online 2010 server hosted on Office 365.

You can use SharePoint Designer to make all the same types of customizations that you can through the SharePoint UI. Everything that you have done so far in this chapter can be accomplished through SharePoint Designer. It is a desktop app so the user experience is very different. While it may take a little more time to get used to it, once you become familiar with it, you'll probably find it to be easier and faster to use.

SharePoint Designer also provides some advanced features, such as designing declarative workflows that are not available in the SharePoint UI. You will use SharePoint Designer in the next chapter to create workflows and I will explain it in more detail there. I will briefly introduce it here as you may prefer to use it for all your SharePoint development.

Launching SharePoint Designer

The easiest way to start SharePoint Designer is to invoke it from the SharePoint site. From the Site Actions menu, click the "Edit in SharePoint Designer" link shown in Figure 4-20.

Figure 4-20. Launching SharePoint Designer

You may see a pop-up dialog box warning you about launching an application from the web site. Just click the Allow button.

Installing SharePoint Design

If you don't already have SharePoint Designer installed, the "Edit in SharePoint Designer" link will automatically download and install the application for you. You'll need to choose either the 32-bit or 64-bit version and then you should see the installation dialog box shown in Figure 4-21.

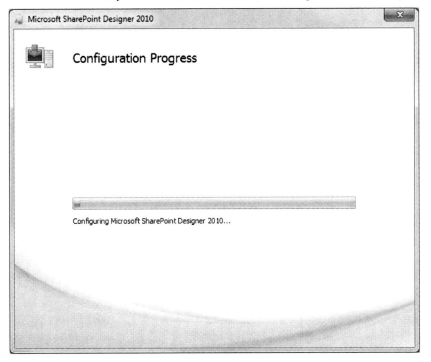

Figure 4-21. Installation progress dialog box

When the installation has finished, you'll see the dialog box shown in Figure 4-22 telling you to close any open Office applications.

Figure 4-22. Installation complete dialog box

You may need to also reboot your workstation. If you see the dialog box shown in Figure 4-23, close any open applications and then click the Yes button.

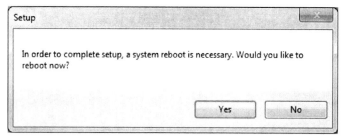

Figure 4-23. Reboot required message

Once your workstation has rebooted, go back to the SharePoint site and click the "Edit in SharePoint Design" link from the Site Actions menu. This will start the SharePoint Designer application.

■ **Note** It may take a few seconds to start the application and you won't see any activity while it is starting.

When you launch SharePoint Designer from the SharePoint site, it will automatically open that site. It will need to authenticate the current user so you may see the login dialog box shown in Figure 4-24.

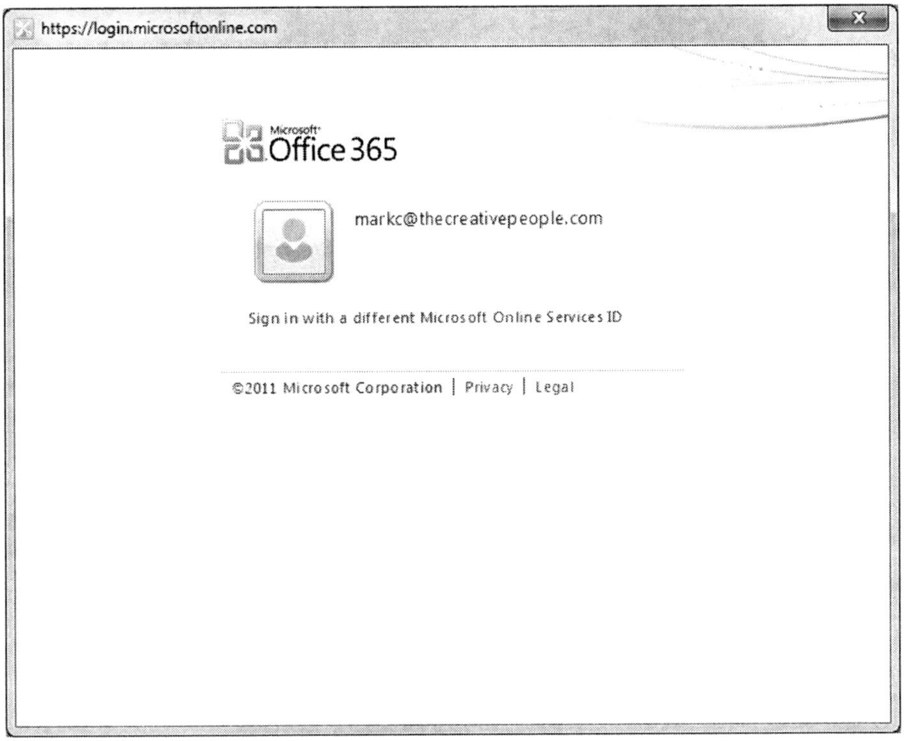

Figure 4-24. Logging in to SharePoint Online

Using SharePoint Designer

The SharePoint Designer uses a typical Office ribbon with different tabs depending on the type of object that is selected. The Navigation pane on the left-hand side enumerates the types of objects that can be viewed and modified. The first item in this pane is the site and there are subsequent items for lists and libraries, workflows, site pages, and so on. In the main section, the selected object or object collection is displayed in a tabbed dialog box, as shown in Figure 4-25.

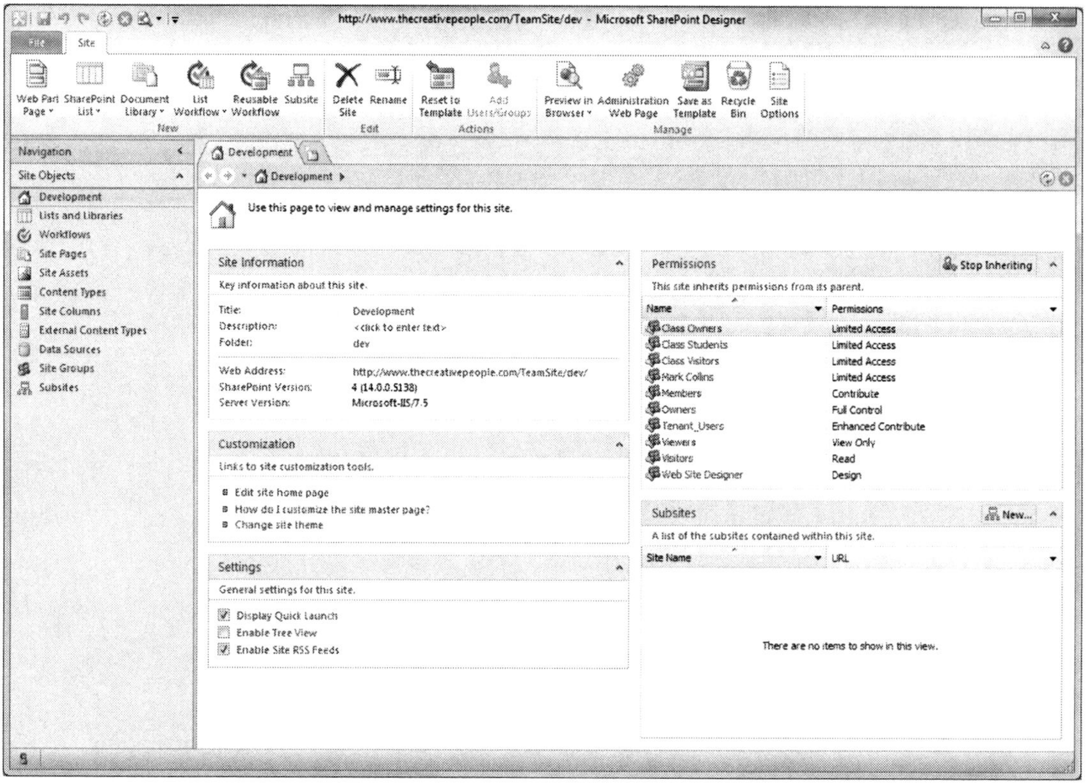

Figure 4-25. The SharePoint Designer displaying site details

Click the Lists and Libraries link in the Navigation pane. You will see all of the lists and document libraries currently installed in that site. Your list should look like Figure 4-26.

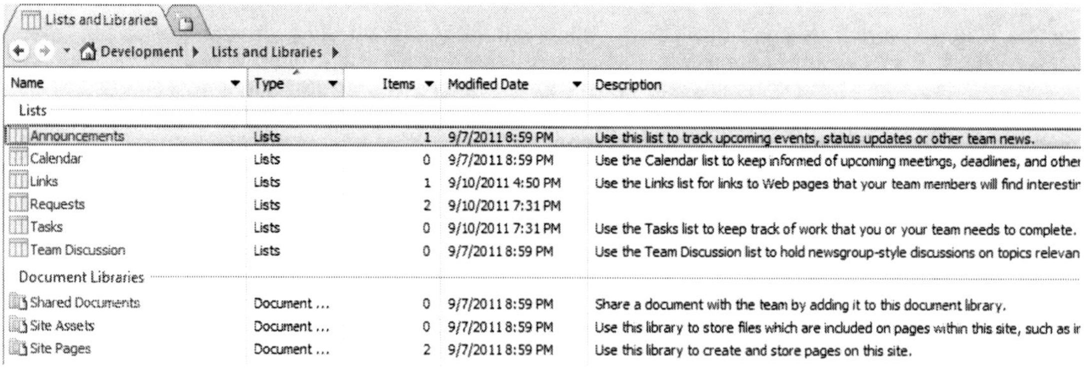

Figure 4-26. Enumerating the Lists and Document libraries

Select the Requests list by clicking the Name column for that item. This will show the details of the Requests list, as shown in Figure 4-27.

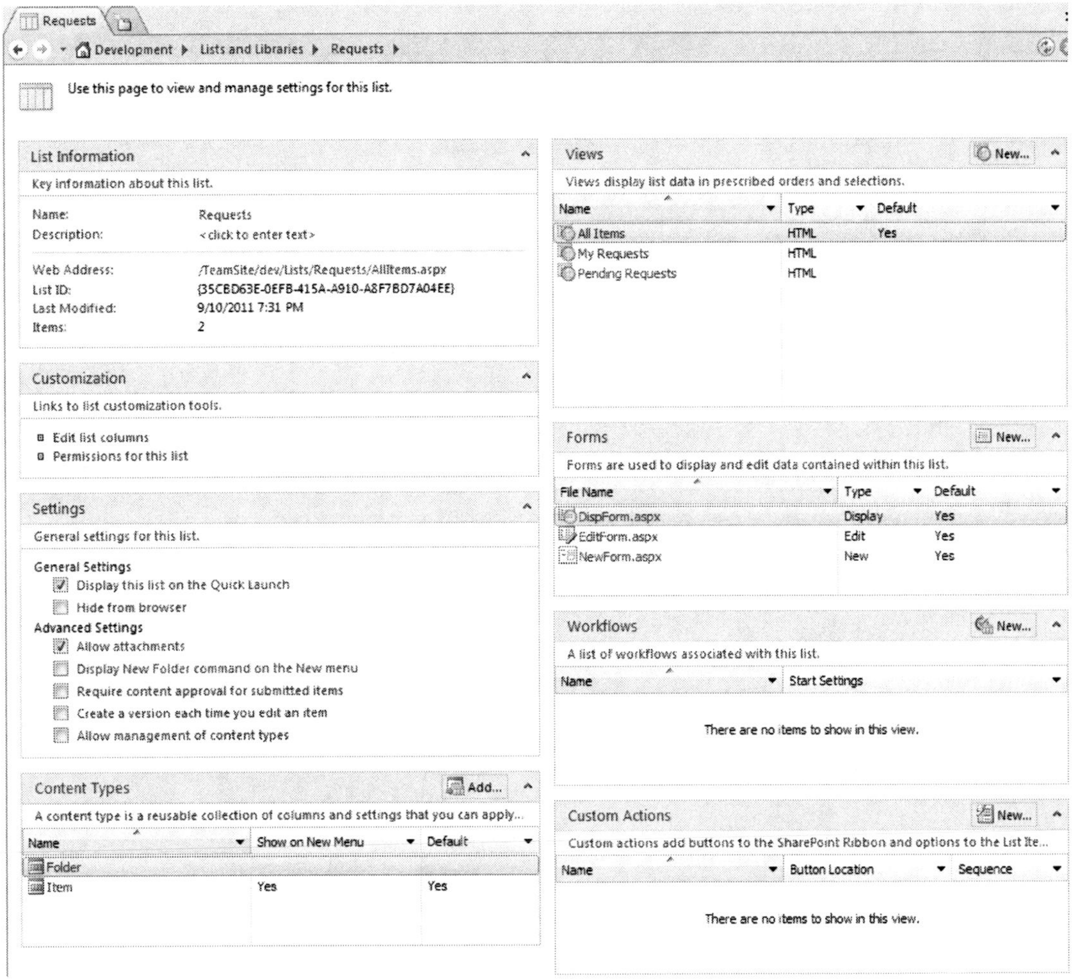

Figure 4-27. Displaying the details of the Requests list

The attributes of this list are grouped into sections including List Information, Settings, and Views. Notice that the All Items view is listed as well as the two custom views that you created. There are some advanced sections such as Workflows and Custom Actions that are not available from the SharePoint UI.

Click the "Edit list columns" link in the Customization section to display the list of columns, which is shown in Figure 4-28. You can use the buttons in the ribbon to add or modify the columns in this list.

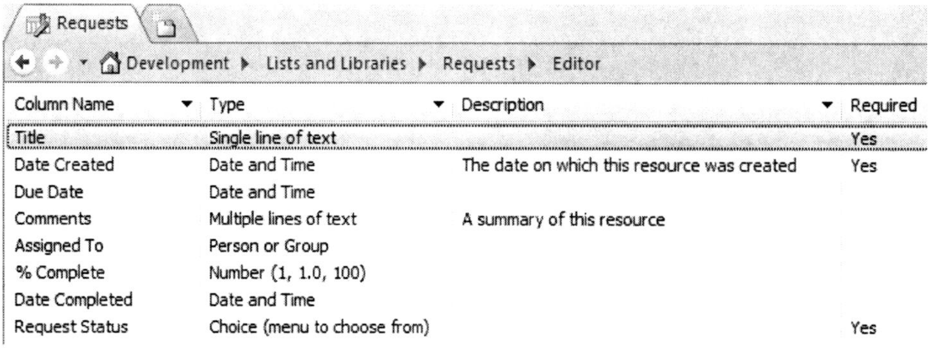

Requests
Development ▸ Lists and Libraries ▸ Requests ▸ Editor
Column Name
Type
Description
Required
Title
Single line of text
Yes
Date Created
Date and Time
The date on which this resource was created
Yes
Due Date
Date and Time
Comments
Multiple lines of text
A summary of this resource
Assigned To
Person or Group
% Complete
Number (1, 1.0, 100)
Date Completed
Date and Time
Request Status
Choice (menu to choose from)
Yes

Figure 4-28. Editing the list columns

Selecting a Site to Open

You can also launch SharePoint Designer from the Start menu and then open the desired SharePoint site from the File tab. In the Open Site dialog box, enter the URL of the site (see Figure 4-29). SharePoint Designer remembers sites that you've visited recently so it's easy to go back to a previous site.

Open Site
Network (INTERNAL) ▸ Web Sites ▸
Search Web Sites
Organize
Desktop
Downloads
Recent Places
SharePoint Sites
Libraries
Documents
Music
Pictures
Videos
Homegroup
Site name:
http://www.thecreativepeople.com/TeamSite/dev
Tools
Open
Cancel

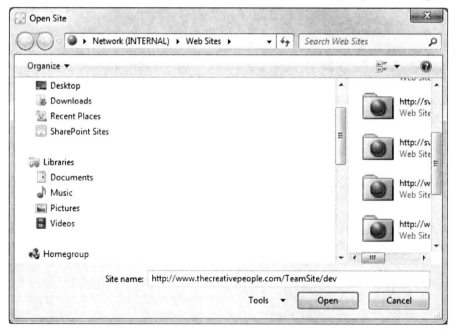

Figure 4-29. Specifying the site URL in the Open Site dialog box

---

■ **Tip** SharePoint Designer can only view one site at a time. To go to a different site you'll need to first close the current site using the File tab of the ribbon. However, you can have multiple copies of SharePoint Designer running if you want to view or edit multiple sites simultaneously.

Designing the Public-Facing Web Site

When setting up an Office 365 Small Business account (Plan P1), a public-facing web site is created for you. I showed you what the default site looks like in Chapter 1. With an Enterprise account, a public-facing web site is not created automatically but I showed you how to add one in Chapter 2. For the remainder of this chapter, I will show you how to design a public-facing web site using SharePoint Online.

For a public-facing web site, SharePoint Online 2010 provides the Website Design Tool, which enables you to easily create a great-looking web site. Designing internal sites is focused primarily on creating lists and libraries for storing and manipulating data and documents. In contrast, public-facing web sites use libraries for storing images and other site assets, but the design activity is mainly involved with creating web pages.

From the Admin page on your Office 365 account, click the "Edit website" link to edit the public-facing web site. The initial page, shown in Figure 4-30, lists the existing web pages that were created for you, which are

- About Us

- Contact Us

- Home

- Site Map

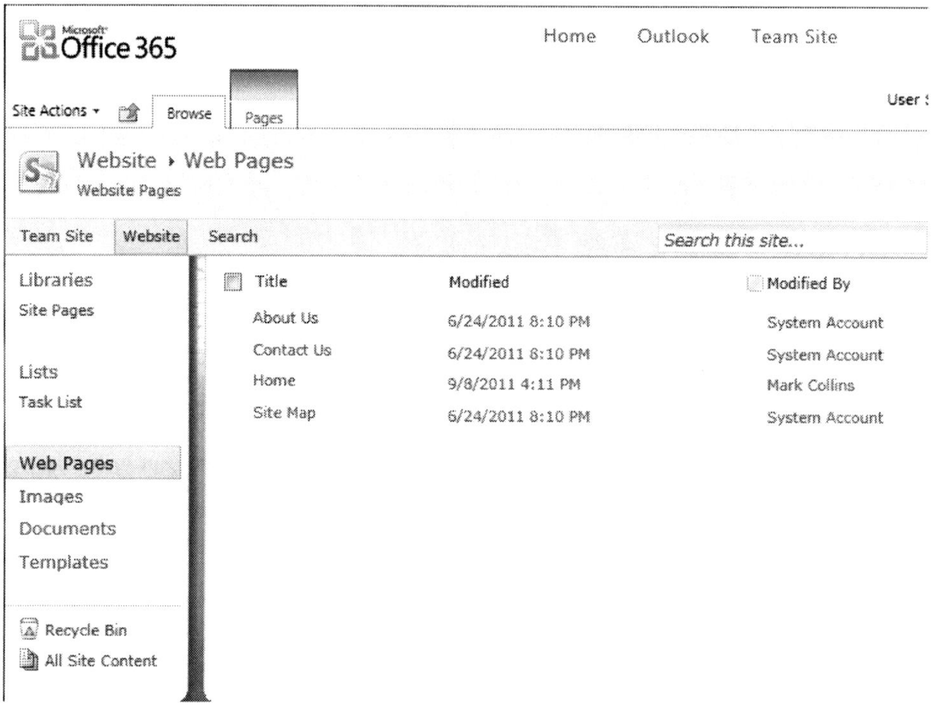

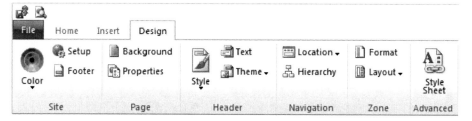

Figure 4-30. The initial set of web pages

Click the Name column of the Home page, which is a link that opens this web page for editing. The Design tab of the ribbon, shown in Figure 4-31, contains buttons for editing the page or site properties.

Figure 4-31. The Design tab of the ribbon

Notice that these buttons are grouped based on the area that the editing will affect:

- **Site:** The buttons in the Site group will affect all of the pages in this web site.

- **Page:** These buttons will affect only the current page.

- **Header:** These buttons will edit the properties of the header (for all pages in this web site).

- **Navigation**: These buttons affect where this page is located in the web site navigation as well as what navigation options are available on the pages.

- **Zone**: These buttons affect the selected zone of the current page.

- **Advanced**: The Style Sheet button is used to edit the style sheet for the entire web site.

Editing the Site Properties

There are three buttons in the Site group.

- **Setup** configures the site options.

- **Footer** designs the content of the page footer.

- **Color** specifies a color scheme for the site.

Configuring the Web Site

The Setup button will display the Setup dialog box shown in Figure 4-32.

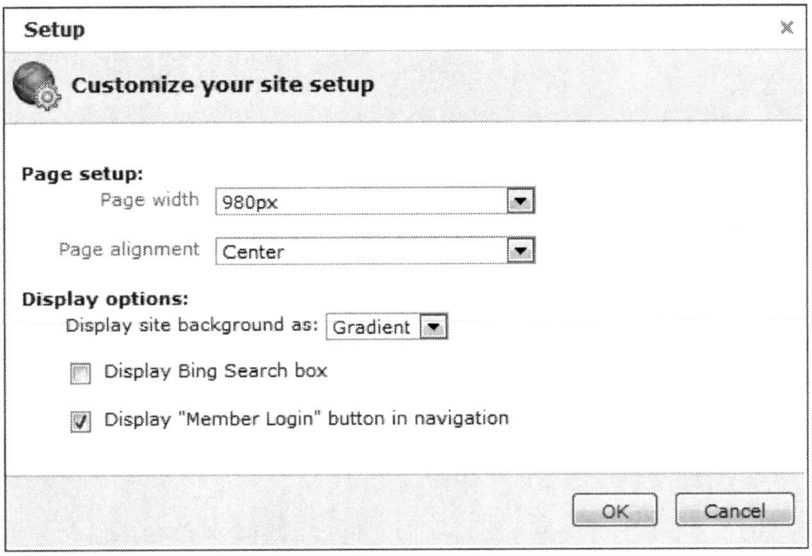

Figure 4-32. Setting the web site attributes

This dialog allows you to specify the page width and its horizontal alignment within the web browser. A wider page will give you more room to display content but may cause users with lower-resolution screens to have to scroll horizontally.

The "Display Bing Search box" option will include a search box in the header of every page. Personally, I don't see why anyone would want to do that since it will navigate them away from your site if they use it. However, the feature is available if you have a need for it.

The final option adds a Member Login button in your site navigation options. If you use your public-facing web site as a portal for your internal users, this is a useful option. When they go to this site, they can use this button to authenticate themselves with the web site, which will then give them access to the internal site(s) as well. In many cases, however, you will want to unselect this check box to prevent the public users from trying to access your internal sites.

Designing the Footer

The Footer button will display the dialog box shown in Figure 4-33.

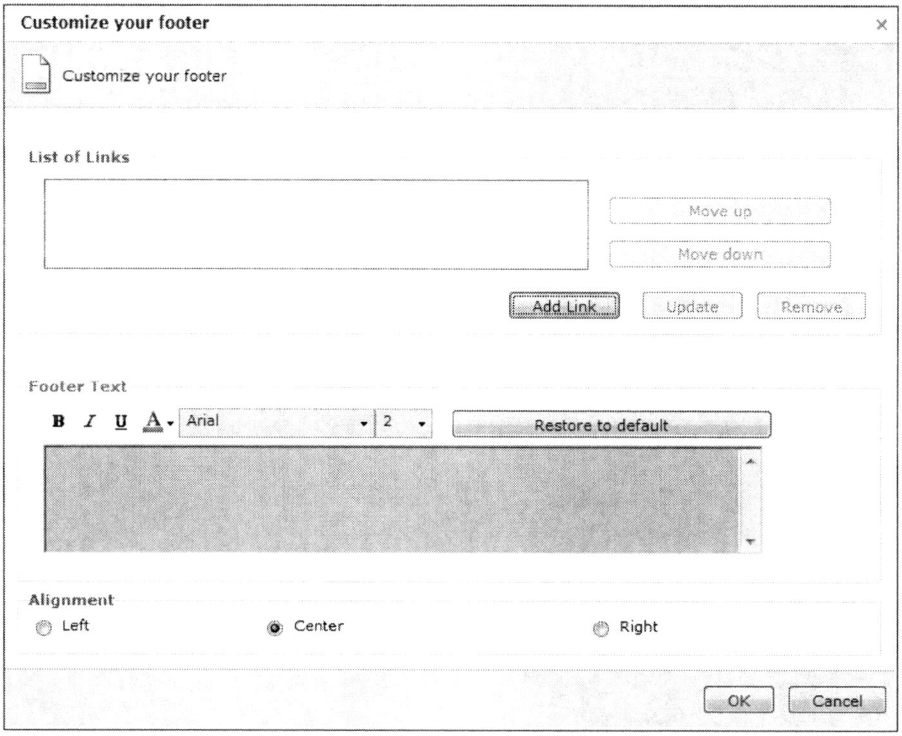

Figure 4-33. Modifying the Footer

You can add one or more links to the footer by using the Add Link button. After clicking the Add button, enter the Name, which is the text that will appear in the footer, as well as the URL that the link should point to (see Figure 4-34).

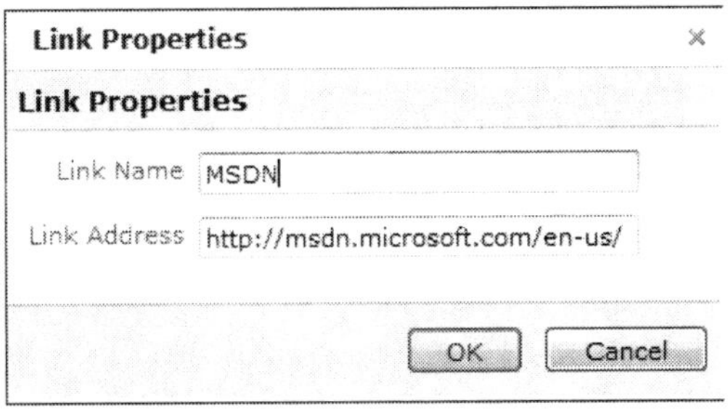

Link Properties ×

Link Properties

Link Name MSDN

Link Address http://msdn.microsoft.com/en-us/

OK   Cancel

Figure 4-34. Adding a footer link

The footer on every page in the web site will contain the links defined here. This will be followed by the static text that you specify. Both of these are optional and the footer will be hidden if neither links nor text are specified.

⬚ **Tip** Normally, the header and footer sections that you design will be included on every page of your web site. Keep this in mind when configuring these options. However, you can disable either the header or footer (or both) from specific pages, when appropriate. Similarly, the navigation controls are normally displayed on every page but can be removed from specific pages. More on this later in the chapter.

Choosing the Color Scheme

You can easily change the site colors by selecting a built-in color scheme. If you click the Color button in the ribbon, a list of available color schemes is displayed, as demonstrated in Figure 4-35.

Figure 4-35. Selecting a built-in color scheme

You can select one of these schemes or use the Create Custom Color Scheme link to create your own. This link will display the dialog box shown in Figure 4-36.

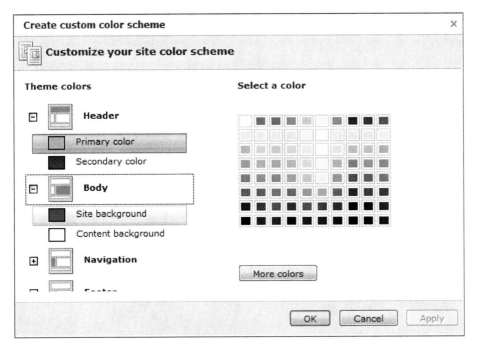

Figure 4-36. Creating a custom column scheme

A color scheme simply specifies a color for each of the various parts of the web page such as header, background, navigation buttons, and so on. These color choices are grouped into related areas. Expand these groups, select an item, and then choose the desired color for that item. You can use the More colors button if you want a color not shown in the dialog box. Repeat this process for each of the items listed.

Setting the Page Properties

There are two buttons in the Page group, which affect the currently selected page only.

- **Background**: Use this to select a background image.
- **Properties**: Set the page configuration options.

The background image is displayed in the page area and is overlaid with the content for that page. You can display the image once or have it repeated (tiled) as often as necessary to fill the page. If it is displayed once, you can chose how you want it aligned on the page.

■ **Tip** Be careful with background images as they can make the site look busy and difficult to read.

The Properties button will display the dialog box shown in Figure 4-37.

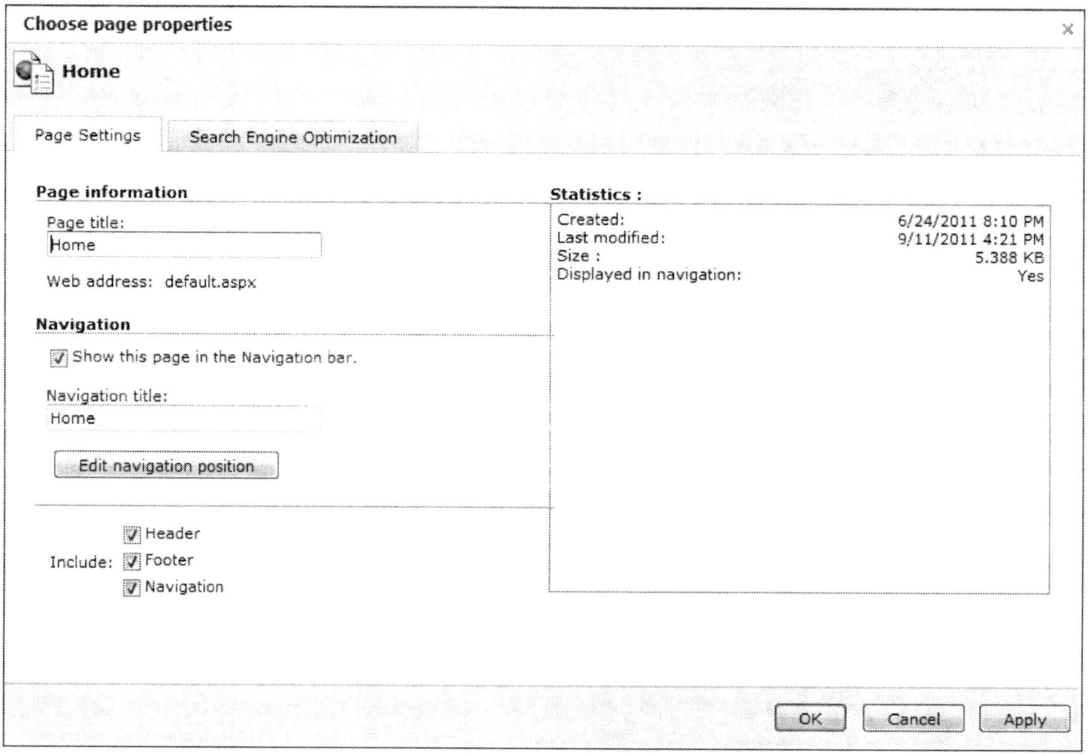

Figure 4-37. Setting the page properties

By default, each page is included in the Navigation bar. You can remove the link to a page from the Navigation bar by unselecting the "Show this page in the Navigation bar" check box. If you leave this option checked, you can specify the text that is displayed for the link to this page. The "Edit navigation position" button will display the Navigation dialog that I will explain later in this chapter.

I said earlier that the page header and footer were displayed on every page and that is the default behavior. However, you can remove the header and/or footer from the page by unselecting the corresponding check box on this dialog box. You can also remove the navigation buttons from this page.

■ **Tip** The Search Engine Optimization tab is used to enter metatags. You can add metatags like keyword, which help search engines determine the how well this page matches their search. The description metatag is often displayed by a search engine so you should specify this as well and keep it current.

Designing the Page Header

There are three buttons available in the Header group.

- **Style** allows you to select from a list of built-in header styles.

- **Theme** specifies a image that is displayed in the header.

- **Text** specifies the text that is included in the header.

The style specifies how the visual elements of the header (including an image, background color, and text) are arranged. Click on the Style button and a list of styles will be displayed. If you hover the mouse over one of these, text will appear describing the style, as shown in Figure 4-38.

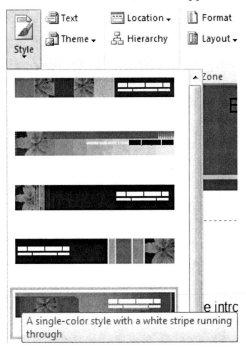

Figure 4-38. Selecting a style

■ **Tip** I did not find the style preview image very useful; the text description may be more helpful. In either case, you can select a style and the page will immediately change based on the selected style. You may have to try a lot of styles before you find one that you like.

In my opinion, the Theme button is mislabeled. It does not select a theme in the same sense as other Office products such as Word or Excel. Instead, it merely selects a stock image to be included in the Header.

Click the Theme button to display a list of images that are grouped into categories, as shown in Figure 4-39. The preview images are fairly small but the hover text is helpful in selecting an appropriate image. The style will determine where the image is displayed and its size.

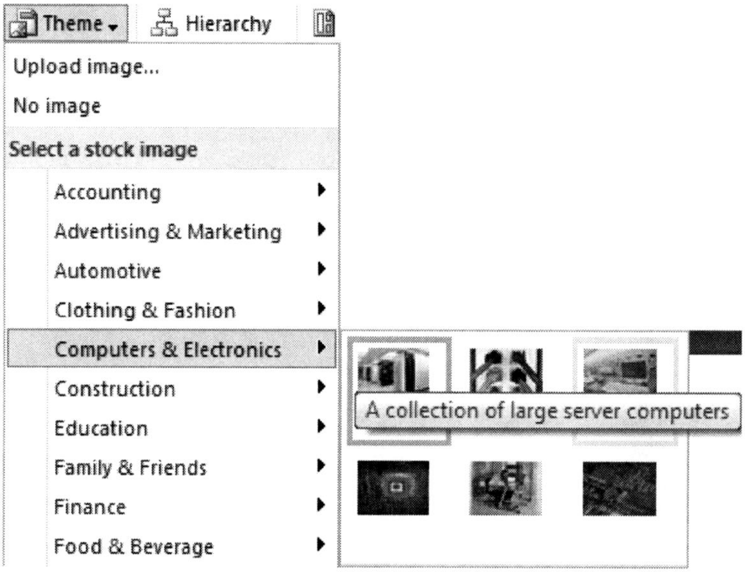

Figure 4-39. Selecting an image (theme)

Click the Text button, which will display the Header dialog box shown in Figure 4-40.

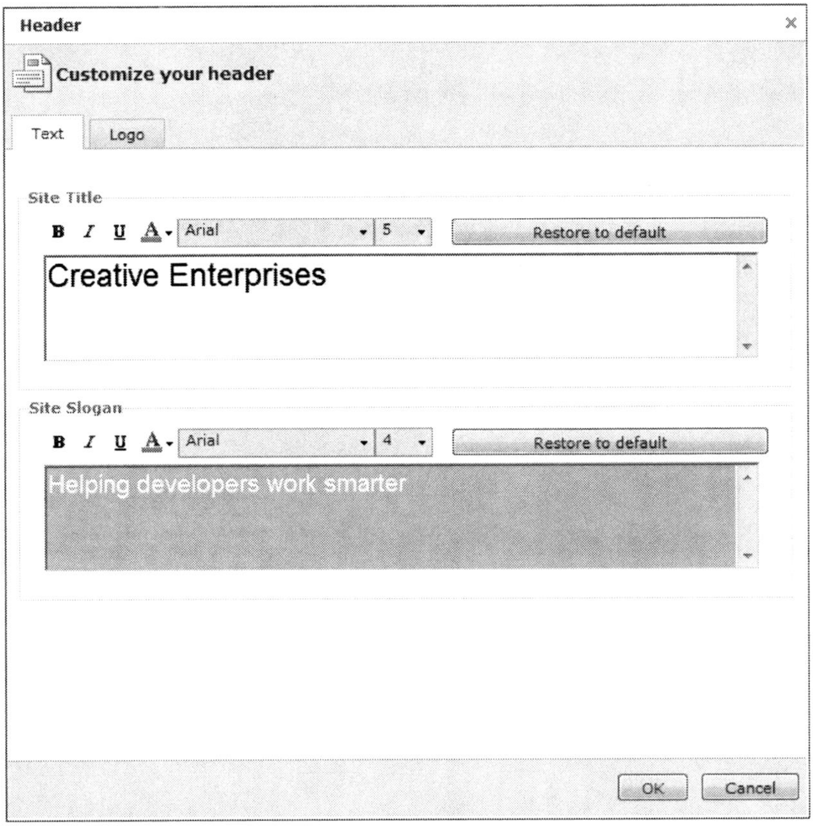

Figure 4-40. Entering the header text

You can enter two lines of text that are referred to as the Title and Slogan. You can also specify font characteristics such as type, size, and color.

■ **Tip** The font color is not controlled by the color scheme. When changing the color scheme, you may need to adjust the font color here. For example, the default color for the Title is Black. If you choose a color scheme that has a dark header background, the title may not be very readable and you may need to select a lighter font color.

Configuring the Navigation Options

As you start adding new web pages to your site, it becomes increasingly important to provide a structure for navigating them. I will explain how to create new pages later in this chapter, but first I will explain the navigation options. There are two buttons in the Navigation group.

- **Hierarchy** allows you to specify where each page belongs in the site's navigation hierarchy.

- **Location** specifies where the navigation buttons are displayed.

Configuring the Page Navigation

Click the Hierarchy button to display the Navigation dialog box shown in Figure 4-41. You can also display this dialog box using the "Edit navigation position" button on the Page Properties dialog box, as mentioned earlier.

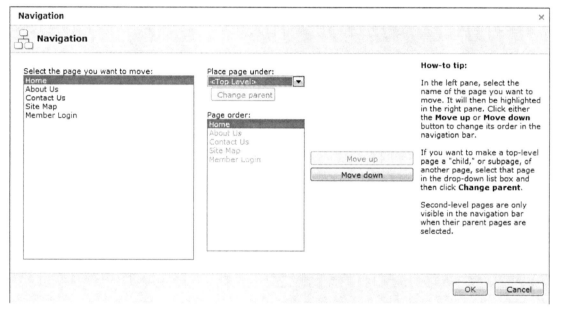

Figure 4-41. Configuring the page hierarchy

The left side of this dialog box lists all of the pages defined in your web site. Select a page to view or change where it belongs in the hierarchy. The "Place page under" drop-down list specifies the parent page. If you want to move a page to a different parent, select the new parent from the drop-down list and then click the Change parent button.

The Page order list box indicates the order of the selected page among its siblings. Use the Move up or Move down buttons to adjust this page's order within this list.

Selecting the Location of the Navigation Controls

The Navigation bar can be at the top (just below the header), to the left of the page area, or in both the top and left locations. Click the Location button and select one of the three options shown in Figure 4-42.

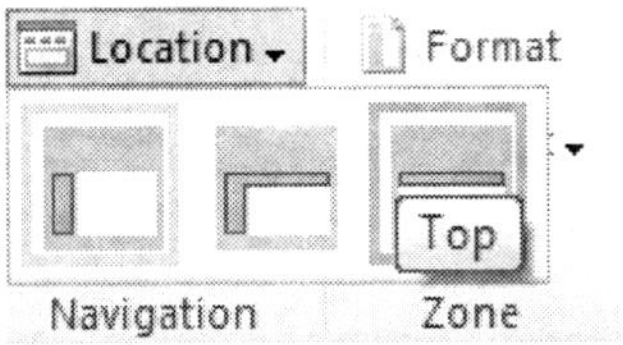

Figure 4-42. Selecting the location of the navigation controls

If you only have a few pages and they are all configured as top-level pages, the navigation controls are aligned in the location specified. It gets a little more interesting when you have pages nested in a hierarchical structure. This scenario is handled differently with each of the location options.

If you put the navigation on the left side, when a page is selected that has child pages, the links to the child pages are listed below the parent and indented. For all the other pages, the parent control is collapsed and its child pages are hidden, as demonstrated in Figure 4-43.

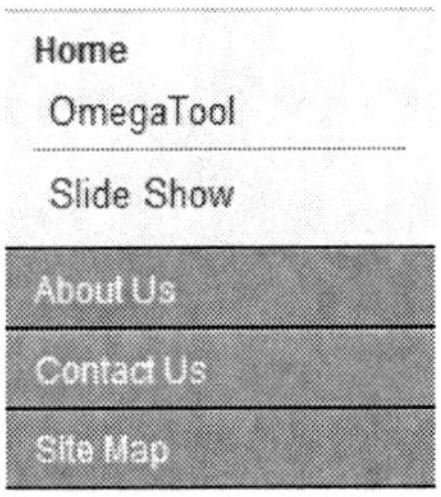

Figure 4-43. Hierarchical navigation using the left side

If you put the Navigation bar at the top, a second bar is used to show the child pages if there are any for the selected top-level page (see Figure 4-44). The second bar is hidden if the selected page doesn't have any child pages.

Figure 4-44. Hierarchical navigation with the bar at the top

If you select the top and left option, links to the top-level pages are shown at the top of the page. Links to the child pages are displayed on the left if there are any for the selected page, as shown in Figure 4-45.

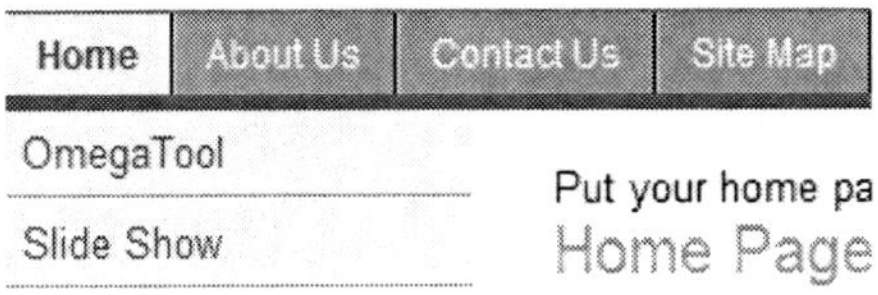

Figure 4-45. Hierarchical navigation when using both the top and left locations

Creating a New Web Page

You can also create additional pages for your web site. You can create a blank page that you'll design from scratch or you can select an existing page template. I'll show you how to add a product information page and upload images to be included on the page.

Creating the Web Page

From the Pages tab of the ribbon, click the New Page button shown in Figure 4-46.

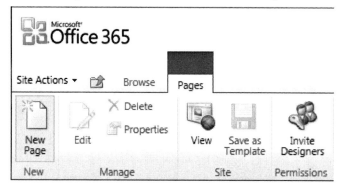

Figure 4-46. Using the New Page button in the ribbon

This will display the Create Web page dialog box. Select the Product or Service template shown in Figure 4-47.

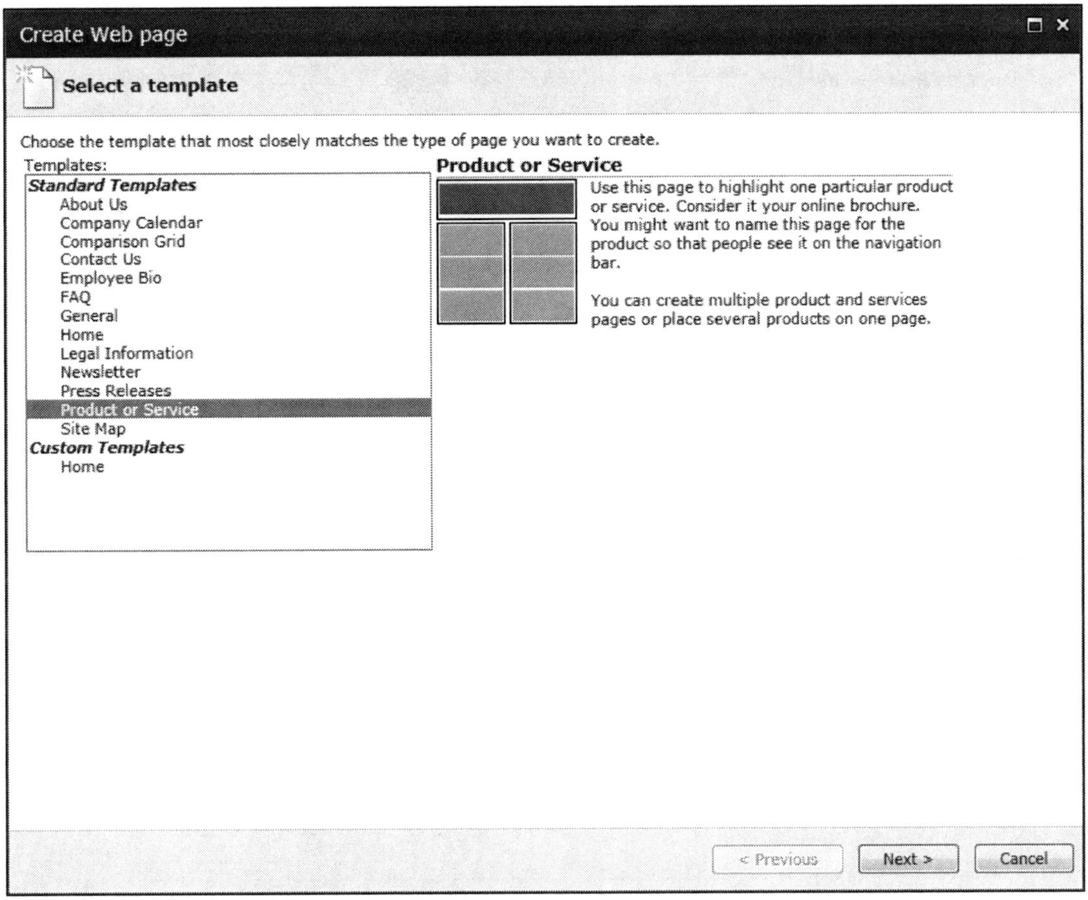

Figure 4-47. *Selecting a page template*

There are several built-in page templates. When you select one, a preview of it is displayed on the right-hand side of the dialog box. Click the Next button to continue, which will display Page Properties dialog box. Enter a page title and URL, as shown in Figure 4-48.

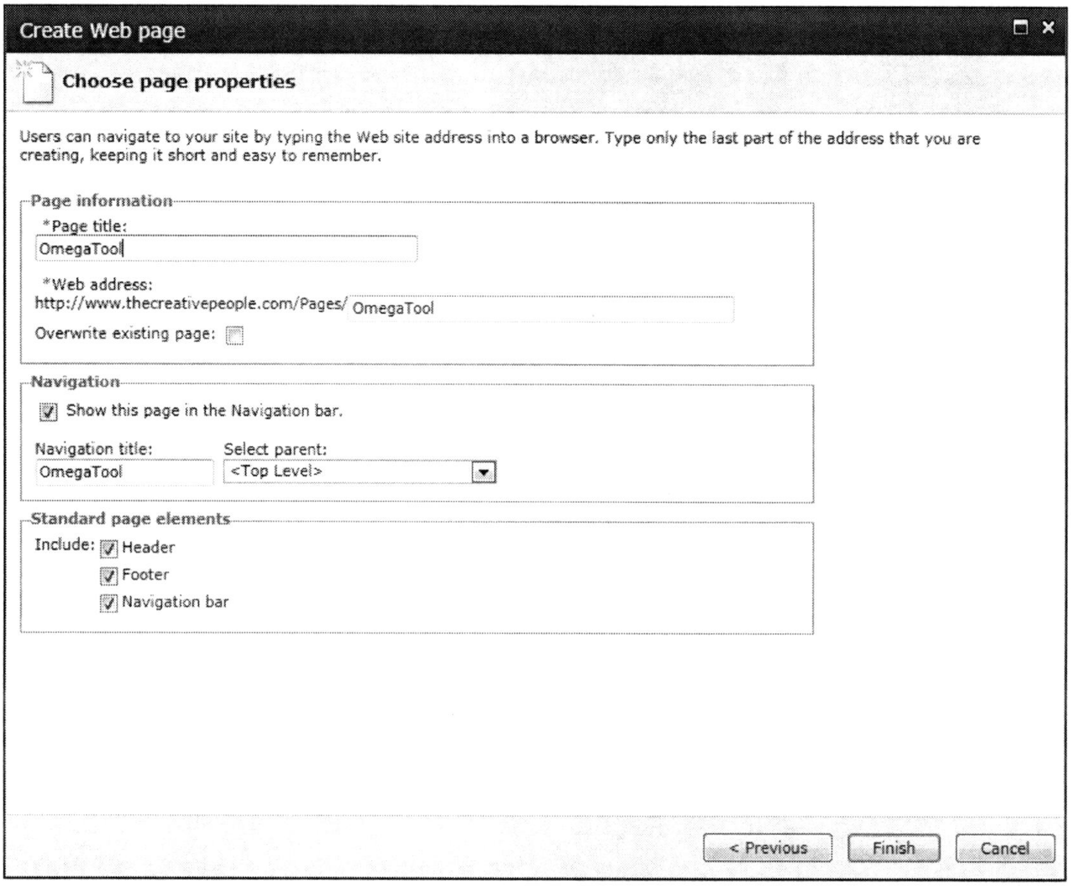

Figure 4-48. Configuring the page properties

This is very similar to the dialog box shown in Figure 4-37. It has the same options for selecting the location within the page hierarchy and whether the header, footer, and/or navigation bar are included on this page.

Editing a Web Page

The template created a page for you; now you need to add content to the page. The page is organized into zones where you can place different pieces of content, such as text, images, and gadgets. Each zone is identified by a red dotted line around it.

The initial arrangement of the zones is defined by the template. You can change the layout of the zones by selecting a different arrangement from the Layout button of the ribbon, as shown in Figure 4-49.

Figure 4-49. Selecting a zone layout

The layout determines the number of zones and their relative placement on the page. You can change the width of each zone by dragging the resize icons. These are located at the top-left and top-right corners of each zone. The height of each zone is determined by the content that you add to it.

The Format button in the ribbon allows you to format the border and fill of the selected zone. By default, zones have no border and no fill. For the zone fill, you can select from the following options:

- **No fill**: Default
- **Solid fill**: The zone has a solid color background.
- **Gradient fill**: The zone is darker at the top and gradually fades to white at the bottom.
- **Image fill**: A background image is used.

Depending on the option you select, other properties can be set, such as color, transparency, and image (see Figure 4-50).

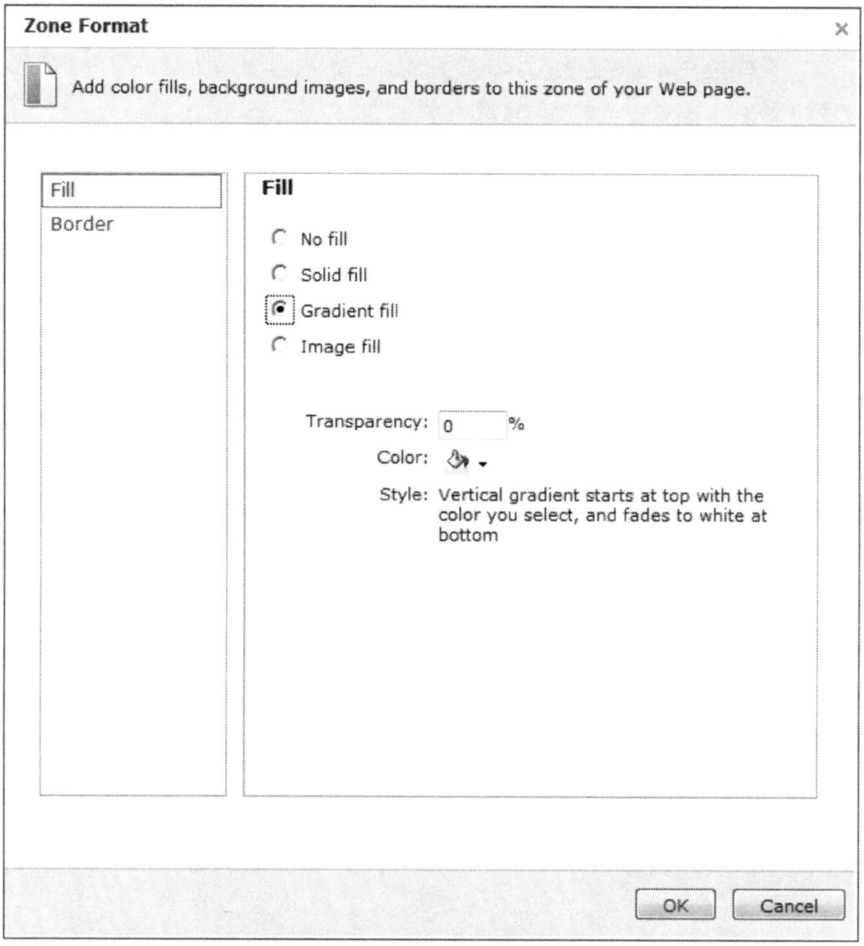

Figure 4-50. *Modifying the zone format*

If you select a border, the red dotted line around the zone will be replaced with a line using the border color that you selected.

The Home tab of the ribbon provides basic text editing controls such as font and paragraph options. You can use these to help format the content. It also includes a View button, as shown in Figure 4-51.

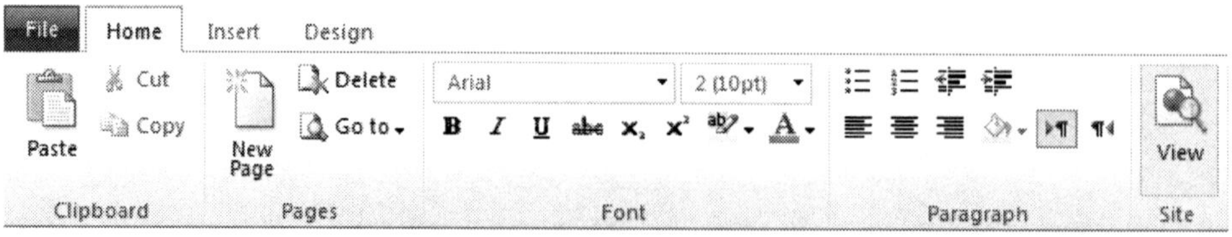

Figure 4-51. *The Home tab of the ribbon*

The View button will display the web site in a new tab so you can see how it will look to the public. This is a useful feature and enables you to easily see how the site is looking so far.

Uploading Files to the Images Library

The web site was created with an Images library, which is used to store images that are included in one or more web pages. Normally, you will upload images to this library and then use these images when designing a web page.

■ **Tip** In most cases, when an image is needed, you can retrieve it directly from the file system (on your workstation) instead of getting it from the Images library. However, the recommended approach is to upload the image to the Images library first and reference it from there. That provides a central location to store all the necessary images. Also, if you need to update an image later, you can simply upload a replacement and all referenced locations will automatically change.

To upload images, go to the Images library and click the Upload button. If you have more than one to upload, click the Upload Multiple Pictures link shown in Figure 4-52.

Figure 4-52. Uploading multiple pictures

You will likely see a dialog box warning you that the web site is trying to access content on your computer. Click the Allow button to continue. This will open the dialog box shown in Figure 4-53. Browse to the appropriate location and select the desired images. Click the "Upload and Close" button, which will upload the selected files.

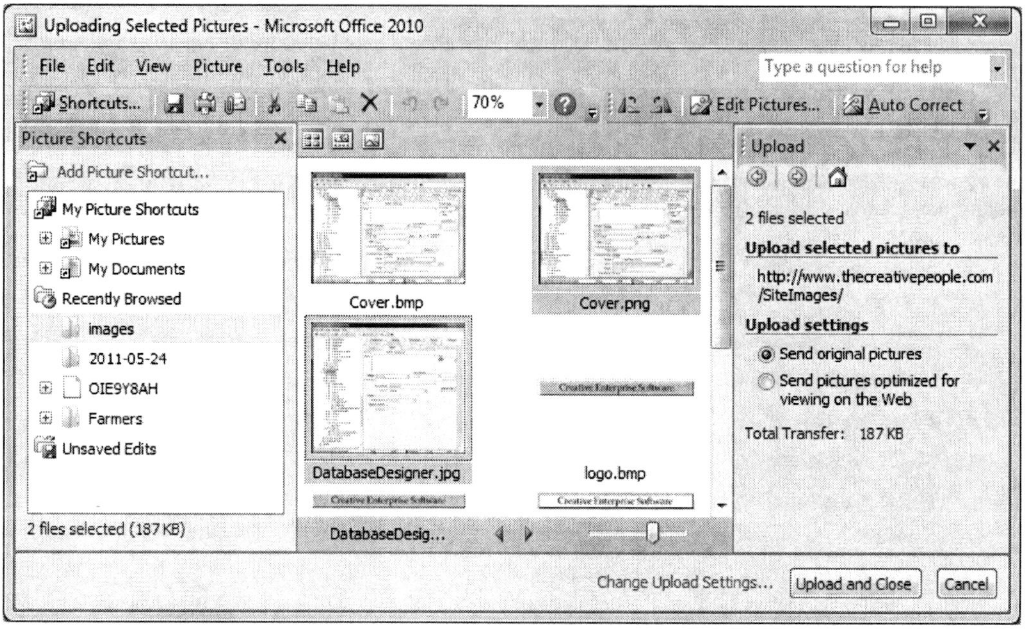

Figure 4-53. Selecting the files to upload

When the upload has completed, these images should be displayed in the Images library, as shown in Figure 4-54.

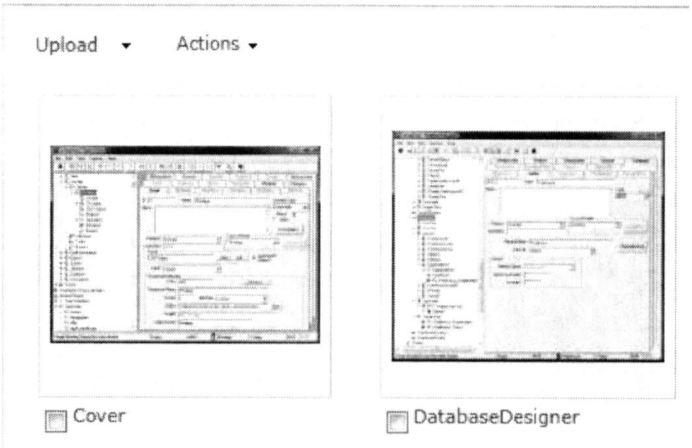

Figure 4-54. The Images library

Adding Images to a Web Page

The product template used to create the new web page includes a pair of images. Initially, these are stock images, which are merely placeholders for the actual images. You will now replace these with the images that you just uploaded.

From the new product page, right-click one of the images and then click the Replace Image link shown in Figure 4-55.

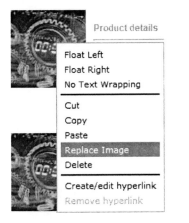

Figure 4-55. Replacing an image

This will display the Insert Image dialog box. Select one of the images from the Images library, as shown in Figure 4-56. Click the Insert image button to update the web page.

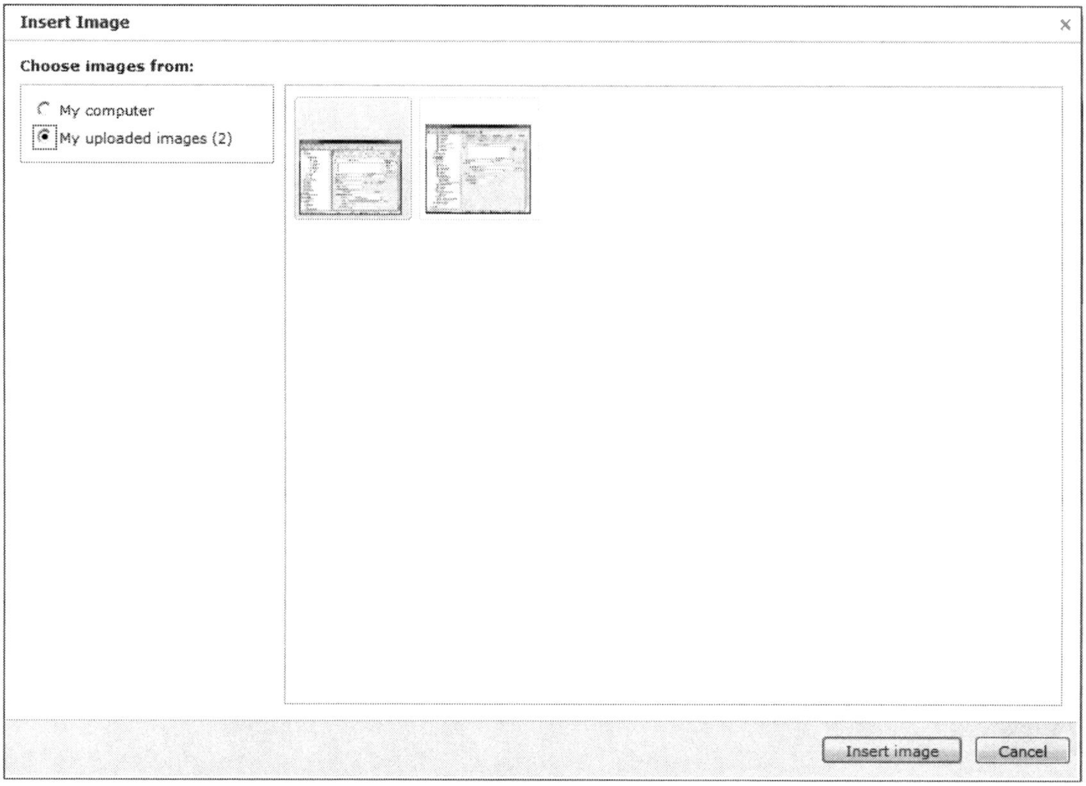

Insert Image   ✕

Choose images from:

○ My computer
◉ My uploaded images (2)

Figure 4-56. Selecting the image to add to a web page

Use the same procedure to replace the other image on this page.

Adding Gadgets to a Web Page

One of the really nice features of the Website Design Tool is that it allows you to easily add gadgets to your web pages. You'll start by adding a map gadget to the Home page. If you have a local business, this is a great way for your customers to find you, literally. I will then show you how to add the following gadgets:

- PayPal "Buy Now" button
- Contact Us form
- HTML block
- Slide show

When you have opened a web page for editing, the Insert tab of the ribbon (Figure 4-57) has buttons for adding several types of gadgets.

File
Home
Insert
Design
Line
Table
Image
Hyperlink
Slide Show
HTML
Map & Directions
Video
Contact Us
More Gadgets
Gadget Properties
Table Properties
Objects
Links
Gadgets
Manage

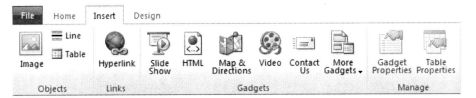

Figure 4-57. The Insert tab of the ribbon

Adding a Map Gadget

Scroll down to the bottom of the `Home` page and put the cursor at the end of the static text. From the Insert tab of the ribbon, click the Map & Directions button. This will display the Map & Directions dialog box. Specify the address that you want mapped in this gadget, as shown in Figure 4-58. Click the OK button when you have finished.

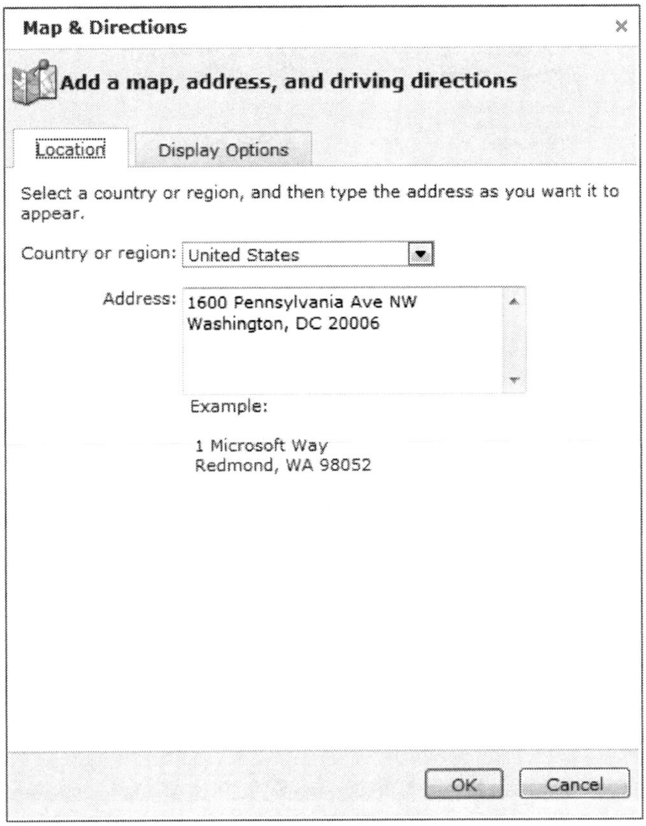
Map & Directions
Add a map, address, and driving directions
Location
Display Options
Select a country or region, and then type the address as you want it to appear.
Country or region: United States
Address: 1600 Pennsylvania Ave NW
Washington, DC 20006
Example:
1 Microsoft Way
Redmond, WA 98052
OK
Cancel

Figure 4-58. Entering the address to be mapped

This will add the gadget at the bottom of the Home page. Save the changes and then go to the public-facing web site to view the Home page. This should look similar to Figure 4-59 depending on the options you selected when configuring your web site.

Put your home page content here.

Home Page

Editing this page

Your Home page introduces your business and your Web site.

Write a summary, including a brief description of your products or services and your value and commitment to customers. This page sets the tone for your site and tells people what they can expect to find on other pages. Give the basics here and provide greater detail on other pages.

Let your customers know why they should explore your site

A business home page is similar to the front window of a retail business. Highlight your best products or services and any special offers here. Present your products or services value to browsers to get them "through the door" or deeper into your site.

Convince customers of your site's value to them

Consider what you might say to people to keep them coming back. You might mention how long you've been in business and how you show your commitment to customers. Be sure to tell visitors about your approach to business, your values, and your abilities.

It's a good idea to also post your contact information on the Home page for people who come to the site to quickly find your phone number or address.

Company Name
Phone number
Fax number
Address
State, ZIP code
E-mail address

Figure 4-59. The Home page with the added Map gadget

⬛ **Tip** There are quick links just above the File tab, as shown in Figure 4-60. You can use the first one to save the changes to the page you're editing. Then use the second button to see how the page will look in a browser.

File
View how your Web site will look to visitors

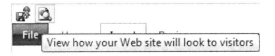

Figure 4-60. Using the quick link to view the page in a browser

There are more gadgets available on the Insert tab of the ribbon. To see all of the available gadgets, click the More Gadgets button shown in Figure 4-61.

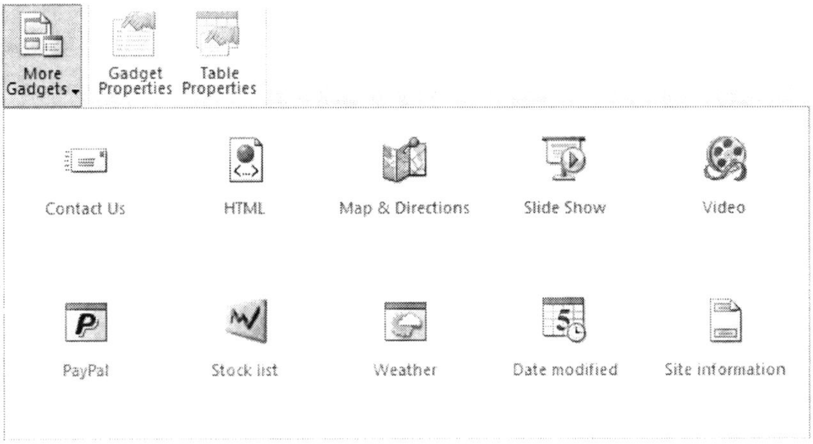
More Gadgets
Gadget Properties
Table Properties
Contact Us
HTML
Map & Directions
Slide Show
Video
PayPal
Stock list
Weather
Date modified
Site information

Figure 4-61. Listing all of the available gadgets

Adding a PayPal "Buy Now" Button

PayPal has a convenient feature that makes it really easy to take a payment from your web site. To use this feature, add a button to your site that has a hyperlink to the PayPal site. The link includes information about your merchant account and the product or service that is being purchased. The PayPal site uses this information to display the pre-configured merchant and product details. The consumer then completes the sale on the PayPal site.

■ **Note** For more information about using PayPal's Buy Now feature, visit `www.paypal.com/pdn-item`.

To add a "Buy Now" button to your site, you'll need a PayPal account. You must first configure the Buy Now button on the PayPal site, which will generate a block of HTML code. From the More Gadgets list, click the PayPal button, which will display the PayPal dialog box shown in Figure 4-62.

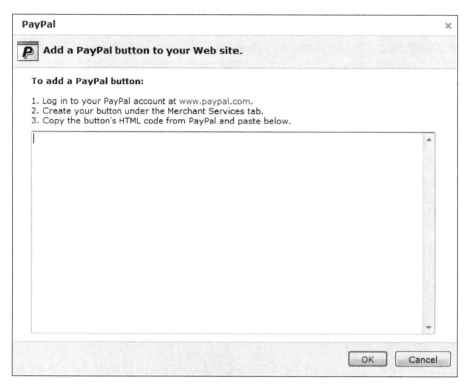

Figure 4-62. Adding a PayPal gadget

Insert the HTML block that was generated on the PayPal site into the PayPal dialog box and click the OK button. This will insert the Buy Now button at the current location.

Adding a Contact Us Form

Another useful gadget is the Contact Us form. This generates a simple form where the user can enter a comment along with their contact information. When the form is submitted, the comment is sent to the specified e-mail address(es).

Open the Contact Us web page and place the cursor at the end of this file. From the Insert tab of the ribbon, click the Contact Us button, which will display the Contact Us dialog box. Enter the e-mail address that the comment should be sent to, as shown in Figure 4-63. You can add multiple addresses; separate them with a semicolon.

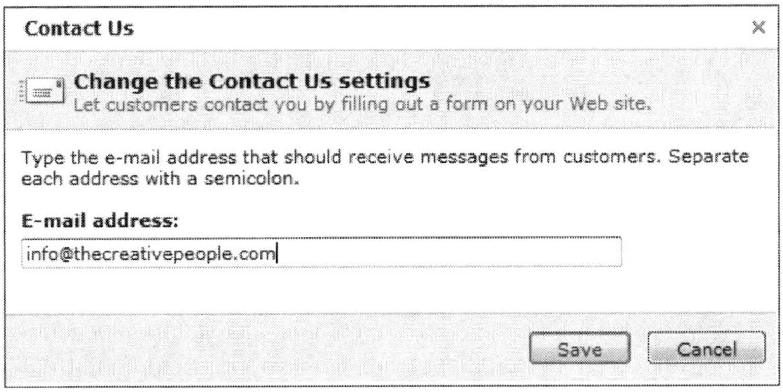
Contact Us
Change the Contact Us settings
Let customers contact you by filling out a form on your Web site.
Type the e-mail address that should receive messages from customers. Separate each address with a semicolon.
E-mail address:
info@thecreativepeople.com
Save
Cancel

Figure 4-63. Configuring the Contact Us form

Save the changes and go to the public-facing web site. Go to the Contact Us page and enter the contact information and comment as shown in Figure 4-64. Click the Submit button to save the comment.

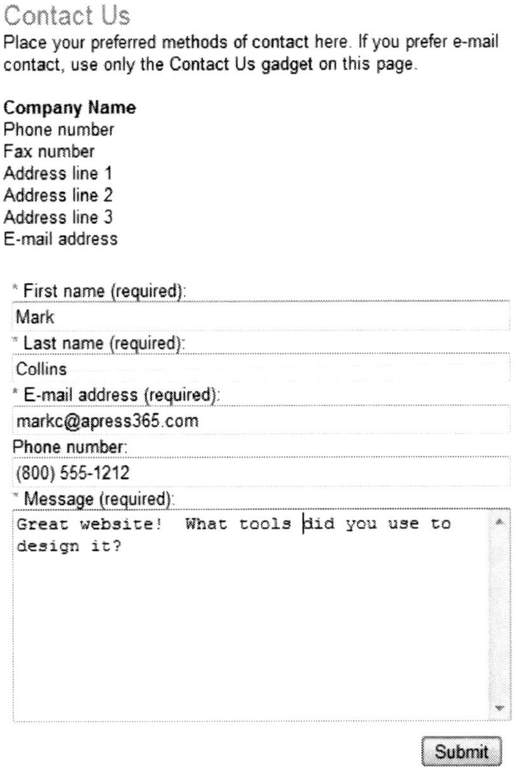
Contact Us
Place your preferred methods of contact here. If you prefer e-mail contact, use only the Contact Us gadget on this page.
Company Name
Phone number
Fax number
Address line 1
Address line 2
Address line 3
E-mail address
* First name (required):
Mark
* Last name (required):
Collins
* E-mail address (required):
markc@apress365.com
Phone number:
(800) 555-1212
* Message (required):
Great website! What tools did you use to design it?
Submit

Figure 4-64. The Contact Us page with the Contact Us gadget

Once the page has been submitted, you should receive an e-mail in the specified mailbox. The e-mail will look something like Figure 4-65.

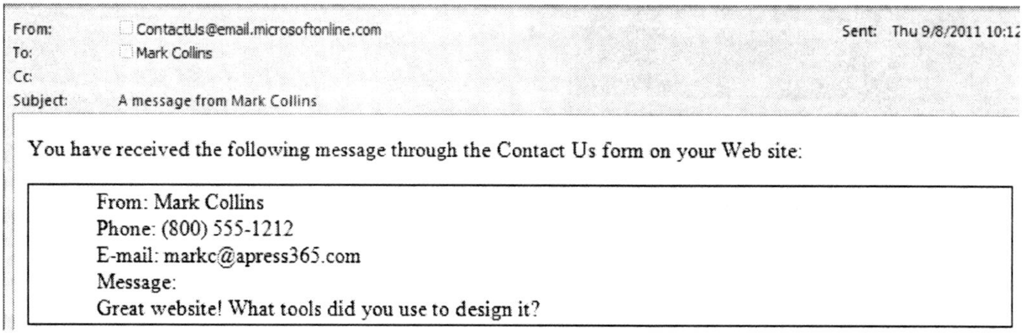
From: ContactUs@email.microsoftonline.com
Sent: Thu 9/8/2011 10:1
To: Mark Collins
Cc:
Subject: A message from Mark Collins
You have received the following message through the Contact Us form on your Web site:
From: Mark Collins
Phone: (800) 555-1212
E-mail: markc@apress365.com
Message:
Great website! What tools did you use to design it?

Figure 4-65. The e-mail generated by the Contact Us gadget

Adding an HTML Block

If you need to write some custom HTML content on a web page, click the HTML button in the Insert tab of the ribbon. In the HTML dialog box shown in Figure 4-66, enter the block of HTML that you want included on this page.

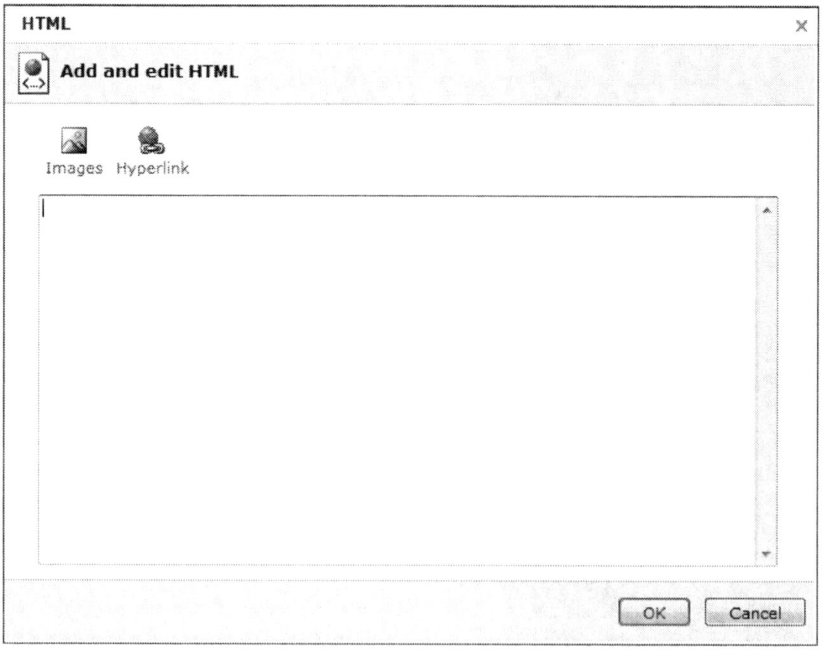
HTML
Add and edit HTML
Images
Hyperlink
OK
Cancel

Figure 4-66. Adding custom HTML code

Using the Slide Show Gadget

The Slide Show gadget is useful if you have several images to display. You'll add all the desired images to this gadget and they will be displayed one at a time. The revolving carousel style will show a thumbnail of all the images that continually rotate on the page. You can hover the mouse over one of the images to see a larger view of it.

Create a new web page using the Blank page template. From the Insert tab of the ribbon, click the Slide Show button, which will open the Slide Show dialog box. Select the desired images from the Images library and drag them to the right-hand side of the dialog box. Enter a name for the slide show and select the carousel type of slide show, as shown in Figure 4-67.

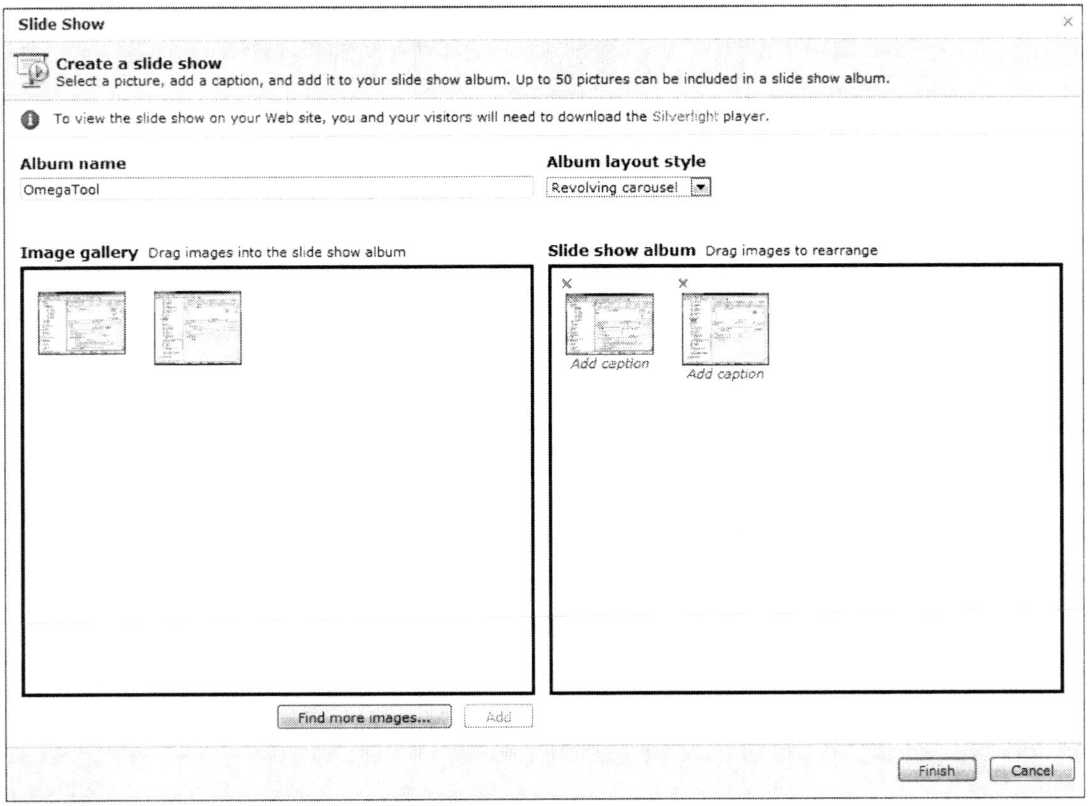

Figure 4-67. Adding images to a Slide Show gadget

Save your changes and view this page using the quick link described earlier. You should see the selected images rotate in a circle. Clicking one of the images causes the rotation to pause and the selected image is enlarged, as shown in Figure 4-68.

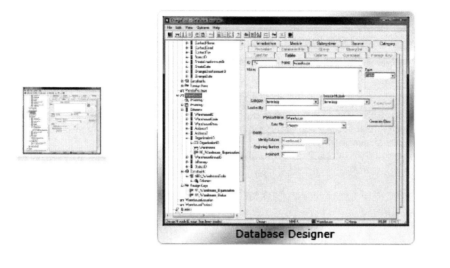

Figure 4-68. The Slide Show gadet in carousel mode with two images included

Summary

In this chapter you used several authoring tools to design an internal and external web site hosted on SharePoint Online 2010. The SharePoint UI enables power users to easily create new sites based on existing templates. They can also create custom lists and views.

I briefly introduced the SharePoint Designer, which is a desktop application that also allows you to create and modify SharePoint sites. This is intended as a developer tool and not as likely to be used by end users. You will use this in subsequent chapters for more advanced editing.

Finally, I showed you how to create a great-looking, content-based, public-facing web site using the Website Design Tool. Using Office 365 and these design tools, you can easily create useful internal and external web sites, which will form the foundation for your office automation solutions.

In the next chapter, I will show you how to design workflows in your SharePoint site to further enhance your office productivity.

CHAPTER 5

Creating Declarative Workflows

As you saw in the last chapter, SharePoint is a versatile repository for all sorts of data including document libraries and various lists of data elements. Workflows are a great way to establish a process around that data. For example, when a new request is created, a workflow can be initiated to automate the processing of that request.

SharePoint workflows are often referred to as *human-centric* workflows (or sometimes *task-centric*) because they are primarily concerned with the tasks that people will perform. When a request is received, for example, some of the typical tasks could be

- Review and approve the request.

- Assign and/or schedule the work.

- Fulfill the request.

- Verify (test) the end result.

- Provide feedback.

The workflow doesn't actually implement these tasks, people do. The workflow, however, enforces the business rules that determine what tasks are needed, what order they are performed in, under what conditions, and by whom.

In this chapter you'll implement a workflow to automate the processing of requests using the custom Requests list created in Chapter 4. I will show you how to

- Create a list template using an existing list.

- Design a workflow in Visio 2010.

- Implement a declarative workflow in SharePoint Designer 2010.

- Customize list forms.

- Create custom forms using InfoPath 2010.

Understanding Workflows in SharePoint Online

If you have created workflows using an on-premise SharePoint 2010 server, you'll notice that there are features that are not available in SharePoint Online. I will briefly explain these limitations up-front as they dictate the design approach used in this chapter.

Using Declarative Workflows

There are two ways to implement a SharePoint workflow. One is considered a code-based implementation that uses Visual Studio and the Workflow Foundation provided in .NET 3.0 and 3.5. These workflows can't run in a sandboxed solution and therefore are not available in Office 365.

The second approach uses *declarative* workflows. These are implemented using the workflow editor in SharePoint Designer to configure a "fixed" set of actions. The available actions provide quite a bit of functionality including:

- Creating or updating a list item.

- Sending an e-mail.

- Checking in a document to a document library.

◼ **Note** You can create custom actions using Visual Studio 2010 and this will be demonstrated in Chapter 10. Once a custom action has been implemented and deployed to SharePoint Online, you can include it in your declarative workflows.

Using the Default Team Site

I mentioned in the previous chapter that the Team Site template includes a Tasks list. This is a key part of most workflows because it stores the tasks that are generated and managed by the workflow. The solution presented here assumes that you have a site that includes a Tasks list. If you don't have a SharePoint site based on the Team Site temple, you should create a new site now and choose the Team Site template, as I explained at the beginning of Chapter 4.

◼ **Tip** You could add a new list to an existing site based on the Tasks list template. Also, you can rename the list that contains the tasks to whatever you wanted to call it. If it is named something other than Tasks, you'll need to override some default values when creating the workflow.

Using Globally Reusable Workflows

SharePoint 2010 provides some useful workflows such as Approval and Collect Feedback that you can use directly or include within a larger workflow. These are called globally reusable workflows and are defined at the site collection level. You will use the Approval workflow in this chapter.

In Chapters 1 and 2, I explained how SharePoint Online is administered for both Small Business and Enterprise plans. The Small Business plan provides a single site collection, while the Enterprise plans allow you to create multiple site collections. Another limitation of the Small Business plans is that you can't manage the site collection features.

This means that you can't activate the globally reusable workflows if you have a Small Business plan. All other aspects of declarative workflows can be used in either plan. Because the solution that is presented in this chapter requires these, I will be using the Enterprise site set up in Chapter 2.

■ **Tip** If you have a Small Business plan, you can implement the techniques presented here as long as you don't use the built-in workflows. You won't be able to complete the exercises in this chapter since they rely heavily on these reusable workflows. However, the workflow concepts explained in this chapter are applicable to Small Business plans.

Activating the Workflows Feature

By default, the Workflows feature is disabled; this must be activated at the site collection level. Go to the SharePoint Online site and, from the Site Actions menu, select the Site Settings link. If this is not the top-level site in the site collection, click the "Go to top level site settings" link in the Site Collection Administration section.

From the top-level site, click the "Site collection features" link. This will display the Features page that lists all of the site collection features that are available. Scroll to the bottom of the list and click the Activate button next to the Workflows feature, as shown in Figure 5-1.

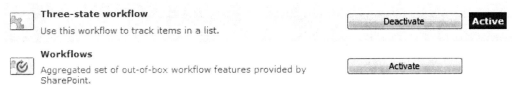

Figure 5-1. Activating the Workflows feature

Once this has been activated, the Active label should appear.

Copying the Requests List

Before getting started designing the workflow, you'll need to implement the Requests lists. This was created in Chapter 4 using a Small Business account and the solution in this chapter requires an Enterprise account. You can save an existing list as a template and then install that template to another SharePoint site. This is a handy technique for replicating an existing list definition.

■ **Note** You can't install a custom list template when using the Small Business plan. Also, this step is not necessary if you created the Requests list in Chapter 4 using an Enterprise Office 365 account. You can also download my template from www.apress.com instead of generating a template yourself.

Generate a List Template

The first step is to create a list template based on the current list definition.

1. Go to the site that contains the existing Requests list and open this list.

2. Go to the List Settings page (click the List Settings button from the List tab of the ribbon). Then click the "Save list as template" link shown in Figure 5-2.

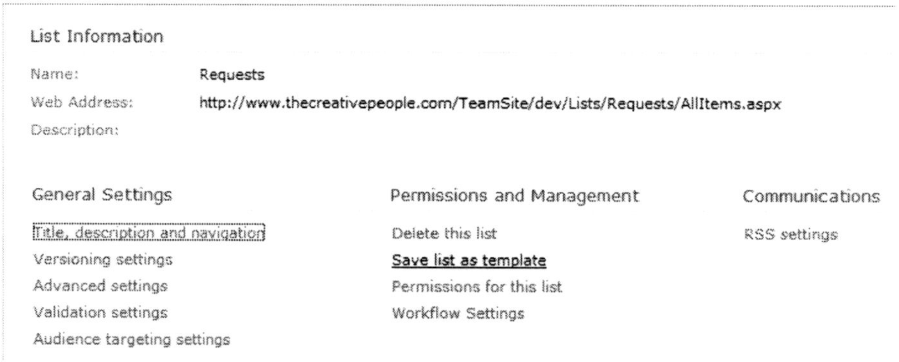

List Information

Name: Requests

Web Address: http://www.thecreativepeople.com/TeamSite/dev/Lists/Requests/AllItems.aspx

Description:

General Settings	Permissions and Management	Communications
Title, description and navigation	Delete this list	RSS settings
Versioning settings	**Save list as template**	
Advanced settings	Permissions for this list	
Validation settings	Workflow Settings	
Audience targeting settings		

Figure 5-2. Saving the Requests list as a list template

3. This will display the Save as Template page. Enter a file name, template name, and description, as shown in Figure 5-3. Leave the Include Content check box unselected. Normally you won't want to include the list data in the template definition; however, this option is available for situations where you need to transfer the data of an existing list.

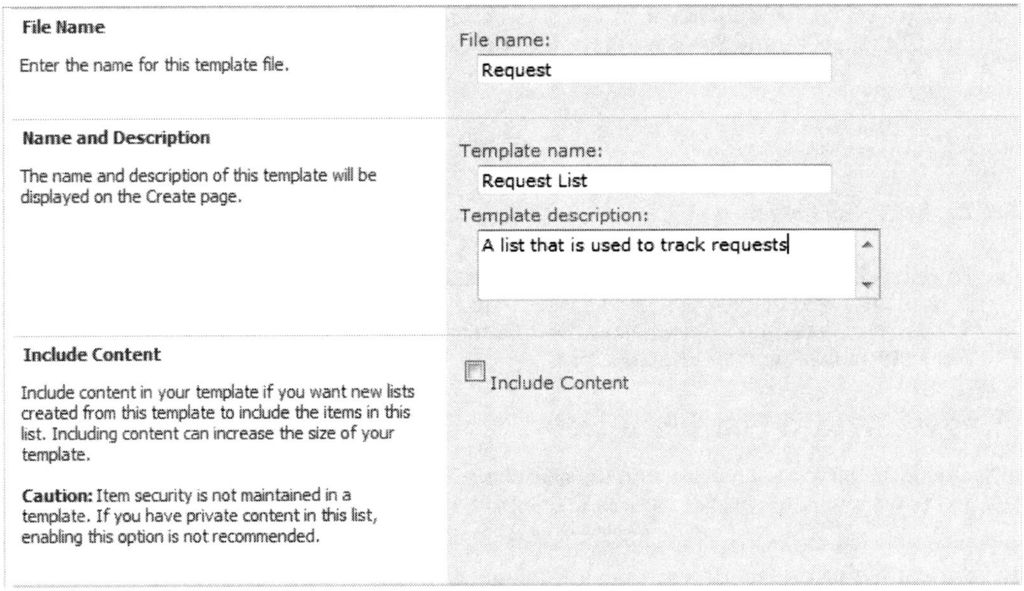

| **File Name** | File name: |
| Enter the name for this template file. | Request |

Name and Description	Template name:
The name and description of this template will be displayed on the Create page.	Request List
	Template description:
	A list that is used to track requests

Include Content	☐ Include Content
Include content in your template if you want new lists created from this template to include the items in this list. Including content can increase the size of your template.	
Caution: Item security is not maintained in a template. If you have private content in this list, enabling this option is not recommended.	

Figure 5-3. Entering the template details

4. Click the OK button to create the template. When this has completed, you'll see the dialog box shown in Figure 5-4, letting you know that the template has been created and where to find it.

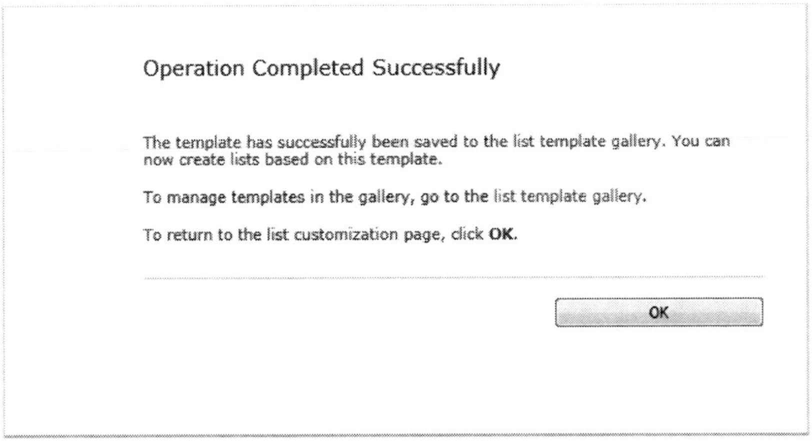

Operation Completed Successfully

The template has successfully been saved to the list template gallery. You can now create lists based on this template.

To manage templates in the gallery, go to the list template gallery.

To return to the list customization page, click **OK**.

[OK]

Figure 5-4. Operation completed dialog box

5. Custom list templates are available from the Site Settings page by using the "List templates" link in the Galleries section. This completion dialog provides a

link that will take you directly to this page by clicking the "list template gallery" link. Click that link and you'll see the new template shown in Figure 5-5.

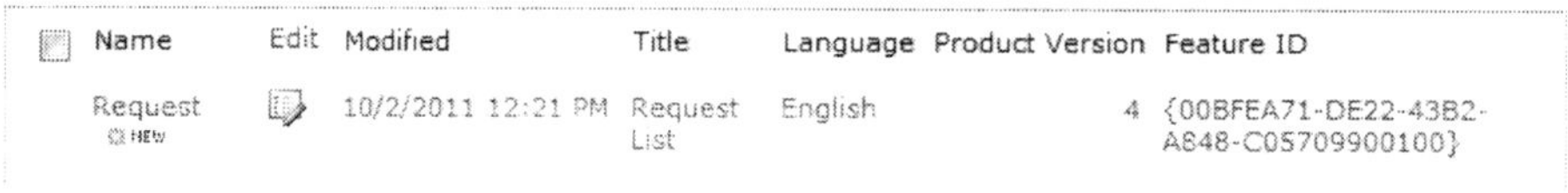

	Name	Edit	Modified	Title	Language	Product Version	Feature ID
☐	Request ✿ NEW	🖉	10/2/2011 12:21 PM	Request List	English	4	{00BFEA71-DE22-43B2-A848-C05709900100}

Figure 5-5. The List Template Gallery

6. To install this template on another site, you'll need to download the template file and then upload it to the new site. When you click on the Request link in the List Template Gallery, you'll have the option to open or save the file. Save the file to a folder on your local machine.

Installing a Custom List Template

Now you'll need to install this list template on the new SharePoint site. This will allow you to create a new list based on this template. You will need to first log out of the existing SharePoint site.

1. Go to the new SharePoint site and navigate to the List Template Gallery from the Site Settings page. List templates are defined for the entire site collection and can only be managed from the top-level site. If your site is a subsite, navigate to the top-level site first or use the "Go to top level site settings" link as I explained earlier.

2. From the Documents tab of the ribbon, click the Upload Document button, which will display the Upload Template dialog box shown in Figure 5-6.

3. Browse to the location where you saved the template file and click the OK button.

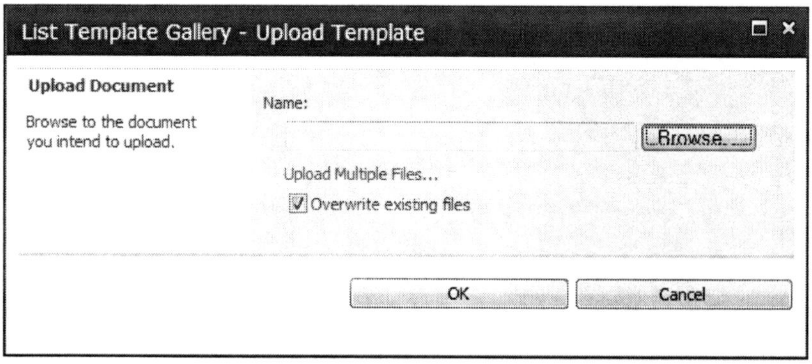

Figure 5-6. Uploading a template file

4. The template details that you entered previously will be displayed and you can edit any of these fields, as shown in Figure 5-7. Click the Save button to install the new list template.

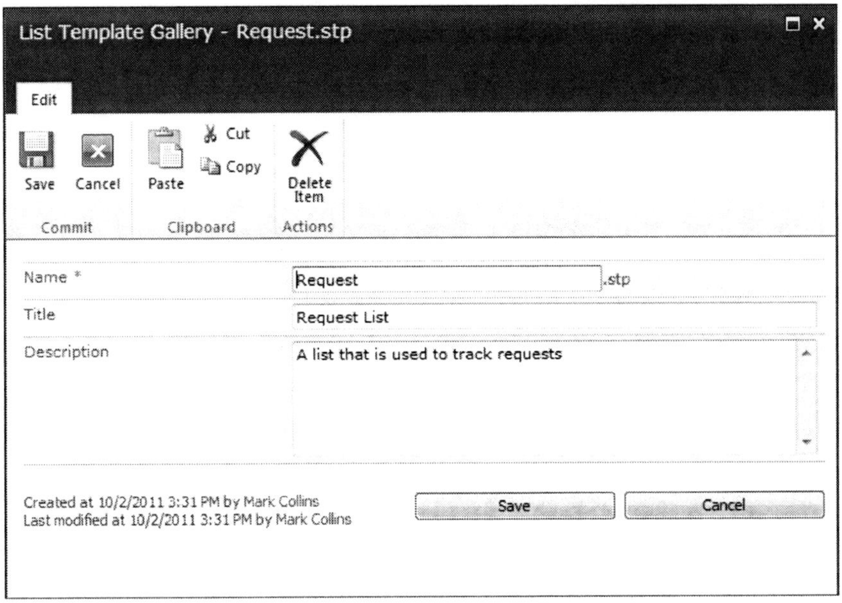

Figure 5-7. Adding the Requests list template

Creating a List

Now that the new template has been installed, you can create a new list based on this template. The list can be created in any site in the site collection that contains the new list template.

1. Go to the Team Site that you will use for this chapter. From the Site Actions menu, click the More Options link.

2. In the Create dialog box, filter the available templates to only List types and Blank & Custom categories, as shown in Figure 5-8. You should see the Request List template; select this and enter the list name **Requests**.

3. Click the Create button to create the Requests list.

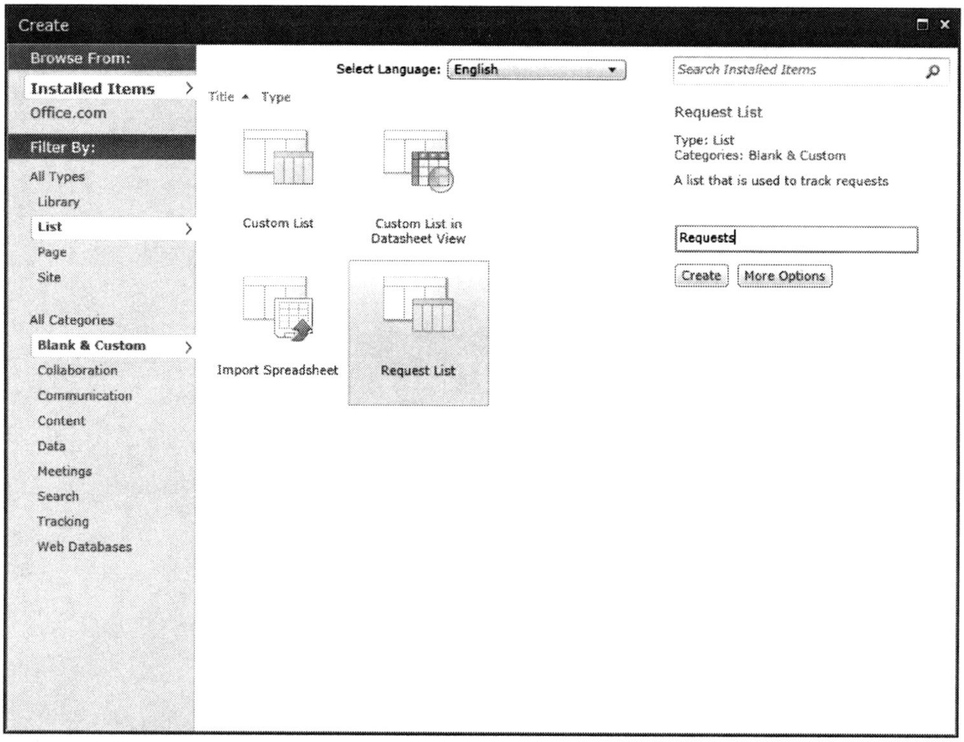

Figure 5-8. Creating the Requests list

Using the SharePoint Designer Workflow Editor

In the previous chapter, I presented a brief introduction to SharePoint Designer. This is a client application that communicates with SharePoint Server (and SharePoint Online) to provide advanced editing capabilities. In this chapter, you'll use its workflow editor to create a declarative workflow. Before getting started, I'll give a basic overview of the workflow editor.

Creating the Workflow Editor Components

The basic building blocks of a declarative workflow are *actions* and *conditions*. Actions are the things a workflow does and conditions define the rules that determine when certain actions are performed. These are often combined into *steps* that help organize the workflow in logical blocks.

Actions

Actions are the things your workflow will do, such as create a task, send an e-mail, or update a variable. Figure 5-9 shows a partial list of the actions that are available to you.

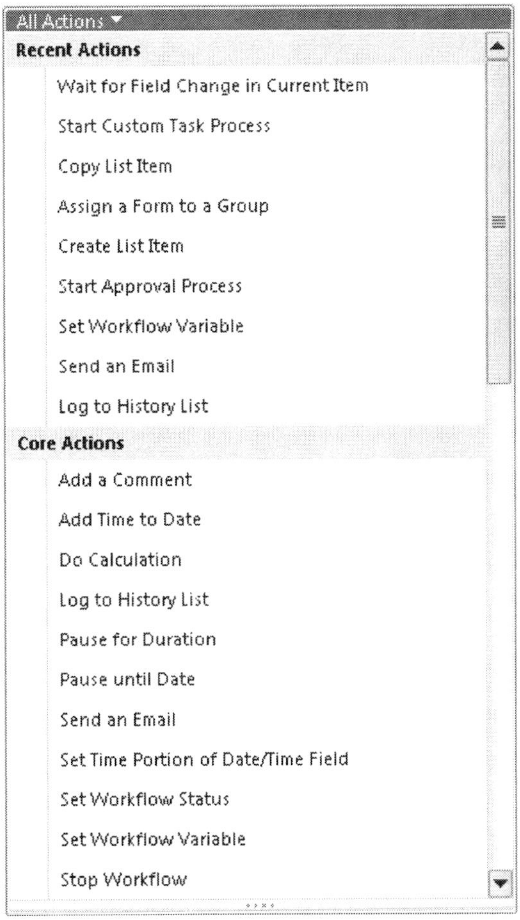

Figure 5-9. *Available actions*

The actions are grouped into categories to help you find the one you need. The first group, called Recent Actions, contains the actions you have used recently. These same actions are also listed in their normal groups. Listing them here makes it easier for you to find actions that you use frequently.

Conditions

Conditions give you the ability to execute actions based on the outcome of previous actions or input parameters. For example, if an item was approved, you may want to perform different actions than if it was rejected. Figure 5-10 shows the list of conditions that you can use.

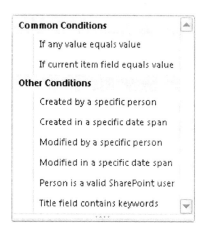

Figure 5-10. Available conditions

When you insert a condition, the designer creates a line in the workflow starting with If and followed by the condition. Subsequent actions are indented to show that they are performed only if the condition is true. You can also add an Else block, which will be executed if the condition is false.

Steps

Steps are used to organize your workflow into blocks that are easy to visualize. When you create a new workflow, the initial implementation contains Step 1. You can add all of your actions and conditions into this step. However, for longer workflows, creating additional steps will make your workflow easier to read. Steps can also be nested so a single step can contain other substeps.

Other Components

Figure 5-11 shows the buttons available on the ribbon for inserting elements.

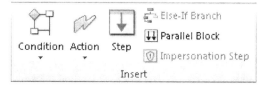
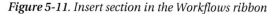

Figure 5-11. Insert section in the Workflows ribbon

I've explained the Condition, Action, and Step buttons, but there are a few smaller buttons that provide some interesting features. The Else-If Branch button will create an Else block for an existing condition. Clicking this button while on a condition will create the corresponding Else block.

The Parallel Block button allows you to create a group of actions that are performed simultaneously. The default logic is to perform actions sequentially (one at a time). As you start entering actions, you'll notice that the wording on the workflow will indicate how the actions are executed. For example, the second action will be prefixed with the word "then," implying that the second action is started after the first action is completed. However, in parallel blocks, the word "and" is used, indicating they are being started at the same time.

The Impersonation Step button creates a new step, just like the Step button, with one important difference. The actions performed in this step are run as the user who designed the workflow (you) instead of the person who started the workflow (the end user). You will usually have more permissions granted to you than most users, so this allows you to perform some actions that the end user might not otherwise have access to. Figure 5-12 shows the help text associated with this button.

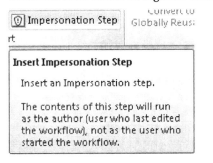

Figure 5-12. The Impersonation Step button

Using the Editor Features

When you design a workflow, you'll add actions, conditions, and steps to your workflow and then configure them. The workflow editor provides some nice features to help you add the necessary components and then to specify how they are to function.

Using the Insertion Point

You will quickly notice the flashing orange bar, which indicates the insertion point. This indicates where actions, conditions, or steps will be inserted when you click one of the buttons in the ribbon. The flashing orange bar indicates the current insertion point. You can move the insertion point by hovering the mouse pointer over where you want to insert an action, condition, or step. If this is a suitable location, a solid faint orange bar will appear where the mouse pointer is, as demonstrated in Figure 5-13.

> **Step 1**
>
> (Start typing or use the Insert group in the Ribbon.)

Figure 5-13. Moving the insertion point

The flashing orange bar (insertion point) is inside step 1. If you hover the mouse just below step 1, a faint orange bar will appear. If you click it, it will start flashing, indicating that this is now the current insertion point. You can generally move the insertion point to any of the following:

- Between existing actions (to insert a new action or condition).

- After the actions for a condition (to create an Else branch).

- After the last action in a step (to add an action or condition).

- Between existing steps (to insert a new step).

- After the last step (to add a new step).

When you click the insertion point, it will open a search box where you can search for the desired action or condition. For example, click the insertion point, and enter **email**. The designer should look like the one shown in Figure 5-14.

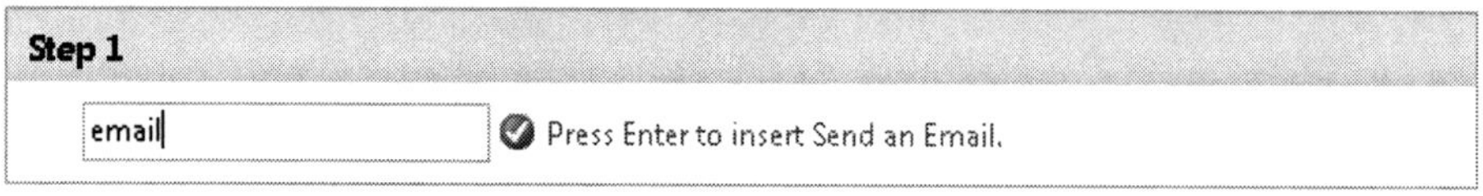

Figure 5-14. Searching for the e-mail action

░ **Tip** You don't have to click the current insertion point. If you just start typing, it will automatically open up the search box.

This is a really handy feature! As you started typing and entered **em**, it would show that it found 12 actions or conditions. If you press Enter at that point, it would list them for you to select one. By the time you typed **ema**, the search was narrowed down to a single result, and it told you to press Enter to select the matching action. So, by only typing **ema** and pressing Enter, you can add an action to send an e-mail.

Defining Parameters

Most actions and conditions have parameters that you can specify to control its execution. In the Send an Email action, for example, you'll need to specify who the e-mail will go to as well as the subject and body of the e-mail. Parameters in an action or condition are underlined and are displayed as links, as shown in Figure 5-15.

Figure 5-15. The Send an Email action with an undefined parameter

When you click one of these parameter links, the display will change to allow you to specify a value for the parameter. The controls that are made available to you will vary greatly depending on the type of parameter. For most simple parameters, the display will look like Figure 5-16.

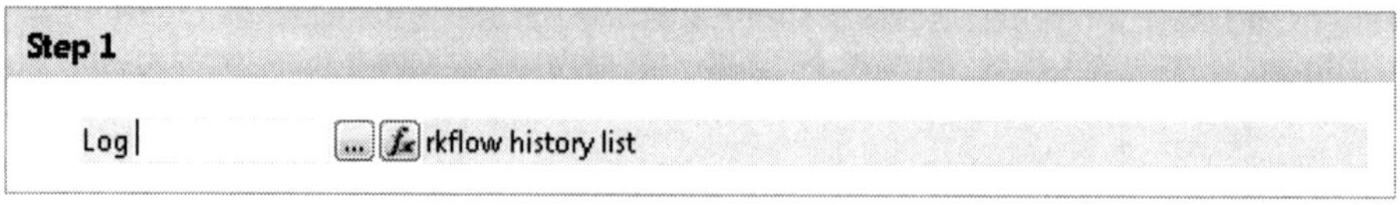

Figure 5-16. Editor changed to accept input

The link has changed into a text box and two buttons. This provides three ways for this information to be entered. For fixed text, you can simply type it in the text box. If you want to use a column, parameter, or variable defined in SharePoint, use the lookup (fx) button to provide a Lookup dialog box, as shown in Figure 5-17.

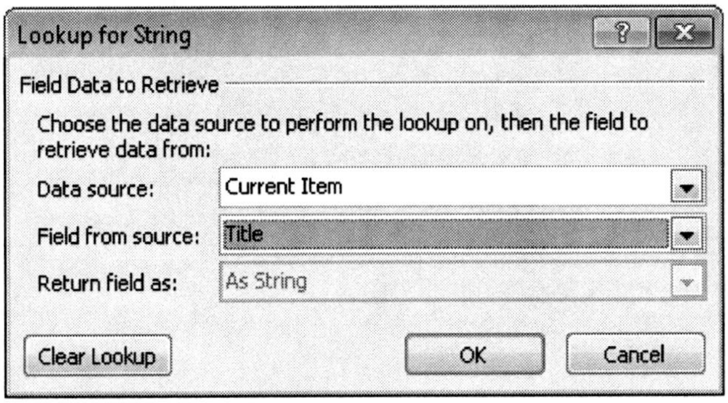

Figure 5-17. The Lookup dialog box

This third option is to click the button with the ellipses. Click this button, and the String Builder dialog box will appear. This allows you to combine static text along with dynamic data stored in SharePoint. To add dynamic data, put the cursor where you want the data inserted and click the Add or Change Lookup button. This will display the same Lookup dialog, as shown in Figure 5-18.

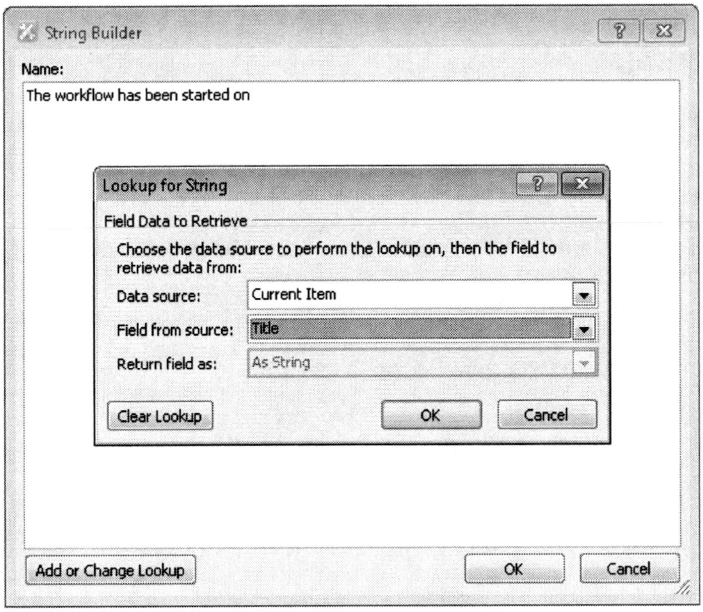

Figure 5-18. Using the String Builder dialog box

Complex parameters will display a dialog box that allows you to define multiple values. The "these users" link in the Send an Email action, for example, will display the Define E-mail Message dialog box shown in Figure 5-19. This is used to specify the recipients as well as the subject and body of the e-mail.

Figure 5-19. The Define E-mail Message dialog box

Using Visio to Define a Workflow

You'll start the workflow design in Visio 2010. Visio is a great tool for creating diagrams and flowcharts, and it allows you to begin your workflow design at a high level. It provides shapes that correspond with many of the common actions and conditions available in SharePoint Designer. You will use Visio to design the steps of the workflow process and then import this design into the SharePoint Designer.

You don't have to use Visio to create a declarative workflow. You can go directly to SharePoint designer and add actions and conditions to implement the workflow logic. For more complicated workflows, however, there are several benefits to using Visio.

- Starting with the big picture is always a good idea.

- A Visio diagram will help you present the workflow design to end users or stakeholders.

- As I will demonstrate later in this chapter, SharePoint can display the current state of a running workflow using the Visio visualization of the workflow steps.

Designing a Workflow in Visio

Let's get started.

1. Start Microsoft Visio 2010.

2. From the File menu, choose New, and select the Microsoft SharePoint Workflow template. Then click the Create button. This template has custom shapes that are recognized by SharePoint Designer. The shapes that you use are very important because they will determine the processing logic.

■ **Tip** If you don't have a template named Microsoft SharePoint Workflow, you can use the Basic template. Then add the SharePoint Workflow Actions and SharePoint Workflow Conditions stencils from the Flowchart group.

---

3. Each workflow begins with a Start shape and ends at a Terminate shape. You will find these shapes on the Quick Shapes collection. Drag a Start shape onto the diagram followed by an Assign item for approval shape. This shape represents the approval process for the request that has been submitted. Change its label to **Approve Request.**

4. Next, drag a Compare data source shape onto the diagram and change the label to **Approved?** This condition will evaluate whether the request was approved.

5. There are two possible outcomes of the Approve Request step: the request is either approved or rejected. So you'll need two branches from the Approved? condition. For each branch, add a Set field shape and change the label to **Set Cancelled Status** and **Set Assigned Status**. You'll also want to send an e-mail to the initiator in each case. For each branch, drag a Send an email shape and change their labels to **Send rejected email** and **Send approved email**.

6. For the final step, when a request is approved you'll need to actually fulfill the request. This will be represented by a Start custom task process shape. Drag this to the approved branch and change its label to **Fulfill Request**. Finally, add a Terminate shape and connect both branches to it.

The completed diagram should look like Figure 5-20.

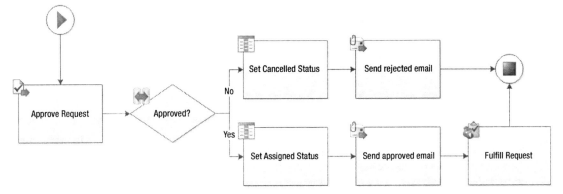

Figure 5-20. The SharePoint Workflow diagram in Visio 2010

Exporting a Visio Workflow

Now that you have designed the workflow, you'll need to export it to a file format that is usable in SharePoint Designer. Go to the Process menu. Click the Check Diagram button. This will verify that the diagram is syntactically correct. Fix any issues that it reports.

Then click the Export button as shown in Figure 5-21 and select a location for the export file. Enter the file name **Workflow**.

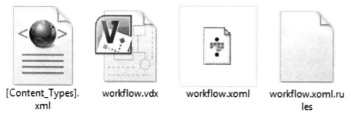

Figure 5-21. Exporting a Visio workflow

The Visio diagram is exported as a Visio Workflow Interchange file using a `*.vwi` extension. This is actually a `.zip` file. If you make a copy of the `Workflow.vwi` file and change the extension to `.zip`, you can inspect the contents using Windows Explorer. Figure 5-22 shows the contents.

[Content_Types].xml workflow.vdx workflow.xoml workflow.xoml.rules

Figure 5-22. Contents of the `Workflow.vwi` file

Importing a Visio Workflow

Now you'll import this workflow design into the SharePoint site that you created based on the Team Site template, which includes the Requests list. As I mentioned in the beginning of the chapter, this workflow will be associated with the Requests list and will require a Tasks list.

1. Go to this SharePoint site and, from the Site Actions menu, click the Edit in SharePoint Designer link. This will start the SharePoint Designer and open the current site.

2. From SharePoint Designer, click the Workflows link in the Navigation pane. You will see a lot of reusable workflows listed here. These are various localized versions of the reusable workflows mentioned earlier and were installed when you activated the Workflows site collection feature.

3. Click the Import from Visio button in the ribbon, as shown in Figure 5-23.

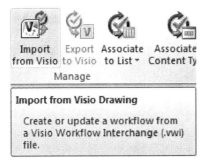

Figure 5-23. Importing a Visio file in SharePoint Designer

4. This will display the dialog box shown in Figure 5-24. Browse to the location of the `Workflow.vwi` file that you just created and click the Next button.

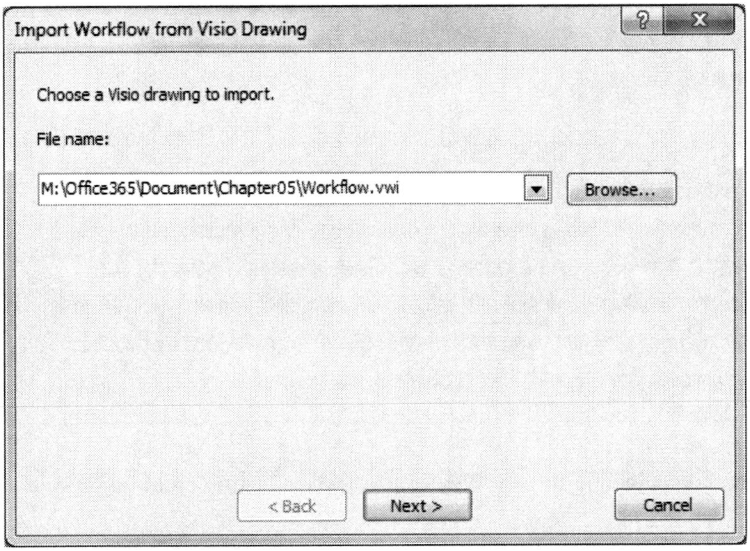

Figure 5-24. Selecting the file location

5. The next dialog box allows you to specify the name of the workflow and to configure its association. Enter the name **Process Request** and select the `Requests` list, as shown in Figure 5-25. Click the Finish button to create the workflow.

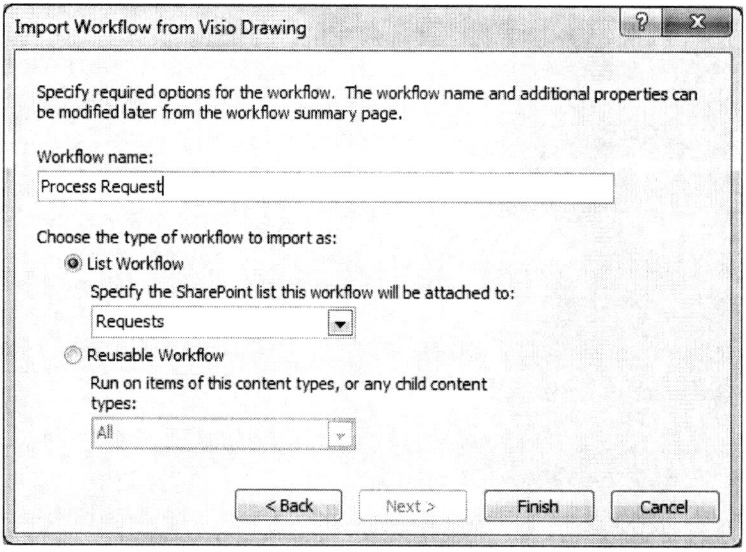

Figure 5-25. Specifying the workflow properties

■ **Note** Generally a workflow is associated with a specific list or document library. (SharePoint 2010 introduces site workflows that are not associated with any list.) When creating a workflow you can either associate it to a specific list or make it a reusable workflow. When creating a reusable workflow, you simply defer the list association. This workflow can then be later associated to multiple lists. If you wanted to make this a reusable workflow, you would need to select the Requests content type since it will use columns defined by this type. This will ensure that the workflow can only be associated to a list that contains Requests items.

This will create the workflow and display it in the workflow editor. The initial implementation will look like Figure 5-26.

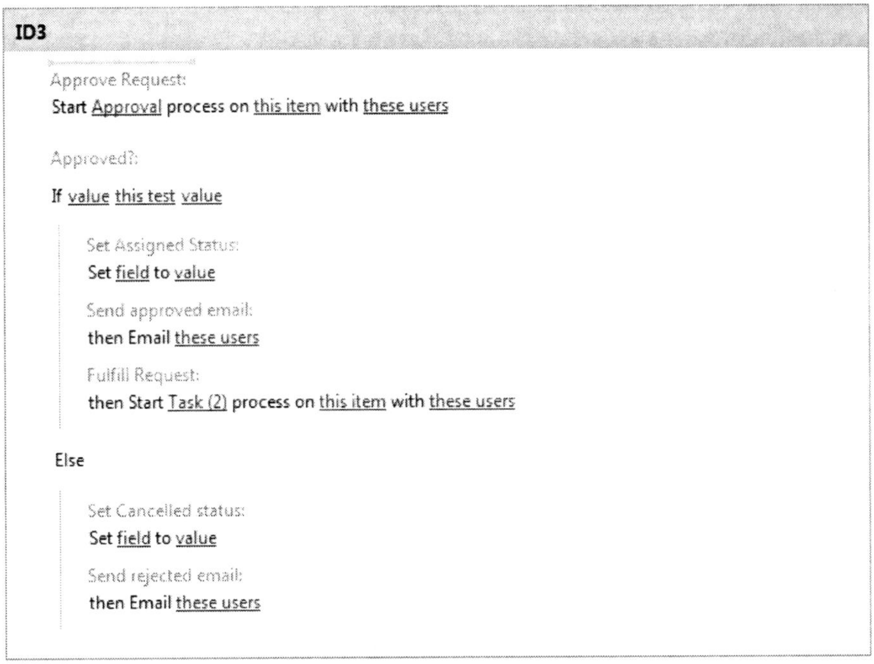

ID3

Approve Request:
Start <u>Approval</u> process on <u>this item</u> with <u>these users</u>

Approved?:

If <u>value</u> <u>this test</u> <u>value</u>

    Set Assigned Status:
    Set <u>field</u> to <u>value</u>

    Send approved email:
    then Email <u>these users</u>

    Fulfill Request:
    then Start <u>Task (2)</u> process on <u>this item</u> with <u>these users</u>

Else

    Set Cancelled status:
    Set <u>field</u> to <u>value</u>

    Send rejected email:
    then Email <u>these users</u>

Figure 5-26. The initial workflow generated from Visio

Implementing the Workflow

Now that you have created the workflow structure, you need to specify the details. Each of the links in the initial implementation represents an action or condition parameter and now you need to specify values for them. I will take you through each of these and show you how to enter them.

Configuring the Approval Task

You'll start with the first action, which will generate a task for someone to review and approve the associated request. The action currently reads

Start *Approval* process on *this item* with *these users*

1. The Approval link is used to configure the task process and I'll explain that later in this chapter. The next parameter, "this item," specifies the list item that the approval process should review. In most cases, this will be the current item, which is the list item that the workflow instance is operating on. Click the "this item" link and a drop-down list will be displayed that enumerates all of the available lists. Select Current Item, as shown in Figure 5-27.

177

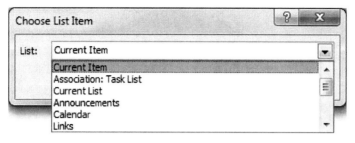

Figure 5-27. *Specifying the item to be approved*

■ **Tip** The drop-down contains all of the available lists including `Calendar`, `Links`, and `Requests`. It also includes a couple of generic references such as `Current Item` and `Association: Task List`. Since this workflow is associated with the `Requests` list, selecting `Current Item` is equivalent to selecting the `Requests` list. However, if you were implementing this as a reusable workflow you would need to use `Current Item`. Then the actual list that is referenced would be defined as whatever list the workflow is associated with.

---

2. The final parameter, these users, is used to configure the task of reviewing the request. When you click the "these users" link, the Select Task Process Participants dialog box is displayed. This in one of the more complex parameters that has several values that can be specified. The first field, `Participants`, indicates who the task should be assigned to. Click the button to the right of this field and the Select Users dialog box, shown in Figure 5-28, is displayed.

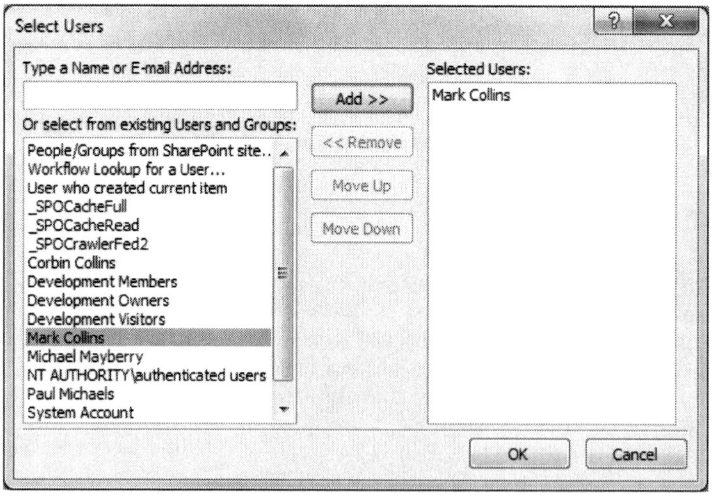

Figure 5-28. *Assigning the task participants*

■ **Note** For this example I just added myself as the approver. You could set up an Approvers group in SharePoint and then select that group. Anyone in that group would then be able to review the request. You can also assign multiple reviewers.

3. After selecting the user(s), you'll also specify the Title and Instructions fields. Keep in mind that you're generating a task that will appear in someone's Tasks list. The Title and Instructions should communicate what they are supposed to do. Since there could be multiple requests that need to be reviewed, it would be useful to include some of the request details in the task. Click the ellipses next to the Title field, which will display the String Builder dialog box. Enter **Review Request –** and then click the "Add or Change Lookup" button. This will allow you to embed data from the associated Requests item in the task's title.

4. In the Lookup for String dialog box, select the Title field of the Current Item list, as shown in Figure 5-29. Click the OK button to add this field to the String Builder.

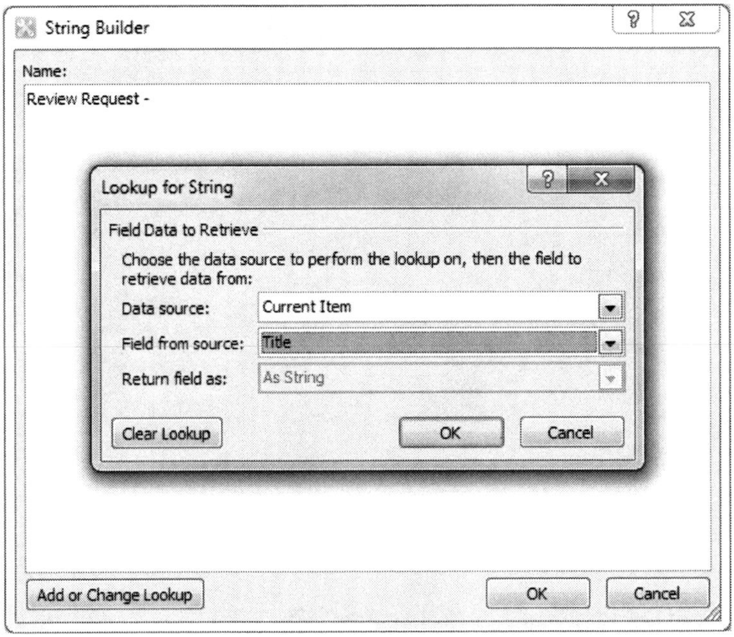

Figure 5-29. Building the task title

5. Click the OK button again to update the Title field. Its value should be

Review Request - [%CurrentItem:Title%]

6.   The Instructions field works a little differently. It is actually like a mini string builder. Enter the static text **Please review this request** and a couple of blank lines. Then click the "Add or Change Lookup" button and select the Comments field from the Current Item. This will include the Comments from the associated request and include them in the workflow task. The completed dialog box should look like Figure 5-30.

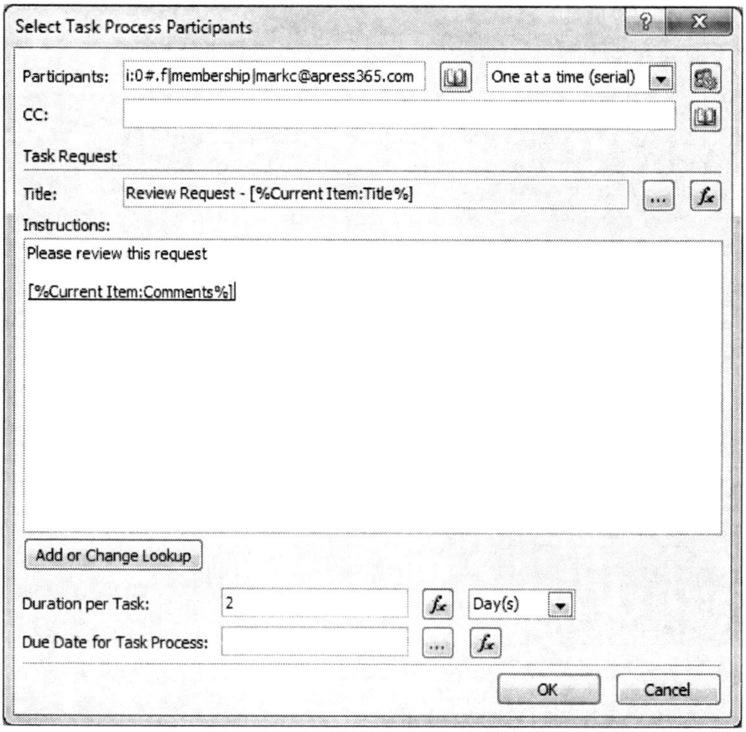

Figure 5-30. The task configuration

The completed action should look similar to

```
Start Approval process on Current Item with i:0#.f|membership|markc@apress365.com
```

Processing the Approval Results

So now the workflow has started the approval process. As I said, this will create a task for someone (me) to review the request. In the meantime, the workflow will be idle waiting for the approval process to complete. The rest of the workflow will take the appropriate actions depending on whether the request was approved.

Designing a Condition

The next line in the workflow reads

If *value* *this test* *value*

1. This condition compares two values, which are specified by the value links. The operation used to compare them is specified by the "this test" link. You'll use this to test the Approval Status column to see if the request was approved. Click the first value link and a text box will appear, as shown in Figure 5-31.

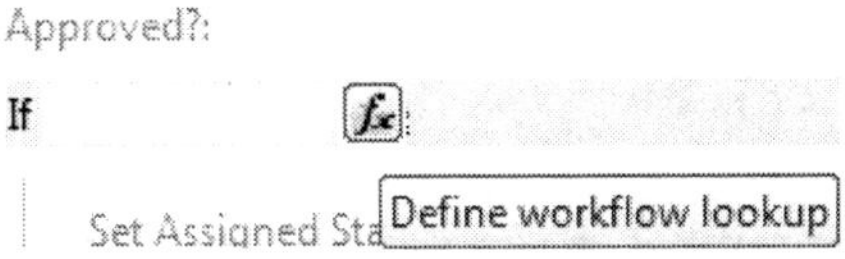

Approved?:

If   *fx* :

Set Assigned Sta | Define workflow lookup |

Figure 5-31. *Specifying the first value*

2. The *fx* button is also displayed, which will launch the Lookup dialog box. Click this button, select the Current Item data source, and then select the Approval Status column, as shown in Figure 5-32. Click the OK button to close the dialog box.

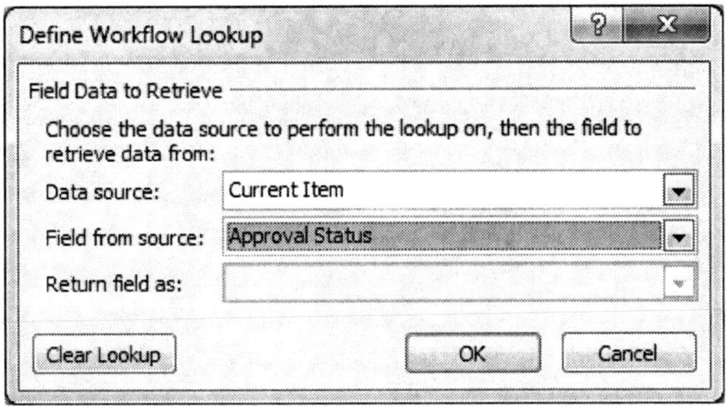

Define Workflow Lookup

Field Data to Retrieve

Choose the data source to perform the lookup on, then the field to retrieve data from:

Data source:	Current Item
Field from source:	Approval Status
Return field as:	

Clear Lookup		OK	Cancel

Figure 5-32. *Selecting the ApprovalStatus column*

3. Click the "this test" link and select the equals operator, as shown in Figure 5-33.

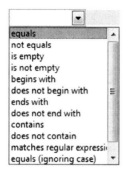

Figure 5-33. Selecting the equals operator

■ **Tip** You can see from this drop-down list all of the available operations such as begins with, contains, and is empty. This dynamic list is based on the column type of the first value that was selected. If you had selected a numeric column you would see operations such as greater than and less than.

---

4. Click the second value link and you'll see a list of values. Because the Approval Status column is defined as a Choice field, it has a fixed set of values that are allowed. These choices are enumerated in the drop-down list. Again, this is dynamic based on the first value that was selected. Select Approved, as shown in Figure 5-34.

Figure 5-34. Specifying the Approved value from a Choice field

The completed condition should now read

If Current Item:Approval Status equals 0;#Approved

Updating the Request Status

In both the If section and the Else clause you'll need to update the Request Status column. The first action in each of these clauses reads

Set *field* to *value*

Click the field link and select the Request Status column, as shown in Figure 5-35.

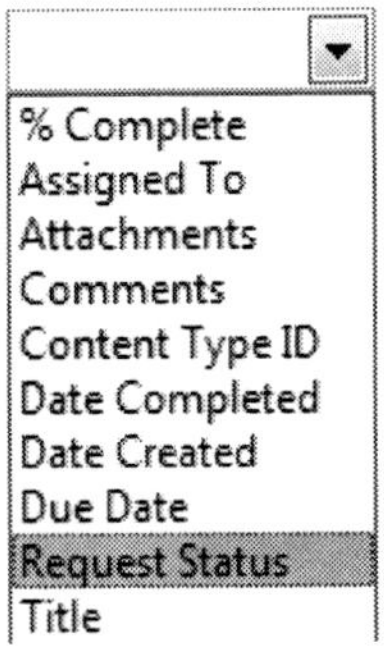

Figure 5-35. Updating the RequestStatus column

Then click the value link and a drop-down will appear listing all of the allowed values. Select Assigned in the If section and Cancelled in the Else clause.

Sending an E-Mail

If the request was approved you'll send an e-mail to the person who created the request. The next action in the workflow reads

then Email *these users*

■ **Tip** As you probably noticed, the workflow editor tries to express the workflow in natural language. Actions such as Set Request Status to Assigned can be easily understood by non-technical users. One of the nice features of this is using the word "then" to express the serialized execution of tasks. This makes it clears that the e-mail is sent after the Request Status is updated. For actions that are in a parallel step, the word "and" is used instead to imply the actions are happening concurrently.

---

1. Click the "these users" link to display the Design E-mail Message dialog box. From this single dialog box you can configure all the e-mail properties. You'll start by defining the recipients. Click the lookup button to the right of the To field, which will display the Select Users dialog box. You used this dialog box before when configuring the approval process.

2. The Select Users dialog box lists the users and groups that are currently defined in your SharePoint site. There are also a couple items that have special handling. Select "User who created current item" and click the Add button, as shown in Figure 5-36.

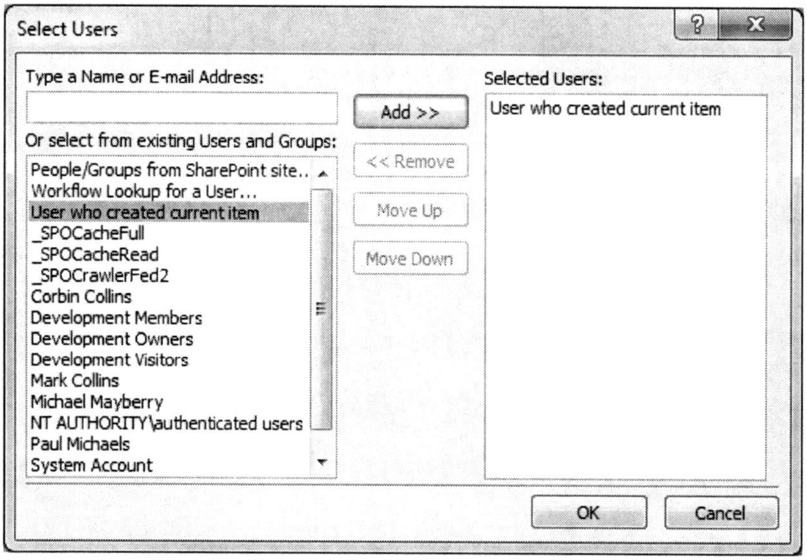

Figure 5-36. Selecting the e-mail recipient

3. For the Subject field, use the String Builder (ellipses button) to build this value. Use the static text **Request is approved –** and then use the "Add or Change Lookup" button to select the Title field of the Current Item. For the e-mail message, enter the static text **Your request has been approved and will be assigned soon**. And then include the Comments field, which will copy the request details in the e-mail. The completed dialog box should look like Figure 5-37.

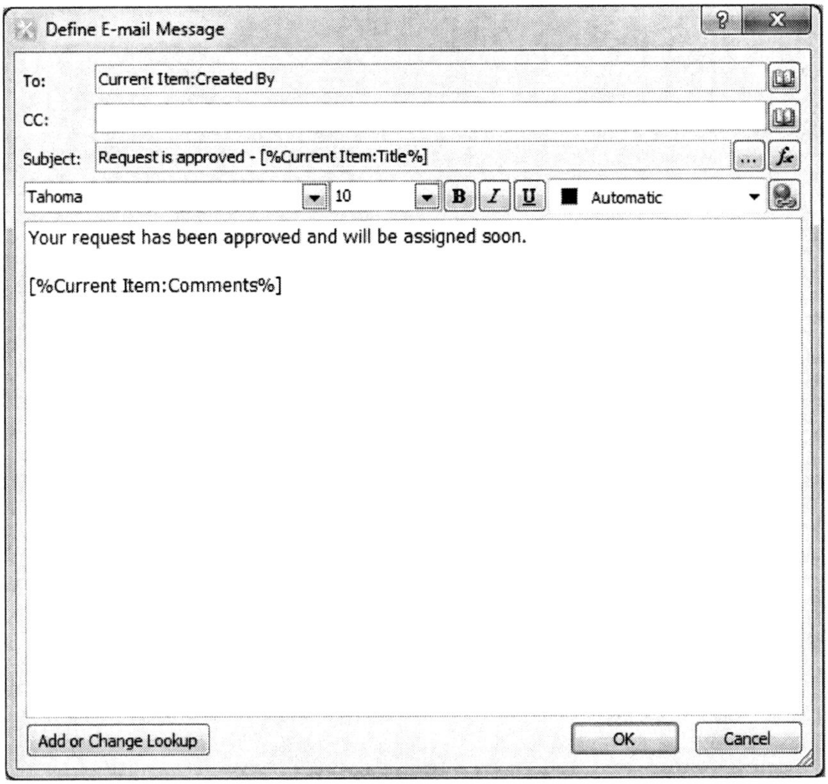

Figure 5-37. Configuring the approved e-mail properties

4. You will send a different e-mail if the request was denied. Click the "these users" link in the second Send an email action and then click the lookup button to the right of the To field. This e-mail will also go to the person who created the initial request. However, I will show you another way to specify that. Select the Workflow Lookup for a User from the list and click the Add button.

5. This will display the Lookup dialog box. Select the Created By column from the Current Item list, as shown in Figure 5-38. This is equivalent to selecting the "User who created current item" option.

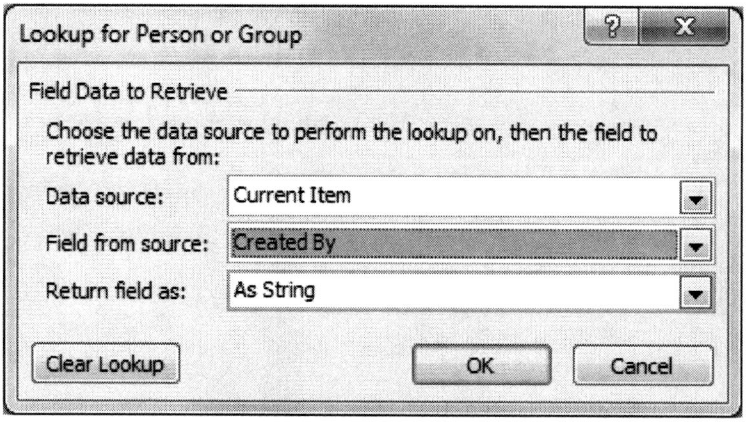

Figure 5-38. Alternate method for selecting the initiator

■ **Tip** The lookup feature is used when you need to send the e-mail to someone else that is defined by data in SharePoint. For example, the `Requests` list might specify an e-mail address to be used for updates. You can use the lookup feature to retrieve that value.

---

6. Specify the `Subject` and message as demonstrated in Figure 5-39. Notice that the message includes the approver's comments instead of the request comments. The approver's comments will, hopefully, explain why the request was denied.

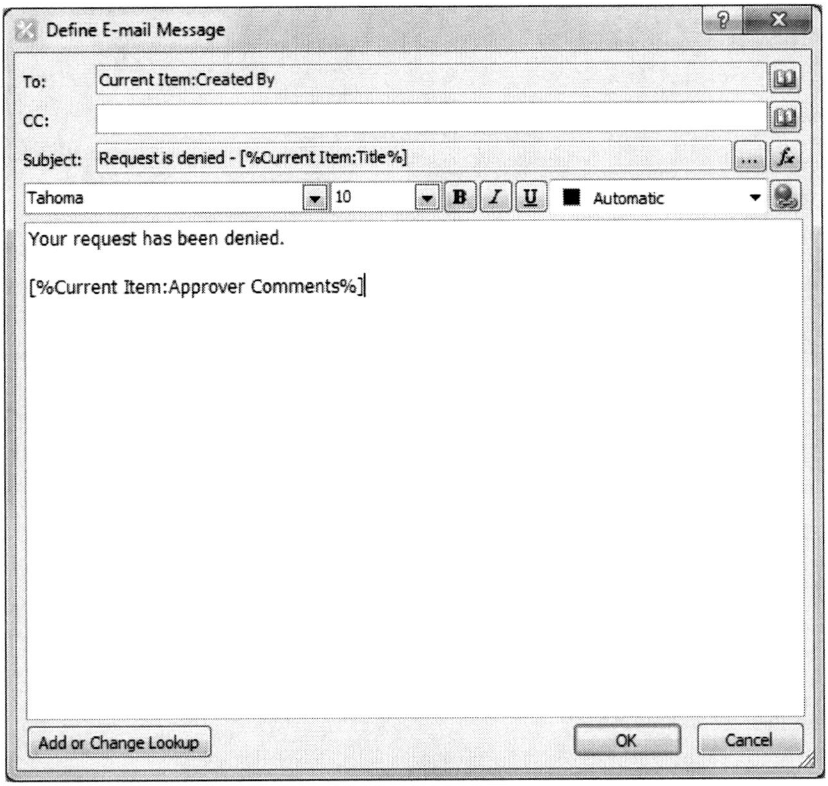

Figure 5-39. *The request denied e-mail message*

The workflow implementation should look similar to Figure 5-40.

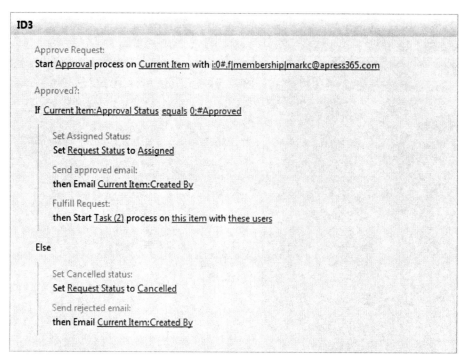

Figure 5-40. The interim workflow implementation

Using a Task Process

As stated, workflows in SharePoint are normally human-centric. While the workflow performs some actions like sending an e-mail or updating a list item, the tasks that people do form the core of the workflow design. The other actions are used to keep everything organized and manageable. This workflow, for example, can be distilled down to the following:

- Review request.

- If approved, fulfill request.

You have already implemented the first task, which is to review and approve (or deny) the request. The second task that you'll implement now is to fulfill the request.

Understanding How a Task Process Works

SharePoint provides a generic task process that you can use for any human task. The approval task that you just implemented uses an Approval workflow, which is a special case of the generic task process. SharePoint also provides two other workflows based on the generic task: Collect Feedback and Collect Signatures. These work in essentially the same way.

The reusable workflow such as Approval is called a *task process* and can contain multiple *tasks*. It is important to understand the distinction between these terms. A task process refers to an action in the workflow such as approve request. A task refers to a single person performing an action such as review a request.

The distinction is more readily apparent when there is more than one approver. Suppose you require three people to review and approve a request. The task process refers to the entire approval process whereas a task refers to one person reviewing a request. This is illustrated in Figure 5-41.

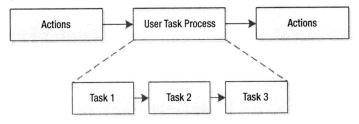

Figure 5-41. User task process with serial execution

SharePoint allows tasks within a task process to be performed concurrently. With this approach, all three approvers are performing their review simultaneously. This is demonstrated in Figure 5-42.

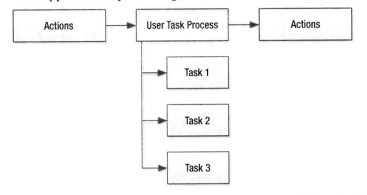

Figure 5-42. User task process with parallel execution

This brings up an interesting question. Suppose the request is reviewed by three people and two approve it but one denies it. Is the request approved? That's up to you; the custom task process allows you to configure this in a number of ways, which I will demonstrate. I'll also show you how to set the completion condition to force the task process to end, if appropriate, based on the results of the tasks completed so far.

To help you configure this generic task process, the workflow exposes events such as before a task is assigned or when the task process completes. You can add your own actions to these event handlers. I will show you how to use these events to enhance your workflow.

Using Custom Task Form Fields

The tasks that are generated by the workflow are placed in the Tasks list. Typically all the workflows in a SharePoint site use the same Tasks list so this becomes a central repository for all the things that someone needs to act on. The Team Site template that generated the Tasks list also created a My Tasks view that only shows the tasks assigned to you. This is a handy view to see what's on your To Do list. You can even synchronize this with Outlook.

While all tasks reside in the same list, they can be of different content types, which means you can provide a different task form for each. When a specific task is opened, the appropriate form will be used depending on the type of task.

In this workflow, you'll let the approver also decide who should fulfill the request. To implement this, you'll add an additional field to the form for the approval task. The person approving the request will use this field to specify the fulfillment user.

From the workflow editor, click the Approval link on the first line of the workflow. This will display the Task Process form shown in Figure 5-43.

> Use this page to define and customize your overall task process. You can add new fields and outcomes to the form, as well as edit the completion conditions that define completing the task process.

Task Information ▲

Key information about this task process.

Name: Approval
Owner: <click to edit>

Customization ▲

Links to task customization tools.

- Return to the workflow
- Change the completion conditions for this task process
- Change the behavior of a single task
- Change the behavior of the overall task process

Settings ▲

General settings for this task.

General Settings
☐ Only allow task recipients and process owners to read and edit workflow tasks
Show the following commands on the task form:
☑ Reassignment
☐ Change Requests

Task Form Fields   📄 New...   🔲 Choose existing field ▲

Fields displayed on the task completion form.

Column Name ▼	Type ▼	F

There are no items to show in this view.

Task Outcomes   🔲 New... ▲

Outcomes define the set of buttons shown on the task completion fo...

Sequence ▼	Name ▼	Task Form... ▼
1	Approved	Approve
2	Rejected	Reject

Figure 5-43. The Task Process form for the approval process

You'll use this form to configure all of the aspects of the task process, including task and task process events, custom form fields, and task outcomes. The Customization section has links for modifying the task events (Change the behavior of a single task) and the task process events (Change the behavior of the overall task process).

Adding a Form Field

You'll now add a field to the form that the approver will use to specify a user to fulfill the request. The Task Form Fields section of the process form lists the existing fields, which is currently empty. Click the New button in this section. In the Add Field dialog box enter the name **Fulfill User** and select Person or Group in the Information type drop-down list, as shown in Figure 5-44.

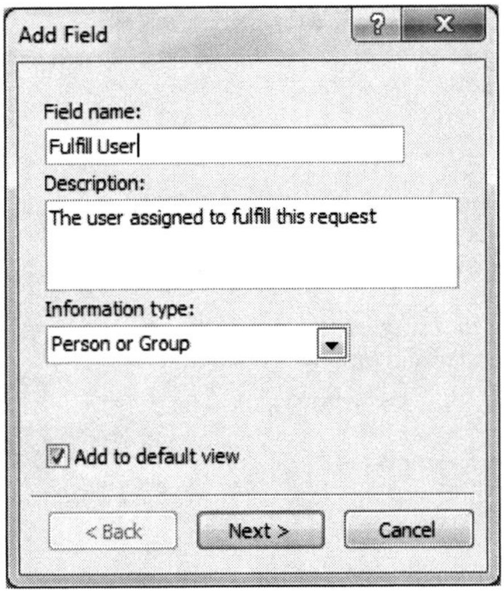

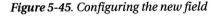

Figure 5-44. *Adding a new form field*

Click the Next button, which will display the Column Settings dialog box shown in Figure 5-45.

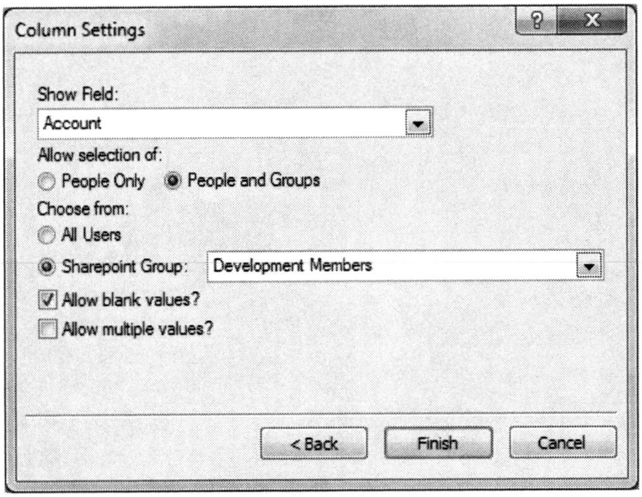

Figure 5-45. *Configuring the new field*

This dialog box is dynamic depending on the type of field being added. Since you selected "People and Groups," there are several properties to configure. The Show Field drop-down list allows you to specify how the user is displayed. I selected to include only people in the Development Members group, which contains all the people I added as members to the Team Site. When assigning a user, only the site members will be allowed. Your list of groups will likely be different; select an appropriate group or allow all users.

Click the Finish button to add the field. Now, whenever an approval task is displayed, the Fulfill User field will be included.

Storing the Assigned User

The next step is to use the value of this field once the user has been chosen. When the approval task has finished, you'll access this custom field. First, you'll update the Requests item setting the Assigned To field and append the reviewer's comments. Then you'll store the selected user in a workflow variable so you can use it later when generating the fulfillment task.

From the Task Process form, click the "Change the behavior of a single task" link. This will allow you to add custom actions to the task events. You can add actions to the following task events:

- Before a task is assigned (this event is raised just before each task is generated).

- When a task is pending (just after the task(s) have been generated).

- When a task expires (an incomplete task passes the due date).

- When a task is deleted.

- When a task completes.

For this scenario you'll use the event that is raised when a task completes and add actions to use the new custom field. The default actions for this event are shown in Figure 5-46.

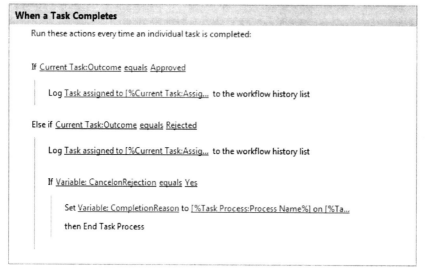

Figure 5-46. The default task completion event

Place the insertion point in the If clause just after the Log action. Add an Update List Item action and the action will read

then Update item in *this list*

1. Click the "this list" link, which will display the Update List Item dialog box. Select Current Item from the drop-down list. This action allows you to update multiple fields at once. You will update the following fields:

   - **Assigned To** stores the user selected in the approval task.

   - **Comments** appends the reviewer's comments.

2. Click the Add button, which will display the Value Assignment dialog box. Select the Assigned To field and for its value, click the *fx* button to display the Lookup dialog box. Select CurrentTask: Approval for the data source and Fulfill User as the source field, as shown in Figure 5-47.

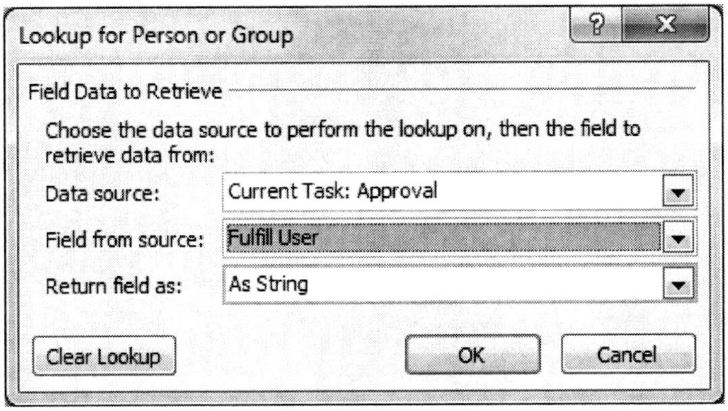

Figure 5-47. Getting the user selected by the reviewers

3. Click the OK button and then click the OK button in the Value Assignment dialog box.

4. Click the Add button again to update another field. Select the Comments field and click the ellipses next to the value field. In the String Builder dialog box, select the Comments field from the Current Item and append the static text **From Approver:** and then add the Comments field from the Current Task. The String Builder dialog box should look like Figure 5-48.

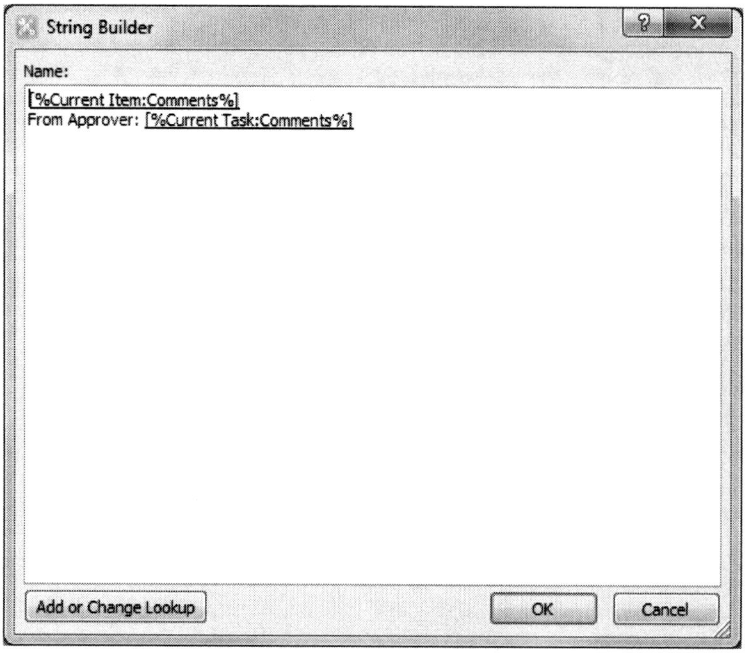

Figure 5-48. Appending the reviewer's comments

5. Click the OK button to add the field. The Update List Item dialog box should look like Figure 5-49.

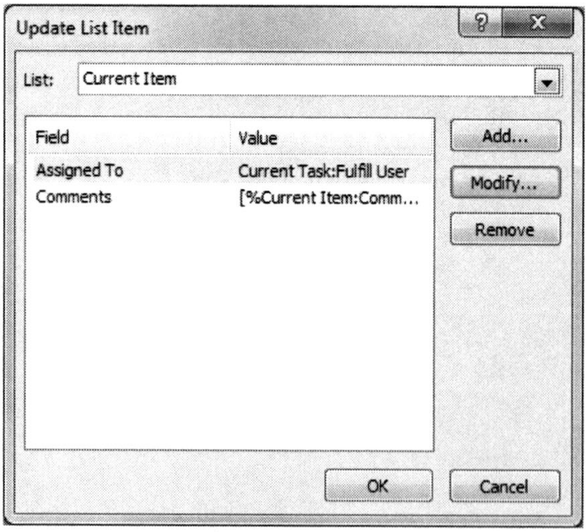

Figure 5-49. Updating the Requests item

Using Workflow Variables

You'll also need to store the selected user in a workflow variable so you can easily get it later in the workflow. Add the Set Workflow Variable action just below the Update List Item action. The action will read

then Set *workflow variable* to *value*

1. Click the "workflow variable" link to display a drop-down list where you can select the desired variable. In this case, it hasn't been defined yet so select "Create a new variable," as shown in Figure 5-50.

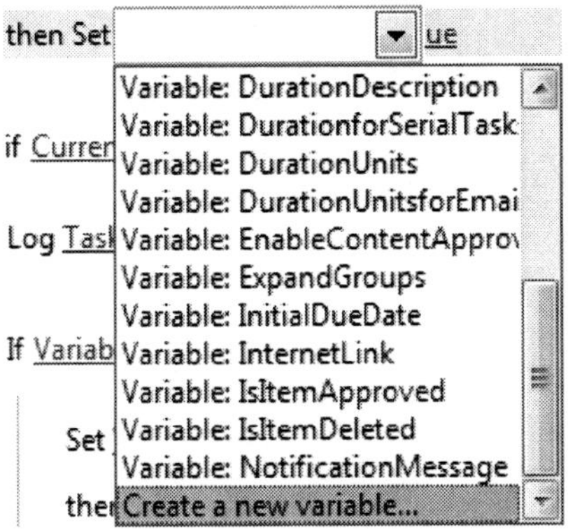

Figure 5-50. Creating a new workflow variable

2. In the Edit Variable dialog box, enter the name **FulfillUser** and select the String type, as shown in Figure 5-51. Click the OK button to add the variable.

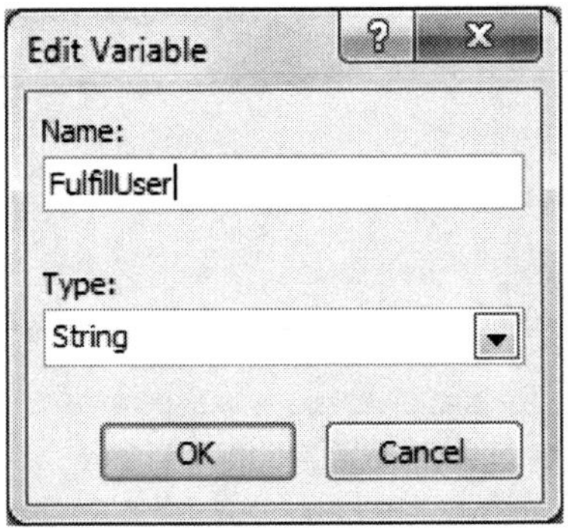

Figure 5-51. Configuring the variable

3. Click the value link and then click the *fx* button. In the Lookup Dialog box, select Fulfill User from the Current Task like you just did to set the Assigned

To column (refer to Figure 5-47). The completed event handler will look like Figure 5-52.

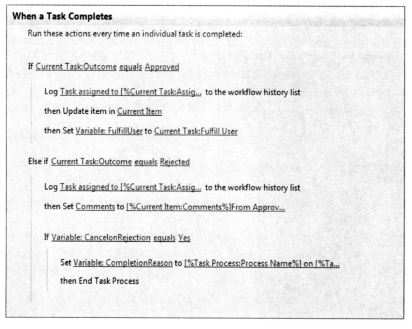

When a Task Completes

Run these actions every time an individual task is completed:

If Current Task:Outcome equals Approved

    Log Task assigned to [%Current Task:Assig... to the workflow history list

    then Update item in Current Item

    then Set Variable: FulfillUser to Current Task:Fulfill User

Else if Current Task:Outcome equals Rejected

    Log Task assigned to [%Current Task:Assig... to the workflow history list

    then Set Comments to [%Current Item:Comments%]From Approv...

    If Variable: CancelonRejection equals Yes

        Set Variable: CompletionReason to [%Task Process:Process Name%] on [%Ta...

        then End Task Process

Figure 5-52. The completed event handler

Creating a Custom Task Process

Next, you'll use the custom task process to generate a task that will be assigned to someone to fulfill the request. The Visio drawing that you imported created an action for this that reads

then Start *Task(2)* process on *this item* with *these users*

This uses the generic task process from which the Approval workflow is derived—the two are very similar.

■ **Caution** The initial name of your task process can be different than mine. The name Task(2) was generated to provide a unique name. Depending on your environment and what work you've already done, a different name may be used.

Assigning the Fulfillment Task

Click the "this item" link and select the Current Item. Click the "these users" link, which will display the Select Task Participants dialog box. For the approval process you selected a static user to perform the review. However, for the fulfillment process you'll need to assign the task to whomever the approver selected. Click the button to the right of the Participants field. In the Select Users dialog box, select the Workflow Lookup for a User option. This will display the Lookup dialog box. Select Workflow Variables and Parameters for the data source and then select the FulfillUser variable, as shown in Figure 5-53.

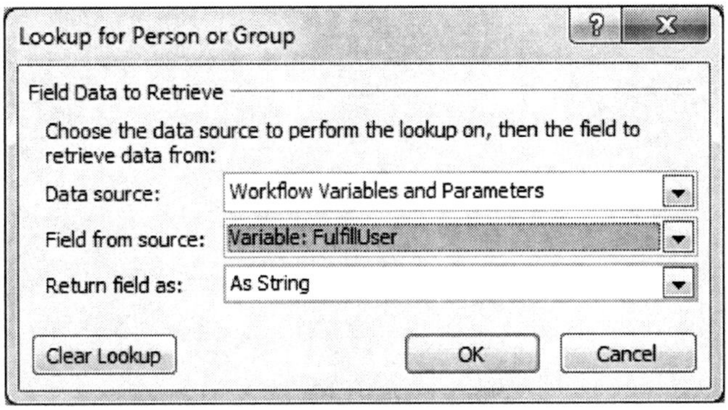

Figure 5-53. Selecting the workflow variables

This is the variable that you just created. Click the OK button to close the dialog box. Specify the Title and Instructions fields like you did for the approval process. The completed form should look like Figure 5-54.

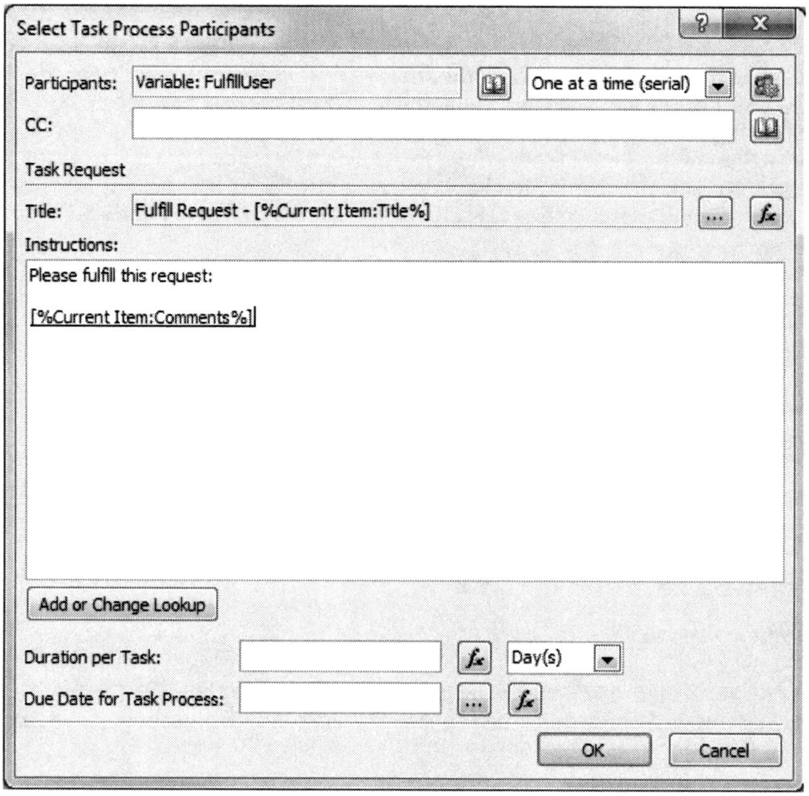

Figure 5-54. The Fulfill Request task properties

Modifying the Task Process Behavior

Now you'll need to modify some additional properties using the Task Process form. You will add actions to some of the task and task process events to configure the fulfillment task and to update the associated Requests item. You'll also need to modify the task outcome options.

Click the Task(2) link to display the task process form shown in Figure 5-55.

Use this page to define and customize your overall task process. You can add new fields and outcomes to the form, as well as edit the completion conditions that define completing the task process.

Task Information

Key information about this task process.

Name: Task (2)
Owner: < click to edit >

Customization

Links to task customization tools.

- ▣ Return to the workflow
- ▣ Change the completion conditions for this task process
- ▣ Change the behavior of a single task
- ▣ Change the behavior of the overall task process

Settings

General settings for this task.

General Settings
☐ Only allow task recipients and process owners to read and edit workflow tasks
Show the following commands on the task form:
☑ Reassignment
☐ Change Requests

Task Form Fields   ▣ New...   ▣ Choose existing field

Fields displayed on the task completion form.

Column Name ▼	Type ▼	F

There are no items to show in this view.

Task Outcomes   ▣ New...

Outcomes define the set of buttons shown on the task completion fo...

Sequence ▼	Name ▼	Task Form Button ▼
1	Approved	Approve
2	Rejected	Reject

Figure 5-55. The Task Process form

Change the Name to **Fulfill Request**.

Changing the Task Outcomes

There will be some buttons at the bottom of the task form that allow the user to select the appropriate task outcome. For example, the approval process includes the Approved and Rejected buttons. These options are appropriate for the approval task but you'll want different outcomes for the fulfillment task. For this workflow you'll just provide options for completing the task or cancelling the request. You could add other options such as "Need more information."

Select the Approved outcome and then click the Delete button in the ribbon. Repeat this step to also delete the Rejected outcome. Click the New button in the Task Outcomes section. This will create a new outcome named Outcome 1. Change both the Name and Task Form Button fields to **Complete**. Add another outcome and change its name and button text to **Cancel**. The Task Outcomes section should look like Figure 5-56.

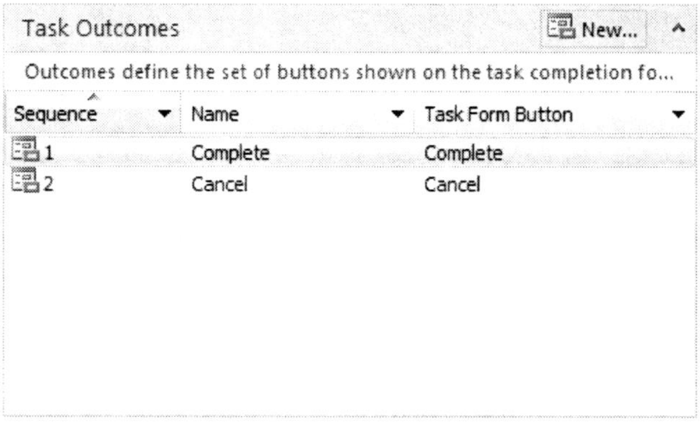

Figure 5-56. The modified Task Outcomes section

■ **Tip** The Sequence field is used to specify the order that the buttons will appear on the form. The Name property is used to logically reference this outcome in subsequent workflow logic as I will demonstrate later. The Task Form Button property specifies the label of the button.

Specifying the Completion Conditions

If a task process contains more than one task, you may want to end the process before waiting for the remainder of the tasks to complete. For example, if there are multiple people reviewing a request and you require all reviewers to approve the request before fulfilling it, the process can stop as soon as one of the reviewers denies the request because there's no need to continue. Regardless of what the other reviewers do, the request will be cancelled.

■ **Note** If there is only a single task in the task process, as is the case for this workflow, there is no need to set the completion conditions. When the task completes, the overall task process also completes. I am going through this step to demonstrate the feature, but it's not necessary for this workflow.

From the task process form, click the "Change the completion conditions for this task process" link. This displays an event handler that is called every time a task is completed. You can add logic to this event handler that checks the results of the tasks that have already been completed. If you determine that the process should end, the event handler should execute the End Task Process action. You'll add logic to cancel the task process if any of the tasks are cancelled.

The default implementation will not have any actions. Add the If any value equals value condition. Click the first value link and click the *fx* button to display the Lookup dialog box. Select Number of Cancel from the Task Process Results data source, as shown in Figure 5-57.

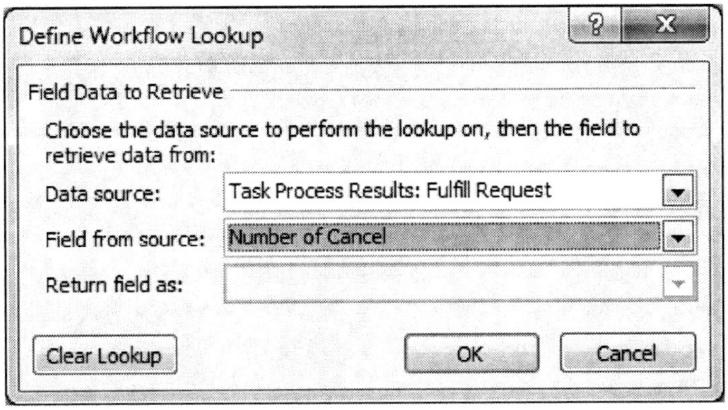

Figure 5-57. Using the process results

Click the equals link and change the operation to "is greater than or equal to." Click the second value link and enter 1. Then add the End Task Process action inside the If clause. The completed event will look like Figure 5-58.

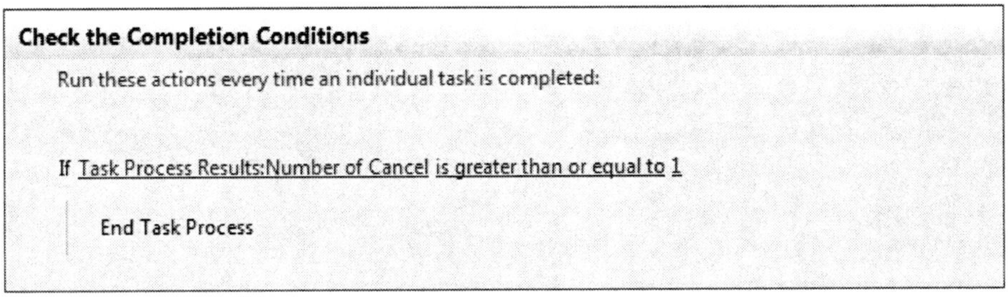

Figure 5-58. Canceling the process when a request is denied

■ **Note** SharePoint Designer provides values such as Number of Cancel and Number of Complete to use in your workflow logic. The values are dynamic based on the task outcomes that you defined. If you were look at the values for the approval process you would see values such as Number of Rejected.

Handling the Task Process Events

The following events are supported by the task process:

- When the task process starts.
- Before the first task is assigned.
- When the task process is cancelled.

- When the task process completes.

The default implementation for these event handlers will be empty. You'll add actions to the cancelled and completed events to update the Requests item to reflect the outcome of the fulfillment task. When the task process in cancelled, you'll set the Request Status to Cancelled and set the Date Completed to the current date and time.

1. In the When the Task Process is Cancelled section, add the Set Field in Current Item action. This action will read

Set *field* to *value*

2. Click the field link and select the Request Status field. Click the value link and select the Cancelled value. Add another Set Field in Current Item action and select the Date Completed field.

3. Click the value link and then click the ellipses to display the Date Value dialog box. Select the current date, as shown in Figure 5-59.

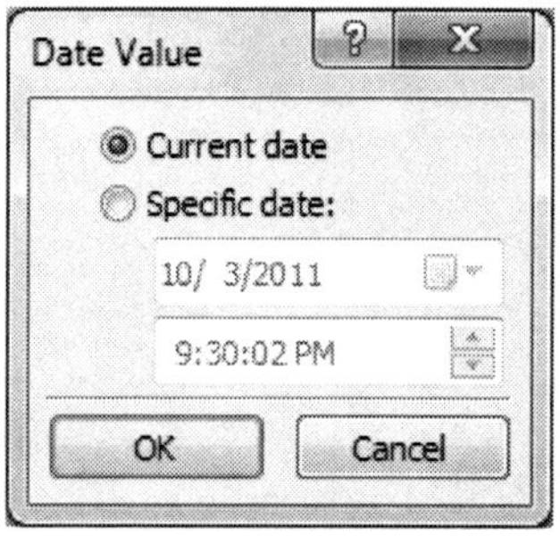

Figure 5-59. Specifying the current date/time

■ **Note** You use the Set Field in Current Item action here instead of the Update List Item action that you used previously. When updating the current item both work equally well; it's just a matter of preference. The Update List Item action can update multiple fields in a single action. However, one of the things I like about the Set Field in Current Item action is that you can see which fields are being updated without having to display the action details.

---

4. Now go to the When the Task Process Completes section. In this event you will set the following columns in the Requests item based on the task outcome:

- Request Status
- % Complete
- Date Completed

5. Add an `If any value equals value` condition and specify the parameters just like you did for the Completion Conditions.

   - `Number of Cancel`

   - `is greater or equal to`

   - 1

6. In the `If` clause, using `Set Field in Current Item` actions, set the `Request Status` to Cancelled and `% Complete` to **0**. Then, using the Else-If Branch button in the ribbon, add an `Else` clause, as shown in Figure 5-60.

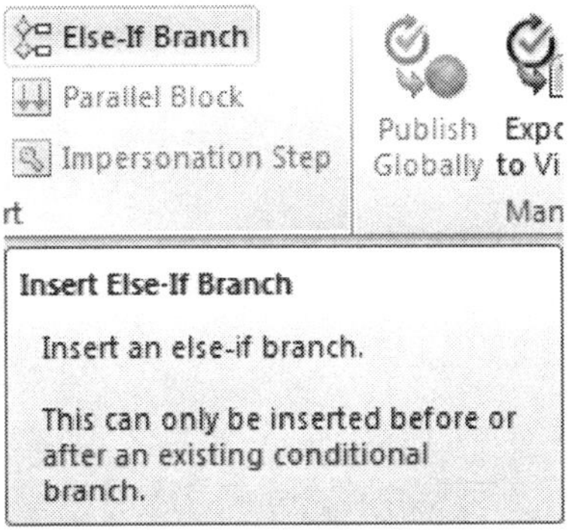

Figure 5-60. Adding an Else branch to a condition

7. In the `Else` clause, set the `Request Status` to Completed and `% Complete` to **1**. Add one more `Set Field in Current Item` action after the `Else` clause (so it is executed in both cases). Set the `Date Completed` field to the current date and time just like you did in the cancelled event. The final event implementations should look like Figure 5-61.

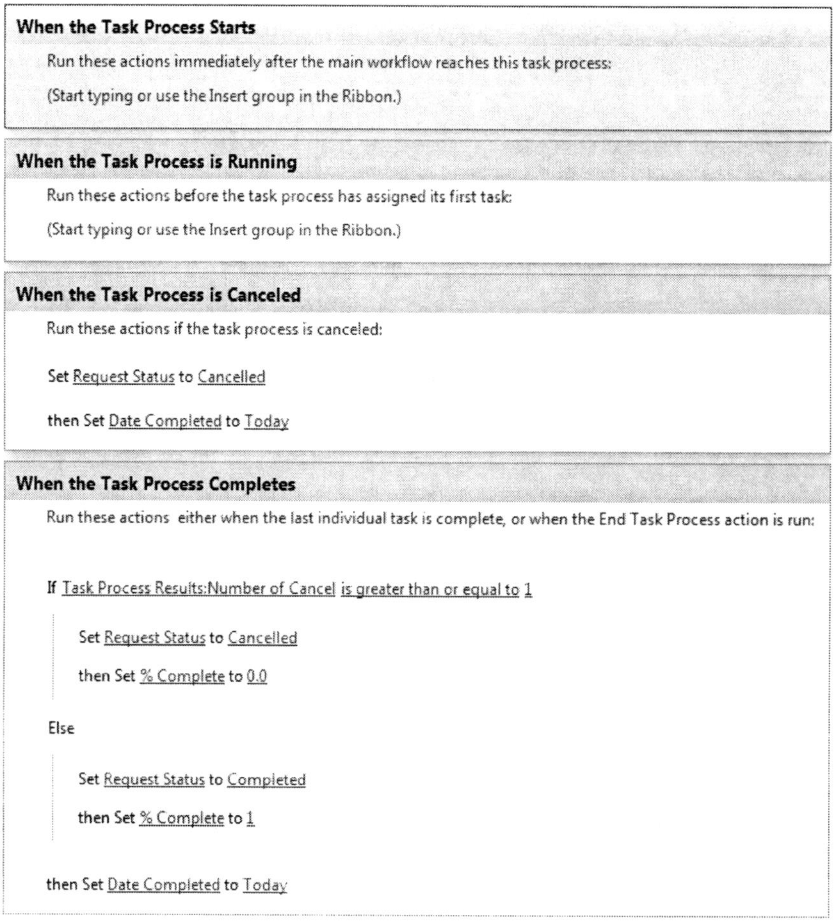

When the Task Process Starts

Run these actions immediately after the main workflow reaches this task process:

(Start typing or use the Insert group in the Ribbon.)

When the Task Process is Running

Run these actions before the task process has assigned its first task:

(Start typing or use the Insert group in the Ribbon.)

When the Task Process is Canceled

Run these actions if the task process is canceled:

Set Request Status to Cancelled

then Set Date Completed to Today

When the Task Process Completes

Run these actions either when the last individual task is complete, or when the End Task Process action is run:

If Task Process Results:Number of Cancel is greater than or equal to 1

    Set Request Status to Cancelled

    then Set % Complete to 0.0

Else

    Set Request Status to Completed

    then Set % Complete to 1

then Set Date Completed to Today

Figure 5-61. The overall task process events

Handling Task Events

Now you'll modify the events for a single task. First, when a task is created you'll add an action to specify the Due Date using the values from the Requests item. Then, when the task is complete you'll append the Comments to the Requests item.

1. From the task process form, click the "Change the behavior of a single task" link to display the existing event handlers, which should be empty. In the Before a Task is Assigned section, add a Set Task Field action. The action will read

Set Task Field *field* to *value*

2. Click the field link and select the Due Date field. Then click the value link, click the ellipses and select the Due Date field from the Current Item. The completed action should look like Figure 5-62.

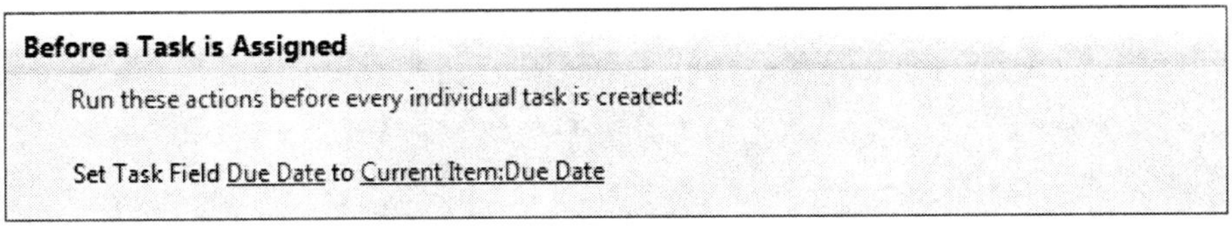

Before a Task is Assigned

Run these actions before every individual task is created:

Set Task Field Due Date to Current Item:Due Date

Figure 5-62. Configuring the task assignment event

3. In the When a Task Completes section, add a Set Field in Current Item action and select the Comments field.

4. Click the value link and click the ellipses to display the String Builder dialog box. Append the task comments like you've done before (see Figure 5-63).

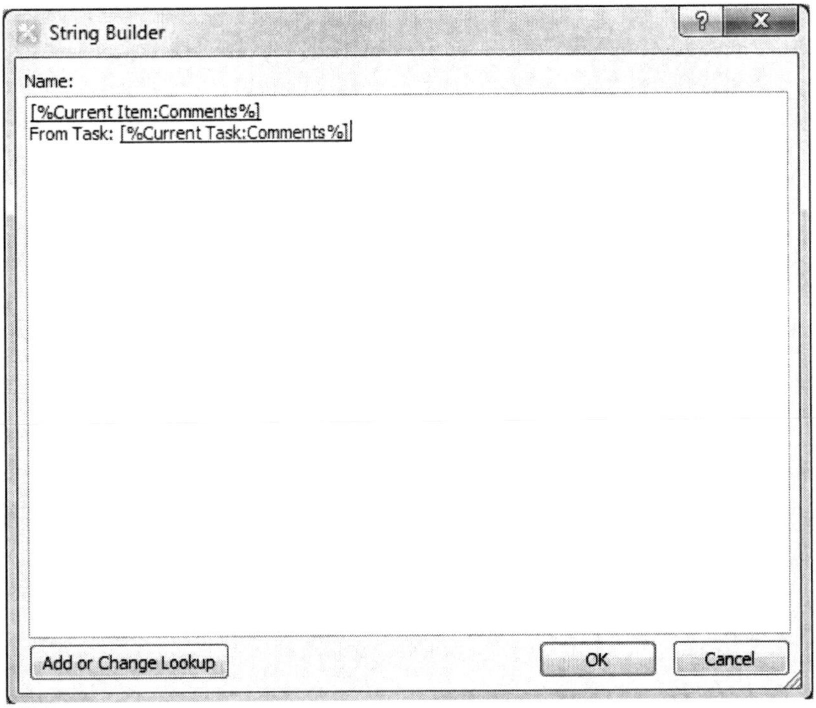

Figure 5-63. Appending the task comments

5. Go back to the workflow editor and the completed workflow should look like Figure 5-64.

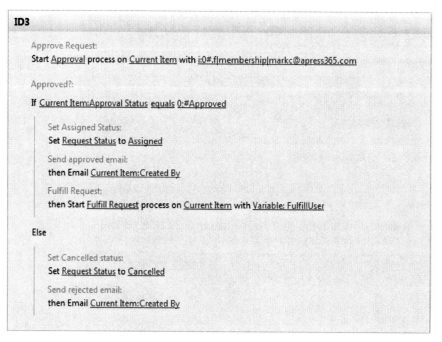

Figure 5-64. The completed workflow

Configuring the Workflow Start Options

There is just one more step to complete before you're ready to test your workflow. You will configure the workflow to start automatically when a new item is added to the Requests list. As soon as someone submits a new request, a workflow will be started and the appropriate tasks added to the Tasks list. Go to the Workflow properties page for your workflow.

■ **Tip** You've probably noticed the breadcrumbs at the top of each SharePoint Designer page. This helps you keep track of where you are and how you navigated there. Your breadcrumbs probably look similar to Figure 5-65. Each of these items is also a link that will take you directly to that object. If you're currently displaying the Task Process Behaviors page, you can click the Process Request link in the breadcrumbs to go to the Workflows property page.

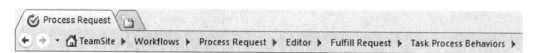

Figure 5-65. The SharePoint Designer breadcrumbs

In the Start Options section, select the "Start workflow automatically when an item is created" check box, as shown in Figure 5-66.

Workflow Information	^
Key information about this workflow.	

Name:	Process Request
Description:	< click to enter text>
Type:	List Workflow
Associated List:	Requests

Customization	^
Links to customization tools.	

- ▫ Edit workflow
- ▫ Open associated list
- ▫ Open task list
- ▫ Open history list

Settings	^
General settings for this workflow.	

Task List:	Tasks	▼
History List:	New History List...	▼

☐ Show workflow visualization on status page

Start Options	^
Change the start options for this workflow.	

☑ Allow this workflow to be manually started
    ☐ Require Manage List permissions
☑ Start workflow automatically when an item is created
☐ Start workflow automatically when an item is changed

Forms	^
A list of the forms used by this workflow.	

File Name ▼	Type ▼	Modified Date ▼
Process Request.xsn*	Initiation	10/3/2011 10:21 PM
Approval.xsn	Task	10/3/2011 10:21 PM
Task_x0028_2_x0029_.xsn	Task	10/3/2011 10:21 PM

Figure 5-66. The workflow settings page

Testing the Initial Workflow

Your workflow is done and ready to be published. Once is has been installed, you'll create a request and watch the workflow generate tasks and update the Requests item.

Publishing the Workflow

Before publishing the workflow, it's a good idea to first check for errors. Click the Check for Errors button in the ribbon, as shown in Figure 5-67.

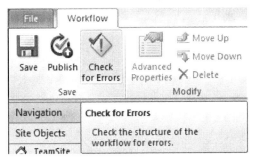

Figure 5-67. The Check for Errors button

Fix any errors that are reported; your workflow should look like Figure 5-64. Once all errors are resolved, click the Publish button to install the workflow. This process can take a few seconds.

Processing a Request

Now you're ready to test the workflow.

1.   Go to the SharePoint site and select the Requests list. Click the "Add new item" link, which will display the New Item form. Enter a request. The only fields you need to enter are as follows (all the other fields should be left blank or have default values). The New Item form will look like Figure 5-68.

   -   Title

   -   Due Date

   -   Comments

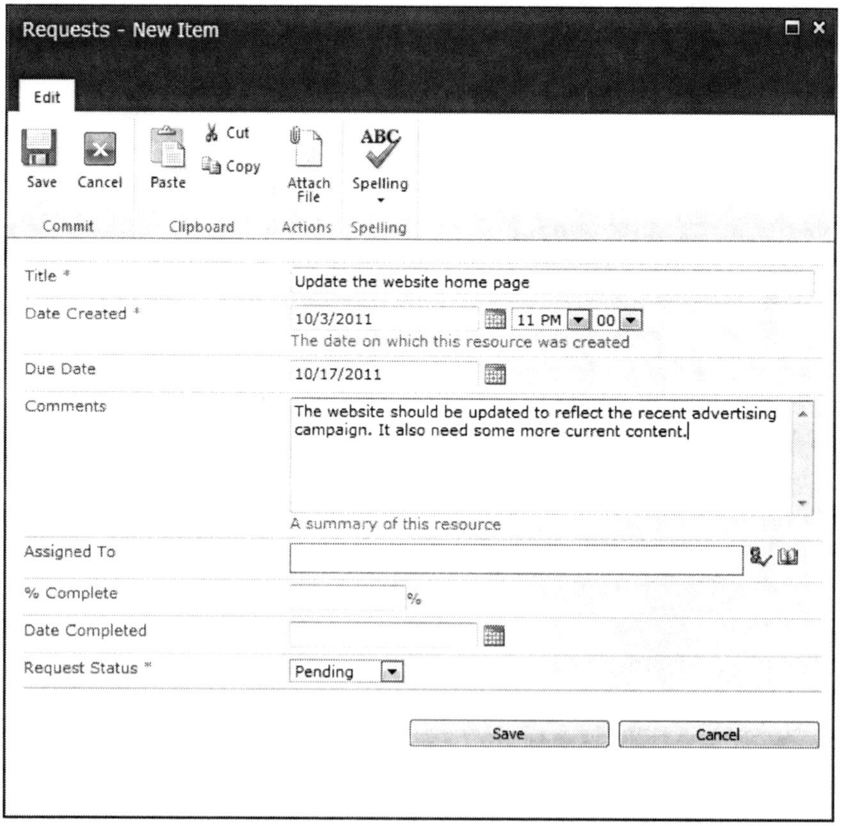

Figure 5-68. The initial New Item form

2. The workflow will start as soon as the request is saved; however, it can take a few seconds before it has generated the first task. It is especially slow the first time it is run. Go to the Tasks list and you will eventually see a new task created.

3. Edit the new task, enter a comment and select Fulfill User. The task form should look like Figure 5-69. Click the Approve button to approve the request.

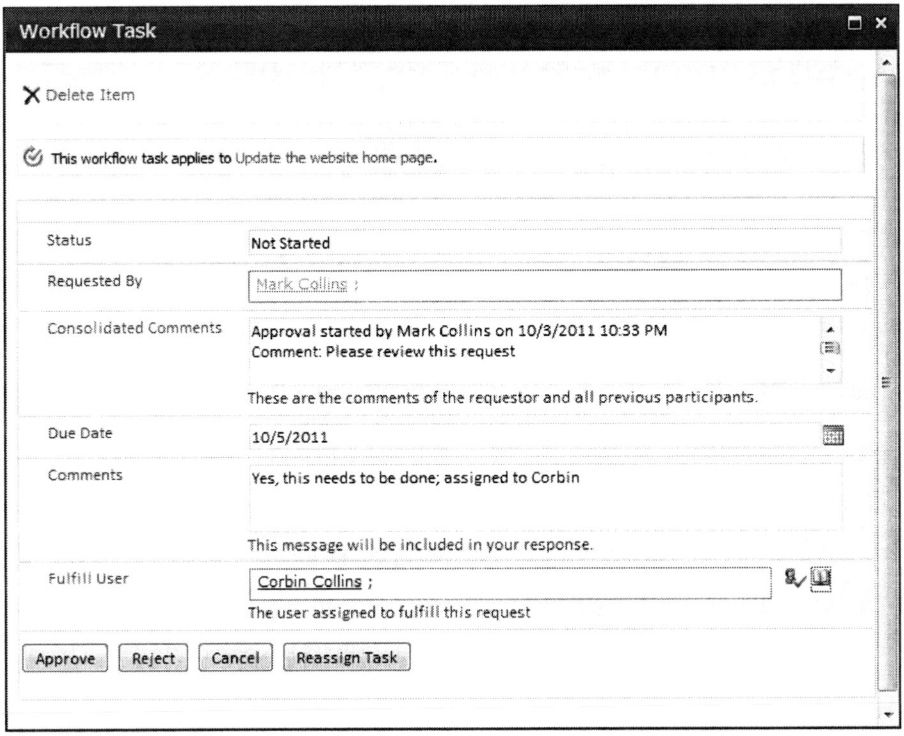

Figure 5-69. The Approval task form

4. After a few seconds another task should be created. This one will be assigned to the user you selected in the approval task. Edit the task and enter a comment. This task form should look like Figure 5-70. Notice that there are different buttons at the bottom and it doesn't have the Fulfill User field. Enter a comment and click the Complete button to complete the task.

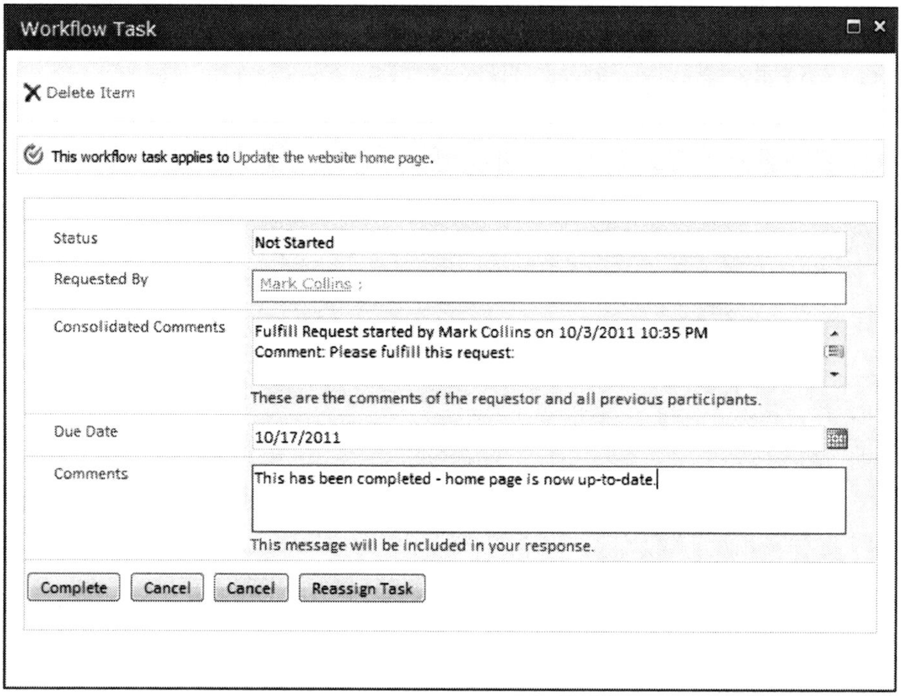

Figure 5-70. The Fulfill Request task form

Reviewing the Results

Now let's look at the artifacts of the workflow process. Open the Requests item that you first created. The Requests item is shown in Figure 5-71.

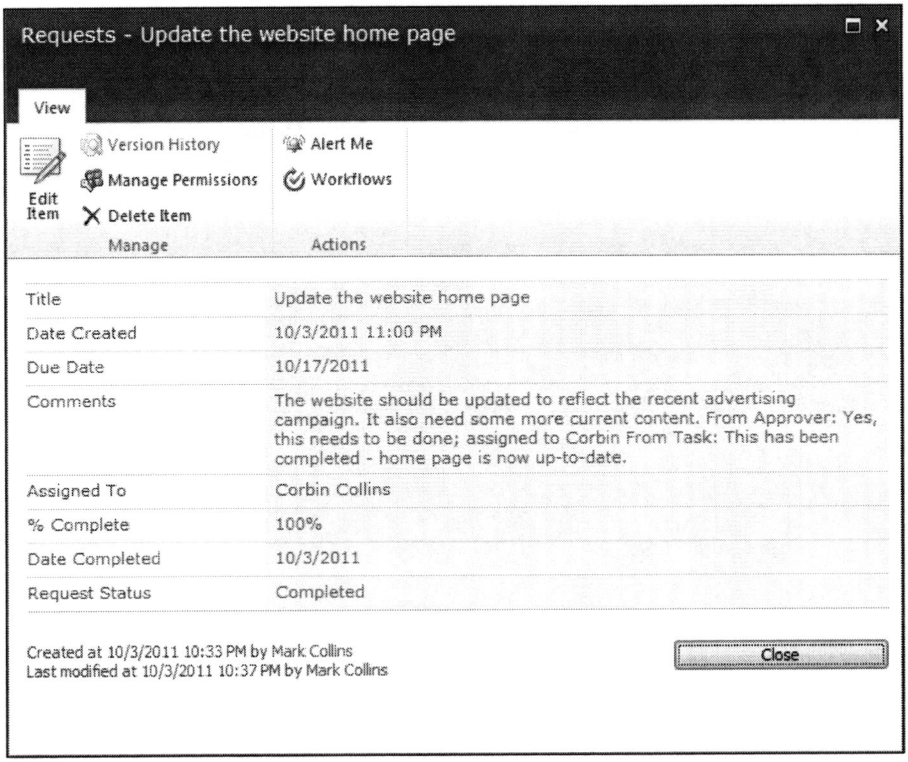

Figure 5-71. *The completed Requests item*

Notice that all of the fields have been populated. The Comments field includes the original request plus the comments made by the approver and the fulfillment users. You can see who the request was assigned to and when it was completed.

Check your inbox and you should see the e-mail letting you know that the request has been approved (Figure 5-72).

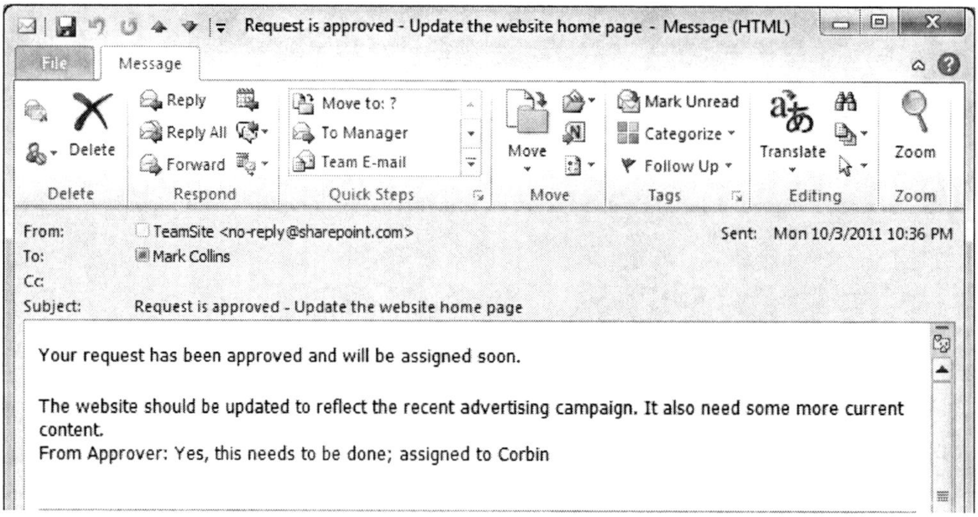

Figure 5-72. The approved notification e-mail

⬛ **Note** There will be other e-mails in your inbox that the Approval workflow generated. These e-mails are generated by the default implementation of the task and task process events.

Customizing the Forms

Now that you have the workflow process implemented, you can enhance the user experience by customizing the forms. The standard forms rendered by SharePoint are fairly generic: each field is displayed on a separate row, the first column contains the label, and the second column contains the data-bound control. Custom forms can implement a more optimal arrangement.

Custom forms can also help implement business rules. For example, when creating a new request, I told you to only specify three fields (Title, Comments, and Due Date). Ideally, the form used to create a request should only have these three fields.

There are three types of forms:

- **New**: Used to add a new list item.

- **Display**: A read-only form for viewing an existing item.

- **Edit**: Used for modifying a list item.

From SharePoint Designer, select the List and Libraries link in the Navigation pane. Then select the Requests list. In the Forms section you'll see three forms, one of each type, as shown in Figure 5-73.

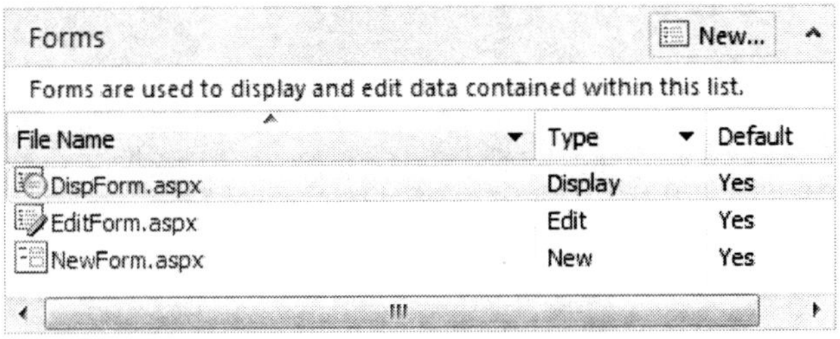

Figure 5-73. Enumerating the existing forms for the Requests list

Modifying the Requests Forms with InfoPath

Now you'll use InfoPath Designer 2010 to generate a new set of forms. InfoPath provides a lot of great features for designing a rich user experience. I will give you a very brief introduction in this chapter.

Open InfoPath Designer 2010. From the New tab of the backstage view, select the SharePoint List template shown in Figure 5-74. Then click the Design Form button to create the form.

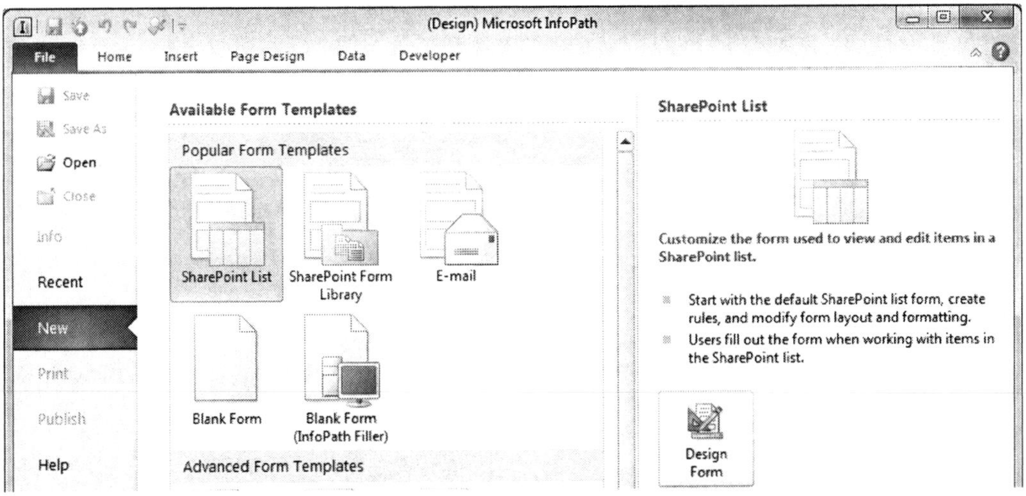

Figure 5-74. Selecting the SharePoint List template

Enter the URL of the SharePoint site in the first dialog box that is displayed.

Activating the Enterprise Services

Using InfoPath forms requires that the Enterprise features are enabled in your site collection. If these have not been activated, you will see the error shown in Figure 5-75.

213

Figure 5-75. Error displayed when the Enterprise features are not activated

---

■ **Caution** You can't use InfoPath if you have a Small Business account.

To activate the Enterprise features, use the Site Actions menu and click the Site Settings link. If this is not the top-level site in this site collection, click the "Go to top level site settings" link on the Site Settings page. Click the "Site collection features" link. Find the SharePoint Server Enterprise Site Collection features and click the Activate button next to it, as shown in Figure 5-76.

SharePoint Server Enterprise Site Collection features

 Features such as InfoPath Forms Services, Visio Services, Access Services, and Excel Services Application, included in the SharePoint Server Enterprise License.

Activate

Figure 5-76. Activating the Enterprise features for the site collection

Once this has been activated for the site collection, you'll need to also activate it for the site. Go back to the SharePoint site and from the Site Actions menu, select the Site Settings link. In the Site Settings page, click the "Manage site features" link. Find the SharePoint Server Site features and click the Activate button next to it, as shown in Figure 5-77.

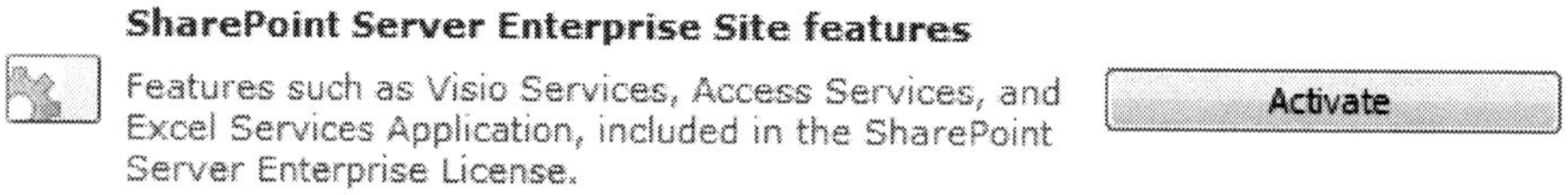

SharePoint Server Enterprise Site features

Features such as Visio Services, Access Services, and Excel Services Application, included in the SharePoint Server Enterprise License.

Activate

Figure 5-77. Activating the Enterprise features for the site

Connecting to the SharePoint Site

In InfoPath Designer, you'll be presented with a series of dialog boxes that will help you connect to the SharePoint site and select the list that you want to generate forms for. In the first dialog box, shown in Figure 5-78, enter the URL of the SharePoint site.

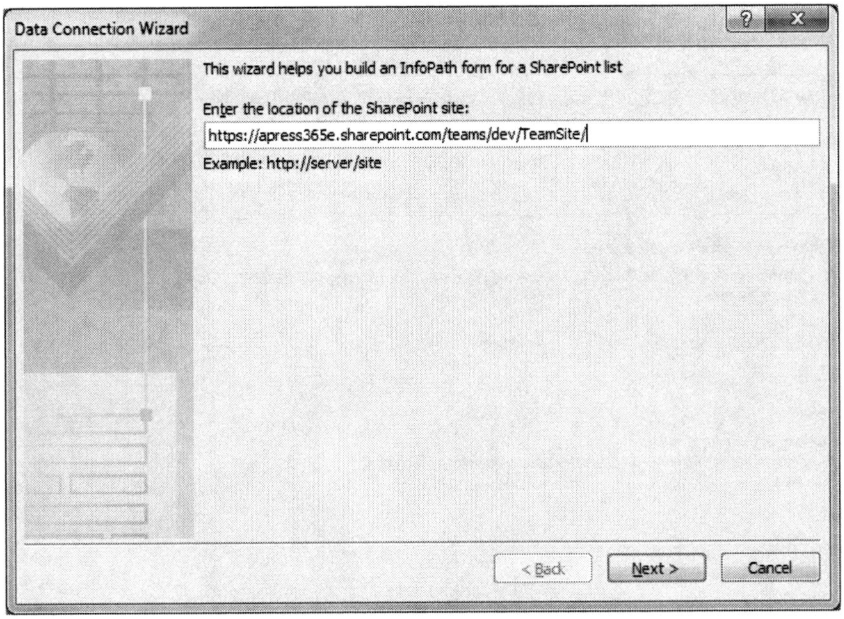

Figure 5-78. Entering the URL of the SharePoint site

In the next dialog box, select the existing Requests list, as shown in Figure 5-79.

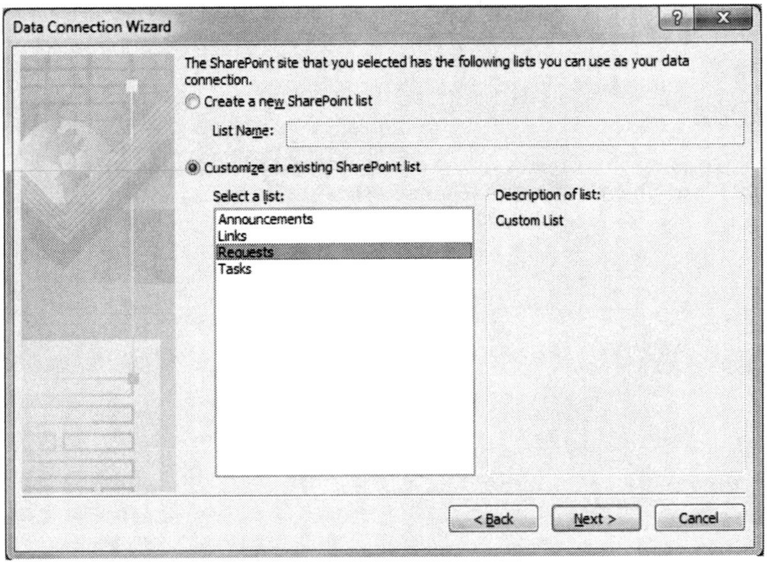

Figure 5-79. Selecting the Requests list

The final dialog box, shown in Figure 5-80, provides some advanced options. Just leave all the default values and click the Finish button.

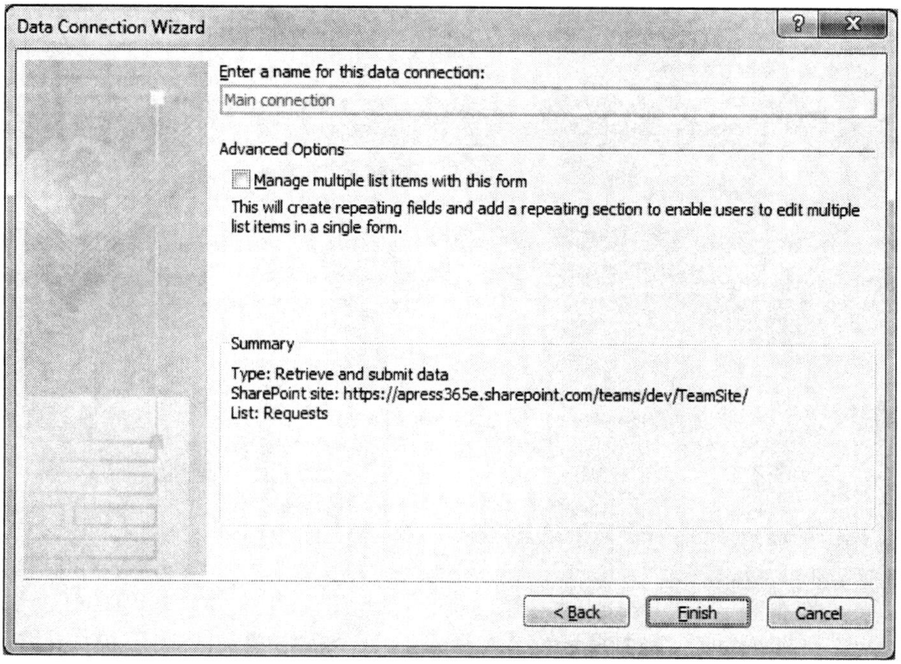

Figure 5-80. Configuring the data connection

Modifying the Requests Form

InfoPath will now connect to the SharePoint site, determine the columns of the Requests list, and generate an initial form implementation, which is shown in Figure 5-81.

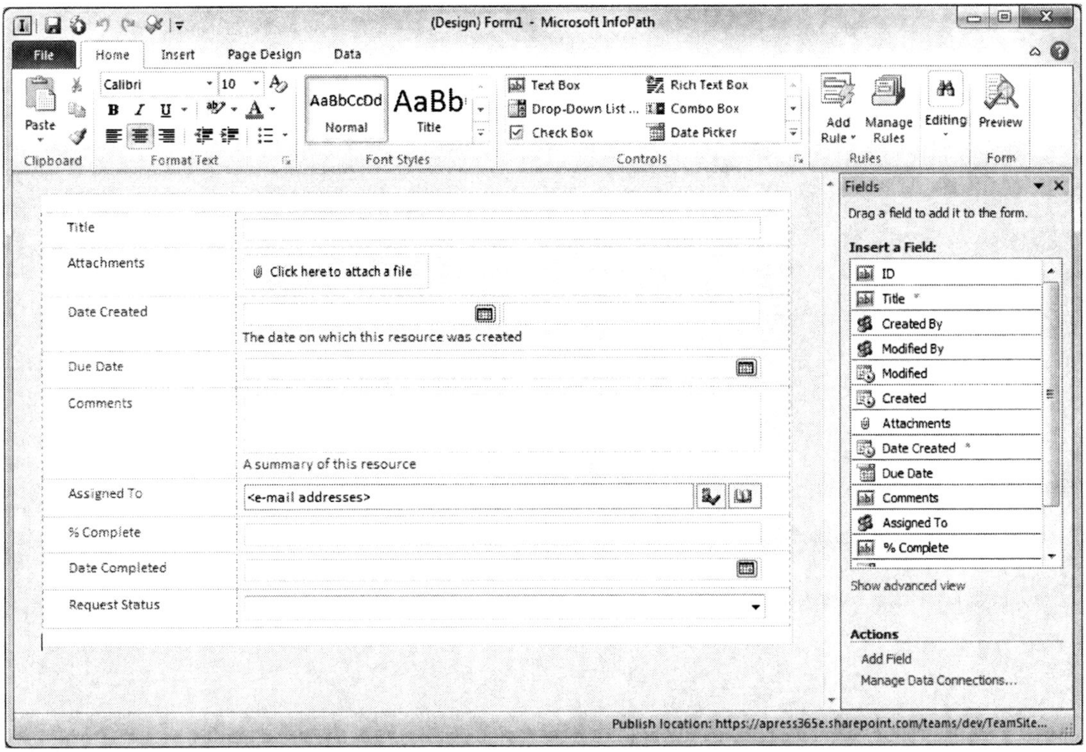

Figure 5-81. The initial InfoPath form design

■ **Note** The specific changes that you make to the InfoPath form are not important for this exercise. I combined some of the shorter fields into a single row. I also changed the Date Created field to a text box control as I will now demonstrate.

Select the data-bound control for the Date Created field. From the Data tab of the ribbon, click the Change Control button and then click the Text Box link, as shown in Figure 5-82.

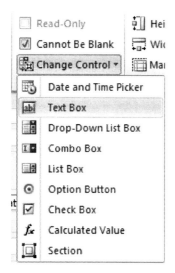

Figure 5-82. Changing the Date Created field to use a text box control

My completed design looks like Figure 5-83.

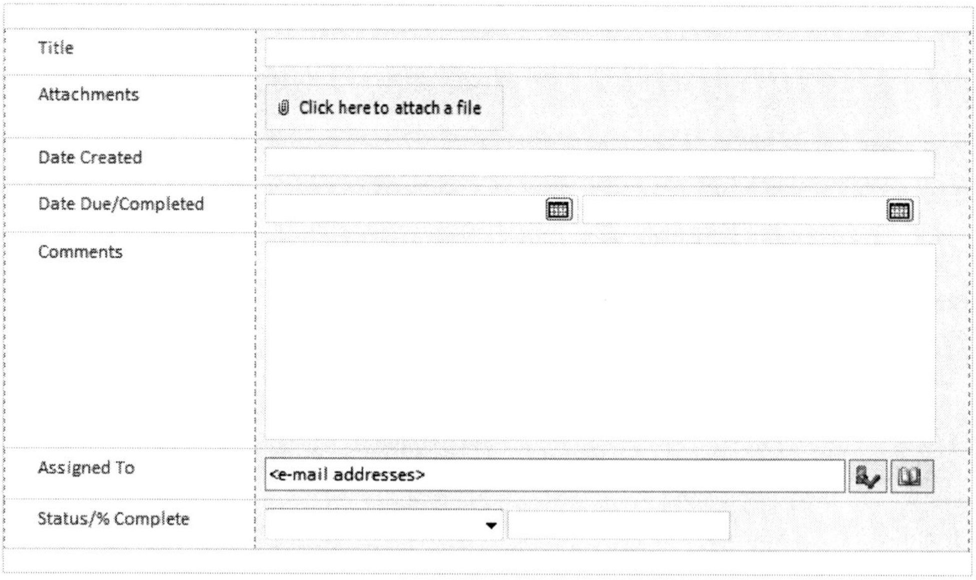

Title	
Attachments	📎 Click here to attach a file
Date Created	
Date Due/Completed	📅 📅
Comments	
Assigned To	<e-mail addresses>
Status/% Complete	▼

Figure 5-83. The updated InfoPath form

Publishing the Form

Now you'll publish these changes to the SharePoint site. InfoPath already knows where the SharePoint site is because you specified this in the beginning and InfoPath used this information to generate the initial form design.

From the Info tab of the backstage view, click the Quick Publish button shown in Figure 5-84. This will deploy the new form to the SharePoint site and make them the default forms.

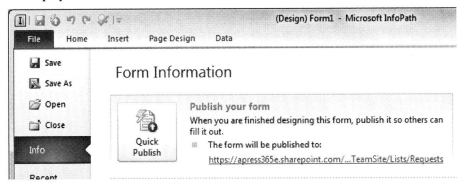

Figure 5-84. Publishing the new InfoPath form

After a few seconds the new form will be published. Display one of the existing Requests items and you should notice that the new form is being used (see Figure 5-85).

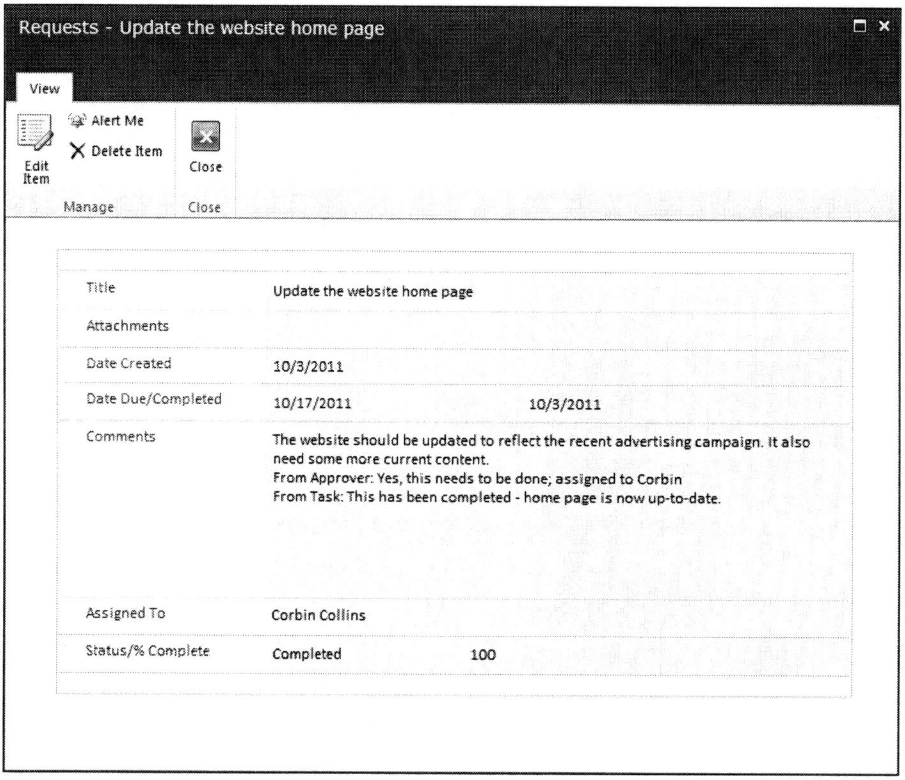

Figure 5-85. The new InfoPath Requests form

Creating the SubmitRequest Form

You'll now create an additional New form that has only the three necessary fields on it. You'll use the SharePoint native form environment for this. You will then make this the default New form so it will be used instead of the InfoPath form (or the initial New form).

1. Open the Requests list in SharePoint Designer. Click the New button in the Forms section and the dialog box shown in Figure 5-86 will appear.

2. Enter the file name **SubmitRequest** since this form will be used to create a new request.

3. Select the New form type and select the "Set as default form for the selected type" check box. Click the OK button to create the form.

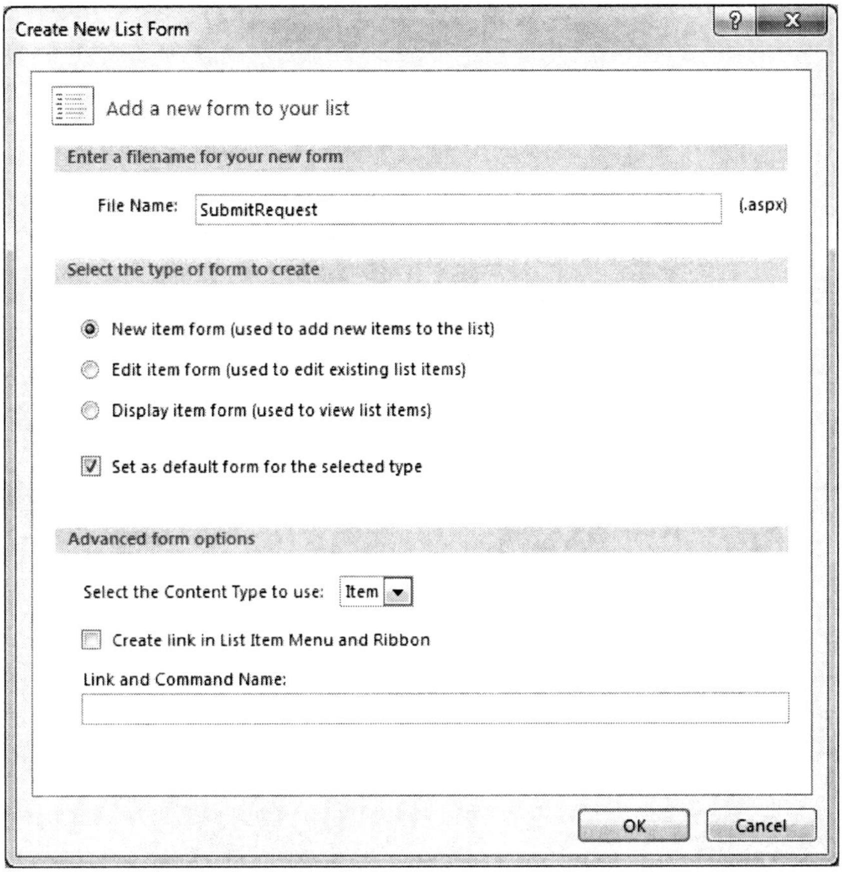

Figure 5-86. *Creating a new form*

4. The form will be displayed in edit mode. Select each of the fields except for the three that you'll keep, right-click the field, and select the Delete Row link. The final design should look like Figure 5-87. Save the form changes.

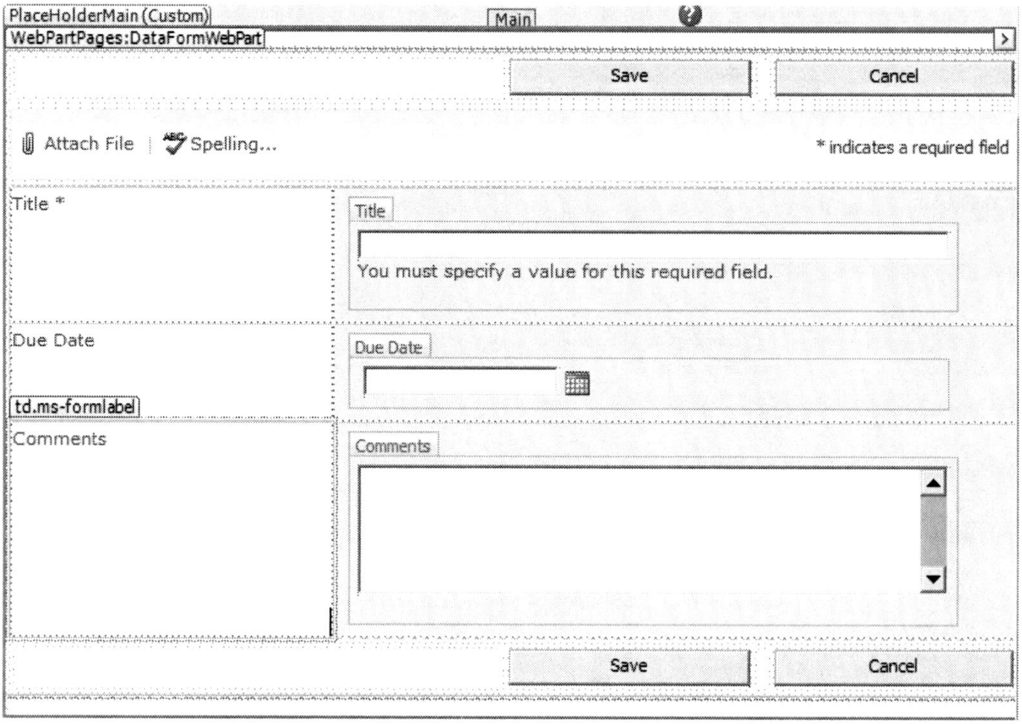

Figure 5-87. The modified from design

Configuring the Default Forms

When I created the InfoPath forms they were set as the default forms. However, when the `SubmitRequest` form was created by SharePoint Designer, the default forms were changed back to the standard forms. You should go to the Forms section and make sure the default forms are set correctly. The default forms should be

- `SubmitRequest`: New
- `Displayifs`: Display
- `Editifs`: Edit

The Forms section will look like Figure 5-88.

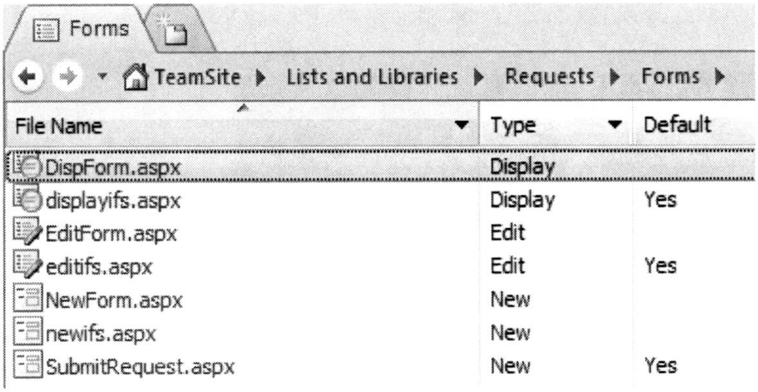

File Name ▲	Type ▼	Default
DispForm.aspx	Display	
displayifs.aspx	Display	Yes
EditForm.aspx	Edit	
editifs.aspx	Edit	Yes
NewForm.aspx	New	
newifs.aspx	New	
SubmitRequest.aspx	New	Yes

Figure 5-88. The Requests list forms

Tip The names of the InfoPath forms all end in "ifs".

Testing the New Forms

Now you'll test the new Requests list forms to make sure they work as expected. Create a new request; the form should only include the three fields, as demonstrated in Figure 5-89.

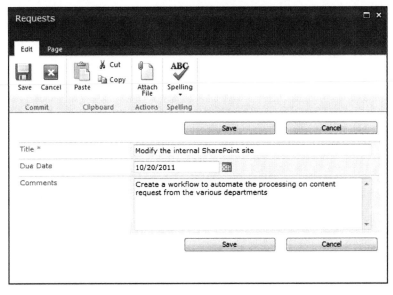

Figure 5-89. Creating a new request using the SubmitRequest form

After saving the request, open the request. The InfoPath version of the display form should look like Figure 5-90.

Figure 5-90. The InfoPath version of the display form

Modifying the Task Forms

For one last comment about custom forms, I want to show you that you can use InfoPath to modify the task forms. You navigate to them a little differently, however. Using SharePoint Designer, go to the Workflow properties page. The Forms section lists the forms that are used by the workflow, as shown in Figure 5-91.

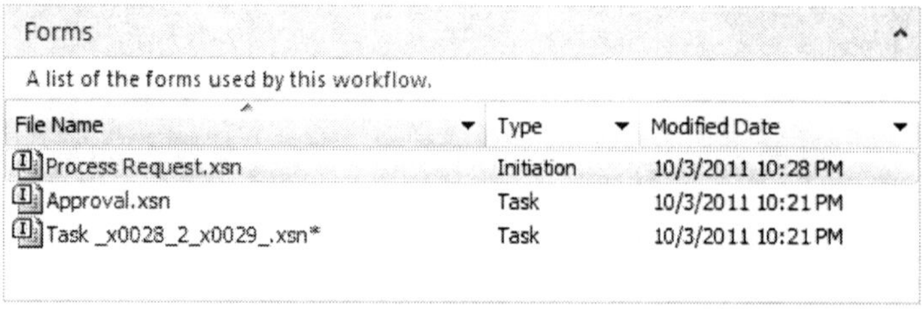

Figure 5-91. The forms used by the Process Request workflow

The first is an initiation form, which is used when starting a workflow manually. The next two are the task forms for the approval and fulfillment tasks. The filename is a link that will open the form using InfoPath. Click either of these and, after a few seconds, InfoPath will start and display the form, as demonstrated in Figure 5-92.

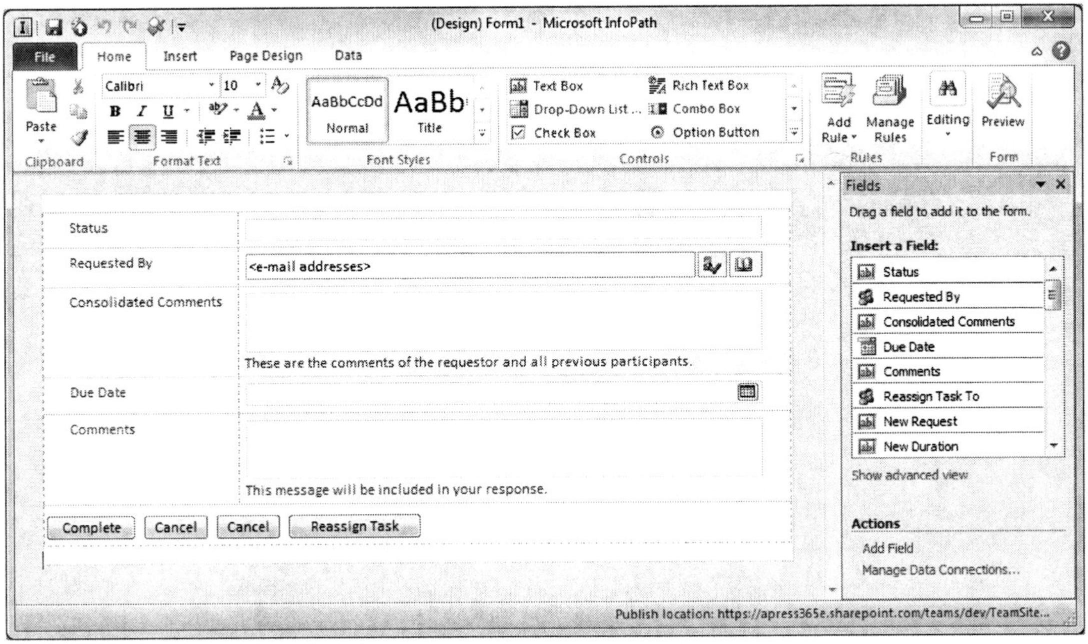

Figure 5-92. The fulfillment task form in InfoPath 2010

You can edit the form as desired. When you're done, use the Quick Publish button on the backstage view to update the form in the SharePoint site.

Using Workflow Visualization

As mentioned, one of the advantages to using Visio to design the workflow is that you can see a visual representation of the workflow process from SharePoint. I'll now demonstrate how to enable that feature.

Enabling the Visualization Option

From the Workflow properties page, select the "Set workflow visualization on status page" check box, as shown in Figure 5-93.

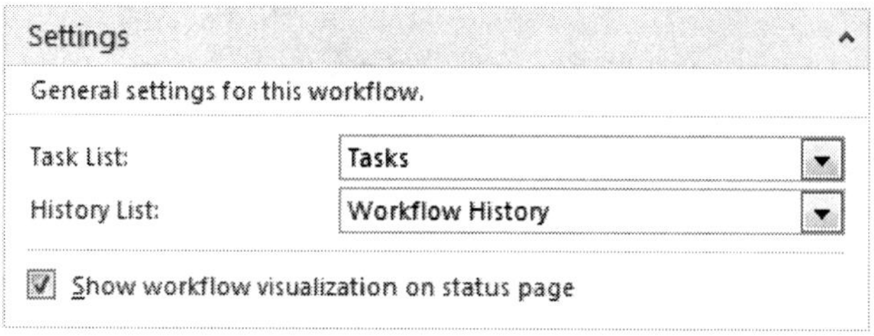

Settings

General settings for this workflow.

Task List: | Tasks | ▼
History List: | Workflow History | ▼

☑ Show workflow visualization on status page

Figure 5-93. Enabling workflow visualization

After making this change, make sure you re-publish the workflow by clicking the Publish button in the ribbon. Create a new request and then approve it once the approval task has been generated.

■ **Note** Workflow supports multiple versions. All of the existing requests were started using the initial workflow version that didn't include the visualization. New requests will use the current workflow version which does includes it. You should keep in mind that if you modify a workflow, the existing instances are not affected.

Displaying the Workflows Page

Select the drop-down next to the request title and click the Workflows link, as shown in Figure 5-94.

Figure 5-94. Selecting the Workflows link

This will display the Workflows page, which allows you to manually start a workflow (if one is available). It also lists the currently running workflows as well as any completed workflows (Figure 5-95).

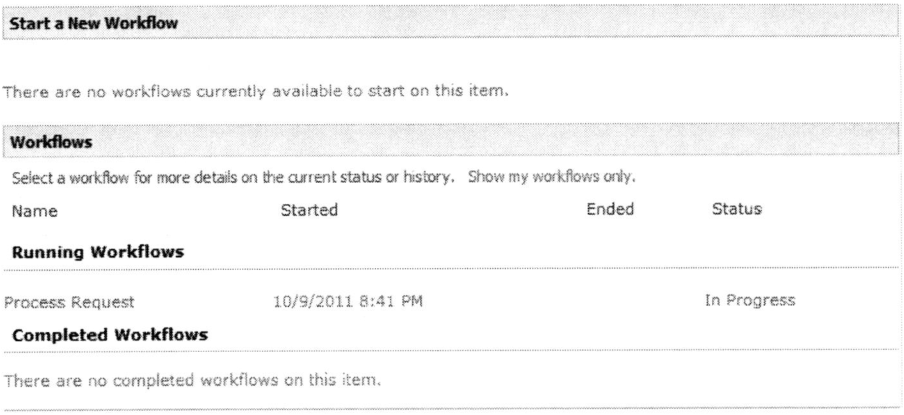

Start a New Workflow

There are no workflows currently available to start on this item.

Workflows

Select a workflow for more details on the current status or history.   Show my workflows only.

Name	Started	Ended	Status
Running Workflows			
Process Request	10/9/2011 8:41 PM		In Progress
Completed Workflows			

There are no completed workflows on this item.

Figure 5-95. The Workflows page showing the running workflows

Viewing the Workflow Visualization

Click the Process Request link to see details of the currently running workflow. Notice the Visio drawing shown in Figure 5-96.

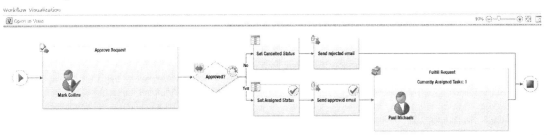

Figure 5-96. The workflow visualization

This is essentially the same Visio drawing that you imported. However, it also includes specific details. Notice the check box added to the actions or tasks that have been completed. The drawing shows that the request was approved by Mark Collins and the fulfillment task is assigned to Paul Michaels. Also, it shows that the fulfillment task has been assigned but not completed yet.

Viewing the Workflow Details

Scroll down this page and you'll see other workflow details, as demonstrated in Figure 5-97.

Tasks

The following tasks have been assigned to the participants in this workflow. Click a task to edit it. You can also view these tasks in the list Tasks.

	Assigned To	Title	Due Date	Status	Related Content	Outcome
	Mark Collins	Review Request - Update the SharePoint forms ⚙ NEW	10/11/2011	Completed	Update the SharePoint forms	Approved
	Paul Michaels	Fulfill Request - Update the SharePoint forms ⚙ NEW	10/26/2011	Not Started	Update the SharePoint forms	

Workflow History

The following events have occurred in this workflow.

	Date Occurred	Event Type		User ID	Description		Outcome
	10/9/2011 8:56 PM	Workflow Initiated		Mark Collins	Approval was started. Participants: Mark Collins		
	10/9/2011 8:56 PM	Task Created		Mark Collins	Task created for Mark Collins. Due by: None		
	10/9/2011 8:57 PM	Task Completed		Mark Collins	Task assigned to Mark Collins was approved by Mark Collins. Comments: Yes, I think that's a great idea		Approved by Mark Collins
	10/9/2011 8:57 PM	Workflow Completed		Mark Collins	Approval was completed.		Approval on Update the SharePoint forms has successfully completed. All participants have completed their tasks.

Figure 5-97. The workflow details

The Tasks section lists the tasks that have been generated. Once again, Mark Collins completed the approval task and the outcome was Approved. Paul Michaels was assigned the fulfillment task but this has not started yet.

The Workflow History section shows the history log for this workflow. The workflow logic logs messages to this history log when certain events occur. This log is a helpful feature for debugging workflows.

Summary

In this chapter I explained how to implement a declarative workflow to automate the processing of requests. Workflows can be used to automate common processes and make them more efficient and manageable. The workflow presented combines the capability of several tools including:

- Visio to provide a visual representation of the workflow.

- SharePoint Designer's workflow editor to implement the workflow logic.

- InfoPath Designer to design custom forms.

As I walked through the implementation I also explained

- Creating and using a list template.

- Using globally reusable workflows.

- Activating the necessary Enterprise features.

- Enabling workflow visualization.

Hopefully I have given you a sense of what you can do with declarative workflows and how to implement them. In the next chapter, I'll show you how to build a web database in SharePoint Online using Access 2010.

CHAPTER 6

Creating Sites with Access 2010

Another powerful technique for creating a web site on SharePoint Online is to use Microsoft Access 2010. For many years Access has been a favorite tool for creating client databases. With SharePoint 2010 and Access 2010 you can use that same familiar database tool to create a web database hosted on SharePoint. You'll use the Access client application to design tables, queries, and forms, and then publish them to SharePoint. This can be used to implement a web application with very little effort.

In Chapter 15, I will show you how to create your own web database from scratch. However, for this chapter you will download an existing Access template. This will get an application up and running quickly. Then I will show you how to publish this to a SharePoint site and explain how web databases work. My purpose in this chapter is to help you see what you can accomplish with a web database created in Access.

Creating a Web Database

You can find several web database templates on Office.com. These are a great way to create your SharePoint site if one of them suits your needs. But more than that, they offer an excellent opportunity to see what you can do in a web database with lots of examples if you want to build your own. Also, once you have created your database using one of these templates, you can customize it as much as you want. So starting with an existing template can be a great way to jump-start your project.

Selecting a Template

You'll begin by downloading the Movie Collection web database template. This is a simple database that allows you to maintain a library of movies that you own or that you would like to add to your collection. After you have created the Access database, I'll give you a quick tour of the included objects and how they work.

1. Start Access 2010 and the New tab of the backstage view should be displayed. From here you can either create a blank database or select an existing database template.

2. In the search box type **web database** and click the search button to the right of the text box. The list of available templates should be similar to Figure 6-1.

Available Templates

← → 🏠 Home ▸ Search Results

Office.com Templates   web database   →

Contacts web database   Assets web database   Projects web database   Issues web database

Northwind web database   Charitable contributions   Family Finances Web   Movie Collection Web
                          web database   Database   Database

Child Development Web   Game Collection Web   Metric Tracking Web
Database   Database   Database

Figure 6-1. Searching Office.com for web database templates

■ **Caution** It's important that you specify a web database template. There are a lot of templates available on Office.com but you want one that is specifically designed to be published on the web.

---

3. Select the template named Movie Collection Web Database. Details of that template will be displayed in the right-hand pane. Select a location on your local machine to save the new database and enter **Movies.accdb** for the filename, as shown in Figure 6-2.

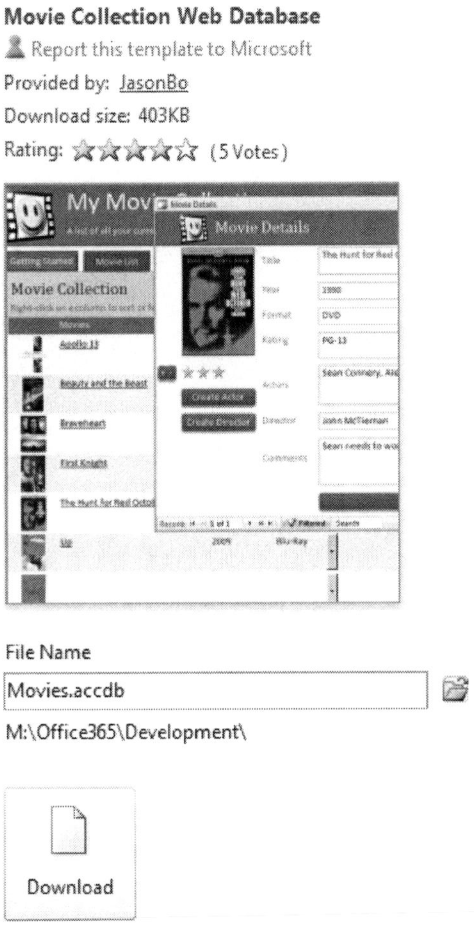

Movie Collection Web Database

👤 Report this template to Microsoft

Provided by: JasonBo

Download size: 403KB

Rating: ⭐⭐⭐⭐☆ (5 Votes)

File Name

Movies.accdb

M:\Office365\Development\

Download

Figure 6-2. Selecting a template and specifying the file location

4. Click the Download button to start the download and creation of your Access database.

5. You will be presented with the license agreement shown in Figure 6-3. The templates are available free of charge with the understanding that they are provided as-is and are not guaranteed to work. After you accept the license agreement, a new Access database will be created based on this template.

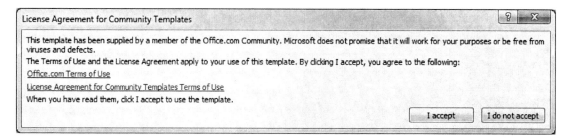

Figure 6-3. License agreement

Using the Application

This database is fairly simple, which makes it a good choice for a demo. It contains two lists.

- **Movies:** The movies that you currently have.

- **Wish List:** The movies that you would like to get.

The home page, shown in Figure 6-4, provides a tab for each list. For each list there is also a button to add a new movie and a button to display a printable version of the list.

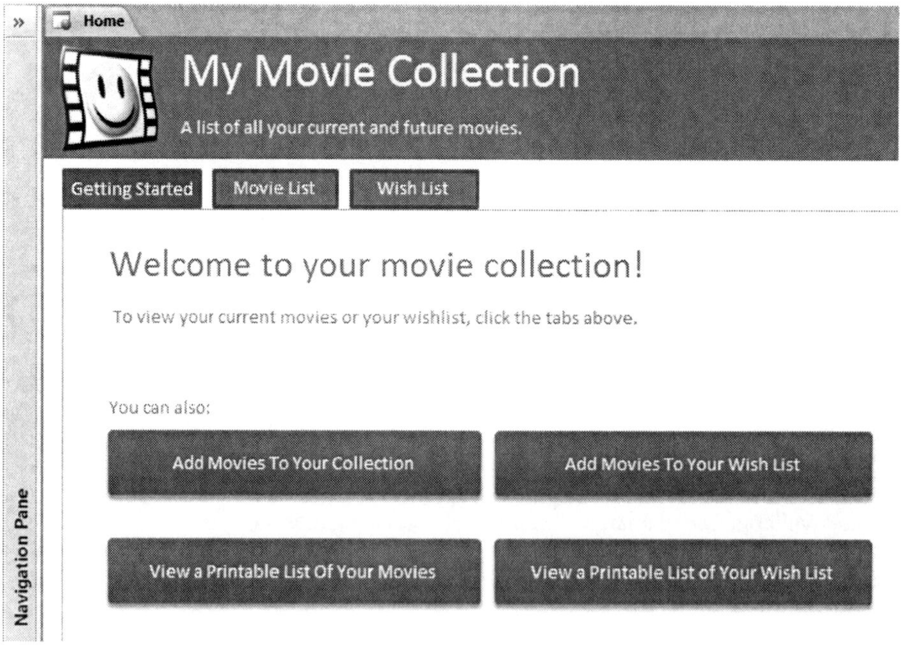

Figure 6-4. The Movies home page

1. Click the "Add Movies To Your Collection" button and a blank Movie Details form will be displayed (see Figure 6-5).

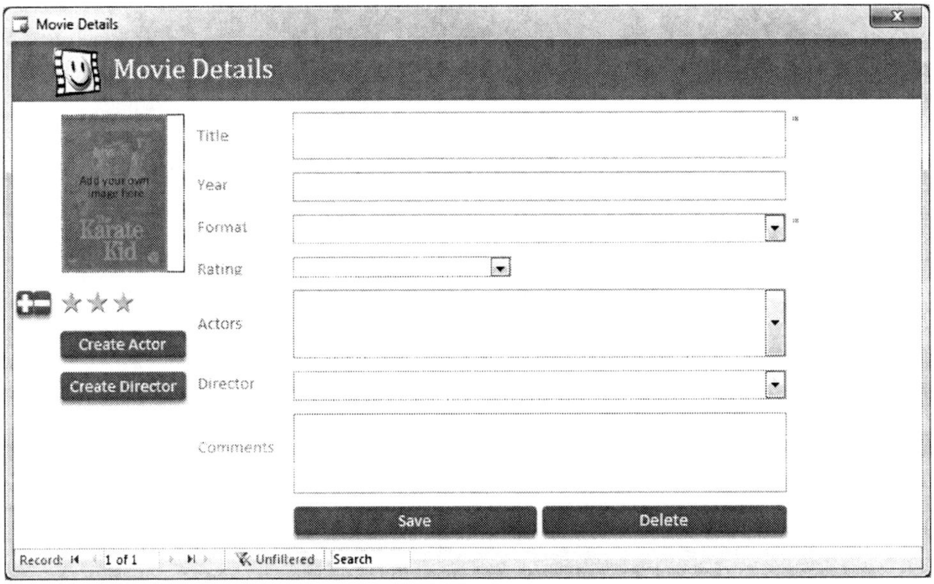

Figure 6-5. Adding a new movie

2. Fill in the various fields. The Format and Rating are drop-down lists that you use to select the appropriate value. The Actors and Director fields are also drop-down list but they allow you to select multiple values. If the actor or director that you want to enter is not in the drop-down, you can add it by using the Create Actor or Create Director button, respectively. Then enter the name in the dialog box, as shown in Figure 6-6. Click the Save button and close the form.

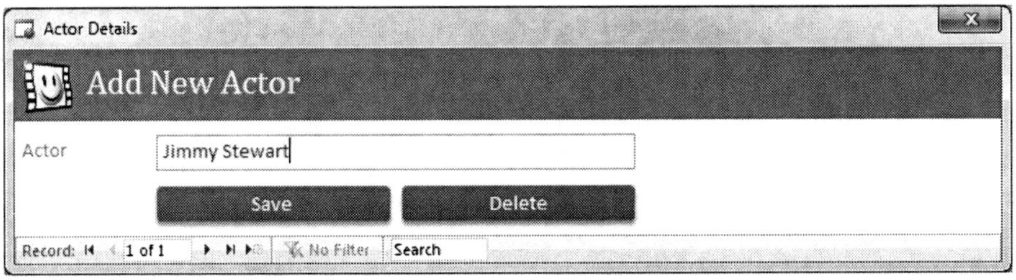

Figure 6-6. Adding a new actor

3. Images are stored as attachments. To add one or more, right-click the sample image and then select the Manage Attachments link. In the Attachments dialog box, shown in Figure 6-7, click the Add button and then browse to the location of the image file. When you're done adding images, click the OK button.

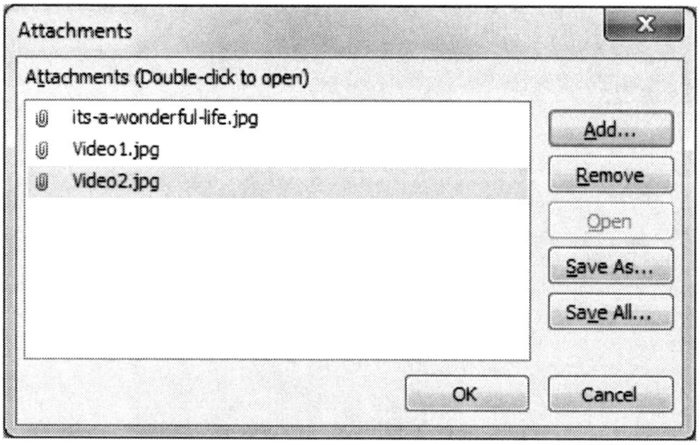

Figure 6-7. Adding attachments (images)

4. Use the plus and minus buttons underneath the image to change the review value. This will add or remove a star to/from the movie review. The completed form will look like Figure 6-8. Click the Save button to add the movie to your list.

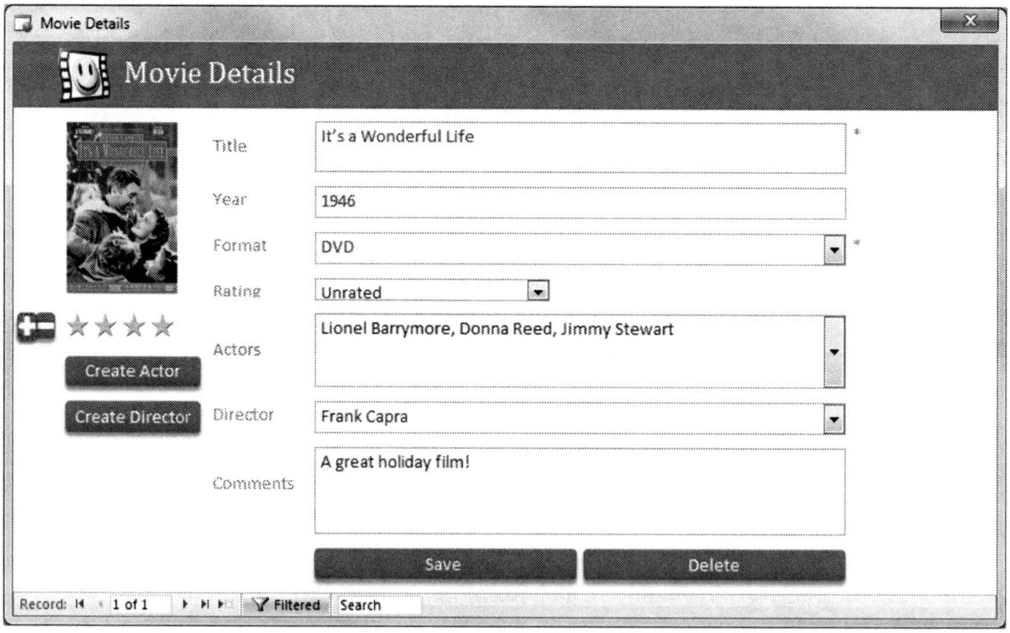

Figure 6-8. The completed Movie Details form

Exploring the Access Database

An Access "database" contains tables to store the data and forms that present this data to the users. A database can also include queries, reports, and macros. If the Navigation pane is hidden, use the >> button to make it visible. The objects included in this database should look like Figure 6-9. As you can see from the Navigation pane, the database contains tables, forms, and reports.

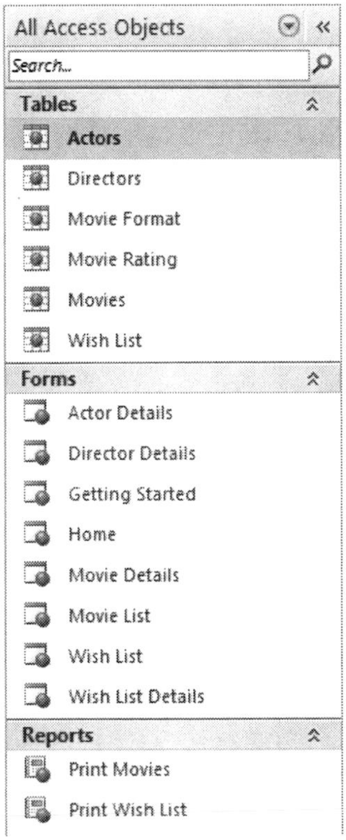

Figure 6-9. The Navigation pane showing all database objects

Using the Tables

The first four tables are used to supply the values for the drop-down lists.

- Actors
- Directors
- Movie Format
- Movie Rating

If you need to add an actor, for example, the dialog box shown in Figure 6-6 adds a record to the Actors table. There is no form for adding ratings and formats since these are fairly static lists. If you need to adjust them, you can open the table and modify the records directly. Double-click the Movie Rating table to open it in the Datasheet View, as demonstrated in Figure 6-10.

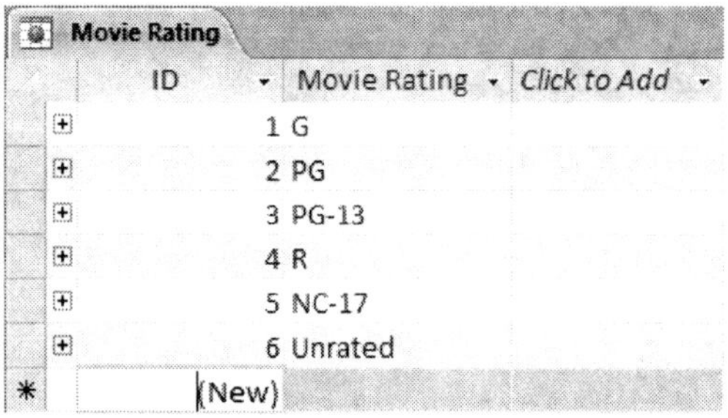

Figure 6-10. The Movie Rating table in Datasheet view

The last two tables, Movies and Wish List, are the main lists that contain the movies you currently own or would like to add.

Understanding the Forms

The Home form is automatically opened when the database is loaded. This is a navigation form that contains three tabs.

- Getting Started
- Movie List
- Wish List

Each of these tabs is implemented by a subform with the same name. The Movie List and Wish List forms display the contents of the Movies and Wish List tables, respectively. These are called *continuous forms* because they display multiple records simultaneously. Each record is formatted in a single row much like a spreadsheet.

In contrast, the Movie Details and Wish List Details forms are used to display a single record at a time. These forms are used to add a new record, to modify an existing record, or to display the details of a single item. The Actor Details and Director Details forms also display a single record from the associated table (Actors or Directors, respectively). They are only used for adding new records.

The Getting Started form has buttons that open the appropriate form or report. Open this form using the Layout View and select the "Add Movie To Your Collection" button. In the Event tab of the Property Sheet, you'll see that the On Click event is implemented by an embedded macro. Click the ellipses next to this event to open the macro editor. The macro implementation is shown in Figure 6-11.

```
OpenForm
        Form Name   Movie Details
   Where Condition
        Data Mode   Add
      Window Mode   Dialog
⊕  Add New Action                    ▼
```

Figure 6-11. The On Click event implementation

This macro contains a single OpenForm action. The form name, Movie Details, is specified as well as the data mode of Add. This will open the Movie Details form and display a new record.

Reviewing the Differences of Web Databases

For those who have used Access to create client databases, I will point out some of the differences when creating a web database.

- There are special web versions of the form, query, and report objects. An Access database can contain both types; however, only the web version can be used from the SharePoint site. As I'll demonstrate later, once published to SharePoint, you can continue to use the Access database as a client application. The client application can use both the client forms and the web forms. But only the web forms are available within SharePoint.

- Web forms must use the layout control. You can use this on the client forms as well, but for web forms it is required.

- Access 2010 introduces a new form view called Layout View. It provides some ability to edit the form without allowing the full capabilities of the Design View. Web forms and reports can't be opened in Design View. Instead you'll use the Layout View. This will be demonstrated in Chapter 15.

- You can't open tables using the Design View; however, you can add and modify the columns from the Datasheet view.

- You can't use VBA in web forms or reports. Instead you will use macros to provide similar functionality. The macro editor in Access 2010 has been enhanced significantly to provide much needed support since VBA is not available.

- Office 365 currently doesn't support Access reports. This is a limitation in Office 365 as web reports will work with an on-premise SharePoint Server. There has been some discussion about adding this ability in future updates to Office 365 but at the time of this writing this was not available. You can still include reports in your database and run them from the Access client, which I will demonstrate later in this chapter.

Using a Web Database in SharePoint

Next, you'll publish the web database to your SharePoint Online site in Office 365. I'll show you how the Access objects are translated into SharePoint objects and demonstrate how the web site works. I will also show you how to use the client and web applications simultaneously.

Publishing to SharePoint

Publishing your web database to a SharePoint site is a fairly simple matter. You'll first run the web compatibility checker to make sure that the database will work with SharePoint and that all the objects are compatible. Then you'll specify the URL of the SharePoint server and indicate the site name.

▪ **Note** When publishing a web database, the process always creates a new site. You can't publish to an existing site.

---

1. Select the Save & Publish tab from the backstage view and then click the Publish to Access Service link. The form will look like Figure 6-12.

Access Services Overview

Share your database with your team, friends, or organization with Access Services and SharePoint.

Use this if you want to:

▪ Make your database available through a Web browser and Access.

▪ Store tables in a central SharePoint location.

▪ Round trip queries, forms, reports, code, and linked tables that are not Web compatible.

Click here to watch a video demo

Check Web Compatibility

Run Compatibility Checker

You can check your database application for Web compatibility to identify items and settings that are not supported on the Web.

Web Compatibility Issues

Publish to Access Services

Full URL: http://www.thecreativepeople.com/TeamSite/Movies

Server URL: http://www.thecreativepeople.com/TeamSite/

Site Name: Movies

Figure 6-12. Publishing the web database to SharePoint Online

2. Click the Run Compatibility Checker button. If this finds any issues, the button will turn red and the Web Compatibility Issues button will be enabled. Click this to show the errors and then resolve them.

3. Once all compatibility issues are corrected, enter the URL of the SharePoint server of your Office 365 account. If you want this site to be connected to an existing subsite, you can add the subsite name as I did. Enter the site name **Movies**. Then click the Publish to Access Services button to start the publishing process.

■ **Note** You can publish a web database to either the Small Business or Enterprise plans. The site collection provided with the Small Business plan is already configured to support Access databases. If you're using an Enterprise plan, you'll need to make sure you have activated the SharePoint Server Enterprise Site Collection features on the site collection that you're using, as I explained in the previous chapter.

The publishing process can take several minutes to complete, especially when there is a lot of data to synchronize. The Actors and Directors tables are pre-populated with a fairly long list of names. When the site has been created, the dialog box shown in Figure 6-13 will be displayed.

Figure 6-13. The Publish Succeeded dialog box

Using the SharePoint Site

The Movies database is now available from the SharePoint site. I'll give you a quick tour of the web applications and then I'll show you how the SharePoint objects were created.

1. Click the link in the Publish Succeeded dialog box shown in Figure 6-13. This will open the SharePoint site that was created for you. The home page should look similar to the default page in Access.

2. Select the Movie List tab and you should see the movie that you entered in the Access client application. Click the title field, which is a link to open the Movie Details form shown in Figure 6-14.

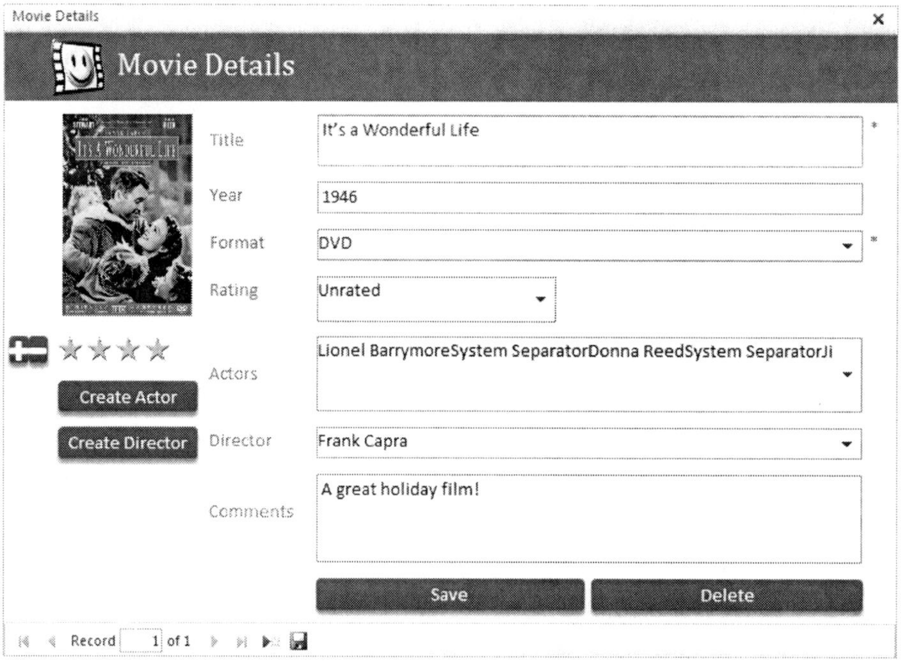

Figure 6-14. The Move Details form in SharePoint

⬚ **Note** The text between each of the actors is "System Separator". I will show you how to correct this later in the chapter.

---

3. Close the form, go back to the Getting Started tab, and click the "Add Movies To Your Collection" button. Fill out the form and click the Save button to add a new movie to your list. The form in SharePoint works pretty much the same way it did within the Access client application.

4. You probably noticed an issue, however, when trying to select actors. When you scroll to the bottom of the list you'll see the text "Not all items are shown..." as demonstrated in Figure 6-15.

☐ April Woodard

☐ Arancha Bonete

☐ Archana

☐ Arden Myrin

☐ Arden Wohl

☐ Ari Folman

☐ Ari Graynor

Not all items are shown...

Figure 6-15. Selecting actors from the list

■ **Caution** Populating a drop-down list with more than 6,000 items is a bad design. While it works from the client application, it's not a good user experience to make the user scroll through 6,000 entries to find the one they want. SharePoint will only include the first 500 items in the drop-down so this doesn't work at all in the web environment. A better design would be to implement a search form, allowing the user to find an actor or director using a partial first or last name.

5. After adding a new movie, select the Movie List tab. The Movie List form will include both movies, as shown in Figure 6-16.

Movies	Year	Format
Movie Collection		
Right-click on a column to sort or filter your movies.		
A Christmas Carol	1984	DVD
It's a Wonderful Life	1946	DVD

Figure 6-16. The Movie List form with an additional item

Exploring the SharePoint Site

When you publish an Access web database, the tables in Access become lists in SharePoint. The actual SharePoint lists are not directly accessible from the normal navigation options. However, there is a back door that you can use to view them. Click the Options drop-down and click the Site Permissions link. The Site Permissions page provides a Site Actions drop-down. Click that and then click the View All Site Content link.

The All Site Content page, shown in Figure 6-17, enumerates all of the lists and document libraries on your SharePoint site.

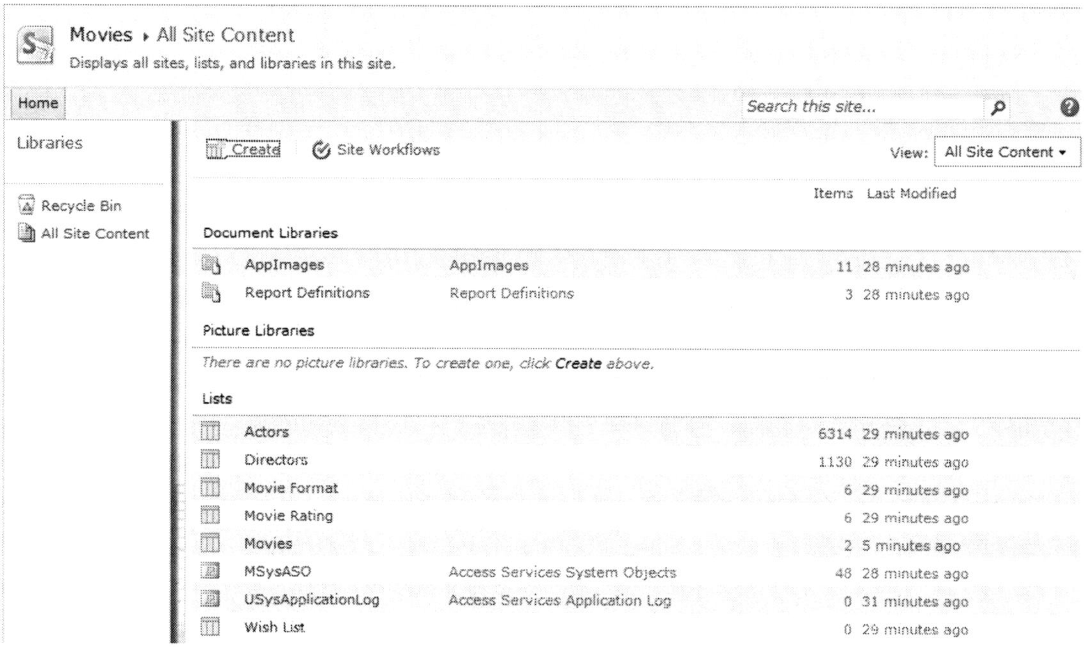

Figure 6-17. The All Site Content page showing the lists created from Access

Notice the lists that correspond to the Access tables such as Actors, Directors, and Movie Format. You can use the links on this page to go directly to the list data without using the Access forms. For example, if you need to adjust movie format, just click the list name, Movie Format, and the list will be displayed using either the Datasheet view or the Standard view (see Figure 6-18).

☐ Type	Title	Movie Format	_OldID
🗋	(no title) ▣ NEW	DVD	1
🗋	(no title) ▣ NEW	Blu-Ray	2
🗋	(no title) ▣ NEW	Digital	3
🗋	(no title) ▣ NEW	VHS	4
🗋	(no title) ▣ NEW	Betamax	5
🗋	(no title) ▣ NEW	Laserdisc	

Figure 6-18. Displaying the contents of the Movie Format list

---

■ **Tip** This is a fully functional SharePoint site and you can use commands in the ribbon to display and edit the data and set up views.

Go back to the All Site Content page and then select the Movies list. You should see the two movies that you have added so far, as demonstrated in Figure 6-19.

☐ Type	📎	_Title	Title	Year	Review	Comments	_OldID	Actors	Director	Format	Rating
🗋	📎	(no title) ▣ NEW	It's a Wonderful Life	1,946	4/5	A great holiday film!		Lionel Barrymore; Donna Reed; Jimmy Stewart	Frank Capra	DVD	Unrated
🗋	📎	(no title) ▣ NEW	A Christmas Carol	1,984	5/5	This is probably my favorite version of the classic Christmas tale.				DVD	PG

Figure 6-19. The Movies list

Click the Title link on one of these movies and you'll see the normal SharePoint view form shown in Figure 6-20.

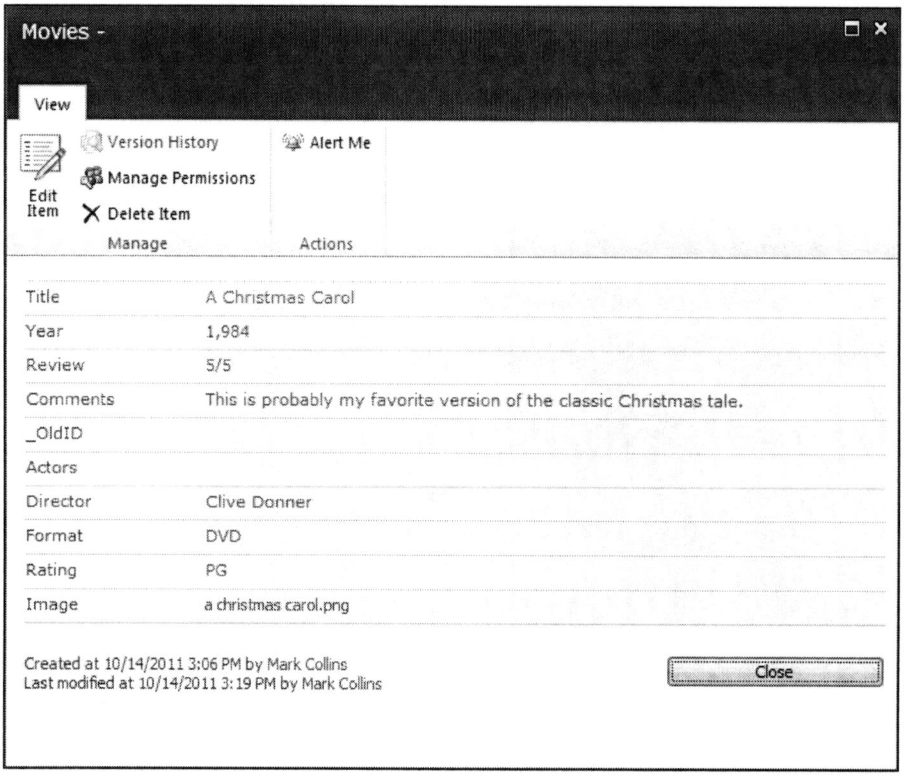

Figure 6-20. The standard SharePoint view form

■ **Tip** Since the data is in SharePoint, you can use SharePoint's security feature to grant or restrict access to each list based on user groups.

Go back to the All Site Content page. Notice that there is document library named AppImages. Access 2010 introduced a new feature called the image gallery. This is a place to store all of the static images used on the forms. The idea is to store an image once and then reference it wherever needed. When the database is published to SharePoint, the image gallery is created as a document library. Select the AppImages library; its contents should look similar to Figure 6-21.

Type	Name	Modified	Modified By
	1_default ☼ NEW	10/14/2011 2:43 PM	Mark Collins
	chkCleared ☼ NEW	10/14/2011 2:40 PM	Mark Collins
	chkDisabled ☼ NEW	10/14/2011 2:40 PM	Mark Collins
	chkSelected ☼ NEW	10/14/2011 2:40 PM	Mark Collins
	default ☼ NEW	10/14/2011 2:43 PM	Mark Collins
	Form Logo ☼ NEW	10/14/2011 2:43 PM	Mark Collins
	LogoBig ☼ NEW	10/14/2011 2:43 PM	Mark Collins
	minus ☼ NEW	10/14/2011 2:43 PM	Mark Collins
	plus ☼ NEW	10/14/2011 2:43 PM	Mark Collins
	Report Logo ☼ NEW	10/14/2011 2:43 PM	Mark Collins
	yellow_star ☼ NEW	10/14/2011 2:43 PM	Mark Collins

Figure 6-21. The contents of the AppImages library

The AppImages library contains the static images such as the smiley face on the Home page and the stars used for the rating. The LogoBig file is the image for the smiley face, for example. If you want to use a different image, you can replace this file and everywhere this image is referenced will be updated.

■ **Note** You can't use SharePoint Designer to edit a site that was created from an Access web database. If you try to open the site with SharePoint Designer, you'll see the error shown in Figure 6-22.

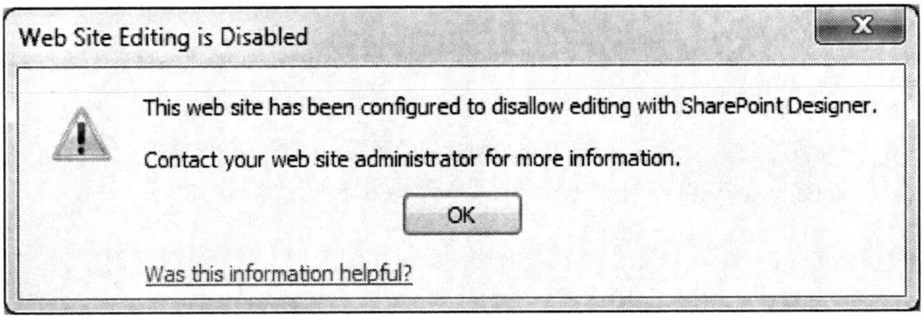

Figure 6-22. Error when trying to use SharePoint Designer

As I mentioned earlier, you can't use Access reports from Office 365. This is a limitation of the Office 365 platform as this is available in an on-premise SharePoint server. If you click either of the two lower buttons on the Home page, you'll see the error shown in Figure 6-23.

Figure 6-23. Error accessing reports

The error message is telling you to use the Access client application to view reports. I will now show you how to do that.

Using the Access Client

When you publish a web database to SharePoint, the data in the tables is moved into SharePoint lists. The Access database is also modified so the tables simply reference the SharePoint site. When you update a record using the Access client application, you are actually updating the SharePoint list. Because of this, you can switch between the web site and the client application, and the data remains consistent.

If you need a form that is too complex to implement as a web form due to their limitations (primarily no VBA code), you can use a client form instead. The user will need to run that form using the Access client, however. The other forms can be used from the web site.

■ **Tip** If the users don't have a copy of Access 2010, they can install the Access 2010 runtime. This is a free application that allows you to open an Access database. You can't edit any of the objects, such as forms, but you can use the forms to view and update the data. You can download the Access Runtime from www.microsoft.com/download/en/details.aspx?id=10910.

The other really nice feature is that the entire contents of the Access database are contained within the SharePoint site. This includes any client objects (forms, queries, etc.) that are contained in the Access database. As a result, SharePoint can produce an Access database from the existing site content. The site members can use either the web site or the Access client without needing the original Access database that was published. So, once the web database has been published, you can delete the original Access database. You don't need to distribute the client database because users can extract it from the SharePoint site. When an update is pushed to the server, which I'll explain later, each user will always have the latest version.

■ **Note** Client objects such as forms and queries can be included in a web database and will be copied to the SharePoint site when it is published. These will be included when an Access database is generated for a web user and can be used from the Access client. However, you can't use the client objects from the web site.

From the Site Actions menu, click the Settings link. The Site Settings page, shown in Figure 6-24, lists all of the Access objects that are included in the site.

 Design With Access
Modify this web database, add new fields, customize forms and reports.

 Settings
Recycle Bin
Delete this Site

Tables

🔘	Actors	Last modified on 10/14/2011 2:43:43 PM by Mark Collins
🔘	Directors	Last modified on 10/14/2011 2:43:44 PM by Mark Collins
🔘	Movie Format	Last modified on 10/14/2011 2:43:44 PM by Mark Collins
🔘	Movie Rating	Last modified on 10/14/2011 2:43:44 PM by Mark Collins
🔘	Movies	Last modified on 10/14/2011 2:43:44 PM by Mark Collins
🔘	USysApplicationLog	Last modified on 10/14/2011 2:41:02 PM by Mark Collins
🔘	Wish List	Last modified on 10/14/2011 2:43:44 PM by Mark Collins

Forms

📋	Actor Details	Last modified on 10/14/2011 2:43:43 PM by Mark Collins
📋	Director Details	Last modified on 10/14/2011 2:43:44 PM by Mark Collins
📋	Getting Started	Last modified on 10/14/2011 2:43:44 PM by Mark Collins
📋	Home	Last modified on 10/14/2011 2:43:44 PM by Mark Collins
📋	Movie Details	Last modified on 10/14/2011 2:43:44 PM by Mark Collins
📋	Movie List	Last modified on 10/14/2011 2:43:44 PM by Mark Collins
📋	Wish List	Last modified on 10/14/2011 2:43:44 PM by Mark Collins
📋	Wish List Details	Last modified on 10/14/2011 2:43:44 PM by Mark Collins

Reports

📊	Print Movies	Last modified on 10/14/2011 2:43:49 PM by Mark Collins
📊	Print Wish List	Last modified on 10/14/2011 2:43:49 PM by Mark Collins

Queries

There are no queries in this application.

Macros

There are no macros in this application.

Figure 6-24. The Site Settings page listing the Access objects

Opening the Access Database

If you select any of these objects, the page will open the Access database so you can edit them there. There is also a link under the "Design With Access" label, which will also open the Access database. However, you can open the Access database from any page in the site by using the Open In Access link in the Options menu, as shown in Figure 6-25.

Figure 6-25. The Open In Access link from the Options menu

Open the Access database using either of these two links. You may see the warning shown in Figure 6-26. This dialog box is letting you know that this Access database is linked to a SharePoint site. When you view data in this database, the data is actually being downloaded from the SharePoint site.

Figure 6-26. Warning that content is being downloaded

The Access database that is being opened is not the same one you created initially. To verify this, you can move it to a different location or rename it. Instead, SharePoint is generating a new database file for you. You will probably see a dialog box similar to Figure 6-27 letting you know that a new file is being created. However, it should look and function just like the one you started with.

Figure 6-27. New database file created

The Home page should be displayed. Click the "View a Printable List Of Your Movies" button. This will run the report that you were not able to run from the Web. The report should look similar to Figure 6-28.

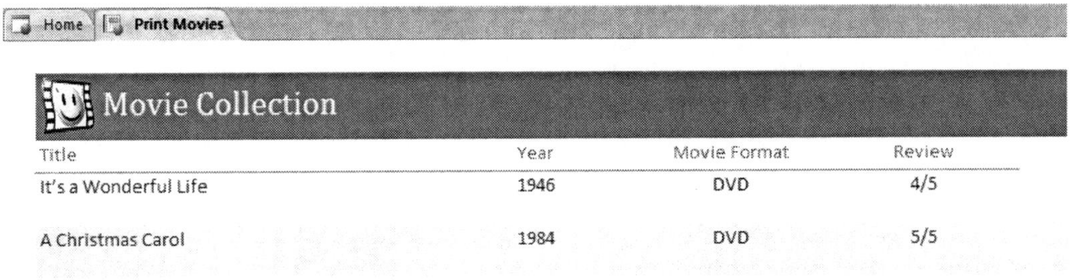

Figure 6-28. The Print Movies report

You can browse the database and verify everything works as it used to. Try adding some move movies to either list and then go to the web site and verify that they are there as well.

Fixing the System Separator

As I promised earlier, I'll now show you how to fix the separator issue. In Access, when you have a Lookup field that allows multiple values, you can specify the character that is displayed between each value. The default setting for this property is System Separator, which tells Access to use the list separator defined by the localization settings. For many regions, this is specified as a comma. However, SharePoint doesn't understand this convention and treats this as a literal string. To resolve this issue, you'll select a different separator. Open the Movie Details form in the Layout view and select the Actors field. In the Format tab of the Property Sheet, change the Separator Characters property to a comma or semicolon, as shown in Figure 6-29.

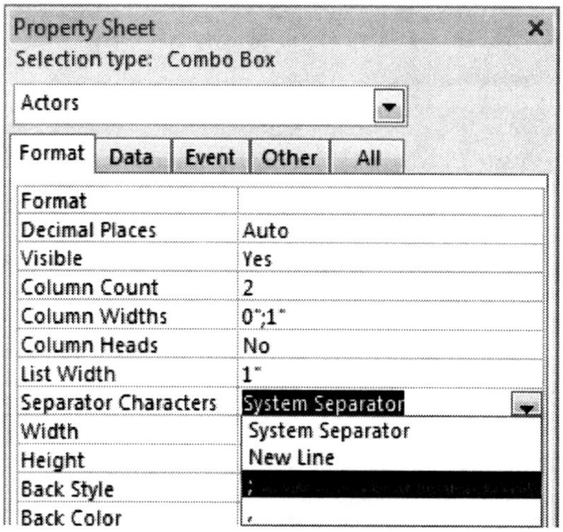

Figure 6-29. *Changing the Separator Characters property*

Make the same change to the Director field. You'll also need to make the same changes to the Movie List form. Save the changes to these forms.

Synchronizing Application Changes

I mentioned earlier that data changes made from the Access client are updated in SharePoint immediately. However, application changes have to be manually synchronized. Go to the Backstage view and click the Check Sync Status button in the Synchronization section. The background should change to red indicating there are unsynchronized changes. The text should indicate there are changes that need to be sent to the server (SharePoint site), as shown in Figure 6-30.

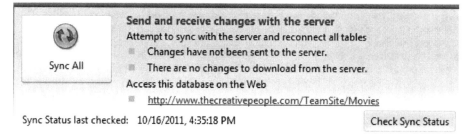

Figure 6-30. *The synchronization status*

Click the Sync All button to push these form changes to the web site. When this has completed, go back to the web site and verify there are commas between the actors in both the Movies and Movie Details forms.

■ **Note** You may need to refresh the current page for these changes to take effect.

Summary

In this chapter, you created an Access web database using a template from Office.com. You tried out the application from the Access client and then published this to your Office 365 account. You then accessed the same forms from the SharePoint site. You also viewed the data using the native SharePoint forms as well. You then opened the Access database from the SharePoint site and data changes made in the client applications were reflected immediately in the SharePoint site.

This chapter was an introduction to web databases. I will explain Access web databases again in Chapter 15. I will show you how to create your own, including the table and query design, implementing forms, and creating macros.

Once you have published a web database to SharePoint, you can view and edit the data using any of the following:

- The SharePoint site using the forms published with the web database.

- The Access client application.

- The SharePoint site using native SharePoint forms.

- As I'll demonstrate in Chapter 16, you can also access this using the SharePoint object model.

In the next chapter, I will show you how to use functionality available in Excel from your SharePoint site.

CHAPTER 7

Excel Services

In this chapter I'll show you how to use some of the collaboration features available when using Microsoft Excel 2010 as part of the Office 365 platform. The Office Web Apps are a great way to view shared documents; you can even edit them with multiple users simultaneously. I'll also show you some of the advance features available when publishing an Excel spreadsheet. Finally, I'll demonstrate how to use the Excel REST services to programmatically extract data from a spreadsheet.

Collaborating with Office Web Apps

Office 365 includes the Office Web Apps, browser-based versions of the familiar Word, Excel, PowerPoint, and OneNote client applications. These, combined with SharePoint document libraries, provide a great way to share data and documents. The file formats of the documents created by the Office Web Apps are identical to the corresponding client counterpart, so you can use either tool when working with a document.

For example, you can create a document with the web app, enter advanced content with the client app, and then view and edit it with the web app. The web apps have a limited feature set for editing a document but can generally display most of the content. I'll give you a brief demonstration of how to take advantage of this capability.

> **Note** For a full description of the features provided by the Office Web Apps, download the product guide from
> http://download.microsoft.com/download/2/6/2/26253C22-D8EC-4230-A3ED-E2DEED9E8EBE/Microsoft
> Office Web Apps Product Guide_Final.xps.

Creating Shared Documents

Figure 7-1 shows the home page of a Small Business (P1 plan) Office 365 account. On this machine all I have is a web browser; none of the Office client applications have been installed.

Microsoft
Office 365   **Home**   Outlook   Team Site

Outlook

Read email and access your Outlook calendar, contacts, and tasks.
Inbox | Calendar | Options

Lync

Use Lync for instant messaging, audio and video calling, and online meetings.
Install Lync 2010

Team site

Collaborate on documents and share information and ideas using SharePoint Online.
Visit team site | Shared documents

Word   Excel   PowerPoint   OneNote

Website

View your public website.
http://www.thecreativepeople.com/

Figure 7-1. The standard Office 365 home page

The links in the Team site section are used to create a new document using the Office Web Apps. When you click one of these links, the corresponding web app opens a blank page for you to start entering data. Click the Excel link and enter the data shown in Figure 7-2.

⚠ **Unsaved Changes**	You are editing an unsaved workbook.		Start Autosaving...		

fx | 1

	A	B	C	D	E	F
1	Team	Wins	Loses	Ties		
2	Tigers	7	2	1		
3	Cougars	6	2	2		
4	Beavers	4	6	0		
5	Frogs	3	6	1		
6	Penguins	1	9	0		

Figure 7-2. Creating a new spreadsheet using Excel Web App

Notice the banner at the top that is warning you that the data is not saved. There is no Save button in the web apps; instead the data is saved automatically. However, when you create a new document you must specify a document name before the autosaving feature can start. Click the Start autosaving link and you'll be prompted to enter a name, as shown in Figure 7-3. Enter **Team Standings** and click the Save button.

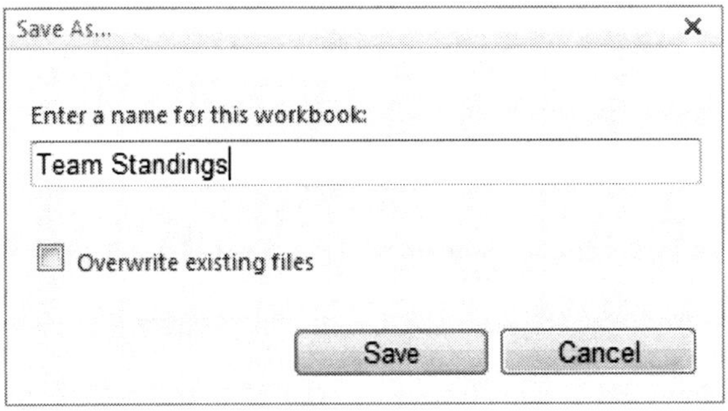

Figure 7-3. Saving the spreadsheet

The specified document is created in the shared document library. You only have to enter a document name once. After a document name has been specified, changes are automatically saved in the document library.

Go back to the home page and select the Shared document link. The new document will be included in this library, as shown in Figure 7-4.

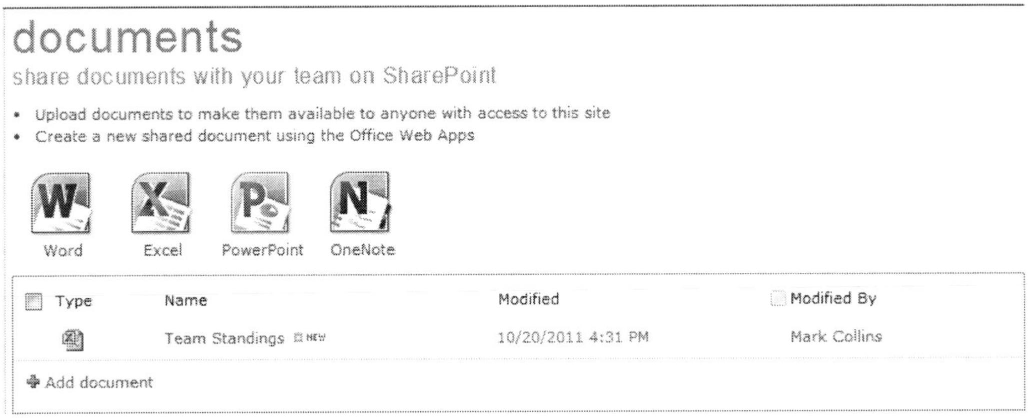

Figure 7-4. The shared documents folder

■ **Tip** The links on the document library page look identical to the links on the home page but they work differently. The links on the home page will always create a new document using the appropriate Office Web App. However, the links on the document library page will create a new document using the client application, if it has been installed on the client machine. If not, the Office Web Apps will be used.

Simultaneous Editing

Perhaps one of the most interesting features in Office 365 is the ability for multiple people to edit the same document simultaneously. There are several scenarios with multiple people sharing the same document and using different applications to view and edit it. I'll explain which scenarios are supported and which ones are not.

The client application can open the document in read-only mode or edit mode. Opening a document for editing requires exclusive access to the document. Once a user has opened a document using the client application in edit mode, no one else may edit the document in either the client app or the web app. However, other users can open the same document in read-only mode with either application.

In contrast, the web apps were designed to allow multiple users to edit the same document simultaneously. If someone is editing a document using the web app, other users can also edit the same document using the web app. I'll demonstrate how that works.

Select the Team Standings.xlsx item from the document library and the document will be opened using the Excel Office Web App in read-only mode. To make some changes, click the Edit in Browser link near the top of the window, as shown in Figure 7-5.

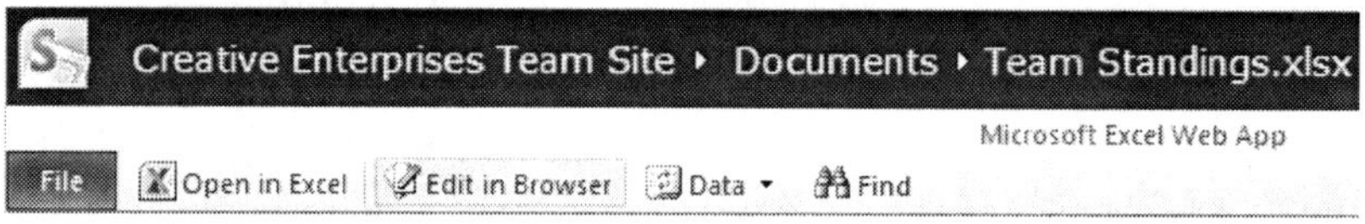

Figure 7-5. Editing an existing spreadsheet

The ribbon will expand to provide some basic editing features. Note that the label at the bottom right-hand corner includes the text "1 person editing" to remind you that the file is opened for edit.

On another machine, log on as a different user and open this document using the web app. When you switch the application to edit mode, the indicator now says "2 people editing" on both machines. If you click the drop-down arrow next to this label, the people who have the document open in edit mode are displayed, as demonstrated in Figure 7-6.

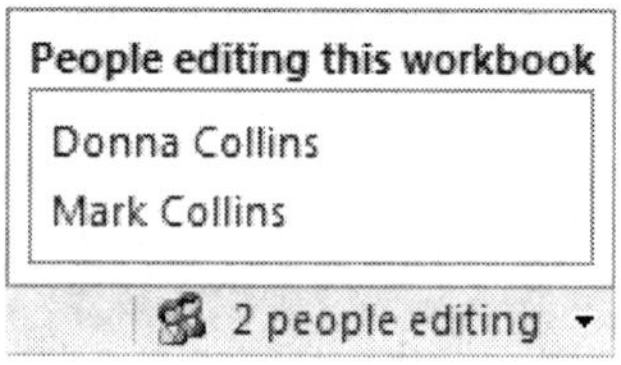

Figure 7-6. Multiple people editing simultaneously

When one person modifies a cell and then tabs off that cell (or selects another cell) the new value is automatically saved and displayed in both applications. If someone else modifies that cell, their change is pushed to everyone else. Essentially, the last change made is applied to all users.

■ **Caution** I have seen situations where the two applications are out of sync. If you suspect this has happened, close all the browser windows and then go back into the document. This clears out all session variables and usually resolves the issue.

Using the Client Applications

The editing capability provided in the Office Web Apps is fairly limited. If you have the Office client applications installed, you can open with Excel and enjoy the full set of Excel features such a charts and pivot tables.

From the Office Web App, you can click the Open in Excel link if the document is open in read-only mode. If it is open for editing, you can use the Open in Excel button in the ribbon. In either case, the Open Document dialog box, shown in Figure 7-7, is displayed.

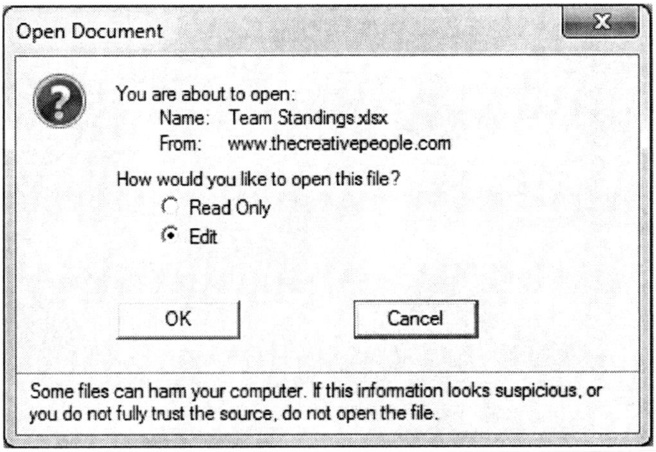

Figure 7-7. Opening the sheadsheet in Excel 2010

■ **Note** If the document library was set up to require documents to be checked out, the second radio button would say "Check Out and Edit" instead of just "Edit."

If you choose to open the document for editing, you will receive the File In Use dialog box (shown in Figure 7-8) if it is still open for editing in the browser. Remember that the Excel client app require exclusive access to be able to edit a document.

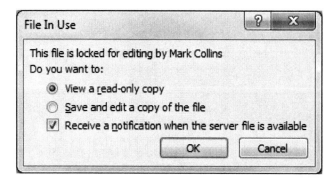

Figure 7-8. The File In Use dialog box

If two or more people have a document open for editing (this is referred to as *collaborating*), and one of them tries to edit the document in Excel, the error message shown in Figure 7-9 is displayed. To open the document in Excel, you must first close it in the web app. Both users would need to stop editing the file before the client app can open it in edit mode.

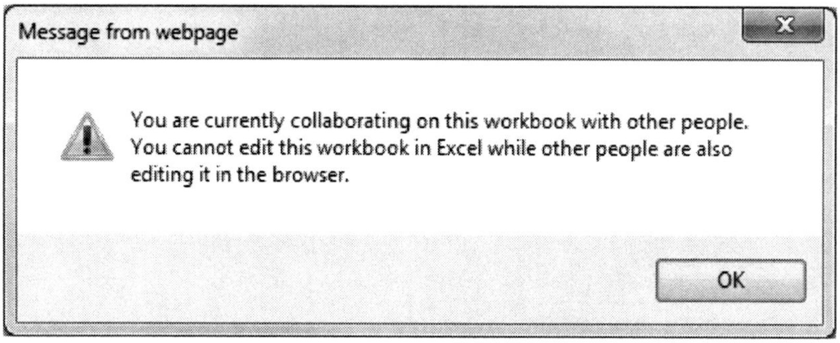

Figure 7-9. Excel editing disabled while collaborating

Once all the collaborators have closed the document, you can then open it in the client app, which is shown in Figure 7-10.

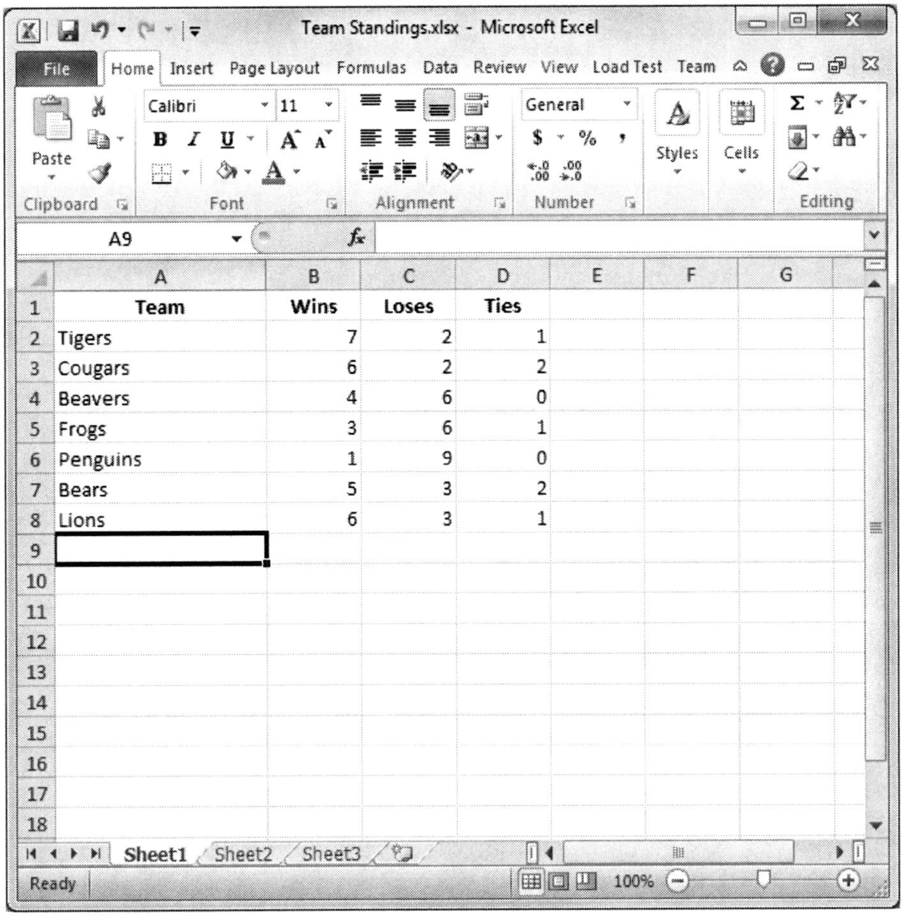

Figure 7-10. Editing the spreadsheet in Excel 2010

In the client app, create a simple PivotTable and PivotChart that shows the numbers of wins, ties, and loses for each team (see Figure 7-11).

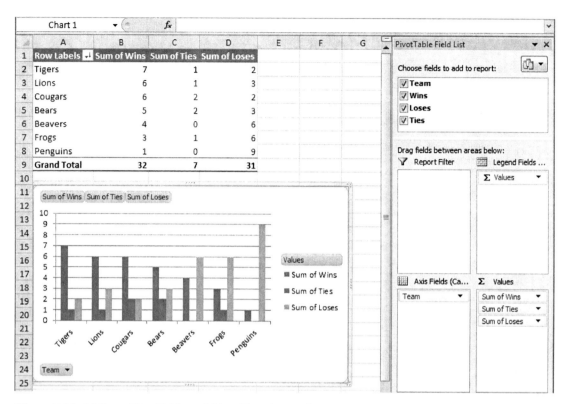

Figure 7-11. Adding a PivotTable and PivotChart in Excel

After these changes are saved, open the document using the web app and select the Chart tab, which displays the PivotTable and PivotChart (see Figure 7-12).

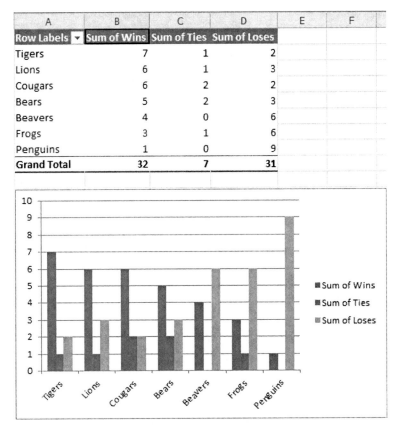

Row Labels	Sum of Wins	Sum of Ties	Sum of Loses
Tigers	7	1	2
Lions	6	1	3
Cougars	6	2	2
Bears	5	2	3
Beavers	4	0	6
Frogs	3	1	6
Penguins	1	0	9
Grand Total	32	7	31

Figure 7-12. Displaying the PivotChart in the web app

While the PivotTable and PivotChart can't be modified in the web app, you can edit the underlying data and refresh the pivot table. Update the standings and add the Squirrels team to the list. The updated data from the web app is shown in Figure 7-13.

Team	Wins	Loses	Ties
Tigers	9	2	1
Cougars	8	2	2
Beavers	6	6	0
Frogs	4	7	1
Penguins	1	11	0
Squirrels	10	1	1
Bears	5	5	2
Lions	6	5	1

Figure 7-13. Updated team standings

■ **Tip** The PivotTable uses a specified range of the Data worksheet. If you had added the new team at the end of the list, the new row would be outside of that range. To include the new team in the PivotTable you would need to open the document using the Excel client and modify the PivotTable. However, by inserting a row in the middle, the range is automatically expanded and will include the new row.

To force the Pivot chart to reflect the new data, click the Data button in the ribbon and select the Refresh All Connections link, as shown in Figure 7-14.

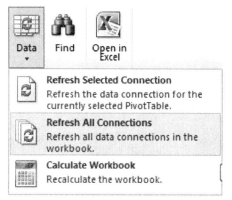

Figure 7-14. Refreshing the PivotTable and PivotChart

The PivotChart is then recalculated to include the new team; the updated data is shown in Figure 7-15.

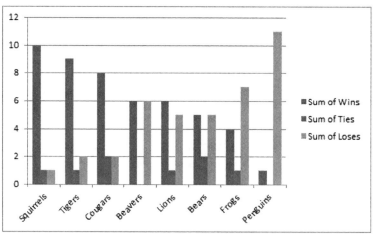

Figure 7-15. The updated PivotChart

Publishing an Excel Document

In the first example, you created a spreadsheet using the Excel Office Web App. Another user later opened the document using the Excel client application and added a PivotChart. However, you could just as easily start with the client application and save the document to a SharePoint library instead of a local file folder. This process is known as *publishing*.

Publishing is simply saving it to SharePoint. When you create a document, instead of saving it to a local file, you can save it in a document library, taking advantage of the same central repository that was used with the web apps. You could also save it to a local file initially and then later decide to publish it and make it available to others.

There are two actions that are available when publishing a document from the client application that you can't do when simply saving the document in the web app.

- You can choose to only show parts of the document.

- You can specify parameters that are linked to specific cells in the spreadsheet.

Showing Parts of a Document

When publishing an Excel document to SharePoint you can choose to only include portions of the document. For example, you may want to hide one or more of the worksheets. Another useful example is to show a chart or PivotTable without showing the supporting data. For this demonstration you will use the same Team Standings.xlsx file and publish it with a different name. This version will only show the PivotChart.

■ **Caution** This technique will restrict the parts of the spreadsheet that are displayed in the Excel Office Web App when viewing a published document. However, if you use the Edit in Browser link, the entire document is available. Likewise, if you use the Open in Excel link, you can see and modify the entire document.

To publish a document, go to the backstage view and select the Save & Send tab, then select the Save to SharePoint link. Since the document that is open is stored in a document library, the Current Location option is provided to you. You will publish this to the same document library so select that option, as shown in Figure 7-16. If you had just created a new document, this option would not be available.

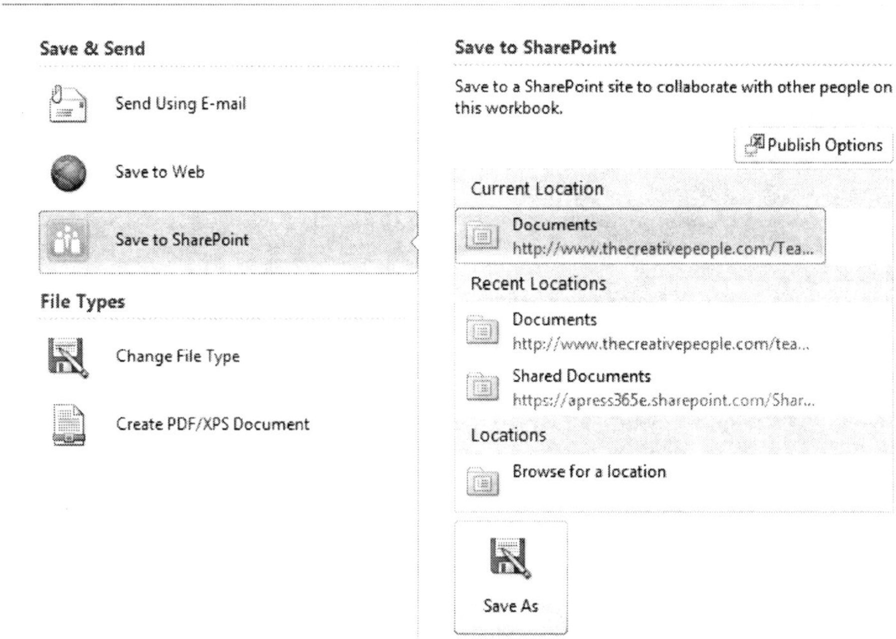

Figure 7-16. *Selecting the current document library*

The Save to SharePoint dialog box has a Publish Options button that opens the Publish Options dialog box. This is where you can configure the advanced features I mentioned. The first tab, labeled Show, is where you can specify what parts of the document should be visible in the web app. Your options are

- Entire Workbook

- Sheets (select one or more sheets in the current document)

- Items in the Workbook (select a specific item such as charts and tables)

In this case, you only want to show the PivotChart so select "Items in the Workbook" and then select Chart 1, as shown in Figure 7-17.

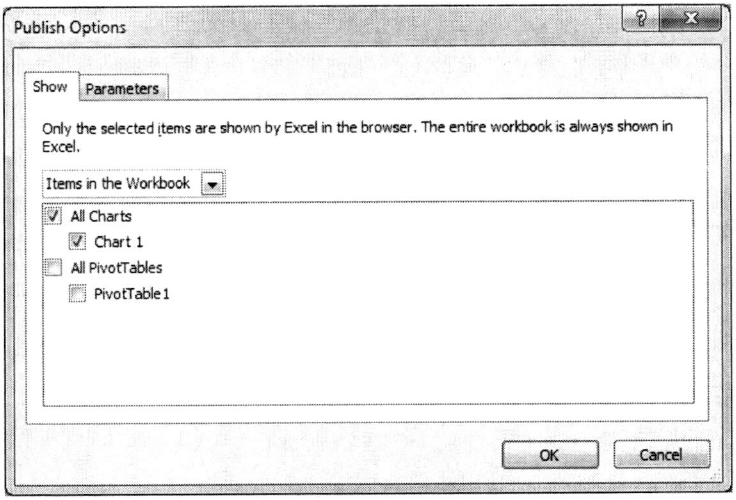

Figure 7-17. Showing only the PivotChart

After clicking the OK button to save these options and close the dialog box, click the Save As button in the Send to SharePoint dialog box. In the Save As dialog box, enter **Published Team Standings.xlsx** for the new file name (see Figure 7-18).

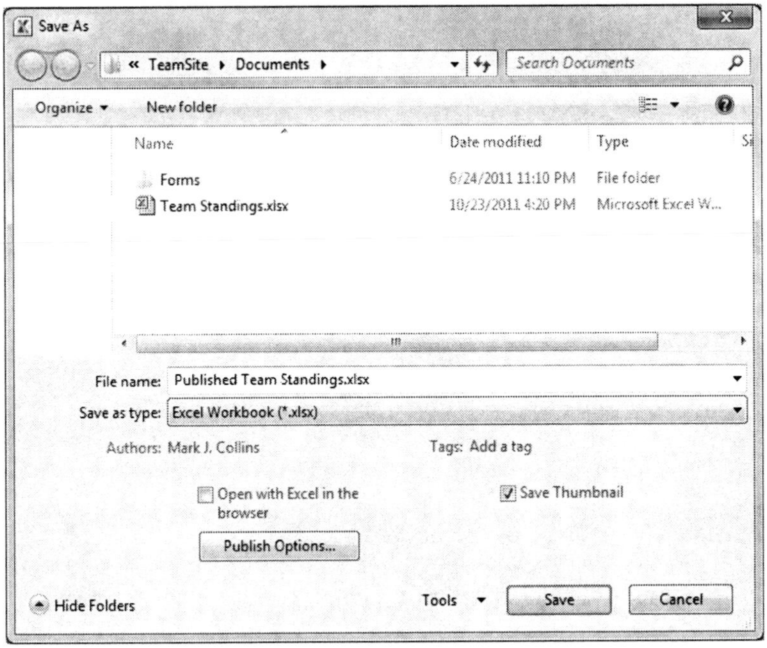

Figure 7-18. Specifying the new filename

■ **Tip** Notice the Publish Options button in the Save As dialog box. This opens the same Publish Options dialog box. You can specify these options from either place.

After clicking the Save button, you are prompted to choose the appropriate content type (see Figure 7-19). Select Excel and click the OK button.

Choose Content Type
The Web server requires you to pick the type of document before it can be saved. Select a type below.
Content Type:
Excel
Description:
A blank Microsoft Excel document.
OK
Cancel

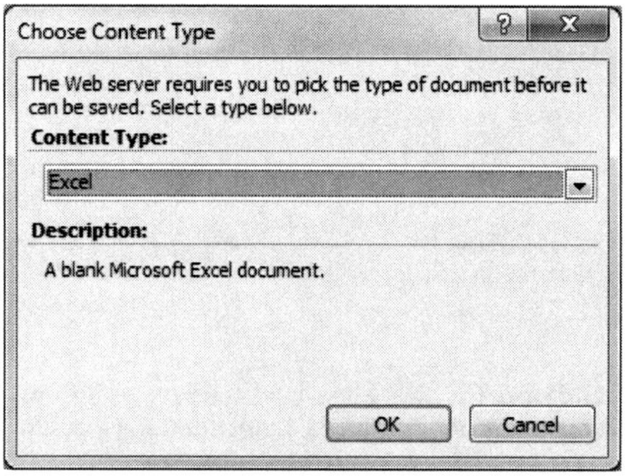

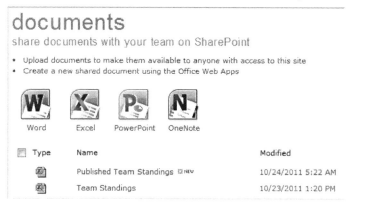

Figure 7-19. Selecting the `Excel` *content type*

The document is now added to the document library, as demonstrated in Figure 7-20.

documents
share documents with your team on SharePoint
Upload documents to make them available to anyone with access to this site
Create a new shared document using the Office Web Apps
Word
Excel
PowerPoint
OneNote
Type
Name
Modified
Published Team Standings NEW
10/24/2011 5:22 AM
Team Standings
10/23/2011 1:20 PM

Figure 7-20. The document library with the `Published Team Standings` *document*

When this document is selected, it is opened in the web app and only the PivotChart is displayed (see Figure 7-21).

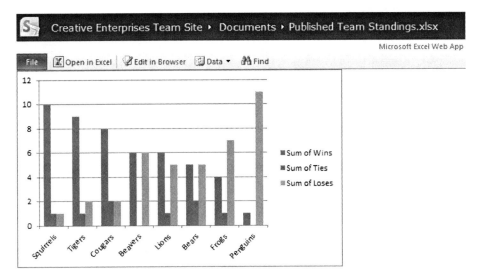

Figure 7-21. Displaying the published document in the Excel Web App

Specifying Parameters

You can also specify parameters when publishing a document. This allows the user to enter values that are configurable and see how the spreadsheet is affected. To use a parameter you must

1. Create a *named* cell.

2. Use that cell in one or more formulas in the spreadsheet.

3. Specify the named cell in the parameter list when publishing the document.

To name a cell, right-click the desired cell and then click the Define Name link. In the New Name dialog box, shown in Figure 7-22, enter the logical name **MinimumWins** for this cell, which you will use to define the number of wins needed to qualify for the playoffs. Specify the entire workbook for the scope so this cell can be referenced from other worksheets.

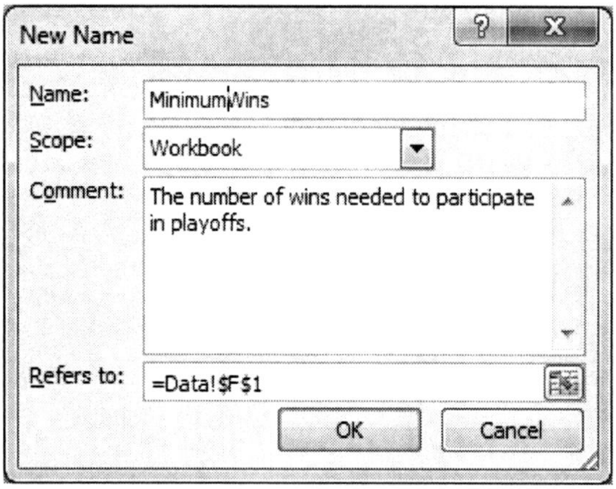

Figure 7-22. Configuring a named cell

In the worksheet that contains the PivotChart, enter the following formula in the cell just below the chart:

```
="Teams must win at least " & MinimumWins & " to participate in the playoffs"
```

This cell simply displays a note reminding the users how many wins are needed to participate in the playoffs. Now you're ready to publish the updated document and specify the parameter. Publish it just like last time and even use the same filename so it will replace the `Published Team Standings.xlsx` document. In order to display the comment, change the Show tab to display the Chart worksheet, as shown in Figure 7-23.

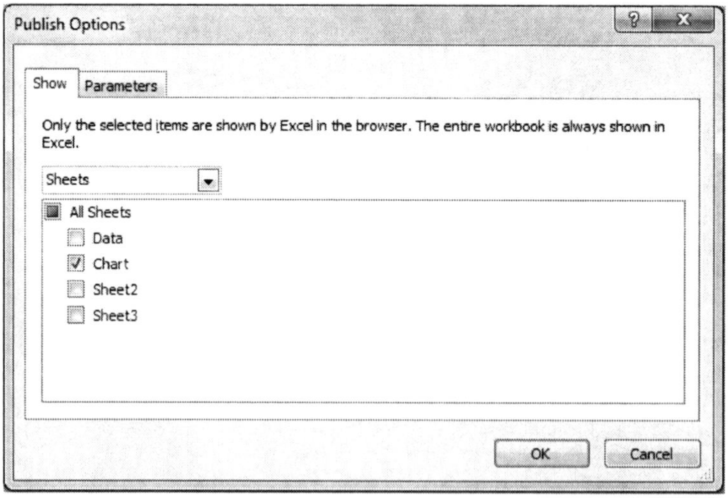

Figure 7-23. Showing the entire Chart worksheet

In the Parameters tab, click the Add button to create a new parameter. In the Add Parameter dialog box, shown in Figure 7-24, select the MinimumWins cell and specify a default value.

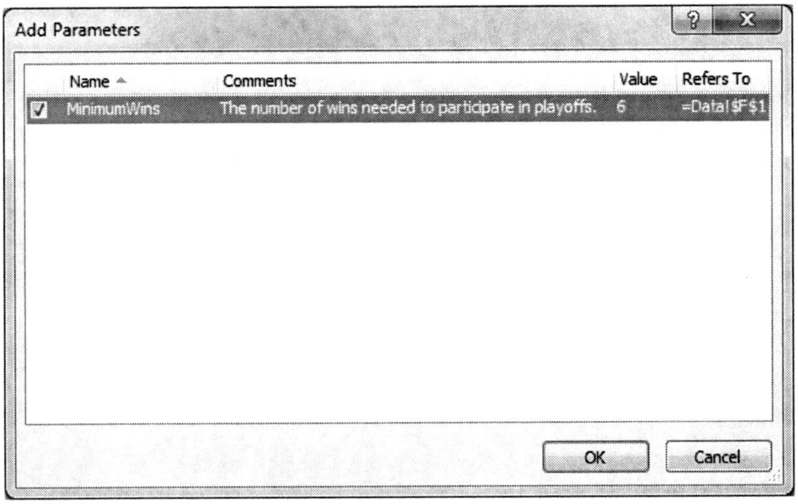

Figure 7-24. Creating a new parameter

The Parameters tab will look like Figure 7-25.

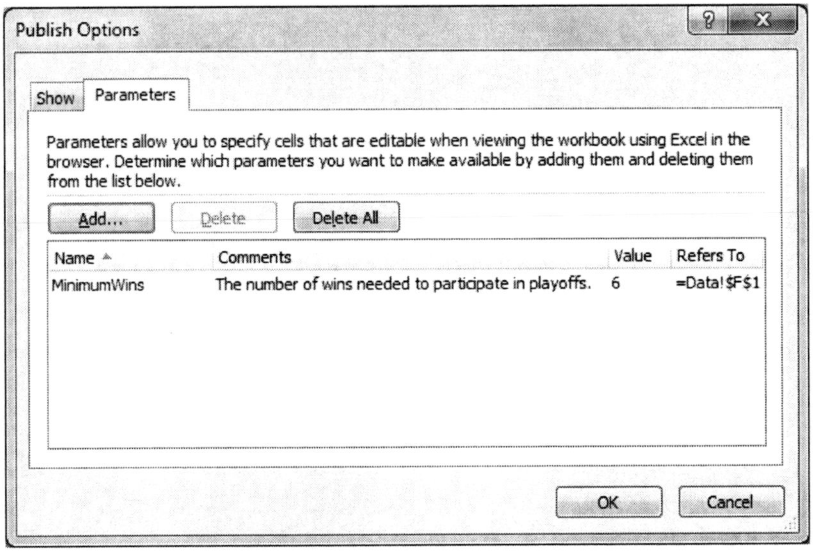

Figure 7-25. The completed Parameters tab

Publish this document to the same location and choose to overwrite the existing file. Now, when someone opens this document, the Parameters pane is displayed (see Figure 7-26).

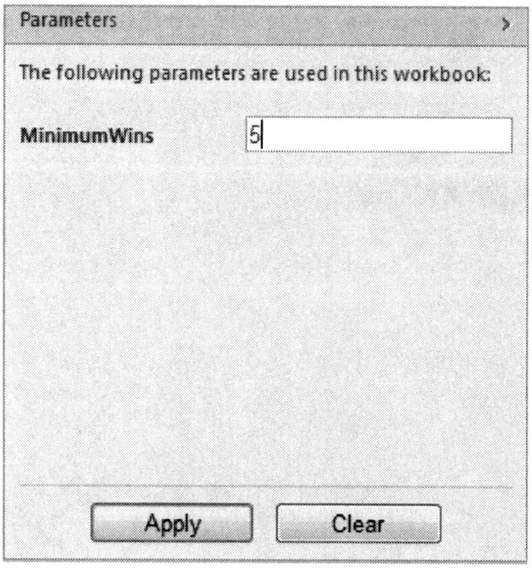

Parameters   >

The following parameters are used in this workbook:

MinimumWins   5|

[Apply]   [Clear]

Figure 7-26. Specifying a value for the `MinimumWins` *parameter*

You can modify this value and click the Apply button, and the text is automatically updated showing the new value, as demonstrated in Figure 7-27.

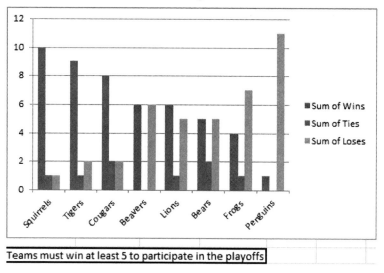

Teams must win at least 5 to participate in the playoffs

Figure 7-27. The PivotChart with dynamic text

While this is a fairly trivial example of using parameters, it demonstrates how to use this feature. You can have any number of named cells and then use them throughout the spreadsheet. Also, the parameter values are not stored in the document so each user can specify a different value, which will not affect other users.

Using REST Services

The Excel REST service is another powerful technique for integrating data into your SharePoint site. The term REST is an acronym for Representational State Transfer. It is an architectural style of exposing data to clients. You access data by providing the address of the data you're looking for. A UNC file location is a good example of a REST-like addressing scheme where the address includes the server, disk drive, folder, sub-folders, and finally the filename.

With the Excel REST services, you can publish an Excel spreadsheet to your SharePoint site and then use the REST API to programmatically extract parts of the document into an existing web page.

■ **Note** The techniques I have demonstrated so far in this chapter are available in both the Small Business (P) and Enterprise (E) plans. However, the Excel REST service is only available in the Enterprise plans. For this demonstration you will need to publish an Excel spreadsheet to an Enterprise account.

Creating the Spreadsheet

For this demonstration you'll create a simple spreadsheet using the Excel client app. I made one to keep track of the progress of completing this book. For each chapter I recorded its current status and the estimated number of pages (see Figure 7-28). Enter similar data in your spreadsheet.

	A	B	C
1	Chapter	Status	# Pages
2	1	Editorial Signoff	28
3	2	Editorial Signoff	30
4	3	Editorial Review	18
5	4	Technical Review	43
6	5	Initial Draft	52
7	6	Initial Draft	18
8	7	In Progress	25
9	8	Not Started	30
10	9	Author Review	29
11	10	Initial Draft	21
12	11	In Progress	20
13	12	Not Started	35
14	13	In Progress	20
15	14	Not Started	25
16	15	Author Review	10
17	16	Technical Review	47
18	17	Not Started	30
19	18	Not Started	25
20	A	Initial Draft	10
21	B	Not Started	10

Figure 7-28. The chapter summary

To provide a more visual representation, try your hand at creating a simple PivotChart, as shown in Figure 7-29. It summarizes the total number of pages in each status.

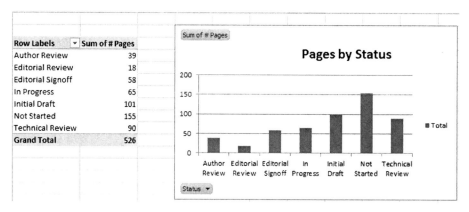

Row Labels	Sum of # Pages
Author Review	39
Editorial Review	18
Editorial Signoff	58
In Progress	65
Initial Draft	101
Not Started	155
Technical Review	90
Grand Total	526

Figure 7-29. The resulting PivotTable and PivotChart

Finally, publish this to Shared Documents library of an Enterprise Office 365 site using the Send to SharePoint tab of the backstage view. If the server you want is not listed, select the Browse for Location option and click the Save As button. In the Save As dialog box, enter the URL of the SharePoint site and then navigate to the Shared Documents library (see Figure 7-30).

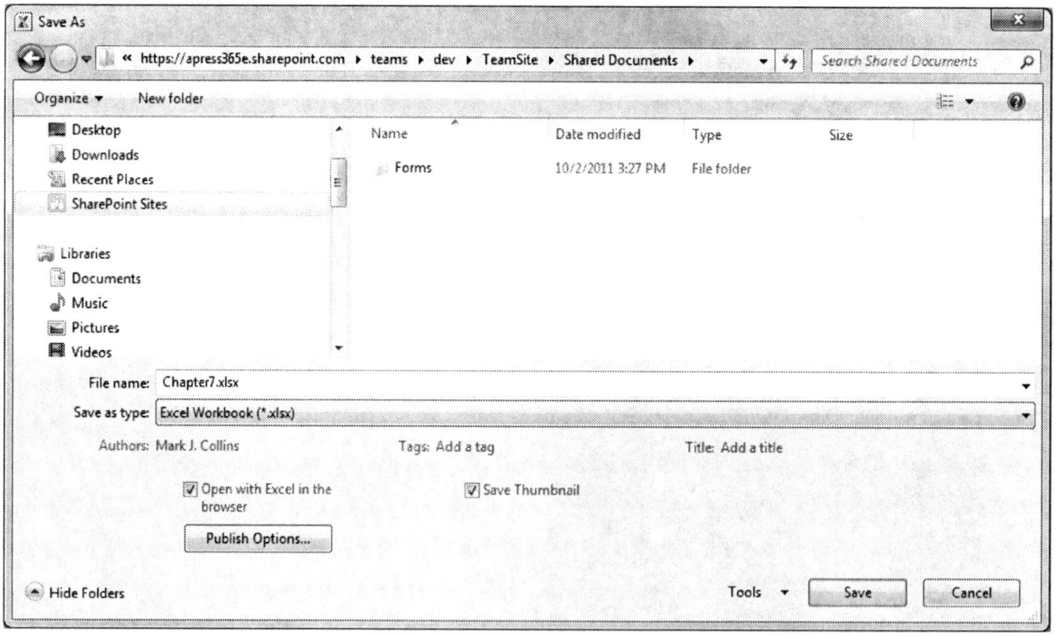

Figure 7-30. Selecting the SharePoint location

For this example, don't modify any of the Publish Options. Leave the "Open with Excel in the browser" check box selected so once the document is published, it's displayed using the web app (see Figure 7-31).

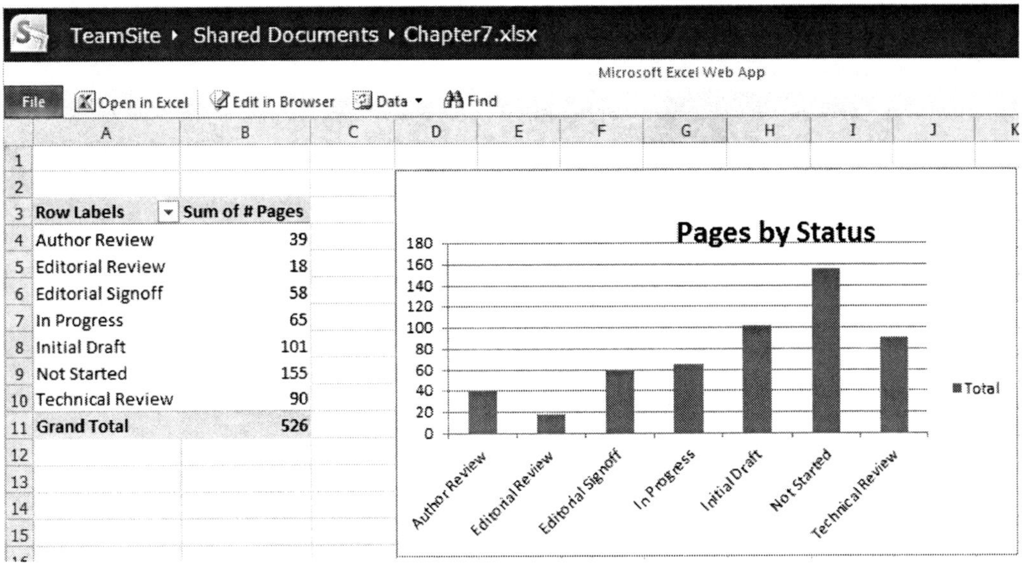

Figure 7-31. The Chapter7.xlsx file in the browser

Now you can edit the Chapters tab using the web app to update the status and page count as the work progresses.

Extracting the Excel Data

Next, you will display the PivotChart on the home page of the Team Site as a visual reminder of your progress. Every time someone goes to the Team Site, the current status will be made visually apparent. To do that, you'll use the Excel REST services to extract the PivotChart.

To access the Excel REST services you must specify a rather long URL that indicates the location of the data. This URL starts with the address of the SharePoint site followed by _vti_bin/ExcelRest.aspx. For example, the address of the service on my Team Site is

```
https://apress365e.sharepoint.com/teams/dev/TeamSite/_vti_bin/ExcelRest.aspx
```

You then append to that the name of the document library (/Shared%20Documents) followed by the document name (/Chapter7.xlsx) and then add /model to access the data elements of this document. Putting all these parts together, my URL would be

```
http://apress365e.sharepoint.com/teams/dev/TeamSite/_vti_bin/ExcelRest.aspx/Shared%20Documents
/Chapter7.xlsx/model
```

If you open a web browser and enter this URL, you'll see the page shown in Figure 7-32.

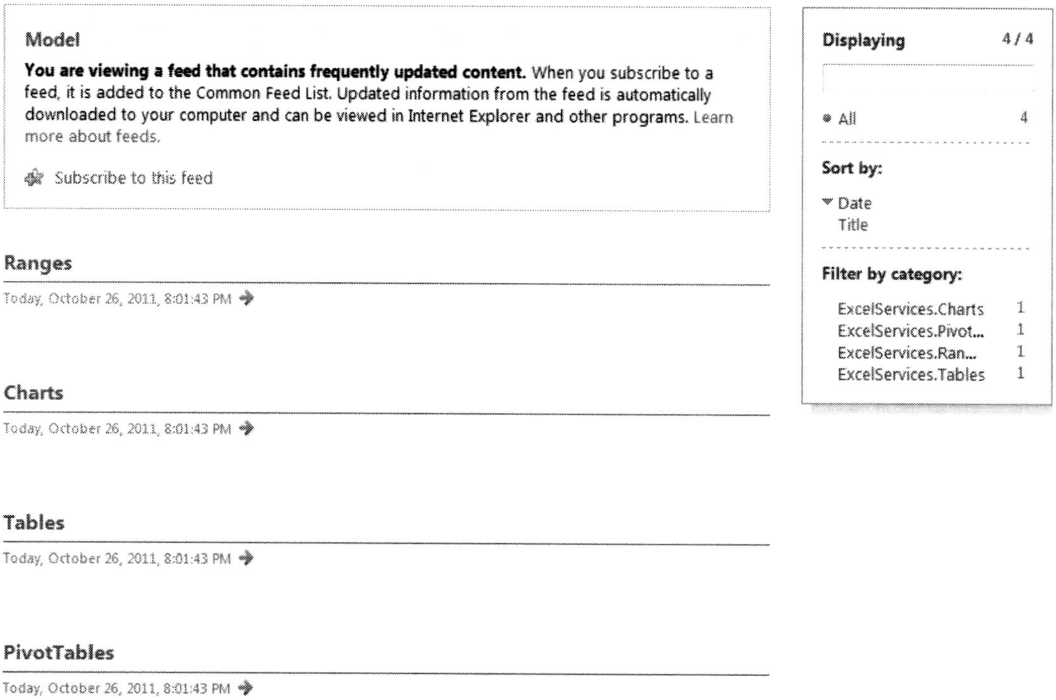

Model

You are viewing a feed that contains frequently updated content. When you subscribe to a feed, it is added to the Common Feed List. Updated information from the feed is automatically downloaded to your computer and can be viewed in Internet Explorer and other programs. Learn more about feeds.

🔖 Subscribe to this feed

Ranges

Today, October 26, 2011, 8:01:43 PM ➡

Charts

Today, October 26, 2011, 8:01:43 PM ➡

Tables

Today, October 26, 2011, 8:01:43 PM ➡

PivotTables

Today, October 26, 2011, 8:01:43 PM ➡

Displaying	4 / 4
• All	4

Sort by:

▼ Date
  Title

Filter by category:

ExcelServices.Charts	1
ExcelServices.Pivot...	1
ExcelServices.Ran...	1
ExcelServices.Tables	1

Figure 7-32. *Displaying the contents of the REST model*

This page shows the elements that can be obtained through the Excel REST services, which include

- Ranges
- Charts
- Tables
- PivotTables

If you click the Charts link, the charts that are included in the document are listed in Figure 7-33.

Charts

You are viewing a feed that contains frequently updated content. When you subscribe to a feed, it is added to the Common Feed List. Updated information from the feed is automatically downloaded to your computer and can be viewed in Internet Explorer and other programs. Learn more about feeds.

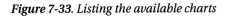 Subscribe to this feed

Chart 1

Today, October 26, 2011, 9:39:30 PM

Displaying	1 / 1
All	1

Sort by:
Date
Title

Filter by category:
ExcelServices.Chart   1

Figure 7-33. Listing the available charts

There is only one chart available and it is named Chart 1. To access this specific object, append the following to the URL:

```
Charts('Chart%201')?$format=image
```

This will specify that you want to access Chart 1 and format it as an image.

▪ **Tip** You can only access named elements through the Excel REST services. Charts, tables, and PivotTables are automatically named for you, even though the default name is not very meaningful (Chart 1). If you want to access a range, you'll need to first name it. This is done just like naming a cell, as demonstrated earlier. Highlight the desired range, right-click it, and select the Define Name link.

Editing the Home Page

Now you'll modify the home page to display this chart. You will insert an Image Viewer web part and specify the REST URL as the source of the image.

From the home page of the Team Site click the Edit button shown in Figure 7-34.

Figure 7-34. Editing the home page

This opens the page in edit mode. Put the cursor where you want to insert the chart and the click the More Web Parts button from the Insert tab of the ribbon. In the Create dialog box that is displayed, select the Media and Content category and then select the Image Viewer web part, as shown in Figure 7-35. Finally, click the Add button to add this web part.

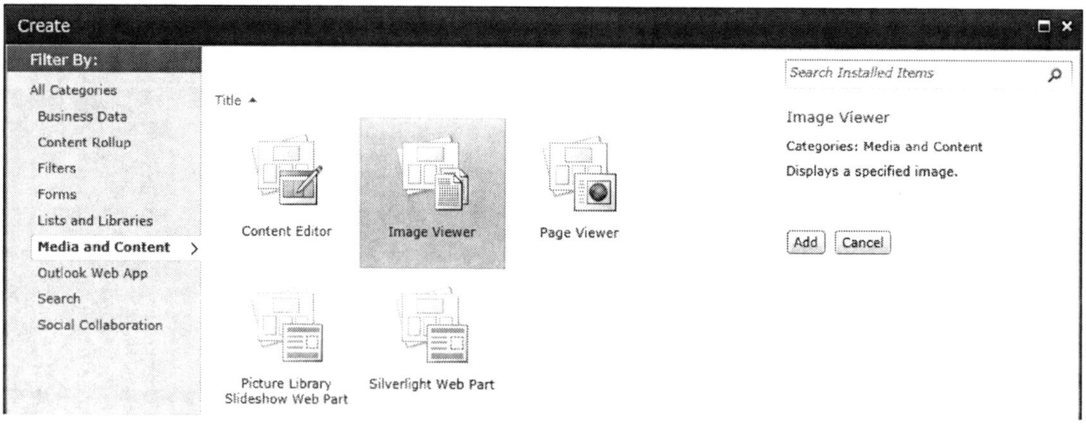

Figure 7-35. Adding an Image Viewer web part

The web part will then be added and will look like Figure 7-36. Now you'll need to configure it to specify the location of the image. Click the "open the tool pane" link.

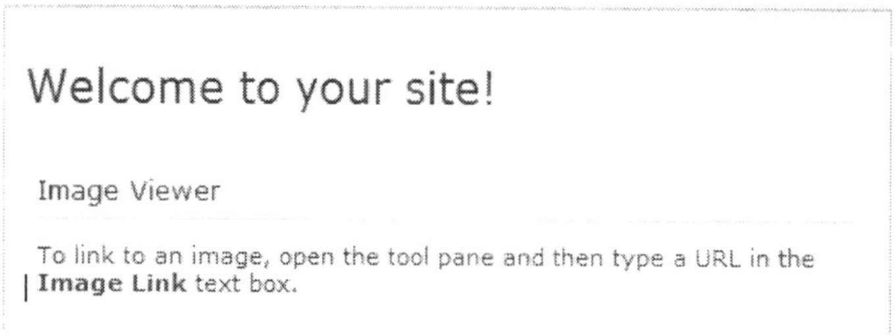

Figure 7-36. Configuring the image viewer

In the Image Viewer pane, for the Image Link property, enter the complete URL for the REST services, which (for my site) is

```
https://apress365e.sharepoint.com/teams/dev/TeamSite/_vti_bin/ExcelRest.aspx/Shared%20Document
s/Chapter7.xlsx/model/Charts('Chart%201')?$format=image
```

After saving these changes and then saving the web page, the modified home page will look like Figure 7-37.

Welcome to your site!

Image Viewer

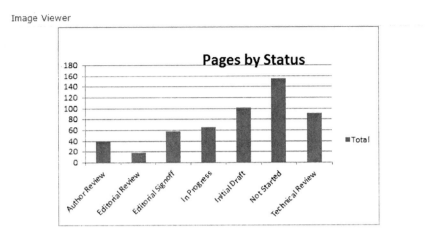

Add a new image, change this welcome text or add new lists to this page by clicking the edit button above. You can click on Shared Documents to add files or on the calendar to create new team events. Use the links in the getting started section to share your site and customize its look.

Shared Documents

	Type	Name	Modified		Modified By
		Chapter7 ◘ NEW	10/26/2011 9:38 PM		Mark Collins

✚ Add document

Figure 7-37. The modified home page

Summary

In this chapter I demonstrated several ways to share data in an Office 365 environment using Microsoft Excel. I presented the following three techniques for sharing data:

- Using the Excel Office Web App to view and edit a shared document, which allows simultaneous editing by multiple users.

- Publishing an Excel spreadsheet to a SharePoint document library. This option enables you to control the parts of the spreadsheet that are displayed. You can also design configurable parameters.

- Using the Excel REST services to programmatically extract data from a published Excel document.

In the next chapter I will show you how to link external data from Windows Azure into your Office 365 SharePoint site using Business Connectivity Services (BCS).

CHAPTER 8

Accessing External Data

The Office 365 platform allows you to access external data from your SharePoint sites using a feature called Business Connectivity Services (BCS). This enables you to integrate corporate data stores into your office automation solution. For example, you may have an Accounting system that you need to extract data from or feed data into from within your team site. In this chapter, I will show you how to implement this functionality.

Note BCS is only available on Enterprise plans; you will need an Enterprise Office 365 account to work through the sample project presented in this chapter.

External data is surfaced in SharePoint as a special type of list called an *external* list. The data doesn't actually reside in SharePoint but the SharePoint server knows how to access the external data source. Once it has been properly configured, you can then use the external list just like you would a native SharePoint list.

In this chapter, you will create a simple WCF web service that exposes some hardcoded data. You will then define an external content type using SharePoint Designer that consumes this web service. Finally, you will create an external list based on the external content type.

Using Business Connectivity Services

The process of integrating external data starts with defining an *external content type*. Like other content types, external content types are used to define a set of fields. However, that is where the similarity stops. The primary focus of an external content type is to define how the external data will be accessed and mapped to SharePoint.

External content types work on the principle of implementing the operations known by the CRUD acronym, which stands for **Create**, **Read**, **Update**, and **Delete**. By implementing these basic operations, the external content type provides complete control over the external data. There are actually two read operations. One returns a single record based on an identifier that is supplied. The other returns a set of records, which may be the entire table or a subset based on filters that are defined. As you create external content types, you will implement one or more of these operations.

Connecting to an External Data Source

SharePoint provides three ways to connect to an external data source; however, only one of these is supported on the Office 365 platform.

- SQL Server (not supported): This allows you to map an external table or view in SQL Server.

- Web Service (supported): You provide a web service that is hosted separately from SharePoint and implements the CRUD services.

- .NET Assembly Connector (not supported): The .NET assembly runs on the SharePoint server and implements the CRUD methods.

The SQL Server connection is the easiest to implement because it doesn't require any coding. You use SharePoint Designer to declare the mapping between a SQL Server table or view and the columns of the content type. The other two methods require you to write code to implement each of the CRUD methods. These methods allow you to access any data that you can reach from .NET code. The primary difference is the .NET assembly runs on the SharePoint server while the web service runs on a separate web server not hosted on Office 365.

In an Office 365 environment, only the web service approach is supported. You will implement a simple WCF web service. This can be hosted on a Windows Azure platform or an on-premise web server. However, it must be reachable from the Office 365 site. You can design your web service to access many sources including databases, file system objects, or other web services. Because you will implement this yourself, you have full control of how the data is access, manipulated, or aggregated.

Creating a Web Service

The web service will define a data contract that defines the properties of an item, which will be mapped to columns in your external content type. For example, this simple class, MyClass, defines two properties, ID and Name:

```
[DataContract]
public class MyClass
{
    [DataMember]
    public int ID { get; set; }

    [DataMember]
    public string Name { get; set; }
}
```

The web service will also define a service contract that defines the methods that are exposed by the web service. Each of these methods implements one of the following:

- Finder returns a collection of items.

- SpecificFinder returns a single item specified by an identifier.

- Creator inserts a new item.

- Updater updates an existing item.

- Deleter removes an existing item.

Note Unfortunately, SharePoint is not consistent with the use of these terms. For example, as you'll see later in this chapter, SharePoint Designer calls the `Finder` operation "Read List" and the `SpecificFinder` "Read Item."

If the external content type is designed to be read-only, you only need to supply the `Finder` and `SpecificFinder` method, as shown in this example:

```
[ServiceContract]
public interface ICustomers
{
    [OperationContract]
    // Finder
    List<MyClass> GetAll();

    [OperationContract]
    // SpecificFinder
    MyClass GetByID(int ID);
}
```

If the external content type supports updates to the data store, the web service will implement the `Creator`, `Updater`, or `Deleter` methods as appropriate.

Once you have defined the data and service contracts you will then implement these methods such as `GetAll()` and `GetByID()`. This is where you will access the data and format it as defined by the data contract. Since this code doesn't run on Office 365 you can implement this web service in any way that is appropriate for your environment.

Defining the External Content Type

Once you have a web service that exposes the external data, you'll use SharePoint Designer to create an external content type. This process will map each of the supported method types (`Finder`, `SpecificFinder`, and so on) to the specific method exposed by the web service. For example, with the contract shown previously, you would indicate the `GetAll()` method as the `Finder` method. You will also map each of the properties of the data contract as columns defined by the external content type.

After the external content has been configured you can use it to create an external list. This list can be used just like the native list but will access the data using your web service.

Providing a Simple Web Service

To simplify the project for this chapter, the web service will return canned data. The service will not actually persist the data, so data changes will not remain true across multiple calls to the service. However, the focus of this chapter is how to connect to a hosted web service, not how to build the web service. For this, you need only a service that includes the proper methods and responds accordingly.

Implementing a Web Service

This service will be deployed to Windows Azure. You will need an active account to accomplish this. They offer a free trial, which was used during the writing of this book. To begin working with Windows Azure, visit `www.windowsazure.com`. Once your Azure account is created, you will need to download the Azure SDK. This resource can be downloaded from `www.microsoft.com/windowsazure/sdk/`.

⬛ **Note** The web services don't have to be hosted in Azure. This was chosen for this book to demonstrate a scenario that doesn't require any local infrastructure and to show how these two cloud services can work together. If you have access to a public web server that can host WCF services, then you can build using the same service code; just bypass the Azure service steps.

Creating the Windows Azure Project

You'll start by creating the Windows Azure Project.

1. Once the Azure SDK is installed, start Visual Studio and start a new project. Select Windows Azure Project template under the Cloud option. Enter the name of the project as **AzureService** and the location as desired. When your screen appears similar to Figure 8-1, click OK.

Figure 8-1. Creating a new Windows Azure Project

2. In the next prompt, select WCF Service Web Role and click the > button to add this role to the Windows Azure solution (see Figure 8-2).

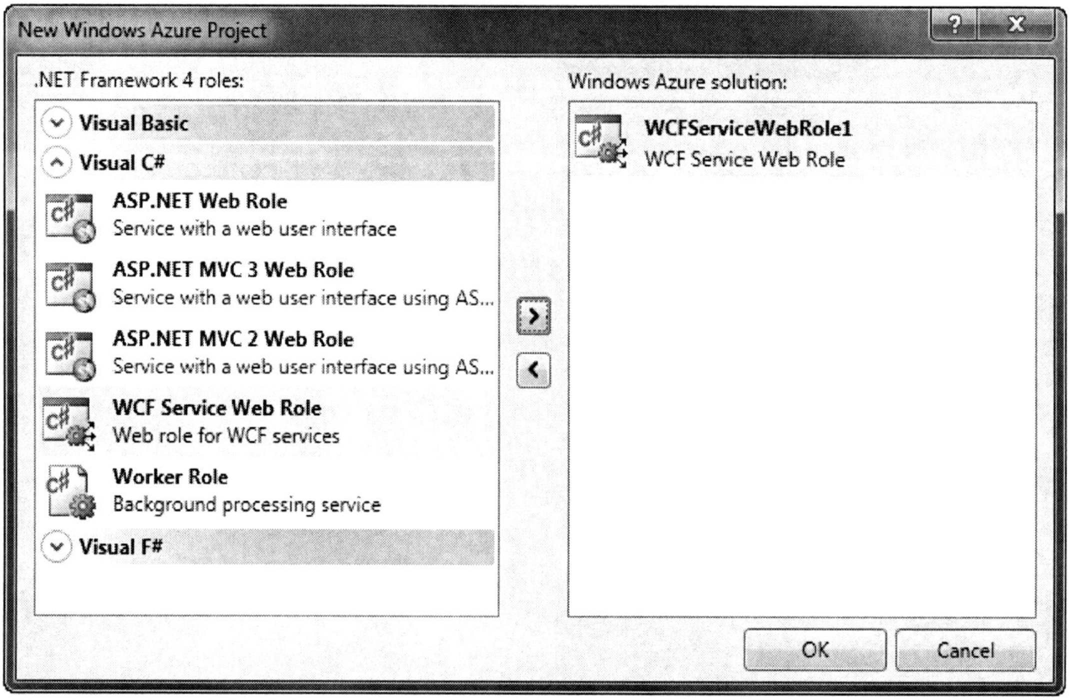

Figure 8-2. Adding WCF Service Web Role to the Windows Azure solution

3.   This creates the Azure Service configuration files as well as the WCF service project. Your screen should appear similar to Figure 8-3.

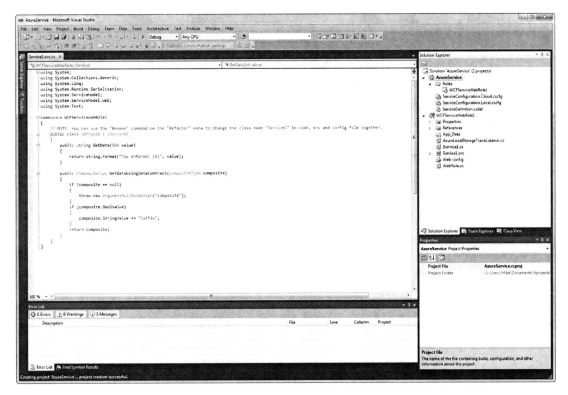

Figure 8-3. Azure Service WCF Service project

Defining the WCF Service Contract

Now you are ready to define the WCF service. Visual Studio created the Service1 service. For simplicity, keep this service and redefine the contract and implementation. Open the IService1.cs file and replace the entire file with the code in Listing 8-1.

Listing 8-1. IService1.cs

```
using System;
using System.Collections.Generic;
using System.Linq;
using System.Runtime.Serialization;
using System.ServiceModel;
using System.ServiceModel.Web;
using System.Text;

namespace WCFServiceWebRole1
{
    [ServiceContract]
    public interface IService1
```

```
{
    [OperationContract]
    Vehicle GetVehicleByID(int vehicleID);

    [OperationContract]
    List<Vehicle> GetAllVehicles();

    [OperationContract]
    string CreateVehicle(Vehicle newVehicle);

    [OperationContract]
    string UpdateVehicle
        (int vehicleID, int year, string make, string model, string color, int mileage);

    [OperationContract]
    bool DeleteVehicle(int vehicleID);
}


[DataContract]
public class Vehicle
{
    [DataMember]
    public int id { get; set; }

    [DataMember]
    public int year { get; set; }

    [DataMember]
    public string make { get; set; }

    [DataMember]
    public string model { get; set; }

    [DataMember]
    public string color { get; set; }

    [DataMember]
    public int mileage { get; set; }
}
}
```

This code defines the service contract (or interface). The CRUD methods are defined. The names of the methods state their function (they are simplified for this demonstration). Listing 8-1 also includes the type of Vehicle, defining the data object for the service (again, simple properties for demonstration).

Adding the Service Implementation

It's now time to add the service implementation. Open the Service1.svc.cs file and replace the entire file with the code from Listing 8-2.

Listing 8-2. Service1.svc.cs

```csharp
using System;
using System.Collections.Generic;
using System.Linq;
using System.Runtime.Serialization;
using System.ServiceModel;
using System.ServiceModel.Web;
using System.Text;

namespace WCFServiceWebRole1
{
    public class Service1 : IService1
    {

        #region IService1 Members

        private List<Vehicle> _vehicles = new List<Vehicle>();
        private List<Vehicle> vehicles
        {
            get
            {
                if (_vehicles.Count == 0)
                {
                    //build new list of vehicles
                    _vehicles.Add(new Vehicle()
                        { id = 1, year = 2012, make = "Ford", model = "Mustang",
                          color = "Blue", mileage = 1000 });
                    _vehicles.Add(new Vehicle()
                        { id = 2, year = 2010, make = "Ford", model = "Focus",
                          color = "Red", mileage = 3000 });
                    _vehicles.Add(new Vehicle()
                        { id = 3, year = 2000, make = "Chevrolet", model = "Camaro",
                          color = "Yellow", mileage = 7000 });
                    _vehicles.Add(new Vehicle()
                        { id = 4, year = 2003, make = "Chevrolet", model = "Silverado",
                          color = "White", mileage = 12000 });
                    _vehicles.Add(new Vehicle()
                        { id = 5, year = 2003, make = "Honda", model = "Accord",
                          color = "White", mileage = 6000 });
                    _vehicles.Add(new Vehicle()
                        { id = 6, year = 2003, make = "Toyota", model = "Camry",
                          color = "Green", mileage = 51000 });
                }

                return _vehicles;
            }
        }


        public Vehicle GetVehicleByID(int vehicleID)
```

```
    {
        //return item by ID
        return (from v in vehicles where v.id == vehicleID select v).SingleOrDefault();
    }

    public List<Vehicle> GetAllVehicles()
    {
        //return full list of items
        return vehicles;
    }

    public string CreateVehicle(Vehicle newVehicle)
    {
        //find max id in list
        int maxID = (from v in vehicles orderby v.id descending select
v.id).FirstOrDefault();

        //add new item
        vehicles.Add(new Vehicle()
        {
            id = maxID++,
            year = newVehicle.year,
            make = newVehicle.make,
            model = newVehicle.model,
            color = newVehicle.color,
            mileage = newVehicle.mileage
        });

        //return item ID
        return maxID.ToString();
    }

    public string UpdateVehicle
        (int vehicleID, int year, string make, string model, string color, int mileage)
    {
        //find item by ID
        Vehicle oldVehicle =
            (from v in vehicles where v.id == vehicleID select v).SingleOrDefault();

        if (oldVehicle != null)
        {
            //remove current item
            vehicles.Remove(oldVehicle);

            //update values
            oldVehicle.year = year;
            oldVehicle.make = make;
            oldVehicle.model = model;
            oldVehicle.color = color;
            oldVehicle.mileage = mileage;

            //add updated item back into list
```

```
                vehicles.Add(oldVehicle);

                //return
                return vehicleID.ToString();
            }
            else
            {
                return "0";
            }
        }

        public bool DeleteVehicle(int vehicleID)
        {
            //find item by ID
            Vehicle vehicle =
                (from v in vehicles where v.id == vehicleID select v).SingleOrDefault();

            if (vehicle != null)
            {
                //remove found item
                vehicles.Remove(vehicle);

                //return
                return true;
            }
            else
            {
                return false;
            }
        }

        #endregion
    }
}
```

The service implementation begins by defining a dataset to work with; this is simply for demonstration. This dataset is in memory only and is recreated each time the service is called. It creates a list of Vehicle objects for the CRUD methods to work with.

The service then consists of the CRUD methods. These are simple implementations of their respective tasks. The code is straightforward by design and simple types are returned, except for the two Finder methods. Build the WCFWebServiceRole1 project to ensure everything has been added correctly.

Deploying the Web Service to Azure

Now that you have your service, you need to deploy it.

1. Right-click the AzureService project and click Package, as shown in Figure 8-4.

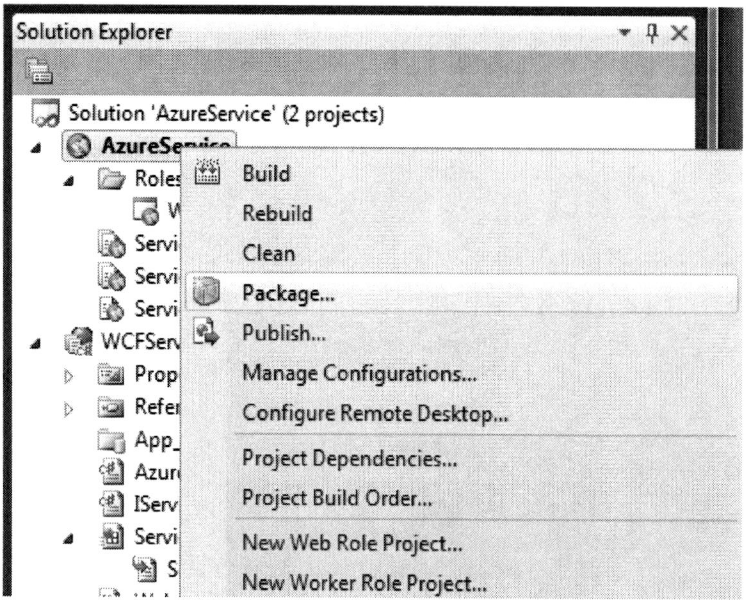

Figure 8-4. Packaging the Azure Service project

2.   Select the package options shown in Figure 8-5.

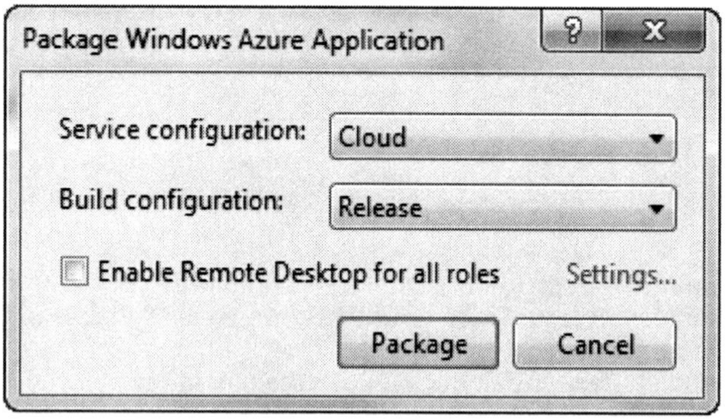

Figure 8-5. Package options

3.   In your browser, navigate to http://windows.azure.com and log in. This will take you to the Windows Azure Management Portal. Click the New Hosted Service button in the top left corner, as shown in Figure 8-6.

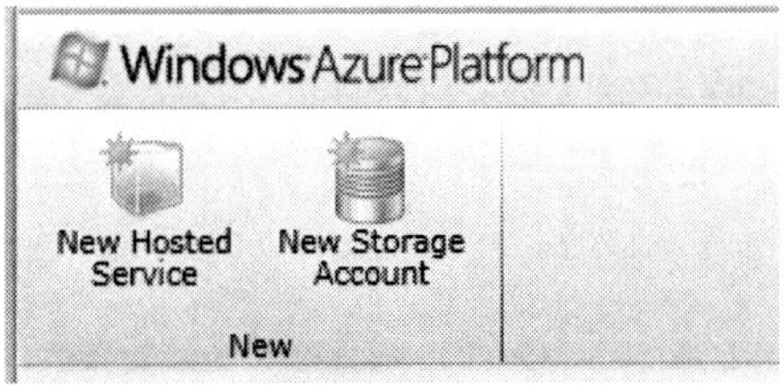

Figure 8-6. Adding a new hosted service in Windows Azure Management Portal

4. This will bring up the Hosted Service configuration screen. Enter the values shown in Figure 8-7. Ensure you select "Deploy to stage environment" under Deployment options.

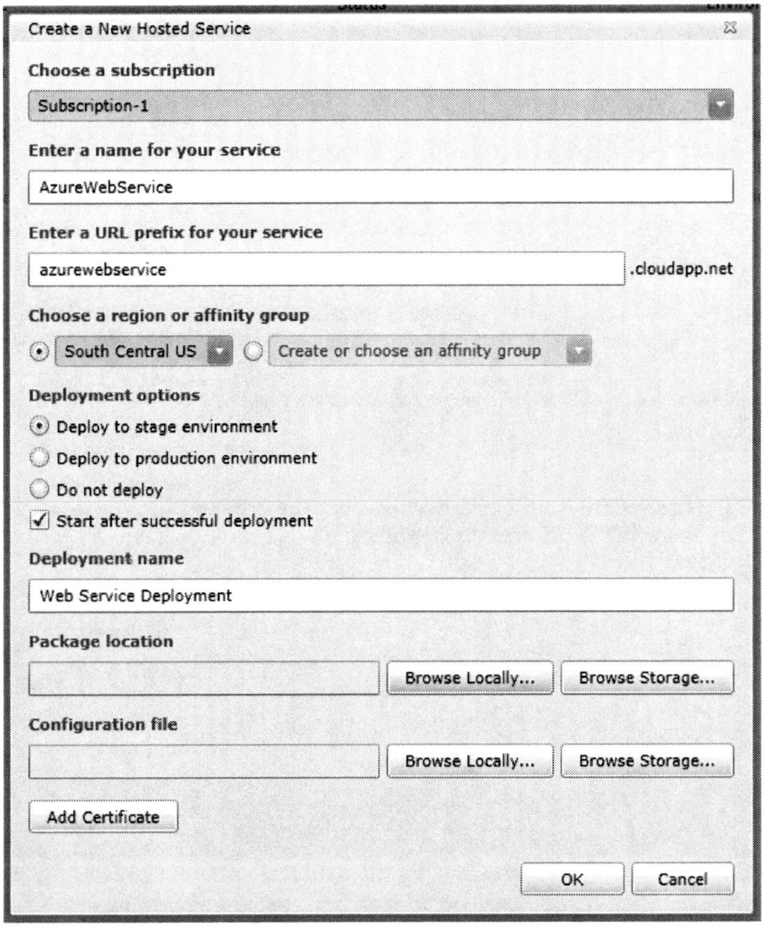

Figure 8-7. Hosted Service options

5. Click the Browse Locally button for the Package location. Browse to the `bin\Release\app.publish` folder under the AzureService project folder. Select the package file, as shown in Figure 8-8.

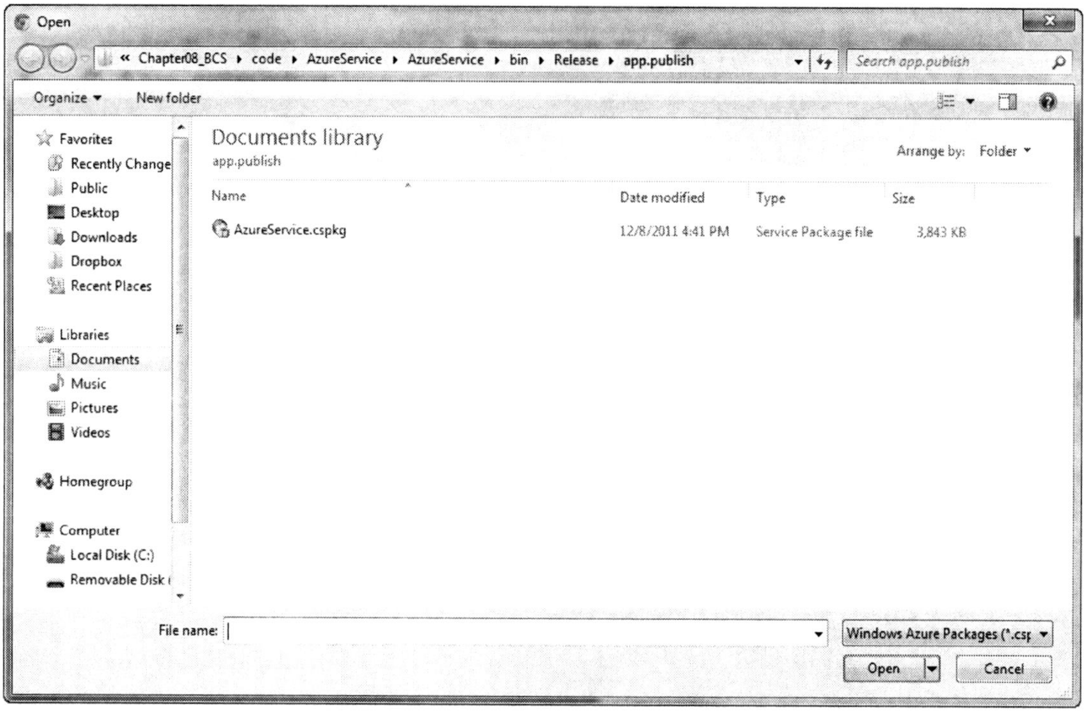

Figure 8-8. *Azure Service package file*

6. Now you'll repeat this step to select the configuration file. Click the Browse Locally button for the configuration file. Select the configuration file, as shown in Figure 8-9, and click Open.

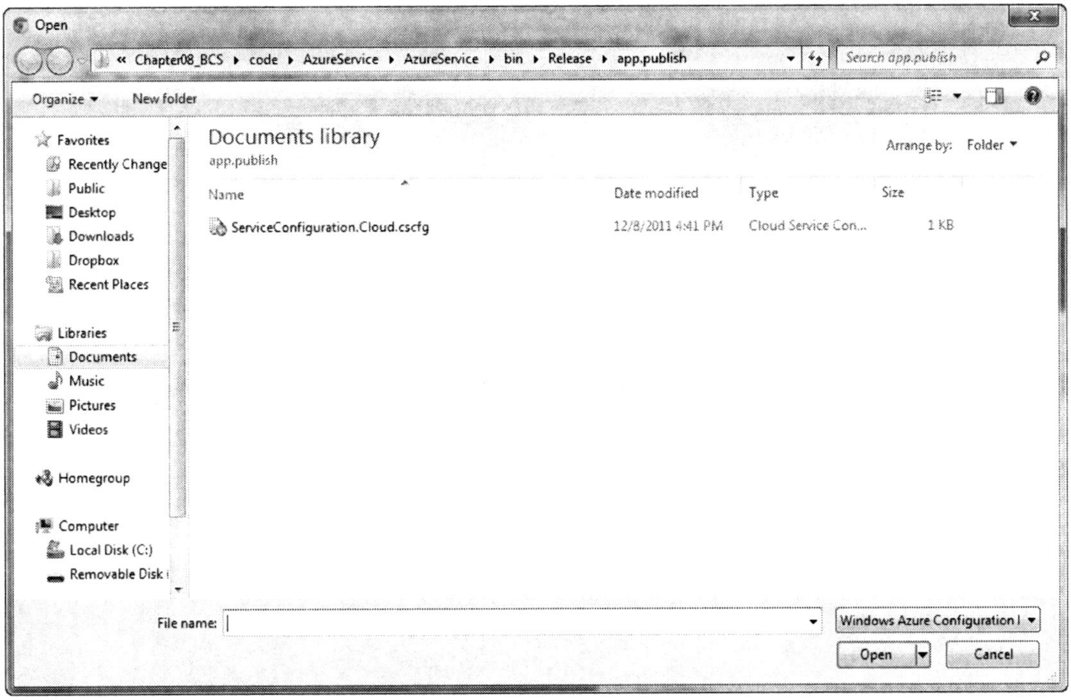

Figure 8-9. Azure Service configuration file

7. Click OK on the hosted service options screen. You will receive a warning about the deployment only creating one instance. For the purposes here, this is fine. For a production service, at least two instances per role is recommended for load balancing and availability. This warning is depicted in Figure 8-10. Click Yes to continue.

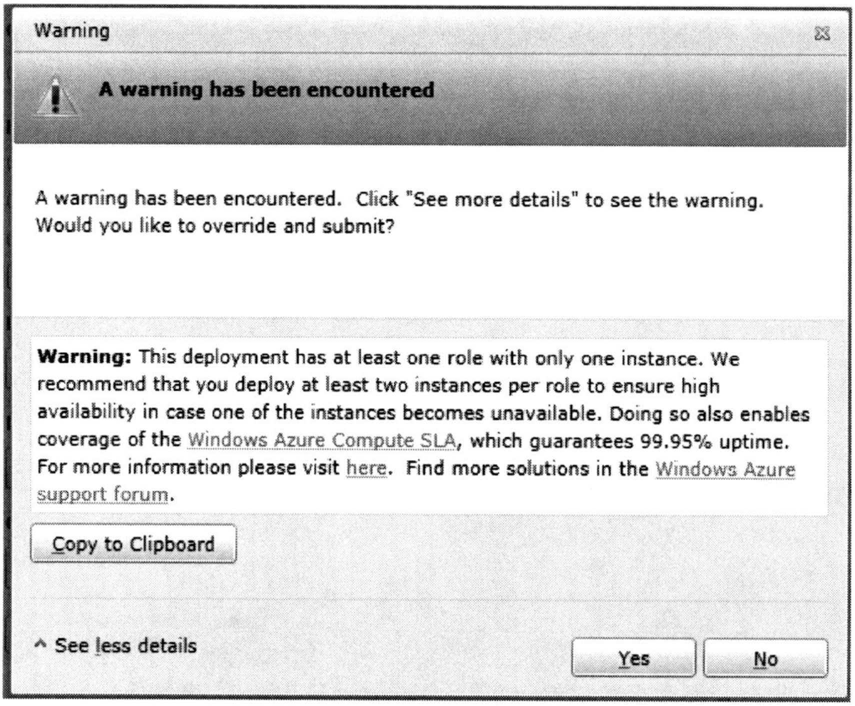

Figure 8-10. Instance-per-role warning for Azure Service

8. This will begin the process of creating the roles and instances and then deploying the service. This will take a few minutes. You will be able to monitor this in the Management Portal. Your screen should appear similar to Figure 8-11.

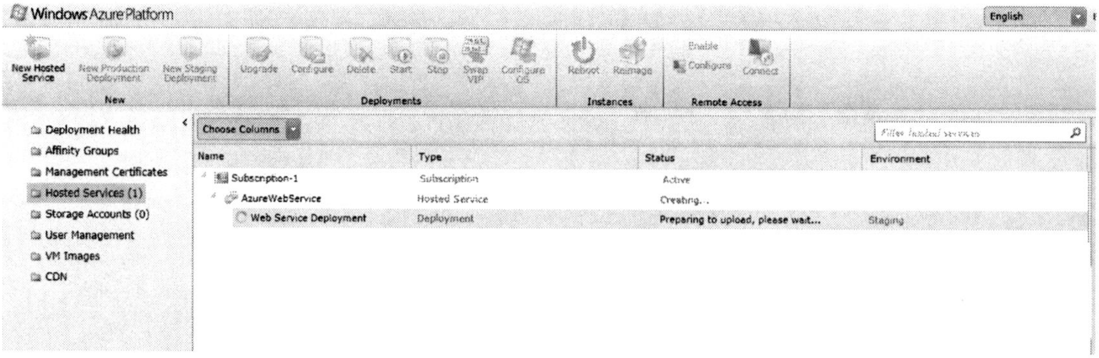

Figure 8-11. Monitoring service deployment in Azure Management Portal

9. Click the Web Service Deployment and you can see the URL for the stage deployment of the service. It has been assigned a GUID as part of the DNS name. The URL for the service will be `http://<GUID>.cloudapp.net/service1.svc`. Use this URL for testing and connecting to the service from SharePoint. The location of this information is shown in Figure 8-12.

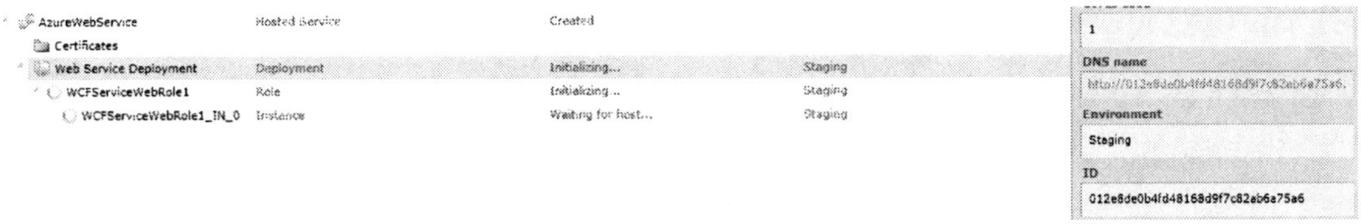

Figure 8-12. DNS name for deployed service to staging environment

Continue to monitor the deployment until everything reports as Ready, as shown in Figure 8-13. Once this is the case, the service is ready for testing.

Figure 8-13. Deployment ready for testing

Testing the Service

Before using your new service in SharePoint it's a good idea to test it first to make sure it works like you expect it to. Visual Studio includes a utility called WCF Test Client that makes it really easy to do this. If you have Visual Studio installed, the application should be located at `C:\Program Files\Microsoft Visual Studio 10.0\Common7\IDE\WcfTestClient.exe`. If you have a 64-bit machine, it will be in the `Program Files (x86)` folder.

■ **Tip** For more information about the WCF Test Client utility, see the article at `http://msdn.microsoft.com/en-us/library/bb552364.aspx`.

---

1. Start this application. You should see a node in the left-hand pane labeled My Service Projects, as shown in Figure 8-14.

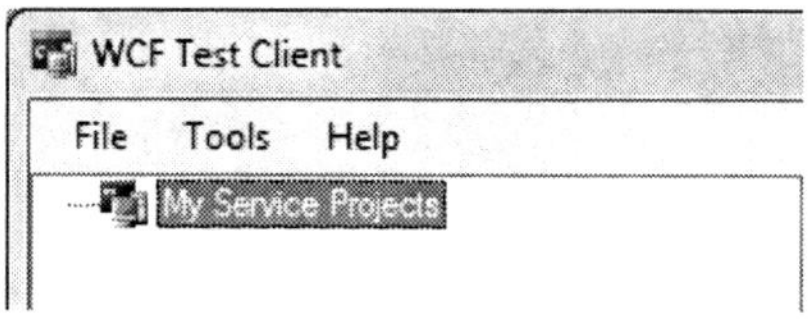

Figure 8-14. The initial WCF Test Client window

    2.   Right-click this node and select the Add Service link. In the Add Service dialog box, enter the URL of your web service, as shown in Figure 8-15. Click the OK button to add this service.

Figure 8-15. Specifying the service URL

After a few seconds the left-hand pane will list all of the methods exposed by this service, as demonstrated in Figure 8-16. When you double-click one of these methods, a tab will be added to the right-hand pane that allows you to invoke this method.

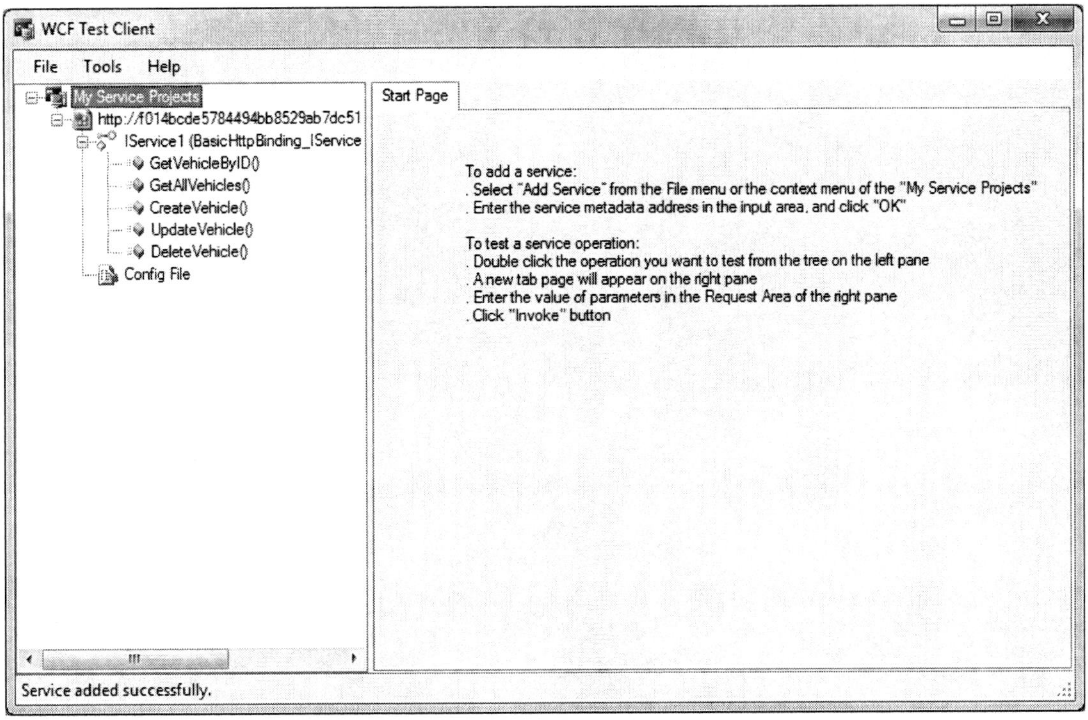

Figure 8-16. Displaying the available methods

3. Double-click the GetAllVehicles() method and you should see the tab shown in Figure 8-17. The top portion allows you to specify the method parameters. In this case there are none. Click the Invoke button and you should see vehicle information displayed, as shown in Figure 8-17.

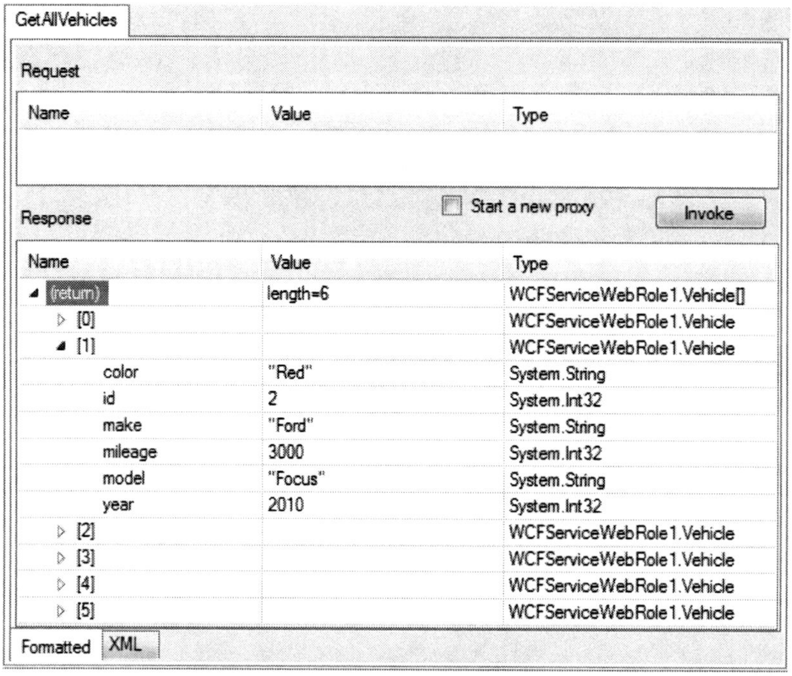

Figure 8-17. Invoking the GetAllVehicles() method

I collapsed all of the records except one so you can more easily see the data being returned. It provides an array of vehicles, each containing several properties.

4. Double-click the GetVehicleByID() method and a new tab will be added. Enter a vehicleID and click the Invoke button. The properties of this specific vehicle will be returned (see Figure 8-18).

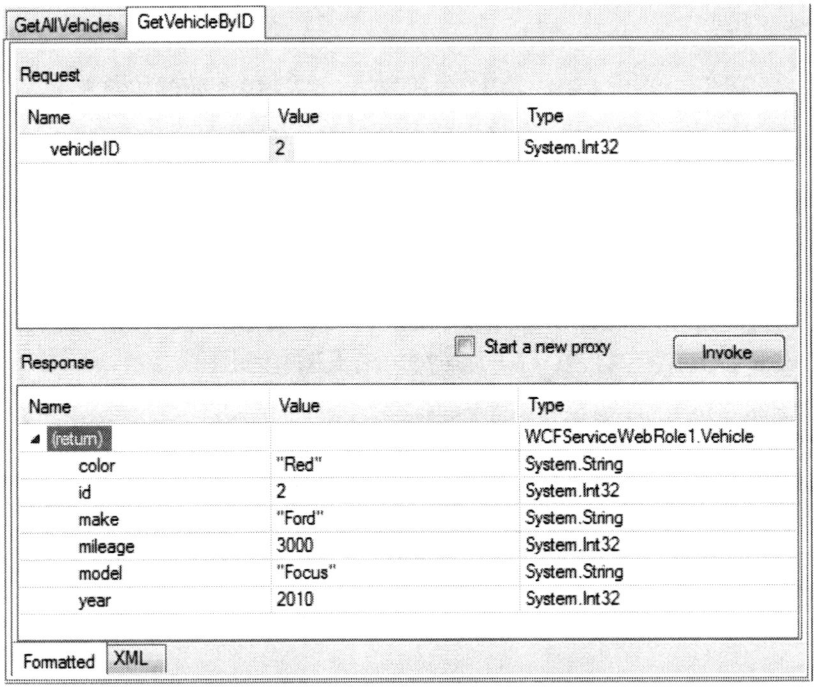

Figure 8-18. Invoking the GetVehicleByID() method

The other methods work the same way. For example, the CreateVehicle() method, shown in Figure 8-19, allows you to add a new vehicle and specify its properties.

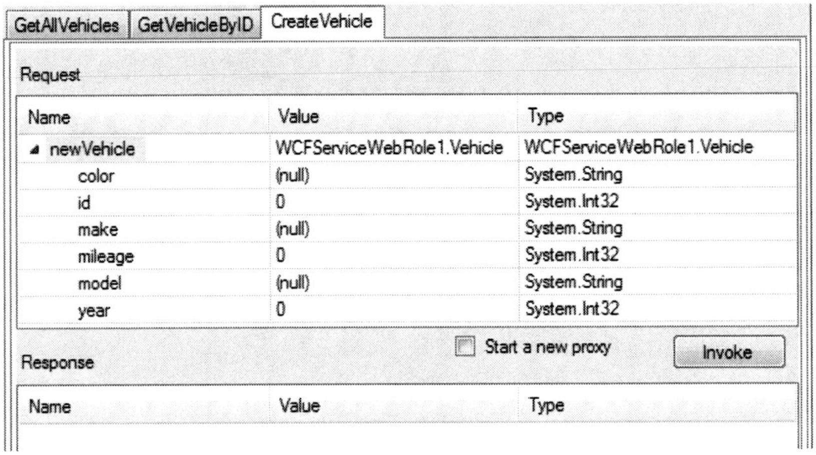

Figure 8-19. The CreateVehicle() method

Defining an External List

To create an external list based on data provided through a web service, you'll perform the following steps:

1. Create an external content type.

2. Define the connection to the external data source (web service).

3. Specify the CRUD operations.

4. Create an external list based on the external content type.

Configuring Business Connectivity Services in Office 365

Before you get started, you'll need to make sure you have permission to access the BCS services.

1. From the home admin page on your Office 365 account, click the Manage link in the SharePoint Online section, which will display the SharePoint Online admin page shown in Figure 8-20.

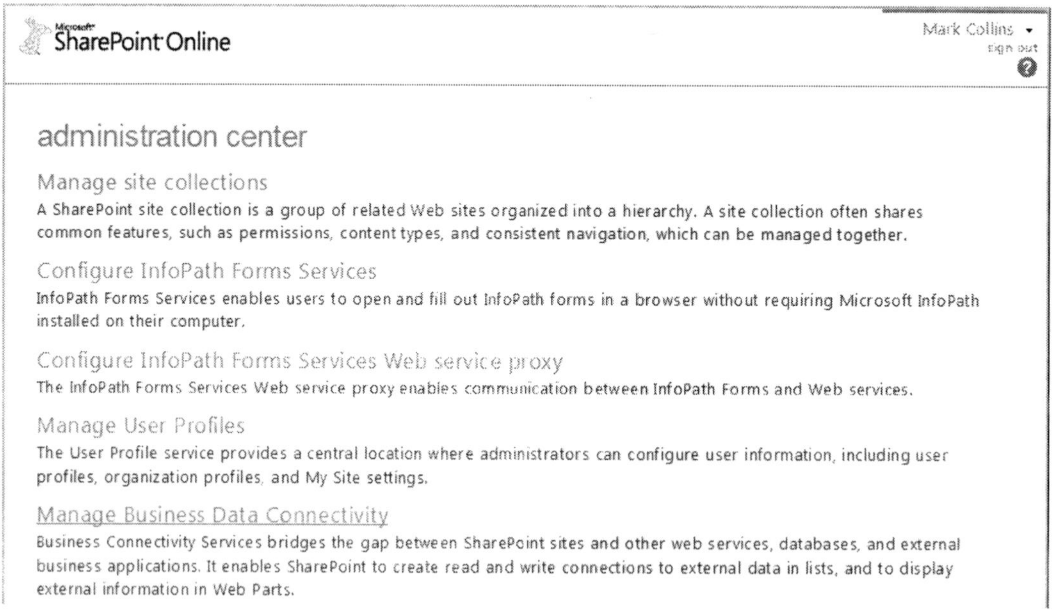

SharePoint Online

Mark Collins ▾
sign out
❷

administration center

Manage site collections
A SharePoint site collection is a group of related Web sites organized into a hierarchy. A site collection often shares common features, such as permissions, content types, and consistent navigation, which can be managed together.

Configure InfoPath Forms Services
InfoPath Forms Services enables users to open and fill out InfoPath forms in a browser without requiring Microsoft InfoPath installed on their computer.

Configure InfoPath Forms Services Web service proxy
The InfoPath Forms Services Web service proxy enables communication between InfoPath Forms and Web services.

Manage User Profiles
The User Profile service provides a central location where administrators can configure user information, including user profiles, organization profiles, and My Site settings.

Manage Business Data Connectivity
Business Connectivity Services bridges the gap between SharePoint sites and other web services, databases, and external business applications. It enables SharePoint to create read and write connections to external data in lists, and to display external information in Web Parts.

Figure 8-20. The SharePoint Online admin page

■ **Tip** Some of the terms and acronyms can be confusing. Business Data Connectivity (BDC) is the feature provided by SharePoint 2010 that allows you to access external data sources. To implement it, you use the BDC services hosted on SharePoint. The acronym for these services drops the word "Data" and is simply Business Connectivity Services (BCS). So the services you will use are called BCS but the overall functionality is referred to as BDC. This should not be confused with Business Data Catalog (BDC), which is the predecessor of BCS.

2.   Click the Manage Business Data Connectivity link and the ribbon shown in Figure 8-21 will be displayed.

Figure 8-21. The Business Data Connectivity ribbon

3.   Click the Set Metadata Store Permission button in the ribbon. In the dialog box that is displayed, enter or select your account and click the Add button (see Figure 8-22).

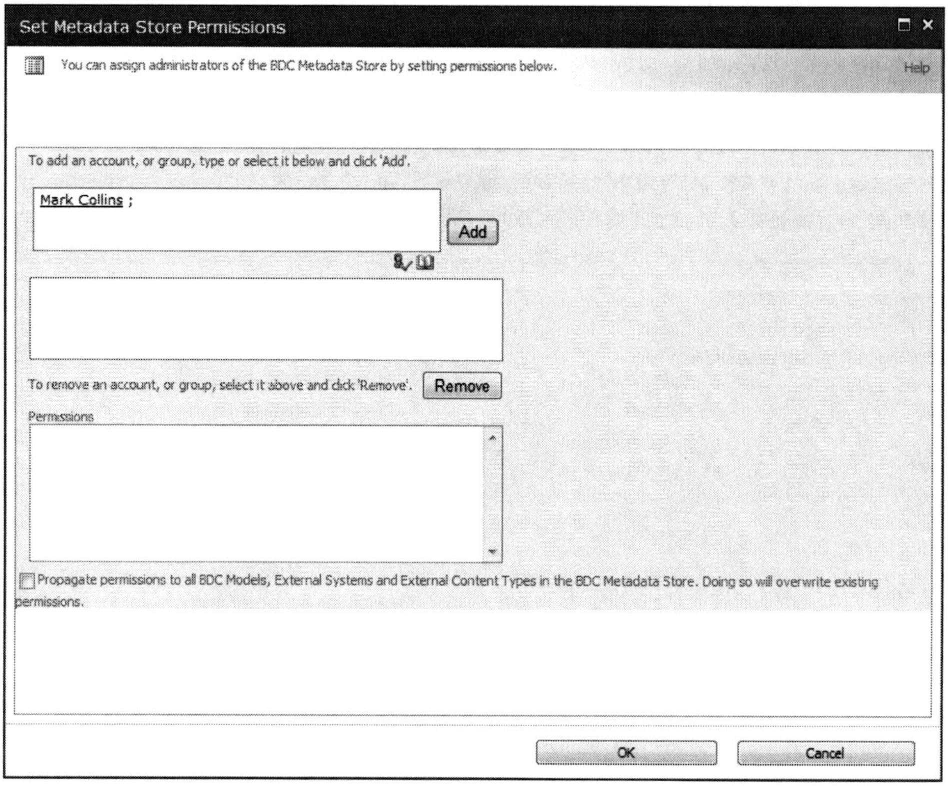

Figure 8-22. Adding an administrator of the BDC metatdata

    4.   Then select all the check boxes (see Figure 8-23). Click the OK button to update the permissions.

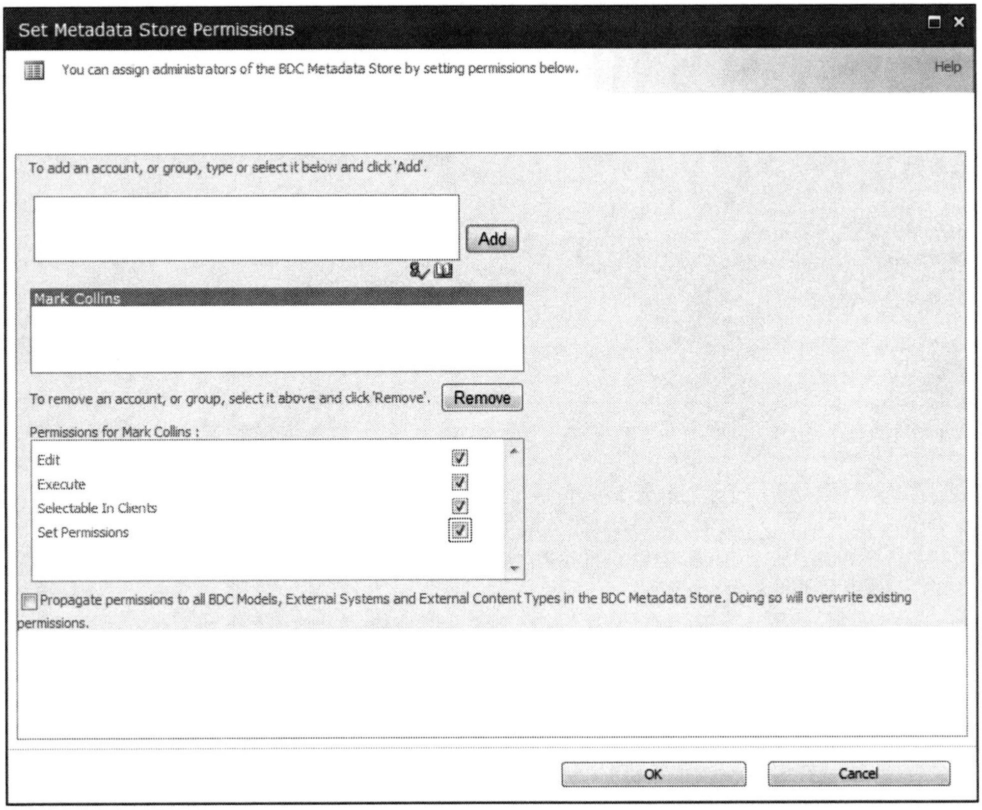

Figure 8-23. *Granting metatdata store permissions*

Creating an External Content Type

Now you're ready to create an external content type (ECT) using SharePoint Designer. This was briefly introduced in Chapter 4 and then used extensively in Chapter 5; you can refer back to either of these chapters if necessary. You can either go to the desired SharePoint site and select the "Edit in SharePoint Designer" link from the Site Actions menu or open SharePoint designer and select or navigate to the desired site.

Once the site has been opened, select the External Content Types link in the Navigation pane. Then click the External Content Type button in the ribbon to create a new ECT, as shown in Figure 8-24.

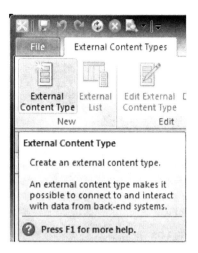

Figure 8-24. The External Content Type button in the ribbon

In the External Content Type Information section, enter the name **Vehicle** and the display name should be updated automatically (see Figure 8-25).

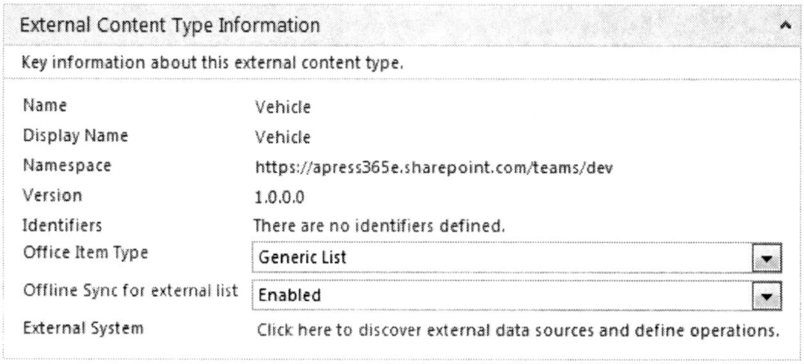

External Content Type Information		^
Key information about this external content type.		
Name	Vehicle	
Display Name	Vehicle	
Namespace	https://apress365e.sharepoint.com/teams/dev	
Version	1.0.0.0	
Identifiers	There are no identifiers defined.	
Office Item Type	Generic List	▼
Offline Sync for external list	Enabled	▼
External System	Click here to discover external data sources and define operations.	

Figure 8-25. Specifying the ECT name

Specifying the Data Source

Now you'll need to configure the connection to the web service.

1. Click the "Click here to discover external data sources and define operations" link, which will switch to the Operation Designer view shown in Figure 8-26.

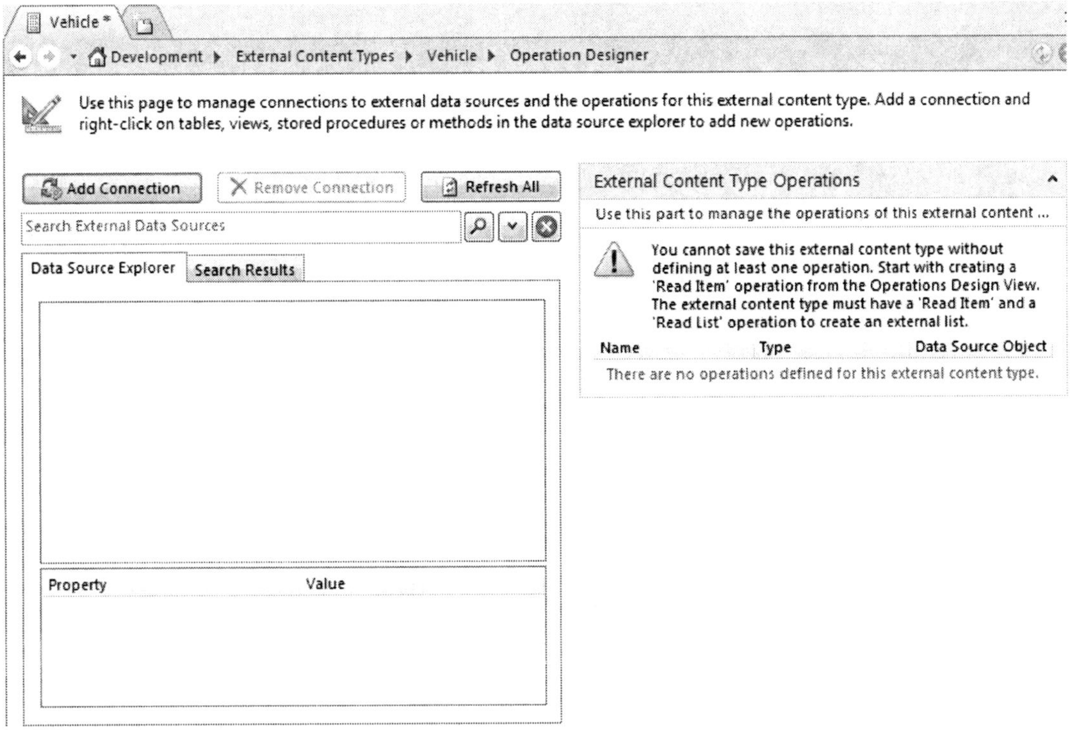

Figure 8-26. The initial Operations view

2. Click the Add Connection button and you'll see a prompt to choose the type of data source to use. As mentioned, only the WCF Service type is supported in Office 365, so choose it (see Figure 8-27).

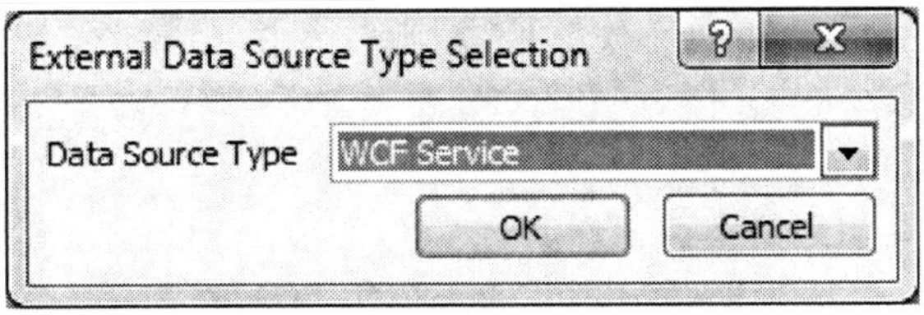

Figure 8-27. Selecting the WCF Service data source type

3. In the WCF Connection dialog box, specify the address of the web service as well as the metadata that defines the service contract. Typically, the metadata URL is the same as the web service except is has the &wsdl parameter. Enter the name **Vehicles** and leave all of the default values. The dialog box will be similar to Figure 8-28.

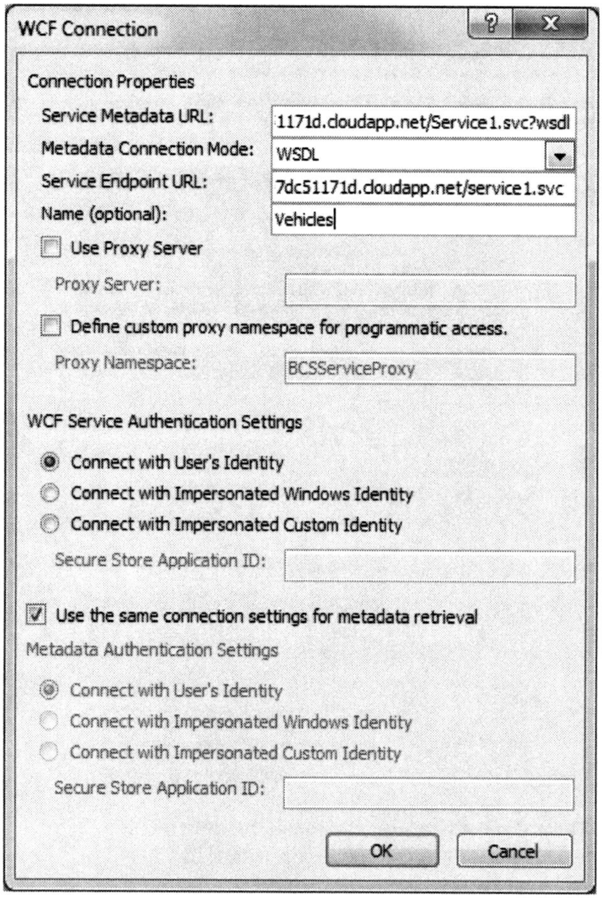

Figure 8-28. Specifying the WCF service details

4. Click the OK button and SharePoint Designer will attempt to access this web
   service and list the existing methods, as shown in Figure 8-29.

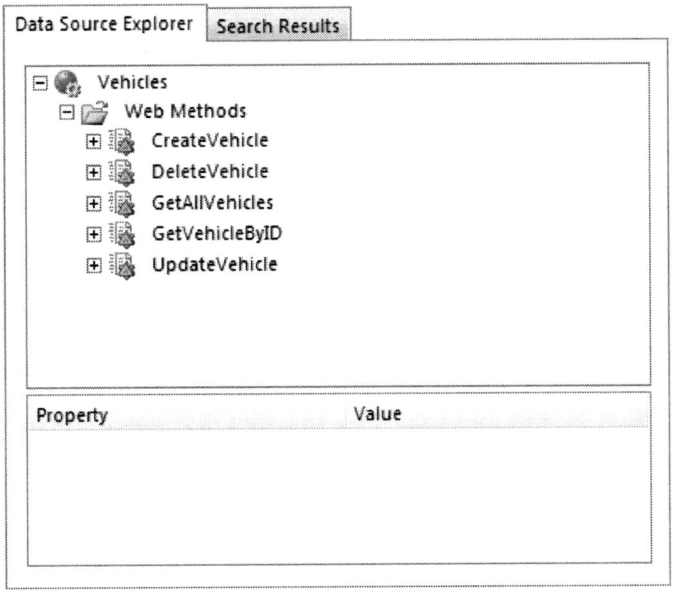

Figure 8-29. The methods provided by the web service

Mapping the Read Operations

Now that you have an ECT connected to a web service data source, you'll need to define the CRUD operations. To create a read-only list, you only need to define the Read List and Read Item operations. You'll start with these and test the list, then you can add the Create, Update, and Delete operations later.

Defining the Read List Operation

To define the Read List operation, follow these steps:

1. Right-click the GetAllVehicles() method and select the "New Read List Operation" link shown in Figure 8-30.

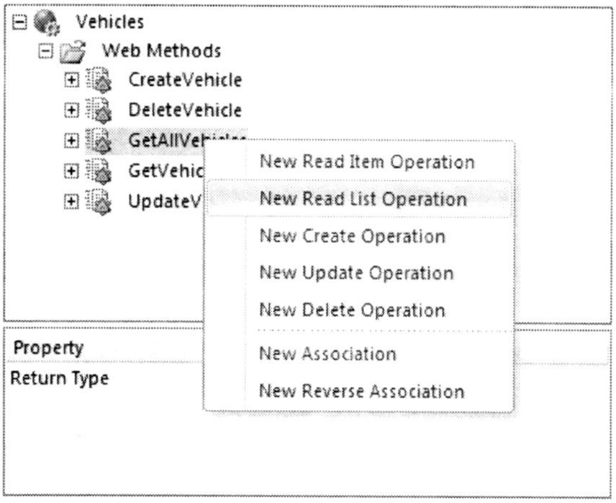

Figure 8-30. *Adding a Read List operation*

2. This will display a series of dialog boxes where you can map the selected method. The first dialog box, shown in Figure 8-31, displays the general operation properties. You can leave all of the default settings and click the Next button.

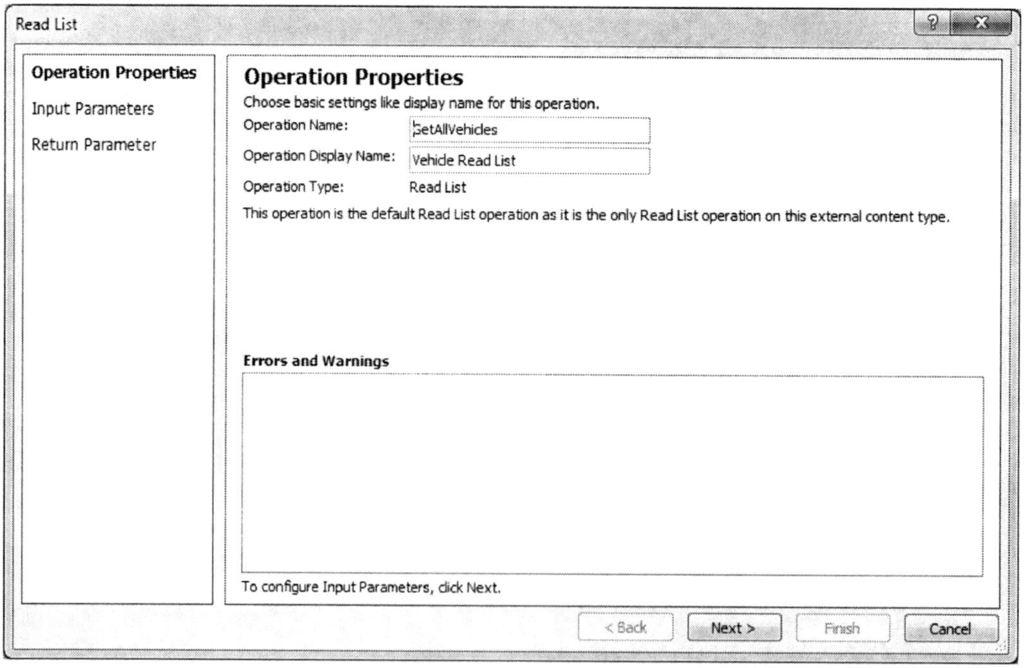

Figure 8-31. *The initial Read List dialog box*

3. The second dialog box, shown in Figure 8-32, is where you configure the input parameters; however, this method doesn't have any so you can just click the Next button.

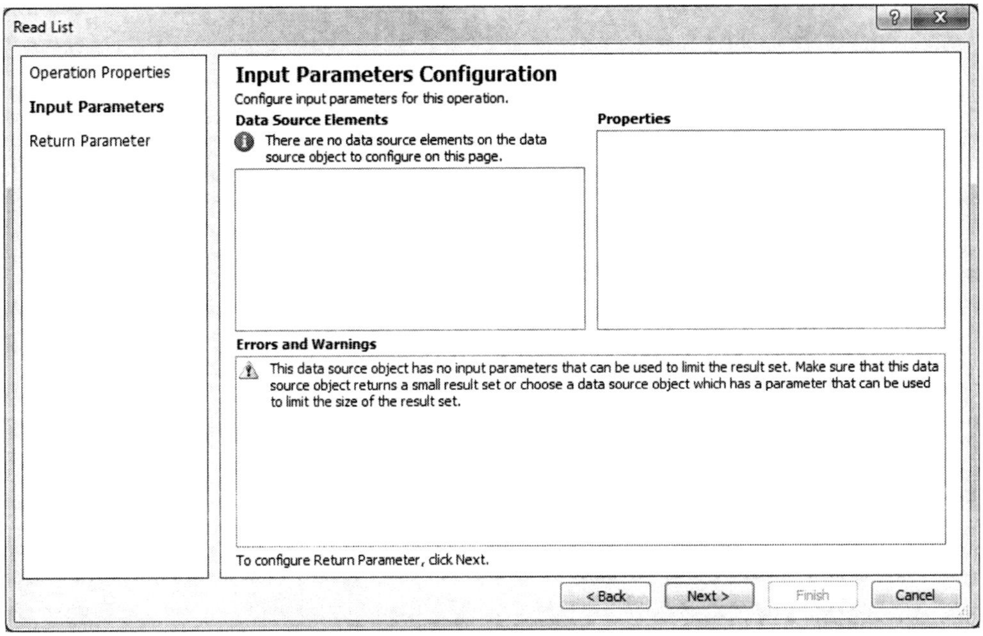

Figure 8-32. The Read List input parameters dialog box

■ **Caution** Notice the warning displayed in Figure 8-32. Since there are no input parameters, there is no way to programmatically filter the items that are returned. This method will literally return all records. SharePoint doesn't handle large amounts of data very well. Since your service uses a very small set of hardcoded data, this is not a concern. In general, you will want to provide a way to filter the list. You should also code the service to return a maximum number of records in case the values provided don't filter the list sufficiently.

---

4. The third and final dialog box is used to configure the return parameter. You can use all of the default settings except you will need to specify which property is used as the unique identifier for this data source. Select the id parameter and select the "Map to Identifier" check box, as shown in Figure 8-33. Click the Finish button to create this operation.

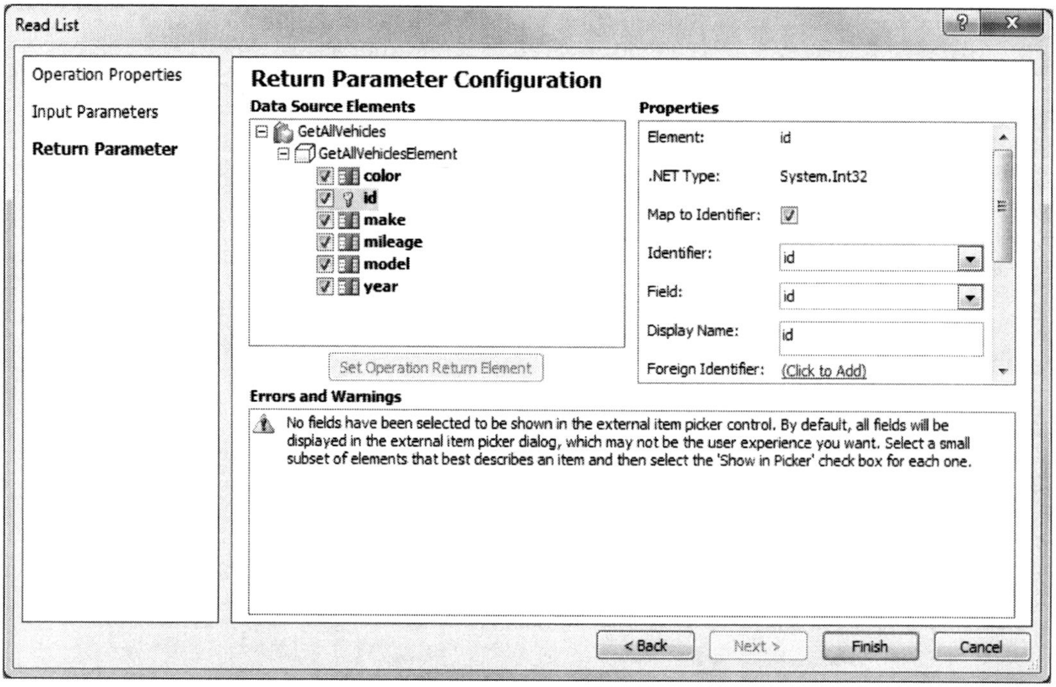

Figure 8-33. Configuring the return parameter

Adding the Read Item Operation

Now you'll create the Read Item (or SpecificFinder) operation.

1. Right-click the GetVehicleByID() method and select the New Read Item
   Operation link. This will display the same three dialog boxes that you used to
   configure the Read List operation.

2. Again, use the default settings for the first dialog box. The second dialog box
   shown in Figure 8-34 shows the vehicleID input parameter.

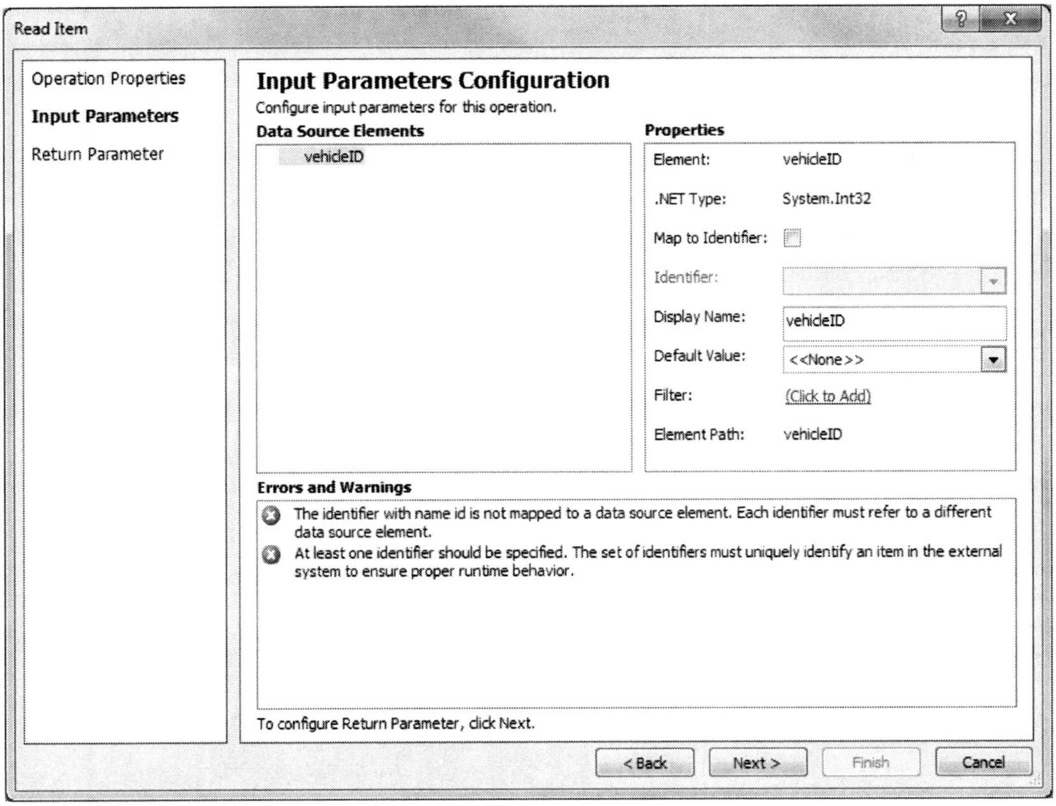

Figure 8-34. *The Read Item input parameters dialog box*

3. Notice the error messages that are displayed. When you created the Read List operation, an identifier was configured for this ECT called id. The Read Item operation returns a single record based on this identifier. For this to work, you will need to map an input parameter to the identifier. To do that, select the vehicleID parameter and then select the "Map to Identifier" check box. The dialog box will look like Figure 8-35 and the error messages will be removed. Click the Next button to go to the next dialog box.

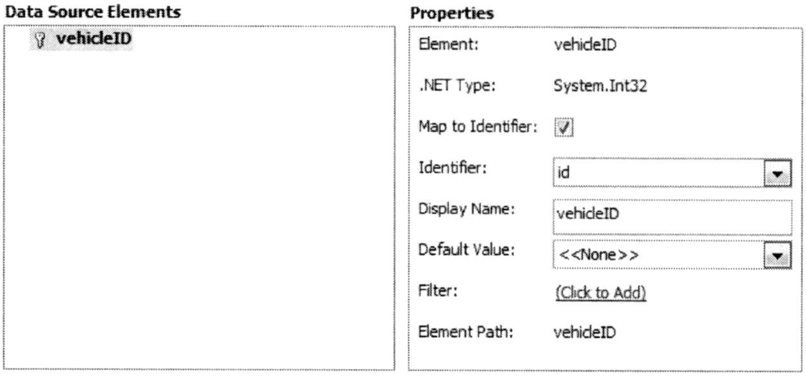

Data Source Elements

♀ **vehicleID**

Properties

Element:	vehicleID
.NET Type:	System.Int32
Map to Identifier:	☑
Identifier:	id ▼
Display Name:	vehicleID
Default Value:	<<None>> ▼
Filter:	(Click to Add)
Element Path:	vehicleID

Figure 8-35. Mapping the identifier

4. In the third dialog box you will need to map the id parameter to the identifier just like you did with the Read List operation. Select the id parameter and select the "Map to Identifier" check box, as shown in Figure 8-36. Click the Finish button to complete the operation.

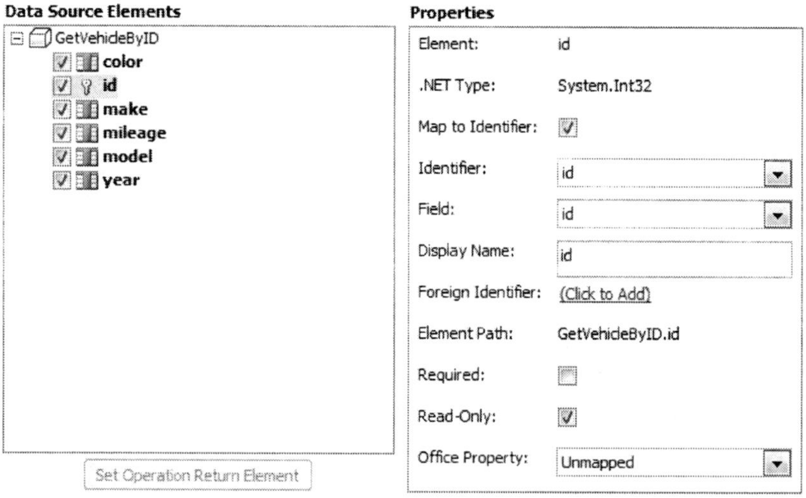

Data Source Elements

- ☐ GetVehicleByID
  - ☑ color
  - ☑ ♀ id
  - ☑ make
  - ☑ mileage
  - ☑ model
  - ☑ year

    Set Operation Return Element

Properties

Element:	id
.NET Type:	System.Int32
Map to Identifier:	☑
Identifier:	id ▼
Field:	id ▼
Display Name:	id
Foreign Identifier:	(Click to Add)
Element Path:	GetVehicleByID.id
Required:	☐
Read-Only:	☑
Office Property:	Unmapped ▼

Figure 8-36. Mapping the identifier

Creating an External List

With the two read operations defined, you have satisfied the minimum requirements for a read-only list. That's what the text in the External Content Type Operations section, shown in Figure 8-37, is telling you.

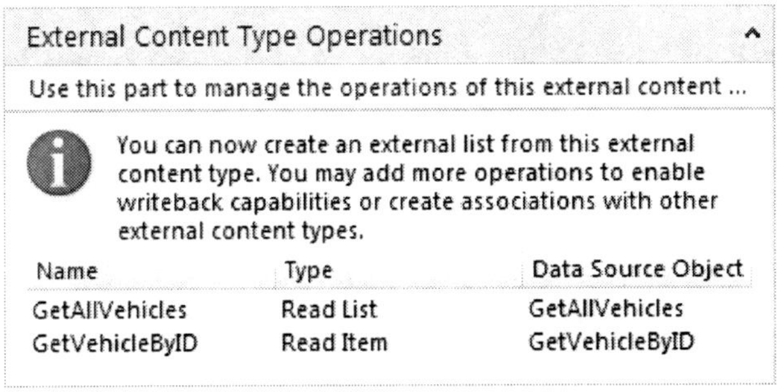

Figure 8-37. The existing operations

At this point you'll create a read-only list so you can see how this works. You will later come back to this and add the remaining operations so the list can also add, update, and delete records. Click the "Create Lists & Form" button in the ribbon, as shown in Figure 8-38.

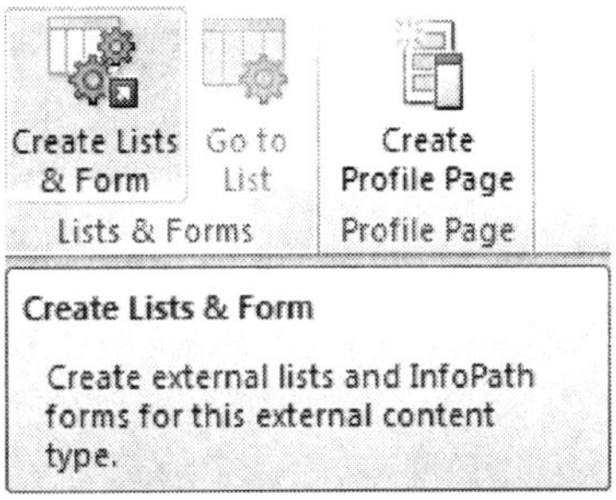

Figure 8-38. The Create Lists & Form button

Before generating the list, the ECT must be saved. If you didn't already save them, you'll see the dialog box shown in Figure 8-39. Click the Yes button to save the ECT and proceed with creating the list.

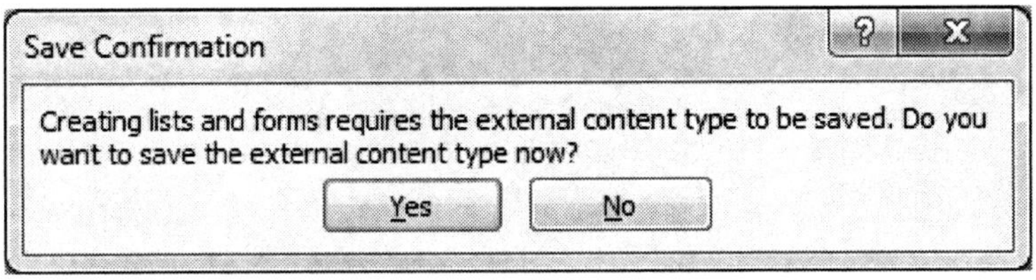

Figure 8-39. Saving the external content type

The dialog box shown in Figure 8-40 will appear; in it you can specify the name of the new list. Enter **Vehicles** and a list description. Click the OK button to continue.

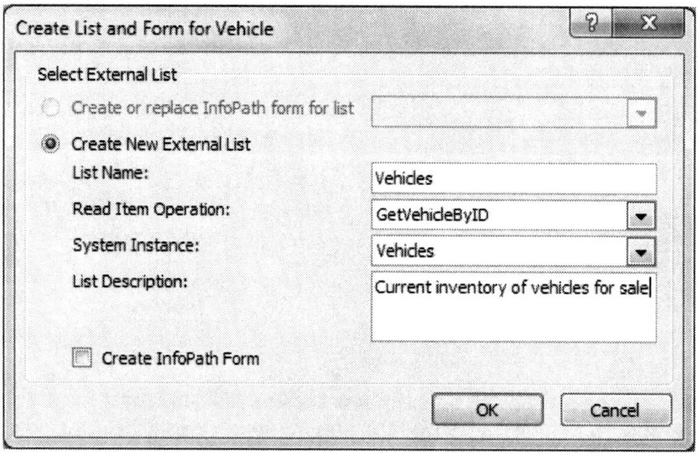

Figure 8-40. Specifying the list properties

After a few seconds the Vehicles list will be generated.

Testing the Initial Vehicles List

Go to the SharePoint site and navigate to the new list, which will look like Figure 8-41.

Figure 8-41. The default All Items view of the Vehicles list

The first column, color, is configured as a link to display a single item. Click one of these records and it will be displayed in the View Item form shown in Figure 8-42.

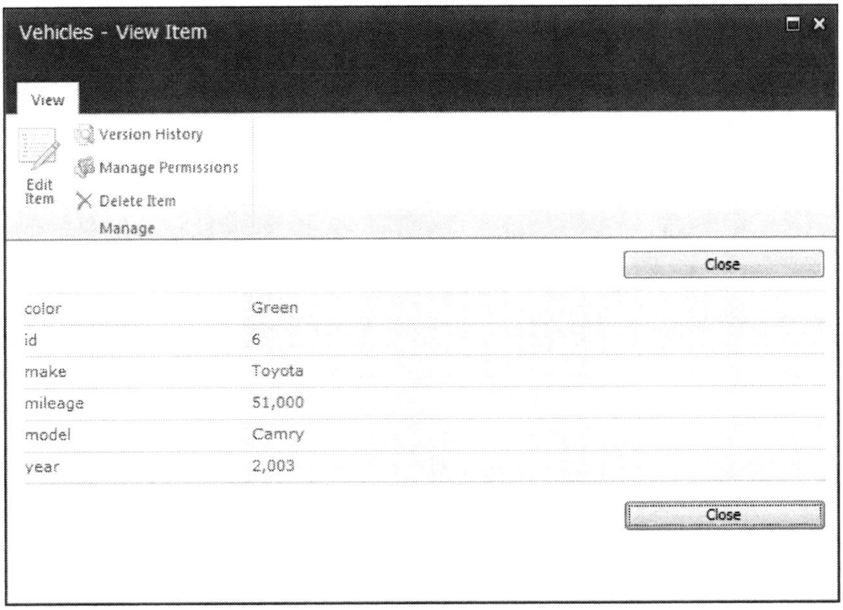

Figure 8-42. Viewing a single item

Normally the identifier is the first column. You can configure this by reordering the columns. From the List tab of the ribbon, click the Modify View button. In the Columns section, set the "Position from Left" value for the id columns to 1, as shown in Figure 8-43. Click the OK button to save the changes.

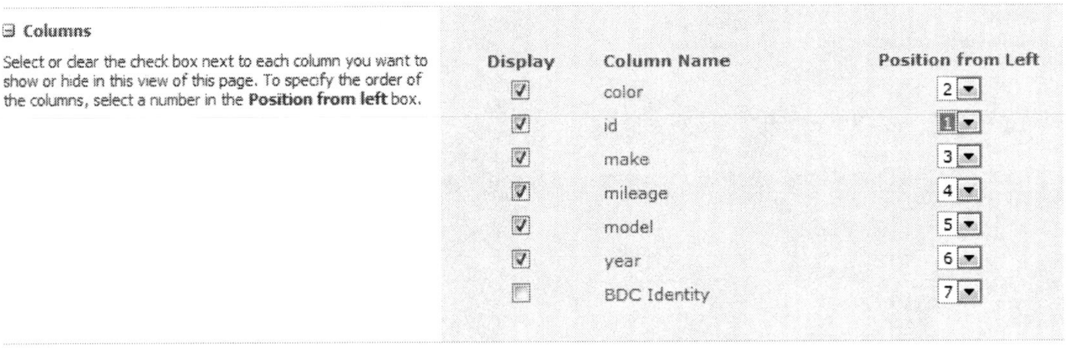

Figure 8-43. Modifying the column order

Specifying the Remaining Operations

Now you'll define the remaining operations (Create, Update, and Delete) so you will be able to modify the external data. These will be defined using the same dialog boxes that you used to configure the read operations. You will use the default settings in most dialog boxes and I'll show you where changes are necessary.

When you display the ECT in SharePoint Designer, it normally displays the Summary View shown in Figure 8-44.

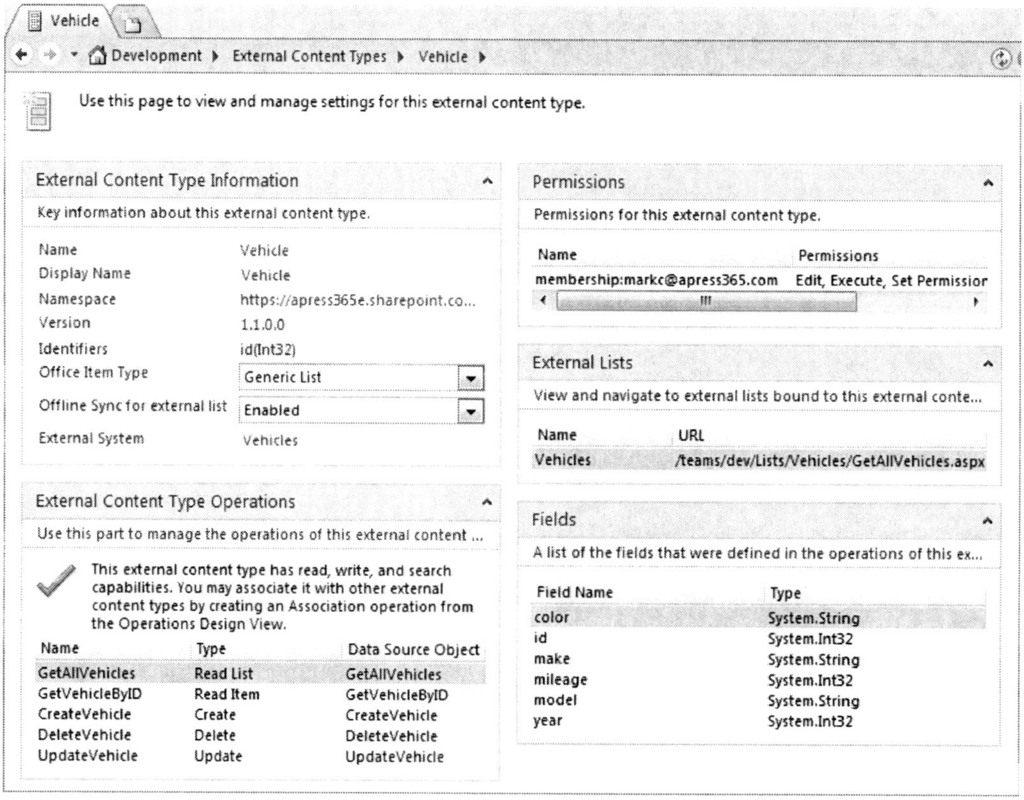

Figure 8-44. The ECT Summary View

To modify the operations, click the "Operations Design View" button in the ribbon, as shown in Figure 8-45.

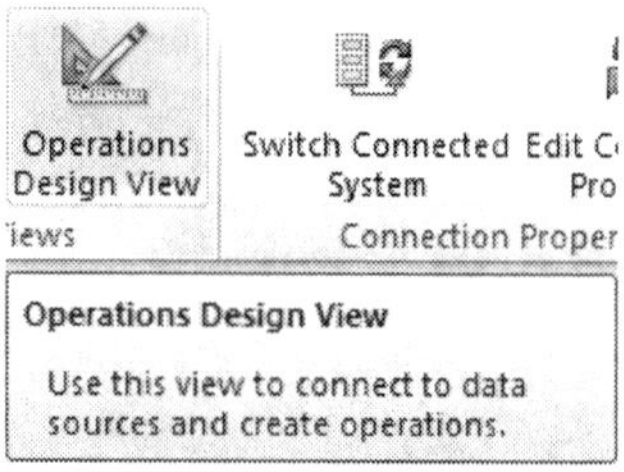

Figure 8-45. Switching to the Operations Design view

Defining the Create Operation

Right-click the CreateVehicle method and select the New Create Operation link, as shown in Figure 8-46.

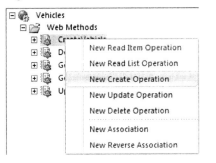

Figure 8-46. Mapping the Create operation

Leave the default values in the first dialog box and click the Next button to display the second dialog box. In the second dialog box, select the id parameter and click the "Map to Identifier" check box, as shown in Figure 8-47.

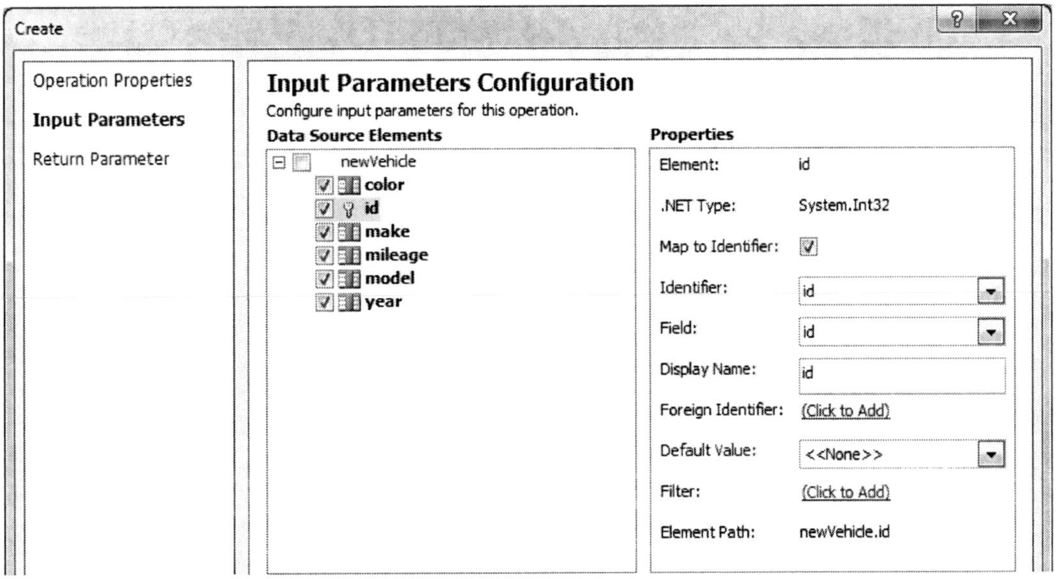

Figure 8-47. Mapping the identifier

Click the Next button to go to the third dialog box and leave it as is. Click the Finish button to create the operation.

Defining the Update Operation

Create the Update operation in the same way: by right-clicking the UpdateVehicle() method and selecting the New Update Operation link. The Update operation only has two dialog boxes. Leave the first one as is. In the second dialog box, select the vehicleID parameter, as shown in Figure 8-48.

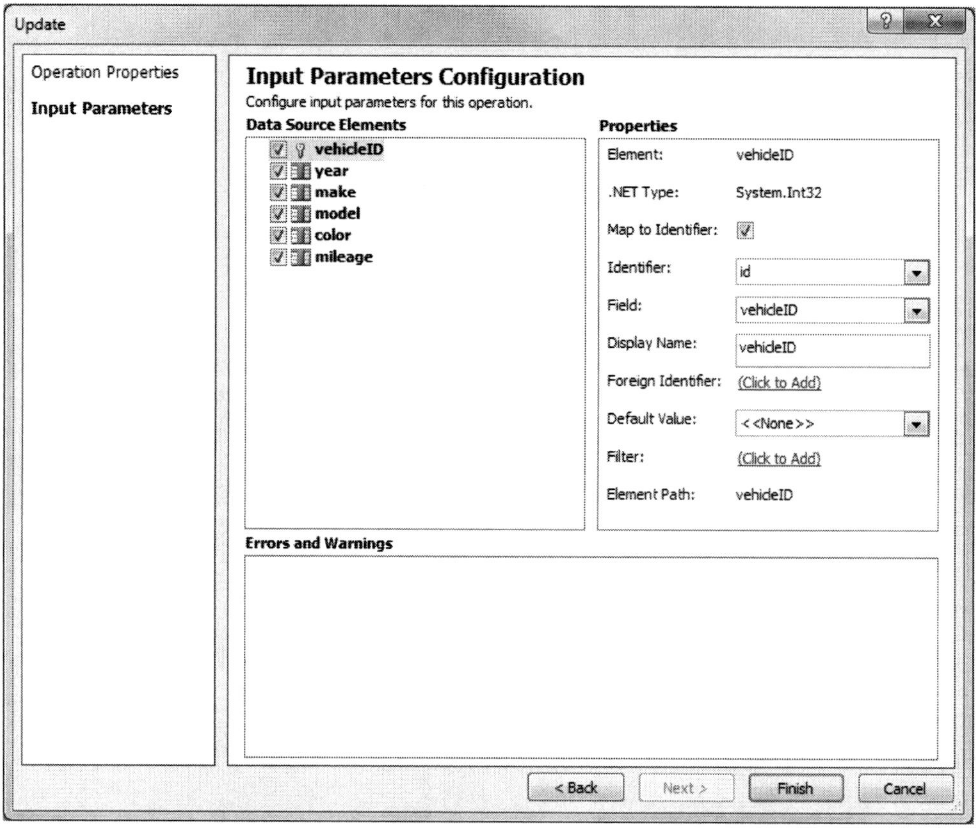

Figure 8-48. Mapping another operation identifier

Select the "Map to Identifier" check box as you did with most of the other operations. There is one more subtle but critical change that you'll need to make. In all the other operations this parameter is called id but in the UpdateVehicle() method it is called vehicleID. If they are named the same, SharePoint Designer maps them correctly. However, in this case, you'll need to explicitly map the vehicleID parameter to the id field. To do that, simply select the id value from the Field drop-down, as shown in Figure 8-49.

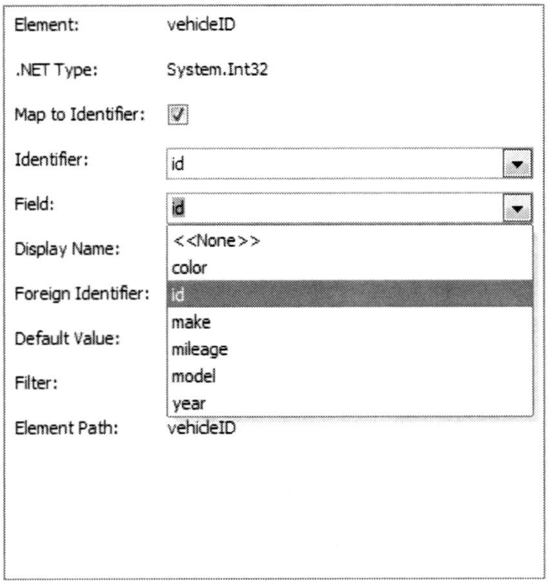

Element:	vehicleID
.NET Type:	System.Int32
Map to Identifier:	☑
Identifier:	id
Field:	id
Display Name:	<<None>>
	color
Foreign Identifier:	id
	make
Default Value:	mileage
	model
Filter:	year
Element Path:	vehicleID

Figure 8-49. Changing the mapped column

> ▪ **Caution** The Update method must map all of the columns provided by the Read Item operation. If you don't, the list will not be updateable. If you fail to make this adjustment, the id field will not be mapped to any of the input parameters. This would make the Update method invalid. When you later try to update the external list you'll get an error similar to Figure 8-50.

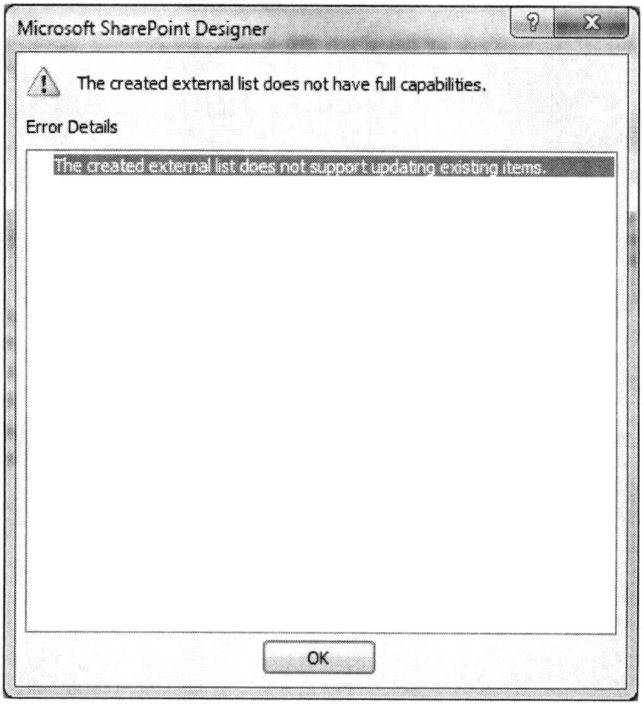

Figure 8-50. Error when the Update operation isn't configured correctly

Defining the Delete Operation

Create a Delete operation just like you did with the other operations except using the New Delete Operation link. In the second dialog box, select the vehicleID input parameter and select the "Map to Identifier" check box, as shown in Figure 8-51.

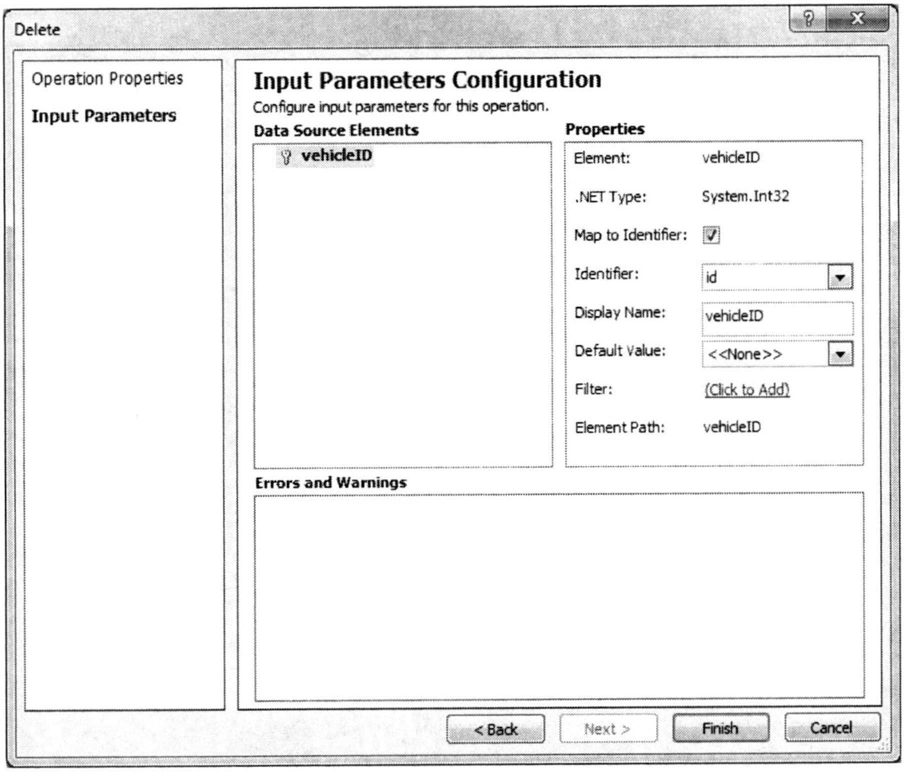

Figure 8-51. Configuring the Delete operation

With all the operations defined, the Operation Designer view should look like Figure 8-52.

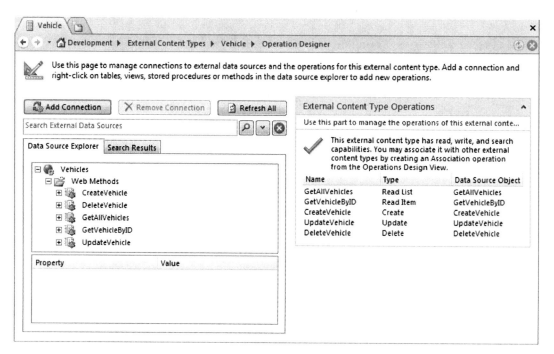

Figure 8-52. The completed external content type

Adding the Edit and New Forms

When you created the Vehicles list, only the read operations were defined and the list was read-only. Consequently, only the display form was generated; the New and Edit forms were not. The ECT now supports read/write operations but the appropriate forms don't exist. You will create those now.

1. In SharePoint Designer, select the Lists and Libraries link in the Navigation pane. Then select the Vehicles list.

2. In the Forms section you'll see that only the DispForm.aspx form is included. Click the New button to create a new form.

3. Enter **EditForm** for the name and select the "Edit item form" radio button. The "Set as default form for the selected type" check box should be checked.

4. Select the "Create link in List Item Menu and Ribbon" check box, as shown in Figure 8-53.

5. Click the OK button to create the form.

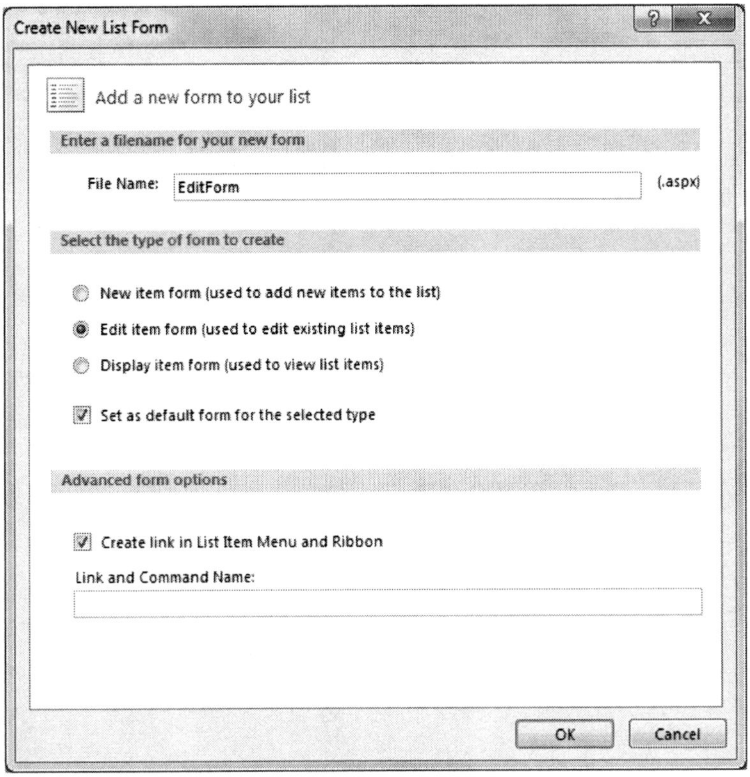

Figure 8-53. Creating an Edit form

6. In the same way, create a new item form. Enter the name **NewForm**, as shown in Figure 8-54.

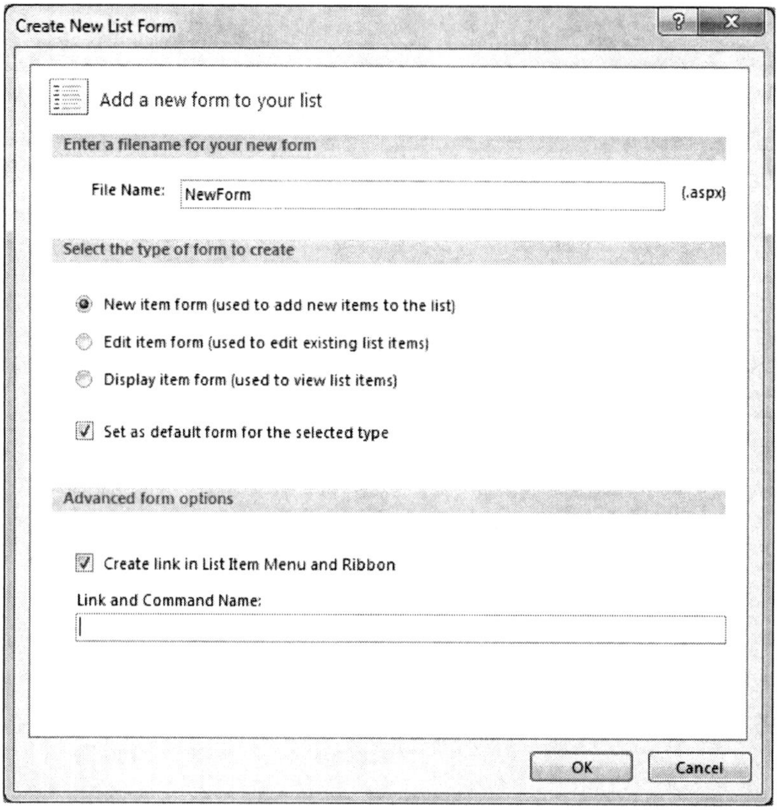

Figure 8-54. Creating a New Item form

The Forms section should now list all three forms (see Figure 8-55).

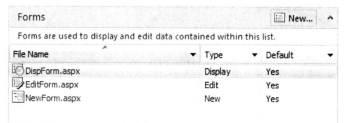

Figure 8-55. The existing forms for the Vehicles list

Testing the Vehicles List

Your Vehicles list should now allow you to add, update, and delete items in the list. Go to the Vehicles list on SharePoint a view a single record. Notice that the Edit Item and Delete Item links are enabled (see Figure 8-56).

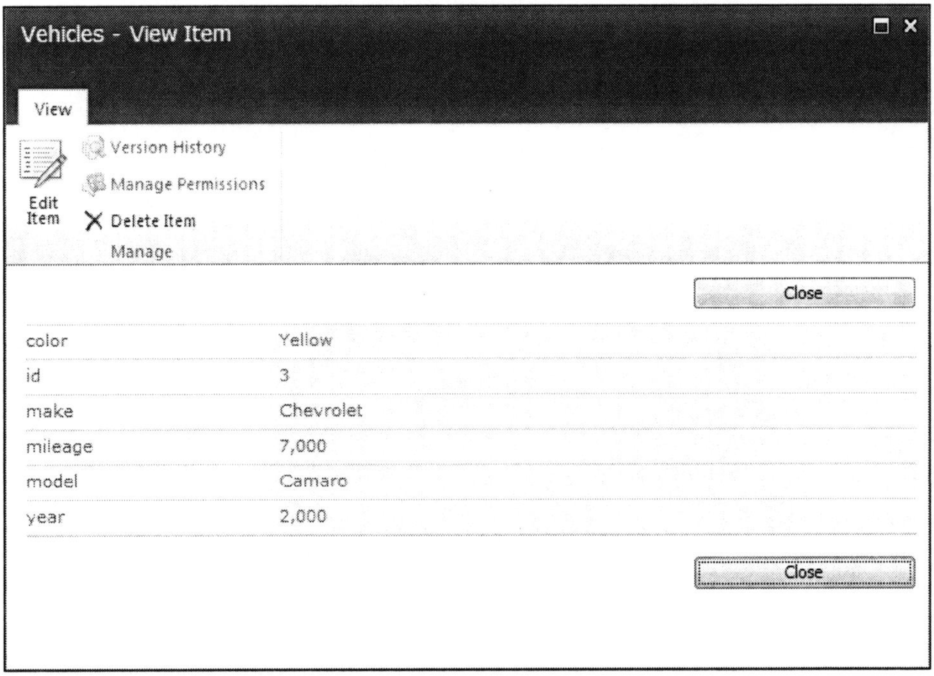

Figure 8-56. The display form with the Edit and Delete links enabled

From the Items tab of the ribbon you can click the New Item button, which will display the New Item form shown in Figure 8-57.

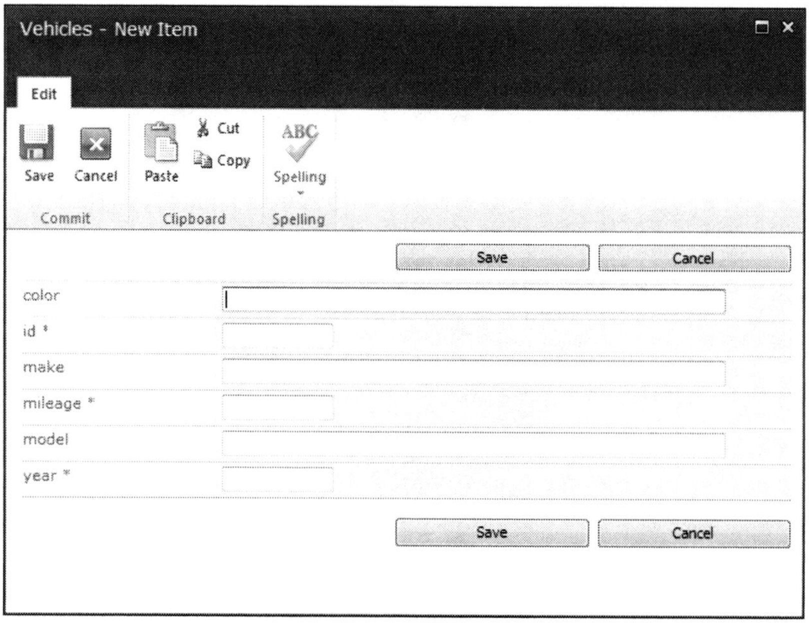

Figure 8-57. The New Item form

You can also edit an existing record using the Edit Form shown in Figure 8-58.

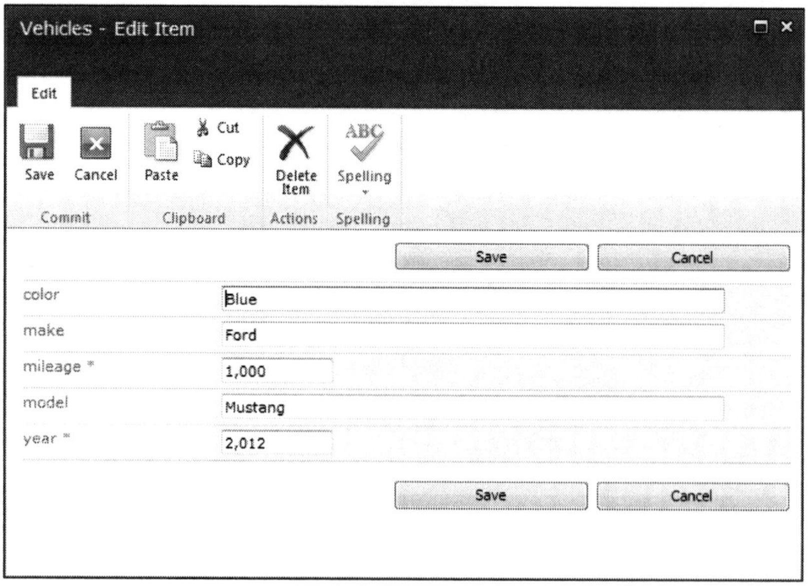

Figure 8-58. The Edit form

Summary

In this chapter you created an external list to access data outside of SharePoint. You used SharePoint Designer to configure an external content type that maps the necessary CRUD operations to methods implemented by a web service. The web service is hosted on a Windows Azure site.

While the specific implementation was somewhat trivial, you can use this same approach to connect to just about any kind of data from within the Office 365 platform. You can use this to access your line of business (LOB) data, providing powerful integration into your office automation solution.

PART 3

Building SharePoint Solutions with Visual Studio

In this section, you'll use Visual Studio to create SharePoint solutions. You'll learn the basic concepts for creating, debugging, packaging, and deploying sandboxed solutions in Chapter 9.

In Chapter 10, you'll create a visual web part and access the SharePoint object model. You'll use LINQ to SharePoint to manipulate the SharePoint objects. You will also create a custom workflow action that can be called in a declarative workflow using SharePoint Designer.

In Chapter 11, you will use the client object model and implement client-side functionality using both JavaScript and Silverlight. This will allow you to implement solutions that can access your SharePoint objects as well as local resources not accessible from server-side implementations.

CHAPTER 9

SharePoint Content

Adding content to your SharePoint site through Visual Studio is a great way to begin looking at developing solutions. You can declaratively create content and deploy it out to your SharePoint site. This chapter will show you how to set up content types, site columns, lists, and event receivers. Together, these can be used to set up the SharePoint content for your site.

Sandboxed Solutions

Developing for SharePoint Online means developing sandboxed solutions. SharePoint Online is based on SharePoint 2010, and as such, provides the sandboxed solution architecture. As I explained in Chapter 3, developers can safely build custom applications and deploy them to the shared environment of SharePoint Online.

Sandboxed solutions are limited in scope. The API is a subset of the `Microsoft.SharePoint` API. However, many powerful options remain, including:

- Site columns
- Content types
- List definitions
- List instances
- Web Parts
- Workflows
- Custom actions
- SharePoint Designer workflow activities
- Event receivers
- Modules/files

Sandboxed solutions run in partial trust. They are only given access to features at the site collection level. This means they can't access web application–scoped features or farm-scoped features. They also can't access the file system. This means you can't create solutions that deploy files up to the server. Sandboxed solutions are not allowed to make external web service calls. The SharePoint solution can't reach outside of the sandbox. However, only code running on the server is sandboxed. Silverlight and JavaScript applications can provide a workaround for some of these limitations.

Visual Studio 2010

The same tools used to develop solutions for on-premise SharePoint sites are used for developing sandboxed solutions. When starting a new SharePoint project in Visual Studio 2010, you must select whether the project scope is sandboxed or not. For SharePoint Online solutions, select the sandboxed option. The development environment will then supply the proper IntelliSense, packaging, and debugging options for your choice.

■ **Caution** SharePoint development requires Visual Studio be installed on a machine that is running SharePoint. Typically this is a Windows Server, although a Windows 7 workstation can be set up to satisfy this requirement. Debugging is performed against the on-premise installation. The solution can then be packaged and installed out to the remote SharePoint site.

List Definition

A good place to start is building a list for the SharePoint site. This can be done declaratively in Visual Studio 2010. The debugging and deployment steps are the same as more complex solutions, so this serves as a good introduction to the process and ensures everything is set up and working properly.

The solution you will build here includes a couple of site columns, a new content type, and a list of those types. Site columns are essentially fields for data collection. They can be used in more than one content type, but they collect a particular type of data and display a specific prompt to the user. Content types are a category of information. They contain a collection of columns and other settings associated with that particular type of data.

■ **Tip** If you're new to SharePoint development check out the SharePoint Primer in Appendix A. This is a quick overview of the basic SharePoint concepts.

Creating a SharePoint Project

Launch Visual Studio 2010 and select an Empty SharePoint Project, as shown in Figure 9-1. Name the project **CustomLists**.

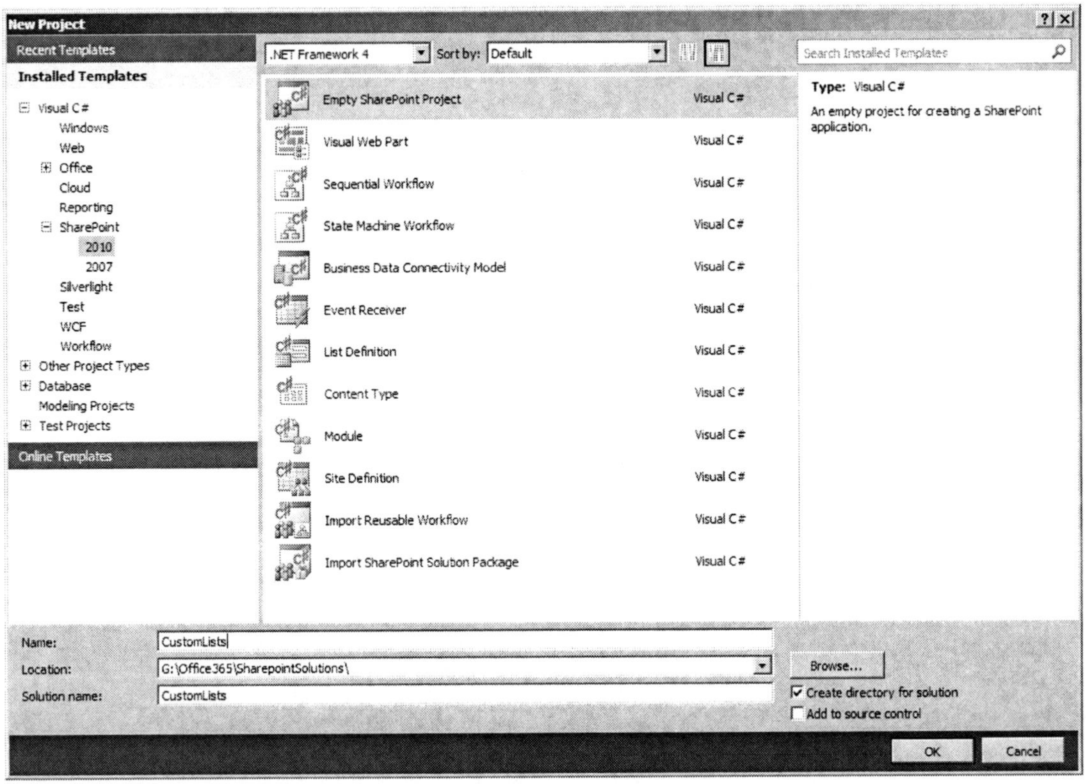

Figure 9-1. Creating an Empty SharePoint project

Visual Studio will prompt for the local SharePoint site for debugging. Enter your local SharePoint site address and select "Deploy as a sandboxed solution," as shown in Figure 9-2.

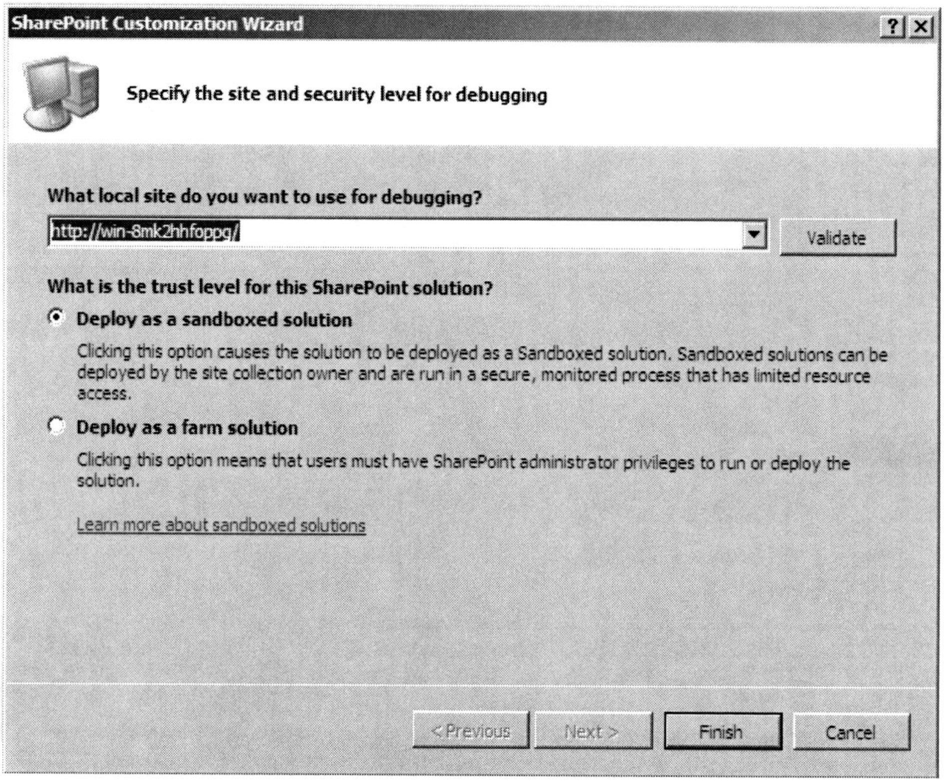

Figure 9-2. Connecting to the local SharePoint site

Adding a Content Type

You will add a content type as the basis of the future list. Right-click the project and click Add Item. Select Content Type 9-and name it **Book** (as shown in Figure 9-3).

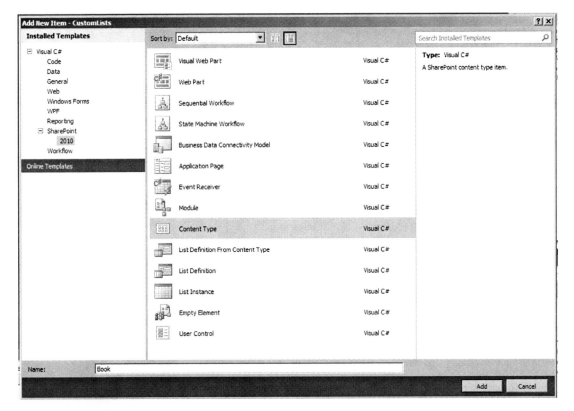

Figure 9-3. Adding a content type

You must select a base content type for your new type. The new content type will inherit the columns and settings from the base type. Figure 9-4 displays the various base types to choose from. Select Item in the drop list and click Finish.

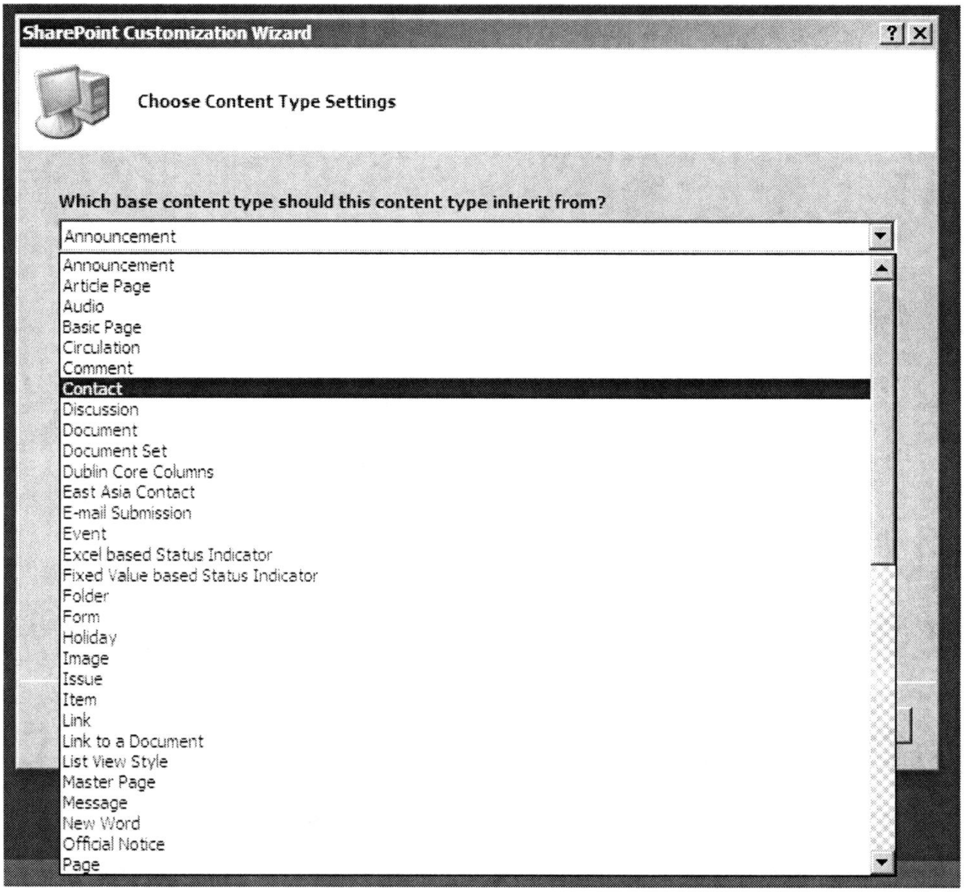

Figure 9-4. Choosing the base content type

A Book item will be added to the project along with an `Elements.xml`, file as seen in Figure 9-5.

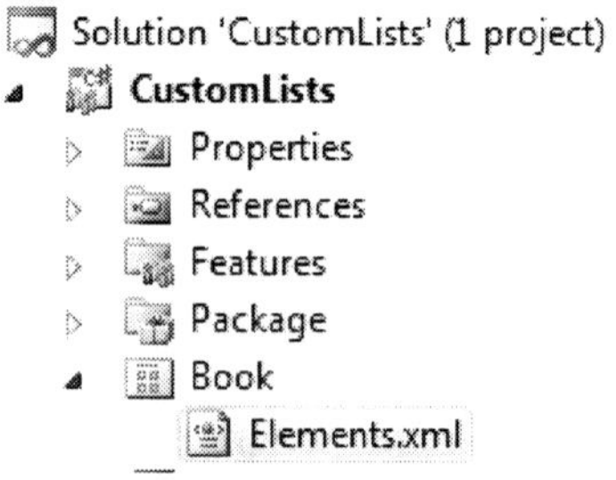

Figure 9-5. The Elements.xml file

The Elements.xml file will be opened in Visual Studio. This file contains the initial information for the new type. Edit the Name value to **Book** to keep things simple.

```xml
<?xml version="1.0" encoding="utf-8"?>
<Elements xmlns="http://schemas.microsoft.com/sharepoint/">

  <!-- Parent ContentType: Item (0x01) -->
  <ContentType ID="0x010058fa1e4c58904b1abcbdf9d569921efa"
               Name="Book"
               Group="Custom Content Types"
               Description="My Content Type"
               Inherits="TRUE"
               Version="0">
    <FieldRefs>
    </FieldRefs>
  </ContentType>
</Elements>
```

Now, add site columns to use as fields in the types. Add the definitions of these columns to the beginning of this Elements.xml file. The field definitions require GUIDs for identification. You will need to generate these GUIDs for use in this file.

ADDING GUIDGEN TO VISUAL STUDIO

To generate GUIDs, you will use the Create GUID tool in Visual Studio. This tool is available under the Tools menu. If this tool is not present in your development environment, add it by clicking Tools ➤ External Tools in Visual Studio. Click the ellipses next to the Command textbox to bring up an Open file dialog window. Navigate to C:\Program Files(x86)\Microsoft SDKs\Windows\v7.0A\Bin and select the guidgen.exe file, as shown in Figure 9-6.

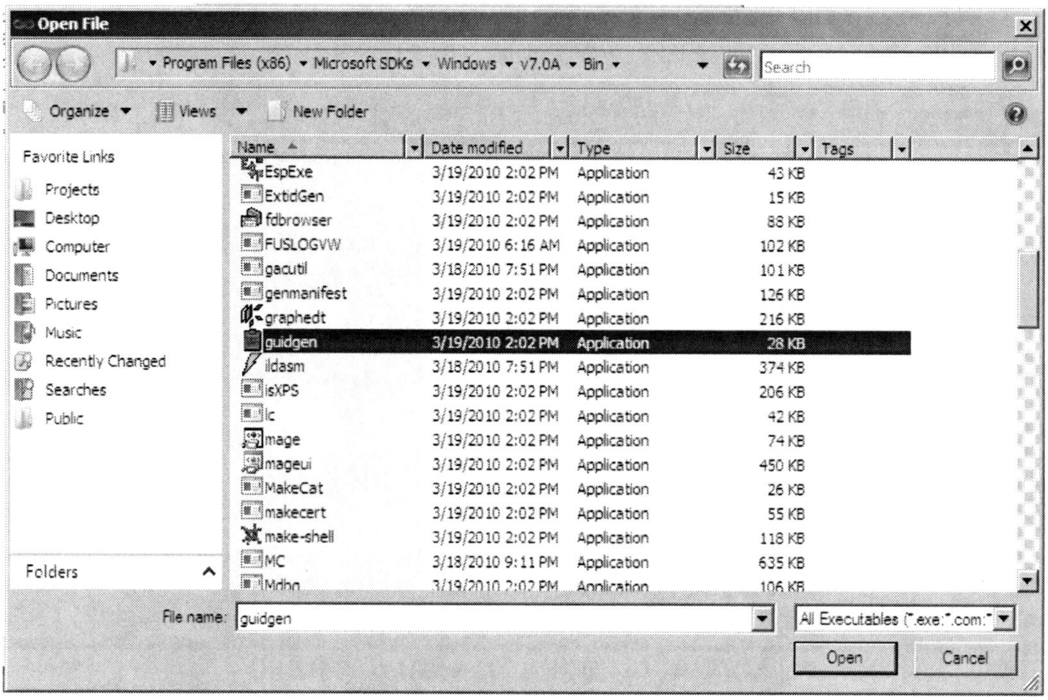

Figure 9-6. *Finding guidgen external tool for Visual Studio*

Enter "Create GUID" into the Title textbox and click OK, as shown in Figure 9-7.

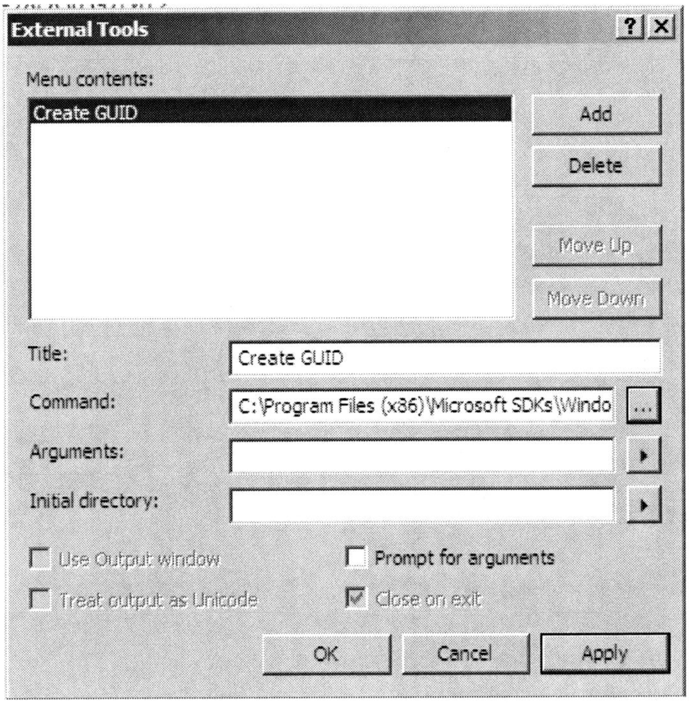

Figure 9-7. Adding Create GUID to the External Tools list

Use this tool to generate all GUIDs necessary in this project.

Figure 9-8 shows how an option called Create GUID is added to the Tools menu.

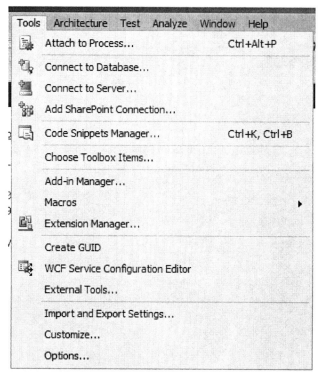

Figure 9-8. The Create GUID menu option

The dialog box shown in Figure 9-9 is displayed with the generated GUID. Click New GUID to generate a new value. Click Copy to place the current value into the clipboard. Use the GUID Format options to choose how this value is generated.

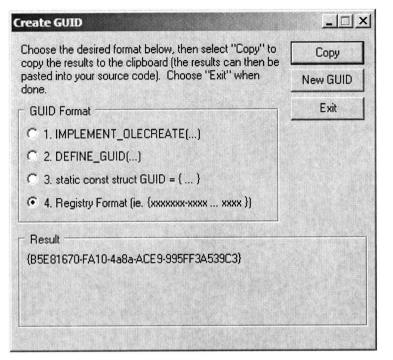

Figure 9-9. The Create GUID tool

Site columns use a Field node in the XML for their definition. You will define the following attributes:

- SourceID: Reference to schema definition.

- ID: GUID for reference within SharePoint.

- Name: Another point of reference with SharePoint files.

- DisplayName: Name shown on web pages and other places when type is shown.

- Group: Group name used in organizing site columns in SharePoint Site Settings pages.

- Type: Data type for field.

- DisplaceOnUpgrade: Controls override of properties if field already exists.

Enter the following code just under the opening Elements node in the `Elements.xml` file:

```
<Field SourceID="http://schemas.microsoft.com/sharepoint/v3"
       ID="{F44EC4B6-0963-4fae-B2D0-9635720A806E}"
       Name="ISBN"
       DisplayName="ISBN"
```

```
          Group="Custom Columns"
          Type="Text"
          DisplaceOnUpgrade="TRUE" />
<Field SourceID="http://schemas.microsoft.com/sharepoint/v3"
       ID="{8D095FEE-0E82-4edf-8F5E-517393690661}"
       Name="BookAuthor"
       DisplayName="Author"
       Group="Custom Columns"
       Type="Text"
       DisplaceOnUpgrade="TRUE" />
<Field SourceID="http://schemas.microsoft.com/sharepoint/v3"
       ID="{30427EC2-E181-4206-8328-F305423932E3}"
       Name="Rating"
       DisplayName="Rating"
       Group="Custom Columns"
       Type="Number"
       DisplaceOnUpgrade="TRUE" />
```

Adding Fields to Content Type

Now that the site columns are defined, they can be used to define the type. These will be used when displaying the prompt for adding new items to the list. They can also be used in defining views for the list. These topics will be covered in detail a little later. Add the following code to the Elements.xml file:

```
<FieldRefs>
  <FieldRef ID="{fa564e0f-0c70-4ab9-b863-0177e6ddd247}"
            Name="Title"
            DisplayName="Book Name" />
  <FieldRef ID="{F44EC4B6-0963-4fae-B2D0-9635720A806E}"
            Name="ISBN" />
  <FieldRef ID="{8D095FEE-0E82-4edf-8F5E-517393690661}"
            Name="BookAuthor" />
  <FieldRef ID="{30427EC2-E181-4206-8328-F305423932E3}"
            Name="Rating"/>
</FieldRefs>
```

The FieldRefs list includes the Title field. This is a base site column inherited by the base content type of Item, chosen when you created the Book type. The GUID for this field remains the same for all installations of SharePoint, so it is safe to copy the GUID from here.

The final Elements.xml file should look like Listing 9-1.

Listing 9-1. The final Elements.xml file

```
<?xml version="1.0" encoding="utf-8"?>
<Elements xmlns="http://schemas.microsoft.com/sharepoint/">
  <Field SourceID="http://schemas.microsoft.com/sharepoint/v3"
         ID="{F44EC4B6-0963-4fae-B2D0-9635720A806E}"
         Name="ISBN"
         DisplayName="ISBN"
         Group="Custom Columns"
         Type="Text"
         DisplaceOnUpgrade="TRUE" />
```

```
<Field SourceID="http://schemas.microsoft.com/sharepoint/v3"
       ID="{8D095FEE-0E82-4edf-8F5E-517393690661}"
       Name="BookAuthor"
       DisplayName="Author"
       Group="Custom Columns"
       Type="Text"
       DisplaceOnUpgrade="TRUE" />
<Field SourceID="http://schemas.microsoft.com/sharepoint/v3"
       ID="{30427EC2-E181-4206-8328-F305423932E3}"
       Name="Rating"
       DisplayName="Rating"
       Group="Custom Columns"
       Type="Number"
       DisplaceOnUpgrade="TRUE" />

<!-- Parent ContentType: Item (0x01) -->
<ContentType ID="0x010058fa1e4c58904b1abcbdf9d569921efa"
             Name="Book"
             Group="Custom Content Types"
             Description="My Content Type"
             Inherits="TRUE"
             Version="0">
  <FieldRefs>
    <FieldRef ID="{fa564e0f-0c70-4ab9-b863-0177e6ddd247}"
              Name="Title"
              DisplayName="Book Name" />
    <FieldRef ID="{F44EC4B6-0963-4fae-B2D0-9635720A806E}"
              Name="ISBN" />
    <FieldRef ID="{8D095FEE-0E82-4edf-8F5E-517393690661}"
              Name="BookAuthor" />
    <FieldRef ID="{30427EC2-E181-4206-8328-F305423932E3}"
              Name="Rating"/>
  </FieldRefs>
</ContentType>
</Elements>
```

Building the List Definition

Now you can define the list based on the Book content type. Right-click the project and click Add Item.
Select the "List Definition From Content Type" shown in Figure 9-10.

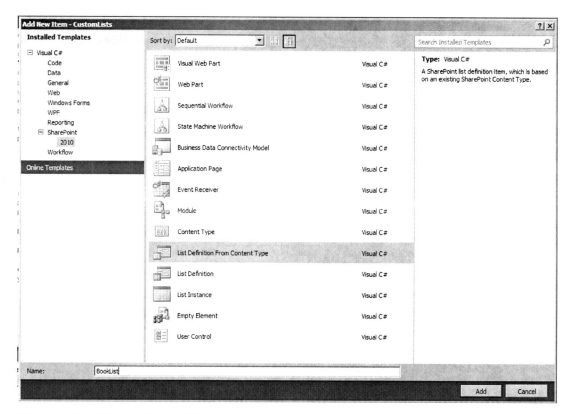

Figure 9-10. Adding the list definition to the project

Visual Studio now prompts for the List Definition Settings seen in Figure 9-11. Enter **BookList** as the display name of the list. Choose Book as the content type to use in the list.

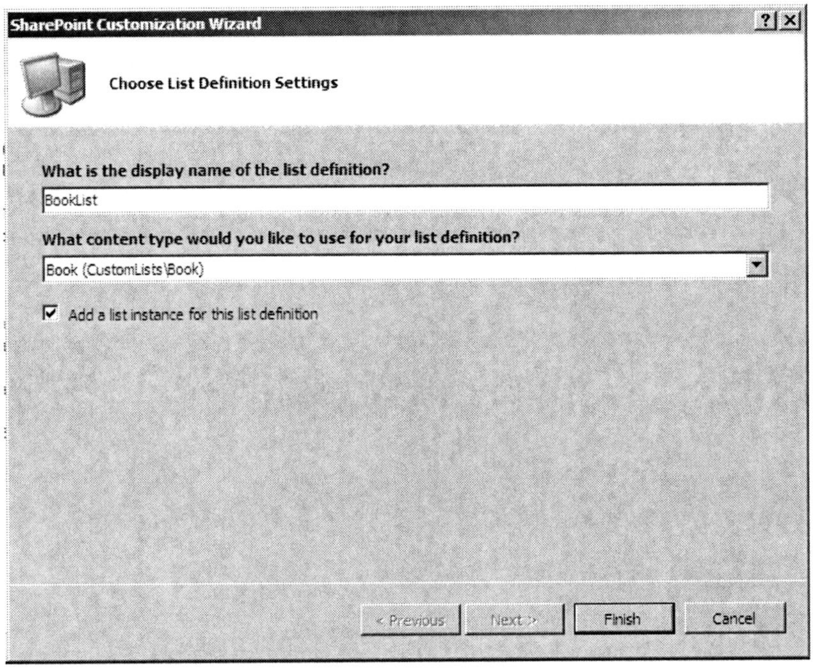

Figure 9-11. List definition settings

The list template will be added to the project. This will consist of some more XML files. To begin, look in the Elements.xml file just under the BookList item. This will contain a ListTemplate node. The primary concern for developers within this file is the Type attribute. The value must be set to something unique, but also over 10,000. The values 10,000 and below are reserved for internal types in SharePoint. For this project, Change the Name to **BookList**, the Type to **10100** and the DisplayName to **BookList**. The final file should appear as the following:

```
<?xml version="1.0" encoding="utf-8"?>
<Elements xmlns="http://schemas.microsoft.com/sharepoint/">
    <!-- Do not change the value of the Name attribute below. If it does not match the folder
name of the List Definition project item, an error will occur when the project is run. -->
    <ListTemplate
        Name="BookList"
        Type="10100"
        BaseType="0"
        OnQuickLaunch="TRUE"
        SecurityBits="11"
        Sequence="410"
        DisplayName="BookList"
        Description="My List Definition"
        Image="/_layouts/images/itgen.png"/>
</Elements>
```

Now, rename the List Instance to **Books,** as shown in Figure 9-12.

Figure 9-12. *Renamed list instance*

Check the `Elements.xml` file just below the `Books` item. This file contains the ListInstance node and its attributes. Ensure the TemplateType value is the same as what was set as the value for the Type of the ListTemplate. Change the Title to **Books,** the TemplateType to **10100** and the Url to **Lists/Books.** This file should contain the following code:

```
<?xml version="1.0" encoding="utf-8"?>
<Elements xmlns="http://schemas.microsoft.com/sharepoint/">
  <ListInstance Title="Books"
                OnQuickLaunch="TRUE"
                TemplateType="10100"
                Url="Lists/Books"
                Description="My List Instance">
  </ListInstance>
</Elements>
```

Open the `Schema.xml` file. When Visual Studio created this file, it copied the content type and columns that were defined in the content type definition. You can see this in the code at the beginning of the file.

```
<ContentTypes>
  <ContentType ID="0x010058fa1e4c58904b1abcbdf9d569921efa"
               Name="Book"
               Group="Custom Content Types"
               Description="My Content Type"
               Inherits="TRUE"
               Version="0">
    <FieldRefs>
      <FieldRef ID="{F44EC4B6-0963-4fae-B2D0-9635720A806E}" Name="ISBN" />
      <FieldRef ID="{8D095FEE-0E82-4edf-8F5E-517393690661}" Name="BookAuthor" />
      <FieldRef ID="{30427EC2-E181-4206-8329-F305423932E3}" Name="Rating" />
    </FieldRefs>
  </ContentType>
</ContentTypes>
```

The GUIDs should be the same as the ones set previously as well as the name attributes. You can also see that the fields were copied across as well.

```
<Fields>
    <Field SourceID="http://schemas.microsoft.com/sharepoint/v3"
           ID="{F44EC4B6-0963-4fae-B2D0-9635720A806E}"
           Name="ISBN"
           DisplayName="ISBN"
           Group="Custom Columns"
           Type="Text"
           DisplaceOnUpgrade="TRUE" />
    <Field SourceID="http://schemas.microsoft.com/sharepoint/v3"
           ID="{8D095FEE-0E82-4edf-8F5E-517393690661}"
           Name="BookAuthor"
           DisplayName="Author"
           Group="Custom Columns"
           Type="Text"
           DisplaceOnUpgrade="TRUE" />
    <Field SourceID="http://schemas.microsoft.com/sharepoint/v3"
           ID="{30427ec2-e181-4206-8329-f305423932e3}"
           Name="Rating"
           DisplayName="Rating"
           Group="Custom Columns"
           Type="Number"
           DisplaceOnUpgrade="TRUE" />
</Fields>
```

Now you can add the fields for display in the views for the list. Find the View where the BaseViewID = 1 and add the following field references just below the existing fields:

```
<FieldRef ID="{F44EC4B6-0963-4fae-B2D0-9635720A806E}"
          Name="ISBN"
          DisplayName="ISBN" />
<FieldRef ID="{8D095FEE-0E82-4edf-8F5E-517393690661}"
          Name="BookAuthor"
          DisplayName="Author" />
<FieldRef ID="{30427ec2-e181-4206-8328-f305423932e3}"
          Name="Rating"
          DisplayName="Rating" />
```

Only this view is changed in the Schema.xml file, so the full file doesn't need to be shown here. Compare the view to the following code to ensure everything is correct:

```
<View BaseViewID="1"
      Type="HTML"
      WebPartZoneID="Main"
      DisplayName="$Resources:core,objectiv_schema_mwsidcamlidC24;"
      DefaultView="TRUE"
      MobileView="TRUE"
      MobileDefaultView="TRUE"
      SetupPath="pages\viewpage.aspx"
      ImageUrl="/_layouts/images/generic.png"
```

```
        Url="AllItems.aspx">
    <Toolbar Type="Standard" />
    <XslLink Default="TRUE">main.xsl</XslLink>
    <RowLimit Paged="TRUE">30</RowLimit>
    <ViewFields>
      <FieldRef Name="Attachments">
      </FieldRef>
      <FieldRef Name="LinkTitle">
      </FieldRef>
      <FieldRef ID="{F44EC4B6-0963-4fae-B2D0-9635720A806E}"
                Name="ISBN"
                DisplayName="ISBN" />
      <FieldRef ID="{8D095FEE-0E82-4edf-8F5E-517393690661}"
                Name="BookAuthor"
                DisplayName="Author" />
      <FieldRef ID="{30427ec2-e181-4206-8328-f305423932e3}"
                Name="Rating"
                DisplayName="Rating" />
    </ViewFields>
    <Query>
      <OrderBy>
        <FieldRef Name="ID">
        </FieldRef>
      </OrderBy>
    </Query>
    <ParameterBindings>
      <ParameterBinding Name="NoAnnouncements" Location="Resource(wss,noXinviewofY_LIST)" />
      <ParameterBinding Name="NoAnnouncementsHowTo"
Location="Resource(wss,noXinviewofY_DEFAULT)" />
    </ParameterBindings>
</View>
```

Debug the Application

The project is now ready for debugging.

1. Press F5 to run the project in Debug mode. This should bring up your browser to your on-premise SharePoint site. First, ensure that the site columns and content type has been added properly.

2. Click Site Actions and navigate to Site Settings, as shown in Figure 9-13.

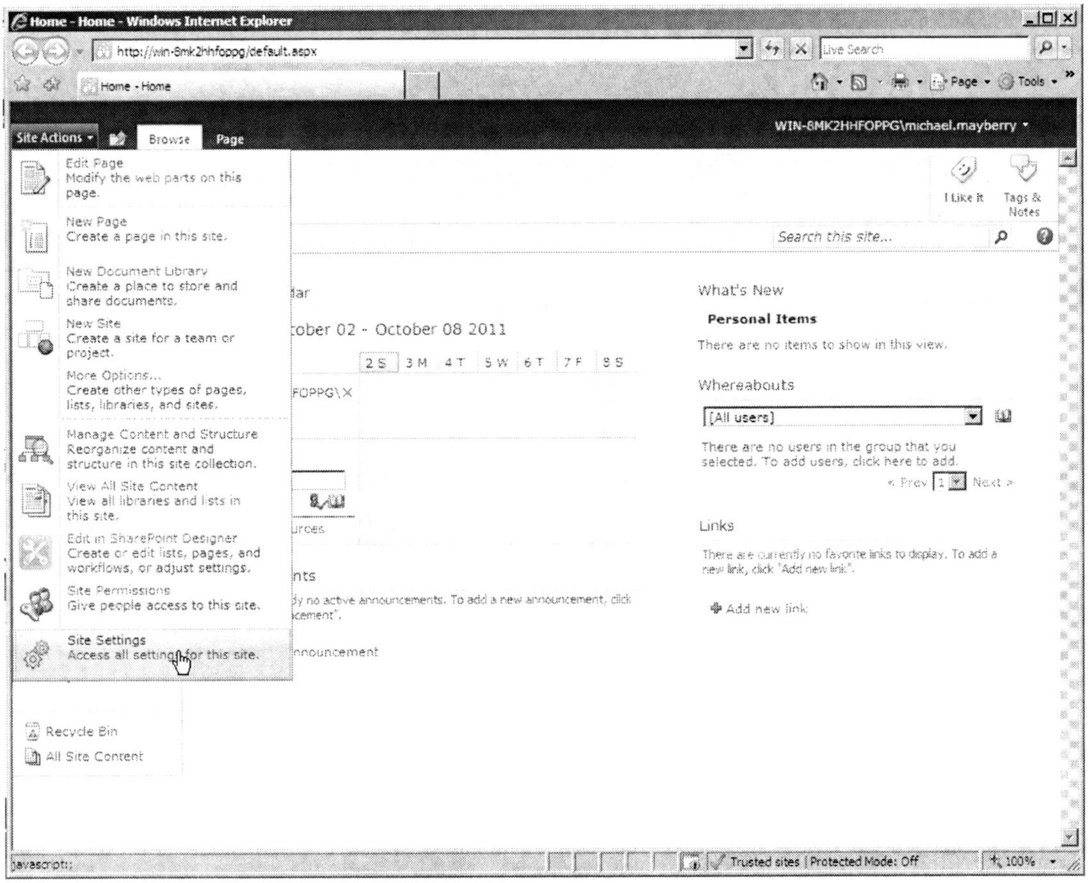

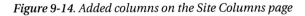

Figure 9-13. Navigating to Site Settings in SharePoint

3. Under the Galleries section, there are options for site columns and site content types. You should find something similar to what is shown in Figures 9-14 and 9-15 on those pages.

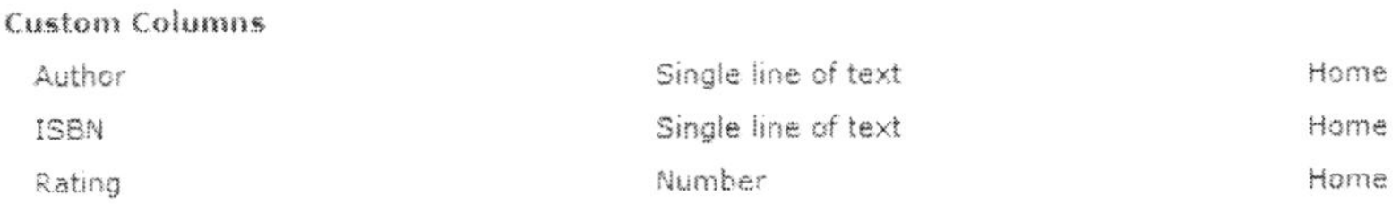

Custom Columns

Author	Single line of text	Home
ISBN	Single line of text	Home
Rating	Number	Home

Figure 9-14. Added columns on the Site Columns page

Custom Content Types

Book   Item   Home

Figure 9-15. Added type on the Content Type page

    4.   You should see the Books list added to the Quick Launch menu, as shown in Figure 9-16.

Lists

Group Calendar

Circulations

Phone Call Memo

Tasks

Links

Books

Figure 9-16. Added list to Quick Launch menu

    5.   Check to ensure the list works properly. Click the Books link. This takes you to the page for the list. It is empty since this is a new list. Now you can add the first item. Ensure the proper columns are requested.

- Title
- ISBN
- Author
- Rating

    6.   Click the "Add new item" link. A prompt similar to Figure 9-17 should appear.

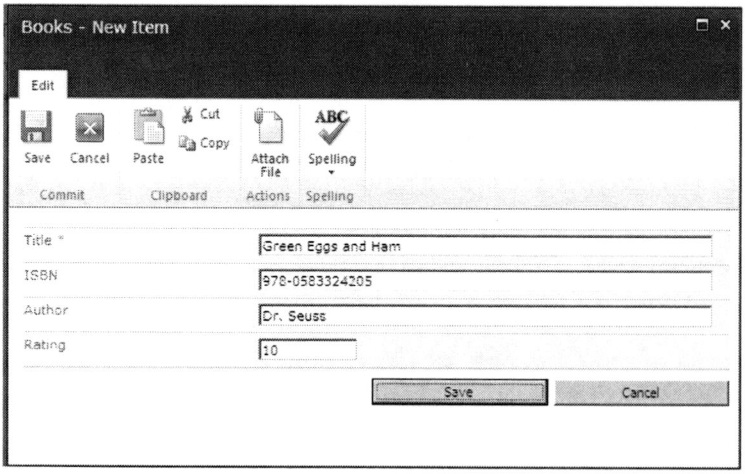

Figure 9-17. The "Add a new item" prompt

7. Click Save and the new book will be added to the list. Confirm the data was added correctly. It should appear as in Figure 9-18.

		Title	ISBN	Author	Rating
☐	🔲	Green Eggs and Ham ✪ NEW	978-0583324205	Dr. Suess	10

➕ Add new item

Figure 9-18. Newly added book to list

Deploying the Application

If everything works properly, the solution is ready for deployment to your remote SharePoint site. The debugging process built a package that can be used to deploy this list to your site.

1. In your browser, access the remote SharePoint site and navigate to the Site Settings page. Click the link for Solutions under the Galleries section on that page, as shown in Figure 9-19.

Galleries
Site columns
Site content types
Web parts
List templates
Master pages
Themes
Solutions

Figure 9-19. SharePoint Solutions link

2. You should now see the Solution Gallery page, so take a look at it. If you haven't uploaded any solutions prior to this one, you will see an empty list like the one in Figure 9-20.

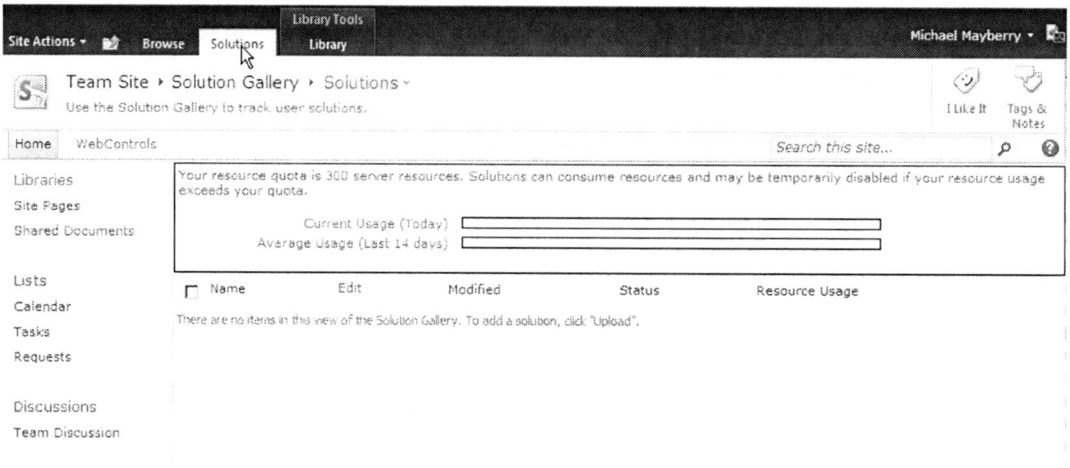

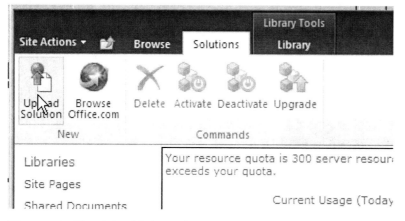

Figure 9-20. SharePoint Solution Gallery

3.   Click the Solutions tab at the top of the page to bring up the Solutions ribbon. Figure 9-21 shows the Upload Solution button to click.

Figure 9-21. The Upload Solution button on the Solutions ribbon

4.   Click the Browse button and navigate to your project folder. The package file you need to upload is in the bin\Debug folder. Choose it, as shown in Figure 9-22.

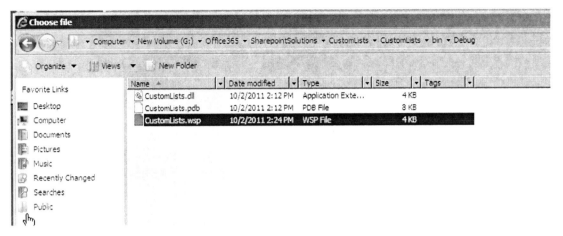

Figure 9-22. Package file for uploading to SharePoint

5. Your screen should look similar to Figure 9-23, with the path to your project. Click OK to upload the solution.

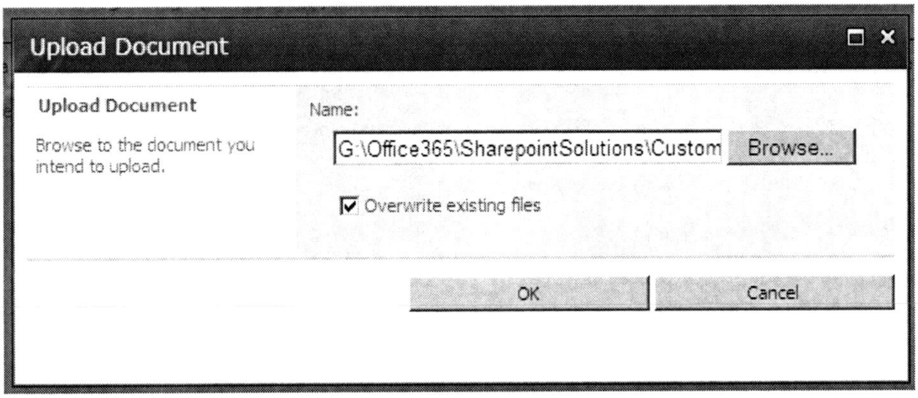

Figure 9-23. Upload Document dialog for solution upload

6. You will be given the opportunity to activate the solution in the next prompt, as shown in Figure 9-24. Click the Activate button.

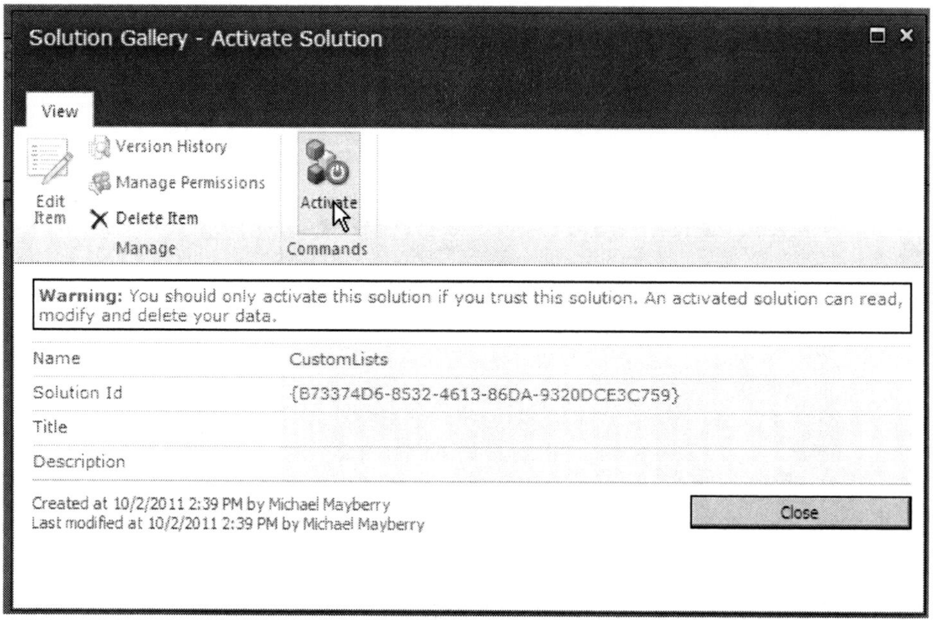

Solution Gallery - Activate Solution ☐ ✕

View

Edit
Item

📋 Version History

🔲 Manage Permissions

✕ Delete Item

Manage

Activate

Commands

Warning: You should only activate this solution if you trust this solution. An activated solution can read, modify and delete your data.

Name	CustomLists
Solution Id	{B73374D6-8532-4613-86DA-9320DCE3C759}
Title	
Description	

Created at 10/2/2011 2:39 PM by Michael Mayberry
Last modified at 10/2/2011 2:39 PM by Michael Mayberry

Close

Figure 9-24. The Activate prompt

7. Now you need to activate the feature that was just uploaded and installed. Navigate to the Site Settings page and look for the Site Actions section shown in Figure 9-25. Click the "Manage site features" link.

Site Actions

Manage site features
Save site as template
Reset to site definition
Delete this site

Figure 9-25. Site Actions options

8. SharePoint now presents the Features page, listing all the features available for your site. You should find the CustomLists Feature1 option, as shown in Figure 9-26. To install the site columns, content type, and list you created, you need to activate the feature. Click the Activate button next to the CustomLists Feature1 item.

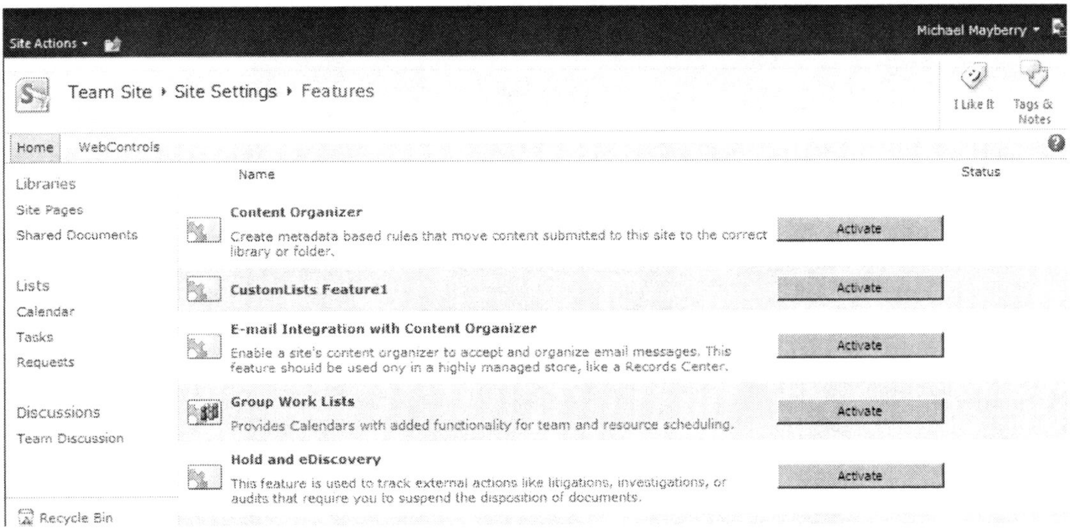

Figure 9-26. SharePoint features page

Using the Application

The application is now available on your remote SharePoint site. You can confirm that the site columns and content type are present by looking at the Site Settings page and following the appropriate links. You should also see the Books list added to your Quick Launch menu, as shown in Figure 9-27.

Lists

Calendar

Tasks

Requests

Books

Figure 9-27. Books list added to the Quick Launch menu

Navigate to the Books list and click the Add new item link to bring up the prompt for a new Book. Ensure the correct fields are requested and enter the book information shown in Figure 9-28.

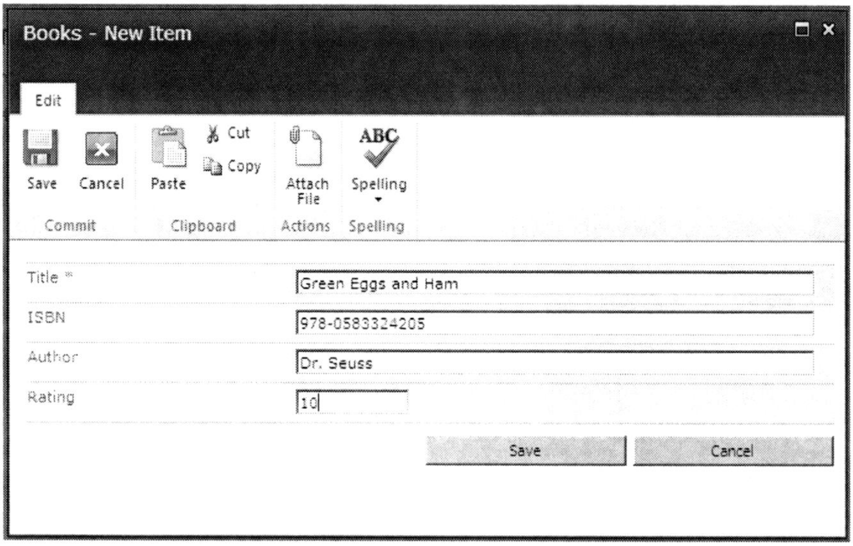

Figure 9-28. New Book item

Confirm that the book has been added correctly. Check the columns and the data to see that everything worked properly. Your screen should appear similar to Figure 9-29. Add a few more books and make sure all is working as expected.

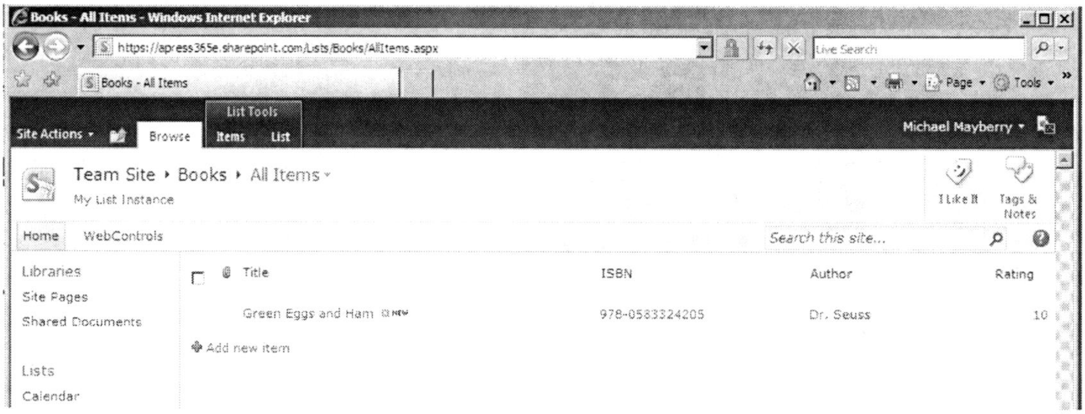

Figure 9-29. New Book added to the list

Your list is now available for all SharePoint users to add to the book collection. You can manage this just like any other list on SharePoint.

■ **TO DO** Repeat the steps for deploying the solution for your on-premise SharePoint site as well. Visual Studio retracts the solution at the end of the debugging session, so the application is not available. You will continue to build solutions that expect this list to be present on the SharePoint site, so you need to deploy the application locally as well.

Populating the List with an Event Receiver

It's helpful that the list is available, but it's empty. One option is to manually enter all of the data into the site through the browser, but that will take time and is prone to error. Another option is to build an event receiver to populate the list for you.

1. Start by creating an Empty SharePoint Project, as shown in Figure 9-30. Enter Events for the project name and set the location on your local drive where you can find the solution once Visual Studio creates the files.

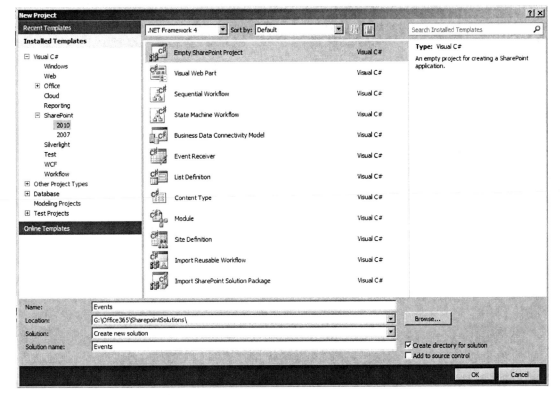

Figure 9-30. Creating the events SharePoint solution

2. Visual Studio will prompt for the SharePoint site to use for debugging. Enter the location for your on-premise site and select "Deploy as a sandboxed solution" option so this can be deployed to SharePoint Online. Once your screen looks similar to Figure 9-31, click Finish.

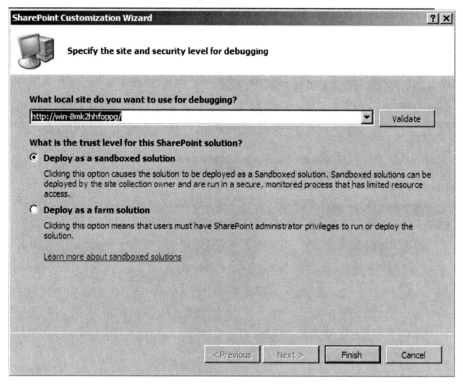

Figure 9-31. Setting up debugging for the sandboxed solution

3. You are going to create an event receiver. These are made available as a part of a feature, so your project needs a feature. Right-click the Features folder and click Add Feature, as shown in Figure 9-32.

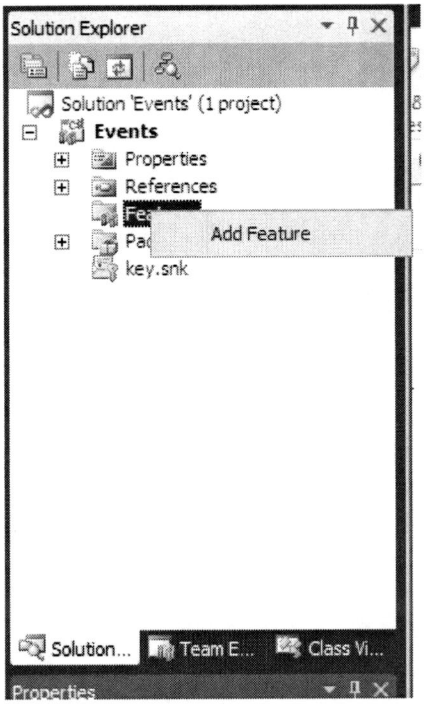

Figure 9-32. Adding a feature to the SharePoint project

4. For this project, you will not adjust the feature settings. Once the feature has been created and is displayed on your screen, right-click the feature in the Solution Explorer and click Add Event Receiver. Figure 9-33 shows where this option is located.

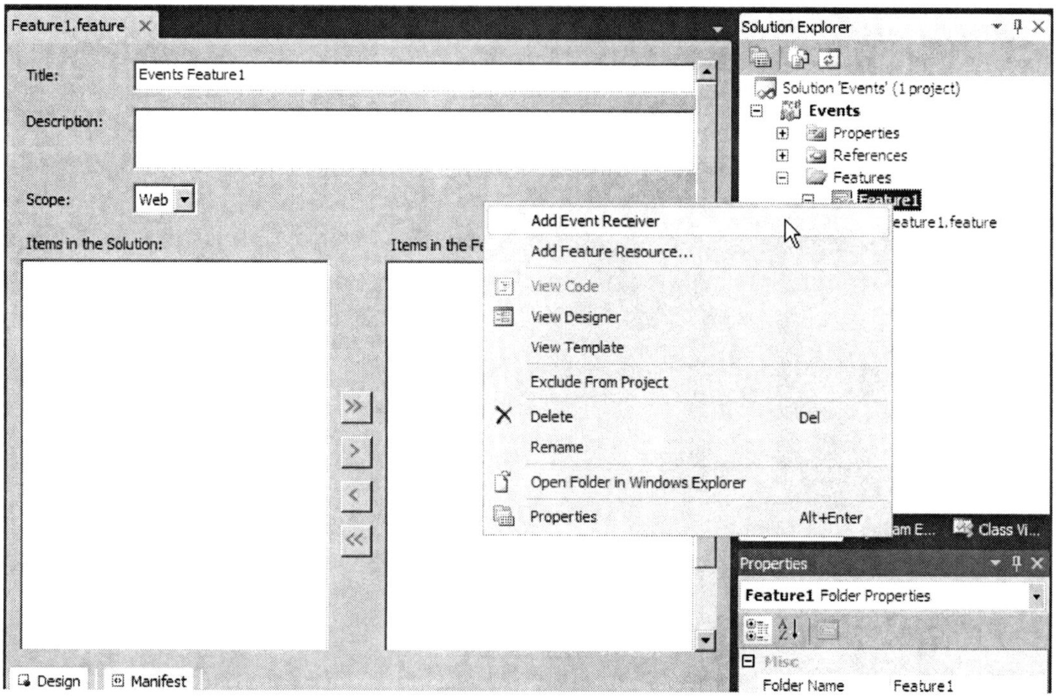

Figure 9-33. Adding an event receiver to a feature in a SharePoint project

5. You should now have Feature1.EventReceiver.cs open in Visual Studio. You will adjust this file to contain the code to populate the Book list you created in the previous section. When first created, this file contains the Feature1EventReceiver class. This class contains multiple commented methods. Uncomment the FeatureActivated method. You will add the code to this method, which will populate the list once the feature has been activated.

Add the following code to the method:

```
using (SPWeb web = (SPWeb)properties.Feature.Parent)
{

}
```

6. This code references the site running the feature. This site contains the list and will allow you to access that list for manipulation. Add the following code to access the list and add an item. SPList is the SharePoint object that refers to lists. The list is referenced by name, "Books." This returns the Books list that was deployed earlier. The Items collection contains any items already contained in the list. That collection also provides the Add() method for inserting additional items. The SPListItem object refers to the items within the

list or a new item as in this case. This code references the columns by name and sets their values. The Update() method saves the changes to SharePoint.

```
SPList bookList = web.Lists["Books"];

SPListItem book1 = bookList.Items.Add();
book1["Title"] = "The Invisble Man";
book1["ISBN"] = "1450517935";
book1["BookAuthor"] = "H.G. Wells";
book1["Rating"] = "7";
book1.Update();
```

7. The list should contain more than one or two items, so add the code shown in Listing 9-2 for the full method implementation:

Listing 9-2. The complete event receiver implementation

```
public override void FeatureActivated(SPFeatureReceiverProperties properties)
        {
            using (SPWeb web = (SPWeb)properties.Feature.Parent)
            {
                SPList bookList = web.Lists["Books"];

                SPListItem book1 = bookList.Items.Add();
                book1["Title"] = "The Invisble Man";
                book1["ISBN"] = "1450517935";
                book1["BookAuthor"] = "H.G. Wells";
                book1["Rating"] = "7";
                book1.Update();

                SPListItem book2 = bookList.Items.Add();
                book2["Title"] = "David Copperfield";
                book2["ISBN"] = "0679783415";
                book2["BookAuthor"] = "Charles Dickens";
                book2["Rating"] = "6";
                book2.Update();

                SPListItem book3 = bookList.Items.Add();
                book3["Title"] = "The Adventures of Sherlock Holmes";
                book3["ISBN"] = "979-0486474915";
                book3["BookAuthor"] = "Sir Arthur Conan Doyle";
                book3["Rating"] = "9";
                book3.Update();

                SPListItem book4 = bookList.Items.Add();
                book4["Title"] = "The Count of Monte Cristo";
                book4["ISBN"] = "979-1613820971";
                book4["BookAuthor"] = "Alexander Dumas";
                book4["Rating"] = "7";
                book4.Update();
```

```
                 SPListItem book5 = bookList.Items.Add();
                 book5["Title"] = "The Jungle Book";
                 book5["ISBN"] = "979-0553211993";
                 book5["BookAuthor"] = "Rudyard Kipling";
                 book5["Rating"] = "6";
                 book5.Update();
             }
         }
```

8. Once the method is complete, you are ready to debug your application. Ensure your project builds without issue, then press F5 to start the debugger. This will package the solution, deploy it to your on-premise SharePoint site, and activate the feature. That activation will call your method, so the list populates without any further action on your part. Your browser should come up and access your local SharePoint site. The Books list should look similar to Figure 9-34.

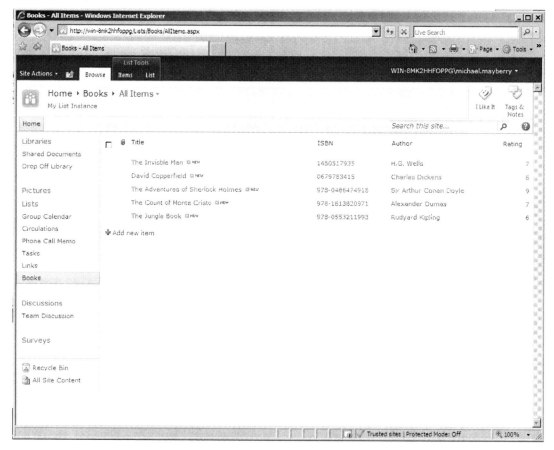

Figure 9-34. Debugging the event receiver that populates the Books list

9. If everything is successful, the solution is ready for deployment to the remote SharePoint site. Figure 9-35 shows where to generate the package to upload.

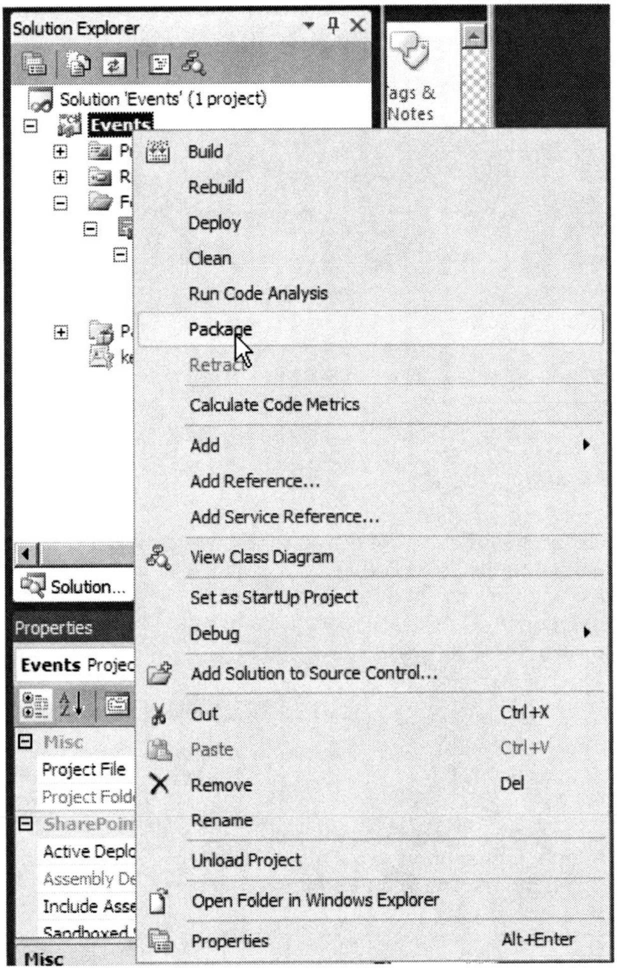

Figure 9-35. Create a package for a SharePoint project

10. Just as in the previous section, bring up your browser and go to your remote SharePoint site. Navigate to the Site Settings page and click on the Solutions option, which takes you to the Solution Gallery. Click the Solutions tab at the top of the page to view the Solution ribbon. Click the Upload Solution button. You will find the package for upload in the Events\bin\Debug folder of your project, as seen in Figure 9-36.

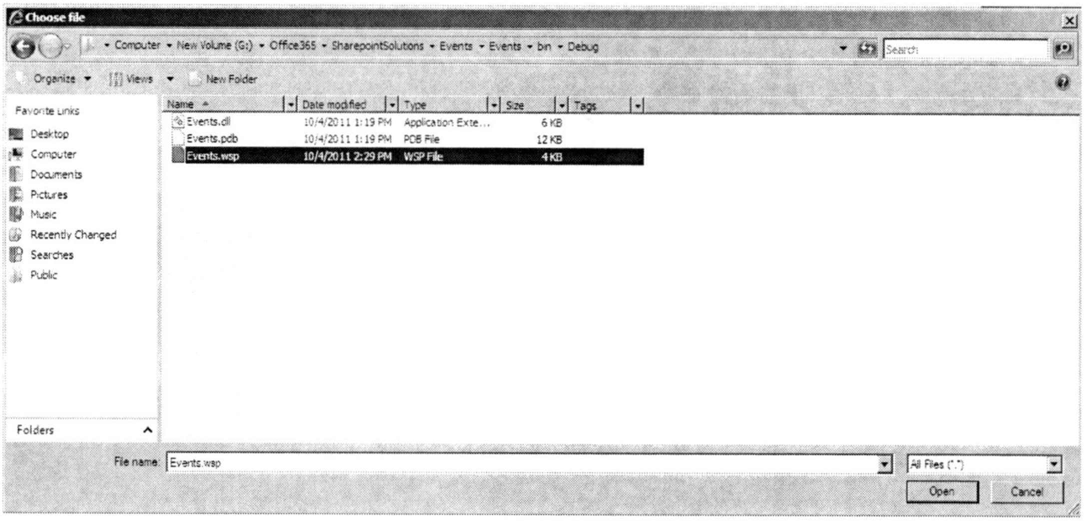

Figure 9-36. Event package for uploading to SharePoint

11. Click the Activate option on the next prompt and close the window. The Events feature has now been uploaded and added to the SharePoint site. It awaits activation. Navigate to the Features list and click the Activate button next to the Events Feature1 item, as shown in Figure 9-37.

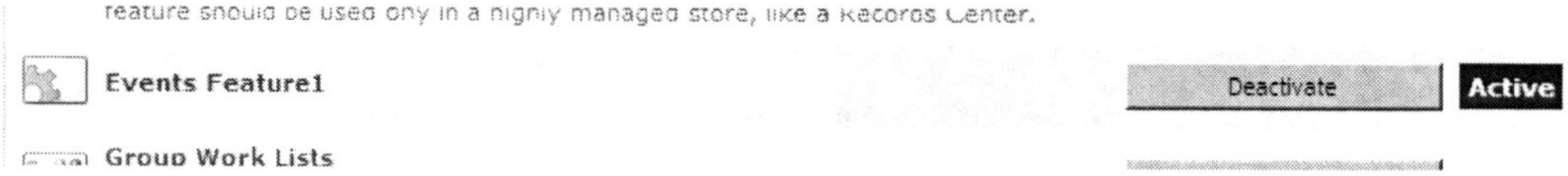

Figure 9-37. Activating the Events Feature

12. Click on the Books list in the Quick Launch menu and view the added items. Figure 9-38 shows the populated list from the remote SharePoint site.

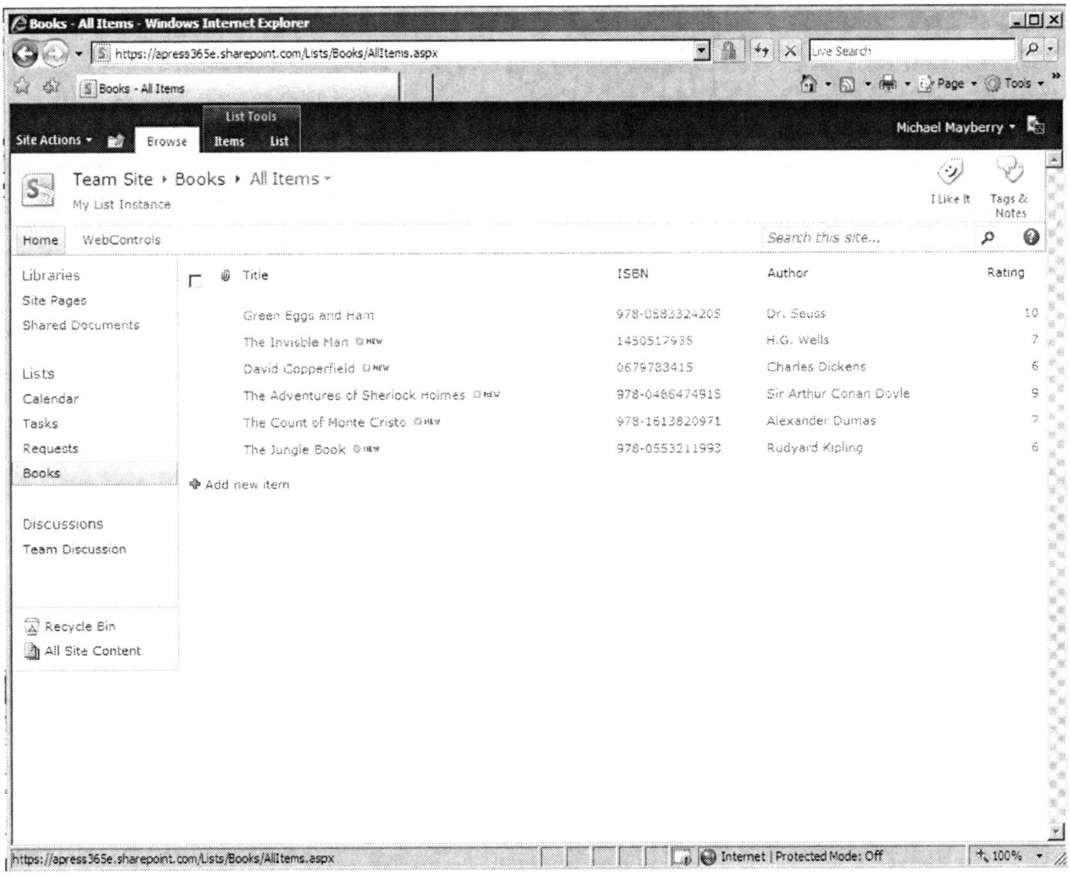

Figure 9-38. Populated Books list

Summary

You have been introduced to SharePoint sandboxed solutions. This chapter showed you how to declaratively create content for your SharePoint site. You created the following types of content:

- Site columns
- Content type
- List

   You debugged the SharePoint sandboxed solution against the local, on-premise site and then deployed the package to your remote SharePoint Online site. You then created an event receiver to populate the list. That sandboxed solution was also debugged and deployed using the same procedure. The next two chapters will discuss more advanced topics, building upon the applications created in this chapter.

Developing SharePoint Applications

Adding content to your SharePoint site is easily done in Visual Studio 2010. However, developers like to make things happen. Code is written to solve problems, and that typically involves action, not just content. Developers are tasked with extending functionality of a given product or set of technologies. SharePoint Online and Visual Studio provide the environment to fulfill that assignment. This chapter will focus on building custom functionality into your SharePoint Online site.

First, you will look at Web Parts. Custom Web Parts allow you to add your own controls to your SharePoint site. You will build a Visual Web Part and deploy it out to your SharePoint Online site. Then you will use LINQ to SharePoint to simplify the code within that project.

Then you will turn your focus to workflows. Workflows can implement business processes or automate communication functions based on data within the SharePoint environment. Adding customized steps within those workflows extends SharePoint to meet very diverse needs. You will build a custom action to implement within a workflow using SharePoint Designer and deploy that out to your SharePoint online site as well.

Note Make sure that Visual Studio 2010 Service Pack 1 is installed on your SharePoint development machine. This update corrects some issues that affect developing against SharePoint.

The Visual Web Part

The Visual Web Part combines a custom UI with functionality. Essentially, it is a user control developed for a SharePoint page, providing the ability to customize the look and feel of your site. Along with the visual effects, functionality is gained as well. This project consists of a filter for the Books list deployed in the previous chapter. This Web Part will allow the user to filter the books by author.

> **Note** Sandboxed Solutions, which must be used for SharePoint Online, do not allow Visual Web Parts directly. There is no item template or project template for Visual Web Parts within Visual Studio 2010. You must install SharePoint Power Tools for Visual Studio 2010. This set of templates and extensions is available online in the Visual Studio Gallery. This allows you to develop a Visual Web Part for a Sandboxed Solution.

Creating the Project

Start by creating an empty SharePoint project. Name the project **VisualWebParts** and set the location where it is easily found, as shown in Figure 10-1.

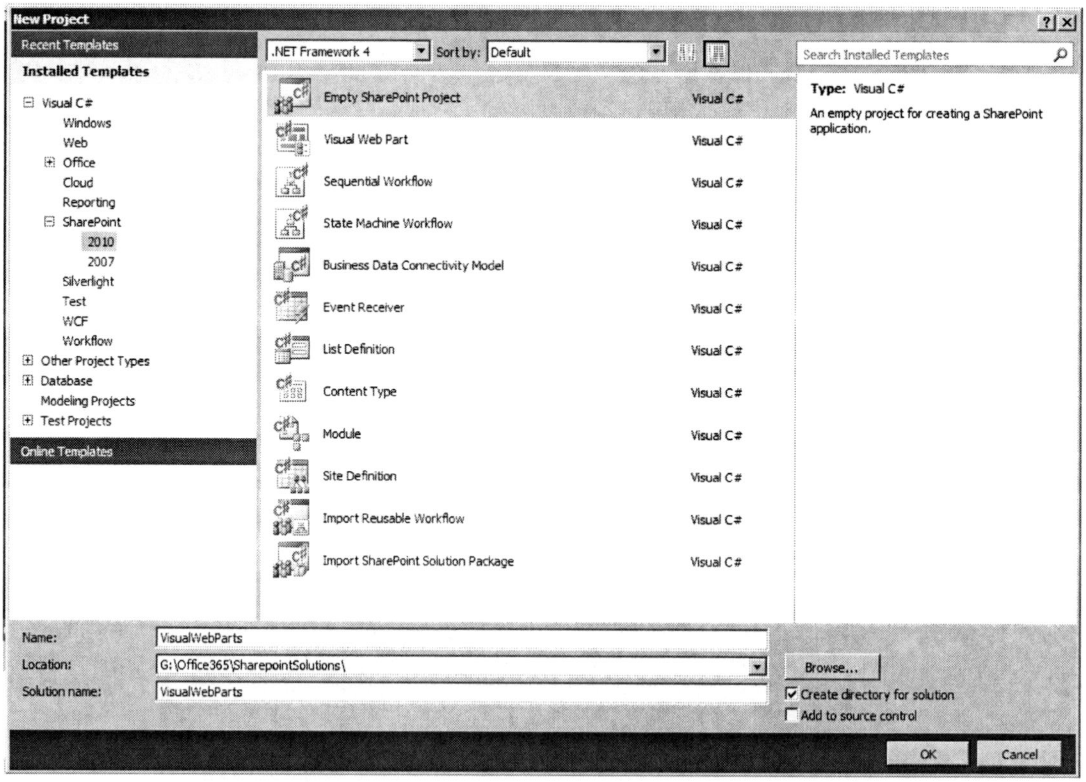

Figure 10-1. Create an empty SharePoint solution.

As mentioned in Chapter 9, Visual Studio needs to be installed on a local SharePoint server for development. Debugging runs against this local installation. When the solution performs as desired, it can be deployed to SharePoint Online. Enter the address of your on-premise SharePoint site and select Sandboxed solution. Your screen should look similar to Figure 10-2. Click Finish.

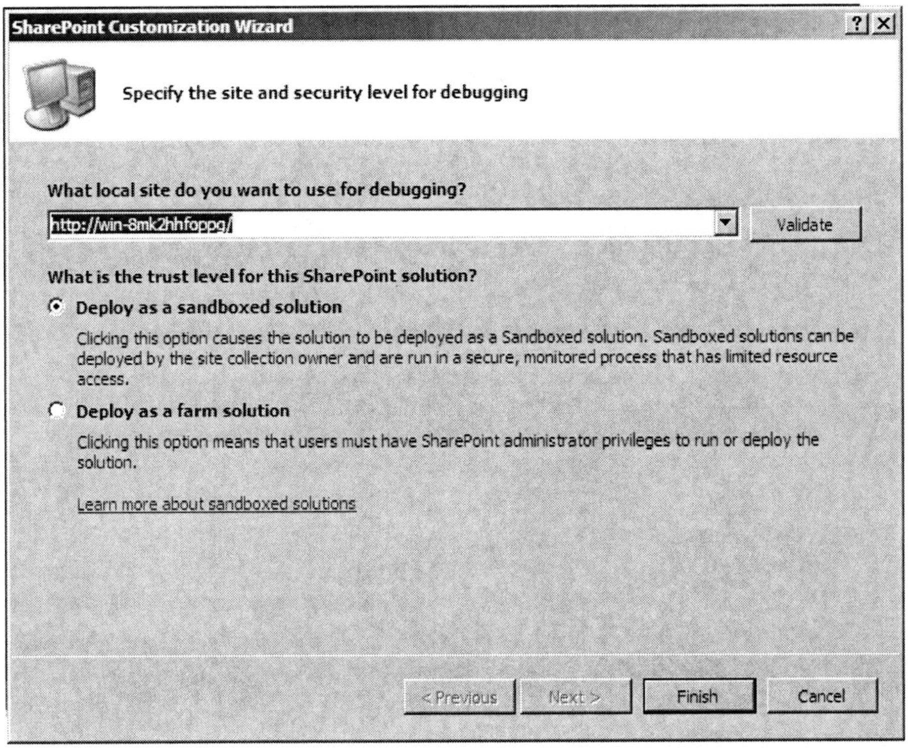

Figure 10-2. Set up the project for debugging.

Adding the Visual Web Part

Right-click the project and click Add New Item. Select the Visual Web Part (Sandboxed) and name the item **FindBooks**, as shown in Figure 10-3.

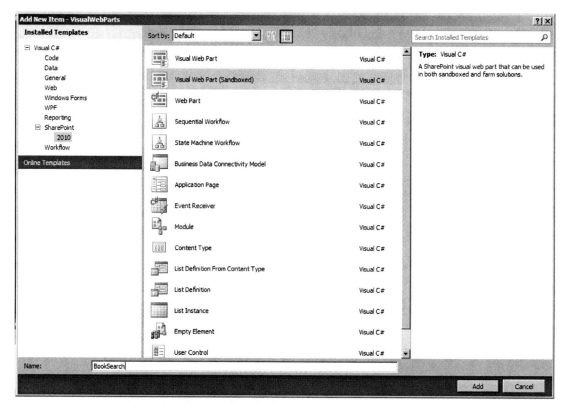

Figure 10-3. Adding a Visual Web Part to a sandboxed solution

Visual Studio has added the FindBooks web part to the project. The added item(s) should look like Figure 10-4.

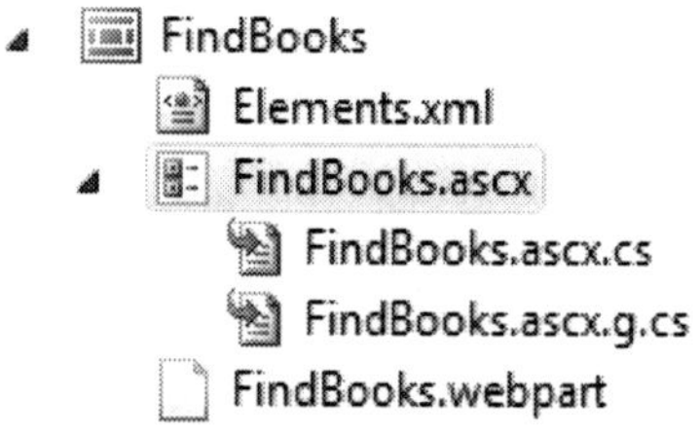

▲ 🔳 FindBooks
  📄 Elements.xml
  ▲ 📄 FindBooks.ascx
      📄 FindBooks.ascx.cs
      📄 FindBooks.ascx.g.cs
    📄 FindBooks.webpart

Figure 10-4. Visual Web Part files added to SharePoint project

The structure of the Web Part is similar to a web control. There is the markup file that ends in `.ascx` and the codebehind file that ends with the `.cs` file extension. Open the `FindBooks.ascx` file. Add the following code:

```
<p>
    Filter Books By Author:
    <asp:DropDownList ID="ddlAuthor" runat="server" />
    <asp:Button ID="btnSearch" runat="server" Text="Get Books" OnClick="btnSearch_Click" />
</p>
<p>
    Results:
    <asp:GridView ID="gvResults" runat="server" />
</p>
```

The Web Part contains a drop-down list called ddlAuthor that will display all of the authors in the Books list. The button, btnSearch, will call the code that searches the list for items with an author that matches the selected item in the drop-down list. The grid view called gvResults will display the found items.

Open the FindBooks.ascx.cs file and add the following code to the Page_Load() method:

```
if (!Page.IsPostBack)
{
    PopulateAuthorList();
}
```

This code calls PopulateAuthorList() on the first call of the page to ensure that the drop-down list contains data for filtering the list. Add the following method definition for populating the ddlAuthor control:

```
protected void PopulateAuthorList()
{
    SPList bookList = SPContext.Current.Web.Lists["Books"];

    SPQuery query = new SPQuery();
    query.ViewFieldsOnly = true;
    query.ViewFields = "<FieldRef Name='BookAuthor' />";
    query.RowLimit = 20;

    DataTable authorTable = bookList.GetItems(query).GetDataTable();
    DataView authorView = new DataView(authorTable);
    DataTable distinctAuthors = authorView.ToTable(true, "BookAuthor");

    gvResults.DataSource = distinctAuthors;
    gvResults.DataBind();
}
```

This code first gets the Books list from the SharePoint hosting the Visual Web Part using the SPContext.Current.Web object. The Lists property of this object contains the lists for the current site. Then a SPQuery object is built. The only field needed is the BookAuthor, so the ViewFields property value limits the results to only include that single field.

The GetItems() method of the bookList (SPList) object then returns the results of the query. The GetDataTable() method returns the results as a DataTable object. The items may not be distinct. If there is more than one book in your list with the same author, they would be listed multiple times. Using a DataView, you can reduce the list to only the distinct values; to do so, you create a new DataView and convert that back to a DataTable, but only bringing over the distinct values. These results are bound to the drop-down list and set to display the author.

■ **Note** The result set from the GetItems() method does not directly bind to a user control. Instead, use the GetDataTable() method to return an object that can bind directly.

Add the following code to provide functionality to the button click event:

```
protected void btnSearch_Click(object sender, EventArgs e)
{
    SPList bookList = SPContext.Current.Web.Lists["Books"];

    SPQuery query = new SPQuery();
    query.ViewFieldsOnly = true;
    query.ViewFields = "<FieldRef Name='Title' /><FieldRef Name='BookAuthor' />";
    query.Query = "<Where><Eq><FieldRef Name='BookAuthor'/><Value Type='Text'>" +
            ddlAuthor.SelectedItem.Text + "</Value></Eq></Where>";
    query.RowLimit = 20;

    gvResults.DataSource = bookList.GetItems(query).GetDataTable();
    gvResults.DataBind();
}
```

This code gets the Books list and builds a SPQuery object just as the previous segment does. However, this time both the Title and BookAuthor fields are returned for display in the grid. The Query property holds the CAML statement to return the items that have a matching BookAuthor to the value selected in the drop-down list. The results are returned to a DataTable and bound to the grid view control.

■ **Note** Collaborative Application Markup Language (CAML) is the XML-based language used to work with SharePoint data. It is used in Microsoft SharePoint Foundation to define the data for SharePoint sites. The Query Schema is used to define queries against list data. Find more information about CAML at http://msdn.microsoft.com/en-us/library/ms426449.aspx.

Debugging the Project

Press F5 to debug the solution. Doing this packages and deploys the Visual Web Part to your on-premise SharePoint site. The Web Part has been deployed, but nothing is using it yet. First, the web part needs to be added to a page.

■ **Note** Remember, Sandboxed Solutions do not allow Visual Web Parts, so this solution has been deployed as a regular Web Part. This will be available to deploy to your SharePoint Online site.

---

1. Pressing F5 should open your browser to your on-premise SharePoint site. To test your solution, start by creating a new page, as shown in Figure 10-5.

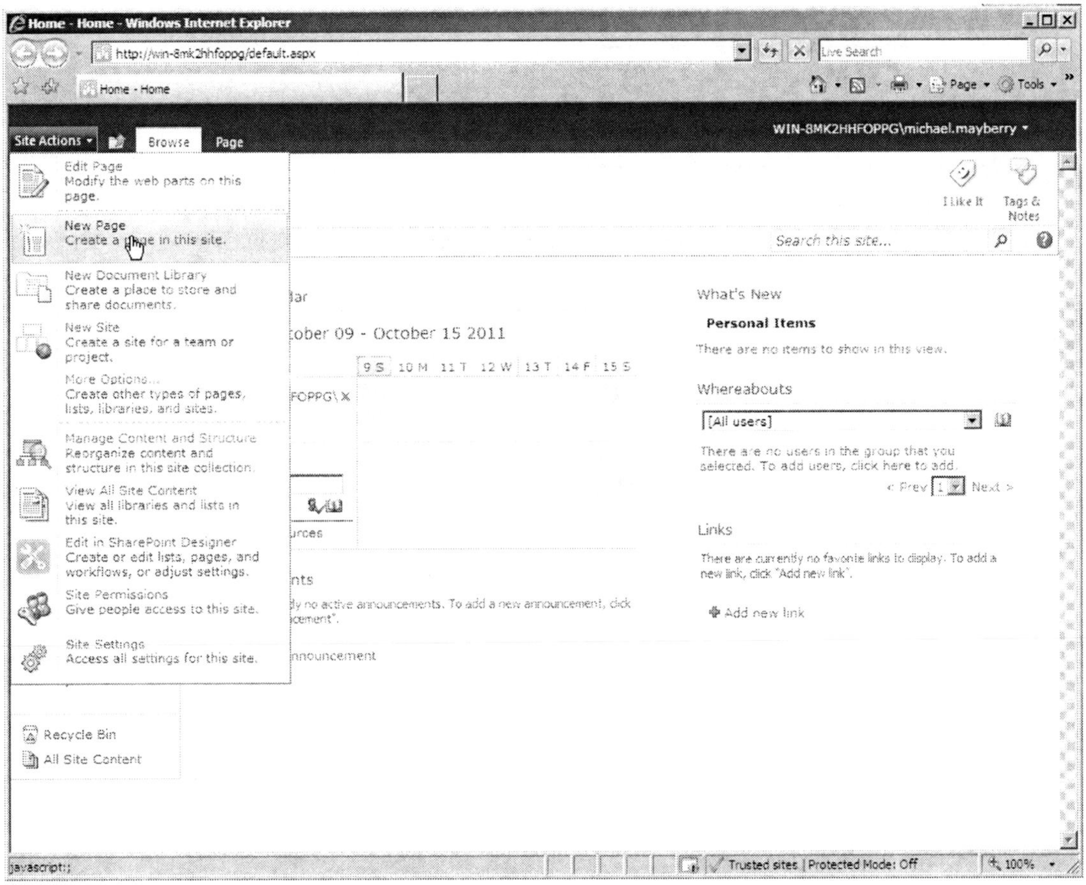

Figure 10-5. Create a new page.

2. Name the page **VisualWebPartTest**, as shown in Figure 10-6.

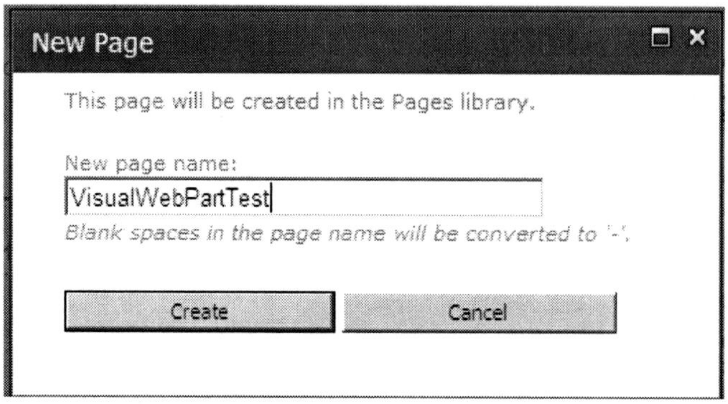

Figure 10-6. New page name prompt

3. Navigate to the Editing Tools in the ribbon and select the Insert tab. This lists all the types of items that can be inserted into a page, including a Web Part. Select the Web Part, as shown in Figure 10-7.

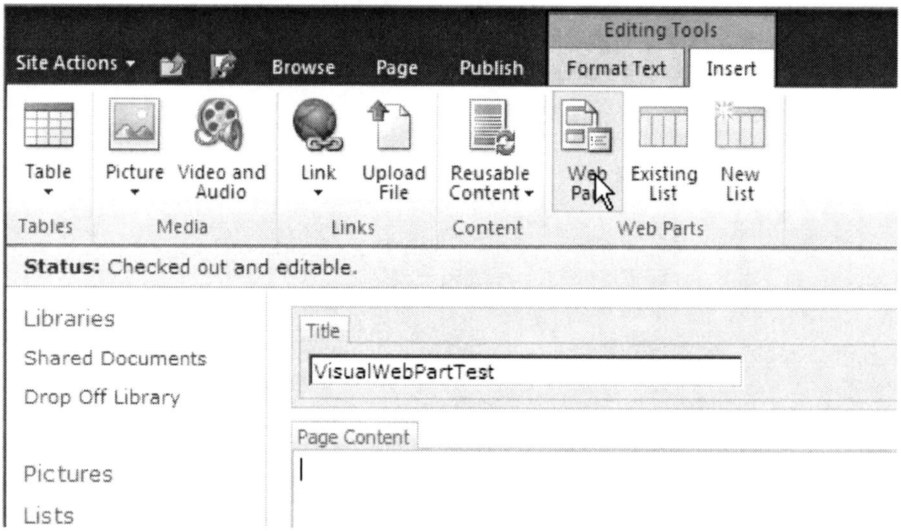

Figure 10-7. Adding a Web Part to a page

4. You will now see the Web Parts available to insert into your page. Select the Custom Category. This will list the FindBooks Web Part deployed when debugging started. You should see something similar to Figure 10-8. Select the FindBooks item and click Add.

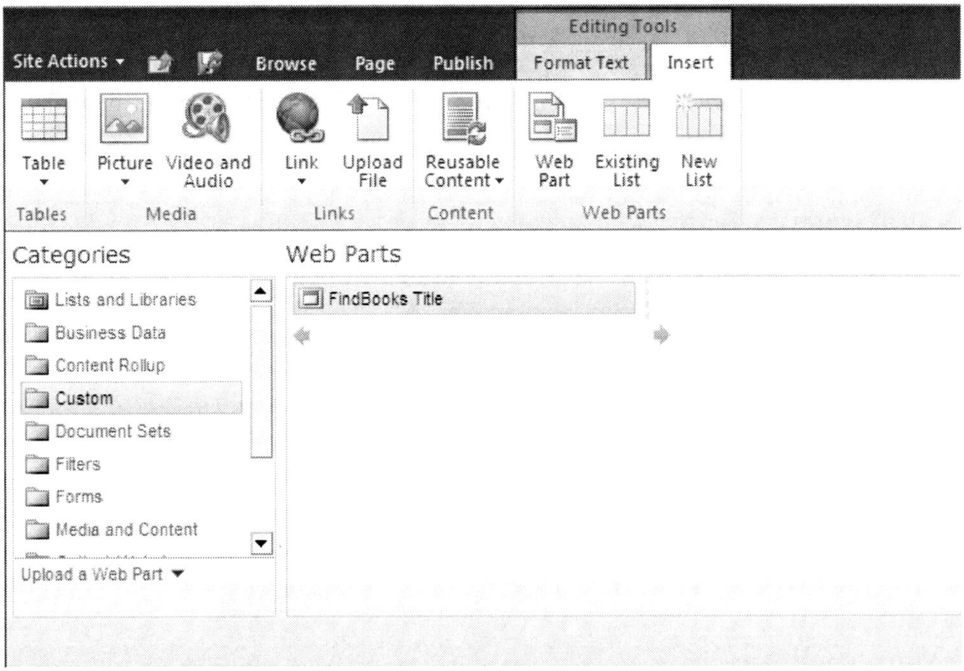

Figure 10-8. *Select the Custom Web Part*

5. Navigate to the page and test the filter you created. The drop-down list should list the authors. Select one and click Get Books. This should return a list of books by the selected author. The results should appear as in Figure 10-9.

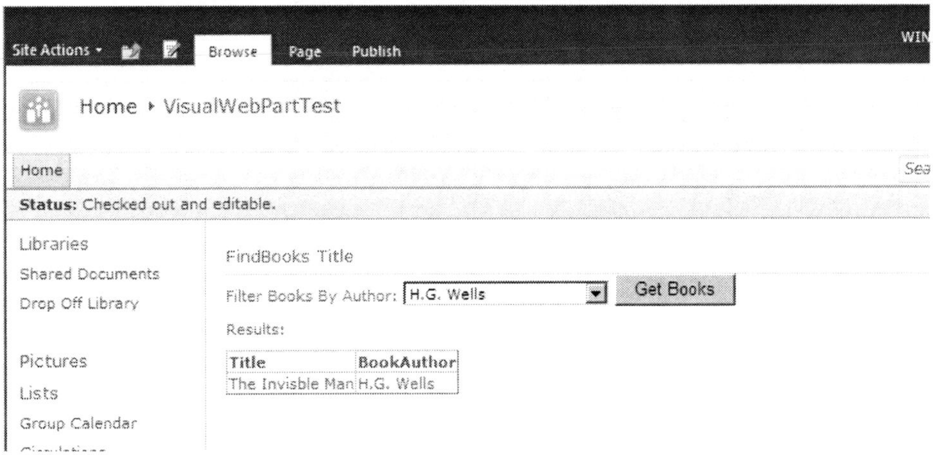

Figure 10-9. *Web Part results*

Deploying the Solution

Once everything works properly, your solution is ready to deploy to your SharePoint Online site. Deploying the solution is similar to the process from the previous chapter, so I will simply mention the steps here:

1. Right-click your solution in Visual Studio and click Package.

2. Open your browser and go to your SharePoint Online site.

3. Navigate to Site Settings and click the Solutions link, shown in Figure 10-10.

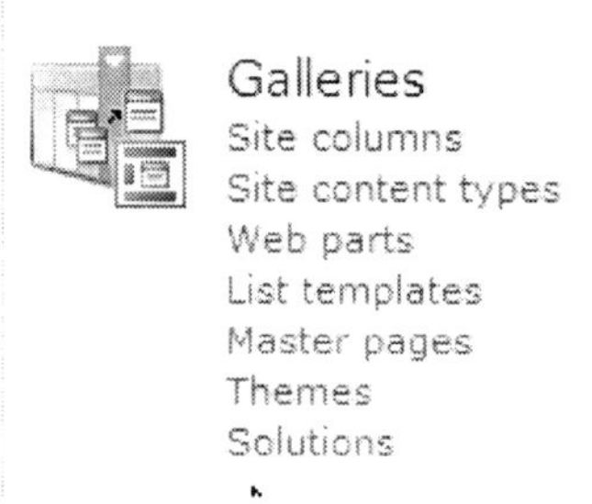

Galleries
Site columns
Site content types
Web parts
List templates
Master pages
Themes
Solutions

Figure 10-10. Solutions link in SharePoint Online

4. Click the Solutions tab on the ribbon and click Upload Solution, shown in Figure 10-11

Figure 10-11. Uploading a solution to SharePoint Online

5. Click Browse and find the package file (`.wsp`) in the solution folder under the `\bin\debug` folder.

6. Activate the solution when prompted.

7. Create a new page. Figure 10-12 illustrates adding the Web Part to the page.

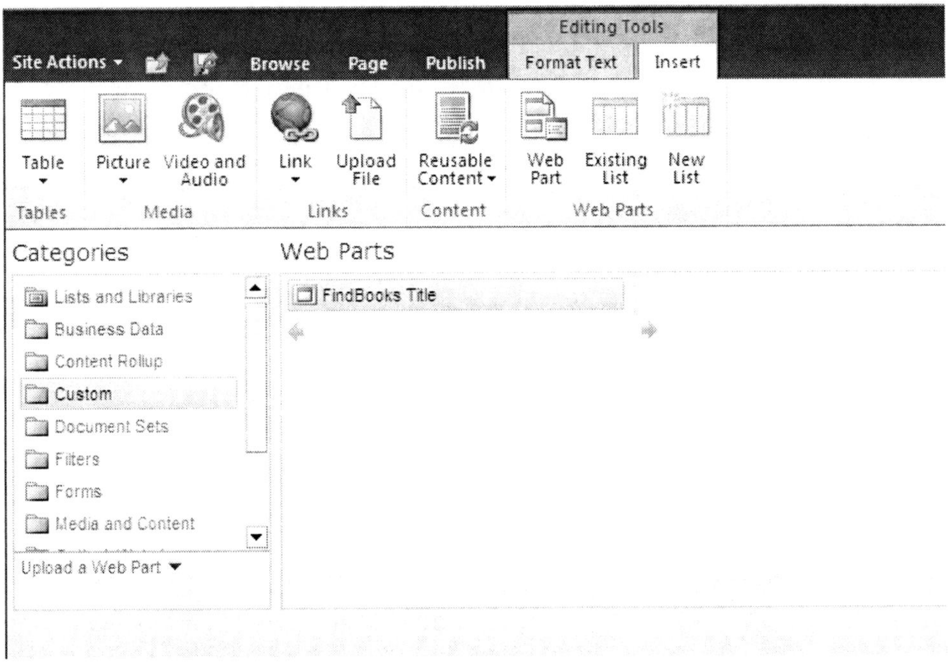

Figure 10-12. Adding the custom Web Part to a page

8. Navigate to the new page and test. The results should look exactly the same as your on-premise site (Figure 10-13).

Figure 10-13. Visual Web Part test in SharePoint Online

LINQ to SharePoint

Language Integrated Query (LINQ) provides the ability to query just about any type of data collection. Uses include LINQ to Objects, LINQ to XML, LINQ to SQL, and now LINQ to SharePoint. Using LINQ to access SharePoint content makes things quite a bit simpler. This next section will demonstrate this point by modifying the previous Visual Web Part to use LINQ to SharePoint to accomplish the exact same functionality.

Using SPMetal

SharePoint provides a command-line tool called SPMetal that generates classes for accessing SharePoint content. This tool is located in %ProgramFiles%\Common Files\Microsoft Shared\web server extensions\14\BIN.

If you run this SPMetal with no parameters, the following instructions are returned:

```
Microsoft (R) SharePoint LINQ Code Generator 2008

for Microsoft (R) .NET Framework version 3.5

Copyright (C) Microsoft Corporation. All rights reserved.



SPMetal [options]



Options

/web:<url>                Specifies absolute URL of the web-site. Host address can be
local, in

                          which case Server OM will be used to connect to the server.

/useremoteapi             Specifies that the web-site URL is remote.

/user:<name>              Specifies logon username (or domain).

/password:<password>      Specifies logon password.

/parameters:<file>        Specifies XML file with code generation parameters.

/code:<file>              Specifies output for generated code (default: console).

/language:<language>      Specifies source code language. Valid options are "csharp" and
"vb"
```

(default: inferred from source code file name).

/namespace:<namespace>   Specifies namespace that is used for source code (default: no

namespace).

/serialization:<type>   Specifies serialization type. Valid options are "none" and

"unidirectional" (default: none).

Generate C# source code from a local SharePoint site:

SPMetal /web:http://localserver:5555/localsite /namespace:nwind /code:nwind.cs

Generate VB source code from a local SharePoint site with specified parameters:

SPMetal /web:http://localserver:5555/localsite /namespace:nwind /code:nwind.vb

 /parameters:parameters.xml

Generate C# source code from a remote SharePoint site using default credentials:

SPMetal /web:http://remoteserver:5555/remotesite /useremoteapi /namespace:nwind
/code:nwind.cs

Generate C# source code from remote SharePoint server using Client OM with specified
credentials:

SPMetal /web:http://remoteserver:5555/remotesite /user:domain\username /password:password

/namespace:nwind /code:nwind.cs

The following are the primary arguments that you'll need to supply:

- /web:<url>: Url is the path to your SharePoint site.

- `/namespace:<namespace>`: Namespace specifies the namespace used in the code file.

- `/code:<file>`: File is the filename of the output file.

The namespace argument specifies the namespace in which the generated classes will be contained. SPMetal can generate the output classes in either C# or Visual Basic, and you can specify this with the `/language:<language>` argument. The allowed values are `csharp` and `vb`. However, you don't generally need to use this because it will determine the language from the extension of the file name.

These additional parameters may be needed to connect to the site depending on your configuration:

- `/useremoteapi`: Use this if the SharePoint site is not on the local machine

- `/user:<user name>`

- `/password:<password>`

You will use this tool to generate classes to access the `Books` list.

1. Start a command prompt and enter a command similar to the one shown in Figure 10-14. You will need to provide the address to your SharePoint site.

```
C:\Program Files\Common Files\Microsoft Shared\Web Server Extensions\14\BIN>spme
tal /web:http://win-8mk2hhfoppg /namespace:booklist /code:booklist.cs
```

Figure 10-14. SPMetal command

2. This will generate all the classes in a `booklist.cs` file in the same folder as the SPMetal program. Move this file to a different location where it can be easily located.

3. Open the VisualWebParts solution in Visual Studio 2010. Right-click the project and select Add Existing Item. Navigate to the `booklist.cs` file and add it to the project, as shown in Figure 10-15.

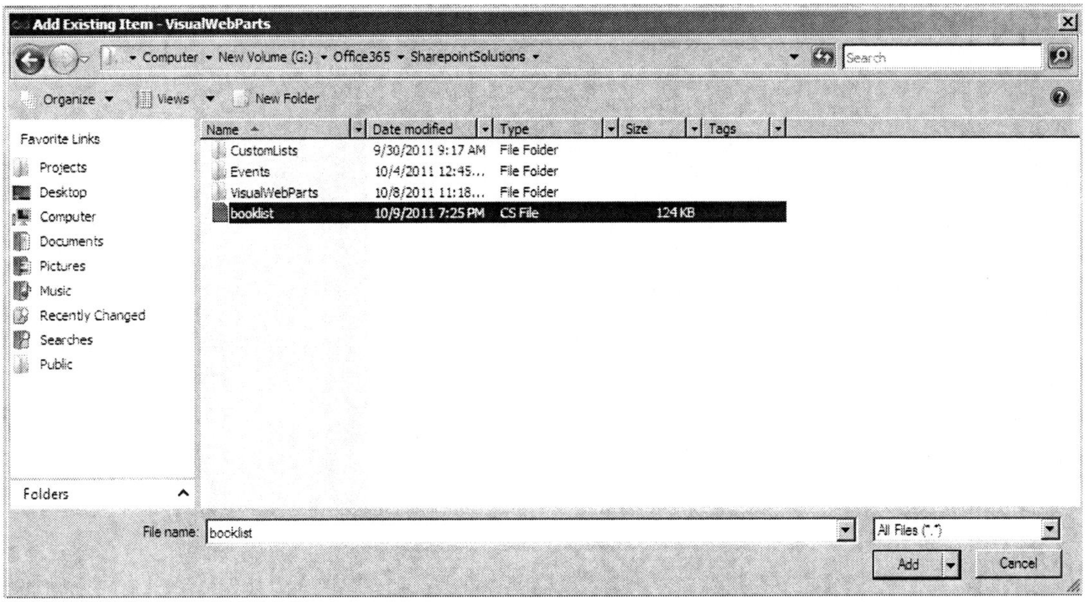

Figure 10-15. Add booklist.cs to the project.

4. You need to add a reference to the project before you can use LINQ to SharePoint. Right-click the References in the Solution Explorer and click Add Reference. Find the `Microsoft.SharePoint.Linq` component, as seen in Figure 10-16, and add it to your project.

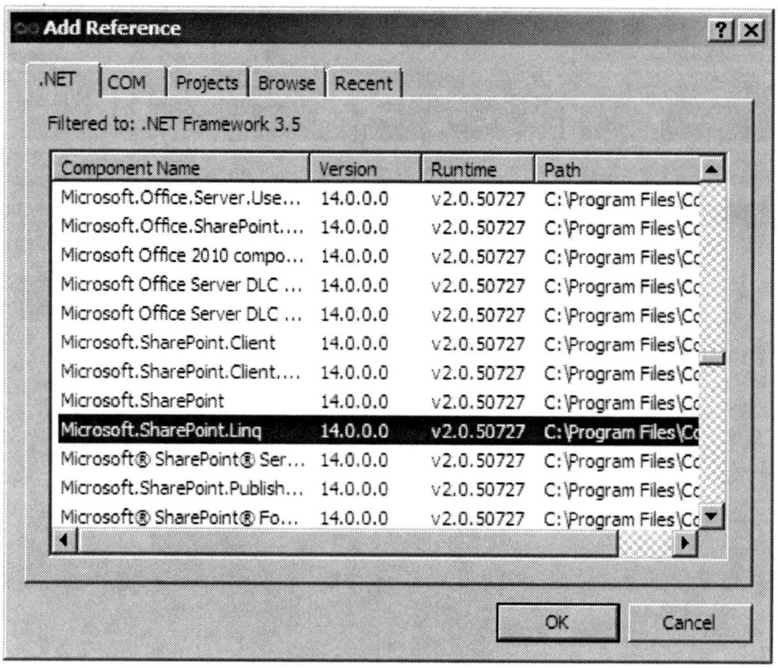

Figure 10-16. Adding LINQ to SharePoint reference

5. Now you are ready to begin modifying the code to use LINQ to SharePoint. Open the FindBooks.ascx.cs file. Add the following using statements to the top of the file:

```
using System.Collections.Generic;
using Microsoft.SharePoint.Linq;
using System.Linq;
```

6. You also need to access the generated classes from SPMetal. Add the following using statement to provide that reference:

```
using booklist;
```

7. Rather than modify the existing methods, add new ones so that you can compare the code and see how the same functionality can be achieved through these different means. Add the following two methods:

```
protected void PopulateAuthorListLINQ()
{
    BooklistDataContext context = new BooklistDataContext(SPContext.Current.Web.Url);
```

```
    var authorList = (from B in context.Books
                       select B.Author).Distinct();

    foreach (string author in authorList)
    {
        ddlAuthor.Items.Add(author);
    }
}

protected void btnSearch_ClickLINQ(object sender, EventArgs e)
{
    BooklistDataContext context = new BooklistDataContext(SPContext.Current.Web.Url);

    List<BookView> bookList = (from B in context.Books
                               where B.Author == ddlAuthor.SelectedValue
                               select new BookView{ Title = B.Title, Author = B.Author
}).ToList();

    gvResults.DataSource = bookList;
    gvResults.DataBind();
}
```

The booklist.cs file generated by SPMetal includes the BooklistDataContext, which provides LINQ the contextual information about the content from SharePoint. The context provides Visual Studio information for IntelliSense, which makes accessing the structural information much easier.

The PopulateAuthorListLINQ() method uses LINQ to return only the Author field from the Books list. The Distinct() method ensures the results are unique. The results are added to the drop-down one at a time rather that bound directly.

The btnSearch_ClickLINQ() method also uses LINQ to return data. The where statement compares the Author field to the selected value from the drop-down.

8. To provide the ability to bind the results, a new type needs to be created. To do this, add a class to the project called BookView.cs that implements the following:

```
public class BookView
{
    public string Title { get; set; }
    public string Author { get; set; }
}
```

LINQ can return anonymous types. However, those can't be bound to the grid view control. Using the BookView type, the grid view control can bind to the results without issue. The code specifically uses the ToList() extension to convert the results into the generic-typed List of BookView. This collection is then used to bind to the GridView control.

Debug and test this project as you did in the previous section of this chapter. Once everything works properly, deploy to your SharePoint Online site. The result should be exactly the same as before, as shown in Figure 10-17.

Figure 10-17. Visual Web Part result

Custom Workflow Action

Visual Studio provides the ability to build custom functionality that can be added to the workflows within SharePoint Online. This project will build a custom action that processes the Title and BookAuthor fields of the Books list into proper casing.

1. Start with an empty SharePoint Project. Name the project **CustomWorkflowActions**, as shown in Figure 10-18, and select a location easily located.

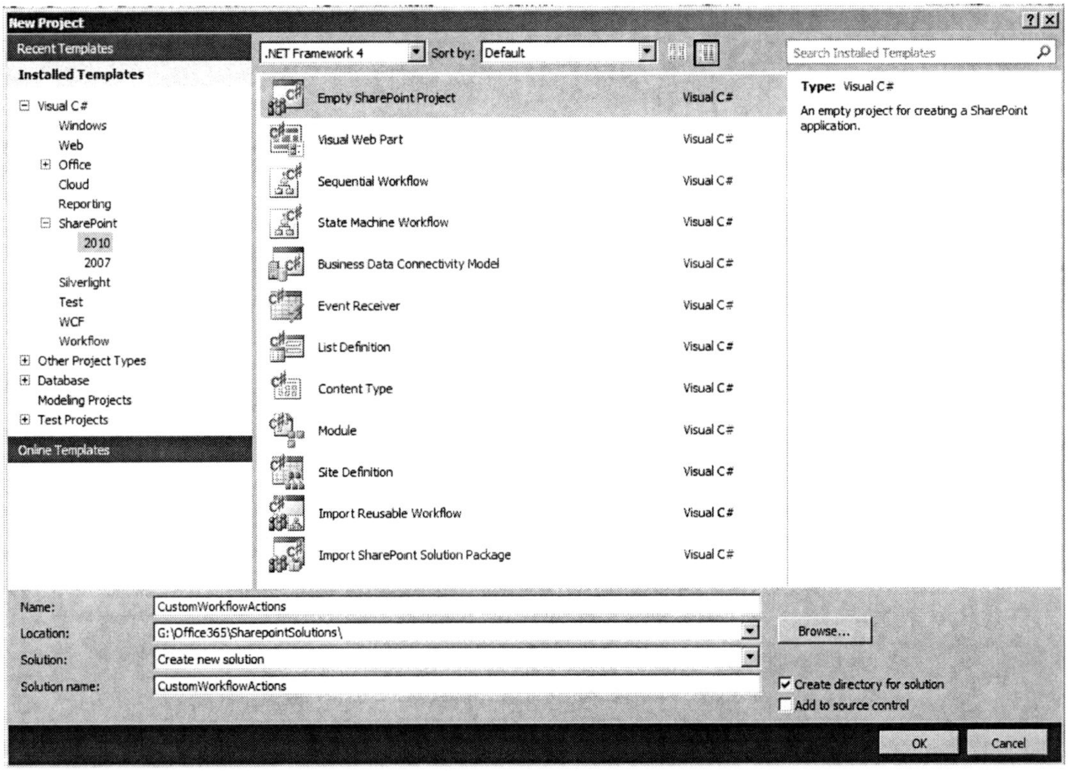

Figure 10-18. Empty SharePoint project for custom workflow action

2. Add a new class called **ProcessNewBookAction**, as seen in Figure 10-19.

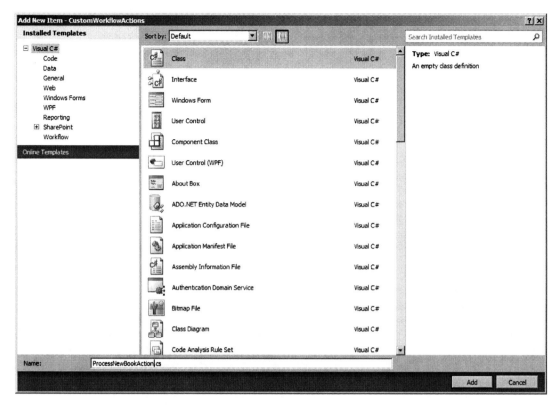

Figure 10-19. New custom action class

3. Add the method shown in Listing 10-1 to the ProcessNewBookAction class:

Listing 10-1. Implementation of the ProcessNeweBook() method

```
public Hashtable ProcessNewBook(SPUserCodeWorkflowContext context)
{
    Hashtable response = new Hashtable();

    try
    {
        using (SPSite site = new SPSite(context.CurrentWebUrl))
        {
            using (SPWeb web = site.OpenWeb())
            {
                SPList bookList = web.Lists[context.ListId];
                SPListItem currentBook = bookList.GetItemById(context.ItemId);
                //proper case title and author
                CultureInfo culture = CultureInfo.CurrentCulture;
                TextInfo textInfo = culture.TextInfo;
```

```
                currentBook["Title"] =
textInfo.ToTitleCase(currentBook["Title"].ToString().ToLower());
                currentBook["BookAuthor"] =
                        textInfo.ToTitleCase(currentBook["BookAuthor"].ToString().ToLower());

                currentBook.Update();

                response["result"] = "success";
            }
        }
    }
    catch (Exception ex)
    {
        response["result"] = "error: " + ex.Message;
    }

    return response;
}
```

The method returns a hashtable to the workflow. This hashtable will hold any return values for the workflow to process. This particular method only returns the status of the action.

The method accepts a SPUserCodeWorkflowContext parameter. This holds the contextual information for the SharePoint site where the workflow is running. Using the context, the method accesses the list and the specific item currently being referenced. The CurrentCulture.TextInfo object is used to set the Title and BookAuthor fields to the proper casing. This only works on lowercased values, so the values use the ToLower() method. The list item is updated and the result is returned.

4. To surface this method to SharePoint, you need to add a new Empty Element item. Name the item **ProcessNewBookDefinition,** as shown in Figure 10-20.

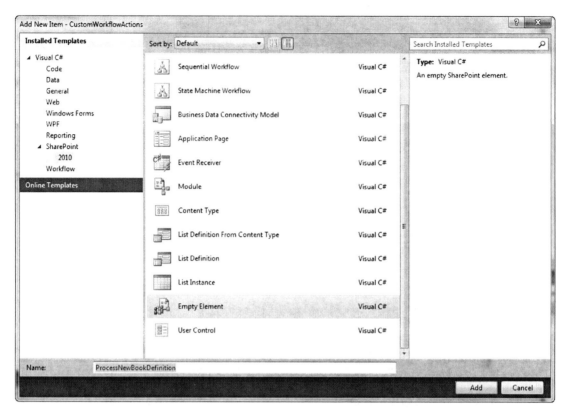

Figure 10-20. *Custom action definition*

    5.   This XML file contains the configuration for the custom action, making the functionality available for use within workflows. Add a `WorkflowActions` node.

```
<WorkflowActions>

</WorkflowActions>
```

    6.   Within that node, add an `Actions` node with the following information:

```
<Action Name="Process New Book"
        SandboxedFunction="true"
        Assembly="$SharePoint.Project.AssemblyFullName$"
        ClassName="CustomWorkflowActions.ProcessNewBookAction"
        FunctionName="ProcessNewBook"
        AppliesTo="all"
        UsesCurrentItem="true"
        Category="Custom Workflow Actions">
```

```
</Action>
```

7. This sets the name of the action and maps to the class and method. Add a
    RuleDesigner node within the Action node.

```
<RuleDesigner Sentence="Process New Book"></RuleDesigner>
```

This sets the sentence that is displayed within workflows when this action is added.

⬛ **Note** Parameters can be used within the Sentence attribute of the RuleDesigner node. When this is done,
FieldBind nodes must also exist to map the parameters. This project does not need them, so inline parameters
are not used.

---

8. Add the Parameters node.

```
<Parameters>
    <Parameter Name="__Context" Type="Microsoft.SharePoint.WorkflowActions.WorkflowContext,
                                Microsoft.SharePoint.WorkflowActions"
            Direction="In"
            DesignerType="Hide" />
</Parameters>
```

This section lists all the parameters for the custom action. The only parameter for this project is the
incoming context. The DesignerType is set to "Hide" as it is not shown within the workflow UI. If other
parameters were accepted in the workflow screens or passed back, they would be defined here.

9. The code and configuration files are complete. The Elements.xml file should
    look like listing 10-2:

Listing 10-2. The complete Elements.xml file

```
<?xml version="1.0" encoding="utf-8"?>
<Elements xmlns="http://schemas.microsoft.com/sharepoint/">
  <WorkflowActions>
    <Action Name="Process New Book"
            SandboxedFunction="true"
            Assembly="$SharePoint.Project.AssemblyFullName$"
            ClassName="CustomWorkflowActions.ProcessNewBookAction"
            FunctionName="ProcessNewBook"
            AppliesTo="all"
            UsesCurrentItem="true"
            Category="Custom Workflow Actions">
      <RuleDesigner Sentence="Process New Book"></RuleDesigner>
```

```
    <Parameters>
        <Parameter Name="__Context"
Type="Microsoft.SharePoint.WorkflowActions.WorkflowContext,
                                    Microsoft.SharePoint.WorkflowActions"
                    Direction="In"
                    DesignerType="Hide" />
    </Parameters>
  </Action>
 </WorkflowActions>
</Elements>
```

10. Check the Feature settings and ensure that the scope is set to Site, as shown in Figure 10-21.

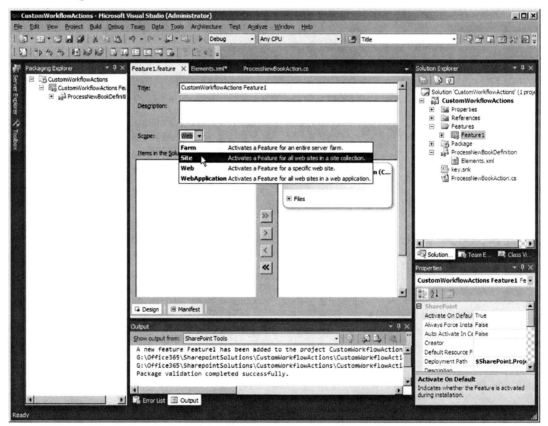

Figure 10-21. Set the scope to Site for the custom action.

Debugging the Project

Press F5 to begin debugging this solution. This will package and deploy the solution to your on-premise SharePoint site. This project is a custom action that works within a workflow, so it is not immediately accessible. First, you must design a workflow and use this action. Then you can run tests against this project.

Designing a Simple Workflow

Start SharePoint Designer and open your on-premise site.

1. Navigate to Workflows. Create a new List Workflow from the button in the ribbon. Name the workflow **Process New Item**, as shown in Figure 10-22.

Figure 10-22. Creating a List Workflow in SharePoint Designer

2. Click Action in the ribbon and look for the Process New Book action (seen in Figure 10-23).

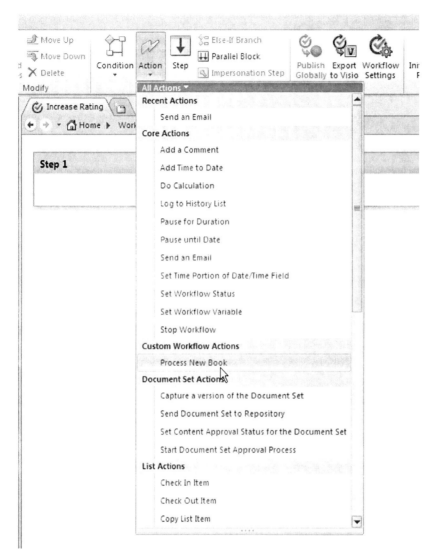

Figure 10-23. Add the custom action to the workflow.

3. There is a Check for Errors button on the Ribbon. Clicking this button checks the workflow and visually notifies you of any issues with the workflow, such as missing parameters or other similar type errors. Use this to check the workflow for errors, then save and publish. Now the workflow is available for the Books list.

4. Navigate to your on-premise SharePoint site and view the Books list. Figure 10-24 shows the form for adding a new test item to the list.

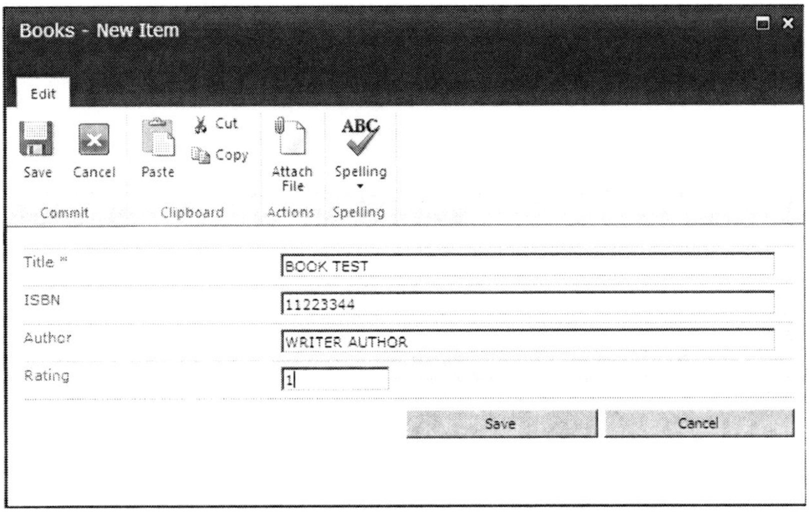

Figure 10-24. Adding a test item to the list

5. Select the newly added item and click the Workflows button in the ribbon. You should see a screen similar to Figure 10-25.

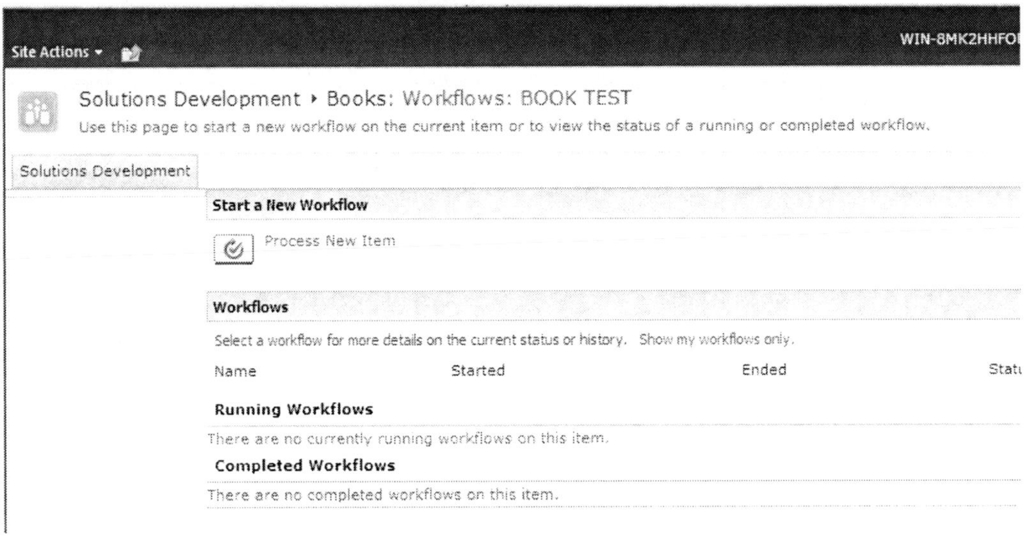

Figure 10-25. Workflow screen

6. Click Process New Item to run the workflow. SharePoint will display a processing screen until the workflow completes. The first time it runs may take a little longer. Once it completes, view the list to ensure the workflow action

processed the new item correctly. You should see results similar to
Figure 10-26.

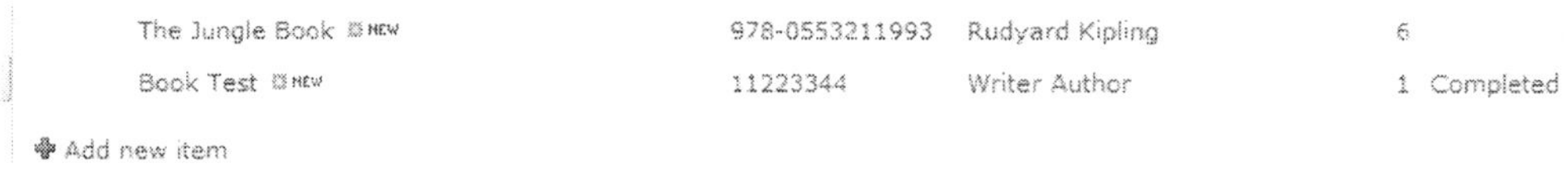

The Jungle Book ⊠ NEW	978-0553211993	Rudyard Kipling	6	
Book Test ⊠ NEW	11223344	Writer Author	1	Completed

✦ Add new item

Figure 10-26. Workflow results

Deploying the Solution

Deployment to you SharePoint Online follows the same process as any other solution.

1. Right-click your solution in Visual Studio and click Package.

2. Open your browser and go to your SharePoint Online site.

3. Navigate to Site Settings and click the Solutions link.

4. Click the Solutions tab on the ribbon and click Upload Solution, as shown in
    Figure 10-27.

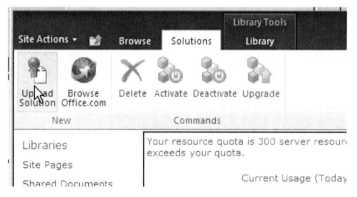

Figure 10-27. Uploading a solution to SharePoint Online

5. Click Browse and find the package file (.wsp) in the solution folder under the
    \bin\debug folder.

6. Activate the solution when prompted.

7. Open SharePoint Designer and Open the SharePoint Online site.

8. Create a new List Workflow using the Books list, as illustrated in Figure 10-28.

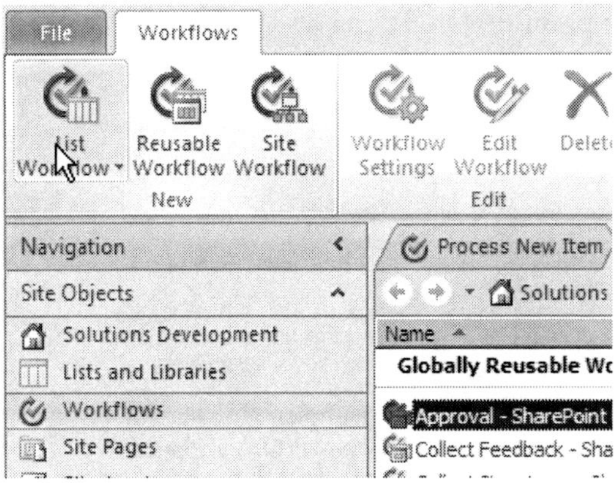

Figure 10-28. Create a new List Workflow in SharePoint Designer.

9. Add the custom Process New Book action to the workflow.

10. Save and publish the workflow.

11. Open your browser and go to your SharePoint online site.

12. Navigate to the Books list and add a new item with improper casing, as demonstrated in Figure 10-29.

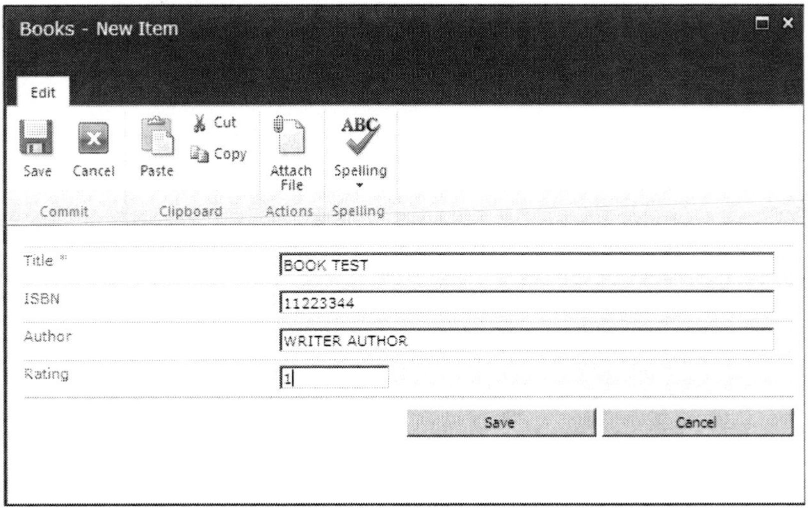

Figure 10-29. Adding an improperly cased test item to the Books list

13. Select the new item and click Workflows from the ribbon.

14. Run the Process New Item workflow and wait for completion.

15. The results should be the same as on your on-premise SharePoint site. The test item should appear similar to the item in Figure 10-30.

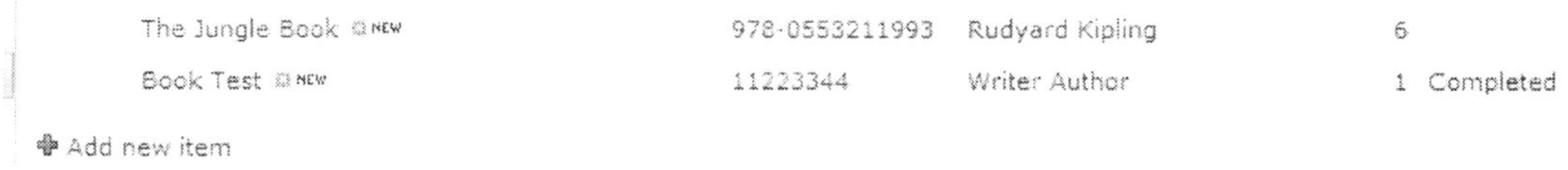

The Jungle Book ✿NEW	978-0553211993	Rudyard Kipling	6
Book Test ✿NEW	11223344	Writer Author	1 Completed

✦ Add new item

Figure 10-30. Custom Workflow Action result

Summary

Visual Studio provides the ability to create complex functionality within SharePoint Online. You have built and deployed a Visual Web Part, simplified that project with LINQ to SharePoint, and added a custom action to a SharePoint workflow. These can be very powerful options when creating business or personal solutions for SharePoint Online.

You will continue into more complex development in the next chapter as you build solutions with Silverlight and JavaScript.

CHAPTER 11

Developing Silverlight and JavaScript Applications

Microsoft SharePoint Foundation 2010 provides developers the Client Object Model for accessing SharePoint from a remote client application. The Client Object Model is available for Silverlight and JavaScript applications. In this chapter, you will build an application in each of these technologies. You will build and deploy solutions that access the Books list that has been used throughout this section, this time using the Client Object Model.

Understanding the Client Object Model

The SharePoint Client Object Model provides an easier method of developing against SharePoint than services. It delivers a consistent way to access SharePoint from various types of client technologies and was designed to be consistent with the server-side object model, making its use intuitive for developers accustomed to coding for SharePoint. The Client Object Model is a subset of the `Microsoft.SharePoint` object model. It is scoped to site collection and lower. It is available for .NET, Silverlight, and JavaScript. The Client Object Model is made available through the classes shown in Table 1-1.

Table 11-1. Client Object Locations

Technology	Location
.NET Managed	Microsoft.SharePoint.Client
Silverlight	Microsoft.SharePoint.Client.Silverlight
ECMAScript	SP.js

The following areas are supported:

- Site collections and sites

- Lists, ListItems, views, and list schemas

- Files and folders

- Web, list, and ListItem properties

- Web Parts

- Security (SPUser)

- Contact types

- Site templates and site collection operations

- All areas restricted to SharePoint Online features

Table 11-2 illustrates how the client-side object model maps to the server-side object model.

Table 11-2. Client-Side Objects Mapped to Server-Side Objects

Server Object Model	Client Object Model
SPContext	ClientContext
SPSite	Site
SPWeb	Web
SPList	List
SPListItem	ListItem
SPField	Field

SharePoint Online only allows sandboxed solutions. This limits access to data within the SharePoint context. However, client applications provide a way to access external data. The client application can call web services not hosted in SharePoint. They can access Azure data as well as on-premise SharePoint installations through the Azure Service Bus.

Choosing Silverlight or JavaScript

To demonstrate the versatility of the Client Object Model, you will develop two client-side applications using two different technologies: Silverlight and JavaScript. The reasons for developing with one over the other are outside the scope of this book. However, it is helpful to regard a few similarities and a few differences here.

Both Silverlight and JavaScript provide web-distributed client applications. The written code is executed on the client machine, with access to client resources. Direct access to server resources is not available in either technology. Both can be used to provide very interactive experiences for the end user since they are running on the client. Both also must take into consideration this user experience when accessing resources from the server.

These two technologies differ in the technical details. JavaScript is a language run in a web browser. Developers have direct access to the browser elements as well as the Document Object Model (DOM) of the hosting web page. There is not an inherent framework, so either everything is written along with the application, or external frameworks like jQuery must be used. The user interface is provided through HTML.

Silverlight, on the other hand, is a .NET technology, which means developers can use C# or VB.NET to write their code. The client .NET framework is available to the developer, providing a rich base of core functionality. The application is distributed in a web page, but more along the lines of a plug-in than embedded code like JavaScript. The user interface is provided through XAML, making the development experience similar to writing a WPF application. The user experience is similar in this regard as well, since the application runs outside of the HTML. The developer doesn't have direct access to the browser elements nor the DOM.

As you can see, there are enough differences between these two technologies to raise questions about how each would be used to connect to the SharePoint site. This chapter will demonstrate that using the Client Object Model is very similar regardless of the client technology.

Building the Silverlight Application

This project will require two Visual Studio projects, the Silverlight application itself and a SharePoint application for deployment. Let's start with the SharePoint application.

1. Open Visual Studio 2010 and select the Empty SharePoint Project.

2. Enter the name **SilverlightSearchDeployment** and the location for your project, as shown in Figure 11-1. Click OK to continue.

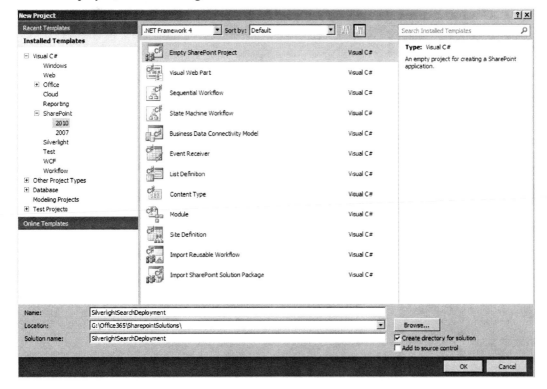

Figure 11-1. Creating a new SharePoint project for deploying the Silverlight application

3. Choose your on-premise SharePoint site at the prompt and select Sandboxed Solution, as you did in the other projects in this book.

4. Now you need to add the Silverlight project to the solution. Right-click the solution in the Solution Explorer and click Add Project. Choose the Silverlight Application template and enter **BookSearchSilverlight** as the name, similar to Figure 11-2.

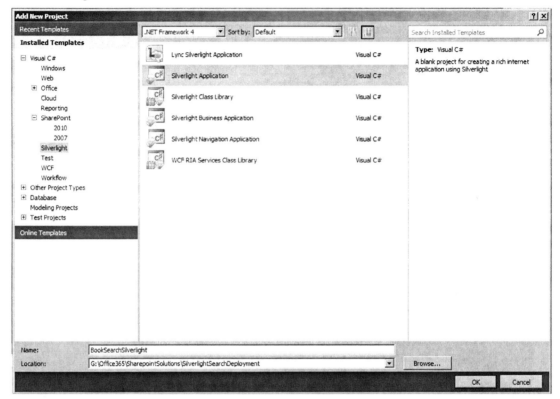

Figure 11-2. Adding a Silverlight application

5. Silverlight applications must be hosted in a web page of some sort. Visual Studio can either create references for the new Silverlight application to a new web site as well or generate a test page for debugging. Make sure the check box is unchecked and that Silverlight 4 is selected as the version. When the dialog box looks like Figure 11-3, click OK.

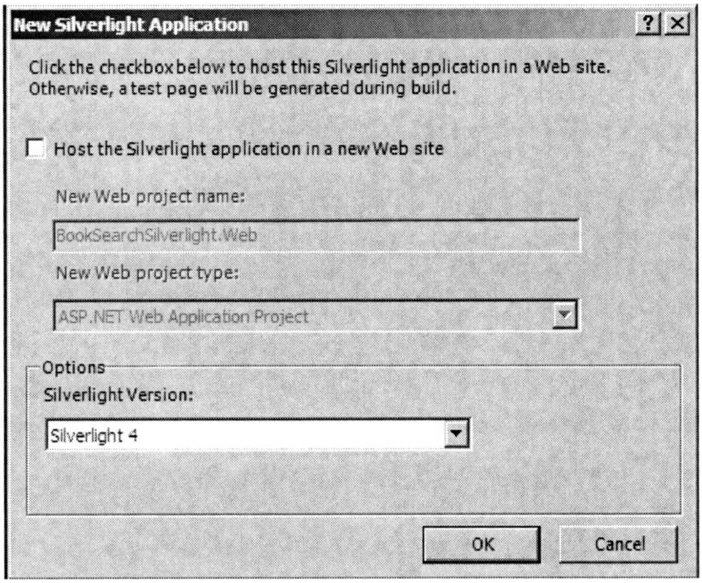

New Silverlight Application

Click the checkbox below to host this Silverlight application in a Web site. Otherwise, a test page will be generated during build.

☐ Host the Silverlight application in a new Web site

New Web project name:

BookSearchSilverlight.Web

New Web project type:

ASP.NET Web Application Project

Options

Silverlight Version:

Silverlight 4

OK   Cancel

Figure 11-3. Silverlight application host settings

6. You need to add the client object model references to the Silverlight project. Right-click References and add the following references:

- `Microsoft.SharePoint.Client.Silverlight`

- `Microsoft.SharePoint.Client.Silverlight.Runtime`

■ **Note** The reference files are located in `C:\Program Files\Common Files\Microsoft Shared\Web Server Extensions\14\Template\Layouts\ClientBin`.

You'll now create a simple UI for searching through the Books list by title. Open the `MainPage.xaml` file and replace the existing code with the code from Listing 11-1.

Listing 11-1. Silverlight XAML Code for Simple Search Through Books List

```
<UserControl x:Class="BookSearchSilverlight.MainPage"
    xmlns="http://schemas.microsoft.com/winfx/2006/xaml/presentation"
    xmlns:x="http://schemas.microsoft.com/winfx/2006/xaml"
    xmlns:d="http://schemas.microsoft.com/expression/blend/2008"
    xmlns:mc="http://schemas.openxmlformats.org/markup-compatibility/2006"
    mc:Ignorable="d"
    d:DesignHeight="300" d:DesignWidth="400">
```

```
    <Grid x:Name="LayoutRoot" Background="White">
        <Grid.RowDefinitions>
            <RowDefinition Height="50"/>
            <RowDefinition />
        </Grid.RowDefinitions>
        <StackPanel Orientation="Horizontal" Grid.Row="0">
            <TextBox x:Name="txtSearch" Height="25" Width="200" />
            <Button x:Name="btnSearch" Height="25" Width="75" Margin="10,0,0,0"
Content="Search"
                                            Click="btnSearch_Click" />
        </StackPanel>
        <StackPanel Orientation="Vertical" Grid.Row="1">
            <TextBlock Height="25" Text="Books Found:" Margin="5" />
            <ListBox x:Name="lstSearchResults" Margin="5,0,5,5" Height="200" />
        </StackPanel>
    </Grid>
</UserControl>
```

This creates a simple grid with two rows. The top row contains a TextBox for the text to search with and a Button to start the search. The bottom row contains a TextBlock for a label and a ListBox for the search results. Now you are ready to add functionality to the application. Open the MainPage.xaml.cs file. Add the following using statement at the beginning of the code:

```
using Microsoft.SharePoint.Client;
```

When the Silverlight application accesses the SharePoint data, it will do so through an asynchronous method call. This application uses private variables at the page level so the event handler method can access the client objects. Add the following variables to the start of the MainPage class:

```
private Web _web;
private List _bookList;
private ListItemCollection _items;
private ClientContext _context = ClientContext.Current;
```

Variables are set up for the Web, List, and ListItemCollection objects that are needed in the application. The primary variable of concern here is the ClientContext _context, set to the current context. The Silverlight application will be hosted within the SharePoint application, so this easily accesses the hosting context.

Next, add the code shown in Listing 11-2 to implement the event handler for the search button click event.

Listing 11-2. Search Button Click Event Handler

```
private void btnSearch_Click(object sender, RoutedEventArgs e)
{
    _web = _context.Web;
    _bookList = _web.Lists.GetByTitle("Books");
    string queryString = "<View><Query><Where><BeginsWith><FieldRef Name='Title'/><Value
                        Type='Text'>" + txtSearch.Text +
                        "</Value></BeginsWith></Where></Query></View>";
    CamlQuery query = new CamlQuery();
    query.ViewXml = queryString;
    _items = _bookList.GetItems(query);
```

```
    _context.Load(_items);
    _context.ExecuteQueryAsync(onQuerySuccess, onQueryFailure);
}
```

This method simply uses the Client object, starting with the _context object, to access the Web, List, and ListItemCollection from the Books list in the SharePoint site. The Text property of the txtSearch TextBox is used to compile a CAML query string for accessing items that match the entered string. All of this code is very similar to how you would code a function within a Visual Web Part using the server-side objects. The final step is to call the ExecuteQueryAsync() method, which passes the query to the SharePoint server and waits for the response. The method takes the event handlers for success and failure as parameters. Implement these by adding the code from Listing 11-3.

Listing 11-3. Success and Failure Event Handlers for SharePoint Query

```
private void onQuerySuccess(object sender, ClientRequestSucceededEventArgs e)
{
    this.Dispatcher.BeginInvoke(new Action(BindBookList));
}

private void onQueryFailure(object sender, ClientRequestFailedEventArgs e)
{
    MessageBox.Show("Error:" + e.Message);
}
```

The event handler for failure simply displays the error message received in the response from the server. The success event handler uses the Dispatcher to call a method for binding the ListItems that are returned from the SharePoint site. Since the BindBookList() will need to access UI objects, the Dispatcher must be implemented. Listing 11-4 shows the implementation of the BindBookList() method.

Listing 11-4. Method for Binding Results from SharePoint into a ListBox

```
private void BindBookList()
{
    List<string> books = new List<string>();

    foreach(ListItem item in _items)
    {
        books.Add(item["Title"].ToString());
    }

    lstSearchResults.ItemsSource = books;
}
```

The application will display the title in the ListBox. The BindBookList() method loops through the _items collection and adds the title to a generic List object to bind to the ListBox.

Building the Deployment Solution

The Silverlight application is now complete. However, it must first be deployed to the SharePoint site so that it can be available for use. To do so you need a deployment solution.

1. Add a module to the `SilverlightSearchDeployment` project, as shown in
    Figure 11-4.

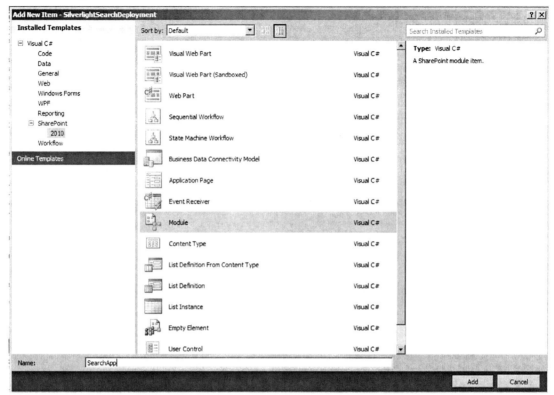

Figure 11-4. Adding a module for deployment

2. This creates a module node in Solution Explorer within the project. Under this
    node, an `Elements.xml` file and a `Sample.txt` file are added as well. You don't
    need the `Sample.txt` file, so delete it, as illustrated in Figure 11-5.

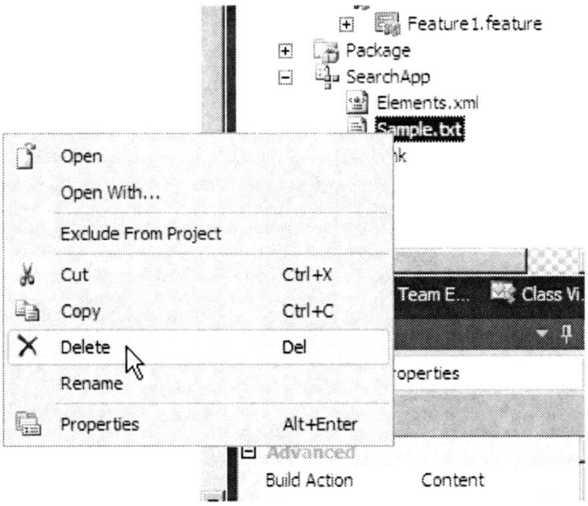

Figure 11-5. Delete the Sample.txt file from the new module

3. Now the module needs to reference the Silverlight application output in order to deploy the XAP file when deploying the solution package. Figure 11-6 shows where to access the Project Output References item within the properties of the SearchApp module.

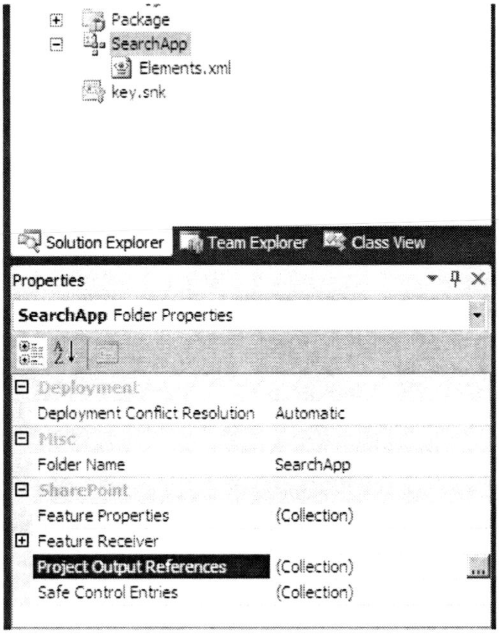

Figure 11-6. Reference properties for deploying the Silverlight application

4. Select the BookSearchSilverlight project from the Members list. Make sure the Deployment Type is set to ElementFile, as shown in Figure 11-7.

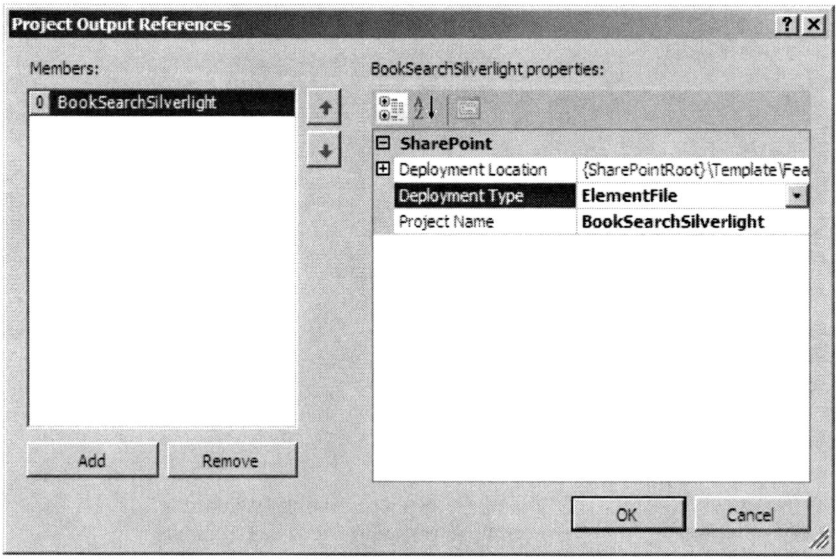

Figure 11-7. Project Output References settings

5. The Elements.xml file should now reflect the XAP file from the Silverlight application project. You need to ensure the file is deployed to a location known to you so that you can access it in your SharePoint site. Ensure the Elements.xml file is similar to Listing 11-5. This configures the module to deploy the XAP file to the documents list, under the SearchApp folder.

Listing 11-5. Elements.xml

```
<?xml version="1.0" encoding="utf-8"?>
<Elements xmlns="http://schemas.microsoft.com/sharepoint/">
  <Module Name="SearchApp">
  <File Path="SearchApp\BookSearchSilverlight.xap"
Url="Documents/SearchApp/BookSearchSilverlight.xap" />
</Module>
</Elements>
```

6. Press F5 to deploy the solution to your on-premise SharePoint site. Create a new page and edit it. In the Edit Tools, select Web Part and choose the Media and Content category. From there, select the Silverlight Web Part option, as shown in Figure 11-8.

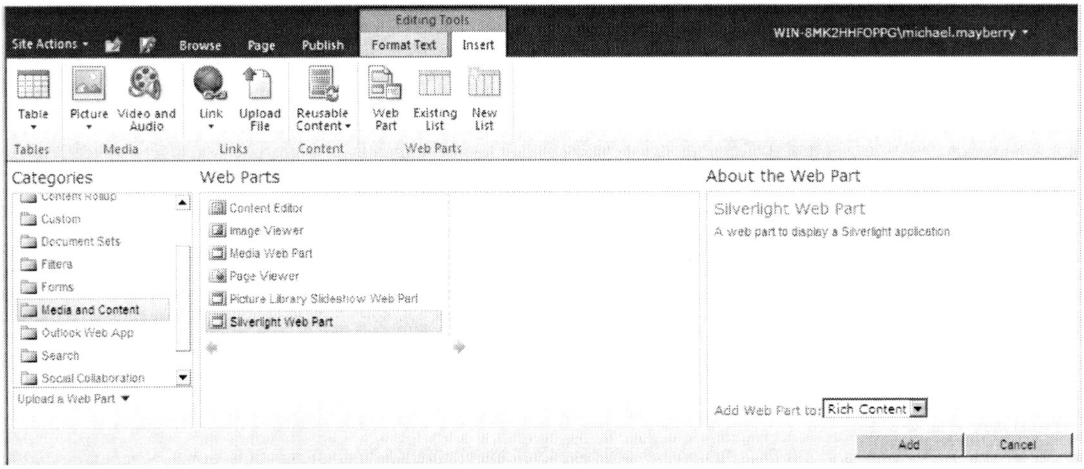

Figure 11-8. Adding a Silverlight Web Part to a SharePoint page

7. Click Add. You are then prompted for the URL for the Silverlight application. Enter the path used in the Elements.xml file earlier. You will most likely need to prefix the path with "/" to ensure SharePoint finds it correctly. When your screen appears similar to Figure 11-9, click OK.

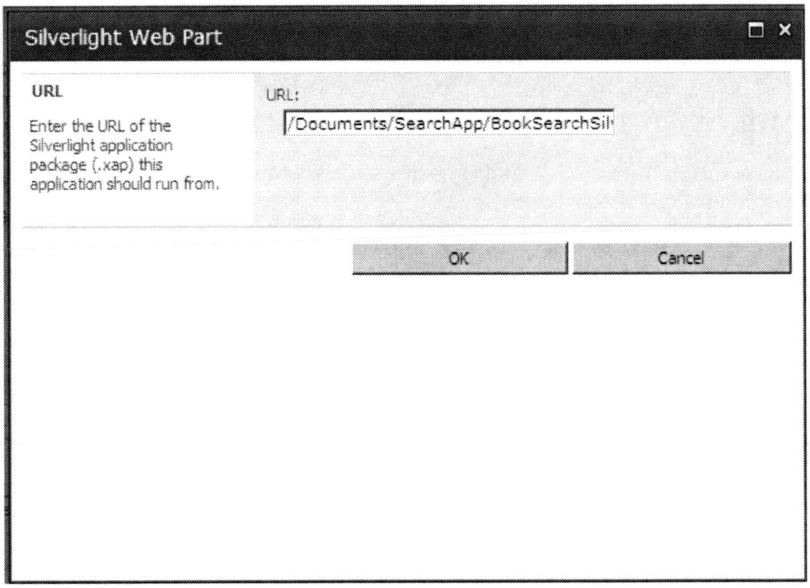

Figure 11-9. URL for the Silverlight Web Part

8. The Web Part is then added to the page. From here, save the page and navigate to the page for testing. Type a phrase in the text box and click Search. You should see results similar to Figure 11-10.

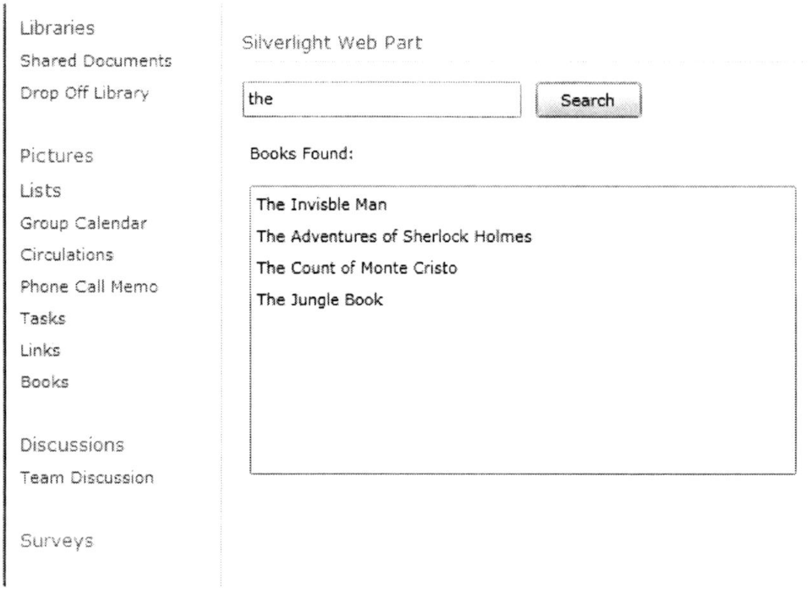

Libraries
Shared Documents
Drop Off Library
Pictures
Lists
Group Calendar
Circulations
Phone Call Memo
Tasks
Links
Books
Discussions
Team Discussion
Surveys
Silverlight Web Part
the
Search
Books Found:
The Invisble Man
The Adventures of Sherlock Holmes
The Count of Monte Cristo
The Jungle Book

Figure 11-10. Silverlight Web Part test results

Deploying the Silverlight Application to SharePoint Online

You are now ready to deploy this solution to your SharePoint Online site. Deploying this solution will be similar to deploying to any other SharePoint application.

1. Right click the `SilverlightSearchDeployment` project and click Package. This will create the `SilverlightSearchDeployment.wsp` needed to upload to the SharePoint server.

2. Navigate to Site Settings and the Solutions list. Click the Upload Solution button, as shown in Figure 11-11.

Library Tools
Site Actions
Browse
Solutions
Library
Upload Solution
Browse Office.com
Delete
Activate
Deactivate
Upgrade
New
Commands

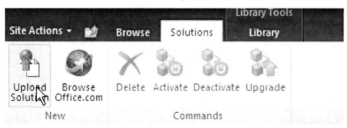

Figure 11-11. Uploading a solution to SharePoint Online

3. Within the following prompt, browse to your project folder and select the SilverlightSearchDeployment.wsp file. Make sure to activate the solution during the upload.

4. Once the solution is uploaded, navigate to the Features list and activate the SilverlightSearchDeployment Feature1 by clicking on the button as illustrated in Figure 11-12.

Figure 11-12. Activating the feature for the Silverlight solution

5. Create a new page or edit an existing one. In the Web Parts section of the Edit ribbon, click the More Web Parts button (see Figure 11-13).

Figure 11-13. More Web Parts option

6. Scroll the resulting list to find the Silverlight Web Part shown in Figure 11-14.

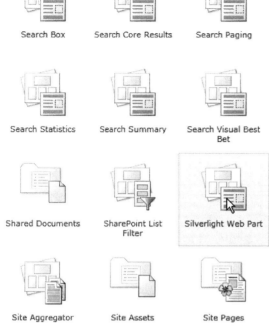

Search Box   Search Core Results   Search Paging

Search Statistics   Search Summary   Search Visual Best
                                                      Bet

Shared Documents   SharePoint List   Silverlight Web Part
                              Filter

Site Aggregator   Site Assets   Site Pages

Figure 11-14. Silverlight Web Part option

7.   You should now have the Silverlight Web Part added, but it needs to be
     configured. When Feature1 was activated, the XAP file was deployed to the
     Documents list, as was done on the on-premise SharePoint site. Your page
     should look similar to Figure 11-15.

Silverlight Web Part   ▾ □
No Silverlight Application (.xap) or Application Definition is specified.

To re-configure the Web Part or to provide a different Silverlight application (.xap), open the tool pane and then click **Configure**.

Figure 11-15. Added Silverlight Web Part before configuration

8.   Click the configure button seen in Figure 11-16.

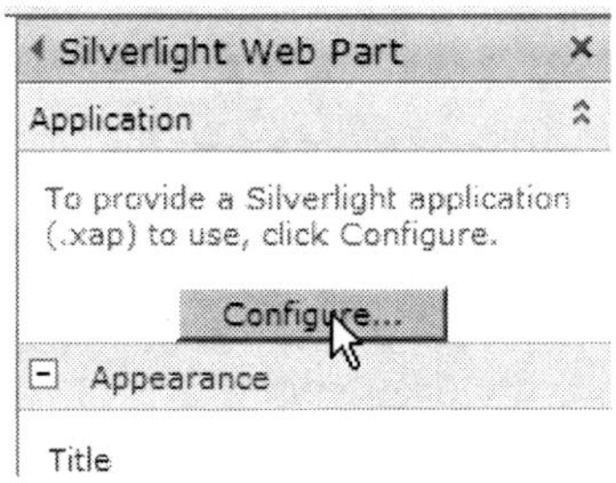

Figure 11-16. Configuring the Silverlight Web Part

9. Enter the URL from the Elements.xml file. Make sure the path begins with "/" in the prompt so the XAP can be found by the SharePoint site.

10. The Silverlight Web Part must have a height defined. Set the height to 400 Pixels, as shown in Figure 11-17.

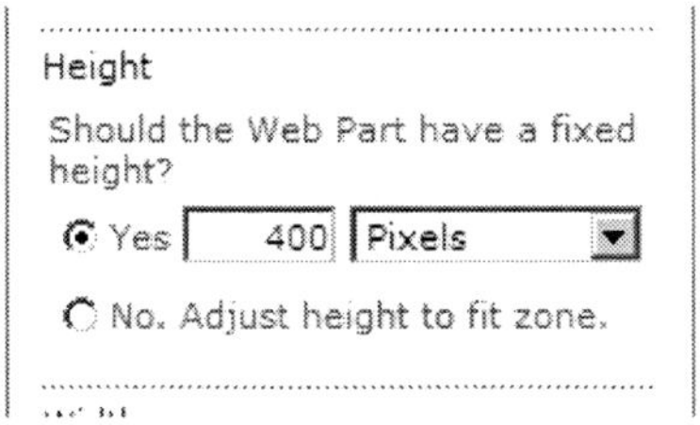

Figure 11-17. Setting display options (height) for a Silverlight Web Part

11. Save the page and navigate to the page for testing. The results should look like those in Figure 11-18.

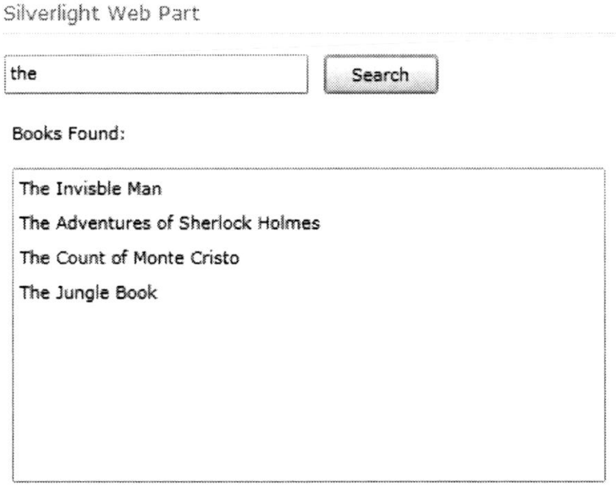

Figure 11-18. SharePoint Online Silverlight Web Part results

Building the JavaScript Application

A primary goal of the Client Object Model is to provide a similar development experience across the various client technologies. Accessing SharePoint through JavaScript is very similar to the way it is done in Silverlight. To demonstrate this, you will build an application that accomplishes the same functionality as the previous example. This time, you will use JavaScript. This project will consist of an ASPX page that includes the JavaScript code to access the SharePoint list. This web page will be deployed through a SharePoint module, just like the Silverlight application from earlier in this chapter.

1. Start with an empty SharePoint project.

2. Enter **BookSearchJavaScript** as the project name and set the location to your SharePoint development folder, as shown in Figure 11-19.

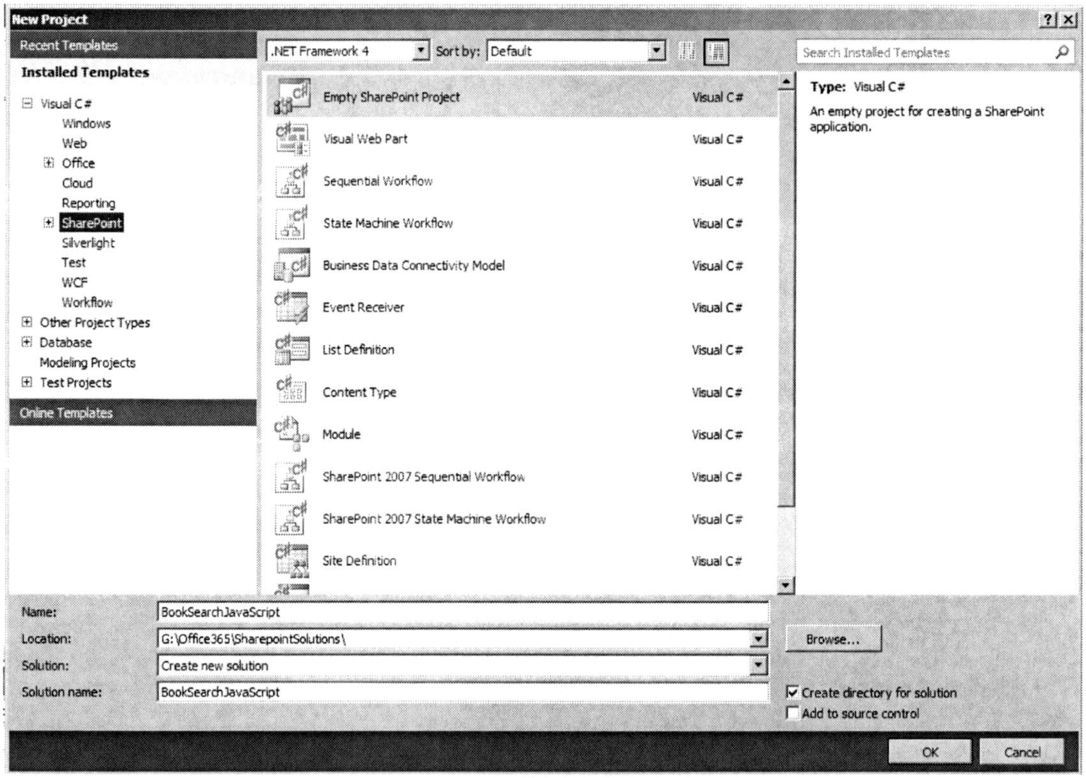

Figure 11-19. Starting the JavaScript application solution

3. Add a new module called CustomPages to the project, as seen in Figure 11-20.

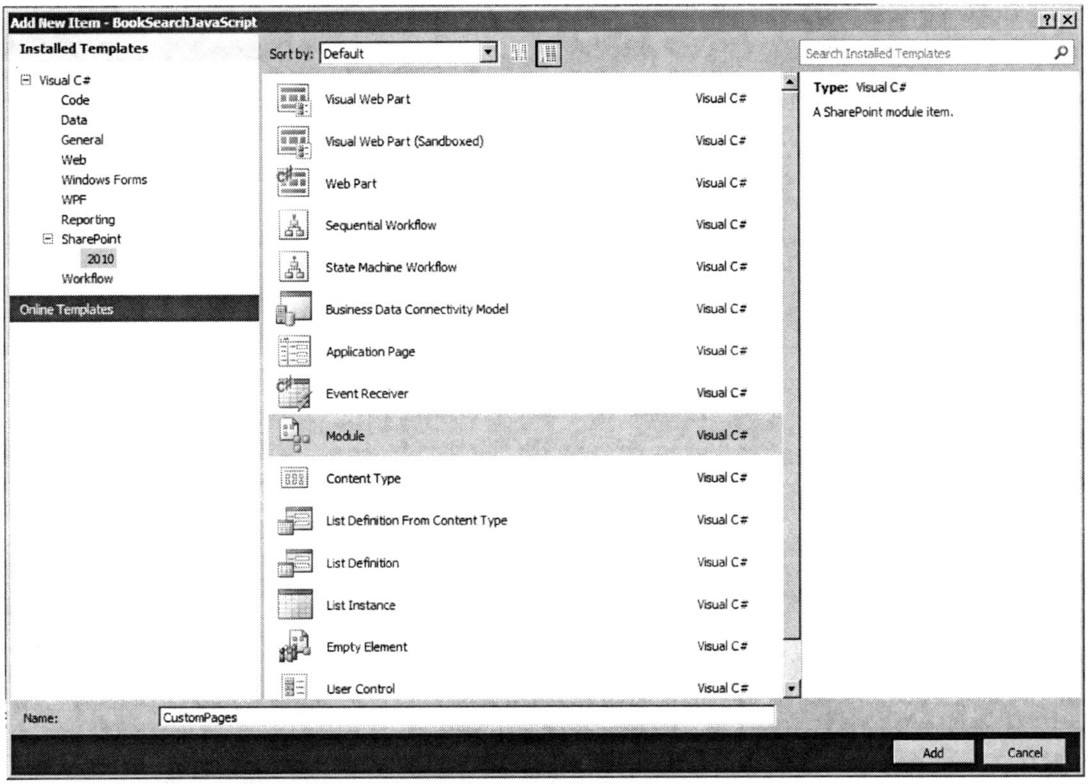

Figure 11-20. Adding a module to the JavaScript SharePoint project

As in the previous section in this chapter, a new module consists of an Elements.xml file and a Sample.txt file. Rename the Sample.txt file to BookSearch.aspx. Replace any text with the following:

```
<%@ Page Language="C#" masterpagefile="~masterurl/default.master" %>

<%@ Import Namespace="Microsoft.SharePoint.ApplicationPages" %>

<%@ Register Tagprefix="SharePoint" Namespace="Microsoft.SharePoint.WebControls"
Assembly="Microsoft.SharePoint, Version=14.0.0.0, Culture=neutral,
PublicKeyToken=71e9bce111e9429c" %>

<%@ Register Tagprefix="Utilities" Namespace="Microsoft.SharePoint.Utilities"
Assembly="Microsoft.SharePoint, Version=14.0.0.0, Culture=neutral,
PublicKeyToken=71e9bce111e9429c" %>

<%@ Register Tagprefix="asp" Namespace="System.Web.UI" Assembly="System.Web.Extensions,
Version=3.5.0.0, Culture=neutral, PublicKeyToken=31bf3856ad364e35" %>

<%@ Import Namespace="Microsoft.SharePoint" %>
```

This code sets up the file as an ASPX page and references the necessary SharePoint assemblies. To add the content for the page, add the code in Listing 11-6.

Listing 11-6. Content Markup for ASPX Page in SharePoint

```
<asp:Content ContentPlaceHolderId="PlaceHolderMain" runat="server">
    <SharePoint:ScriptLink ID="scriptLink1" runat="server" />

    <script language="javascript" type="text/javascript">
    </script>

    <div>
        <label>Search:</label><input type="text" id="txtSearchQuery" />
        <input type="button" id="btnSearch" value="Search" onclick="searchList()" />
        <br />
        <br />
        <br />
        Results:<br />
        <div id="result"></div>
    </div>
</asp:Content>
```

This code defines the page structure with a text box and button for searching plus a div for presenting the results. The SharePoint:ScriptLink will render the necessary link to the SP.js file for accessing the JavaScript Client Object. The starting event will be the button click, which is coded to call the searchList() method.

▪ **Note** Visual Studio doesn't provide an easy way to add a basic ASPX page to a SharePoint project. In this chapter, you will write one from scratch. You could copy a file from a Web Application project or from any other source; remember to add the SharePoint references into the ASPX code.

Adding the JavaScript

The script section of the ASPX page is meant to contain the JavaScript code for the SharePoint functionality. Start by adding a variable to store the items from the search.

```
var items;
```

Add the code in Listing 11-7 to define the searchList() method that is called when the button is clicked.

Listing 11-7. searchList() Implementation

```
function searchList()
{
    //get client context
    var context = new SP.ClientContext.get_current();
```

```
    //get the current site
    var bookList = context.get_web().get_lists().getByTitle('Books');

    var queryString = "<View><Query><Where><BeginsWith><FieldRef Name='Title'/><Value
Type='Text'>"
                        + document.getElementById('txtSearchQuery').value +
                        "</Value></BeginsWith></Where></Query></View>";

    var camlQuery = new SP.CamlQuery();
    camlQuery.set_viewXml(queryString);

    items = bookList.getItems(camlQuery);
    context.load(items);

    context.executeQueryAsync(
            Function.createDelegate(this, this.onSuccess),
            Function.createDelegate(this, this.onFailure));
}
```

Aside from the syntax, this code is essentially the same as the code in the Silverlight application. The steps are the same and the method calls are very similar. The Books list is accessed through the Web in the current context. A CAML query is submitted to SharePoint through an asynchronous call. The success and failure events are handled through delegate methods. The implementation for these is found in Listing 11-8.

Listing 11-8. Success and Failure Methods

```
function onSuccess(sender, args) {
    //show items
    var resultString = '';

    var itemsList = items.getEnumerator();
    while (itemsList.moveNext())
    {
        var item = itemsList.get_current();
        resultString += item.get_item('Title') + '<br />';
    }

    document.getElementById('result').innerHTML = resultString;
}

function onFailure(sender, args){
    alert('Error!');
}
```

The failure method simply displays the error. The success method loops through the items found from SharePoint and builds HTML to insert into the result div. This completes the coding. The final step is to adjust the Elements.xml to configure where the page should deploy. Open the Elements.xml file under the CustomPages node and ensure it is similar to Listing 11-9.

Listing 11-9. Elements.xml for Deploying the JavaScript Application

```xml
<?xml version="1.0" encoding="utf-8"?>
<Elements xmlns="http://schemas.microsoft.com/sharepoint/">
  <Module Name="CustomPages" Url="Pages">
<File Path="CustomPages\BookSearch.aspx" Url="CustomPages/BookSearch.aspx" />
</Module>
</Elements>
```

Testing the JavaScript Application

Right-click the solution and click Package to build the deployment package. Upload and activate the solution in the SharePoint Online site. Navigate to the Features list and activate Feature1, as shown in Figure 11-21.

Name	Status
BookSearchJavaScript Feature1	Activate
Content Organizer	

Figure 11-21. Activate JavaScript project feature

The page has been deployed to /Pages/CustomPages/BookSearch.aspx. Navigate to this URL and you should see a page similar to Figure 11-22.

Search: [   ] [Search]

Results:

Figure 11-22. ASPX page containing JavaScript to access SharePoint

This page is ready to search through the Books list using client-side JavaScript. Enter some text for searching and click the Search button. This should present the results shown in Figure 11-23.

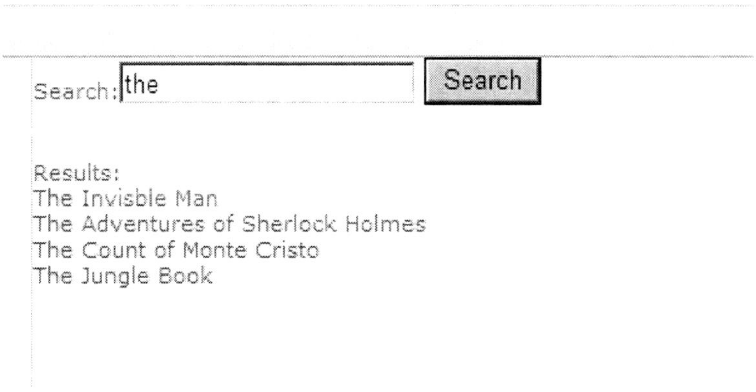

Search: the   Search

Results:
The Invisble Man
The Adventures of Sherlock Holmes
The Count of Monte Cristo
The Jungle Book

Figure 11-23. JavaScript application results

Summary

Accessing SharePoint data from client-side applications offers possibilities to get around the limitations of sandboxed solutions. The client-side applications can access web services and data sources outside of SharePoint and provide the functionality of other systems working with custom SharePoint solutions.

The SharePoint Client Object Model allows for a consistent way to develop against SharePoint data elements using client-side applications. You have built applications using Silverlight and JavaScript. While these examples only accessed the SharePoint and not external applications, they did demonstrate how simple it is to develop client-side applications using the Client Object Model.

PART 4

Developing Messaging Applications

Exchange Online and Lync Online are important components of the Office 365 platform. In this section, you'll learn how to leverage them using custom client applications.

Chapter 12 shows you how to use the Exchange Web Services (EWS) to implement a custom messaging application. Chapter 13 explains how to implement a custom Lync application. You will embed the Lync controls in a custom WPF application. You'll also pass contextual information in the Lync conversation and use Lync automation to embed the complete UI experience in your custom application.

CHAPTER 12

Developing Exchange Online Solutions

In this chapter you'll create a client application that accesses the Exchange Online server in your Office 365 account. Exchange Online 2010 exposes a lot of features through Exchange Web Services (EWS) to client applications such as Outlook and Outlook Web App. Your custom application can use these same features as well. I will show you how to

- Connect to the Exchange Online server using the *autodiscover* process. The actual server that is hosting your Exchange instance can change, so you should always use the autodiscover process instead of hard-coding the connection string.

- Access the mailbox items stored in Exchange. Think of Exchange as a specialized database containing objects such as e-mails, appointments, tasks, and contacts, which are organized in a hierarchy of folders. You can view, modify, and create these objects programmatically.

- Determine the availability of someone or a group of people. Exchange provides a feature that allows you to see when people will be available based on their calendars. You can also use this feature to suggest windows of time when the specified group of people and resources will be available.

- Subscribe to notifications when certain events occur, such as the arrival of a new message. Your custom application can receive these notifications and take appropriate actions. I will show you both push- and pull-type subscriptions.

You'll create a Windows Presentation Foundation (WPF) application that will communicate with Exchange. To save you some time in designing the form, you can download the XAML file from www.apress.com and paste it into your project. This simply defines the visual controls that are used on the form. I will explain how to write the code-behind for each of the functions that you'll implement. Along the way, I'll explain how each works.

Creating the Visual Studio Project

Launch Visual Studio 2010 and create a new project and solution. Enter the project name **ExchangeApp**, as shown in Figure 12-1.

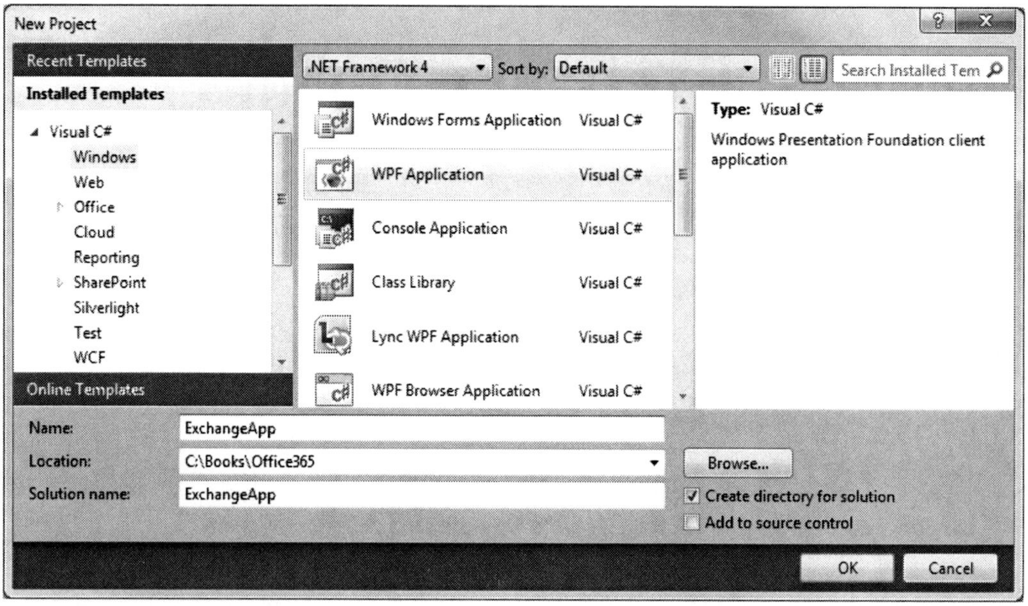

Figure 12-1. Creating a Visual Studio project

Click the OK button to create the project and solution. The MainWindow.xaml file will be opened and show a blank form.

Designing the Form

Select the XAML tab to see all of the code. Download the MainWindow.xaml file from www.apress.com and paste the XAML code from it into your local file. Switch to the Design tab, and the form should look like Figure 12-2.

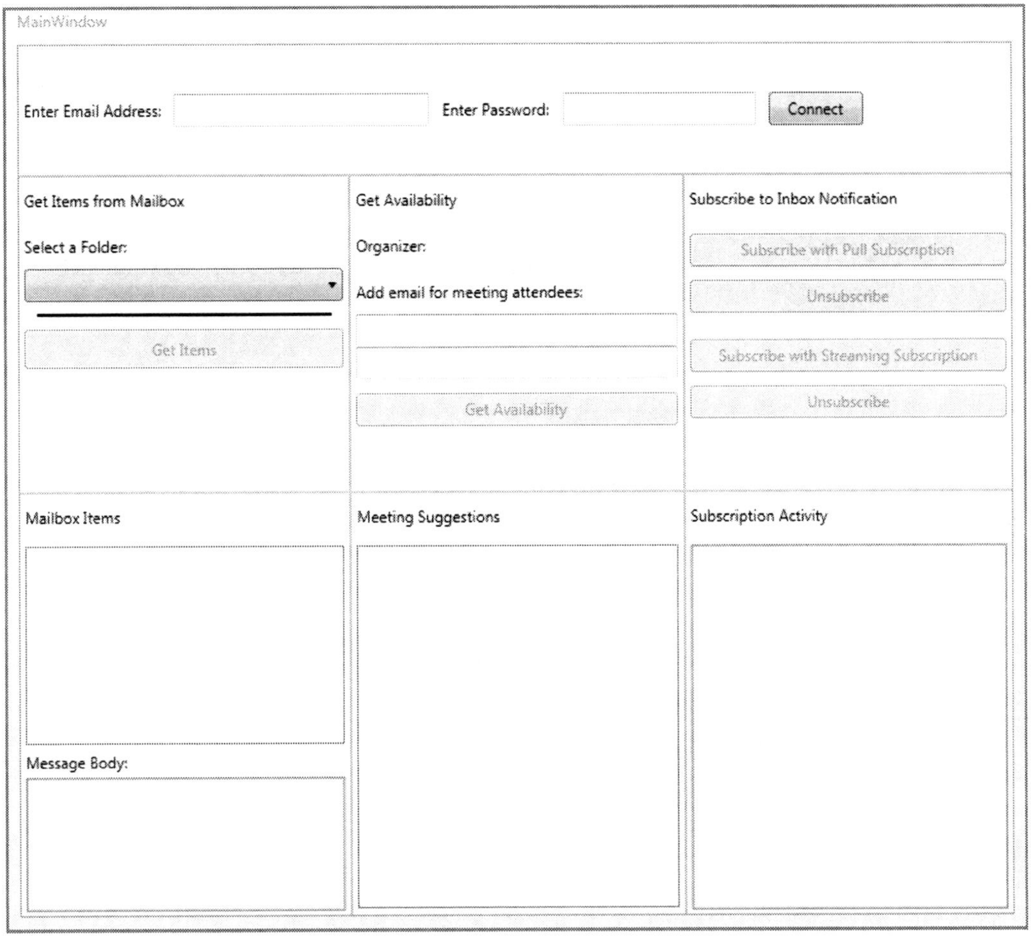

Figure 12-2. The main window form design

The form is divided into four areas that correspond to the four basic functions that you will implement in this chapter. The section across the top contains the controls you'll use to connect to the Exchange server. The other areas of the form consist of three columns that will be used to implement the remaining functions. From left to right the columns are for:

- Querying the mailbox contents

- Checking for availability

- Subscribing to inbox notifications

Preparing the Visual Studio Project

Before I explain the coding that is required, you'll first make some changes in the project's environment. You'll install the managed API, add the necessary reference, and configure .NET.

Installing the EWS Managed API

The features in Exchange Online are exposed to client applications through EWS. However, instead of calling the web service directly, you'll use a managed API. You'll need to install the API on your client machine. You can download the installation file (.msi) at www.microsoft.com/download/en/details.aspx?id=13480.

■ **Note** The term *managed API* refers to the fact that the assemblies are written in .NET and run under the same management processes as any other .NET-based coding. This results in the code being compiled into the Common Language Runtime (CLR) and then compiled further upon the first execution. The alternative would be *native* code, which is compiled to machine language and run directly against the core services of the OS.

When you run this installation file, you'll see the dialog box shown in Figure 12-3.

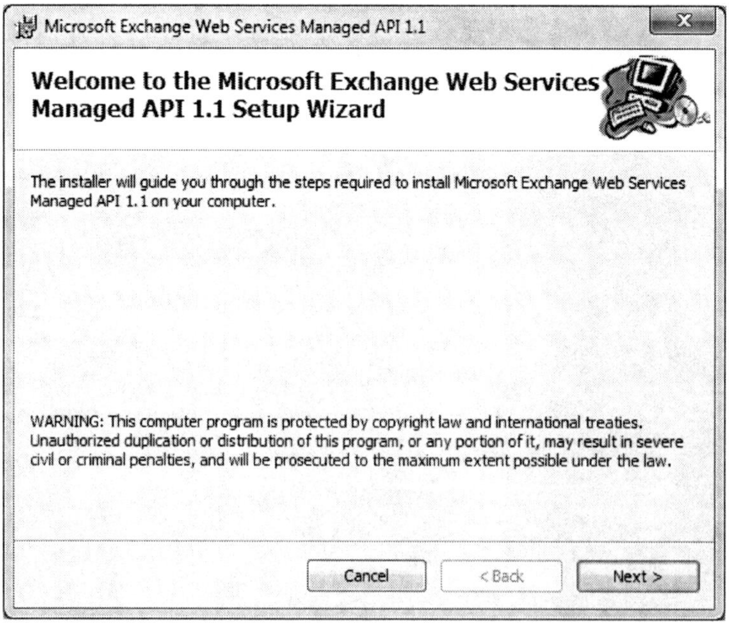

Figure 12-3. Installing the EWS Managed API

You'll be presented with several more dialog boxes; you can use all the default values to complete the installation.

Adding a Reference

When it has finished, you'll need to add a reference to your project.

1. Right-click the ExchangeApp project in Solution Explorer and click the Add Reference link.

2. Select the Browse tab and browse to the C:\Program Files\Microsoft\Exchange\Web Services\1.1 folder.

3. Select the Microsoft.Exchange.WebServices.dll file, as shown in Figure 12-4.

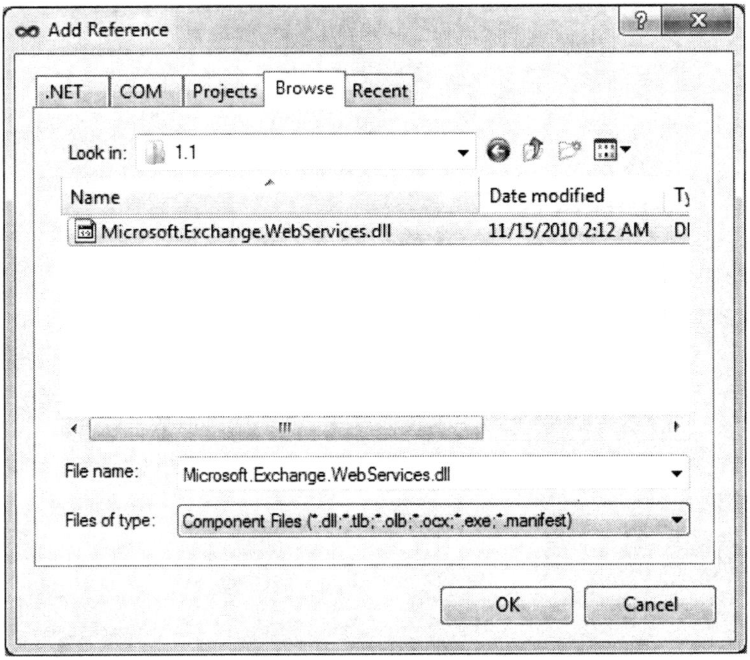

Figure 12-4. Adding a reference to the EWS Managed API

Adding the Full .NET Profile

In many cases, when you create a project for a client application, such as a WPF desktop application, only the .NET client profile is used. However, this project needs the full .NET 4.0 Framework. Right-click the ExchangeApp project and select the Properties link. If the target framework is .NET Framework 4 Client Profile, change it to .NET Framework 4, as shown in Figure 12-5.

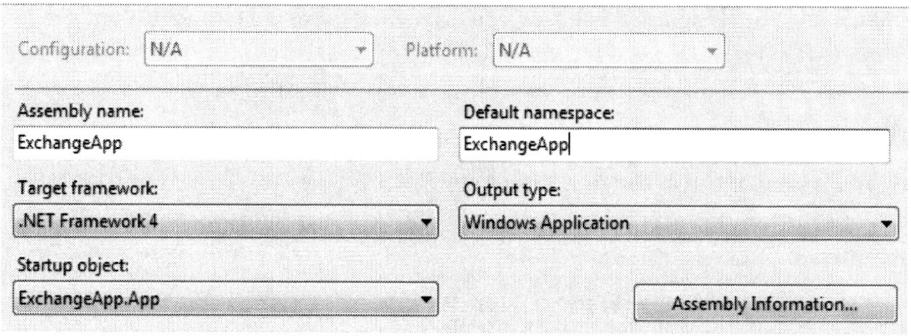

Figure 12-5. Changing the target .NET Framework

You will probably see the warning shown in Figure 12-6. Click the Yes button to continue.

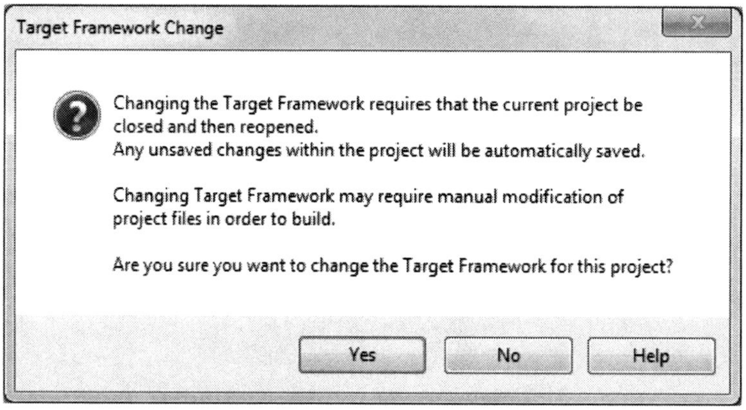

Figure 12-6. Warning about changing the target framework

Creating the Data Class

To help organize the code, you'll create a separate class that contains the code used to communicate with Exchange via the managed API. The logic in the code-behind class, MainWindow.xaml.cs, provides the glue for moving the Exchange data to the form controls.

Right-click the ExchangeApp project in Solution Explorer and select Add ➤ Class. In the Add New Item dialog box, enter the class name **ExchangeDataContext**. Then click the Add button to create the class. Add the following namespaces to this file:

```
using Microsoft.Exchange.WebServices.Data;
using Microsoft.Exchange.WebServices.Autodiscover;
using System.Windows;
```

Open the MainWindow.xaml.cs code-behind file and add the following namespaces:

```
using System.Web;
using Microsoft.Exchange.WebServices.Data;
using System.Windows.Threading;
```

Connecting to Exchange with Autodiscover

Now you're ready to implement the four functions I listed at the beginning of the chapter:

- Connecting to the Exchange Online server

- Accessing mailbox items

- Determining availability

- Subscribing to notifications

Before you can do anything else, you'll need to connect to the Exchange server. I'll start with that feature. You will first add the logic in the ExchangeDataContext class that calls the autodiscover process. Then you'll implement the click event in the code-behind class.

Implementing the ExchangeDataContext Class

Go to the ExchangeDataContext class and add the code shown in Listing 12-1 to the class definition.

Listing 12-1. Connecting to the Exchange Server

```
private ExchangeService _service;

public ExchangeDataContext(string emailAddress, string password)
{
    _service = GetBinding(emailAddress, password);
}

public ExchangeService GetService()
{
    return _service;
}

static ExchangeService GetBinding(string emailAddress, string password)
{
    // Create the binding.
    ExchangeService service =
        new ExchangeService(ExchangeVersion.Exchange2010_SP1);

    // Define credentials.
    service.Credentials = new WebCredentials(emailAddress, password);

    // Use the AutodiscoverUrl method to locate the service endpoint.
    try
    {
        service.AutodiscoverUrl(emailAddress, RedirectionUrlValidationCallback);
```

```
        }
        catch (AutodiscoverRemoteException ex)
        {
            MessageBox.Show("Autodiscover error: " + ex.Message);
        }
        catch (Exception ex)
        {
            MessageBox.Show("Error: " + ex.Message);
        }

        return service;
    }

    static bool RedirectionUrlValidationCallback(String redirectionUrl)
    {
        // Perform validation.
        // Validation is developer dependent to ensure a safe redirect.
        return true;
    }
```

This code is used to return an ExchangeService class. This defines a private _service member that is created by the class constructor. The GetService() method simply returns this private member.

The real work is done in the GetBinding() method. This method first creates an instance of the ExchangeService class. Notice that the constructor takes a version parameter. The managed API allows you to specify which version of Exchange you want to use. It then supplies the credentials, which consist of the e-mail address associated with the inbox and a password.

Finally, the AutodiscoverUrl() method is called. This is where the API does the work of finding the appropriate Exchange server and setting up the connection. This method takes a few seconds to complete. The code also handles exceptions. Finally, a callback is created to validate any redirects that may be configured for this inbox.

Modifying the Code-Behind Class

Add the following methods to the MainWindow.xaml.cs code-behind file:

```
private ExchangeDataContext _context;
private void btnConnect_Click(object sender, RoutedEventArgs e)
{
    _context = new ExchangeDataContext(txtEmailAddress.Text, txtPassword.Password);
    EnableButtons();
}

protected void EnableButtons()
{
    btnGetAvailability.IsEnabled = true;
    btnGetItems.IsEnabled = true;
    btnPullSubscribe.IsEnabled = true;
    btnStreamSubscribe.IsEnabled = true;
}
```

When the Connect button is clicked, this code will create an instance of the `ExchangeDataContext` class, passing in the credentials that were specified on the form. Now that the application is connected to the Exchange server, the `EnableButtons()` method enables the other buttons that you will implement shortly.

Accessing the Folder Contents

The next function that you will implement is displaying the contents of the selected folder.

Retrieving Items from Exchange

Add the methods shown in Listing 12-2 to the `ExchangeDataContext` class.

Listing 12-2. Reading the Mailbox Items

```
public List<Folder> GetFolders(FolderId parentFolderID)
{
    return _service.FindFolders(parentFolderID, null).ToList();
}

public List<Item> GetMailboxItems(WellKnownFolderName folder)
{
    return _service.FindItems(folder, new ItemView(30)).ToList();
}

public Item GetItem(ItemId itemId)
{
    List<ItemId> items = new List<ItemId>() { itemId };

    PropertySet properties = new PropertySet(BasePropertySet.IdOnly,
        EmailMessageSchema.Body, EmailMessageSchema.Sender,
        EmailMessageSchema.Subject);
    properties.RequestedBodyType = BodyType.Text;
    ServiceResponseCollection<GetItemResponse> response =
        _service.BindToItems(items, properties);

    return response[0].Item;
}
```

These methods retrieve the various Exchange objects from the service.

- `GetFolders()` returns all child folders for the given parent.
- `GetMailboxItems()` returns all items within the given folder.
- `GetItem()` returns an item for the given ItemId.
  - This method uses the `BindToItems()` method to populates only the properties specified in the `PropertySet` type parameter.

- The RequestedBodyType attribute is set to BodyType.Text since the application will display the information in a TextBox. HTML is returned by default.

Displaying the Mailbox Items

Add this code to the MainWindow class constructor, which will set up the event handler for the OnLoaded event:

```
this.Loaded += MainWindow_Loaded;
```

Then add the methods shown in Listing 12-3 to the MainWindow.xaml.cs code-behind class.

Listing 12-3. Displaying the Mailbox Contents

```
void MainWindow_Loaded(object sender, RoutedEventArgs e)
{
    BindWellKnownFolderList();
}

protected void BindWellKnownFolderList()
{
    //bind the known folders to the list box
    foreach(WellKnownFolderName folderName in
        Enum.GetValues(typeof(WellKnownFolderName)))
    {
        cboWellKnownFolders.Items.Add(folderName);
    }
}

private void btnGetItems_Click(object sender, RoutedEventArgs e)
{
    //check for given values
    if (string.IsNullOrWhiteSpace(txtEmailAddress.Text))
    {
        MessageBox.Show("You must enter an email address to proceed.");
        return;
    }

    if (cboWellKnownFolders.SelectedIndex < 0)
    {
        MessageBox.Show("You must select a folder to proceed");
        return;
    }

    //get items for the given folder and bind them to the list box
    lstItems.ItemsSource = _context.GetMailboxItems
        ((WellKnownFolderName)cboWellKnownFolders.SelectedItem);
}
```

```
private void lstItems_SelectionChanged(object sender, SelectionChangedEventArgs e)
{
    Item email = _context.GetItem(((Item)lstItems.SelectedItem).Id);

    txtMessageBody.Text = "From:" + ((EmailMessage)email).Sender
                                  + Environment.NewLine;
    txtMessageBody.Text += Environment.NewLine;
    txtMessageBody.Text += email.Body;
}

private void btnGetAvailability_Click(object sender, RoutedEventArgs e)
{
}

private void btnPullSubscribe_Click(object sender, RoutedEventArgs e)
{
}

private void btnPullUnsubscribe_Click(object sender, RoutedEventArgs e)
{
}

private void btnStreamSubscribe_Click(object sender, RoutedEventArgs e)
{
}

private void btnStreamUnsubscribe_Click(object sender, RoutedEventArgs e)
{
}
```

A ComboBox is populated when the application is loaded through the BindWellKnownFolderList() method. This ComboBox displays the default folders for Exchange. This method simply iterates through the WellKnownFolders enum and adds each item.

When the GetItems button is clicked, the GetMailboxItems() method is called from the DataContext class, and the results are bound to the lstItems ListBox. When an item is selected from the ListBox, the GetItem() method is called, and the results are used to populate the TextBox to display the sender and the body.

■ **Note** The last five methods provide an empty event handler for each of the remaining command buttons on the form. You will need these to prevent compiler errors. You will implement these later.

Testing the Application

Now is a good time to pause and test the functions that you have already implemented. Press F5 to compile and launch the application. Enter the e-mail address for a mailbox that is hosted on Office 365 and the corresponding password, and then click the Connect button, as shown in Figure 12-7. It will take a few seconds for the autodiscover process to obtain the correct address.

Figure 12-7. Connecting to Exchange Online

When the application has connected, most of the command buttons will be enabled. Select a folder and click the Get Items button. The items in that folder should be shown in the Mailbox Items list. Select one of these items and the message box will be displayed below it. The form will look similar to Figure 12-8.

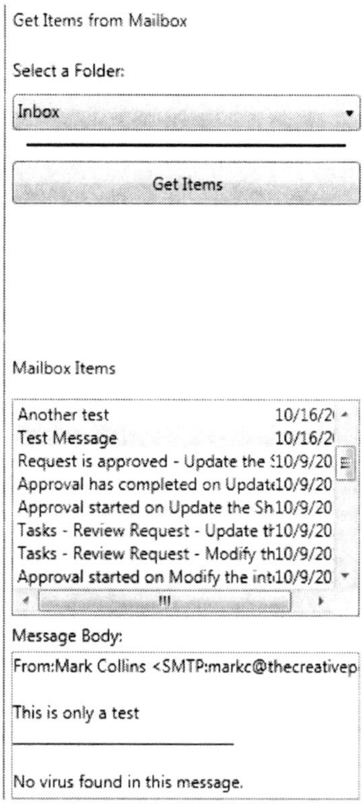

Figure 12-8. Displaying the mailbox items

Checking Availability

Exchange Online provides the ability to query the server for the availability of accounts based on their calendar. This provides the information necessary to schedule meetings when the primary stakeholders are free. The meeting parameters, including the attendees, the time, and the duration of the meeting, are sent to the server. The service returns a list of possible meeting times with a quality setting based on the settings of the query.

■ **Note** Availability is only provided for users with accounts on the Exchange Online server. This service does not query calendars outside of the Exchange server.

Retrieving the Availability Results

Add the method shown in Listing 12-4 to the ExchangeDataContext class.

Listing 12-4. Querying Availability from Exchange

```
public GetUserAvailabilityResults GetAvailability
    (string organizer,
     List<string> requiredAttendees,
     int meetingDuration,
     int timeWindowDays)
{
    List<AttendeeInfo> attendees = new List<AttendeeInfo>();

    //add organizer
    attendees.Add(new AttendeeInfo()
    {
        SmtpAddress = organizer,
        AttendeeType = MeetingAttendeeType.Organizer
    });

    //add required attendees
    foreach(string attendee in requiredAttendees)
    {
        attendees.Add(new AttendeeInfo()
        {
            SmtpAddress = attendee,
            AttendeeType = MeetingAttendeeType.Required
        });
    }

    //setup options
    AvailabilityOptions options = new AvailabilityOptions()
    {
        MeetingDuration = meetingDuration,
```

```
        MaximumNonWorkHoursSuggestionsPerDay = 4,
        MinimumSuggestionQuality = SuggestionQuality.Good,
        RequestedFreeBusyView = FreeBusyViewType.FreeBusy
    };

    GetUserAvailabilityResults results = _service.GetUserAvailability
        (attendees,
         new TimeWindow(DateTime.Now, DateTime.Now.AddDays(timeWindowDays)),
         AvailabilityData.FreeBusyAndSuggestions,
         options);

    return results;
}
```

This code provides the method for getting the availability suggestions for given e-mail addresses. The attendees are added using the AttendeeInfo object. The account used to connect to the Exchange service is used as the organizer. The e-mail addresses added in the form are added as required attendees. The AttendeeOptions object is used to set the options for the search against the service, setting the following properties:

- MeetingDuration: How long the open window needs to be

- MaximumNonWorkingHoursSuggestionsPerDay : Whether the search should include suggestions during non-working hours

- MinimumSuggestionQuality: Only returns items of this value and above

- RequestedFreeBusyView: What type of data is returned

The attendees' options are passed into the GetUserAvailabilityResults() service call along with the AvailabilityData setting. This property indicates whether to include suggestions in the result data.

Displaying the Results

Add the following code to the btnConnect_Click() method. This simply defaults the meeting organizer to the same inbox that you connected to.

```
lblOrganizer.Text += " " + txtEmailAddress.Text;
```

Replace the blank implementation of the Get Availability button with the code shown in Listing 12-5.

Listing 12-5. Implementing the Get Availability Button

```
private void btnGetAvailability_Click(object sender, RoutedEventArgs e)
{
    List<string> attendees = new List<string>();
    if (!string.IsNullOrWhiteSpace(txtAttendee1.Text))
    {
        attendees.Add(txtAttendee1.Text);
    }
```

```
    if (!string.IsNullOrWhiteSpace(txtAttendee2.Text))
    {
        attendees.Add(txtAttendee2.Text);
    }

    if (attendees.Count == 0)
    {
        MessageBox.Show("You must add at least one attendee to proceed.");
        return;
    }

    GetUserAvailabilityResults results =
        _context.GetAvailability(txtEmailAddress.Text, attendees, 30, 2);

    foreach (Suggestion suggestion in results.Suggestions)
    {
        foreach (TimeSuggestion time in suggestion.TimeSuggestions)
        {
            lstSuggestions.Items.Add(time);
        }
    }
}
```

When the Get Availability button is clicked, the attendees are added and passed into the GetUserAvailabilityResults() method in the DataContext. The returned suggestions are added to the lstSuggestions ListBox for display.

Testing the Availability Feature

Let's test the availability feature:

1. Press F5 to compile and start the application.

2. Enter an e-mail address and password, and click the Connect button as you did before. Once the buttons are enabled, the meeting organizer will be set using the e-mail address that was used to log in.

3. Specify another user or two and click the Get Availability button. The available time slots will be displayed in the suggestions list, as shown in Figure 12-9.

Get Availability

Organizer: markc@apress365.com

Add email for meeting attendees:

michaelm@apress365.com

corbinc@apress365.com

Get Availability

Meeting Suggestions

10/18/2011 10:00:00 PM	Good
10/18/2011 10:30:00 PM	Good
10/18/2011 11:00:00 PM	Good
10/18/2011 11:30:00 PM	Good
10/19/2011 9:00:00 AM	Excellent
10/19/2011 9:30:00 AM	Excellent
10/19/2011 10:00:00 AM	Excellent
10/19/2011 10:30:00 AM	Excellent
10/19/2011 11:00:00 AM	Excellent
10/19/2011 11:30:00 AM	Excellent
10/19/2011 12:00:00 PM	Excellent
10/19/2011 12:30:00 PM	Excellent
10/19/2011 1:00:00 PM	Excellent
10/19/2011 1:30:00 PM	Excellent

Figure 12-9. Displaying the availability results

Subscribing to Notifications

For the final function, you will set up a subscription to be notified when a new item is added to the inbox. There are three types of subscriptions:

- The first, called a *pull notification*, happens when the client makes periodic calls to check for updates since the last call. This works by subscribing to the notification service and then polling that service for changes. A *watermark* is set each time the service is polled. Any changes that occurred since the last watermark are returned. This can easily be done in application code, but it does require polling the service. Notifications are not sent back to the subscription object automatically. Either some type of user event must be used to trigger the application to check the service or some sort of timer must be used.

- The second is called *streaming notification*. With this type of notification, an event is raised automatically. This works by opening a constant connection with the Exchange service. Notifications occur automatically. An event handler is used to respond to any notifications that are received from the subscription. A streaming subscription can only be open for 30 minutes or less. Any application designed to be open longer than this must either restart a streaming subscription after 30 minutes or use another type of subscription.

- The third is called *push notification*. Push notification works by subscribing to a notification service, similarly to a pull notification, except that a listener service is set up to receive notification events. This typically involves a WCF service, or some other type of web service that can receive the online event. This requirement for a listening service means that our WCF application does not demonstrate push notification.

Setting Up Pull Notification

Replace the blank implementations of the Pull Subscribe and Pull Unsubscribe buttons with the code shown in Listing 12-6.

Listing 12-6. Implementing Pull Notification

```
private PullSubscription _pullSubscription;
private StreamingSubscription _streamSubscription;
DispatcherTimer _timer;

private void btnPullSubscribe_Click(object sender, RoutedEventArgs e)
{
    ExchangeService service = _context.GetService();

    _pullSubscription = service.SubscribeToPullNotifications
        (new FolderId[] {WellKnownFolderName.Inbox}, 10, null, EventType.NewMail);
    txtSubscriptionActivity.Text
        += "Pull Subscription Created" + Environment.NewLine;

    //set up polling
    _timer = new DispatcherTimer();
    _timer.Interval = TimeSpan.FromSeconds(10);
    _timer.Tick += timer_Tick;
    _timer.Start();

    btnPullSubscribe.IsEnabled = false;
    btnPullUnsubscribe.IsEnabled = true;
}

void timer_Tick(object sender, EventArgs e)
{
    GetEventsResults results = _pullSubscription.GetEvents();

    txtSubscriptionActivity.Text
        += "Pull Subscription checked for new items" + Environment.NewLine;
```

```
    foreach (ItemEvent itemEvent in results.ItemEvents)
    {
        switch (itemEvent.EventType)
        {
            case EventType.NewMail:
                txtSubscriptionActivity.Text
                    += "Pull Subscription: New email received"
                    + Environment.NewLine;
                break;
        }
    }
}

private void btnPullUnsubscribe_Click(object sender, RoutedEventArgs e)
{
    _timer.Stop();

    _pullSubscription.Unsubscribe();

    txtSubscriptionActivity.Text
        += "Pull Subscription Unsubscribed" + Environment.NewLine;

    btnPullSubscribe.IsEnabled = true;
    btnPullUnsubscribe.IsEnabled = false;
}
```

When the Pull Subscribe button is clicked, a PullSubscription object is created. The WellKnownFolderName.Inbox enum is passed, along with a timeout of 10 (minutes) and the EventType.NewMail enum to sent the subscription to be notified of any new items that are received in the inbox. The 10-minute timeout allows the subscription to expire if it is not polled within 10 minutes.

A DispatchTimer is set up to poll the PullSubscription object every 10 seconds. It uses the timer_Tick() method. This code calls the GetEvents() method, which checks for notifications and sets a new watermark. An event is recorded in the txtSubsctiptionActivity TextBox, and any notifications are processed. Each notification is recorded in the txtSubscriptionActivity TextBox as well.

The Pull Unsubscribe button stops the timer and calls the Unsubscribe() method, which ends the subscription. An event is recorded in the activity TextBox.

Using Streaming Notification

Replace the blank implementations of the Stream Subscribe and Stream Unsubscribe buttons with the code shown in Listing 12-7.

Listing 12-7. Implementing Streaming Notification

```
private void btnStreamSubscribe_Click(object sender, RoutedEventArgs e)
{
    ExchangeService service = _context.GetService();

    _streamSubscription = service.SubscribeToStreamingNotifications
```

```
        (new FolderId[] { WellKnownFolderName.Inbox }, EventType.NewMail);

    StreamingSubscriptionConnection connection =
        new StreamingSubscriptionConnection(service, 10);

    connection.AddSubscription(_streamSubscription);
    connection.OnNotificationEvent += connection_OnNotificationEvent;

    connection.Open();

    txtSubscriptionActivity.Text
        += "Stream Subscription Created" + Environment.NewLine;

    btnStreamSubscribe.IsEnabled = false;
    btnStreamUnsubscribe.IsEnabled = true;
}

void connection_OnNotificationEvent(object sender, NotificationEventArgs args)
{
    foreach(NotificationEvent notification in args.Events)
    {
        switch (notification.EventType)
        {
            case EventType.NewMail:
                Dispatcher.Invoke(new Action(
                    delegate()
                    {
                        txtSubscriptionActivity.Text
                            += "Stream Subscription: New email received"
                            + Environment.NewLine;
                    }));
                break;
        }
    }
}

private void btnStreamUnsubscribe_Click(object sender, RoutedEventArgs e)
{
    _streamSubscription.Unsubscribe();

    txtSubscriptionActivity.Text
        += "Stream Subscription Unsubscribed" + Environment.NewLine;

    btnStreamSubscribe.IsEnabled = true;
    btnStreamUnsubscribe.IsEnabled = false;
}
```

When the Stream Subscribe button is clicked, a streaming subscription is created using
WellKnownFolderName.Inbox and EventType.NewMail parameter values to set up the service to notify the
subscription object when a new item is received in the inbox. A StreamingSubscriptionConnection object

is created and set to use the connection_OnNotificationEvent() method as its even handler. The connection is opened and the event is recorded in the activity TextBox.

Since this is a streaming subscription, it will receive notifications automatically from the service. It will then call the specified event handler. In this case, that is the connection_OnNotification() method. This method simply records the event into the activity TextBox. The Dispatcher.Invoke() method is used because the event handler is running on a different thread than the UI. To manipulate UI objects, the dispatcher must be used.

When the Stream Unsubscribe button is clicked, the Unsubscribe() method is called, which ends the subscription. The event is recorded in the activity TextBox.

Testing the Subscription Functions

Start the application and connect to the Exchange server as you have done before:

1. After it has connected, click the Subscribe with Pull Subscription button.

2. Then send an e-mail to this inbox (the one you just connected with).

3. After a few minutes you should see the "New e-mail received" text appear in the Subscription Activity list, as shown in Figure 12-10. Click the Unsubscribe button to stop the polling.

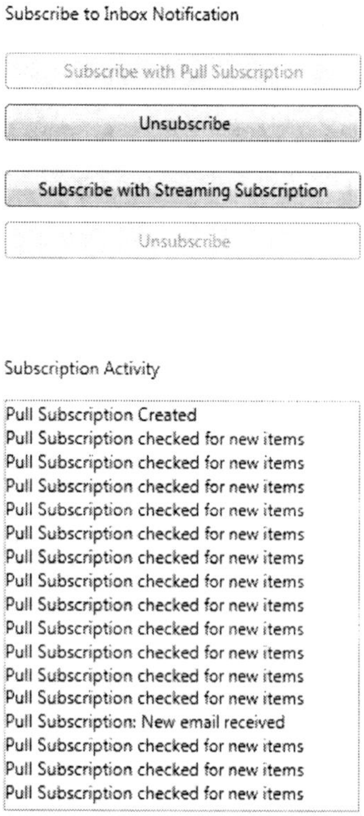

Figure 12-10. Testing the pull notification

4. Now click the Subscribe with Streaming Subscription button and send another e-mail to this inbox.

5. You should see the "New e-mail received" text appear shortly after the e-mail arrives. The form will look like Figure 12-11. Click the Unsubscribe button to stop the polling.

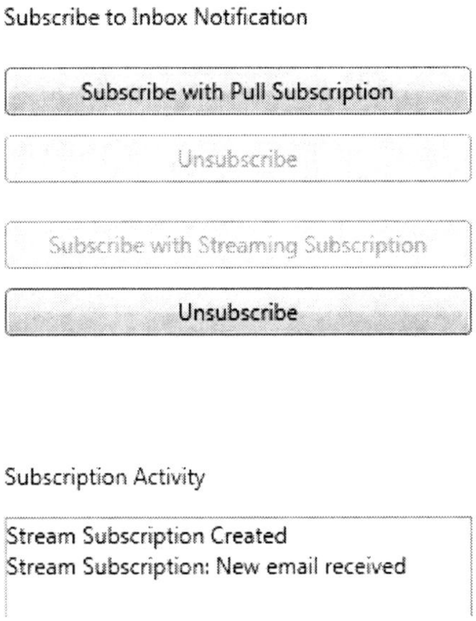

Subscribe to Inbox Notification

Subscribe with Pull Subscription

Unsubscribe

Subscribe with Streaming Subscription

Unsubscribe

Subscription Activity

Stream Subscription Created
Stream Subscription: New email received

Figure 12-11.Testing the stream notification

Summary

In this chapter, you created a WPF application that does the following, for the purposes of demonstrating the features offered by EWS:

- Uses the autodiscover service to dynamically connect to Exchange Online by determining which service is currently used to host the specified mailbox

- Queries a mailbox and return all items within a specified folder

- Checks availability of accounts for a requested meeting, displaying suggested times returned by the service

- Subscribes to notification services to respond programmatically to events occurring within the Exchange service

This type of development allows features typically found in Outlook to be included in your custom applications. This type of functionality has been available for a long time, and could be used as long as Exchange server was hosted within your network. Now this powerful set of features is available to you through the cloud.

CHAPTER 13

Developing Lync Applications

The Lync features are provided to developers to make custom Lync applications or embed Lync features within an existing application. In this chapter I will show you how to build a custom Lync application. You'll start out with a simple application that includes a presence indicator in a WPF application. You'll then use more of the standard Lync controls to enhance the application by adding a contact search feature and a custom contact list. Finally, you'll use Lync automation to start a conversation and dock the conversation window in your custom application.

I introduced these in Chapter 3, but as a brief review, the Lync components that you'll use in this chapter are

- **Lync controls**: You will add controls such as PresenceIndicator and ContactSearch to integrate Lync functionality directly into the WPF application.

- **Lync automation**: You will call Lync automation to control the running Lync client on the local machine and send conversation information.

These are shown in Figure 13-1.

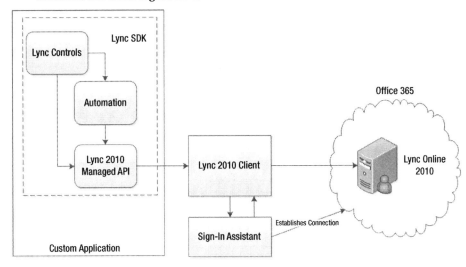

Figure 13-1. Lync architecture

The Lync 2010 client application has a key role in the overall architecture. It manages the connection to the server component (Lync Online 2010). It uses the Online Services Sign-In Assistant to provide the credentials to the server and establish this connection.

■ **Caution** Lync is the only Office 365 feature that requires a client installation. In order to use any of the Lync features, you must install the Lync 2010 client. A custom Lync application does not replace the need for the Lync client. Rather, the custom application will expect a running instance of the Lync client on the client machine.

If you have not already done so, you will need to download and install the Lync 2010 SDK. You can download this at www.microsoft.com/download/en/details.aspx?id=18898. This will download the LyncSdkSetup.exe application. Run this to install the SDK on your machine. This will provide the necessary assemblies as well as add project templates to Visual Studio for Lync development.

Using the Lync Project Template

Visual Studio 2010 includes a project template that will create a Lync-enabled WPF application. You will use this to create the initial application.

Creating the Visual Studio Project

Let's start the example:

1. Start Visual Studio 2010 and create a new project.

2. Select the Lync WPF Application project template, as shown in Figure 13-2.

3. Enter the project name **LyncApp** and click the OK button to create the project.

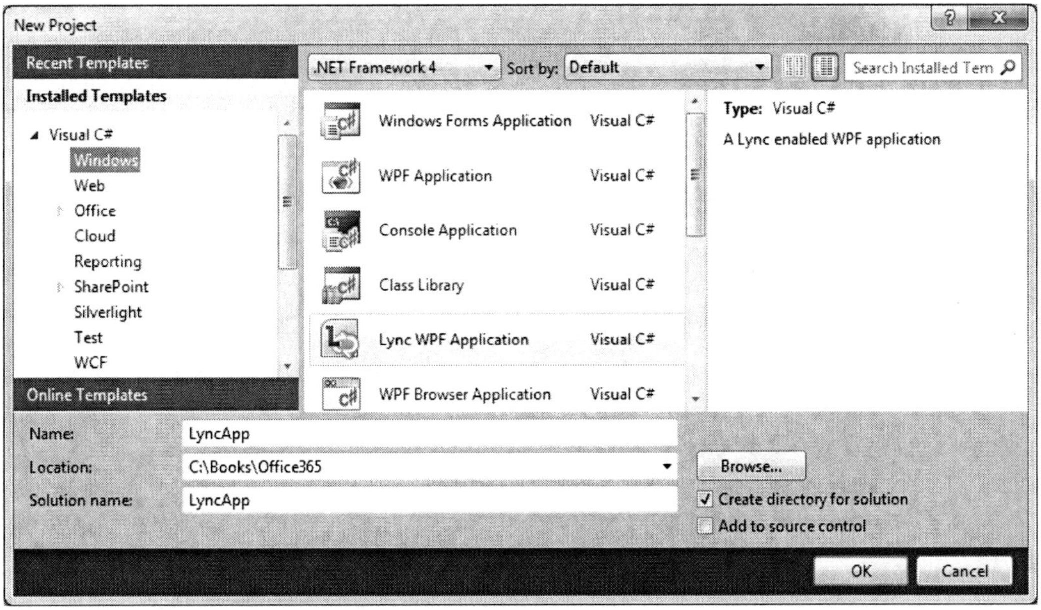

Figure 13-2. Creating a Lync-enabled WPF application project

This project template creates a standard WPF application, but it performs two other steps that will help you get started with Lync. First, it adds the following references:

- `Microsoft.Lync.Controls`
- `Microsoft.Lync.Controls.Framework`
- `Microsoft.Lync.Model`
- `Microsoft.Lync.Utilities`

Second, the template adds a presence indicator control to the initial window. The `Window1.xaml` file will look like Figure 13-3, and the XAML code is shown in Listing 13-1.

Figure 13-3. The initial window design

Listing 13-1. The Initial XAML Implementation

```
<Window x:Class="LyncApp.Window1"
    xmlns="http://schemas.microsoft.com/winfx/2006/xaml/presentation"
    xmlns:x="http://schemas.microsoft.com/winfx/2006/xaml"
    xmlns:controls
        ="clr-namespace:Microsoft.Lync.Controls;assembly=Microsoft.Lync.Controls"
    Title="Window1" Height="Auto" Width="Auto">
    <Grid>
        <StackPanel Orientation="Horizontal"
                    HorizontalAlignment="Center"
                    VerticalAlignment="Center">
            <!--
                Show the presence indicator. Hover over the icon to see the contact
                card. Set Source to a valid SIP URI in your organization.
            -->
            <controls:PresenceIndicator
                x:Name="Presence"
                Source="sip:john@contoso.com"
                PhotoDisplayMode="Large"
                />
            <!-- Use the DisplayName property from PresenceIndicator to show
                the user's name -->
            <TextBlock
                Text="{Binding DisplayName, ElementName=Presence}"
                Margin="4,0,0,0"
                VerticalAlignment="Center"
                />
        </StackPanel>
    </Grid>
</Window>
```

The following line makes all of the Lync controls available to the application:

```
xmlns:controls
        ="clr-namespace:Microsoft.Lync.Controls;assembly=Microsoft.Lync.Controls"
```

And this line includes a presence indicator in the window:

```
<controls:PresenceIndicator
    x:Name="Presence"
    Source="sip:john@contoso.com"
    PhotoDisplayMode="Large"
    />
```

Testing the Initial Application

This initial application does not require any implementation in the code-behind file, Window1.xaml.cs. However, you will need to specify a valid Lync address. Edit the Window1.xaml file and replace john@contoso.com with your Office 365 login name. Make sure the Lync client is installed and you are signed in to the Lync server.

Press F5 to build and run the application. The window will show you presence status, as demonstrated in Figure 13-4.

Figure 13-4. Running the initial application

Hover over the presence indicator control to view the contact information and then click the Expand button in the bottom-right corner. The expanded view may look similar to Figure 13-5, depending on how the user was set up in Office 365.

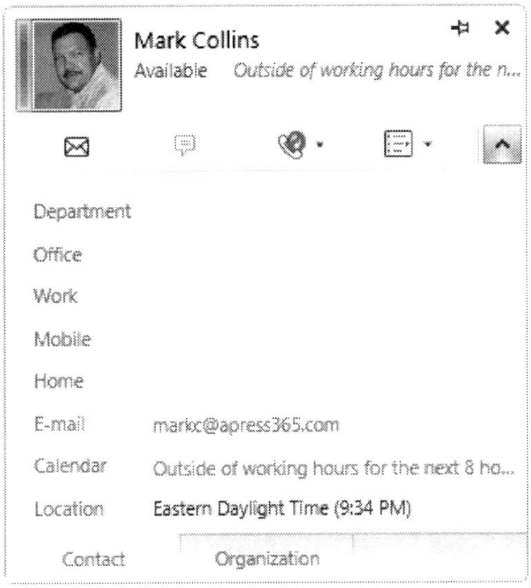

Figure 13-5. Viewing the contact card

While this application is still running, use the Lync client to change your status. Your WPF application should reflect the status change. Also try entering a note using the Lync client and then hovering over the presence indicator in your custom application to see the new note, as shown in Figure 13-6.

Figure 13-6. Displaying the status note

Using Lync Controls

The Lync SDK provides several controls that you can drag and drop onto your application. This allows you to easily embed these Lync features into a custom application. You already used one of these, PresenceIndicator, in the initial implementation. From the Visual Studio project, select the Window1.xaml file and you should see all of the available Lync controls in the toolbox, as shown in Figure 13-7.

```
Toolbox                         ▼ ⏸ ×
  ▷ Common WPF Controls
  ▷ All WPF Controls
  ▲ Lync SDK Controls
     ▶   Pointer
     ▦   ContactSearch
     ▦   ContactSearchInputBox
     ▦   ContactSearchResultList
     ▦   MyNoteBox
     ▦   MyPresenceChooser
     ▦   MyStatusArea
     ▦   ScheduleMeetingButton
     ▦   SendEmailButton
     ▦   SendFileButton
     ▦   ShareDesktopButton
     ▦   StartVideoCallButton
     ▦   ContactCard
     ▦   ContactList
     ▦   CustomContactList
     ▦   CustomContactListItem
     ▦   PresenceIndicator
     ▦   StartAudioCallButton
     ▦   StartInstantMessagingButton
  ▷ General
```

Figure 13-7. Listing all of the Lync controls

Dynamically Adjusting the Presence Indicator

Admittedly, displaying the presence of a hard-coded Lync address is not very useful. You'll extend the application to allow the user to select a contact from a drop-down list. The presence of the selected contact will then be displayed. The code-behind class will control the Lync address of the presence indicator based on the contact that was selected. You'll also provide an option to start a conversation with the selected contact.

Edit the Window1.xaml file and replace the entire contents with the code shown in Listing 13-2.

Listing 13-2. Revised XAML Implementation

```
<Window x:Class="LyncApp.Window1"
    xmlns="http://schemas.microsoft.com/winfx/2006/xaml/presentation"
    xmlns:x="http://schemas.microsoft.com/winfx/2006/xaml"
    xmlns:controls
        ="clr-namespace:Microsoft.Lync.Controls;assembly=Microsoft.Lync.Controls"
    Title="Window1" Height="Auto" Width="Auto">
    <Grid>
        <Grid.RowDefinitions>
            <RowDefinition Height="54" />
            <RowDefinition />
        </Grid.RowDefinitions>
        <StackPanel Orientation="Horizontal" Grid.Row="0">
            <TextBlock Margin="15" Text="View Presence of Selected Contact:" />
            <ComboBox x:Name="cboContacts" Width="200" Height="25" Margin="0,0,20,0"
                    SelectionChanged="cboContacts_SelectionChanged" />
            <!-- Presence Indicator -->
            <controls:PresenceIndicator PhotoDisplayMode="Large" x:Name="lyncPresence" />
            <!-- Start Instant Message -->
            <controls:StartInstantMessagingButton x:Name="lyncStartMessage" Height="25"
                                        Margin="20,10,10,10" />
        </StackPanel>
    </Grid>
</Window>
```

The Design tab should look like Figure 13-8.

Figure 13-8. The design of the revised window

In addition to the PresenceIndicator control, the window now has a ComboBox that will contain the available contacts and a StartInstantMessagingButton control that will be used to start a conversation with the selected contact.

To populate the ComboBox, you'll need a class to represent the values of each contact. This simple class has two members, name and sipAddress. From Solution Explorer, right-click the LyncApp project and click New ➤ Class. Enter the class name **Contact.cs**. Then enter the following code for its implementation:

```
using System;
using System.Collections.Generic;
using System.Linq;
using System.Text;

namespace LyncApp
{
    public class Contact
    {
        public string name { get; set; }
        public string sipAddress { get; set; }
    }
}
```

The initial application did not require any implementation in the code-behind class. However, now you'll need to provide code to update the presence indicator based on the selected contact. Enter the code shown in Listing 13-3.

Listing 13-3. Implementation ofWindow1.xaml.cs Code-Behind Class

```
using System;
using System.Collections.Generic;
using System.Text;
using System.Windows;
using System.Windows.Controls;
using System.Windows.Data;
using System.Windows.Documents;
using System.Windows.Input;
using System.Windows.Media;
using System.Windows.Media.Imaging;
using System.Windows.Navigation;
using System.Windows.Shapes;

namespace LyncApp
{
    /// <summary>
    /// Interaction logic for Window1.xaml
    /// </summary>
    public partial class Window1 : Window
    {
        public Window1()
        {
            InitializeComponent();
            this.Loaded += MainWindow_Loaded;
        }

        void MainWindow_Loaded(object sender, RoutedEventArgs e)
        {
            BuildContactList();
```

```
        LoadContacts();
    }

    private List<Contact> _contacts = new List<Contact>();

    protected void BuildContactList()
    {
        // Build collection of valid contacts -- using Contact class
        _contacts.Add(new Contact()
        {name = "Mark Collins", sipAddress = "sip:markc@apress365.com"});
        _contacts.Add(new Contact()
        {name = "Michael Mayberry", sipAddress = "sip:michaelm@apress365.com"});
        _contacts.Add(new Contact()
        {name = "Corbin Collins", sipAddress = "sip:corbinc@apress365.com"});
        _contacts.Add(new Contact()
        {name = "Paul Michaels", sipAddress = "sip:paulm@apress365.com"});
        _contacts.Add(new Contact()
        {name = "Jonathan Hassel", sipAddress = "sip:jonathanh@apress365.com"});
        _contacts.Add(new Contact()
        {name = "Martina Grom", sipAddress = "sip:martinag@apress365.com"});
    }

    protected void LoadContacts()
    {
        // Bind collection to combo box
        cboContacts.ItemsSource = _contacts;
        cboContacts.DisplayMemberPath = "name";
        cboContacts.SelectedValuePath = "sipAddress";
    }

    private void cboContacts_SelectionChanged
        (object sender, SelectionChangedEventArgs e)
    {
        // Set the sipAddress of the selected item as the
        // source for the presence indicator
        lyncPresence.Source = cboContacts.SelectedValue;

        // Set the start instant message button
        lyncStartMessage.Source = cboContacts.SelectedValue;
    }

}
}
```

This code creates a collection of Contact classes. The BuildContactList() method populates this collection using hard-coded values. You will need to change this implementation to use contacts that are reachable from your client. The LoadContacts() method binds this collection to the ComboBox.

The cboContacts_SelectionChanged() event handler is where the real work is done. This simply sets the Source property on both of the Lync controls. This will specify the Lync address used for determining the presence of the selected contact and the participant when starting a conversation.

Press F5 to build and run the application. Select a contact and their status will be displayed by the presence indicator, as shown in Figure 13-9.

Figure 13-9. Displaying the status of the selected contact

Click the button next to the presence indicator and a new conversation window will appear. A sample conversation is shown in Figure 13-10.

Figure 13-10. A conversation window lauched by the custom application

Searching for Contacts

The Lync controls include a couple that are useful for searching for a contact:

- ContactSearch: Searches for contacts
- ContactList: Displays the standard Lync client contact lists

This functionality is identical to what you'll find on the standard Lync 2010 client. To include these controls in your application, add the following code to the `Windows1.xaml` file, just after the current `StackPanel` control:

```
<!-- Contact controls -->
<StackPanel Orientation="Horizontal" Grid.Row="1">
    <controls:ContactSearch Width="300" />
    <controls:ContactList Width="300" />
</StackPanel>
```

■ **Tip** The `ContactSearch` control is actually a combination of two controls. The `ContactSearchInputBox` control is used to receive the search criteria and the `ContactSearchResultList` control displays the contacts that were found. You can enter these a separate controls, which will allow you to control where each is placed in the application. You would need to bind the two controls together so the results will be automatically displayed when the input is changed. The code will be similar to this:

```
<controls:ContactSearchInputBox x:Name="search"/>


<controls:ContactSearchResultList


    ItemsSource="{Binding Results, ElementName=search, Mode=OneWay}"


    ResultsState="{Binding SearchState, ElementName=search, Mode=OneWay}" />
```

There is no need to add any implementation to the code-behind class. Press F5 to build and run the application. In the search box, start typing a contact's name, and the matching contacts will be displayed, as shown in Figure 13-11.

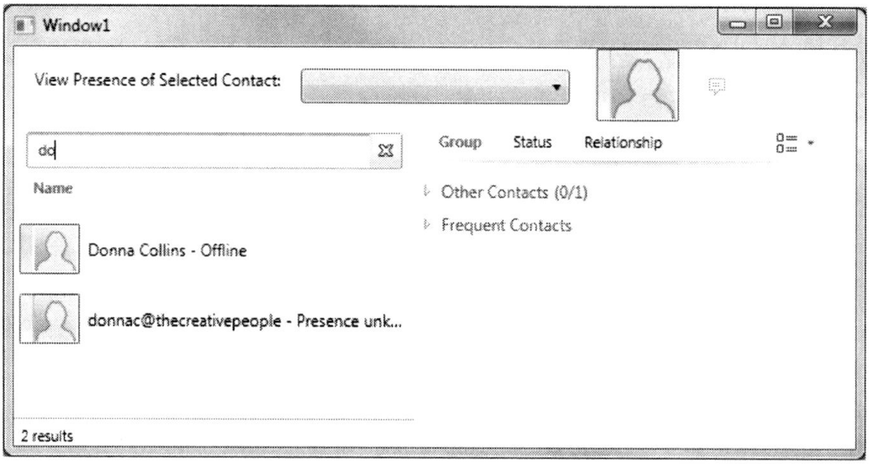

Figure 13-11. Searching for a contact

■ **Note** The search feature looks for people in your contact list. It also searches for all other people in your organization. Generally this is limited to users defined in your Office 365 account. If you have configured Active Directory federation, the search can include these federated domains as well.

The second control you added displays your contact list, and this is identical to the way the Lync 2010 client displays these. There are several ways to organize the contacts. I chose to group by relationship, so colleagues are listed first, followed by friends and family, as shown in Figure 13-12.

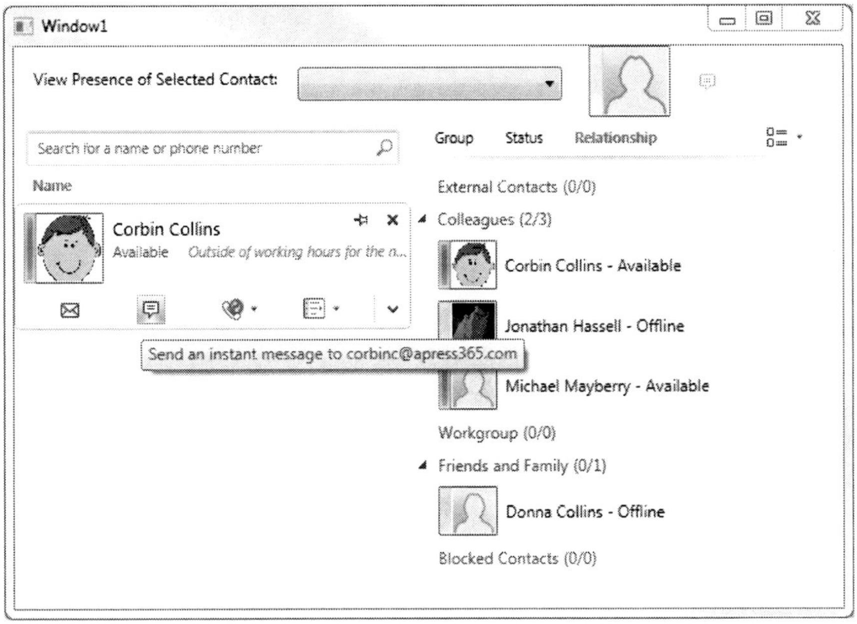

Figure 13-12. Displaying the standard contact list

If you hover the mouse over a contact, the contact card is displayed. This provides links for starting a conversation.

Adding a Custom Contact List

In a custom application, you might need to control the contacts that are listed based on other application data and/or business rules. For example, you might want the user's immediate supervisor to be included, as well as other specific individuals for certain escalation rules. Whatever the reason may be, you'll want to provide a list of contacts that are application driven and not based on the user's contact list.

This is easy to do by using the CustomContactList control. You add this control to the application and then set its list of contacts in the code-behind class. In the Window1.xaml file, replace the ContactList control with the CustomContactList control, as shown here:

```
<StackPanel Orientation="Horizontal" Grid.Row="1">
    <controls:ContactSearch Width="300" />
    <!--<controls:ContactList Width="300" />-->
    <controls:CustomContactList x:Name="lyncCustomList" Width="300" />
</StackPanel>
```

You will use Language Integrated Query (LINQ) in this application, so add the following namespace to the file:

```
using System.Linq;
```

In the code-behind class, `Window1.xaml.cs`, add the `LoadCustomContacts()` method using the following code:

```
protected void LoadCustomContacts()
{
    lyncCustomList.ItemsSource = (from C in _contacts select C.sipAddress);
}
```

Then call the `LoadCustomContacts()` method in the `MainWindow_Loaded()` event handler. Press F5 to build and run the application. Your custom contact list should include the same people that were included in the `ComboBox`, as shown in Figure 13-13.

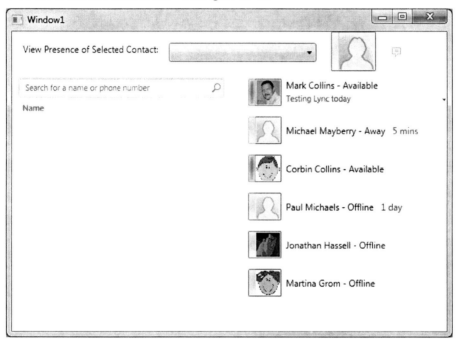

Figure 13-13. Using the custom contact list

Using Contextual Conversations

Lync allows you to embed information in a conversation to provide some *context* for the conversation. This is particularly useful in a custom Lync application. Suppose your application was viewing or editing some business data; a customer order, for example. If you needed to ask someone a question, the specific customer order could be provided in the conversation. The other participants in the conversation could then display the background information (context) when they receive your question.

There are two ways to do this:

- **Launch Link**: This allows you to include a link to launch an application from the conversation window. In this example, the link would start the business application and pre-load the specific customer order.

- • **Context Window Extensibility (CWE):** This allows you to host Silverlight application code inside the conversation window. In this case, this Lync client application could display details of the product in question inside the conversation window.

You can use both of these techniques in the same conversation. You can include the details directly in the conversation window as well as a link to launch the application. The recipient can then view the details already provided while still having the option to use the application to browse for more information.

I will now demonstrate how to use the Launch Link feature. The second approach, CWE, will be explained in Chapter 16.

Creating the Launch Application

With the Launch Link approach, the Lync client that is receiving the conversation request will include a link that will launch another application and pass the contextual information to it. The application will use this to display the appropriate data.

You'll now create the launch application. For this demo, the launch application will simply display the contextual information that was passed to it.

From Solution Explorer, right-click the LyncApp solution and click Add ➤ New Project. Select the WPF Application template and enter the name **ContextDemo**, as shown in Figure 13-14.

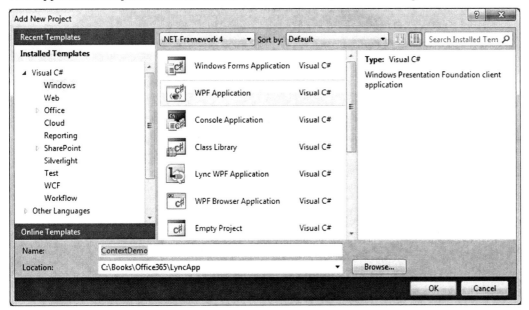

Figure 13-14. Adding the ContextDemo project

Replace the XAML code with the following:

```
<Window x:Class="ContextDemo.MainWindow"
        xmlns="http://schemas.microsoft.com/winfx/2006/xaml/presentation"
```

```
        xmlns:x="http://schemas.microsoft.com/winfx/2006/xaml"
        Title="MainWindow" Height="350" Width="525">
    <Grid>
        <TextBlock x:Name="lblData" Text="Hello!" VerticalAlignment="Center"
                   HorizontalAlignment="Center" FontSize="24"/>
    </Grid>
</Window>
```

This window has a single TextBlock control that contains the greeting "Hello!" In the code-behind class, add the following event handler:

```
void MainWindow_Loaded(object sender, RoutedEventArgs e)
{
    lblData.Text = Application.Current.Properties["testData"].ToString();
}
```

This code replaces the static text with the data that was supplied. Then link this event handler by adding the following code to the constructor:

```
this.Loaded += MainWindow_Loaded;
```

Finally, add the following method to the App.xaml.cs code-behind class:

```
protected override void OnStartup(StartupEventArgs e)
{
    if (e.Args != null && e.Args.Count() > 0)
    {
        this.Properties["testData"] = e.Args[0];
    }

    base.OnStartup(e);
}
```

This code receives the contextual data that is passed in as a command-line parameter and stores it as an application property so the window can display it.

Registering the Launch Application

You will need to register this application on all the clients that may receive the contextual Lync request. Create a .reg file using the code shown in Listing 13-4. You should generate a new Guid for the name of the context package. You might also need to adjust the path of the launch application.

Listing 13-4. Installation .reg File

```
Windows Registry Editor Version 5.00

[HKEY_CURRENT_USER\Software\Microsoft\Communicator\ContextPackages\
    {F03A7197-5E52-49FF-B28C-3ADA7636D02F}]]
"DefaultContextPackage"=dword:00000000
"Path" ="C:\\Books\\Office365\\LyncApp\\ContextDemo\\bin\\Debug\\ContextDemo.exe"
"InternalURL"=""
"ExternalURL"=""
"Name"="Contextual Demo"
"ExtensibilityWindowSize"=dword:00000001
```

```
"Parameters"="%AppData%,%AppId%"
```

■ **Note** The launch application will run on a different machine, not the one you're developing on. Once this application has been built, you'll need to copy the .exe file to the other machines that will be used. The path in the .reg file should point to where this application will be installed.

Modifying the Lync Application

Now, you'll go back to the custom Lync application and modify this to pass the contextual information. Open the Window1.xaml.cs code-behind class (in the LyncApp project). Add the following namespaces:

```
using Microsoft.Lync;
using Microsoft.Lync.Controls;
using Microsoft.Lync.Model;
using Microsoft.Lync.Model.Extensibility;
```

Then modify the cboContacts_SelectionChanged() event handler as shown in Listing 13-5, entering the additional code shown in bold.

Listing 13-5. The Modify Selection Changed Event Handler

```
private void cboContacts_SelectionChanged
    (object sender, SelectionChangedEventArgs e)
{
    // Set the sipAddress of the selected item as the
    // source for the presence indicator
    lyncPresence.Source = cboContacts.SelectedValue;

    // Set the start instant message button
    lyncStartMessage.Source = cboContacts.SelectedValue;

    // Set up the contextual information
    ConversationContextualInfo info = new ConversationContextualInfo();
    info.ApplicationId = "{F03A7197-5E52-49FF-B28C-3ADA7636D02F}";
    info.ApplicationData = "\"Can you see this?\"";
    info.Subject = "Hello " + ((Contact)cboContacts.SelectedItem).name +
                    ", take a look at this program!";

    lyncStartMessage.ContextualInformation = info;
}
```

459

Testing the Application

Build the ContextDemo project and copy the ContextDemo.exe and installation .reg files to one or more client machines. You can test this launch application by executing the following from a command prompt:

ContextDemo "Hello, World!"

Make sure the path in the .reg file points to the location of the launch application. Run the .reg file to register this application with Lync. You will probably see the warning shown in Figure 13-15.

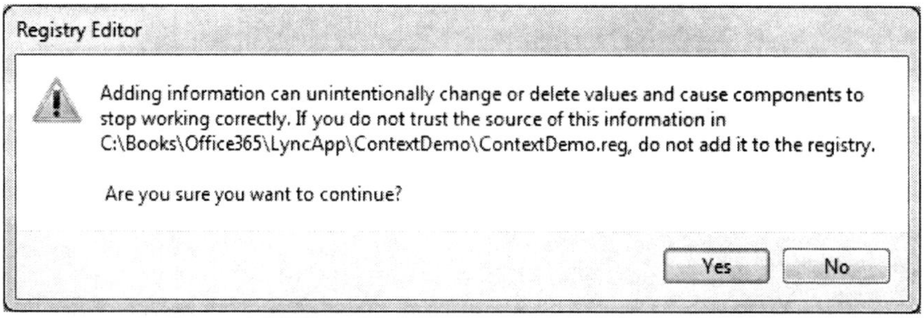

Figure 13-15. Warning about running .reg files

Press F5 to run the application. Select a contact in the drop-down list and click the icon to begin a Lync conversation, as shown in Figure 13-16.

Figure 13-16. Starting the contextual conversation

A conversation window will open. The contextual information will appear once the initial message has been sent. Type in **Hello** or a similar greeting to begin, and press Enter. The contextual information should appear as in Figure 13-17.

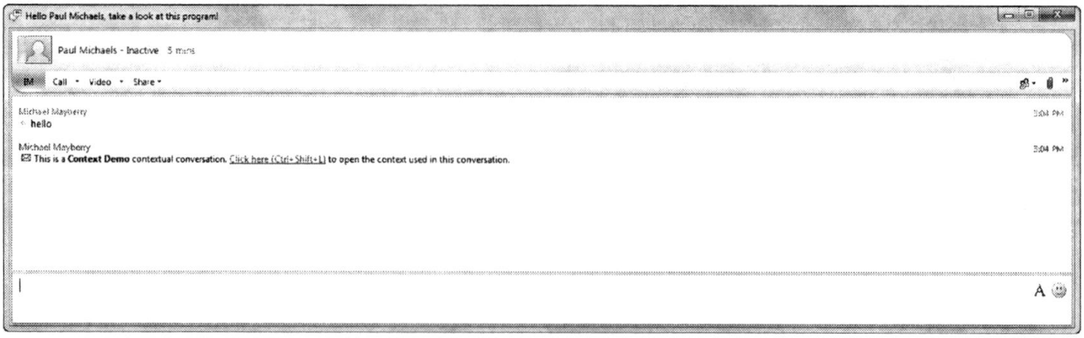

Figure 13-17. Contextual information within a Lync conversation

Click the link to start the WPF application associated with the contextual information. You should see what is illustrated in Figure 13-18.

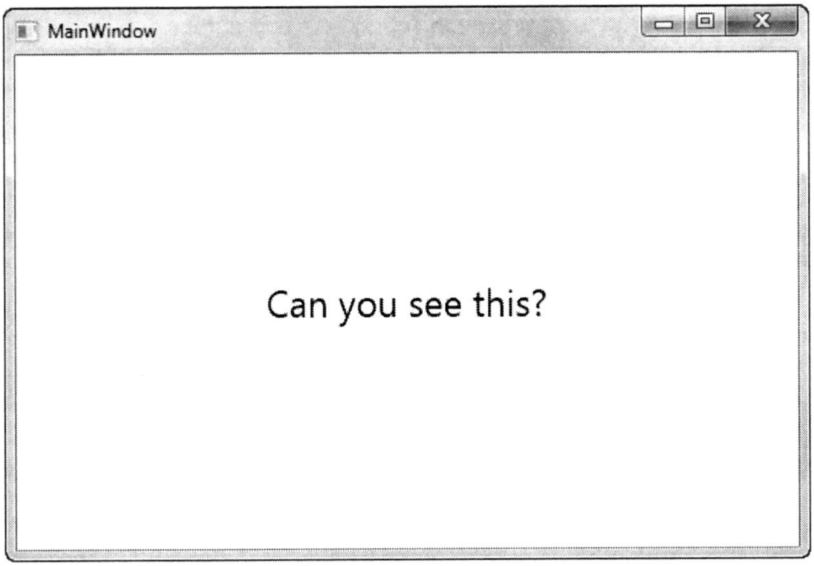

Figure 13-18. WPF application associated with the contextual conversation

Using Lync Automation

For the final exercise I'll show you how to use Lync automation to start a conversation and dock the window inside your custom application. This process requires interoperation between your custom WPF application and the Lync application. Open the `Window1.xaml.cs` file and add the following namespace:

```
using System.Windows.Interop;
```

Adding the Docking Host Location

Your application will need to include UI elements to interoperate with Lync. You will need to reference the classes in the XAML code needed for this and add a place for the Lync conversation to dock. Start by adding the following namespaces:

```
xmlns:interop="clr-
namespace:System.Windows.Forms.Integration;assembly=WindowsFormsIntegration"
xmlns:forms="clr-namespace:System.Windows.Forms;assembly=System.Windows.Forms"
```

Now you need to add the UI elements to accept the conversation window during docking. Add an additional row to the main grid by adding the following to the `Grid.RowDefinitions` section:

```
<RowDefinition />
```

Just before the closing `Grid` tag, add the following XAML code:

```
<interop:WindowsFormsHost x:Name="formHost" Grid.Row="2">
```

```
        <forms:Panel x:Name="formPanel"></forms:Panel>
</interop:WindowsFormsHost>
```

This adds the host and panel elements for the docking process. When the automation code is called to start the application and dock the window within your application, the conversation window will be displayed in this Panel control.

Calling Lync Automation

Using Lync automation requires the application to respond to an event within the custom programming rather than the Lync controls. For this requirement, you will adjust the user interface to include a button to start the conversation. Open the Window1.xaml file and add the following code just after the StartInstantMessagingButton control:

```
<!-- Automation Button -->
<Button x:Name="btnConversationStart" Content="Start Conversation" Margin="10"
Click="btnConversationStart_Click" />
```

The Design tab should appear similar to Figure 13-19.

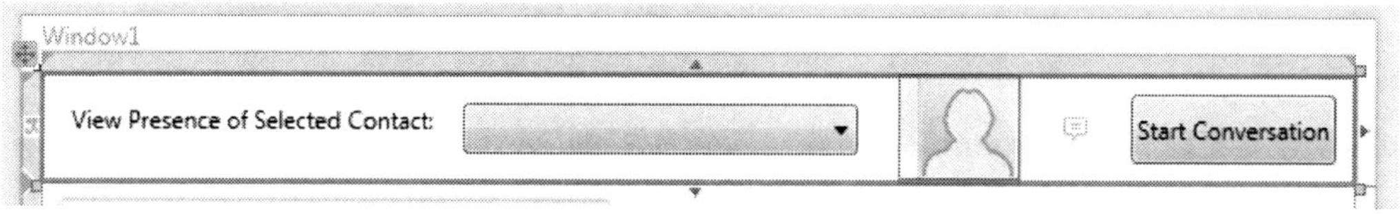

Figure 13-19. Adding a custom button for Lync automation

Double-click the new button on the Design tab to automatically create the event handler in the Window1.xaml.cs file. Modify the btnConversationStart_Click() method to include the code in Listing 13-6.

Listing 13-6. The Start Conversation Button Event Handler

```
private void btnConversationStart_Click(object sender, RoutedEventArgs e)
{
    // Create an Automation object.
    Automation automation = LyncClient.GetAutomation();

    List<string> participants = new List<string>();
    participants.Add(cboContacts.SelectedValue.ToString());

    // Declare instance of Dictionary to pass the conversation context data.
    Dictionary<AutomationModalitySettings, object> automationSettings =
    new Dictionary<AutomationModalitySettings, object>();

    // Provide Conversation context: First IM Message.
    automationSettings.Add(AutomationModalitySettings.FirstInstantMessage, "Hello!");

    // Provide Conversation context: Send first IM message immediately after the
```

```
    // conversation starts.
    automationSettings.Add(AutomationModalitySettings.SendFirstInstantMessageImmediately,
true);

    // Start the conversation.
    IAsyncResult beginconversation =
        automation.BeginStartConversation(AutomationModalities.InstantMessage,
            participants,
            automationSettings,
            onConversationStart,
            automation);
}
```

This code creates the Lync automation object and configures the settings for the conversation. The final step is to call BeginStartConversation() and pass in the settings. This method call identifies a callback event handler to run when the conversation is started. First add the following private variables to the Window1 class:

```
private delegate void FocusWindow();
private delegate void ResizeWindow(Size newSize);
private WindowInteropHelper _windowHelper;
private Int32 _handle;
private ConversationWindow _conversationWindow;
```

This sets up the necessary methods and variables needed for the event handlers for docking the conversation window within the custom application. Now add the following code to provide the event handler for the start of the conversation:

```
private void onConversationStart(IAsyncResult result)
{
    if (result.IsCompleted)
    {
        // get conversation window
        _conversationWindow = ((Automation)result.AsyncState).EndStartConversation(result);

        // wire up events
        _conversationWindow.NeedsSizeChange += _conversationWindow_NeedsSizeChange;
        _conversationWindow.NeedsAttention += _conversationWindow_NeedsAttention;

        // dock conversation window
        _conversationWindow.Dock(formHost.Handle);
    }
}
```

This code gets the conversation window object and wires up the NeedsSizeChange and NeedsAttention events necessary for docking the window. Then the Dock() method is called. This passes in the Handle parameter from the host element added earlier. Now add the event handler methods shown in Listing 13-7:

Listing 13-7. The automation event handlers

```
private void _conversationWindow_NeedsAttention(object sender,
    ConversationWindowNeedsAttentionEventArgs e)
{
    FocusWindow focusWindow = new FocusWindow(GetWindowFocus);
    Dispatcher.Invoke(focusWindow, new object[] { });
}

private void _conversationWindow_NeedsSizeChange(object sender,
    ConversationWindowNeedsSizeChangeEventArgs e)
{
    Size windowSize = new Size();
    windowSize.Height = e.RecommendedWindowHeight;
    windowSize.Width = e.RecommendedWindowWidth;
    ResizeWindow resize = new ResizeWindow(SetWindowSize);
    Dispatcher.Invoke(resize, new object[] { windowSize });
}

private void SetWindowSize(Size newSize)
{
    formPanel.Size = new System.Drawing.Size(
    (int)newSize.Width, (int)newSize.Height);
}

private void GetWindowFocus()
{
    Focus();
}
```

These event handlers allow the main application to work with the Lync conversation window. Size changes and attention events are wired up and handled in a straightforward fashion. This completes the changes to the code.

Testing the Application

Press F5 to build and run the application. Select the desired contact from the drop-down list and click the Start Conversation button. The Lync client will begin the conversation and present the window within your custom application, as shown in Figure 13-20.

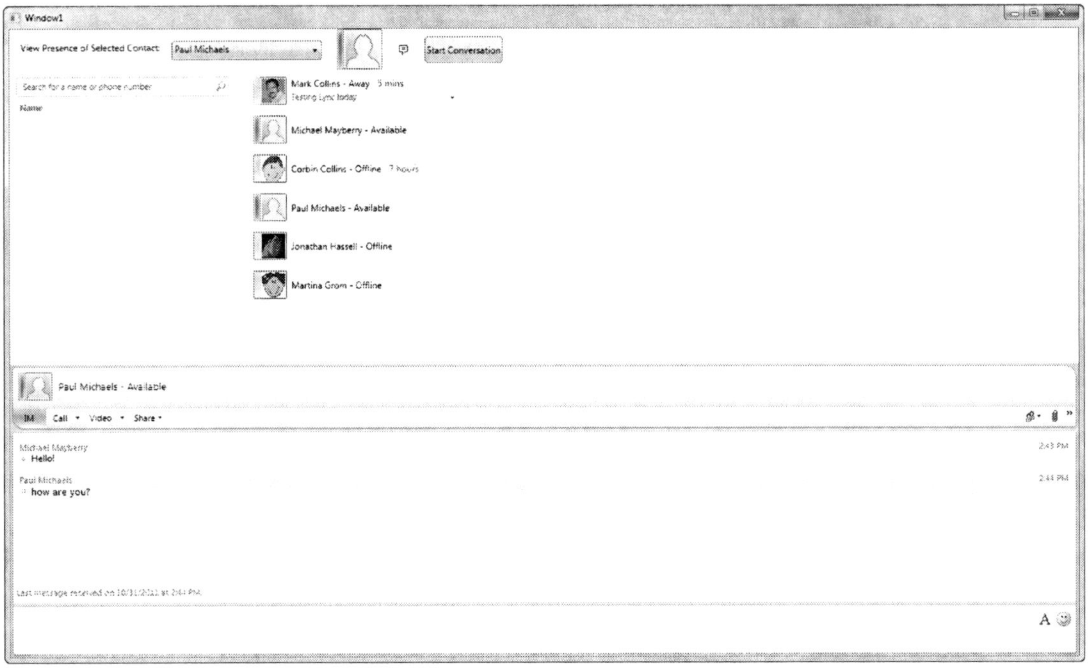

Figure 13-20. Using Lync automation to dock a conversation window in a WPF application

Summary

This chapter showed how to incorporate the functionality of the Lync client into a custom WPF application.

- You used the controls provided by the Lync SDK, simply providing communication functionality without much coding.

- You extended the out-of-the-box functionality using contextual conversation information to launch your own application through a conversation window, even passing information.

- You used Lync automation to provide access to the Lync communication window, presented within your custom application UI space.

Adding real-time communication functionality can greatly extend the usability of your custom applications. The techniques covered in this chapter provide you the ability to deliver a great experience to your users.

PART 5

Developing Messaging Applications

So far in this book you have explored the many customization opportunities available in Office 365. Using both coded and non-code approaches you have learned how to provide custom features using SharePoint Online, Exchange Online, and Lync Online. Now, you'll combine several of these techniques together to create an integrated solution.

Chapter 14 explains the solution and the architectural approach that you'll implement in the remaining three chapters. In Chapter 15, you'll create a web database using Access and publish it to SharePoint Online. Chapter 16 shows you how to write an application using Exchange and Lync to provide a fully integrated office automation solution based on this web database. Finally, you'll implement a public-facing web site using SharePoint online in Chapter 17. This site will demonstrate some advanced SharePoint techniques including video hosting. The Contact Us page on this site will feed directly into the solution developed in Chapters 15 and 16.

CHAPTER 14

Solution Overview

Office365 includes many powerful services for businesses and developers. Each component has been covered individually in this book. The technologies of Office 365 provide unique benefits when they work together. Businesses have relied on this collaboration for decades, but offering Office in the cloud presents new opportunities.

Software development often involves allowing multiple systems to interact with each other to achieve a common business goal. Here and in the next three chapters, you will take what you have learned about each of the Office services from the previous chapters and blend them into a single solution. This solution will combine the web hosting abilities of SharePoint Online with the messaging functionality of Exchange Online and Lync.

Combining Technologies

Integration is the key. Each of the services offered through Office365 is powerful on its own. Each provides extensibility to developers—rich APIs to develop against. This book has gone to great lengths to examine the features of these technologies. The focus for this section is getting some of these services to work together and interact with one another. This allows the developer to extend the functionality of Office365 and create new possibilities. In the coming chapters you will use

- **Exchange Online**: Microsoft extends the power of Exchange to the developer through Exchange Web Services. This set of services allows the developer to connect to the e-mail server and brings the messaging abilities into custom solutions to meet unique needs. Sending and receiving e-mails is only the beginning.

- **SharePoint Online**: SharePoint provides possibly the most beneficial element within the Office365 set of services. The abilities of SharePoint extend in so many directions that it's difficult to think of scenarios that can't be improved using this one tool. The majority of this book is dedicated to the functionality within SharePoint. Of the many aspects available, this section will narrow your focus to two of them.

  - **Public web sites**: SharePoint makes going to the Web easy. There is no need for a separate hosting environment, either local to your company or elsewhere. Accessing Office365 allows you to build and manage your public web presence alongside your e-mail and other services. This topic is covered more extensively in Chapter 4.

- **Access Data Services**: Imagine having your database hosted in a safe and secure environment, but accessible to any client software you can write with access to the Internet. The possibilities are endless. SharePoint Online will host your database. You build it in Access and deploy it out to SharePoint. It's that simple. This functionality is discussed in more detail in Chapter 6.

- **Lync**: Speed is vital. A real-time communication tool like Lync can add real value when used to get information where it is needed. For the developer, Lync includes extensibility through access to the Lync client and controls available for WPF and Silverlight. Lync also provides the ability for contextual conversations where access to information is provided either through links in messaging or directly in the Conversation Window Extension.

Over the next three chapters, you will build a solution that integrates these three technologies. Your application will get these separate services to work together toward a common business goal. In this chapter, you will examine the overall design of the solution and how the technologies are integrated. You will look at how to approach development for Office365 from a design perspective.

- In Chapter 15, you will learn how to implement the database in SharePoint. You will work through designing and creating the database in Access on your local machine. You will then deploy this to SharePoint Online.

- In Chapter 16, you will integrate Exchange Web Services and Lync with the online SharePoint database. You will access messages in the Exchange inbox and extract customer information. You will also use Lync controls and automation to send information through Lync conversations.

- Chapter 17 will cover the public-facing web site. You will build the site navigation and design the layout and artwork. You will add the Contact Us form to collect customer information.

In Figure 14-1, the desktop application is used to integrate the three Office365 services. As the software communicates with each set of services, information flows from one to another.

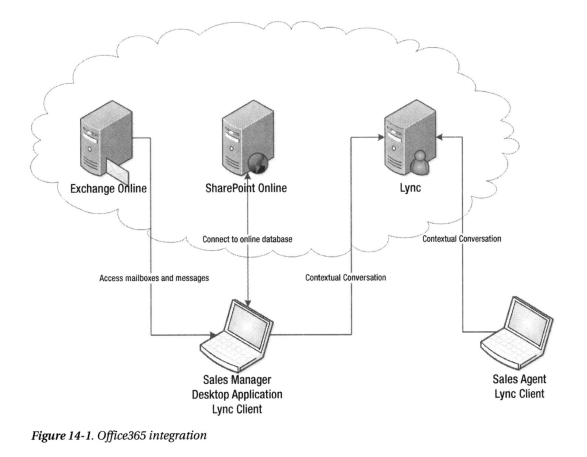

Figure 14-1. Office365 integration

▨ **Note** Development against cloud services is different than using resources on the local network. Special considerations must be taken that affect the design and approach of the application. Authentication, bandwidth, and asynchronous processing are a prime example of these concerns.

Integration Development

You will build a solution that manages sales leads for the fictional company Apress Remodeling, which offers interior design services and custom remodeling. This application will involve a public-facing web site hosted in SharePoint Online that provides information about the company and allows visitors to contact the company through e-mail. Your project will download the e-mails from an inbox in Exchange Online and process them into an online database. That database will be designed in Access and deployed and hosted in SharePoint Online. After the information from the e-mail is stored in the database, the e-mail is archived and an instant message is sent through Lync. This uses contextual conversation and Silverlight to present the contact information to a sales agent. The agent will be allowed to either enter follow-up information directly into the Silverlight application or navigate to the SharePoint application to view and record information online.

To begin, build a flowchart of how the data will move through the application. Decide the starting event—how the data will initially get collected. Then decide where the information is stored and how it becomes most accessible to your users.

Figure 14-2 depicts the public web site as the starting point of the data collection. The customer can enter their information on the Contact Us form, which will be sent by e-mail to the company. The goal is to deliver the customer information to a sales agent, but not all contacts will be sent to the same agent. So the inbox is just the starting point. The sales agents will not access the mailbox directly. Instead, the customer information will be delivered to them through other means.

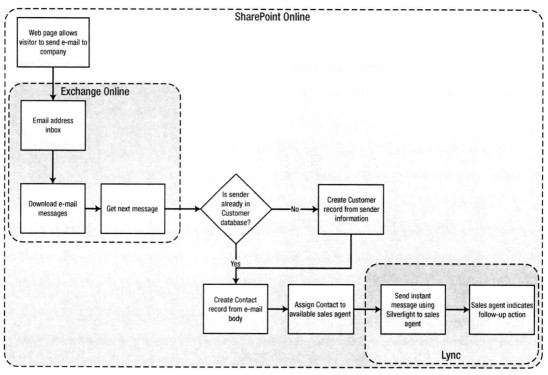

Figure 14-2. Logical design

The application will access Exchange Online and download the e-mail messages. Ultimately, the customer's contact information is stored in a database, not in e-mails. The application searches that database for the sender e-mail address to find out if a record of that customer exists. If not, a record is created. Once the customer record is determined, a contact record is also created, which is related to the customer.

Then the next available agent is found and the contact information is sent through Lync. This will utilize the contextual conversation and host a Silverlight application that will allow the agent to indicate their follow-up action directly back to the database.

■ **Note** This application downloads the e-mails in order to process the information according to some simple business logic. This approach could be expanded in a production environment to utilize more complicated processing. Exchange Online provides Inbox Rules for simple filtering and handling messages, but it doesn't allow custom rules to be applied.

SharePoint Online Public Web Site

The information flow starts with a public-facing web site hosted in SharePoint Online. This web site will host the content for the online presence for the company, such as display samples from previous remodels and information about the company in general. SharePoint offers design capabilities to make this process easier. The web site can be built without coding. Layout choices include the ability to choose colors and themes to achieve a custom look for the company. Figure 14-3 depicts the home page of the public web site.

Figure 14-3. Public web site home page

The web site will provide a Contact Us form, shown in Figure 14-4. This form allows the visitor to contact the organization. This will utilize the built-in SharePoint functionality that makes it easier to build an online web presence. The form will simply send an e-mail to a specific e-mail address that you set up in Exchange Online. It will collect the information you specify in the design wizard.

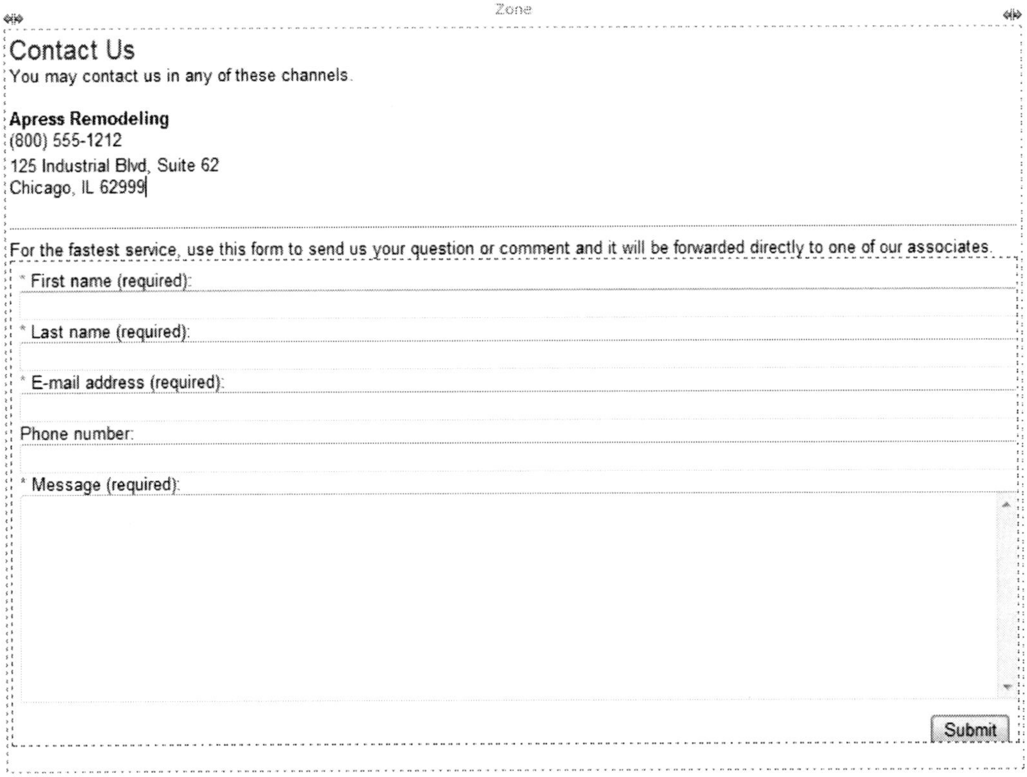

Figure 14-4. *Contact Us form*

The idea is to get the information from the potential customer to the sales agent as quickly as possible. You could have all agents access the same inbox, but the agents would find it difficult to determine which leads need attention and which ones are being handled by other agents. Here is where integrating the services is necessary. Exchange Inbox Rules can process received mail and even forward items to other mailboxes. However, the online solution doesn't allow custom code to run within the rules. To provide custom processing, your code will need to run outside the Exchange server and access the information through Exchange Web Services.

SharePoint Online Access Data Services

The information begins in e-mail. However, it needs to move into a database for easier access and manipulation by the application. You will design an online database, created in Access and hosted in SharePoint Online. The database stores information about the customers and the various products and services offered by Apress Remodeling. The application in this chapter is primarily concerned with Agents, Customers, and Contacts. The public-facing web site provides a web presence for the company for information and marketing.

Figure 14-5 includes part of the database design: those tables that hold information important for sales leads. The full database schema can be seen in Chapter 15.

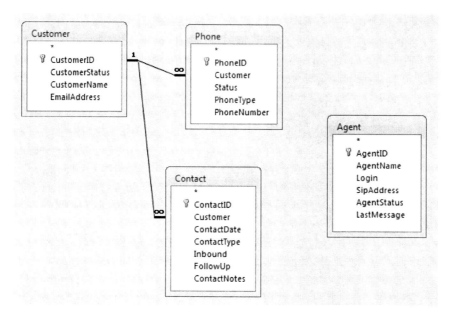

Figure 14-5. Database design

The sales agents access the SharePoint Online database directly to enter information about remodeling jobs and services offered through Apress Remodeling. Customers and contact information can also be entered directly by the agents. The online database provides access to the data anywhere anInternet connection is available. At the same time, SharePoint Online protects that data with its high level of security. SharePoint also allows developers access to that data for their custom projects using the ClientContext API.

Exchange Web Services

You will use WPF to build a Windows desktop application that will connect to Exchange Online to "read" the e-mails sent to the specified inbox. Figure 14-6 shows the user interface design. The application will also connect to SharePoint Online and will be able to start Lync conversations with sales agents. This desktop application will provide some information on how it is processing the information but will not require any interaction from the sales manager. It will essentially automate the process while it is running.

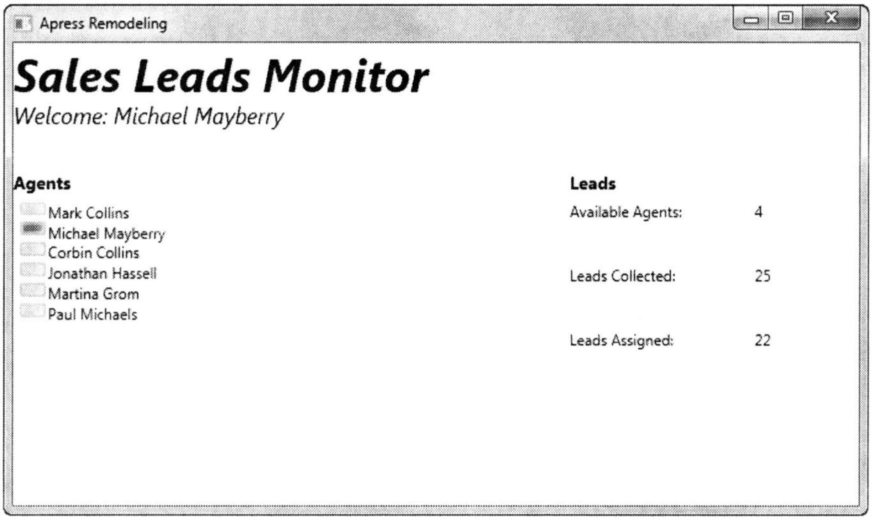

Figure 14-6. *WPF desktop user interface*

The desktop application displays a list of the agents and their current online presence in Lync. Some monitoring information is also shown, including how many agents are available, how many leads have been processed, and how many leads have been assigned. The user interface is minimal. The real function of the application is in the collaboration of the Office365 services and the automation of information processing.

SERVICE AUTOMATION

The information stored in Exchange Online can only be accessed through the Exchange Web Services. This requires an application that can call the service methods and process the results returned from the service. This example uses the WPF application as that anchor point for accessing the Office365 services. While this is a good choice and works well, a production environment might take advantage of WCF services for automation. Web services allow the monitoring pieces to run around the clock. Some features of Exchange Web Services, such as subscriptions, work well with web services to handle events such as received mail. Figure 14-7 shows how WCF service might integrate the Office365 technologies.

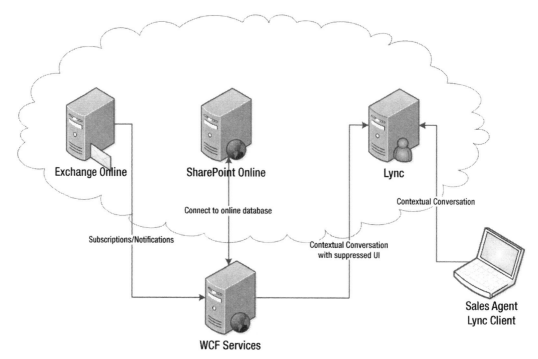

Figure 14-7. WCF Service Integration

While SharePoint does host a public web site and can even host Silverlight web parts, it does not provide an environment for hosting web services. These must be hosted in a separate environment.

As with all cloud-based development, authentication may behave differently for WCF services over WPF desktop applications. Accessing client-based technologies, such as Lync, also presents different challenges when connecting from a server.

Lync Conversation Window Extension

The application processes the e-mails and determines the next available sales agent. The contact information is sent to the agent through Lync using a contextual conversation. To provide the ability for interaction with the sales agent, it is decided to use Silverlight within Lync's Conversation Window Extension. This Silverlight application needs to be hosted on a web server. Rather than deploy a separate web environment, it is also decided to host this Silverlight application as a web part in SharePoint Online. The Silverlight web part, shown in Figure 14-8, displays the customer information and contact details; it also provides the ability to submit the follow-up action back to the online database.

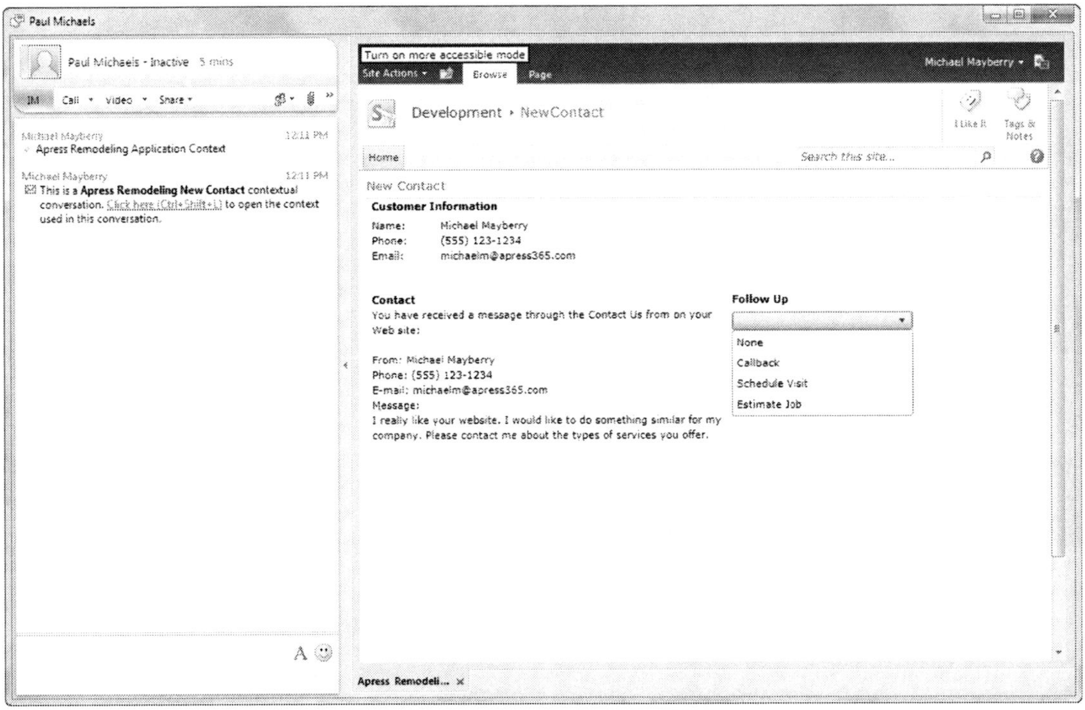

Figure 14-8. Lync Conversation Window Extension

Summary

The services available in Office365 provide the extensibility for integration. The chapter begins to look into how this integration can be done. An application has been designed to integrate the following technologies:

- Exchange Online

- SharePoint Online

- Lync Online

This chapter discussed the design of the solution that you will build in the next three chapters. The next step is to build the database and deploy to SharePoint, which is covered in the next chapter. The remaining chapters will cover integration with Lync, Exchange, and the public web site.

CHAPTER 15

Creating a Web Database

In this chapter you'll create a web database using Access 2010, which will be published to SharePoint Online in your Office 365 platform. This database implements a simple job tracking application that allows you to create, estimate, and track customer jobs. This will be used by the Exchange and Lync applications that you will build in the next chapter.

In Chapter 6, I explained how to create a SharePoint site by publishing a special type of Access database. This is probably the easiest way to create a form-based SharePoint site. In this chapter you will employ the same basic concepts and techniques that you learned in Chapter 6. You will create a fully working web site with numerous tables (lists) and forms (pages).

Out of necessity, I will cover this briefly without explaining every detail as much of it is fairly repetitive. Refer to Chapter 6 for more explanations as necessary. You can also download the complete Access database from `www.apress.com` and then follow along as you read this chapter.

Note For a more though explanation of developing solutions with Access 2010, check out my previous book, *Pro Access 2010 Development.*

You will implement this application using the typical approach of designing the tables first. Then you'll add a few queries (views) that will simplify some of the form development. You'll also create a fairly complex data macro that will compute the estimated job total by adding up the products and services included. You will then develop the forms for each of these tables. Finally, you'll implement a form for navigating each of the top-level forms. After you have verified the application is functioning properly, you will publish it to a new SharePoint site on Office 365.

Designing the Tables

Start Access 2010 and create a new database using the Blank web database template. When using this template, Access will create new objects such as tables and forms that are compatible with SharePoint.

Data Model Overview

The logical starting place for creating a web database is to design the tables. You will need the following tables to support the job tracking application:

- **Customer** contains current or potential customers.

- **Phone** stores customer phone numbers.

- **Address** stores customer and job addresses.

- **Product** defines products that may be included in a job.

- **Service** defines services offered.

- **Job** contains job or proposal summaries.

- **JobProduct** specifies products included in a job.

- **JobService** specifies services included in a job.

- **Contact** records incoming or outgoing contacts (phone calls, e-mails, etc.).

- **Agent** lists agents that are available for responding to incoming contacts.

Figure 15-1 shows how these tables are related.

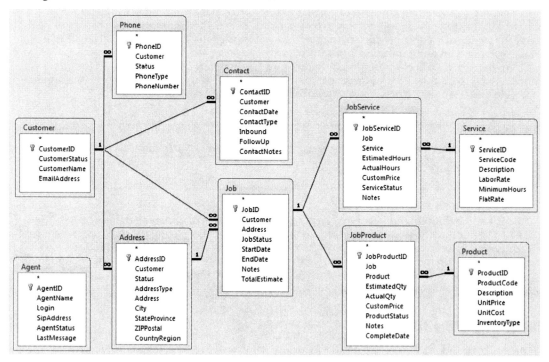

Figure 15-1. Data model diagram

To summarize Figure 15-1 and the structure of the database:

- Addresses and phone numbers are stored in separate tables, Address and Phone, which allows each customer to have more than one. The Job table also references the Address table to indicate the location of a particular job. The Contact table records correspondence with a customer.

- A job is a collection of products and services. The Product and Service tables provide static information about each product or service such as description and price. The JobProduct and JobService tables are used to indicate when these are included in a specific job and provide job-specific details as well.

- The Agent table is needed to support the Exchange and Lync applications and is not actually used by the job tracking application directly.

Creating the Customer Table

You'll start by creating the Customer table.

1. From the Create tab of the ribbon, click the Table button. This will create a blank table, as shown in Figure 15-2.

Figure 15-2. *Starting with a blank table*

2. Right-click on the ID column, select the Rename link, and change the column name to **CustomerID**.

3. The next column will indicate the current status of this customer, such as Prospect or Active. To add another column, click the Click to Add link and select the Lookup & Relationship link, as shown in Figure 15-3.

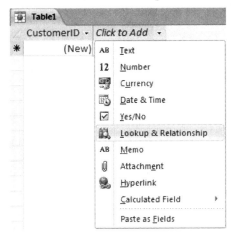

Figure 15-3. *Adding a lookup column*

Defining Static Lookup Values

The Lookup wizard provides two options for providing values for a lookup column. The first is to get the values from another table. This will create a foreign key relationship between the tables. The second option is to specify a static list of allowed values.

1. For this column, you will use the second option, so select it in the first dialog box, as shown in Figure 15-4.

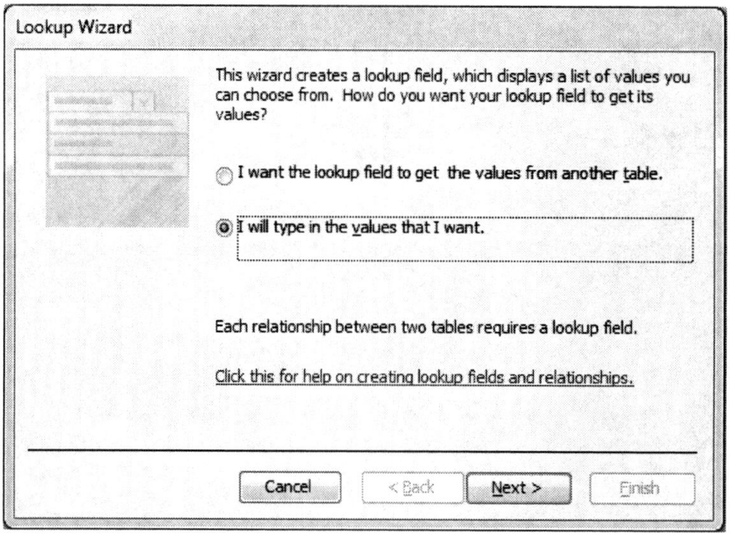

Figure 15-4. Providing fixed values

2. In the next dialog box, enter the following values (also shown in Figure 15-5):

- Prospect
- Active
- Inactive
- Removed

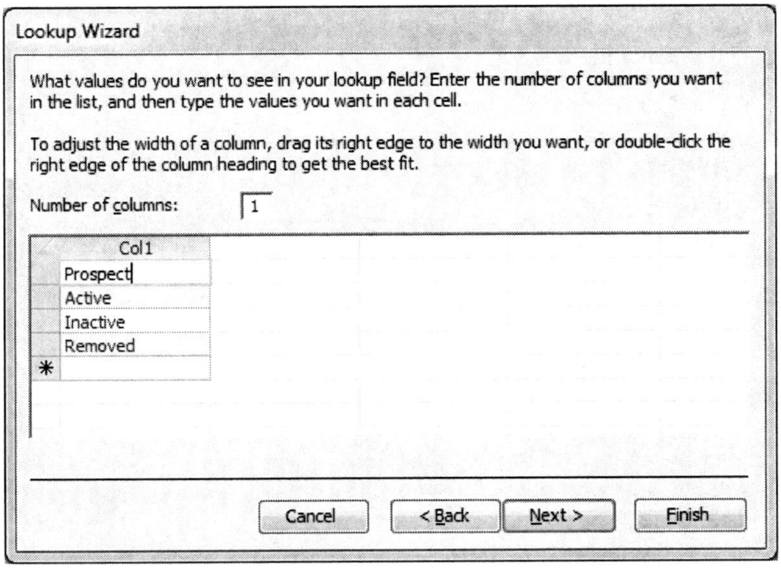

Figure 15-5. Specifying the CustomerStatus values

3. In the final dialog box, enter **CustomerStatus** for the column label and select the "Limit To List" check box, as shown in Figure 15-6. The "Limit To List" option prevents the user from entering anything in this column other than one of the specified values.

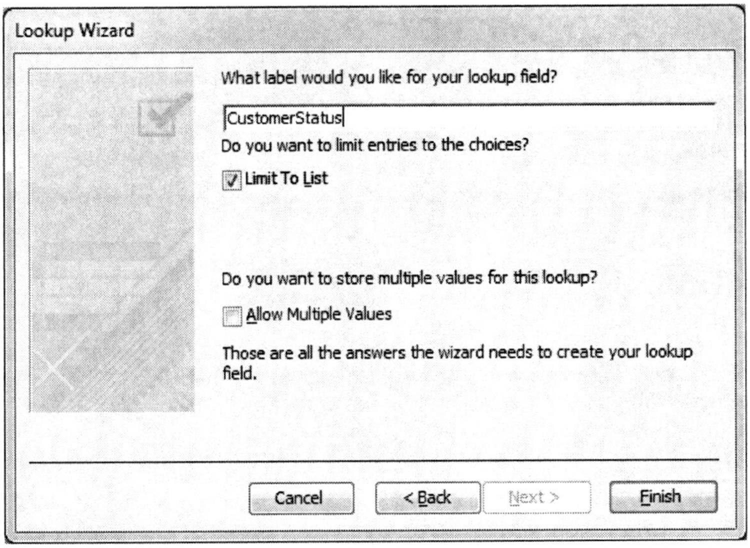

Figure 15-6. Finalizing the CustomerStatus column

4. When you complete the Lookup wizard, you need to save the table. Since this is a new table, you will be prompted to specify the table name. When prompted, enter **Customer**.

Creating the Remaining Columns

Add the following additional columns to the `Customer` table:

- **CustomerName** (text)
- **EmailAddress** (text)

The completed table should look like Figure 15-7.

Customer				
CustomerID ▾	CustomerStatus ▾	CustomerName ▾	EmailAddress ▾	Click to Add ▾
1	Prospect	John Smith	jsmith@gmail.com	
* (New)				

Figure 15-7. The completed Customer table

Creating the Phone Table

The `Phone` table contains customer phone numbers. By placing these in a separate table, each customer can have more than one. The `Phone` table will have the following columns:

- **PhoneID**, the primary key
- **Customer**, a lookup field using the `Customer` table as its source
- **Status**, a lookup field with a static list
- **PhoneType**, a lookup field indicating the type of phone (cell, home, fax, etc.)
- **PhoneNumber**, the actual phone number

Create a new blank table just like you did for the `Customer` table and rename the ID field to **PhoneID**.

Creating a Foreign Key Relationship

Now that you have your table, you can add columns and a foreign key.

1. For the next field, `Customer`, click the Click To Add link and select the Lookup & Relationship link. This time, in the Lookup wizard, select the first option (see Figure 15-8).

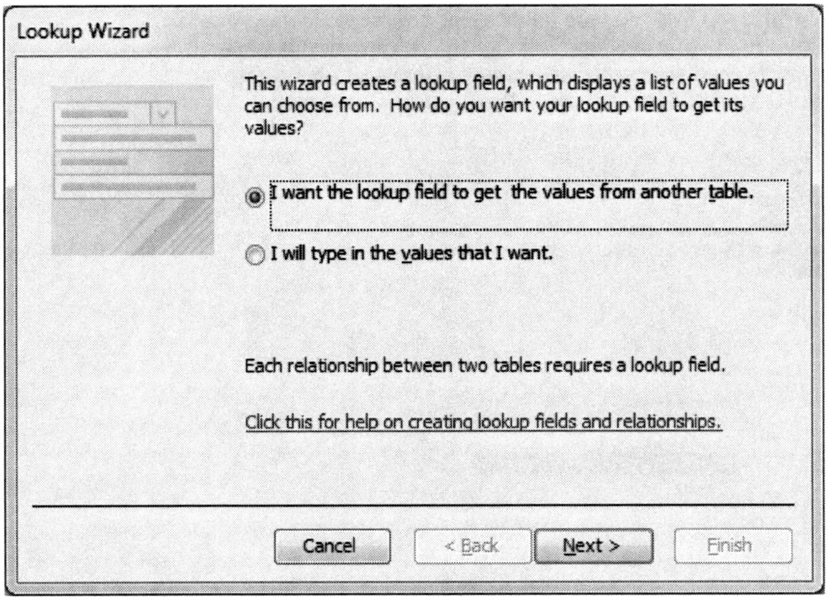

Figure 15-8. Choosing values from another table

2. In the next dialog box, shown in Figure 15-9, select the Customer table as the source of this lookup column.

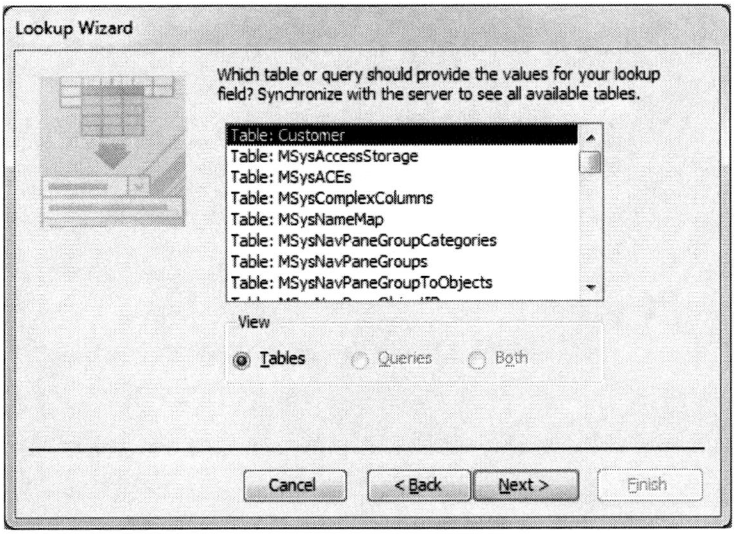

Figure 15-9. Selecting the Customer table as the lookup source

3. In the next dialog box, you'll specify the fields in the source table that should be used. In addition to the primary key, which is the column that the actual foreign key relationship will use, you can include other columns for display purposes. Add the CustomerID and CustomerName columns, as shown in Figure 15-10.

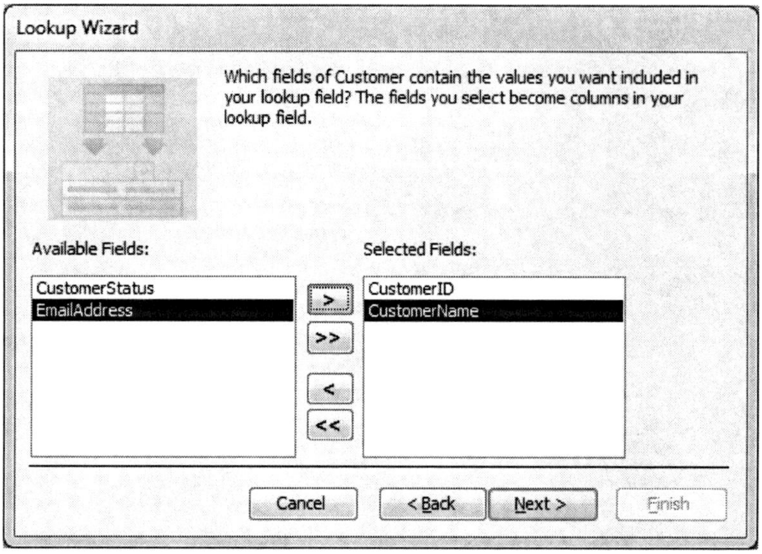

Figure 15-10. Selecting the lookup fields

4. You can specify how the values should be sorted. Select the CustomerName column, as shown in Figure 15-11.

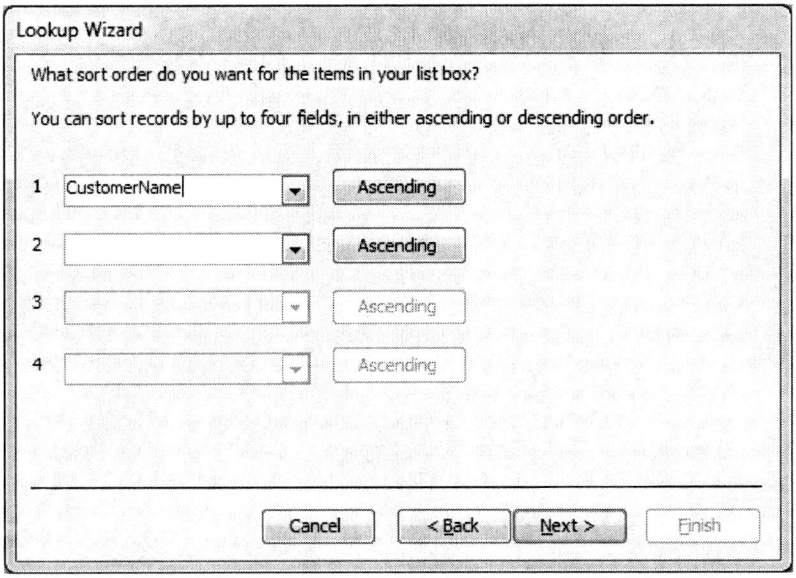

Figure 15-11. *Sorting by the CustomerName*

5. In the Phone table or in a form based on the Phone table, the Customer field will be presented as a drop-down list. As mentioned, you can have multiple fields from the linked table. In the next dialog box, you can specify how the column(s) are displayed in the drop-down list. By default, if there are other columns included, the key field is hidden, as demonstrated in Figure 15-12. To include the key field (CustomerID in this case), unselect the "Hide key column" check box. You can also change the order of these columns as well as the width of each column. The default configuration works fine in this scenario so you can leave this dialog box as it is.

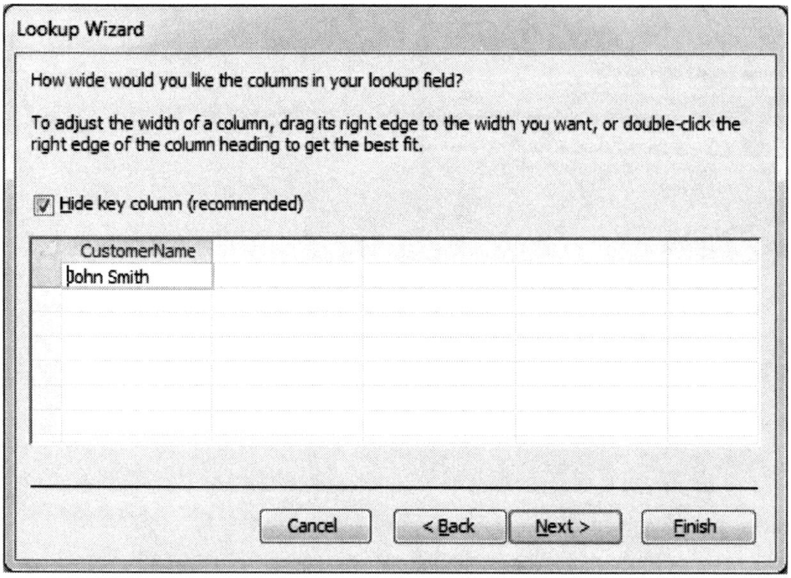

Figure 15-12. *Formating the lookup column*

> 6. In the final dialog box, enter the column name **Customer** and select the "Enable Data Integrity" check box, as shown in Figure 15-13.

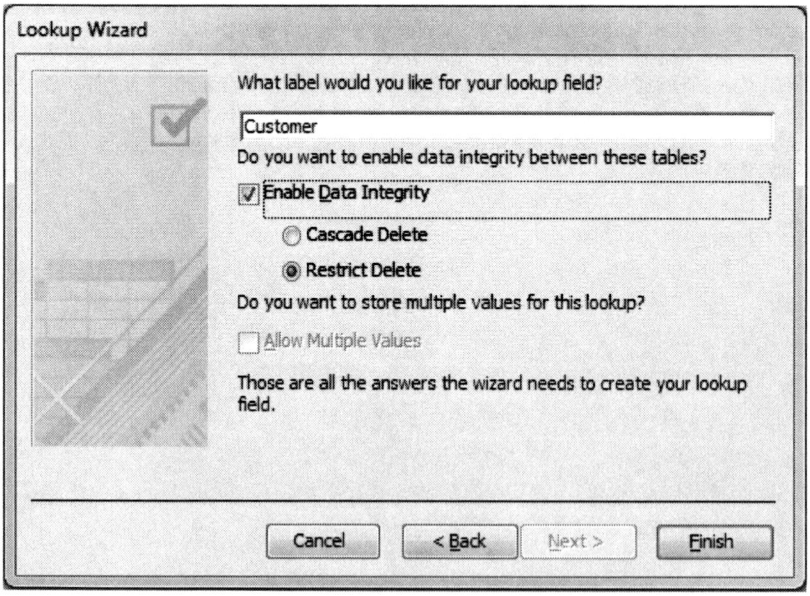

Figure 15-13. *Enabling referential integrity*

▪ **Note** The Data Integrity feature in Access is roughly equivalent to defining a foreign key relationship in SQL Server. The Restrict Delete option that you will use here ensures that a record can't be deleted if it is being referenced by another record. In contrast, the Cascade Delete option will also remove any records that reference the record being deleted. This is useful for parent-child relationships such as an `Order` and an `OrderItem` table. When an `Order` record is deleted, the `OrderItem` records that refer to this order would be deleted as well.

Creating the Remaining Columns

The next two columns, `Status` and `PhoneType`, will each use a static list of values.

1. Create these columns using the Lookup & Relationship link and select the second option in the Lookup wizard, like you did for the `Customer` table. Set up the allowed values as illustrated in Figure 15-14 and Figure 15-15, respectively.

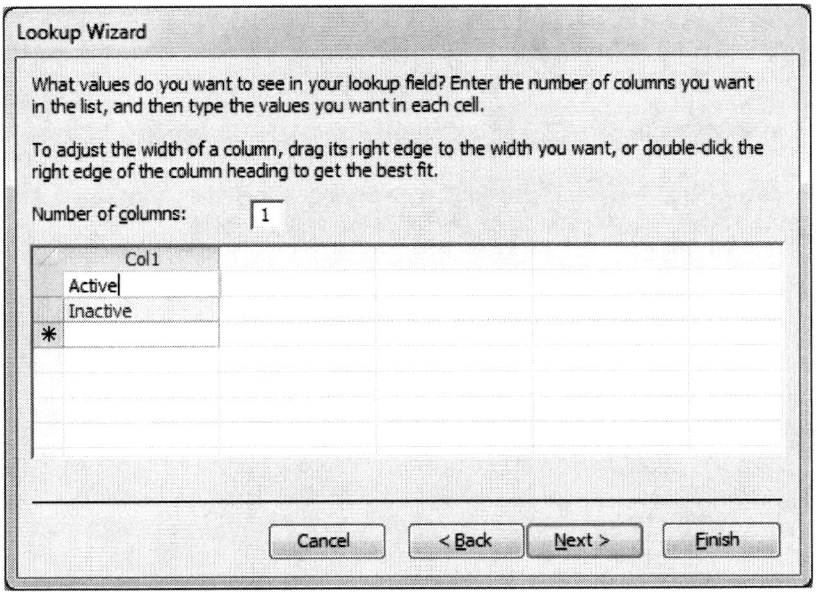

Figure 15-14. Specifying the Status values

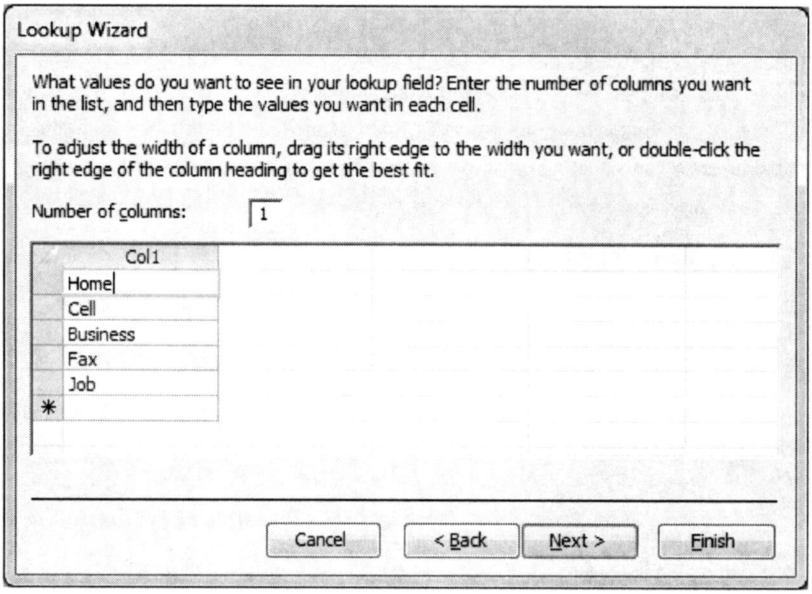

Figure 15-15. Specifying the PhoneType values

2. After creating the Status field, you should provide a default value. Open the Phone table, select the Status column, and from the Fields tab of the ribbon, click the Default Value button.

3. In the Expression wizard, enter ="**Active**" as the default value. This will default all new records to the Active status.

The completed Phone table should look like Figure 15-16. Notice that the Customer column displays the CustomerName field of the linked record.

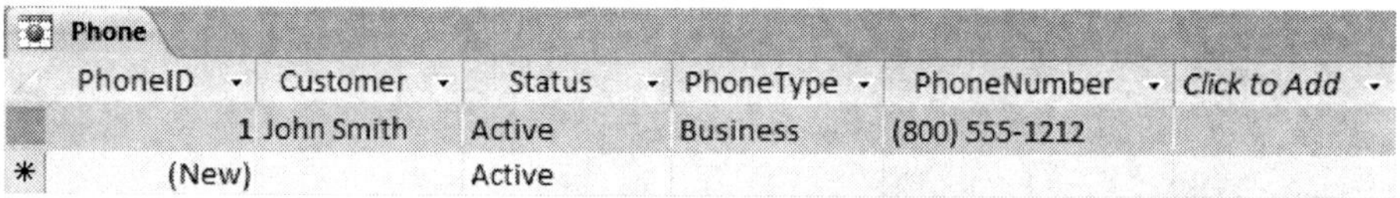

Figure 15-16. The completed Phone table

■ **Note** Notice that the empty row of the table, which is used to add a new record, has the Status column pre-populated to Active. This is because you defined this as the default value. The (New) in the PhoneID column indicates that a new unique ID will be generated automatically when the new record is saved.

Creating the Address Table

The Address table is similar to the Phone table. The first four columns are

- **AddressID**, the primary key

- **Customer**, a lookup field using the Customer table

- **Status**, a static list of values (Active and Inactive)

- **AddressType**, a static list of values (Billing, Job, Shipping)

Let's create it.

1. Create a blank table just like the previous tables and set up the first four columns just like you did for the Phone table. Remember to set the default value for the Status column. For the AddressType column, enter the possible values shown in Figure 15-17.

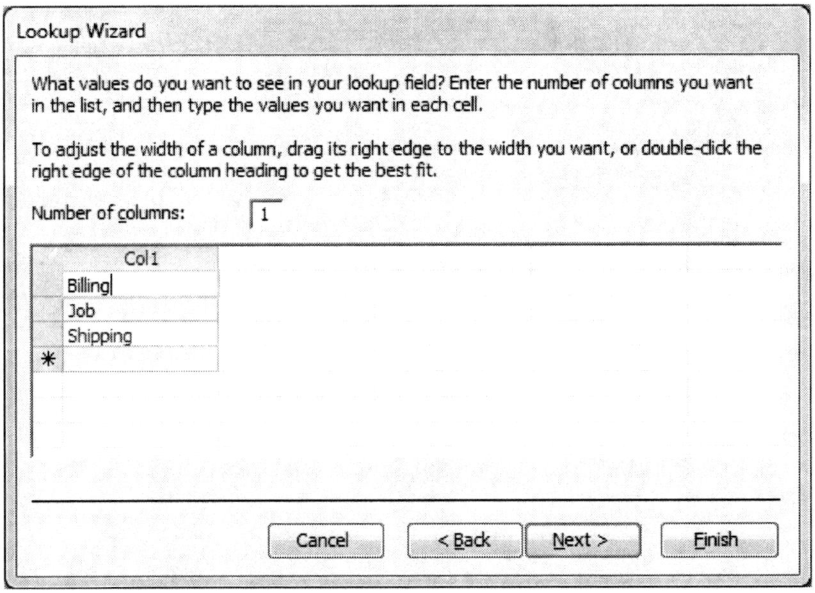

Figure 15-17. Specifying the AddressType values

2. For the remaining columns use the Quick Start field definitions. From the Field tab of the ribbon, select the More Fields drop-down list and then click the Address link, as shown in Figure 15-18.

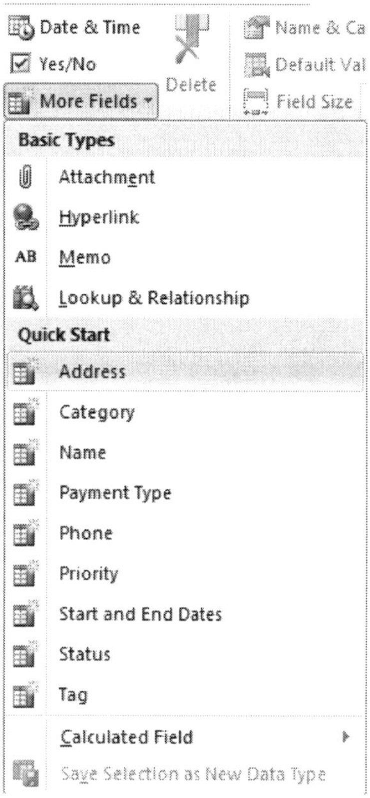

Figure 15-18. Using the Address quick start field

3. The Address quick start field defines a set of columns that collectively define an address. When you add this field, Access will automatically add the following columns:

    -   City

    -   State Province

    -   ZIP Postal

    -   Country Region

4. I added a default value for the Country Region column so the users would not have to enter this. You can choose to leave this without a default value or enter a different value as appropriate. The completed Address table should look like Figure 15-19.

AddressID ▾	Customer ▾	Status ▾	AddressType ▾	Address ▾	City ▾	State Province ▾	ZIP Postal ▾	Country Region ▾
⊞ 1	John Smith	Active	Billing	123 Maple St	Anywhere	IL	60145	United States
* (New)		Active						United States

Figure 15-19. The completed Address table

Creating the Product and Service Tables

Next you'll create the Product and Service tables that will store static information about the products and services that can be included in a job or job estimate. You'll create these much like the previous tables.

The Product table will contain the following columns:

- **ProductID**, the primary key

- **ProductCode**, a text column containing a user-recognizable identifier such as a UPC code

- **Description**, a text column containing a short description.

- **UnitPrice**, currency column type

- **UnitCost**, currency column type

- **InventoryType**, a static list of values that define if/how this item is maintained in inventory

When creating the InventoryType column, enter the possible values shown in Figure 15-20.

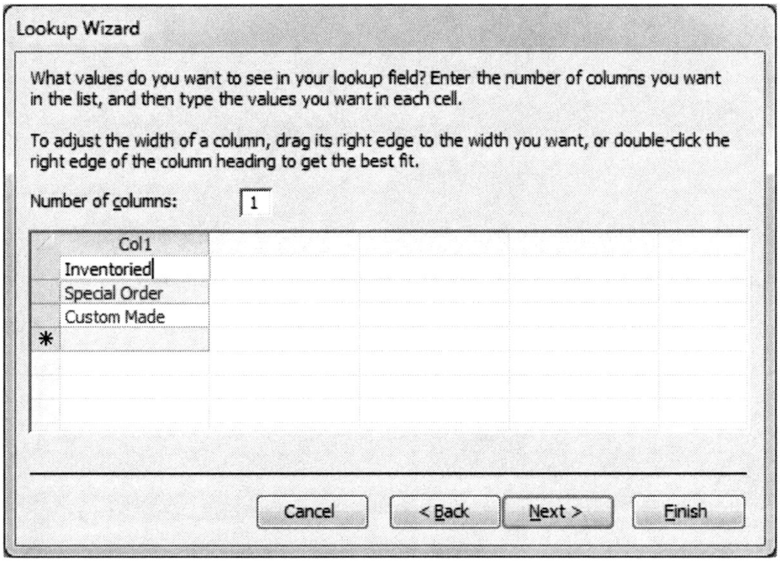

Figure 15-20. Specifying the InventoryType values

The completed Product table should look like Figure 15-21.

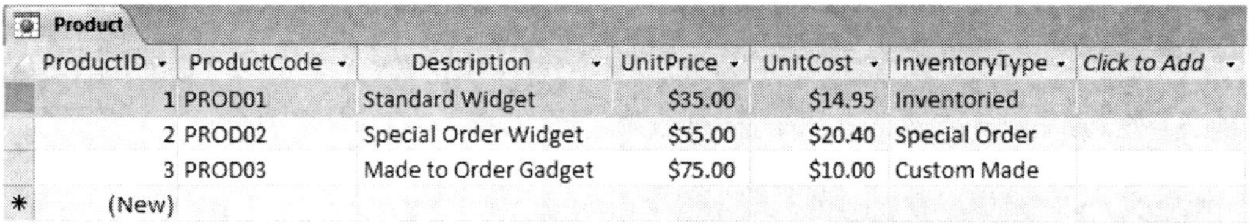

ProductID ▾	ProductCode ▾	Description ▾	UnitPrice ▾	UnitCost ▾	InventoryType ▾	Click to Add ▾
1	PROD01	Standard Widget	$35.00	$14.95	Inventoried	
2	PROD02	Special Order Widget	$55.00	$20.40	Special Order	
3	PROD03	Made to Order Gadget	$75.00	$10.00	Custom Made	
*	(New)					

Figure 15-21. The completed Product table

The Service table will have the following columns:

- **ServiceID**, the primary key

- **ServiceCode**, a text column that contains a user recognizable identifier

- **Description**, a text column that contains a short description

- **LaborRate**, a currency column that defines the hourly rate charged for this service.

- **MinimumHours**, a numeric field indicating the minimum hours that will be charged (0 indicates that there is no minimum).

- **FlatRate**, a Boolean column that indicates if this service is charged at a flat rate. If it is, the LaborRate column specifies the flat rate instead of an hourly rate. When adding this field, select the Yes/No column type, as shown in Figure 15-22.

Figure 15-22. Adding a Yes/No column

■ **Tip** To define a default value for a Yes/No column, enter the expression as **False** or **True** (no equal sign or quotes).

The completed Service table should look like Figure 15-23.

ServiceID ▾	ServiceCode ▾	Description ▾	LaborRate ▾	MinimumHours ▾	FlatRate ▾	Click to Add ▾
1 INITIAL		Initial Consultation	$35.00	0	☑	
2 ONSITE		On-site work	$100.00	2	☐	
3 OFFSITE		Off-site work	$75.00	1	☐	
(New)					☐	

Figure 15-23. The completed Service table

Creating the Job Table

The Job table will contain the proposed, active, and completed jobs. It will generally start out as an estimate. When the job is completed the actual values will replace the estimates, and this will be then used for billing purposes.

1. Create the Job table as you have the previous tables. It will contain the following columns:

   - `JobID`, the primary key

   - `Customer`, a lookup column using the `Customer` table

   - `Address`, a lookup column using the `Address` table

   - `JobStatus`, a static list of allowed valued, defaults to New

   - `StartDate`, a date column indicating the expected date the job will start

   - `EndDate`, a date column indicating the expected or actual completion date

   - `Notes`, a memo column for storing notes and comments

   - `TotalEstimate`, a currency column that will be computed by a data macro

2. When specifying the lookup definition for the `Address` column, include the following columns:

   - `AddressID`

   - `Address`

   - `City`

   - `AddressType`

497

3. Then when you get to the dialog box shown in Figure 15-24, make sure the key field is hidden and columns are formatted as shown.

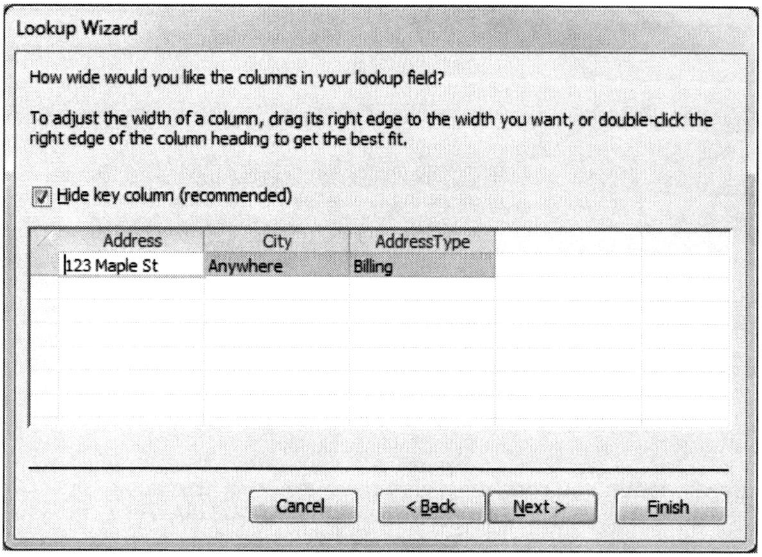

Figure 15-24. Defining the Address drop-down list

4. When defining the JobStatus column, enter the choices shown in Figure 15-25.

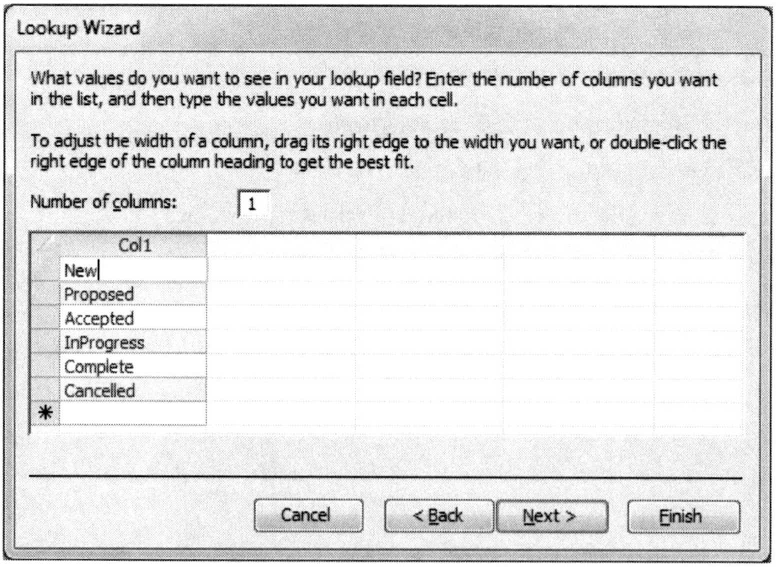

Figure 15-25. Specifying the JobStatus values

5. After the columns have been added, select the EndDate column and change the format to Short Date, as shown in Figure 15-26. This will cause the time portion to be ignored. Do the same for the StartDate column.

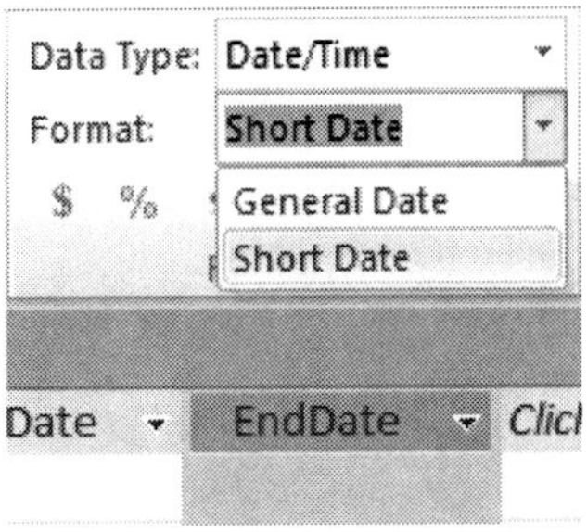

Figure 15-26. Specifying the date format

When adding a new record, notice that the Address drop-down list includes three columns, as shown in Figure 15-27.

Figure 15-27. The Address drop-down list

The completed Job table should look like Figure 15-28.

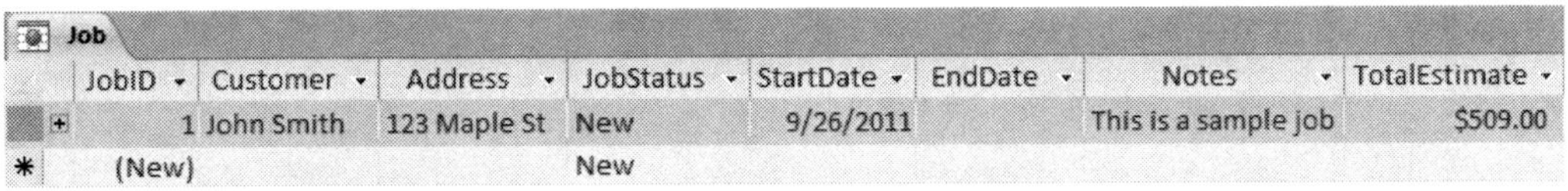

Figure 15-28. The completed Job table

Creating the JobProduct and JobService Tables

The JobProduct and JobService tables specify the products and services that are included in a job. The referenced tables, Product and Service, respectively define the static properties such as price and description. The JobProduct and JobService tables supply the job-specific details such as quantity and status. These tables also allow for a custom price to be assigned that is applicable for this job only.

Create the JobProduct table and include the following columns:

- **JobProductID**, the primary key
- **Job**, a lookup column using the Job table
- **Product**, a lookup column using the Product table
- **EstimatedQty** (numeric)
- **ActualQty** (numeric)

- **CustomPrice**, of currency type, used to override the price for this job only
- **ProductStatus**, a static list of allowed values
- **Notes**, a memo field
- **CompleteDate**, a date column indicating when the product was delivered

When defining the ProductStatus column, enter the following for the allowed values. Set New as the default value.

- **New**
- **Waiting**
- **Delivered**
- **Cancelled**

The completed JobProduct table should look like Figure 15-29.

JobProductID ▾	Job ▾	Product ▾	EstimatedQty ▾	ActualQty ▾	CustomPrice ▾	ProductStatus ▾	Notes ▾	CompleteDate ▾
1	1	PROD01	2			Waiting		
2	1	PROD03	3		$50.00	New		
3	1	PROD02	1			Delivered		
(New)						New		

Figure 15-29. The completed JobProduct table

Create the JobService table and include the following columns:

- **JobServiceID**, the primary key
- **Job**, a lookup column using the Job table
- **Service**, a lookup column using the Service table
- **EstimatedHours** (numeric)
- **ActualHours** (numeric)
- **CustomPrice**, of currency type, used to override the price for this job only
- **ServiceStatus**, a static list of allowed values
- **Notes**, a memo field
- **CompleteDate**, a date column indicating when the product was delivered

When defining the ServiceStatus column, enter the following for the allowed values. Set Planned as the default value.

- **Planned**
- **Waiting**
- **Completed**

- **Cancelled**

The completed table should look like Figure 15-30.

JobServiceID ▾	Job ▾	Service ▾	EstimatedHours ▾	ActualHours ▾	CustomPrice ▾	ServiceStatus ▾	Notes ▾	CompleteDate ▾
6	5	INITIAL				Planned		
7	5	ONSITE	1			Planned		
8	5	OFFSITE	3		$99.00	Planned	This is an advertisec	
(New)						Planned		

Figure 15-30. The completed JobService table

Creating the Contact Table

The Contact table is used to record correspondence with a customer. Incoming e-mails are automatically added to this table by the Exchange application that you will build in the next chapter. Contacts can also be added or updated from the SharePoint site as well as the Lync extension window.

Create the Contact table and add the following columns:

- **ContactID**, the primary key

- **Customer**, a lookup column using the Customer table

- **ContactDate**, the date/time that the contact occurred

- **ContactType**, a static list of allowed values such as e-mail or phone

- **Inbound**, a Boolean column indicating if the customer initiated the contact

- **FollowUp**, a static list of values, specifying an appropriate action

- **ContactNotes**, a memo field, recording the contents of the contact

When specifying the ContactType column, include the following values:

- **Email**

- **Phone**

- **Mail**

- **InPerson**

- **Other**

When specifying the FollowUp column, include the following values:

- **None**

- **Callback**

- **Schedule Visit**

- **Estimate Job**

For the `ContactDate`, set the `Default Value` as **=Now()**, which will default to the current date and time. The completed table will look like Figure 15-31.

ContactID	Customer	ContactDate	ContactType	Inbound	FollowUp	ContactNotes
1	John Smith	9/14/2011 10:32:23 PM	Email	✓	Schedule Visit	Schedule an onsite consultation fo
* (New)		9/14/2011 10:34:11 PM		■		

Figure 15-31. The completed Contact table

Creating the Agent Table

The Agent table is used by the Exchange and Lync applications that you will develop in the next chapter. This table defines the agents that are available for responding to incoming e-mails. This will be explained in more detail in the next chapter.

Create an Agent table and include the following columns:

- **AgentID**, the primary key
- **AgentName** (text)
- **Login** (text; this is their Office 365 account)
- **SipAddress**, the address of their Lync client; in your scenario, this will be the same as their login.
- **AgentStatus**, a static list of allowed values
- **LastMessage**, a date/time column that records when the last incoming message was assigned to the agent

For the `AgentStatus` column, enter the following values:

- **Available**
- **Offline**
- **Inactive**

The completed table should look like Figure 15-32.

AgentID	AgentName	Login	SipAddress	AgentStatus	LastMessage
1	Michael Mayberry	michaelm@apress365.com	michaelm@apress365.com	Offline	
* (New)				Available	

Figure 15-32. The completed Agent table

Creating the Queries

A select query can be used to combine the fields of two or more tables into a single view. This technique is often used to simplify form development since a form can use a query just like it would a table. The form can then be developed from the query, which combines the fields for each table.

For example, the `JobProduct` table provides the job-specific details but the `Product` table contains some important static details such as product code and description. You'll combine these two tables into a single, de-normalized view (query). The form will use the query and can include columns from both tables.

You will create the following queries:

- **qryJobProduct** combines the `JobProduct` and `Product` tables.

- **qryJobService** combines the `JobService` and `Service` tables.

- **qryJobSummary** combines the `Job`, `Customer`, and `Address` tables.

Implementing the qryJobProduct Query

Let's start with `qryJobProduct`.

1. From the Create tab of the ribbon, click the Query button. This displays the Show Table dialog box, which allows you to select the tables to be included in the query.

2. Select the `JobProduct` and `Product` tables, as shown in Figure 15-33.

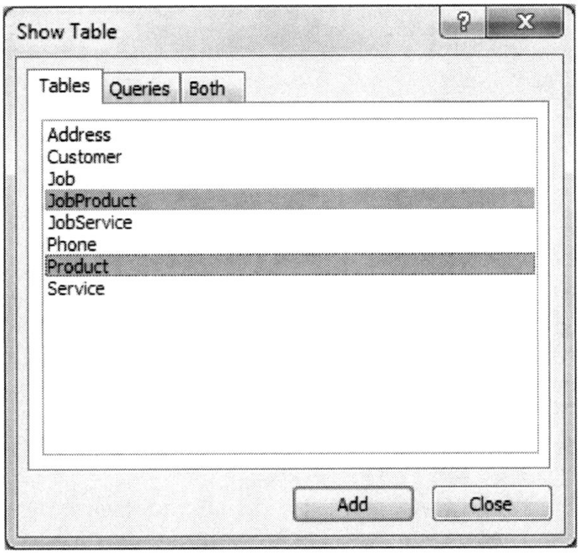

Figure 15-33. Adding the JobProduct and Product tables

3. Click the Add button to add these tables and then click the Close button to close the dialog box. These tables will be displayed in the upper pane of the query window. Because of the foreign key relationship that exists between these two tables, there is already a join relationship shown.

Tip You can remove or edit these joins in the query window without affecting the table relationships.

---

4. Double-click the following fields, one at a time, to add them to the query definition:

- JobProduct.JobProductID
- JobProduct.Job
- JobProduct.Product
- JobProduct.EstimatedQty
- JobProduct.ActualQty
- JobProduct.ProductStatus
- JobProduct.CompleteDate
- JobProduct.CustomPrice
- Product.ProductCode
- Product.Description
- Product.UnitPrice
- Product.UnitCost
- Product.InventoryType
- JobProduct.Notes

5. It will save a few steps when creating the forms to rename the Job column to **JobID**. Remember when creating the JobProduct table, the lookup column was named simply Job. However, the matching field in the Job table is called JobID. When creating subforms, it will be easier to link them together if both forms use the same column name. Edit the Field row for the Job column as **JobID: Job**. This will expose the Job column with the name JobID.

Save the query and enter the name **qryJobProduct** when prompted. The completed query should look like Figure 15-34.

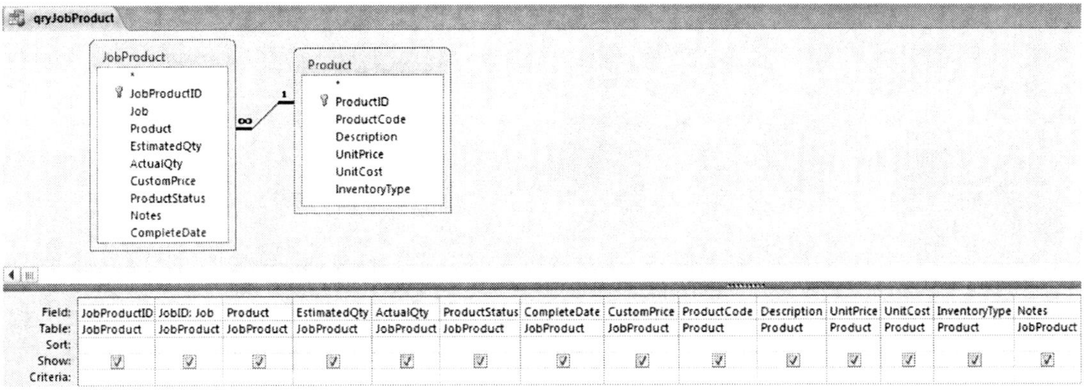

Figure 15-34. The completed qryJobProduct query

Implementing the qryJobService Query

Implement the qryJobService query the same way except use the JobService and Service tables. Include the following columns:

- JobService.JobServiceID
- JobService.Job (again, rename the Job column as **JobID**)
- JobService.Service
- JobService.EstimatedHours
- JobService.ActualHours
- JobService.ServiceStatus
- JobService.CompleteDate
- JobService.CustomPrice
- Service.ServiceCode
- Service.Description
- Service.LaborRate
- Service.MinimumHours
- Service.FlatRate
- JobService.Notes

Save the query and specify the name **qryJobService**. The completed query should look like Figure 15-35.

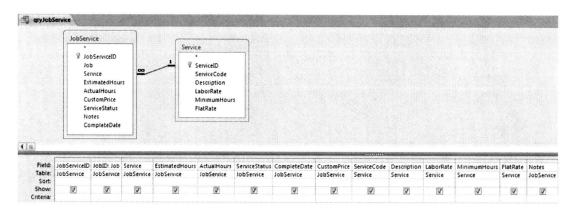

Figure 15-35. The completed qryJobService query

Creating the qryJobSummary Query

Create a new query and add the following tables:

- Customer
- Job
- Address

The initial query will look similar to Figure 15-36.

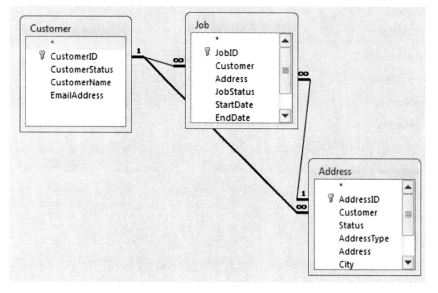

Figure 15-36. The initial query design

Notice that the Address table is linked to both the Customer and Job tables. A customer can have multiple addresses but a job can only have one address. For this query, the Job table is the main table; you'll want to keep the join between Job and Address but remove the one between Customer and Address. Click this join and then press the Delete key to remove it. This will have no effect on the table relationships.

Double-click the following columns to add them to the query:

- Job.JobID

- Customer.CustomerID

- Customer.CustomerName

- Customer.EmailAddress

- Job.TotalEstimate

- Address.Address

- Address.City

- Address.StateProvince

- Address.ZIPPostal

- Address.CountryRegion

- Job.Notes

Save the query and enter the name **qryJobSummary**. The completed query should look like Figure 15-37.

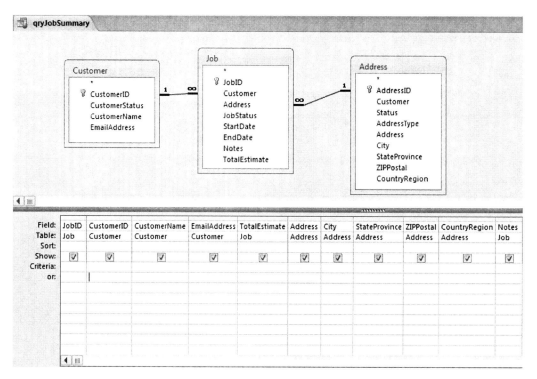

Figure 15-37. The completed qryJobSummary query

Implementing a Data Macro

Data macros are a handy place to implement data processing procedures. They can be automatically executed when certain data events occur, such as a record being added or modified. Because of this, they are particularly useful for keeping related tables in sync and enforcing business rules. A data macro can be assigned to a data event directly, or you can create a named macro that can be called by data events. Named macros can also be called manually from a form.

For this application, you'll create a named macro that calculates the total amount of the job and updates the TotalEstimate column of the Job table. You can then call this macro from all the data events that could potentially affect the total, such as when a record is added to the JobProduct table. However, to simply this project, you'll add a Recalculate button on the Job form that will call this data macro.

Creating the Data Macro

All data macros, including named macros, must be associated with a table. For event macros, the table is the one generating the event. For named macros, the assignment can be somewhat arbitrary depending on the nature of the macro. In this case, since it will update the Job table, you will add it to that table.

Open the Job table. From the Table tab of the ribbon, click the Named Macro button and the click the Create Named Macro link, as shown in Figure 15-38.

Figure 15-38. Creating a named macro

The macro will need to know which job should be updated so you'll create a parameter that will be passed in when the macro is called. Click the Create Parameter link in the upper right-hand corner of the macro editor. Enter the name **jobID** and a description, as shown in Figure 15-39.

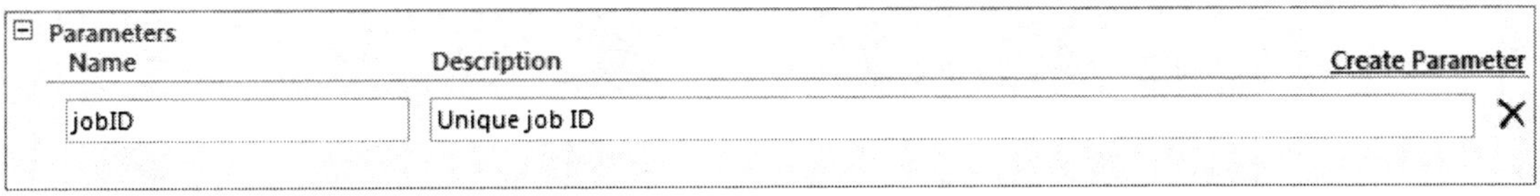

Parameters		
Name	Description	Create Parameter
jobID	Unique job ID	✕

Figure 15-39. Adding the jobID parameter

Computing the Job Total

The macro will compute the job total by adding up the products and services included in the job. The macro is fairly long so I will describe it in pieces. The first macro action creates a local variable, jobTotal, and initializes it to 0. Then the macro iterates through all of the JobProduct records, accumulating the price multiplied by the quantity, as shown in Figure 15-40.

```
SetLocalVar
              Name   jobTotal
        Expression   = 0
☐   For Each Record In   JobProduct
        Where Condition   = [JobProduct].[Job]=[JobID] And [JobProduct].[ProductStatus]<>"Cancelled"
                  Alias   JobProduct

    ☐  If   [JobProduct].[CustomPrice]>0   Then
            SetLocalVar
                      Name   jobTotal
                Expression   = [jobTotal]+[JobProduct].[CustomPrice]

    ☐  Else
        ☐  Look Up A Record In   Product
                Where Condition   = [Product].[ProductID]=[JobProduct].[Product]
                          Alias   Product
            SetLocalVar
                      Name   quantity
                Expression   = [JobProduct].[ActualQty]

            ☐  If   IsNull([quantity]) Or [quantity]<=0   Then
                SetLocalVar
                          Name   quantity
                    Expression   = [JobProduct].[EstimatedQty]
            End If
            SetLocalVar
                      Name   jobTotal
                Expression   = [jobTotal]+[quantity]*[Product].[UnitPrice]

        End If
```

Figure 15-40. Designing the data macro – Part 1

If a price has been specified in the CustomPrice column, this value is used instead. It is assumed that this value will be an extended amount and does not need to be multiplied by the quantity to get the total amount for this product.

■ **Note** The JobProduct table contains both a EstimatedQty column as well as an ActualQty column. If the actual value is populated, the formula will use that field instead of the estimated quantity.

The next step is to accumulate the JobService records. The first portion of this, shown in Figure 15-41, handles the special cases.

Figure 15-41. *Designing the data macro – Part 2*

If a CustomPrice is specified, that value will be used for the JobService record. Otherwise, if this is a flat rate service, the FlatRate amount from the Service record is used and the quantity is ignored. The remainder of this logic, shown in Figure 15-42, handles the normal case, which computes the product of the hourly rate times the number of hours.

```
□ Else
    SetLocalVar
                Name    hours
                Expression    = [JobService].[ActualHours]

    □ If   IsNull([hours]) Or [hours]<=0   Then
        SetLocalVar
                    Name    hours
                    Expression    = [JobService].[EstimatedHours]
    End If
    □ If   IsNull([hours]) Or [hours]<[Service].[MinimumHours]   Then
        SetLocalVar
                    Name    hours
                    Expression    = [Service].[MinimumHours]
    End If
    □ If   IsNull([hours])   Then
        SetLocalVar
                    Name    hours
                    Expression    = 0
    End If
    SetLocalVar
                Name    jobTotal
                Expression    = [jobTotal]+[hours]*[Service].[LaborRate]
End If
End If
```

Figure 15-42. Designing the data macro – Part 3

If the service defines a minimum number of hours, this is used when the actual (or estimated) hours are less than the minimum amount.

Updating the Job Table

The last step is to update the Job table, storing the computed job total. Figure 15-43 shows the actions used to perform the update.

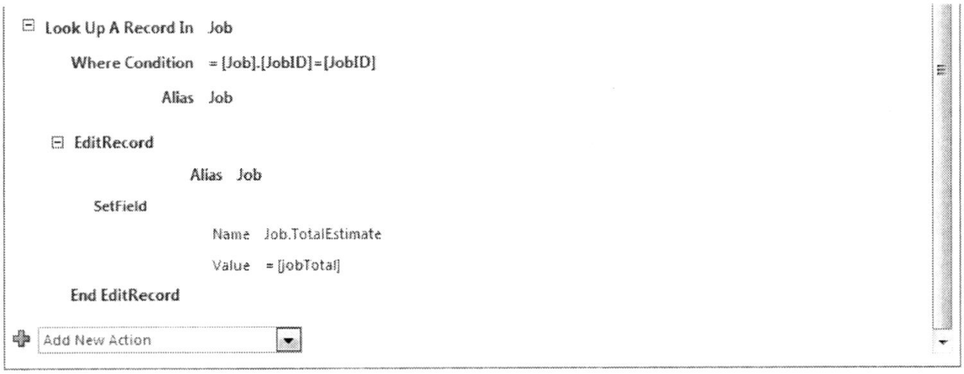

```
⊟  Look Up A Record In   Job
        Where Condition    = [Job].[JobID]=[JobID]
                   Alias   Job

    ⊟  EditRecord
                   Alias   Job
        SetField
                     Name   Job.TotalEstimate
                    Value   = [jobTotal]
        End EditRecord
⊕  Add New Action                  ▼
```

Figure 15-43. Designing the data macro – Part 4

When you have entered all this logic, save the data macro. Enter the name **CalculateJobTotal** when prompted.

Testing the Macro

The easiest way to test a named data macro is to create a UI macro with a single RunDataMacro action.

1. From the Create tab of the ribbon, click the Macro button.

2. In the macro editor, add the RunDataMacro action, as shown in Figure 15-44. For this test, you can hardcode the jobID parameter.

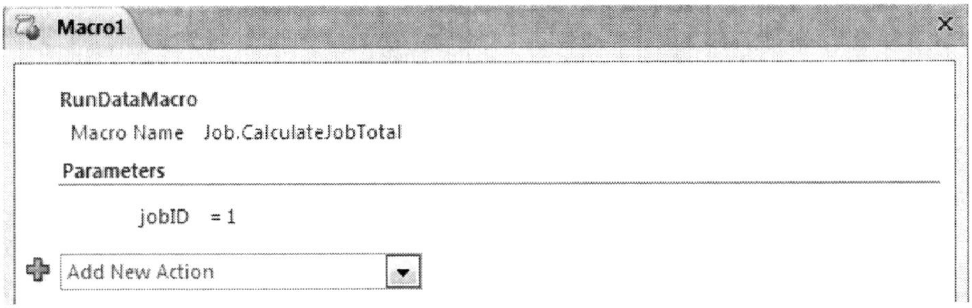

```
⊡  Macro1                                             ✕

    RunDataMacro
      Macro Name   Job.CalculateJobTotal
    Parameters
           jobID   = 1
⊕  Add New Action               ▼
```

Figure 15-44. Creating a test macro

3. Save this macro, which should add it to the Navigation pane.

4. You can either click the Run button in the ribbon or double-click the macro in the Navigation pane.

5. Open the Job table and verify that the TotalEstimate column has the correct value.

Designing Forms

Now that you have the tables designed you can implement forms that allow the users to view and edit the data contained in them. Generally, you will create a form for each table. In some cases you'll use a query that combines the data from multiple tables. When there is a parent-child relationship such as with the Customer and Phone tables, you will embed a subform within the parent form that displays the child table.

■ **Caution** You can't use VBA in a web form as this is not supported with SharePoint. Instead you'll use macros to perform advanced features such as form manipulation. Fortunately, in Access 2010, the macro editor has been significantly improved.

Creating the Phone and Address Forms

I find it easier to create the child forms first. Then as you design the parent forms, the subforms are available to be included in the parent. You'll start with the Phone and Address forms.

Using the Form Templates

Access provides three primary ways to create a web form.

- Blank Form creates a blank form where you can add controls to design the form.

- Form creates a form based on the selected table that displays a single record at a time.

- Multiple Items creates a form based on the selected table that displays multiple records, much like a spreadsheet.

The Create tab of the ribbon contains a button for each of these options, as you can see in Figure 15-45.

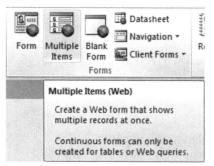

Figure 15-45. Buttons in the ribbon for creating a web form

The last two options are quick ways to get a form started. Both of them create a data-bound control as well as a label for each column in the table or query. The Form template puts the labels and data-bound controls in the Detail section of the form. The label and associated form are displayed side-by-side on the form. The Multiple Items template puts the labels in the Form Header section and all of the controls are arranged in a single row. This looks like a spreadsheet where the labels become the column headings. You will use the Multiple Items template to create the Phone and Address forms. This will allow you to view several records at the same time.

■ **Caution** When using either the Form or Multiple Items template, make sure you select the table before creating the form. There is no dialog box to select the source table or query. Once you click the button in the ribbon, the form will be created immediately.

Creating the Phone Form

Select the Phone table in the Navigation pane and then click the Multiple Items button, as shown in Figure 15-45. After a few seconds, the form will be created and displayed in the Layout view.

■ **Tip** The value of the primary key field is auto-generated and in many cases is not meaningful to the end users. In most forms you will remove the associated control and label to save real estate. The notable exceptions to this rule are the CustomerID and JobID columns. These are often used in documents such as invoices.

Delete the PhoneID and Customer controls and the associated labels. The primary key, PhoneID, is not important to the end user. Since the Phone form will only be used as a child form of the Customer form, displaying the customer name here would be redundant. Arrange the controls to look like Figure 15-46.

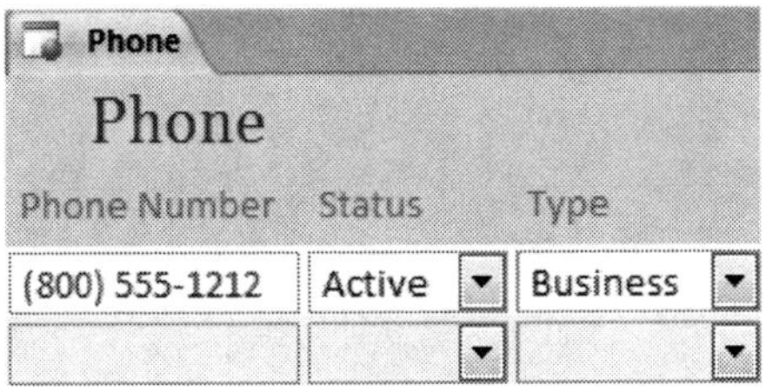

Figure 15-46. The layout of the Phone form

■ **Note** When saving the forms that you'll create in this chapter, use the table name for the form name. For example, with this form, enter the name **Phone** when prompted. For forms that are based on a query such as qryJobProduct, drop the qry prefix and save the form as **JobProduct**, for example.

Creating the Address Form

Create the Address form in the same way, by selecting the Address table and clicking the Multiple Items button in the ribbon. You will also delete the AddressID control and its label. However, for this form, you'll need to leave the Customer control. You will hide it instead of deleting it.

The Address form will be used in another place and you'll need to use the Customer column, which I'll explain later. Delete the Customer label and then resize the Customer control to make it as narrow as possible. Also, set the Visible property to No.

■ **Caution** From the Access client, simply resizing the control is sufficient to effectively hide it. However, when published to SharePoint, if the Visible property is not turned off, the web form will still display its contents.

Arrange the controls to look like Figure 15-47.

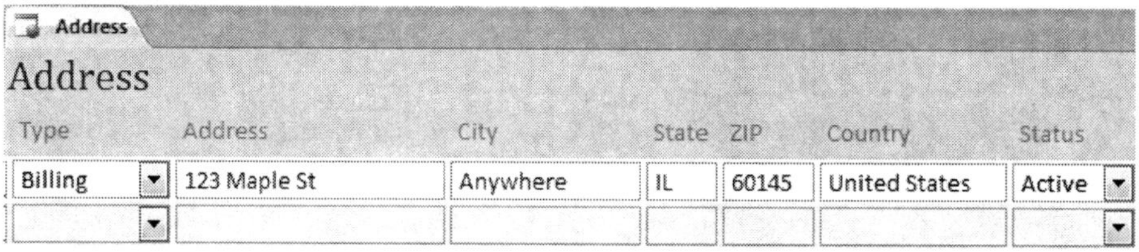

Figure 15-47. The layout of the Address form

Using TempVar Variables

Access 2010 provides a really useful feature called *TempVars*. These are variables that you can use to store information that is available throughout the application. You can set a TempVar in a form and then access that variable from other forms, queries, reports, or macros. In this sense they are similar to session variables in a web application.

You will create a TempVar called CustomerID to remember the current customer. This TempVar is set when a customer is loaded. Then wherever you need to know the current customer you can simply get it from the TempVar. You will also use a TempVar to remember the current job. TempVars will make more sense as you start to use them.

Defaulting the Customer

The Address form will be used by the Job form when the user needs to create a new address for the job. This will be a pop-up window, which does not provide the parent-child relationship that subforms do. You'll want the new address to be associated to the current customer without the user needing to select that customer.

To accomplish this, you will define a default value for the Customer control. When a new record is created, you'll default this value so when the address is saved, it will be linked to the current customer.

In the Property Sheet, select the Customer control. In the Data tab, enter the Default Value property as =**[TempVars]![CustomerID]**, as shown in Figure 15-48.

Property Sheet	
Selection type: Combo Box	
Customer	▾

Format	Data	Event	Other	All

Control Source	Customer
Row Source	SELECT [Customer].[CustomerID], [Customer].[Custc
Row Source Type	Table/Query
Limit To List	Yes
Allow Value List Edits	No
List Items Edit Form	
Inherit Value List	Yes
Default Value	=[TempVars]![CustomerID]
Enabled	Yes
Locked	No

Figure 15-48. Setting the default value for the Customer column

The Default Value property it set by using the CustomerID TempVar. I'll show you later how to set this; for now, you can assume that CustomerID has been set to the current customer.

Create the Products and Services Forms

Next, you'll create the subforms that will display the products and services included in a job. These will be similar to the Phone and Address forms, with a few differences:

- You will use a query instead of a table as the data source.

- The controls will be displayed on two rows instead of one.

- The controls associated with columns from the linked tables (Product or Service) will be locked to prevent editing.

Select the qryJobProduct query in the Navigation pane. This query includes columns from both the JobProduct table as well as the Product table. From the Create tab of the ribbon, click the Multiple Items button. This will generate a new form that will include controls for each of these columns. Remove the JobProductID and JobID controls and their associated labels.

Adding a New Layout Row

There are too many controls to fit them all on one row so you'll create a second row where you'll move some of the controls. Select any one of the controls and from the Arrange tab of the ribbon, click the Insert Below button (see Figure 15-49).

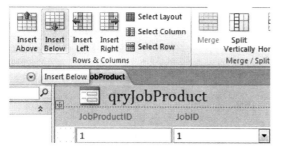

Figure 15-49. Ading a row to the form layout

This creates a second row in the form layout for the Detail section. You'll place the controls for the JobProduct table on the first row and the Product control on the second row. I also deleted many of the labels for the columns of the Product table.

■ **Tip** If you want a second row in the Form Header section, select one of the labels and use the same Insert Below button. I deleted many of the labels so they fit on one row. However, you could use a two-row header and leave all the labels on the form.

Arrange the controls to look like Figure 15-50. From the Arrange tab of the ribbon, you can use the Split Horizontally to split a single cell into two. You can also use the Merge button to combine cells.

JobProduct							
Products							
Est	Actual	Status	Custom $	Complete Dt		Notes	
2		Waiting ▾					
PROD01 ▾		Standard Widget			$35.00	$14.95	Inventoried ▾
1		Delivered ▾					
PROD02 ▾		Special Order Widget			$55.00	$20.40	Special Order ▾
3		New ▾	$50.00				
PROD03 ▾		Made to Order Gadget			$75.00	$10.00	Custom Made ▾
		▾					
▾							

Figure 15-50. The layout of the JobProduct form

Locking Read-Only Controls

The user needs to be able to edit the columns in the JobProduct table such as EstimatedQty, Status, and CompleteDate. However, the Product columns like UnitPrice and Description should not be editable. Select the following controls:

- Description

- UnitPrice

- UnitCost

- InventoryType

With these controls selected, from the Data tab of the Property Sheet, set the Locked property to Yes. This will prevent these values from being modified.

Creating the JobService Form

Create the JobService form in the same way as the JobProduct form except you'll use the qryJobService query. Remove the JobServiceID and JobID controls and associate labels. Create a second row and move the controls from the Service table to the second row. Arrange the controls to look like Figure 15-51.

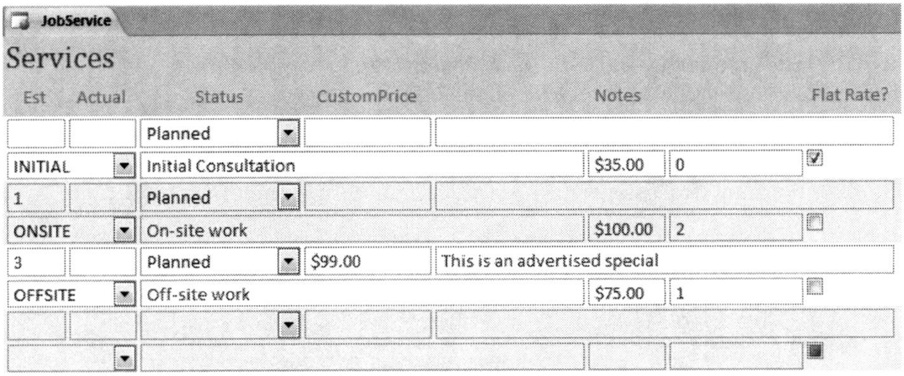

Figure 15-51. The layout of the JobService form

Set the Locked property on the Description, LaborRate, MinimumHours, and FlatRate controls.

Designing the Job Form

The Job form will display a single job so you'll use the Form template to create it. You will embed the JobProduct and JobService forms as subforms to display the products and services included in the job. You will add some command buttons to the form that will be implemented by macros. You will also use macros to implement some advanced features.

Select the Job table in the Navigation pane and then click the Form button in the Create tab of the ribbon. Arrange the controls to look like Figure 15-52. Notice the empty cells where you will later place command buttons.

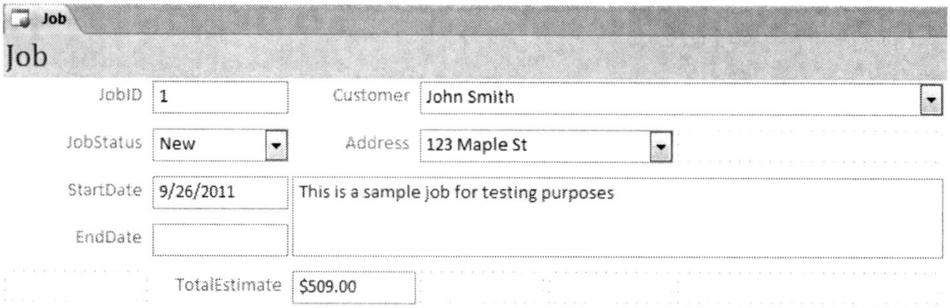

Figure 15-52. The initial layout of the Job form

Adding the Subforms

To add a subform you'll first need to create a cell in the form layout to put it in.

1. Select the TotalEstimate control, which should be on the last row of the form layout.

2. From the Arrange tab of the ribbon, click the Insert Below button. This will create a new row of cells.

3. Select all of the cells on this row and click the Merge button to combine them into a single cell. Increase the height of the cell to about 2".

4. In the Design tab of the ribbon, click the Subform button and then select the new empty cell. This will insert a Subform control in this cell and also insert a new column for the label. You can delete the label and the column that was created.

5. The Subform control is a wrapper that contains a form object. Now you'll need to specify which of the existing forms should be used. Select the Subform control and in the Data tab of the Property Sheet, select the JobProduct form in the Source Object property.

6. You'll then need to specify how the subform is linked to the parent form. This linkage will allow Access to automatically display the correct child records when the parent record is changed. Click the ellipses next to the Link Master Fields property to display the Subform Field Linker dialog box. Select the JobID column as both the master and child link fields, as shown in Figure 15-53.

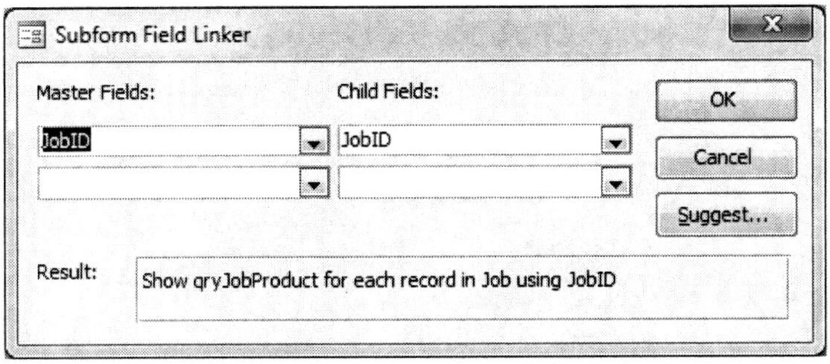

Figure 15-53. Setting the master and child link fields

7. Add another row to the form layout and add the JobService form, linking it just
   like you did the JobProduct form. The Job form should look like Figure 15-54.

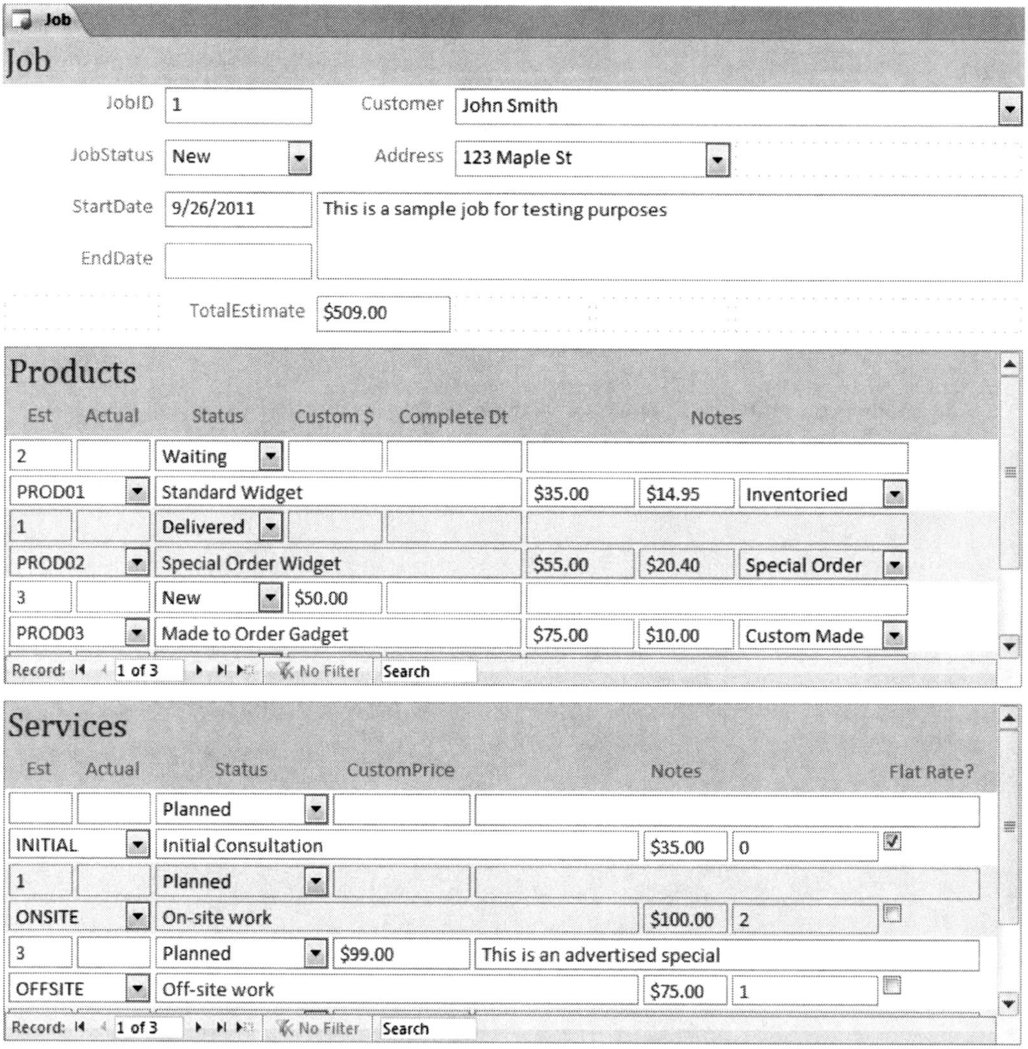

Figure 15-54. The Job form with the subforms added

Adding Command Buttons

Now you'll add three command buttons to the Job form, creating macros for their implementations. You will add the following buttons:

- **Recalculate** calls the data macro to recalculate the job total.

- **New Address** opens the Address form to insert a new address for this job.

- **Save** saves the current Job record and all subrecords.

Let's get started.

1. From the Design tab of the ribbon, click the Button button and then select the empty cell to the left of the TotalEstimate label. Enter the **Recalculate** for the Caption property.

2. In the Event tab of the Property Sheet, select the OnClick event and click the ellipses to start the macro editor.

3. Enter the macro actions shown in Figure 15-55. This macro sets the JobID TempVar and then calls the CalculateJobTotal data macro that you implemented earlier in this chapter. It then calls the RefreshRecord action to force the form to update the TotalEstimate control.

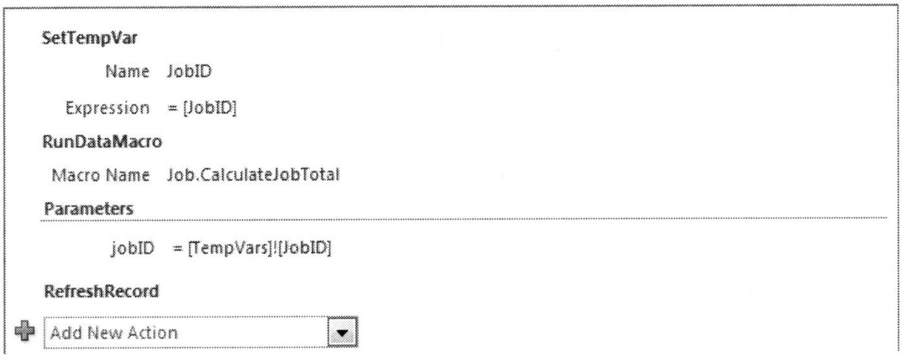

```
SetTempVar
          Name    JobID
     Expression   = [JobID]
RunDataMacro
     Macro Name   Job.CalculateJobTotal
Parameters
          jobID   = [TempVars]![JobID]

RefreshRecord
➕ Add New Action          ▼
```

Figure 15-55. The Recalculate macro

4. In the same way, add a command button to the empty cell to the right of the Address control. Set the Caption property to **New Address...** Click the ellipses next to the OnClick event and enter the macro actions shown in Figure 15-56. This macro opens the Address form. The Data Mode is set to Add so the form will create a new record in the Address table. The Window Mode is set to Dialog so this will be a modal dialog window.

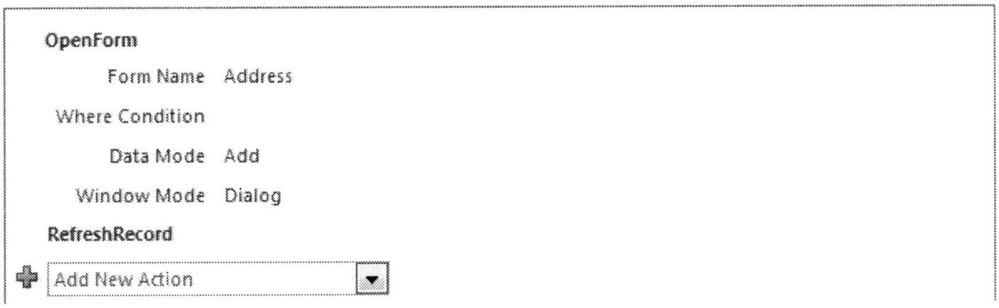

```
OpenForm
     Form Name     Address
Where Condition
     Data Mode     Add
    Window Mode    Dialog
RefreshRecord
➕ Add New Action          ▼
```

Figure 15-56. The New Address macro

5. You can also add a picture that will be displayed on the button. From the Format tab of the Property sheet, click the ellipses next to the Picture property. Scroll through the existing images and select an appropriate one. In Figure 15-57, I picked the Builder image.

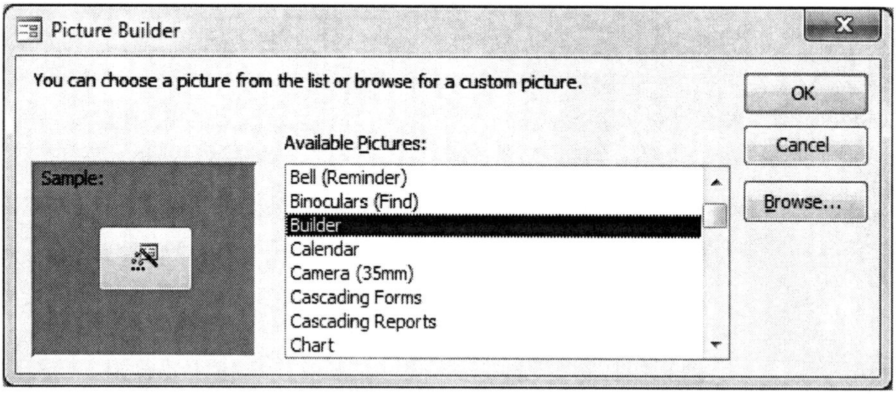

Figure 15-57. Selecting an image for the command button

6. After selecting the Picture property, change the Picture Caption Arrangement property to Right. This will cause the caption to be displayed to the right of the image.

7. Add another command button to an empty cell to the right of the TotalEstimate control. Set the Caption property to Save, select an appropriate image, and set the Picture Caption Arrangement property to Right. For the event implementation, enter the macro actions shown in Figure 15-58. This macro calls the SaveRecord menu command and also sets the JobID TempVar.

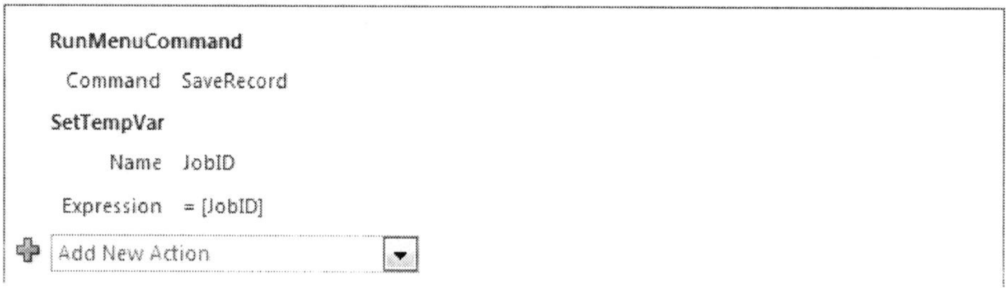

Figure 15-58. The Save macro

The top portion of the Job form should now look like Figure 15-59.

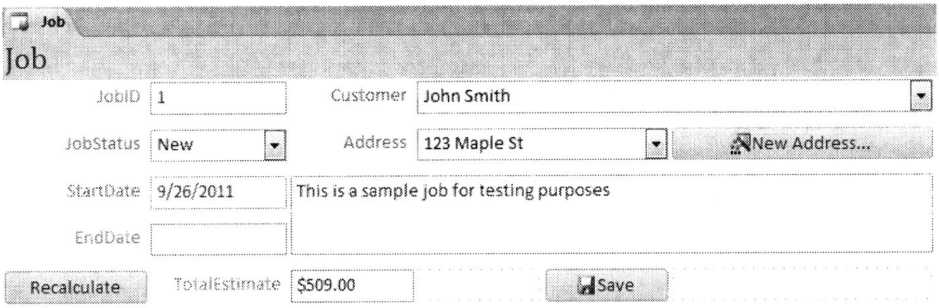

Figure 15-59. The completed Job form

Setting and Using TempVars

As mentioned earlier, one of the key components of integrating these forms is the use of the TempVars, CustomerID and JobID. In order for these forms to work properly, the variables need to be kept up-to-date so they reflect the currently selected record. Fortunately, this is pretty easy to do because there are only two places where they change.

The first is when a record is displayed. This occurs when a form is loaded and the first record is displayed or when the form navigates to a different record. In both cases, the form's OnCurrent event is raised. From the Property Sheet, select the Form object and the Event tab. Define a macro for the OnCurrent event, as shown in Figure 15-60.

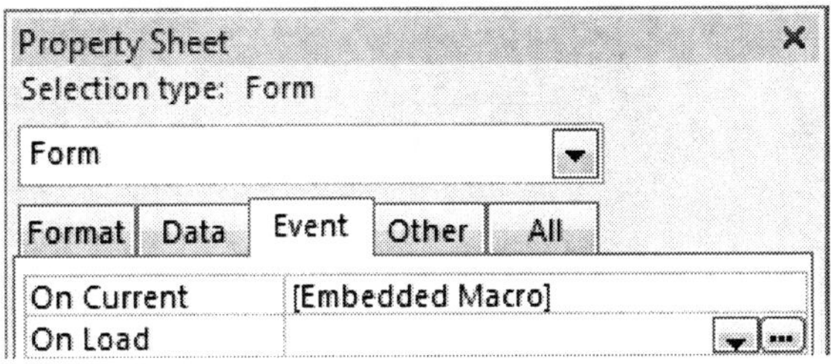

Figure 15-60. Implementing the OnCurrent event

This macro uses the SetTempVar action to set the value of the JobID TempVar, as shown in Figure 15-61.

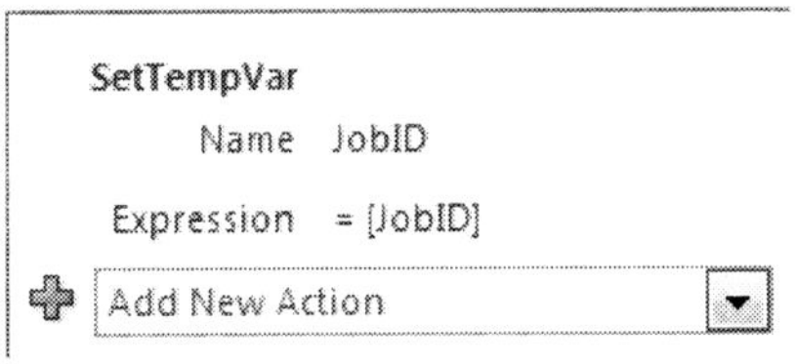

Figure 15-61. Setting the JobID TempVar

The second place where the TempVar should be updated is when a new record is created. When inserting a new record, the primary key is not defined until the record is saved. To obtain this, implement a macro for the AfterUpdate event on the JobID control, as shown in Figure 15-62. The implementation of this macro is identical to the OnCurrent macro. It sets the JobID TempVar.

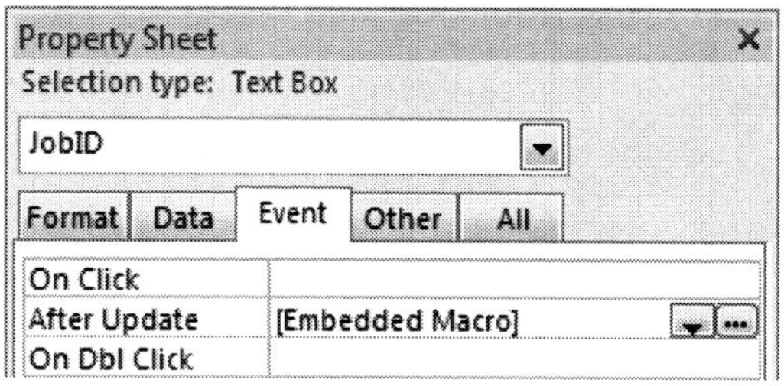

Figure 15-62. Implementing the AfterUpdate event

Just like you did with the Address form, the Job form needs to default the customer. When creating a new job, the customer is set by default and the user doesn't need to select one. For the Customer control, set the Default Value property to =**[TempVars]![CustomerID]**, as shown in Figure 15-63.

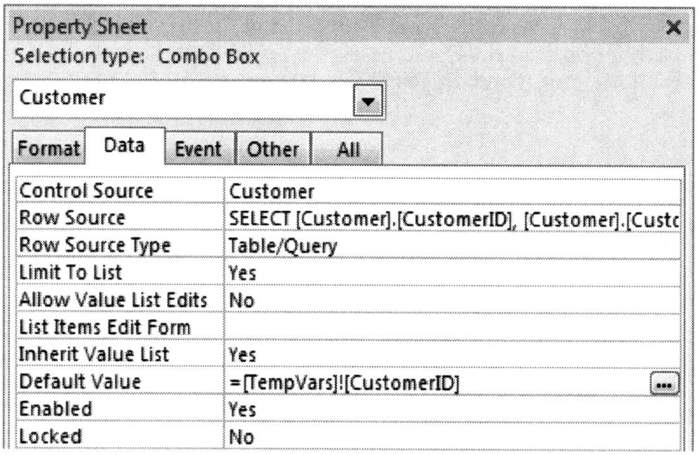

Figure 15-63. Defaulting the customer when creating a new job

Selecting the Job Address

The Job form has an Address drop-down list to select an existing address for the job. This drop-down should only include addresses from the current customer. To accomplish that, you'll define a custom Row Source for this control.

In the Property Sheet, select the Address control. In the Data tab, click the ellipses next to the Row Source property. This will display the Query Builder. Currently, the control is selecting from the Address table with no criteria so it is including all records. Enter **[TempVars]![CustomerID]** for the criteria of the Customer column, as shown in Figure 15-64. This will limit the list to only addresses on the current account.

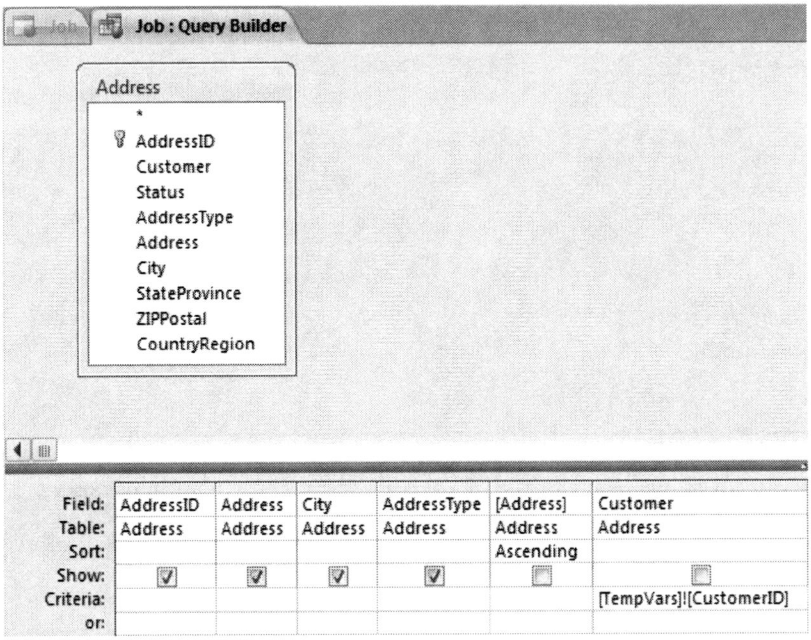

Figure 15-64. Specifying the Customer criteria

Creating the Customer Form

The Customer form will be used to view and update customer information. This is where you'll view and add phone numbers and address for a customer. This form will also allow you to add and modify customer jobs. You'll also record correspondence (contacts) with a customer from here.

You have already implemented the Phone and Address forms that will be included here but you need to create the Contact and JobSummary forms.

Designing the Contact Form

The Contact form will display a single contact with the customer. This can record incoming contacts such as an e-mail from the customer or outbound contacts such as notes about a follow-up call that was made. You'll use the Form template since the form will display one contact at a time.

Select the Contact table in the Navigation pane and click the Form button in the Create tab of the ribbon. Remove the ContactID and Customer controls and their associated labels. Arrange the controls to look like Figure 15-65.

Contact

Contact

Date	Type	Inbound	Follow Up

9/13/2011 | Email ▾ | ☑ | Schedule Visit ▾

Schedule an onsite consultation for the latter part of next week

Figure 15-65. The Contact form layout

Designing the JobEstimate Form

Before creating the JobSummary form, you'll first create the JobEstimate form. This is a printer-friendly, view-only form that displays the details of a job. It will use the qryJobSummary query so it can include customer and address details. You'll also modify the format to remove control borders so it looks more like a printed report.

1. Select the qryJobSummary query in the Navigation pane and click the Form button in the Create tab of the ribbon.

2. Select all of the controls, and from the Arrange tab of the ribbon, set the Control Padding to None, as shown in Figure 15-66.

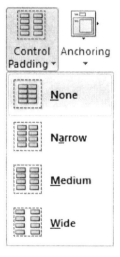

Control Padding ▾   Anchoring ▾

- ▦ **N**one
- ▦ **Na**rrow
- ▦ **M**edium
- ▦ **W**ide

Figure 15-66. Removing the spaces between controls

3. While all the controls are still selected, in the Format tab of the Property Sheet, set the Border Style to Transparent, as shown in Figure 15-67.

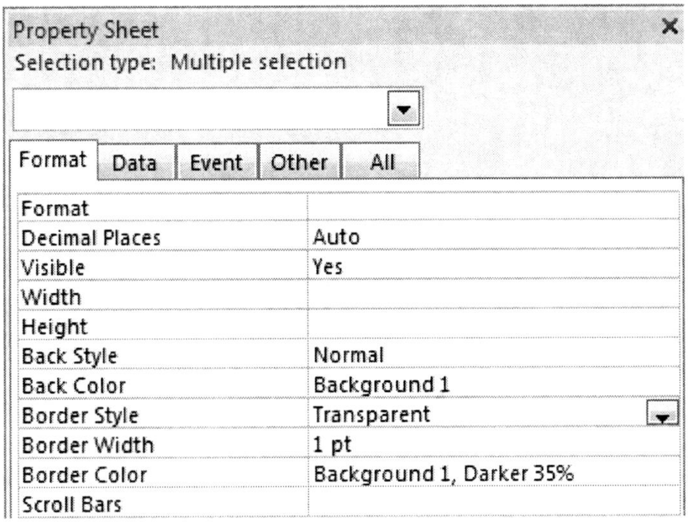

Figure 15-67. Removing the control borders

4.   Arrange the controls to look like Figure 15-68. You will delete most of the labels.

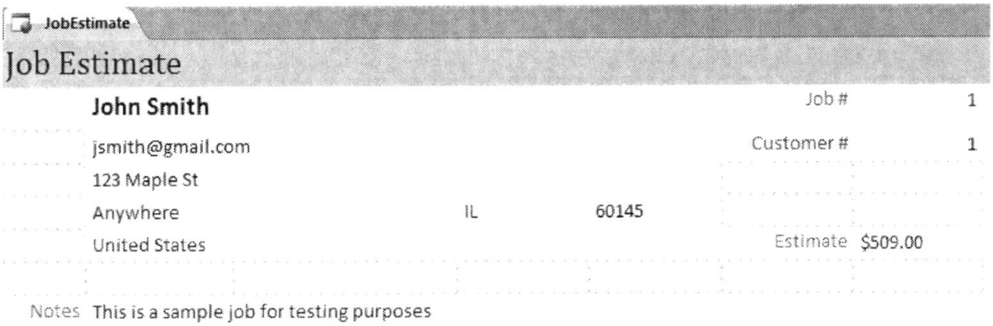

Figure 15-68. The JobEstimate form layout

5.   To make this form only display the selected job, set the Filter property of the Form object to **JobID = TempVars!JobID**. Also set the Allow Additions, Allow Deletions, and Allow Edits properties to No, as shown in Figure 15-69.

Property Sheet		×
Selection type: Form		

Form	▼

Format	Data	Event	Other	All

Record Source	qryJobSummary
Recordset Type	Dynaset
Filter	JobID = TempVars!JobID
Order By	
Wait for Post Processing	No
Data Entry	No
Allow Additions	No
Allow Deletions	No
Allow Edits	No

Figure 15-69. Configuring the form filter

Designing the JobSummary Form

Now you're ready to create the JobSummary form, which is a multiple-item form that lists all of the jobs for the current customer. This form will have a command button to open the Job form, which will allow the user to view and modify the selected job. It will also have a button that will display the JobEstimate form that you just created.

1. Select the Job table in the Navigation page and then click the Multiple Items button in the Create tab of the ribbon.

2. Remove the labels for the JobID and Customer controls, shrink these controls to make them as narrow as possible, and set their Visible property to No. You will need these controls but they should not be visible.

3. Arrange the remaining controls on a single row, leaving an empty cell at both the far left and right of the row. You will add command buttons here to display the Job and JobEstimate forms, respectively.

4. For the left button, select the Pencil image. For the OnClick event, enter the macro actions shown in Figure 15-70. This macro opens the Job form in Edit mode. Notice that the Where Condition selects the current job using the JobID TempVar.

```
OpenForm
        Form Name   Job
   Where Condition   = [JobID]=[TempVars]![JobID]
        Data Mode   Edit
      Window Mode   Dialog
   RefreshRecord
➕  Add New Action        ▼
```

Figure 15-70. The macro for the Job Edit button

5. For the right button, choose the Printer image and add the macro actions shown in Figure 15-71. This macro opens the JobEstimate form in read-only mode.

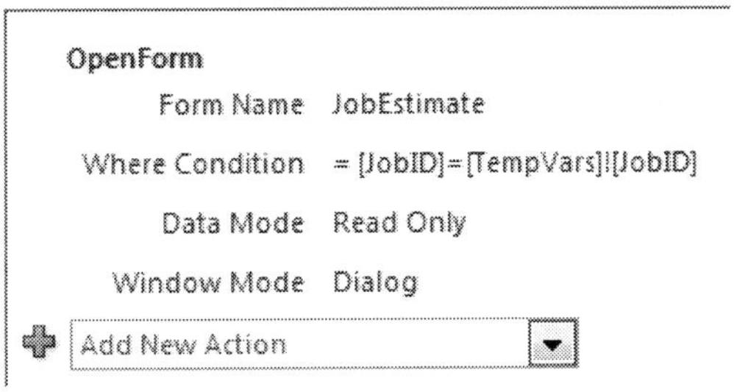

```
OpenForm
        Form Name   JobEstimate
   Where Condition  = [JobID]=[TempVars]![JobID]
        Data Mode   Read Only
      Window Mode   Dialog
⊕ | Add New Action                    ▼ |
```

Figure 15-71. The macro for the Job Estimate button

The final layout of the JobSummary form should look like Figure 15-72.

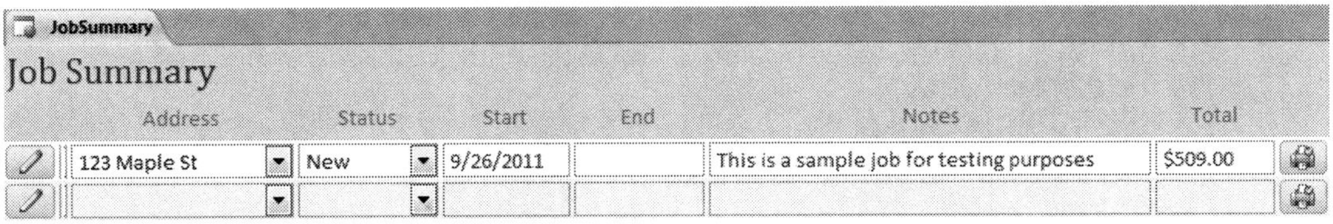

		Address	Status	Start	End	Notes	Total	
Job Summary								
🖉		123 Maple St	New	9/26/2011		This is a sample job for testing purposes	$509.00	🖨
🖉								🖨

Figure 15-72. The JobSummary form layout

Implement the form's OnCurrent event with a macro that sets the JobID TempVar, just like you did for the Job form.

Designing the Customer Form

Now you're ready to create the Customer form. You'll use the Form template since it will display a single record. You'll also add the following subforms:

- Phone
- Address
- Contact
- JobSummary

To do this, follow these steps:

1. Select the Customer table in the Navigation pane and then click the Form button in the Create tab of the ribbon.

2. Add the Phone and Contact subforms and set up the Master-Child links using the CustomerID field.

3. Leave an empty cell in the middle of the form, which you'll later use for a command button. Arrange the controls to look like Figure 15-73.

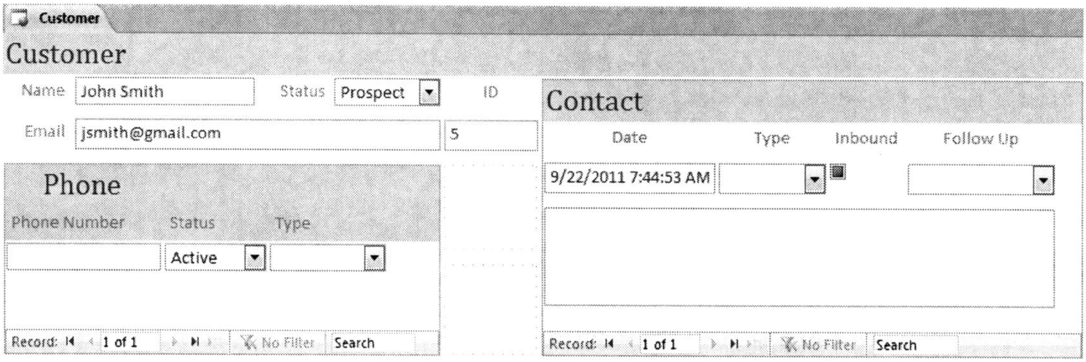

Figure 15-73. The preliminary Customer form

4. Add the Address subform at the bottom of the Customer form using the entire width of the form.

5. In the same way, add the JobSummary form beneath the Address form. Link both of these forms to the master form using the CustomerID field.

6. From the Customer form you can view a summary of that customer's job by using the JobSummary subform. The JobSummary form has a button to display the Job form to see and modify the job details. Now you'll add a command button on the Customer form to create a new job for that customer. Add a command button to the empty cell in the middle of the form and set the Caption to **Create Job**. For the OnClick event, enter the macro actions shown in Figure 15-74. This macro sets the CustomerID TempVar and then opens the Job from in Add mode.

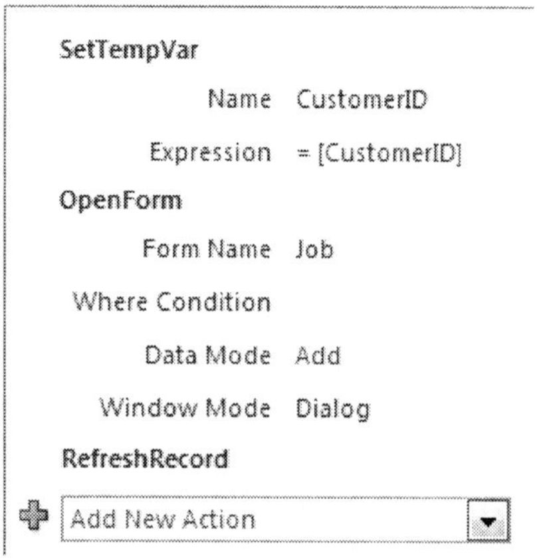

Figure 15-74. The Create Job macro

The final `Customer` form should look like Figure 15-75.

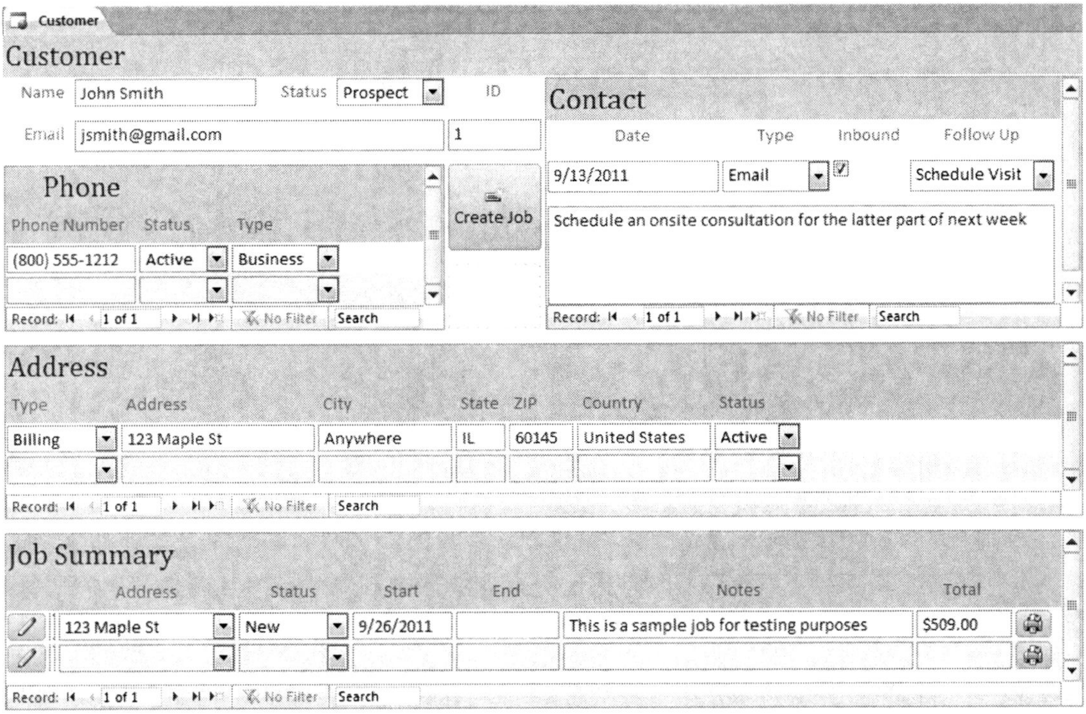

Figure 15-75. The final Customer form layout

Just like you did with the `Job` form, implement the form's `OnCurrent` event with a macro that sets the `CustomerID` TempVar. Also implement the `AfterUpdate` event for the `CustomerID` control. This also sets the `CustomerID` TempVar.

Creating the CustomerSummary Form

The `Customer` form displays a single customer. Now you'll need a form that lists summary information for all of the customers. This will be the form you will normally start with. After selecting a customer, the `Customer` form can then be displayed to show all of the details of that customer.

Designing the Form Details

Select the `Customer` table in the Navigation pane and then click the Multiple Items button in the Create tab of the ribbon. Shrink the `CustomerID` controls as small as possible, set its `Visible` property to No, and delete the associated label. Arrange the controls to look like Figure 15-76. Leave an empty cell to the left of the `CustomerName` control.

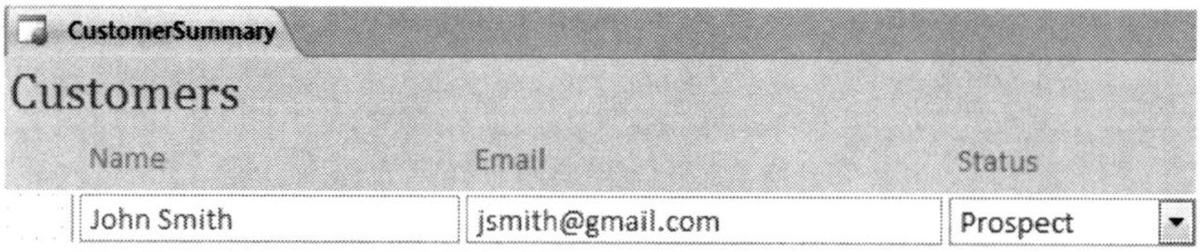

Figure 15-76. The initial CustomerSummary layout

Now you'll add a button that will open the Customer form to display the selected customer. Add a command button to the empty cell. Select the Pencil image for the control's picture. Implement the OnClick event using the actions shown in Figure 15-77.

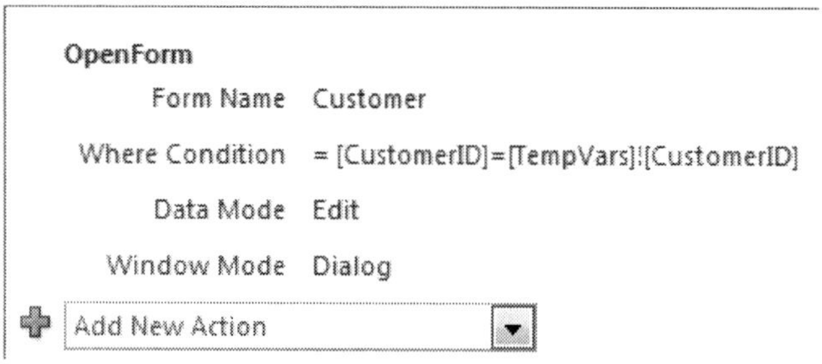

Figure 15-77. The Customer Edit macro

This macro opens the Customer form in Edit mode. Notice that the Where Condition causes this form to display the currently selected record.

Adding a New Customer Button

Just like with the JobSummary form, you'll now add a button to create a new customer. In the Form Header section, split the cell containing the form caption. Add a command button in the empty cell to the right of the caption. Set the Caption to **NewCustomer…** and implement the OnClick event using the actions shown in Figure 15-78.

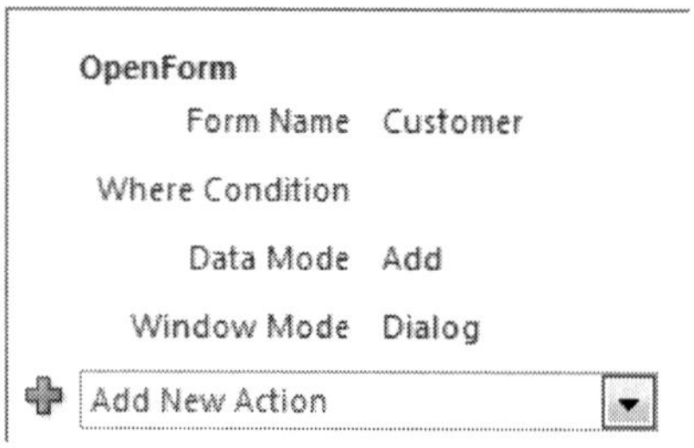

Figure 15-78. The New Customer macro

This macro opens the Customer form in Add mode, which will allow the user to create a new Customer record. The final form layout should look like Figure 15-79.

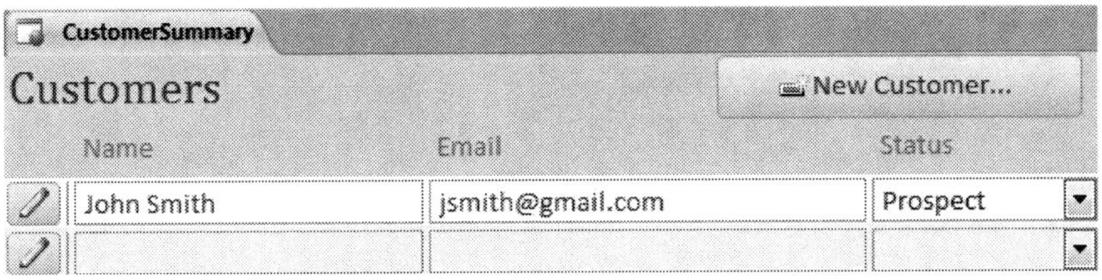

Figure 15-79. The final CustomerSummary form layout

Creating the Remaining Forms

There are three more forms that you'll need to complete this application.

- **Product** adds and configures products sold as part of a job.

- **Service** manages services included in customer jobs.

- **Agent** configures agents that will respond to incoming e-mails.

These are simple forms that don't require any macros. Create these forms using the Form or Multiple Items templates based on the associated table. Remove the primary key from the form. The layout I used is shown in Figure 15-80, Figure 15-81, and Figure 15-82.

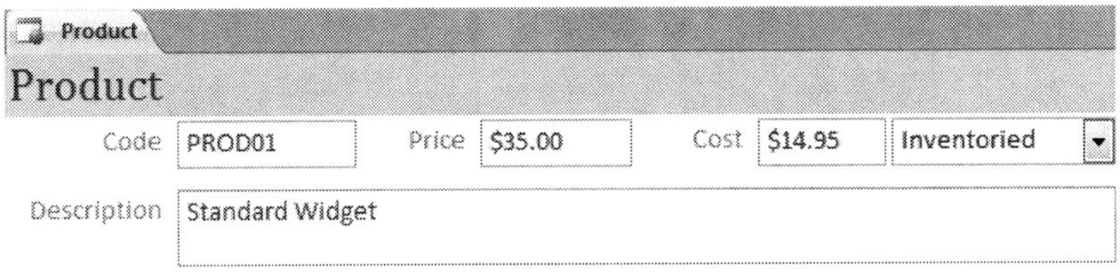

Figure 15-80. The Product form layout

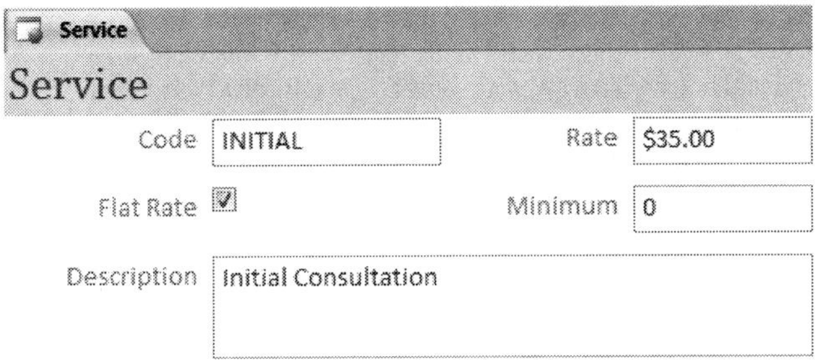

Figure 15-81. The Service form layout

Figure 15-82. The Agent form layout

Creating the Main Form

You have created all of the forms you will need for the application. As a final step you'll create a form that provides a menu of forms for the user. When the Access database is published to the SharePoint server, the standard ribbons and Navigation pane will not be available so you'll need to provide a way for the user to see what forms are available and select the appropriate one.

Many of the forms that you designed are used as subforms or are accessed from a command button on another form. The only forms that you'll need to add to the menu are

- CustomerSummary

- Product

- Service

- Agent

Using the Navigation Form Template

Access provides a convenient way to create a main form that is used as a menu. You create a form using the Navigation template and then drag the other forms onto it.

There are several options for configuring how the tabs for other forms are arranged. If there are only a few items, you can use a single level menu. The tabs can either go across the top of the page, down the left side, or down the right side. If there are a lot of items, you should use a two-level menu. When a top-level tab is selected, the second-level menu shows the tabs associated with that selection. With a two-level menu, the top-level tabs are displayed across the top. The second-level tabs can either be in a second row across the top, down the left side, or down the right side.

From the Create tab of the ribbon, click the Navigation button and then select the desired tab configuration, as shown in Figure 15-83. Since there are only four items, a single level is sufficient. I used the Horizontal tabs option.

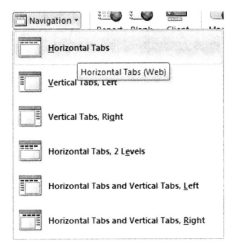

Figure 15-83. Creating the Navigation form

The form is generated with single empty tab, as illustrated in Figure 15-84.

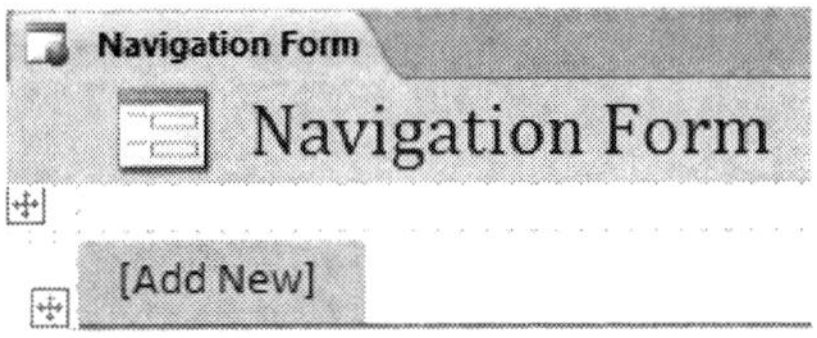

Figure 15-84. The initial empty Navigation form

Adding the Menu Items

The [Add new] text is a placeholder where you can drop a form onto. Drag the CustomerSummary form to this empty tab. The tab label will change to CustomerSummary and a new empty tab will be created. Edit the tab label and change it to **Customers**.

In the same way, add the remaining forms:

- Product
- Service
- Agent

When you're done, the Navigation form should look like Figure 15-85.

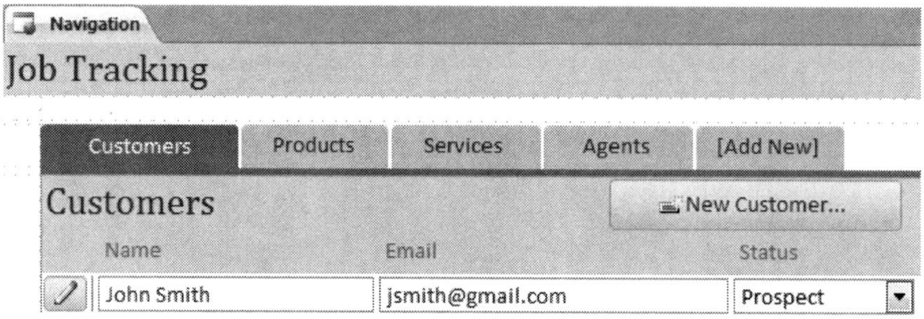

Figure 15-85. The final Navigation form

Defining the Home Page

Next, you'll configure the Access database to display the Navigation form when the application is started. This is done in the backstage view (File tab).

From the Backstage view, click the Options button, which will display the Access Options dialog box. Select the Current Database tab. The Application Option section has options for the Display Form and the Web Display Form. Set these both to Navigation, as shown in Figure 15-86.

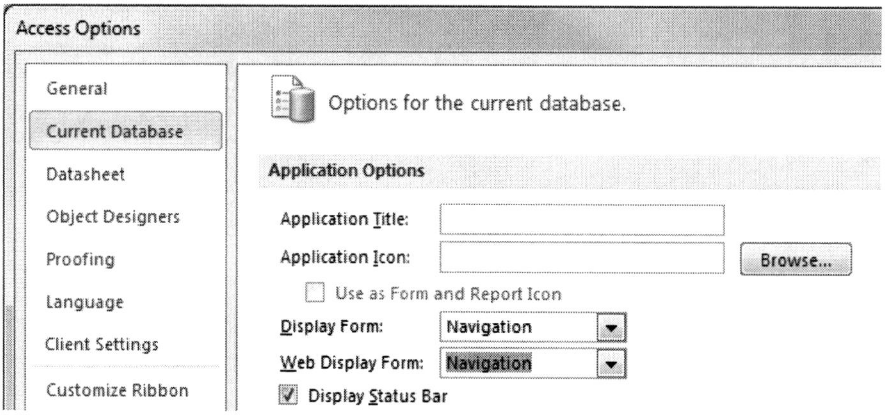

Figure 15-86. Setting the initial display form

The Display Form property specifies which form to load on startup when using the Access client application. The Web Display Form option specifies the initial form to use in SharePoint. If you close Access and then reload this database, you'll see that the Navigation form is loaded automatically.

Publishing the Web Database

Your Access application (database) is now complete and you're ready to publish it to a SharePoint site on your Office 365 account. You'll first run the compatibility checker to make sure the database is ready for the web. Then you'll publish the database to SharePoint.

■ **Caution** I strongly recommend that you make a copy of it before you publish it. Once you have published the Access database to a SharePoint site, the Access database is modified so its contents are irreversibly linked to objects in SharePoint. For example, the `Customer` table is copied to a SharePoint list and the object in Access simply references that list. You will no longer be able to use the Access database as a local database nor can you re-publish it to a different SharePoint site.

Checking for Web Compatibility

Only Access databases that were designed for the web are compatible with SharePoint. By starting with the Blank web database template, Access' default behavior is to create web-compatible objects, so you shouldn't have any issues. However, it's a good idea to run the compatibility check anyway.

From the Backstage view, click the "Publish to Access Services" button in the Info tab. This will display the page shown in Figure 15-87.

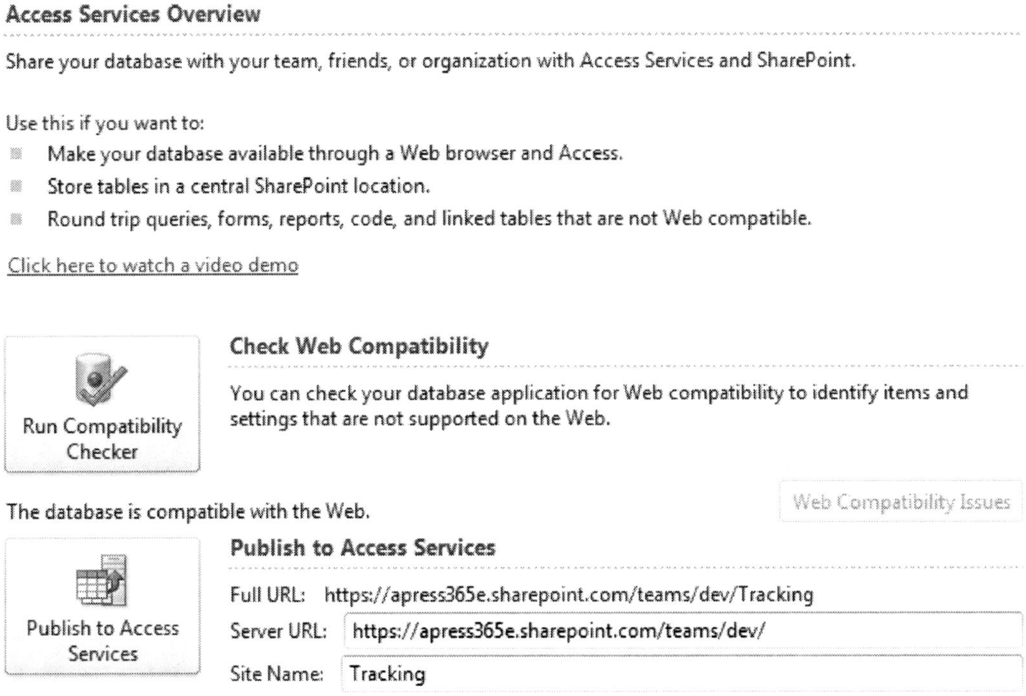

Access Services Overview

Share your database with your team, friends, or organization with Access Services and SharePoint.

Use this if you want to:

■   Make your database available through a Web browser and Access.

■   Store tables in a central SharePoint location.

■   Round trip queries, forms, reports, code, and linked tables that are not Web compatible.

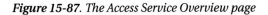
Click here to watch a video demo

Check Web Compatibility

Run Compatibility Checker

You can check your database application for Web compatibility to identify items and settings that are not supported on the Web.

The database is compatible with the Web.   Web Compatibility Issues

Publish to Access Services

Publish to Access Services

Full URL: https://apress365e.sharepoint.com/teams/dev/Tracking

Server URL: https://apress365e.sharepoint.com/teams/dev/

Site Name: Tracking

Figure 15-87. *The Access Service Overview page*

Click the "Run Compatibility Check" button. If any issues are detected, make the necessary corrections.

Publishing the Database

To publish the database, you'll need to specify the URL of the SharePoint Online server. This URL should point to a site collection that you have already created.

■ **Note** If you're using one of the enterprise plans, refer to Chapter 2 for details on creating a site collection. If you're using the small business plan, a single site collection was created for you.

Enter the URL of the site collection that you want to use and specify the site name **Tracking**. Then click the "Publish to Access Services" button. After several seconds you should see the dialog box shown in Figure 15-88.

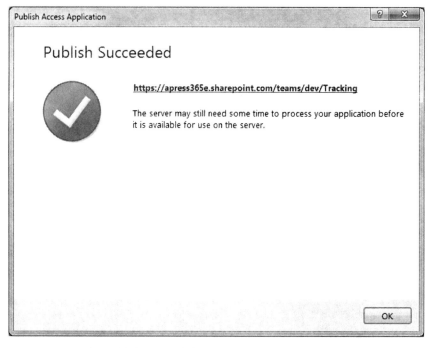

Figure 15-88. The publish succeeded message

This dialog box also specifies the URL of the new SharePoint site. This is the link the users will use to access this application.

Testing the SharePoint Site

Click the link in the Publish Succeeded dialog box, which will go to the new SharePoint site. You should see the Navigation form shown in Figure 15-89.

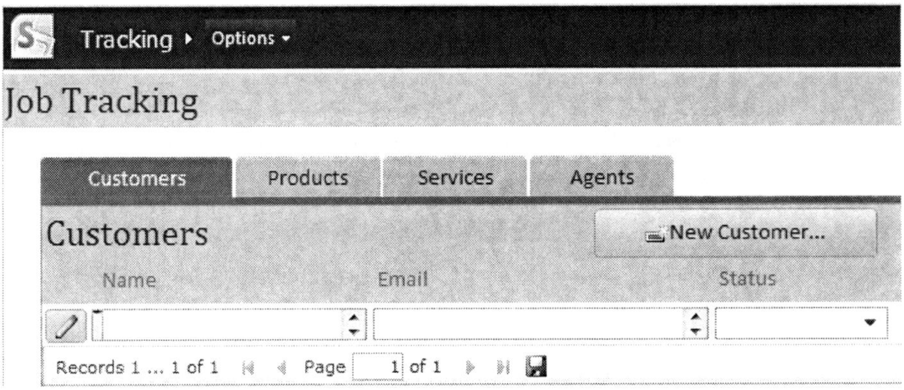

Figure 15-89. The Navigation form as the default web page

Since the Customers tab is listed first, this will be the initial form. If there was data in your Access tables when you published it, this will be copied to the SharePoint site. Select an existing customer and click the Edit button, or create a new customer using the New Customer button. The Customer form will be displayed as a modal dialog box, as demonstrated in Figure 15-90.

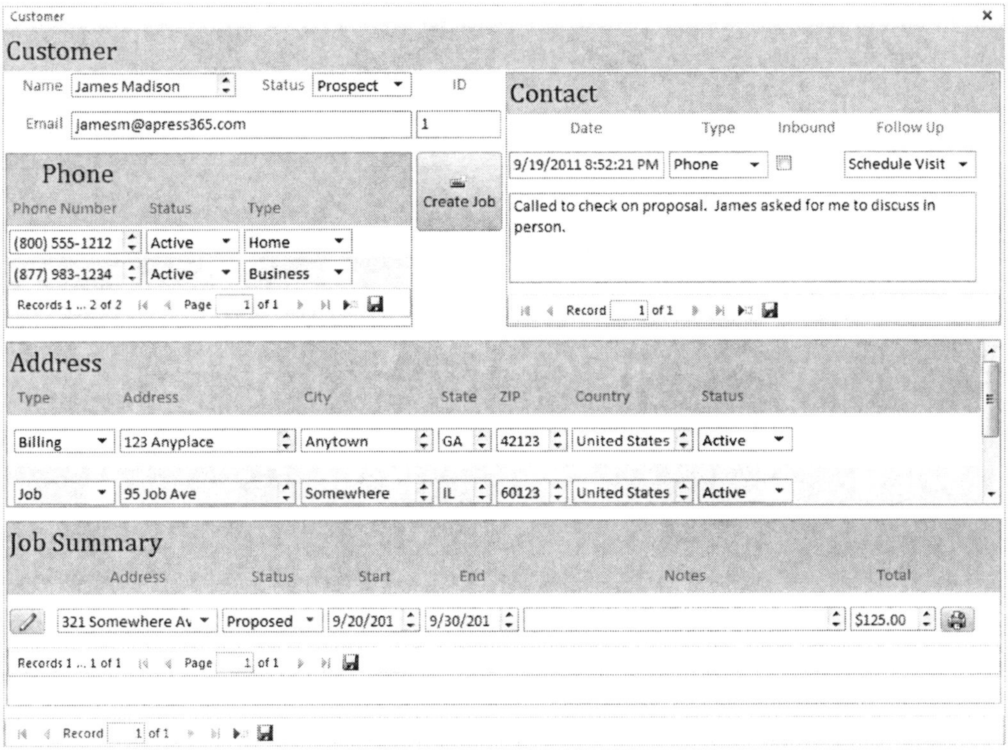

Figure 15-90. The Customer form as a modal dialog box

Test out all of the forms by creating new customers, adding phone numbers and addresses, and creating new jobs. You should also define some products and services. Also populate the Agents list, shown in Figure 15-91. This will be needed by the applications in the next chapter.

Customers	Products	Services	Agents	

Agents

Name	Login	Sip Address	Status	Last Message
Mark Collins	markc@apress365.com	markc@apress365.com	Available ▾	
Michael Mayberry	michaelm@apress365.com	michaelm@apress365.com	Available ▾	
Corbin Collins	corbinc@apress365.com	corbinc@apress365.com	Offline ▾	
Jonathan Hassell	jonathanh@apress365.com	jonathanh@apress365.com	Inactive ▾	
Martina Grom	martinag@apress365.com	martinag@apress365.com	Available ▾	

Records 1 ... 5 of 5 ⏮ ◀ Page 1 of 1 ▶ ▶ ▶◻ 💾

Figure 15-91. The Agents form

Summary

In this chapter, I took you on a whirlwind tour of Access web databases. You built fairly sophisticated application, which is now hosted on your Office 365 account. The application consists of

- Tables
- Queries
- A data macro for calculating the job total
- Web forms (that use macros for navigation)
- A navigation form

With relative ease and essentially no coding, you have created a cloud-based web application. In the next chapter you'll use Exchange Online and Lync Online to further enhance this application.

CHAPTER 16

Integrating Office365 Technologies

So far, this book has focused on parts of Office365. This chapter brings them together as it walks you through an application that integrates three of the primary technologies of Office365:

- SharePoint Online

- Exchange Online

- Lync

The approach of this chapter is a practical one. The application developed here attempts to accomplish a real-world type of scenario, keeping the task of demonstration in mind. This application is not designed for production use, but does attempt to approach a real problem with a real solution. A few technical goals were part of the approach for this application:

- **Development on a workstation, not a SharePoint server**: This application uses the Client Object Model and does not use SharePoint directly. The solution presented in this chapter is intended to be built without the need for SharePoint Server to be installed locally.

- **Client application running locally**: The main application is a WPF application. There is a hosted part of this, but once it is hosted on SharePoint, the desktop application can be run on any machine.

- **No servers needed outside of Office365**: This application only uses Office365 servers. There is no dependency upon additional servers or hosting environments.

The application in this chapter consists primarily of a WPF application that integrates with Lync and pulls data from Exchange Online and SharePoint Online. Part of the integration with Lync is using a contextual conversation to pass information through instant messaging. A Silverlight application is used in this process. It will be hosted on a SharePoint page and displayed within the conversation window. This will allow a clear presentation as well as interaction with the data.

Prerequisites

This application includes a few dependencies from external sources. They are listed here, at the beginning, so that everything can be gathered prior to starting development. This will make it simpler when adding references or projects to the solution later. Download each of the following resources and have them ready for reference. If you have been working the projects in each chapter of this book you will already have installed most of these.

SharePoint Foundation 2010

Since the project was designed for development on a workstation, it will use the SharePoint Client Object. This is included in SharePoint Foundation 2010. That resource can be found here: `www.microsoft.com/download/en/details.aspx?id=5970`. Once downloaded, run to install.

Exchange Web Services Managed API

This application will connect to Exchange Online using the Exchange Web Services Managed API. That resource can be found here: `www.microsoft.com/download/en/details.aspx?id=13480`. Once downloaded, run to install.

Lync 2010 SDK

The Lync 2010 SDK is used to access Lync functionality. That resource can be found here: `www.microsoft.com/download/en/details.aspx?id=18898`. Once downloaded, run to install.

Claims-Based Authentication for SharePoint

Part of this application will access SharePoint data, but from the client, not the server. Authentication becomes an issue for this scenario. Microsoft developed a sample application that accomplishes this type of authentication. A portion of this sample will be used in your application. This resource can be found here: `http://code.msdn.microsoft.com/windowsdesktop/Remote-Authentication-in-b7b6f43c`

Building the Desktop Application

To start building the desktop application, we need to add the necessary references:

1. Open Visual Studio 2010 and start a new project. Choose a WPF Application template and select the location for your project. Name the project **SalesManagement**. Your screen should appear similar to Figure 16-1.

Figure 16-1. New project in Visual Studio 2010

2. Reference Lync assemblies. Right-click References and click Add Reference. On the Browse tab, navigate to the location shown in Figure 16-2.

Figure 16-2. Lync SDK location

3. Add the assemblies highlighted in Figure 16-3.

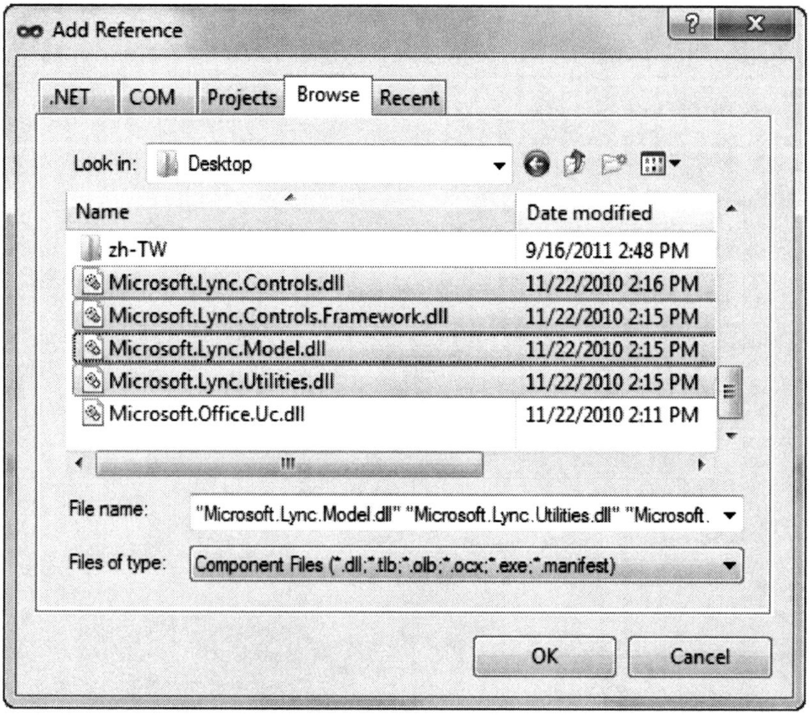

Add Reference
.NET
COM
Projects
Browse
Recent
Look in:
Desktop
Name
Date modified
zh-TW
9/16/2011 2:48 PM
Microsoft.Lync.Controls.dll
11/22/2010 2:16 PM
Microsoft.Lync.Controls.Framework.dll
11/22/2010 2:15 PM
Microsoft.Lync.Model.dll
11/22/2010 2:15 PM
Microsoft.Lync.Utilities.dll
11/22/2010 2:15 PM
Microsoft.Office.Uc.dll
11/22/2010 2:11 PM
File name:
"Microsoft.Lync.Model.dll" "Microsoft.Lync.Utilities.dll" "Microsoft.
Files of type:
Component Files (*.dll;*.tlb;*.olb;*.ocx;*.exe;*.manifest)
OK
Cancel

Figure 16-3. *Lync assemblies for reference*

4. Add the Exchange Web Services Managed API. The assemblies can be found in the location shown in Figure 16-4.

Computer
Local Disk (C:)
Program Files
Microsoft
Exchange
Web Services
1.1

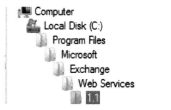

Figure 16-4. *Exchange Web Services assemblies location*

5. Select `Microsoft.Exchange.WebServices.dll` from the Browse tab and click OK.

6. Change the target framework. WPF applications default to use the client framework. This application needs the full framework. Right-click the project and click Properties. On the Application tab, locate the "Target framework" option and select .NET Framework 4, as shown in Figure 16-5.

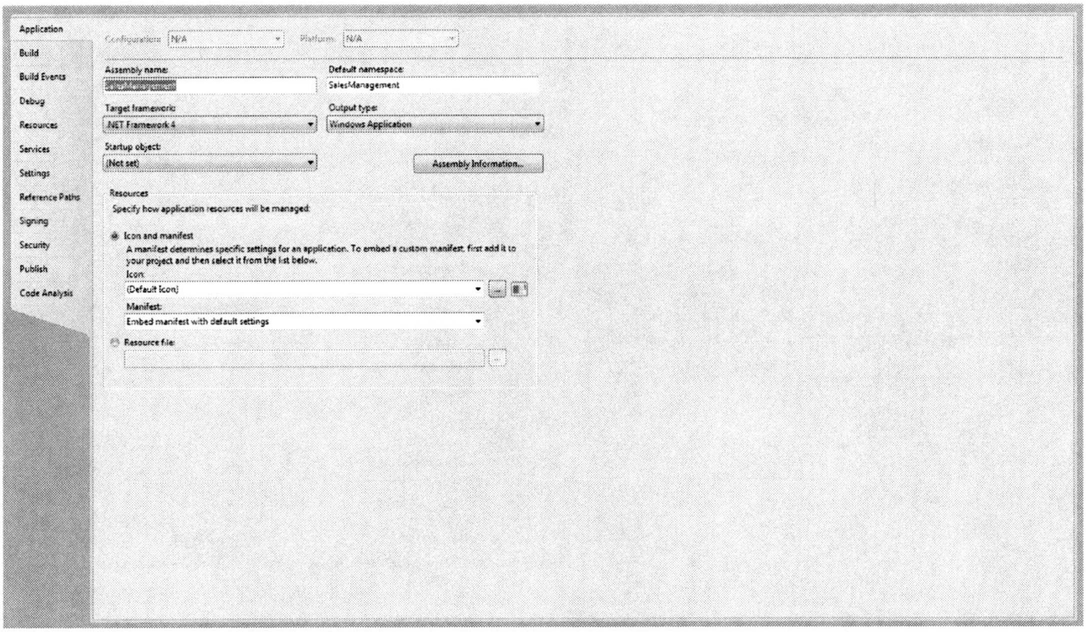

Figure 16-5. Setting the target framework

■ **Note** Making this change will result in a prompt for confirmation. Visual Studio will update the application and close the current project. The project will automatically reopen and all unsaved changes will be saved. Click Yes when the warning dialog appears.

Adding Claims-Based Authentication

The concept of authentication is beyond the scope of this sample application. Rather than developing an authentication module, you will use one developed by Microsoft. This is the ClaimsAuth project you downloaded earlier.

1. Right-click the solution and click Add Existing Item, as shown in Figure 16-6.

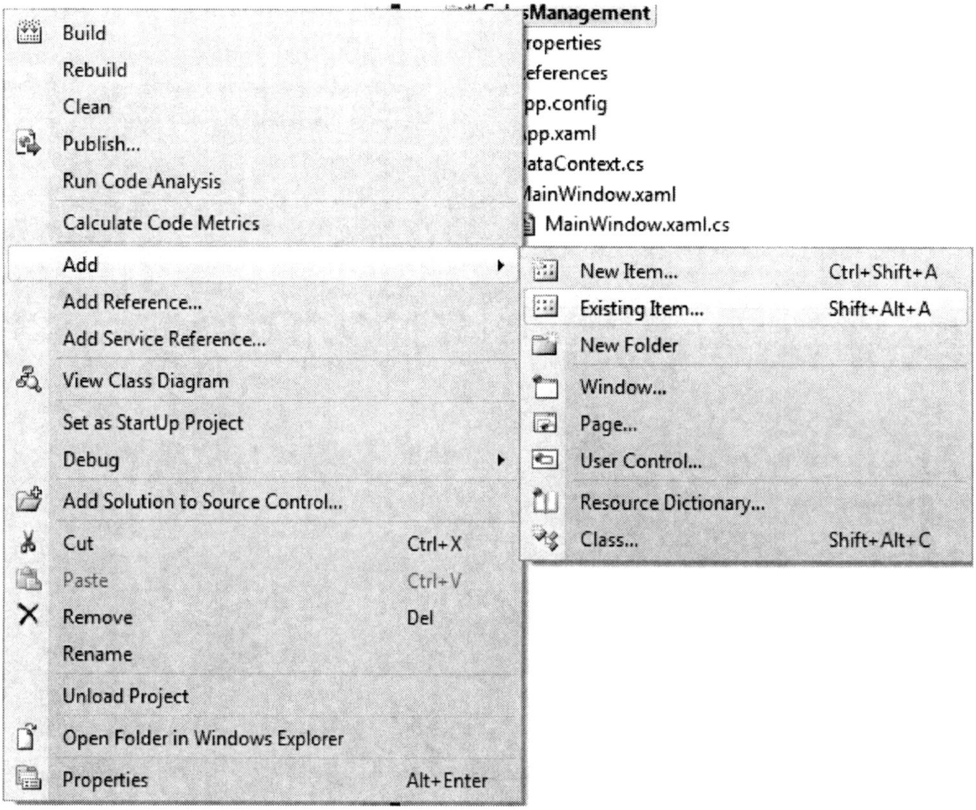

Figure 16-6. Adding an existing project to a solution

2. Navigate to the folder where the code was downloaded and unzipped. Look for the folder and file shown in Figure 16-7 and click Open.

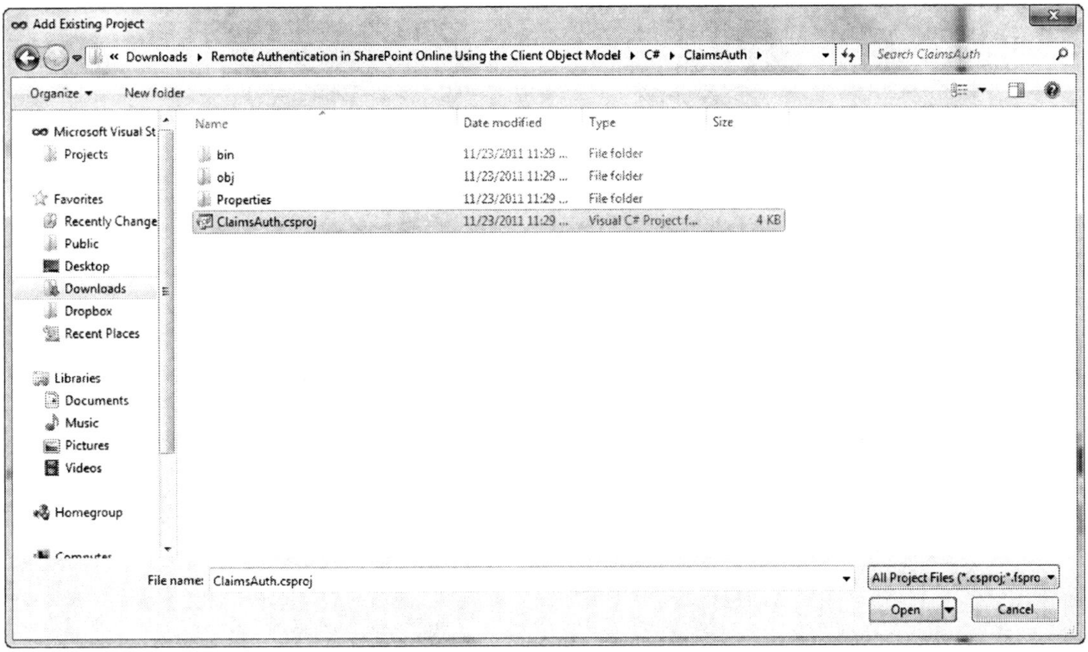

Figure 16-7. Adding the ClaimsAuth project to the solution

3. Reference the newly added project in the SalesManagement project. Right-click References and click Add Reference…. Select ClaimsAuth from the Projects tab and click OK. Figure 16-8 shows what this should look like.

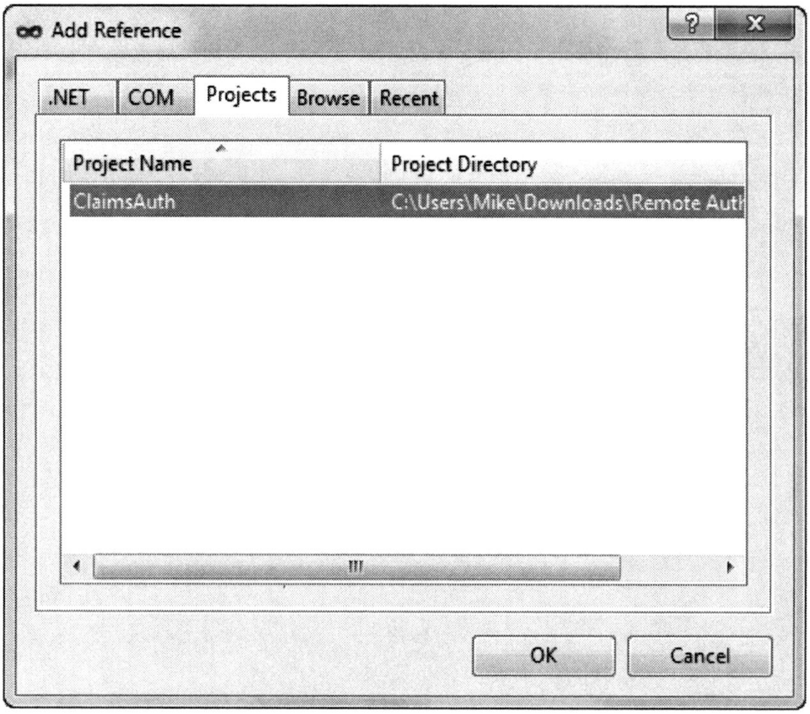

Figure 16-8. Adding a ClaimAuth project reference

Defining the DataContext Class

The application will not access a traditional database, but it will access external services. To abstract the access code from the application, you will include a class called DataContext. This class will include the necessary code to interact with the service. This will help keep the code behind the page cleaner and easier to follow.

    1.   Add a new class to the project called **DataContext.cs**, as shown in Figure 16-9.

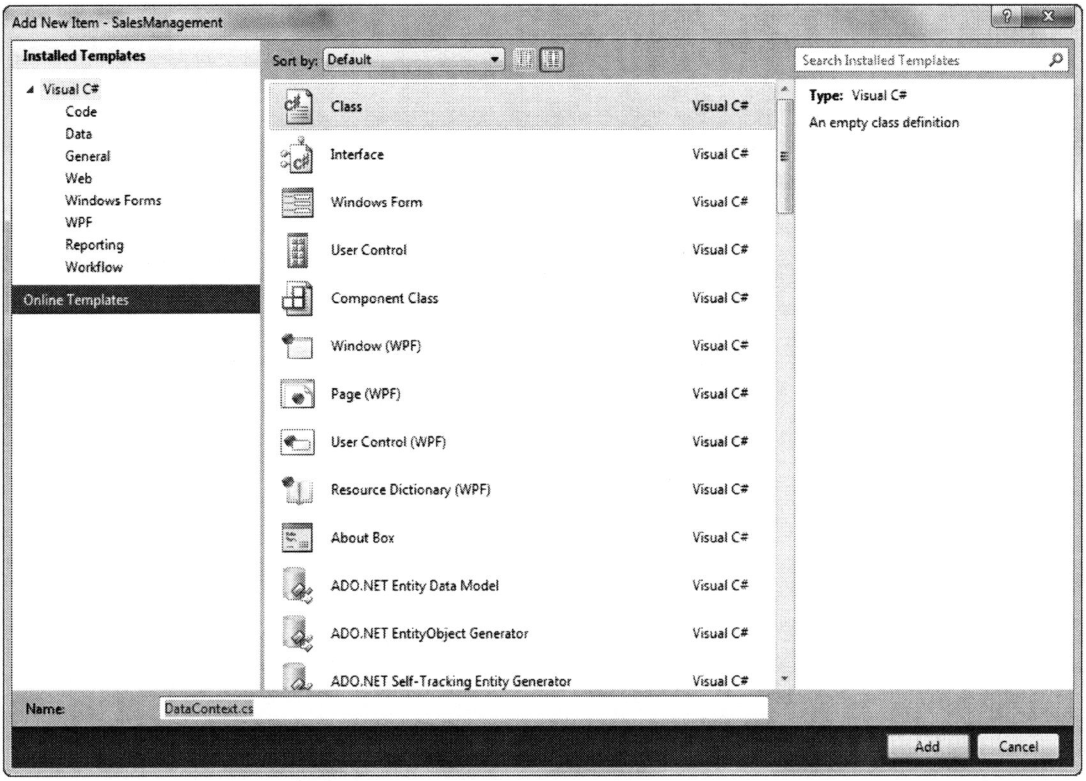

Figure 16-9. Adding the DataContext class to the project

2. Open DataAccess.cs and add the following namespaces:

```
using Microsoft.SharePoint;
using Microsoft.SharePoint.Client;
using MSDN.Samples.ClaimsAuth;
```

3. Define the full class using Listing 16-1.

Listing 16-1. DataContext Class

```
public class DataContext
    {
        private ClientContext _clientContext = ClaimClientContext.GetAuthenticatedContext
            ("https://apress365e.sharepoint.com/teams/dev/Tracking");

        /// <summary>
        /// Returns list of SalesAgents from Sharepoint
        /// </summary>
        /// <returns></returns>
```

```csharp
public List<SalesAgent> GetAgents()
{
    List<SalesAgent> agents = new List<SalesAgent>();

    try
    {
        foreach (ListItem listItem in GetListItems("Agent", ""))
        {
            SalesAgent newAgent = new SalesAgent()
            {
                displayName = listItem["AgentName"].ToString(),
                email = listItem["SipAddress"].ToString(),
                login = listItem["Login"].ToString(),
                lastMessage = (listItem["LastMessage"] ?? string.Empty).ToString()
            };

            agents.Add(newAgent);
        }
    }
    catch (Exception ex)
    {
        throw new Exception(ex.Message);
    }

    return agents;
}

/// <summary>
/// Returns Customer from Sharepoint based on Email
/// </summary>
/// <param name="email"></param>
/// <returns></returns>
public Customer GetCustomerByEmail(string email)
{
    string query = "<View><Query><Where><Contains><FieldRef Name='EmailAddress'/>" +
        "<Value Type='Text'>" + email + "</Value></Contains></Where></Query></View>";
    ListItemCollection listItems = GetListItems("Customer", query);

    //return first found
    if (listItems.Count > 0)
    {
        ListItem foundItem = listItems[0];
        Customer newCustomer = new Customer()
        {
            customerID = foundItem["ID"].ToString(),
            name = foundItem["CustomerName"].ToString(),
            email = foundItem["EmailAddress"].ToString(),
            status = foundItem["CustomerStatus"].ToString()
        };

        return newCustomer;
    }
```

```
            return null;
        }

        public Customer CreateNewCustomer(Customer newCustomer)
        {
            List list = _clientContext.Web.Lists.GetByTitle("Customer");

            ListItemCreationInformation itemCreateInfo = new ListItemCreationInformation();

            ListItem listItem = list.AddItem(itemCreateInfo);
            listItem["CustomerName"] = newCustomer.name;
            listItem["EmailAddress"] = newCustomer.email;
            listItem["CustomerStatus"] = newCustomer.status;

            listItem.Update();

            _clientContext.ExecuteQuery();

            newCustomer.customerID = listItem.Id.ToString();

            return newCustomer;
        }

        private ListItemCollection GetListItems(string listName, string query)
        {
            CamlQuery q = new CamlQuery();
            q.ViewXml = query; //no query needed

            ListItemCollection listItems =
_clientContext.Web.Lists.GetByTitle(listName).GetItems(q);
            _clientContext.Load(listItems);
            _clientContext.ExecuteQuery();

            return listItems;
        }

        public Contact CreateContact(Contact newContact)
        {
            List list = _clientContext.Web.Lists.GetByTitle("Contact");


            ListItemCreationInformation itemCreateInfo = new ListItemCreationInformation();
            ListItem listItem = list.AddItem(itemCreateInfo);
            listItem["Customer"] = new SPFieldLookupValue(newContact.customerID);
            listItem["ContactDate"] = newContact.contactDate;
            listItem["ContactType"] = newContact.contactType;
            listItem["ContactNotes"] = newContact.contactNotes;


            listItem.Update();
            _clientContext.Load(listItem);
```

```
        _clientContext.ExecuteQuery();

        newContact.contactID = listItem.Id.ToString();

        return newContact;
    }
}
```

The `DataContext` code begins with a private member of type `ClientContext`. This object opens a connection to the site at the stated URL. Enter the URL for the SharePoint Online site used in the previous chapter to host the Access database.

The class contains four public methods and one private one. The methods are as follows:

- `List<SalesAgent> GetAgents()`: Returns the agent records from the SharePoint database and uses the data to create a list of `SalesAgent` records. This list is returned.

- `Customer GetCustomerByEmail()`: Accepts `email` as a parameter, builds a CAML query, and retrieves customer records from SharePoint. These are used to create a list of Customer records, which is returned.

- `Customer CreateNewCustomer()`: Accepts `Customer` as a parameter and inserts the information into the SharePoint `Customer` list. The same `Customer` record is returned.

- `ListItemCollection GetListItems()`: Private helper method for returning items from SharePoint. Accepts the list name and a CAML query as a string. This is used by the other public methods to access the SharePoint data.

- `Contact CreateContact()`: Accepts `Contact` as a parameter and inserts the information into the SharePoint `Contacts` list.

This code uses local types for `Customer`, `Contact`, and `SalesAgent`. These are simple types with the properties needed for the application. Now you'll define these types. Add the code from Listing 16-2 to the `DataContext.cs` file but outside of the `DataContext` class definition.

Listing 16-2. Data Type Definitions

```
public class Customer
{
    public string customerID { get; set; }
    public string name { get; set; }
    public string email { get; set; }
    public string status { get; set; }
}

public class Contact
{
    public string contactID { get; set; }
    public string customerID { get; set; }
    public string contactDate { get; set; }
    public string contactType { get; set; }
```

```
        public string contactNotes { get; set; }
}

//Data Types
public class SalesAgent
{
    public string login { get; set; }
    public string lastMessage { get; set; }
    public string email { get; set; }
    public string phone { get; set; }
    public string onlineStatus { get; set; }
    public string Uri
    {
        get
        {
            return email;
        }
    }

    public string displayName
    {
        get;

        set;
    }
}
```

Building the User Interface

Listing 16-3 includes the XAML for the WPF application in its entirety. The application serves as the means to access the Office365 technologies. WPF is beyond the scope of this book, so the user interface is not deeply discussed.

Modify MainWindow.xaml to match the code from Listing 16-3.

Listing 16-3. WPF XAML for MainWindow.xaml

```
<Window x:Class="SalesManagement.MainWindow"
        xmlns="http://schemas.microsoft.com/winfx/2006/xaml/presentation"
        xmlns:x="http://schemas.microsoft.com/winfx/2006/xaml"
        xmlns:lyncuc="clr-namespace:Microsoft.Lync.Controls;assembly=Microsoft.Lync.Controls"
        Title="Apress Remodeling" Height="400" Width="700">
    <Window.Resources>
        <DataTemplate x:Key="MessageItem">
            <Grid>
                <Grid.ColumnDefinitions>
                    <ColumnDefinition Width="225" />
                    <ColumnDefinition Width="125"/>
                </Grid.ColumnDefinitions>
                <TextBlock Grid.Column="0" Width="220" Text="{Binding Path=Subject}" />
```

```xml
                        <TextBlock Grid.Column="1" Width="120" Text="{Binding Path=DateTimeReceived}"
    />
                </Grid>
        </DataTemplate>
        <DataTemplate x:Key="AgentItem">
            <Grid VerticalAlignment="Center">
                <Grid.ColumnDefinitions>
                    <ColumnDefinition Width="25" />
                    <ColumnDefinition Width="100"/>
                </Grid.ColumnDefinitions>
                <lyncuc:PresenceIndicator Grid.Column="0" Source="{Binding Path=Uri}"
    Width="20" />
                <TextBlock Grid.Column="1" Width="100" Text="{Binding Path=displayName}" />
            </Grid>
        </DataTemplate>

    </Window.Resources>
    <Grid>
        <Grid.ColumnDefinitions>
            <ColumnDefinition Width="250" />
            <ColumnDefinition Width="200" />
            <ColumnDefinition Width="250" />
        </Grid.ColumnDefinitions>
        <Grid.RowDefinitions>
            <RowDefinition Height="100" />
            <RowDefinition Height="175" />
            <RowDefinition Height="125" />
        </Grid.RowDefinitions>
        <TextBlock Grid.Column="0" Grid.Row="0" Grid.ColumnSpan="3" FontSize="36"
                FontStyle="Italic" FontWeight="Bold">Sales Leads Monitor</TextBlock>
        <TextBlock Grid.Column="0" Grid.Row="0" Grid.ColumnSpan="2" FontSize="18"
                FontStyle="Italic" Margin="0,45,0,0">Welcome: Michael Mayberry</TextBlock>
        <StackPanel Grid.Column="2" Grid.Row="0">
            <Button x:Name="btnCurrentItems" Content="Process Current Items"
    Margin="30,10,30,10"
                    Click="btnCurrentItems_Click" />
            <Button x:Name="btnNewItems" Content="Listen for New Items" Margin="30,10,30,10"
                    Click="btnNewItems_Click" />
        </StackPanel>
        <StackPanel Grid.Row="1" Grid.Column="0" Grid.ColumnSpan="2">
            <TextBlock Text="Agents" FontSize="14" FontWeight="Bold"/>
            <!--<lyncuc:ContactList Width="225" />-->
            <ListBox x:Name="lstAgents" Margin="0,5,0,0" BorderThickness="0" Height="150"
                    ItemTemplate="{StaticResource AgentItem}">
            </ListBox>
        </StackPanel>
        <StackPanel Grid.Row="1" Grid.Column="2">
            <TextBlock Text="Leads" FontSize="14" FontWeight="Bold" />
            <Grid Height="150" Margin="0,5,0,0">
                <Grid.ColumnDefinitions>
                    <ColumnDefinition Width="150" />
                    <ColumnDefinition />
```

```
                    </Grid.ColumnDefinitions>
                    <Grid.RowDefinitions>
                        <RowDefinition Height="50" />
                        <RowDefinition Height="50" />
                        <RowDefinition />
                    </Grid.RowDefinitions>
                    <TextBlock Grid.Row="0" Grid.Column="0" Text="Available Agents:" />
                    <TextBlock Grid.Row="0" Grid.Column="1" x:Name="txtAvailableAgents" Text="" />
                    <TextBlock Grid.Row="1" Grid.Column="0" Text="Leads Collected:" />
                    <TextBlock Grid.Row="1" Grid.Column="1" x:Name="txtLeadsCollected" Text="" />
                    <TextBlock Grid.Row="2" Grid.Column="0" Text="Leads Assigned:" />
                    <TextBlock Grid.Row="2" Grid.Column="1" x:Name="txtLeadsAssigned" Text="" />
                </Grid>
            </StackPanel>
        </Grid>
    </Window>
```

The user interface is quite simple, so the XAML is fairly straightforward. There are few things to point out. First, there are a couple of Lync controls used, so the namespace indicated by the following line is included.

```
xmlns:lyncuc="clr-namespace:Microsoft.Lync.Controls;assembly=Microsoft.Lync.Controls"
```

Second, a DataTemplate simply defines how the list box items will display. This allows each item to consist of more than one control. Once MainWindow.xaml is updated, the designer window in Visual Studio should appear similar to Figure 16-10.

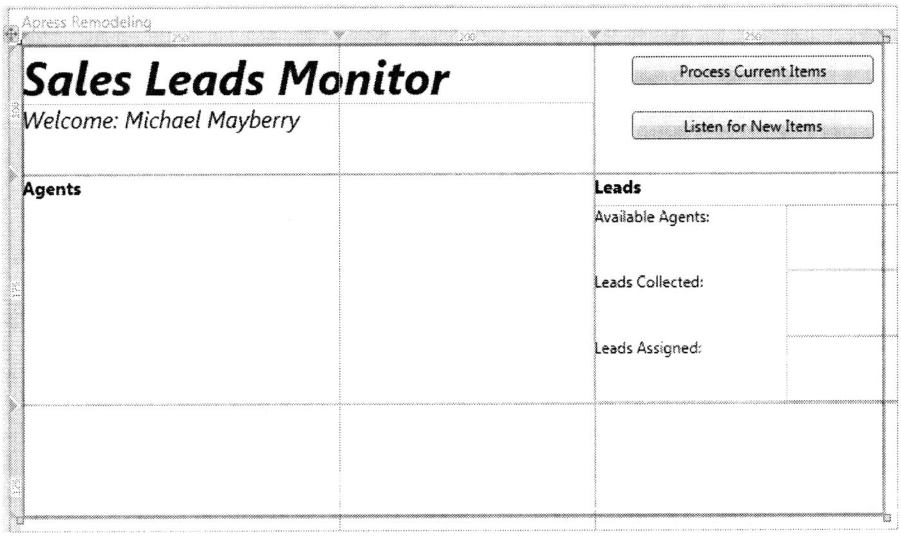

Figure 16-10. MainWindow.xaml

The user interface lists the current agents from the SharePoint Online database along with their Lync online status. Their status is displayed using a Lync PresenceIndicator control. The user interface includes areas that list the number of agents, how many leads have been collected since the application started, and how many of those leads have been assigned to agents. This provides a little bit of feedback to the user about what the application is doing. The two buttons provide the control for the application. The button Process Current Items will process any items currently in the Exchange inbox. The button Listen for New Items starts a notification subscription to respond to any new items that come in. This subscription is set to last for five minutes.

Building the Application Code

Now you will add the code to make this application function. You will only modify MainWindow.xaml.cs.

1. Add these namespaces to reference the proper assemblies:

```
using Microsoft.Exchange.WebServices.Data;
using Microsoft.Exchange.WebServices.Autodiscover;
using Microsoft.Lync.Model;
using Microsoft.Lync.Controls;
using Microsoft.Lync.Model.Extensibility;
using Microsoft.Lync.Model.Conversation;
```

2. Define the variables needed for the application:

```
private DataContext _context = new DataContext();
private ExchangeService _service = GetBinding();
private ConversationWindow _conversationWindow;

private List<SalesAgent> _agents;
private int _leadCount = 0;
private int _collectCount = 0;
```

3. Add a method to handle the Loaded event. This method uses the DataContext class to call the GetAgents() method. This returns the list of SalesAgent objects from the SharePoint site. It then calls the BindAgents() method to display the agents on the screen. The GetBinding() method is called to retrieve the ExchangeService object. The application then uses the service object to get the count of items in the inbox of the Exchange Online account. Finally, a couple of methods are called to display count information on the screen.

```
void MainWindow_Loaded(object sender, RoutedEventArgs e)
{
    //load agents
    _agents = _context.GetAgents();

    //bind agents to List Box with presence
    BindAgents();

    //Connect to Exchange and check for items in Inbox
    _service = GetBinding();
```

```
    _collectCount = _service.FindItems(WellKnownFolderName.Inbox, new
ItemView(10)).TotalCount;

    UpdateCollectCount();
    UpdateLeadCount();
}
```

4. Modify the MainWindow() method to set the Loaded event handler. Add the following line to existing method:

```
this.Loaded += MainWindow_Loaded;
```

5. Define the BindAgents() method called by MainWindow_Loaded(). This method binds the full agent list to the list box. That list box uses a PresenceIndicator control, which will display the current Lync status of each agent. This method also presents the count of the agents that are currently available according to their status in the SharePoint Online database.

```
protected void BindAgents()
{
    lstAgents.ItemsSource = _agents;
    txtAvailableAgents.Text = (from a in _agents
        where a.onlineStatus == "Available"
        select a).Count().ToString();
}
```

6. Define the GetBinding() method called in MainWindow_Loaded():

```
static ExchangeService GetBinding()
{
    // Create the binding.
    ExchangeService service = new ExchangeService(ExchangeVersion.Exchange2010_SP1);

    // Define credentials.
    service.Credentials = new WebCredentials("websales@apress365.com", "@press365");

    // Use the AutodiscoverUrl method to locate the service endpoint.
    try
    {
        service.AutodiscoverUrl("websales@apress365.com", RedirectionUrlValidationCallback);
    }
    catch (AutodiscoverRemoteException ex)
    {
        MessageBox.Show("Autodiscover error: " + ex.Message);
    }
    catch (Exception ex)
    {
        MessageBox.Show("Error: " + ex.Message);
    }

    return service;
```

```
}
```

This method uses the `AutodiscoverUrl()` method to access the Exchange Online account. This service method will determine the proper URL for the server currently hosting the mailbox for the account requested. The method returns the `ExchangeService` object for use by the application.

▨ **Note** This method uses the e-mail address `websales@apress365.com`. Enter the email address you will use for testing this application. This is the account you will need to send test messages to when you are ready to test the application.

---

7. Define the `RedirectionUrlValidationCallback()` method needed for the `AutodiscoverUrl()` method.

```
static bool RedirectionUrlValidationCallback(String redirectionUrl)
{
    // Perform validation.
    // Validation is developer dependent to ensure a safe redirect.
    return true;
}
```

8. Define the `UpdateCollectCount()` and `UpdateLeadCount()` methods needed in `MainWindow_Loaded()`. These are used to update the user interface with counts.

```
protected void UpdateCollectCount()
{
    txtLeadsCollected.Text = _collectCount.ToString();
}

protected void UpdateLeadCount()
{
    txtLeadsAssigned.Text = _leadCount.ToString();
}
```

9. Define the button click events. These simply call other methods, which will be defined next.

```
private void btnCurrentItems_Click(object sender, RoutedEventArgs e)
{
    ProcessMailItems();
}

private void btnNewItems_Click(object sender, RoutedEventArgs e)
{
    SetStreamingNotifications();
}
```

10. Define the `ProcessMailItems()` method for the `btnCurrentItems` button. This method finds the items in the inbox of the Exchange Online account. It then iterates through each item to perform the following tasks:

- Use the `DataContext.GetCustomerByEmail()` method to see if the current item came from an e-mail that is already in the database.

- If a customer is not returned, then a new object is defined and passed to SharePoint through the `DataContext.CreateNewCustomer()` method.

- The item is used to create a new `Contact` object. It is passed to SharePoint through the `DataContext.CreateContact()` method.

- An available agent is selected from the list according to the `onlineStatus` property. If one is found, then the `BeginConversation()` method is called to start the Lync conversation and pass the agent and contact information.

- Once all of the items have been processed, they are then moved to the Archive folder in the Exchange Online mailbox. This will keep them from being processed again in the future.

```
protected void ProcessMailItems()
    {
        //Get mailbox items
        ItemView itemView = new ItemView(10);
        itemView.PropertySet = PropertySet.IdOnly;

        FindItemsResults<Item> mailItems =
            _service.FindItems(WellKnownFolderName.Inbox, itemView);
        PropertySet emailProperties = new PropertySet(
                                        EmailMessageSchema.Sender,
                                        EmailMessageSchema.DateTimeReceived,
                                        EmailMessageSchema.Body,
                                        EmailMessageSchema.Subject);
        emailProperties.RequestedBodyType = BodyType.Text;
        if (mailItems.TotalCount > 0)
            _service.LoadPropertiesForItems(mailItems.Items, emailProperties);

        List<ItemId> emailItemIDs = new List<ItemId>();

        //process each mailbox item
        foreach (Item mailItem in mailItems)
        {
            if (mailItem is EmailMessage)
            {
                //find or create customer in sharepoint database
                EmailMessage email = (EmailMessage)mailItem;
                Customer customer = _context.GetCustomerByEmail(email.Sender.Address);
                if (customer == null)
                {
                    Customer newCustomer = new Customer()
                    {
                        name = email.Sender.Name,
```

561

```
                    email = email.Sender.Address,
                    status = "Prospect"
                };

                customer = _context.CreateNewCustomer(newCustomer);
            }

            //create contact record from e-mail
            Contact newContact = new Contact()
            {
                customerID = customer.customerID,
                contactDate = email.DateTimeReceived.ToShortDateString(),
                contactType = "Email",
                contactNotes = "Subject: " + email.Subject + "\n\n" + email.Body.Text
            };

            Contact savedContact = _context.CreatContact(newContact);

            //assign agent
            SalesAgent assignedAgent = (from A in _agents
                                        where A.onlineStatus == "Available"
                                        orderby A.lastMessage descending
                                        select A).FirstOrDefault();

            if (assignedAgent != null)
            {
                //start lync conversation with contactid
                BeginConversation(assignedAgent, savedContact);

                //update lead count
                _leadCount++;

                //display updated lead count
                Dispatcher.BeginInvoke(new Action(UpdateLeadCount));
            }

            //add item to list of items to get moved to Archive folder
            emailItemIDs.Add(email.Id);
        }
    }

    if (emailItemIDs.Count > 0)
    {
        //move e-mails to archive folder
        //create search filter to find specific folder
        SearchFilter filter = new SearchFilter.IsEqualTo
            (FolderSchema.DisplayName, "Archive");

        //use Exchange Web Service to search for folder
        Folder folder = _service.FindFolders
            (WellKnownFolderName.Inbox, filter, new FolderView(1)).Folders[0];
```

```
            //move e-mail items to found folder
            _service.MoveItems(emailItemIDs, folder.Id);
        }
    }
```

11. Define the `BeginConversation()` method called by the `ProcessMailItems()` method.

```
protected void BeginConversation(SalesAgent agent, Contact contact)
{
    // Conversation participant list.
    List<string> participantList = new List<string>();
    participantList.Add(agent.Uri);

    Dictionary<AutomationModalitySettings, object> conversationContextData =
        new Dictionary<AutomationModalitySettings, object>();

    // initial IM message
    conversationContextData.Add(AutomationModalitySettings.FirstInstantMessage,
        "Apress Remodeling Application Context");

    // send initial IM immediately
    conversationContextData.Add
        (AutomationModalitySettings.SendFirstInstantMessageImmediately, true);

    // set application ID
    conversationContextData.Add(AutomationModalitySettings.ApplicationId,
        "{A07EE104-A0C2-4E84-ABB3-BBC370A37636}");

    string appData = "ContactID=" + contact.contactID + "|CustomerID=" + contact.customerID;

    // set application data
    conversationContextData.Add(AutomationModalitySettings.ApplicationData, appData);

    Automation auto = LyncClient.GetAutomation();

    // start the conversation.
    IAsyncResult beginconversation = auto.BeginStartConversation(
    AutomationModalities.InstantMessage
    , participantList
    , conversationContextData
    , null
    , null);
}
```

This method defines the conversation contextual information and uses Lync automation to start a new conversation with the selected sales agent. This conversation window includes the call to a web page that hosts a Silverlight application for interacting with the contact information. This application is explained later in this chapter.

12. Define the BeginConversationCallBack() method to handle the response from Lync automation once the conversation has begun:

```
private void BeginConversationCallBack(IAsyncResult ar)
{
    Automation _automation = ar.AsyncState as Automation;
    _conversationWindow = _automation.EndStartConversation(ar);
}
```

13. Define the SetStreamingNotifications() method called by the btnNewItems button:

```
protected void SetStreamingNotifications()
{
    // Subscribe to streaming notifications on the Inbox folder, and listen
    // for "NewMail", "Created", and "Deleted" events.
    StreamingSubscription streamingsubscription = _service.SubscribeToStreamingNotifications(
        new FolderId[] { WellKnownFolderName.Inbox },
        EventType.NewMail);

    StreamingSubscriptionConnection connection=new
StreamingSubscriptionConnection(_service,5);

    connection.AddSubscription(streamingsubscription);
    // Delegate event handlers.
    connection.OnNotificationEvent += OnNewItemEvent;

    connection.Open();
}
```

This method defines a new streaming subscription to listen for new items sent to the inbox of the Exchange Online account. The subscription will remain open for 5 minutes. The subscription will receive a notification when a new item arrives. This method then calls the OnNewItemEvent() to handle the notification.

14. Define the OnNewItemEvent() method:

```
protected void OnNewItemEvent(object sender, NotificationEventArgs args)
{
    StreamingSubscription subscription = args.Subscription;

    // Loop through all item-related events.
    foreach (NotificationEvent notification in args.Events)
    {
        object[] emptyArgs = new object[0];

        switch (notification.EventType)
        {
            case EventType.NewMail:
                _collectCount++;
                Dispatcher.BeginInvoke(new Action(UpdateCollectCount));
                ProcessMailItems();
```

```
                break;
        }
    }
}
```

This method responds to new item notifications. If the event is NewMail, then the UpdateCollectCount() method is called to update the screen count of collected leads. The application then calls ProcessMailItems(), previously defined in this chapter.

This completes the application code for the WPF application. The code in MainWindow.xaml.cs is included fully in Listing 16-4.

Listing 16-4. MainWindow.xaml.cs

```csharp
using System;
using System.Collections.Generic;
using System.Windows;
using System.Windows.Documents;
using System.Linq;

using Microsoft.Exchange.WebServices.Data;
using Microsoft.Exchange.WebServices.Autodiscover;
using Microsoft.Lync.Model;
using Microsoft.Lync.Controls;
using Microsoft.Lync.Model.Extensibility;
using Microsoft.Lync.Model.Conversation;

namespace SalesManagement
{
    /// <summary>
    /// Interaction logic for MainWindow.xaml
    /// </summary>
    public partial class MainWindow : Window
    {
        private DataContext _context = new DataContext();
        private ExchangeService _service = GetBinding();
        private ConversationWindow _conversationWindow;

        private List<SalesAgent> _agents;
        private int _leadCount = 0;
        private int _collectCount = 0;

        public MainWindow()
        {
            InitializeComponent();

            this.Loaded += MainWindow_Loaded;
        }

        void MainWindow_Loaded(object sender, RoutedEventArgs e)
        {
            //load agents
```

```
            _agents = _context.GetAgents();

            //bind agents to List Box with presence
            BindAgents();

            //Connect to Exchange and check for items in Inbox
            _service = GetBinding();

            _collectCount = _service.FindItems
                (WellKnownFolderName.Inbox, new ItemView(10)).TotalCount;

            UpdateCollectCount();
            UpdateLeadCount();
        }

        protected void BindAgents()
        {
            lstAgents.ItemsSource = _agents;
            txtAvailableAgents.Text =
                (from a in _agents where a.onlineStatus == "Available" select
    a).Count().ToString();
        }

        static ExchangeService GetBinding()
        {
            // Create the binding.
            ExchangeService service = new ExchangeService(ExchangeVersion.Exchange2010_SP1);

            // Define credentials.
            service.Credentials = new WebCredentials("websales@apress365.com", "@press365");

            // Use the AutodiscoverUrl method to locate the service endpoint.
            try
            {
                //service.Url = new Uri("https://ch1prd0402.outlook.com/EWS/Exchange.asmx");
                service.AutodiscoverUrl("websales@apress365.com",
    RedirectionUrlValidationCallback);
            }
            catch (AutodiscoverRemoteException ex)
            {
                MessageBox.Show("Autodiscover error: " + ex.Message);
            }
            catch (Exception ex)
            {
                MessageBox.Show("Error: " + ex.Message);
            }

            return service;
        }

        static bool RedirectionUrlValidationCallback(String redirectionUrl)
        {
```

```csharp
        // Perform validation.
        // Validation is developer dependent to ensure a safe redirect.
        return true;
    }

    protected void UpdateCollectCount()
    {
        txtLeadsCollected.Text = _collectCount.ToString();
    }

    protected void UpdateLeadCount()
    {
        txtLeadsAssigned.Text = _leadCount.ToString();
    }

    private void btnCurrentItems_Click(object sender, RoutedEventArgs e)
    {
        ProcessMailItems();
    }

    private void btnNewItems_Click(object sender, RoutedEventArgs e)
    {
        SetStreamingNotifications();
    }

    protected void ProcessMailItems()
    {
        //Get mailbox items
        ItemView itemView = new ItemView(10);
        itemView.PropertySet = PropertySet.IdOnly;

        FindItemsResults<Item> mailItems = _service.FindItems(WellKnownFolderName.Inbox,
itemView);
        PropertySet emailProperties = new PropertySet(
                                        EmailMessageSchema.Sender,
                                        EmailMessageSchema.DateTimeReceived,
                                        EmailMessageSchema.Body,
                                        EmailMessageSchema.Subject);
        emailProperties.RequestedBodyType = BodyType.Text;
        if (mailItems.TotalCount > 0)
            _service.LoadPropertiesForItems(mailItems.Items, emailProperties);

        List<ItemId> emailItemIDs = new List<ItemId>();

        //process each mailbox item
        foreach (Item mailItem in mailItems)
        {
            if (mailItem is EmailMessage)
            {
                //find or create customer in sharepoint database
                EmailMessage email = (EmailMessage)mailItem;
                Customer customer = _context.GetCustomerByEmail(email.Sender.Address);
```

```
if (customer == null)
{
    Customer newCustomer = new Customer()
    {
        name = email.Sender.Name,
        email = email.Sender.Address,
        status = "Prospect"
    };

    customer = _context.CreateNewCustomer(newCustomer);
}

//create contact record from e-mail
Contact newContact = new Contact()
{
    customerID = customer.customerID,
    contactDate = email.DateTimeReceived.ToShortDateString(),
    contactType = "Email",
    contactNotes = "Subject: " + email.Subject + "\n\n" + email.Body.Text
};

Contact savedContact = _context.CreatContact(newContact);

//assign agent
SalesAgent assignedAgent = (from A in _agents
                            where A.onlineStatus == "Available"
                            orderby A.lastMessage descending
                            select A).FirstOrDefault();

if (assignedAgent != null)
{
    //start lync conversation with contactid
    BeginConversation(assignedAgent, savedContact);

    //update lead count
    _leadCount++;

    //display updated lead count
    Dispatcher.BeginInvoke(new Action(UpdateLeadCount));
}

//add item to list of items to get moved to Archive folder
emailItemIDs.Add(email.Id);
    }
}

if (emailItemIDs.Count > 0)
{
    //move emails to archive folder
    //create search filter to find specific folder
    SearchFilter filter = new SearchFilter.IsEqualTo(FolderSchema.DisplayName,
"Archive");
```

```
            //use Exchange Web Service to search for folder
            Folder folder = _service.FindFolders
                (WellKnownFolderName.Inbox, filter, new FolderView(1)).Folders[0];

            //move e-mail items to found folder
            _service.MoveItems(emailItemIDs, folder.Id);
        }
    }

    protected void BeginConversation(SalesAgent agent, Contact contact)
    {
        // Conversation participant list.
        List<string> participantList = new List<string>();
        participantList.Add(agent.Uri);

        Dictionary<AutomationModalitySettings, object> conversationContextData =
            new Dictionary<AutomationModalitySettings, object>();

        // initial IM message
        conversationContextData.Add(AutomationModalitySettings.FirstInstantMessage,
            "Apress Remodeling Application Context");

        // send initial IM immediately
        conversationContextData.Add
            (AutomationModalitySettings.SendFirstInstantMessageImmediately, true);

        // set application ID
        conversationContextData.Add(AutomationModalitySettings.ApplicationId,
            "{A07EE104-A0C2-4E84-ABB3-BBC370A37636}");

        string appData = "ContactID=" + contact.contactID + "|CustomerID=" +
contact.customerID;

        // set application data
        conversationContextData.Add(AutomationModalitySettings.ApplicationData, appData);

        Automation auto = LyncClient.GetAutomation();

        // start the conversation.
        IAsyncResult beginconversation = auto.BeginStartConversation(
        AutomationModalities.InstantMessage
        , participantList
        , conversationContextData
        , null
        , null);
    }


    // notify the automation object and conversationWindow
    // that the conversation started.
    private void BeginConversationCallBack(IAsyncResult ar)
```

```
    {
        Automation _automation = ar.AsyncState as Automation;
        _conversationWindow = _automation.EndStartConversation(ar);
    }

    protected void SetStreamingNotifications()
    {
        // Subscribe to streaming notifications on the Inbox folder, and listen
        // for "NewMail", "Created", and "Deleted" events.
        StreamingSubscription streamingsubscription =
            _service.SubscribeToStreamingNotifications(
                new FolderId[] { WellKnownFolderName.Inbox },
                EventType.NewMail);

        StreamingSubscriptionConnection connection =
            new StreamingSubscriptionConnection(_service, 5);

        connection.AddSubscription(streamingsubscription);
        // Delegate event handlers.
        connection.OnNotificationEvent += OnNewItemEvent;

        connection.Open();
    }

    protected void OnNewItemEvent(object sender, NotificationEventArgs args)
    {
        StreamingSubscription subscription = args.Subscription;

        // Loop through all item-related events.
        foreach (NotificationEvent notification in args.Events)
        {
            object[] emptyArgs = new object[0];

            switch (notification.EventType)
            {
                case EventType.NewMail:
                    _collectCount++;
                    Dispatcher.BeginInvoke(new Action(UpdateCollectCount));
                    ProcessMailItems();
                    break;
            }
        }
    }
    }
}
}
```

Building the Silverlight Application

For the sales agent to respond to the assigned lead, this application includes a Silverlight application to display the contact information. The sales agent can also provide a follow-up action and update the SharePoint data directly from the Lync window. To conform to the prerequisite of not using additional web servers outside of Office365, this Silverlight application is written as a web part and will be hosted on a SharePoint Online page.

1. Right-click the solution and click Add New Project. Select the Silverlight Application template and choose the proper location. Name the project AgentResponse. Click OK when your screen is similar to Figure 16-11.

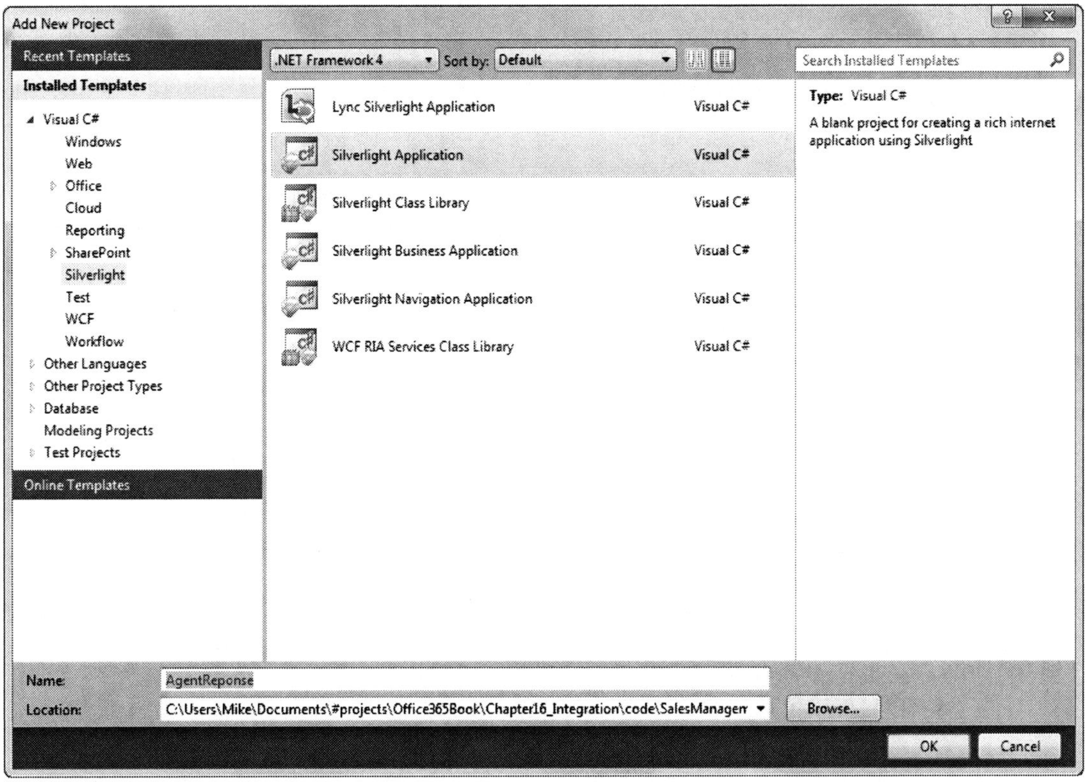

Figure 16-11. New Silverlight application project

2. Visual Studio will prompt you with a dialog box to set the options of how the Silverlight application should be hosted. This application will not actually use a locally defined host. You can keep the default, pictured in Figure 16-12, and click OK. This will create a web application that will not be used.

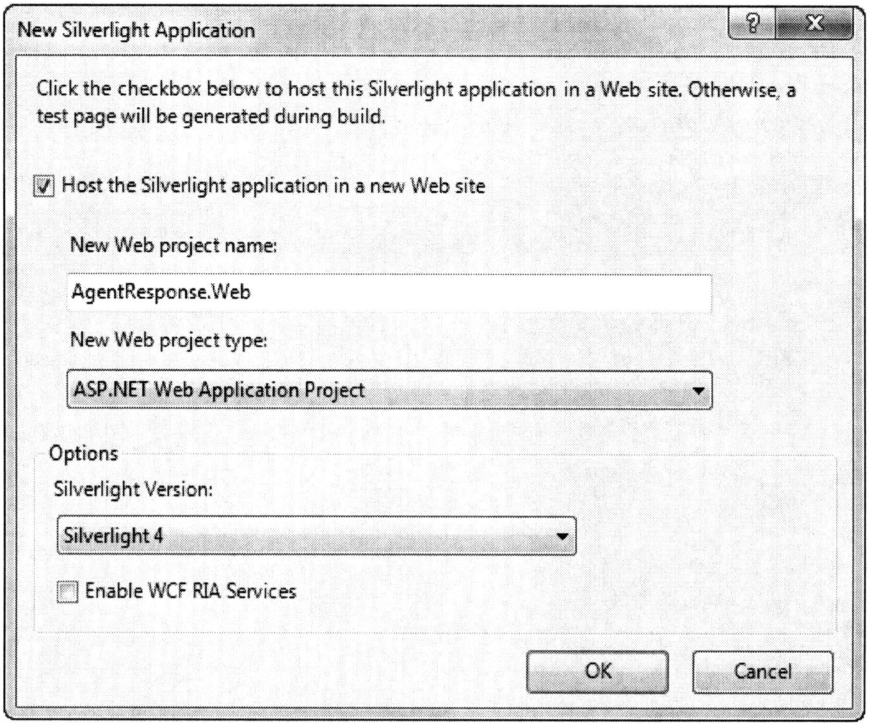

New Silverlight Application

Click the checkbox below to host this Silverlight application in a Web site. Otherwise, a test page will be generated during build.

☑ Host the Silverlight application in a new Web site

New Web project name:

AgentResponse.Web

New Web project type:

ASP.NET Web Application Project ▾

Options

Silverlight Version:

Silverlight 4 ▾

☐ Enable WCF RIA Services

OK   Cancel

Figure 16-12. Silverlight Application hosting options

3. Add the necessary references. Right-click References in Solution Explorer for the AgentResponse project and click Add Reference. Browse to the location where the SharePoint Foundation classes are located and select the items shown in Figure 16-13.

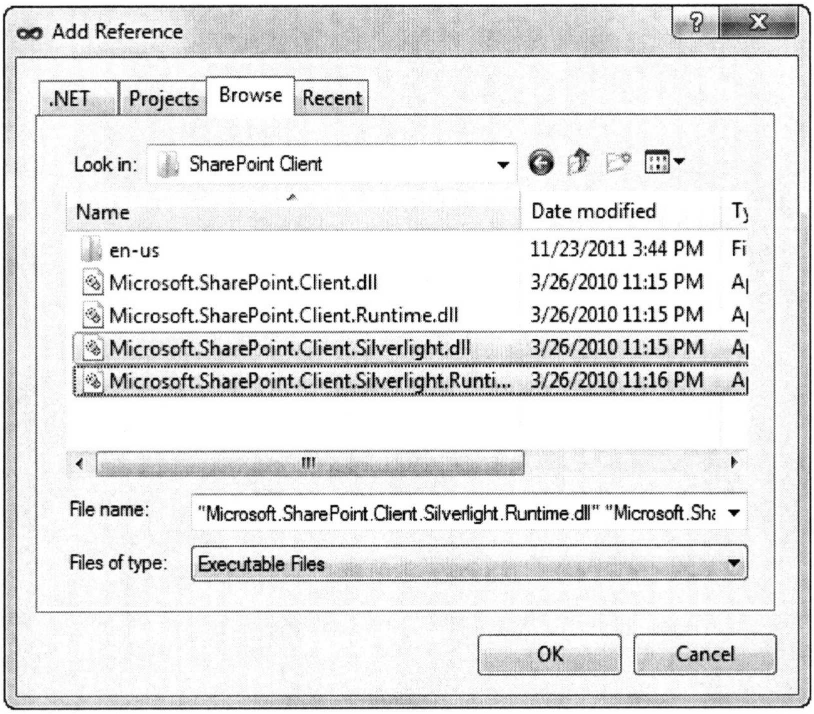

Figure 16-13. References for Silverlight application to access SharePoint

4. Define the user interface in `MainPage.xaml`. Replace the existing XAML markup with the code from Listing 16-5.

Listing 16-5. MainPage.xaml

```
<UserControl x:Class="AgentResponse.MainPage"
    xmlns="http://schemas.microsoft.com/winfx/2006/xaml/presentation"
    xmlns:x="http://schemas.microsoft.com/winfx/2006/xaml"
    xmlns:d="http://schemas.microsoft.com/expression/blend/2008"
    xmlns:mc="http://schemas.openxmlformats.org/markup-compatibility/2006"
    mc:Ignorable="d"
    d:DesignHeight="300" d:DesignWidth="600">

    <Grid x:Name="LayoutRoot" Background="White" VerticalAlignment="Stretch"
        HorizontalAlignment="Stretch">
        <Grid.RowDefinitions>
            <RowDefinition Height="100" />
            <RowDefinition Height="200" />
        </Grid.RowDefinitions>
        <Grid.ColumnDefinitions>
            <ColumnDefinition Width="400" />
            <ColumnDefinition Width="200" />
```

```xml
                    </Grid.ColumnDefinitions>
                    <StackPanel Grid.Row="0" Grid.Column="0" Margin="5,0,0,0">
                        <TextBlock Text="Customer Information" Grid.Row="0" Grid.Column="0"
                                    Grid.ColumnSpan="2" FontWeight="Bold" />
                        <Grid Margin="0,5,0,0">
                            <Grid.ColumnDefinitions>
                                <ColumnDefinition Width="75"/>
                                <ColumnDefinition />
                            </Grid.ColumnDefinitions>
                            <Grid.RowDefinitions>
                                <RowDefinition />
                                <RowDefinition />
                                <RowDefinition />
                            </Grid.RowDefinitions>
                            <TextBlock Grid.Row="0" Grid.Column="0" Text="Name:" />
                            <TextBlock x:Name="txtCustomerName" Grid.Row="0" Grid.Column="1" />

                            <TextBlock Grid.Row="2" Grid.Column="0" Text="Email:" />
                            <TextBlock x:Name="txtCustomerEmail" Grid.Row="2" Grid.Column="1" />
                        </Grid>
                    </StackPanel>
                    <Button Grid.Row="0" Grid.Column="1" MaxHeight="30" Content="Load Contact --"
                        Click="Button_Click" Visibility="Collapsed" />
                    <StackPanel Grid.Row="1" Grid.Column="0" Margin="5,0,0,0">
                        <TextBlock Text="Contact" FontWeight="Bold" />
                        <TextBlock x:Name="txtContactNotes" TextWrapping="Wrap">

                        </TextBlock>
                    </StackPanel>

                    <StackPanel Grid.Row="1" Grid.Column="1">
                        <TextBlock Text="Follow Up" FontWeight="Bold" />
                        <ComboBox x:Name="cboFollowUp" Margin="0,5,0,0">

                        </ComboBox>
                        <Button x:Name="btnComplete" Content="Update Contact" Margin="0,30,0,0"
                                Click="btnComplete_Click" />
                        <TextBlock x:Name="txtAppData" TextWrapping="Wrap" Visibility="Visible"
Height="40" />
                    </StackPanel>
                </Grid>
            </UserControl>
```

When MainPage.xaml has been updated, it should appear similar to Figure 16-14 in the designer window.

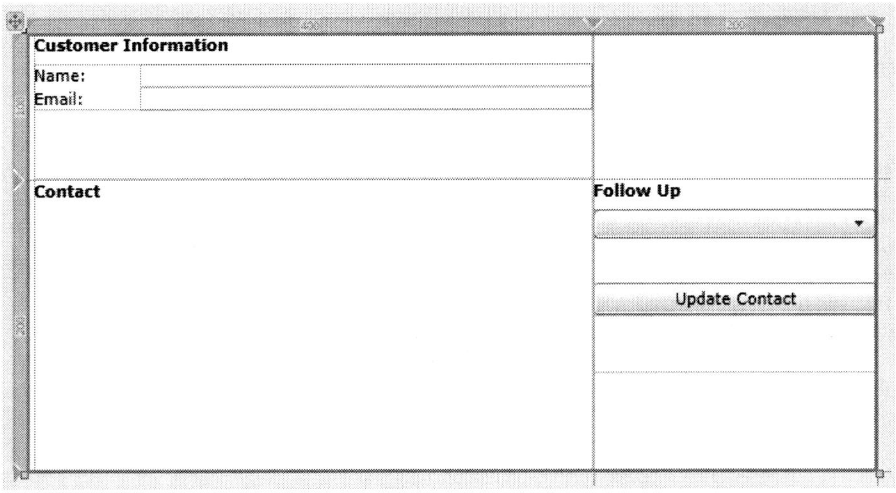

Figure 16-14. MainPage.xaml in the Visual Studio designer window

5. Define the application code. All of the code will exist in `MainPage.xaml.cs`. Start with the `using` statements:

```
using Microsoft.Lync.Model.Conversation;
using Microsoft.Lync.Model;
using Microsoft.Lync.Model.Extensibility;
using Microsoft.SharePoint.Client;
```

6. Add the following application variables to the beginning of the `MainPage` class:

```
Conversation _conversation = LyncClient.GetHostingConversation() as Conversation;
string _appID = "{A07EE104-A0C2-4E84-ABB3-BBC370A37636}";

private Web _web;
private List _list;
private ClientContext _context;

private List _customerList;
private ListItemCollection _customerItems;

private ListItem _contact;
```

7. Modify the `Initialize()` method with the following statements and replace the URL with your Office 365 SharePoint site:

```
_context = new ClientContext("https://apress365e.sharepoint.com/teams/dev/tracking");
// _context = ClientContext.Current;
cboFollowUp.Items.Add("None");
cboFollowUp.Items.Add("Callback");
cboFollowUp.Items.Add("Schedule Visit");
```

```
cboFollowUp.Items.Add("Estimate Job");

//display contact/customer information
LoadContact();
```

8. Define the LoadContact() method called in Initialize(). This method begins
    by accessing the contact list. It then checks for an active conversation, since
    this is written to be hosted within a Lync contextual conversation. If the
    conversation is found, the application data is retrieved and parsed to find the
    contact ID and the customer ID. SharePoint is then queried to get the contact
    data by ID. Since this is Silverlight, the call to the SharePoint service must be
    an asynchronous one. The success and failure methods are indicated for that
    call. Then the method GetCustomerInformation() is called to perform similar
    tasks to get the customer information.

```
private void LoadContact()
{
    try
    {
        //ClientContext context = ClientContext.Current;
        _web = _context.Web;
        _list = _web.Lists.GetByTitle("Contact");

        string appData;
        string customerID = "";
        string contactID = "";

        if (_conversation != null)
        {
            appData = _conversation.GetApplicationData(_appID);
            string[] data = appData.Split('|');
            contactID = data[0].Replace("ContactID=", "");
            customerID = data[1].Replace("CustomerID=", "");

            txtAppData.Text = "contactID = " + contactID + Environment.NewLine;
            txtAppData.Text += "customerID = " + customerID + Environment.NewLine;
        }
        else
        {
            txtAppData.Text = "appData not populated!";
        }

        _contact = _list.GetItemById(contactID);
        _context.Load(_contact);

        //execute request async
        _context.ExecuteQueryAsync(GetItemsSucceeded, GetItemsFailed);

        this.GetCustomerInformation(customerID);
    }
    catch (Exception ex)
```

```
    {
        txtAppData.Text = ex.Message;
    }
}
```

9. Define the GetItemsSucceeded() and GetItemsFailed() methods called as event handlers in LoadContact(). The success method calls the BindList() method to display the results on the screen. This is done through the Dispatcher to access the UI thread. The event handler is not running on that thread and cannot access user controls. The failure method displays the error in a text box on the screen.

```
private void GetItemsSucceeded(object sender, ClientRequestSucceededEventArgs e)
{
    try
    {
        Dispatcher.BeginInvoke(new Action(BindList));
    }
    catch (Exception ex)
    {
        Dispatcher.BeginInvoke(() => txtAppData.Text += ex.Message);
    }
}

private void GetItemsFailed(object sender, ClientRequestFailedEventArgs e)
{
    //log error
    Dispatcher.BeginInvoke(() => txtAppData.Text += "contact failure");
        // + Environment.NewLine + e.Message + Environment.NewLine + e.StackTrace);
}
```

10. Define the BindList(), which is called by GetItemsSucceeded(). This simply displays the ContactNotes field to the Contact Notes text box on the screen.

```
private void BindList()
{
    txtContactNotes.Text = _contact["ContactNotes"].ToString();
}
```

11. Define the GetCustomerInformation() method called in LoadContact(). This method performs similar tasks to LoadContact(). It accesses the SharePoint Customer list and queries that list by ID. This time, a CAML query is used simply to show a different way to accomplish the same thing. The query is again called asynchronously, indicating the methods to handle success and failure.

```
private void GetCustomerInformation(string customerID)
{
    _web = _context.Web;
    _customerList = _web.Lists.GetByTitle("Customer");
```

```
    //create query
    CamlQuery query = new Microsoft.SharePoint.Client.CamlQuery();
    string camlQueryXml = "<View><Query><Where><Contains><FieldRef Name='ID'/>" +
        "<Value Type='Text'>" + customerID + "</Value></Contains></Where></Query></View>";

    //string camlQueryXml = "";
    query.ViewXml = camlQueryXml;

    _customerItems = _customerList.GetItems(query);
    _context.Load(_customerItems);

    //execute request async
    _context.ExecuteQueryAsync(GetCustomerItemsSucceeded, GetCustomerItemsFailed);
}
```

12. Define `GetCustomerItemsSucceeded()` and `GetCustomerItemsFailed()`, which
    are called as event handlers in `GetCustomerInformation()`. The success method
    calls `BindCustomerList()`, which displays the customer information on the
    screen. Again, this is called with the `Dispatcher` to access the user controls in
    the UI. The failure method displays the error in a text box on the screen.

```
private void GetCustomerItemsSucceeded(object sender, ClientRequestSucceededEventArgs e)
{
    try
    {
        Dispatcher.BeginInvoke(new Action(BindCustomerList));
    }
    catch (Exception ex)
    {
        Dispatcher.BeginInvoke(() => txtAppData.Text += ex.Message);
    }
}

private void GetCustomerItemsFailed(object sender, ClientRequestFailedEventArgs e)
{
    //log error
    Dispatcher.BeginInvoke(() => txtAppData.Text += "customer failure");
        // + Environment.NewLine + e.Message + Environment.NewLine + e.StackTrace);
}
```

13. Define `BindCustomerList()`, which is called in `GetCustomerItemsSucceeded()`.
    This method displays the customer name and e-mail address on the screen.

```
private void BindCustomerList()
{
    foreach (ListItem item in _customerItems)
    {
        txtCustomerName.Text = item["CustomerName"].ToString();
        txtCustomerEmail.Text = item["EmailAddress"].ToString()
    }
```

```
}
```

14. Define the Update Contact button click event handler. This method updates the FollowUp field with the current option in the Follow Up drop-down list and calls the methods to update the SharePoint data. As with the other SharePoint service methods, the call is asynchronous and the success and failure event handlers are indicated.

```csharp
private void btnComplete_Click(object sender, RoutedEventArgs e)
{
    _contact["FollowUp"] = cboFollowUp.SelectedItem.ToString();
    _contact.Update();

    _context.ExecuteQueryAsync(UpdateContactSucceeded, UpdateContactFailed);
}
```

15. Define the UpdateContactSucceeded() and UpdateContactFailed() methods, which are called as event handlers in btnComplete_Click(). Both methods simply report their action by displaying a message on the screen. This completes the application code for the Silverlight project.

```csharp
private void UpdateContactSucceeded(object sender, ClientRequestSucceededEventArgs e)
{
    Dispatcher.BeginInvoke(() => txtAppData.Text = "Contact Updated Successfully!");
}

private void UpdateContactFailed(object sender, ClientRequestFailedEventArgs e)
{
    Dispatcher.BeginInvoke(() => txtAppData.Text = "Contact Update Failed: " +
e.Exception.Message);
}
```

The complete code for MainPage.xaml.cs can be found in Listing 16-6.

Listing 16-6. MainPage.xaml.cs

```csharp
using System;
using System.Collections.Generic;
using System.Linq;
using System.Net;
using System.Windows;
using System.Windows.Controls;
using System.Windows.Documents;
using System.Windows.Input;
using System.Windows.Media;
using System.Windows.Media.Animation;
using System.Windows.Shapes;

using Microsoft.Lync.Model.Conversation;
using Microsoft.Lync.Model;
```

```
using Microsoft.Lync.Model.Extensibility;
using Microsoft.SharePoint.Client;

namespace AgentResponse
{
    public partial class MainPage : UserControl
    {
        Conversation _conversation = LyncClient.GetHostingConversation() as Conversation;
        string _appID = "{A07EE104-A0C2-4E84-ABB3-BBC370A37636}";

        private Web _web;
        private List _list;
        private ClientContext _context;

        private List _customerList;
        private ListItemCollection _customerItems;

        private ListItem _contact;

        public MainPage()
        {
            InitializeComponent();
            Initialize();
        }

        private void Initialize()
        {
            //txtAppData.Text = "Page Loaded!";
            _context = new
ClientContext("https://apress365e.sharepoint.com/teams/dev/tracking");
            //_context = ClientContext.Current;
            cboFollowUp.Items.Add("None");
            cboFollowUp.Items.Add("Callback");
            cboFollowUp.Items.Add("Schedule Visit");
            cboFollowUp.Items.Add("Estimate Job");

            //display contact/customer information
            LoadContact();
        }

        private void LoadContact()
        {
            try
            {
                //ClientContext context = ClientContext.Current;
                _web = _context.Web;
                _list = _web.Lists.GetByTitle("Contact");

                string appData = "9";
                string customerID = "";
                string contactID = "";
```

```csharp
        if (_conversation != null)
        {
            appData = _conversation.GetApplicationData(_appID);
            string[] data = appData.Split('|');
            contactID = data[0].Replace("ContactID=", "");
            customerID = data[1].Replace("CustomerID=", "");

            txtAppData.Text = "contactID = " + contactID + Environment.NewLine;
            txtAppData.Text += "customerID = " + customerID + Environment.NewLine;
        }
        else
        {
            txtAppData.Text = "appData not populated!";
        }

        _contact = _list.GetItemById(contactID);
        _context.Load(_contact);

        //execute request async
        _context.ExecuteQueryAsync(GetItemsSucceeded, GetItemsFailed);

        this.GetCustomerInformation(customerID);
    }
    catch (Exception ex)
    {
        txtAppData.Text = ex.Message;
    }
}

private void GetItemsSucceeded(object sender, ClientRequestSucceededEventArgs e)
{
    try
    {
        Dispatcher.BeginInvoke(new Action(BindList));
    }
    catch (Exception ex)
    {
        Dispatcher.BeginInvoke(() => txtAppData.Text += ex.Message);
    }
}

private void GetItemsFailed(object sender, ClientRequestFailedEventArgs e)
{
    //log error
    Dispatcher.BeginInvoke(() => txtAppData.Text += "contact failure");
        // + Environment.NewLine + e.Message + Environment.NewLine + e.StackTrace);
}

private void BindList()
{
    txtContactNotes.Text = _contact["ContactNotes"].ToString();
}
```

```csharp
private void GetCustomerInformation(string customerID)
{
    _web = _context.Web;
    _customerList = _web.Lists.GetByTitle("Customer");


    //create query
    CamlQuery query = new Microsoft.SharePoint.Client.CamlQuery();
    string camlQueryXml = "<View><Query><Where><Contains><FieldRef Name='ID'/>" +
        "<Value Type='Text'>" + customerID +
"</Value></Contains></Where></Query></View>";

    //string camlQueryXml = "";
    query.ViewXml = camlQueryXml;

    _customerItems = _customerList.GetItems(query);
    _context.Load(_customerItems);

    //execute request async
    _context.ExecuteQueryAsync(GetCustomerItemsSucceeded, GetCustomerItemsFailed);
}

private void GetCustomerItemsSucceeded(object sender, ClientRequestSucceededEventArgs
e)
{
    try
    {
        Dispatcher.BeginInvoke(new Action(BindCustomerList));
    }
    catch (Exception ex)
    {
        Dispatcher.BeginInvoke(() => txtAppData.Text += ex.Message);
    }
}

private void GetCustomerItemsFailed(object sender, ClientRequestFailedEventArgs e)
{
    //log error
    Dispatcher.BeginInvoke(() => txtAppData.Text += "customer failure");
        // + Environment.NewLine + e.Message + Environment.NewLine + e.StackTrace);
}

private void BindCustomerList()
{
    foreach (ListItem item in _customerItems)
    {
        txtCustomerName.Text = item["CustomerName"].ToString();
        txtCustomerEmail.Text = item["EmailAddress"].ToString();
    }
}
```

```
        private void Button_Click(object sender, RoutedEventArgs e)
        {
            this.LoadContact();
        }


        private void btnComplete_Click(object sender, RoutedEventArgs e)
        {
            _contact["FollowUp"] = cboFollowUp.SelectedItem.ToString();
            _contact.Update();

            _context.ExecuteQueryAsync(UpdateContactSucceeded, UpdateContactFailed);
        }

        private void UpdateContactSucceeded(object sender, ClientRequestSucceededEventArgs e)
        {
            Dispatcher.BeginInvoke(() => txtAppData.Text = "Contact Updated Successfully!");
        }

        private void UpdateContactFailed(object sender, ClientRequestFailedEventArgs e)
        {
            Dispatcher.BeginInvoke(() => txtAppData.Text = "Contact Update Failed: " +
                e.Exception.Message);
        }

    }
}
```

In the next steps, you will upload the Silverlight application to SharePoint and create a page for hosting.

Hosting the Silverlight Application in SharePoint Online

Now you will perform the tasks to host the application in SharePoint Online. This will allow the application to be hosted publicly on the Web. Then Lync can access this page within a contextual conversation to present the contact information to a sales agent.

1. Right-click the AgentResponse project and click Build, as shown in Figure 16-15.

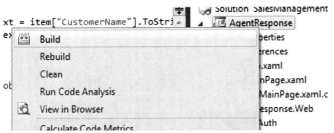

Figure 16-15. Building the Silverlight application

2. Navigate to the SharePoint Online site that is the parent to the hosted Access database. Click All Site Content at the bottom of the left window, as shown in Figure 16-16.

Figure 16-16. All Site content in SharePoint Online

3. Click Create at the top of the Site Content page, as shown in Figure 16-17.

Figure 16-17. The Create option on the SharePoint Online Site Content page

4. Choose Document Library as the type and enter **WebControls** as the name. This is illustrated in Figure 16-18.

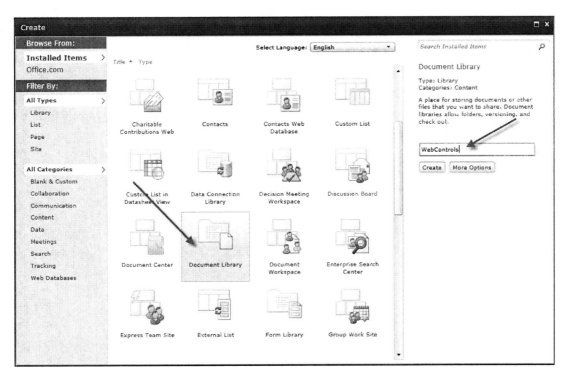

Figure 16-18. Creating the WebControls document library in SharePoint Online

5. Navigate to the WebControls library. Click the "Add document" option. This brings up a dialog to choose the file for upload, as shown in Figure 16-19.

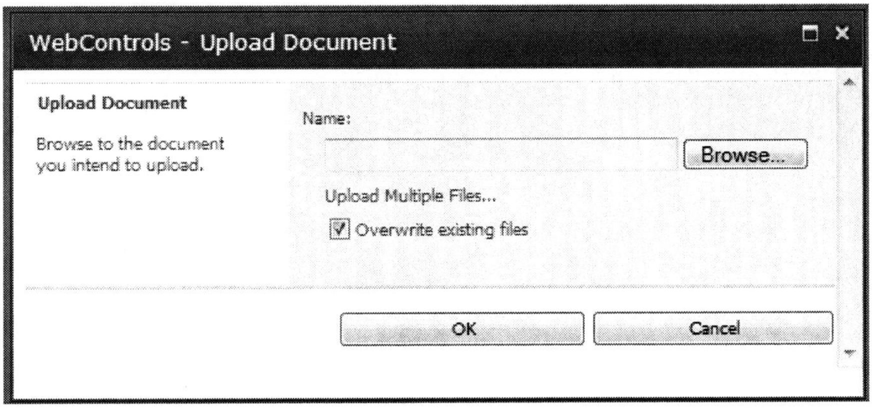

WebControls - Upload Document

Upload Document

Browse to the document you intend to upload.

Name:

Browse...

Upload Multiple Files...

☑ Overwrite existing files

OK   Cancel

Figure 16-19. Uploading a file to the WebControls document library

6. Click Browse and navigate to the project folder for the SalesManagement project. Then navigate to the folder \AgentResponse\bin\Debug. Choose the file AgentResponse.xap and click Open, as shown in Figure 16-20.

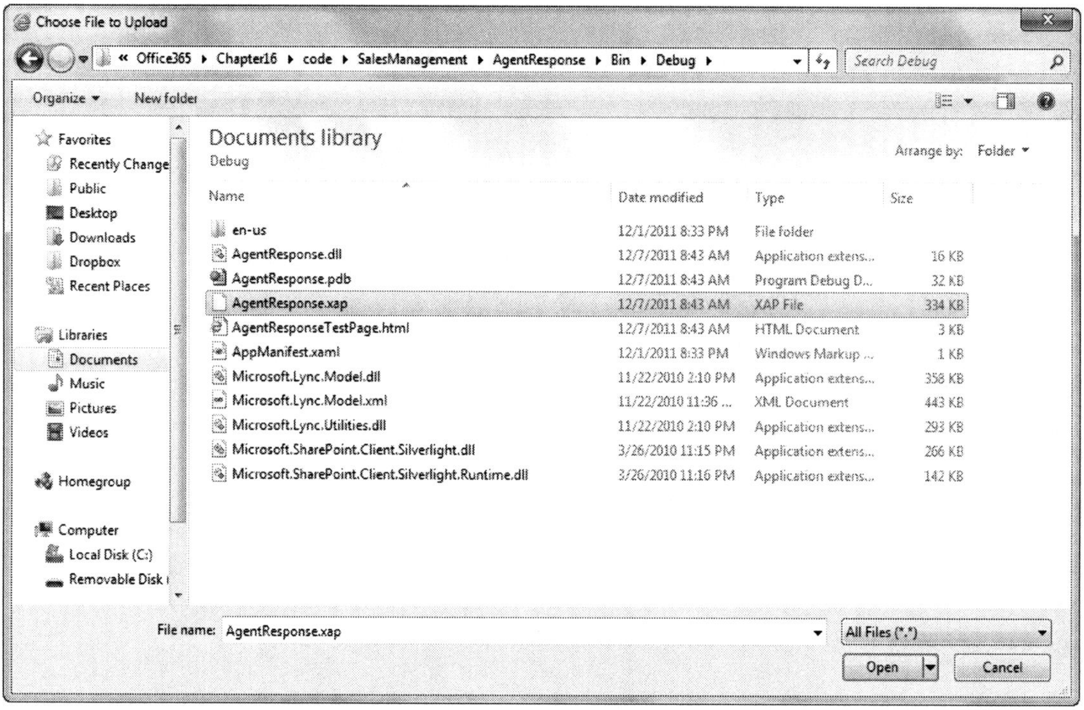

Figure 16-20. Choosing the Silverlight XAP file for upload to SharePoint Online

7. Now the control is available to SharePoint pages. Navigate back to the parent site. Click Create again, and this time select Web Part Page as the type. Click the Create button, as shown in Figure 16-21.

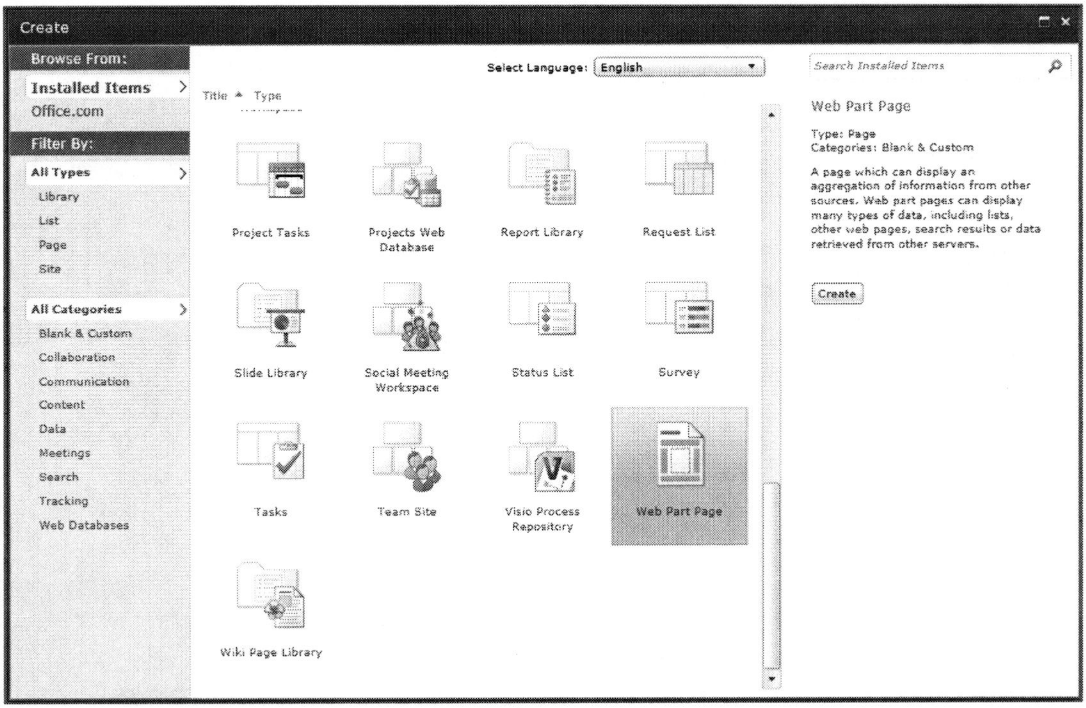

Figure 16-21. Creating a Web Part page in SharePoint Online

8. Enter **NewContact** as the page name and choose Full Page, Vertical for the page layout template. Your screen should look like Figure 16-22. Click Create to generate the new page.

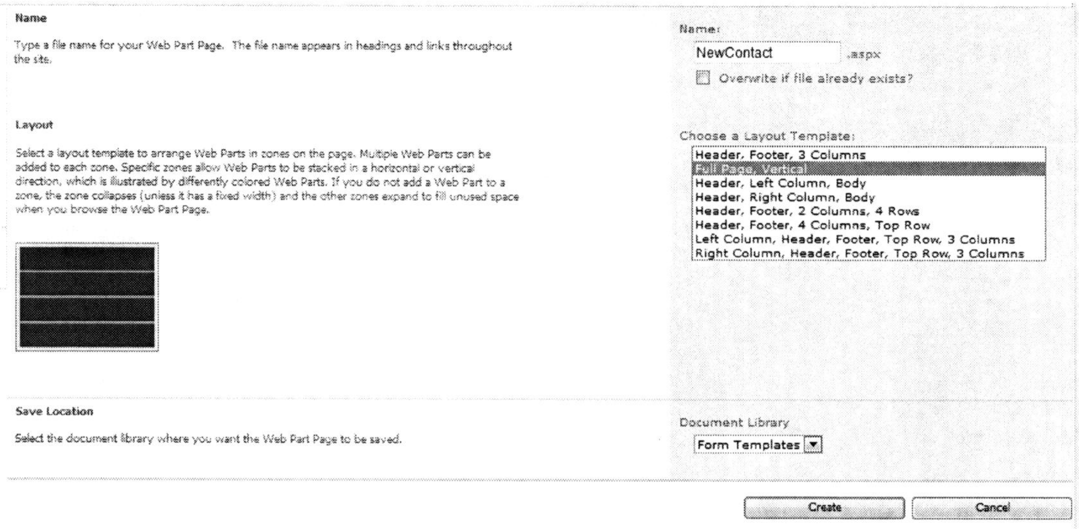
Name
Type a file name for your Web Part Page. The file name appears in headings and links throughout the site.
Name:
NewContact
.aspx
Overwrite if file already exists?
Layout
Select a layout template to arrange Web Parts in zones on the page. Multiple Web Parts can be added to each zone. Specific zones allow Web Parts to be stacked in a horizontal or vertical direction, which is illustrated by differently colored Web Parts. If you do not add a Web Part to a zone, the zone collapses (unless it has a fixed width) and the other zones expand to fill unused space when you browse the Web Part Page.
Choose a Layout Template:
Header, Footer, 3 Columns
Full Page, Vertical
Header, Left Column, Body
Header, Right Column, Body
Header, Footer, 2 Columns, 4 Rows
Header, Footer, 4 Columns, Top Row
Left Column, Header, Footer, Top Row, 3 Columns
Right Column, Header, Footer, Top Row, 3 Columns
Save Location
Select the document library where you want the Web Part Page to be saved.
Document Library
Form Templates
Create
Cancel

Figure 16-22. Setting a name and layout for the Silverlight host page

9. The page created is empty. Click the Add Web Part option on the page. Select Silverlight Web Part, as shown in Figure 16-23.

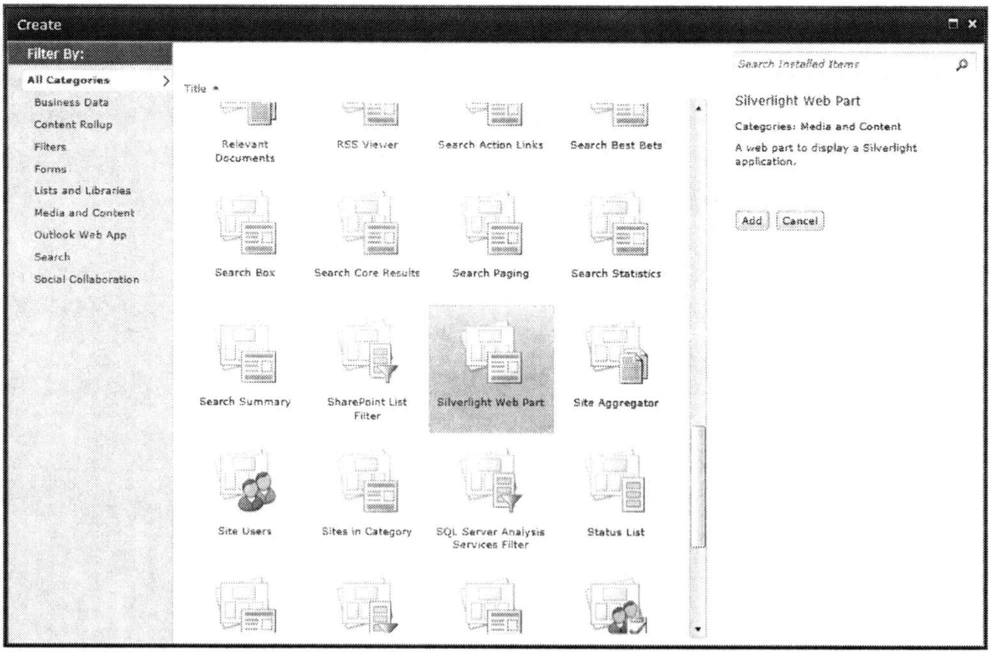
Create
Filter By:
All Categories
Business Data
Content Rollup
Filters
Forms
Lists and Libraries
Media and Content
Outlook Web App
Search
Social Collaboration
Title
Relevant Documents
RSS Viewer
Search Action Links
Search Best Bets
Search Box
Search Core Results
Search Paging
Search Statistics
Search Summary
SharePoint List Filter
Silverlight Web Part
Site Aggregator
Site Users
Sites in Category
SQL Server Analysis Services Filter
Status List
Search Installed Items
Silverlight Web Part
Categories: Media and Content
A web part to display a Silverlight application.
Add
Cancel

Figure 16-23. Adding the Silverlight Web Part to the host page

10. Your page should now look like Figure 16-24. The Silverlight Web Part needs to be configured. Click the "open the tool pane" link to configure this.

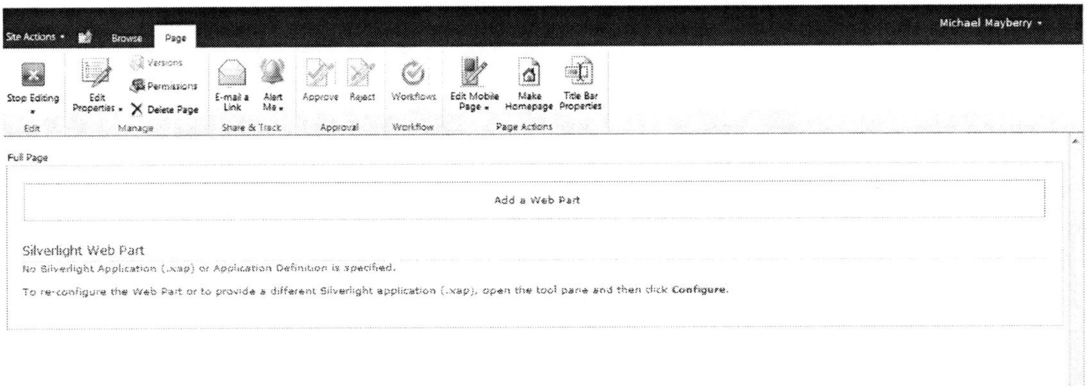

Figure 16-24. Silverlight Web Part added to the page, but not configured

11. The top portion of the tool pane contains a button for providing the URL for the Silverlight application. It looks like Figure 16-25. Click the Configure button.

Figure 16-25. Configuring the Silverlight tool pane

12. This brings up the prompt for the URL for the application (the .xap file). You need to enter the location in SharePoint that this was just uploaded to. This URL is relative to the top SharePoint site. I created the WebControls folder on the \teams\dev site, so the URL entered on this page is /teams/dev/WebControls/AgentResponse.xap. Adjust yours appropriately and enter the proper value. Figure 16-26 shows this prompt. Click OK.

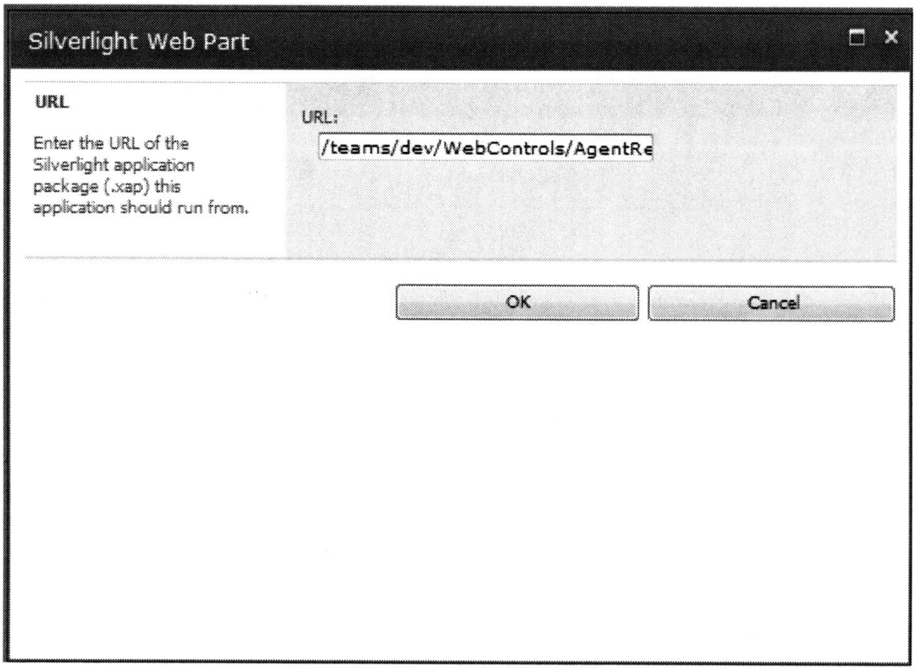

Figure 16-26. Entering the URL for the Silverlight application

13. Configure the other options for the Silverlight Web Part. Enter the title as **New Contact** and **400** as the height. Your screen should look similar to Figure 16-27. Click OK.

Figure 16-27. Configuring the Silverlight Web Part

▒ **Note** The Silverlight Web Part requires that height be specified. You will receive an error if you do not provide a value for height.

---

14. Once the Web Part is configured properly, it should appear on the screen. Your page should appear like Figure 16-28.

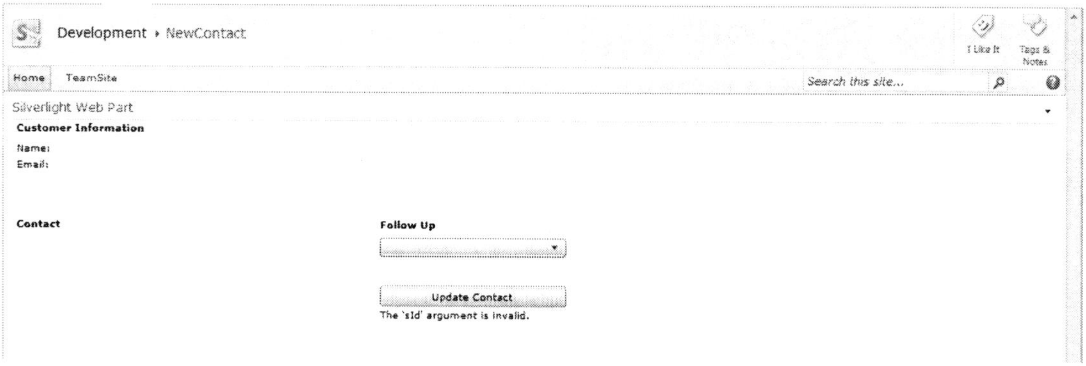

Figure 16-28. Silverlight Web Part fully configured

■ **Note** You may notice the error "The 'sld' argument is invalid." This error results when the application cannot find an active Lync conversation. Since this page is being served to your browser, this error is expected.

Registering the Contextual Application

For Lync to securely call another application in the contextual context, the hosting machine needs to be aware of the called application. This is most easily done through the local registry.

1. Create a text file called SalesManagement.reg and add the text from Listing 16-7. You will need to modify the GUID if your application is using a different one. You will also need to modify the InternalURL and ExternalURL values to point to your Office 365 SharePoint Online site. You will also need to modify the Path value similarly.

Listing 16-7. SalesManagement.reg

```
Windows Registry Editor Version 5.00

[HKEY_CURRENT_USER\Software\Microsoft\Communicator\ContextPackages\{A07EE104-A0C2-4E84-ABB3-
BBC370A37636}]
"DefaultContextPackage"=dword:00000000
"InternalURL"="https://apress365e.sharepoint.com/teams/dev/FormServerTemplates/NewContact.aspx
"
"ExternalURL"="https://apress365e.sharepoint.com/teams/dev/FormServerTemplates/NewContact.aspx
"
"Name"="Apress Remodeling New Contact"
"ExtensibilityWindowSize"=dword:00000001
"Parameters"="%AppData%,%AppId%"
"Path"="https://apress365e.sharepoint.com/teams/dev/tracking"
```

2. Save the `SalesManagement.reg` file. Right-click the resulting file and click `Merge`. This will add the registry key so that it is available for Lync. This needs to be done on all of the machines that will use the Silverlight part of the application.

Testing the Sales Management Application

Everything is now ready for testing. Ensure you have access to two machines for both ends of the conversations that are started by the application. Before you start the application, send at least one test e-mail to the address you are using for this application. Press F5 to start the application in debug mode. The WPF application will load to the screen.

The first screen that should appear is a login page for Office365. This looks like Figure 16-29.

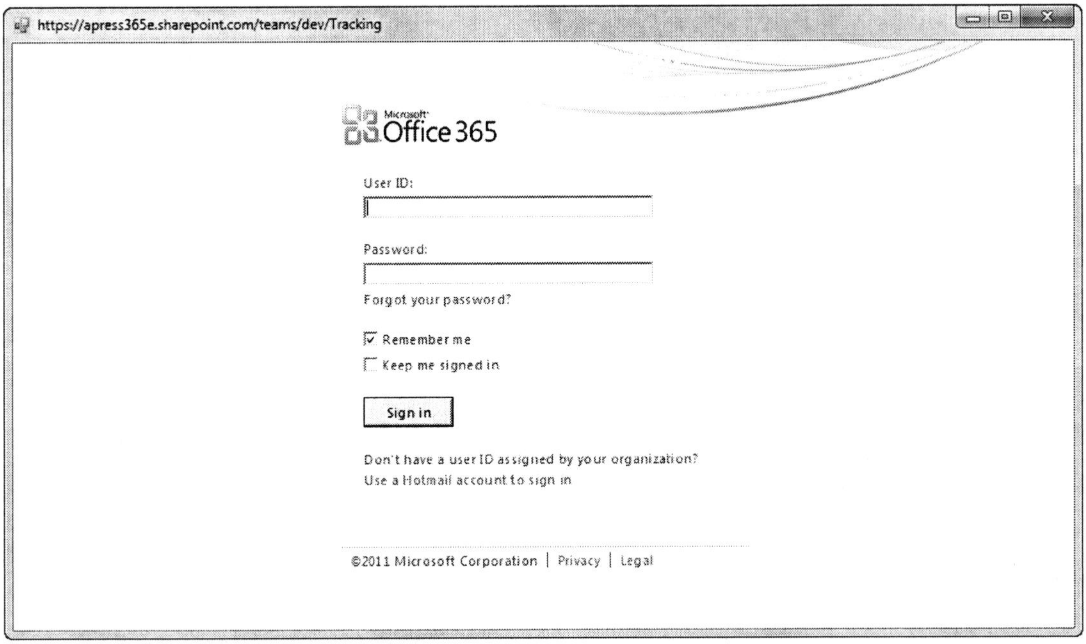

Figure 16-29. Claims-based authorization login page

This is the result of the claims-based authorization module you included from the Microsoft project. This part of the application works by looking for a cookie that is returned when you log in to Office365. If you log in through your browser and keep it open or choose the "Keep me signed in" option, this page will not fully appear. You might see this window flash and disappear. As long as the cookie can be found, your application will bypass this login screen.

Enter the Office365 credentials and the desired options and click "Sign in." This will take you to the WPF application screen, as shown in Figure 16-30.

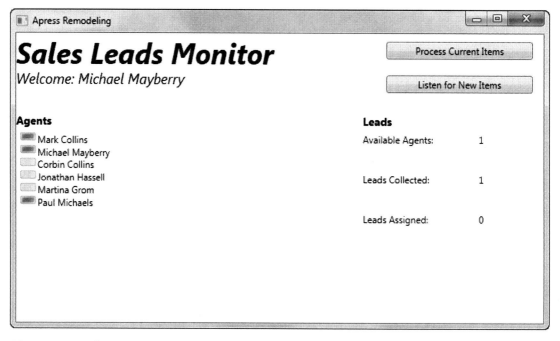

Figure 16-30. SalesManagement application screen

Notice the presence indicators of the other agents, as well as the Available Agents count and the Leads Collected count. The Available Agents count is based on the SharePoint data, not the real-time Lync status. The Leads Collected count starts out with the number of items in the inbox of the Exchange Online account used in the application code.

Make sure you are signed into the Lync client, and click the Process Current Items button to assign the lead from the e-mail in the inbox. A new conversation will begin with the attached contextual window. Your screen should appear similar to Figure 16-31.

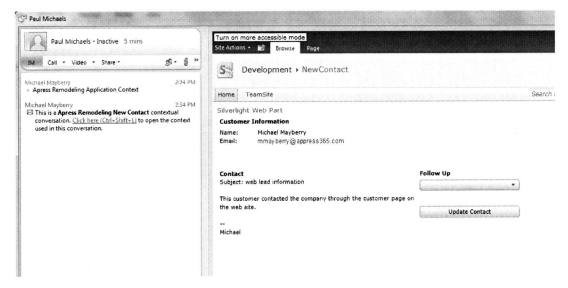

Figure 16-31. Lync contextual window with assigned lead information

Notice the conversation begins with the instant message coded in the application. The contextual window appears with the Silverlight application, hosted in SharePoint, populated with the information from the e-mail. This control populates from the SharePoint database, so the fact that it displays means that the desktop application has done its job of submitting this information into the hosted Access database.

Select an option from the Follow Up drop-down list and click Update Contact, as shown in Figure 16-32.

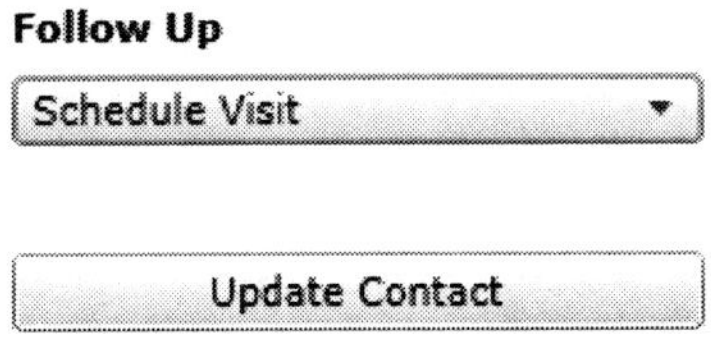

Follow Up

Schedule Visit ▼

Update Contact

Figure 16-32. The Follow Up drop-down list in the Silverlight application

Clicking Update Contact updates the information in the SharePoint Online database. You can access the site directly to ensure the record was indeed updated. Figure 16-33 shows the updated record.

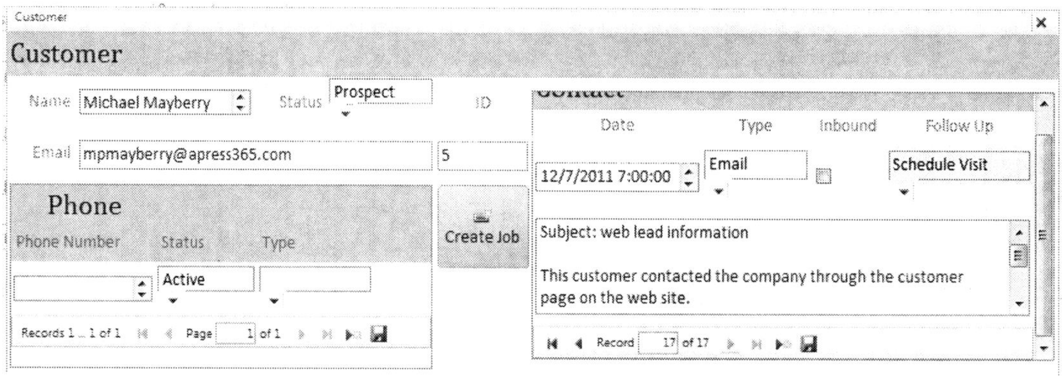

Figure 16-33. Updated Contact record

The Lync conversation can now close. You can click the Listen for New Items button, which will start a 5-minute notification subscription to Exchange. Send another test e-mail to the e-mail address and the application will automatically process the information once it is received into the mailbox. While this processing occurs, you will see the counts adjust accordingly, as demonstrated in Figure 16-34.

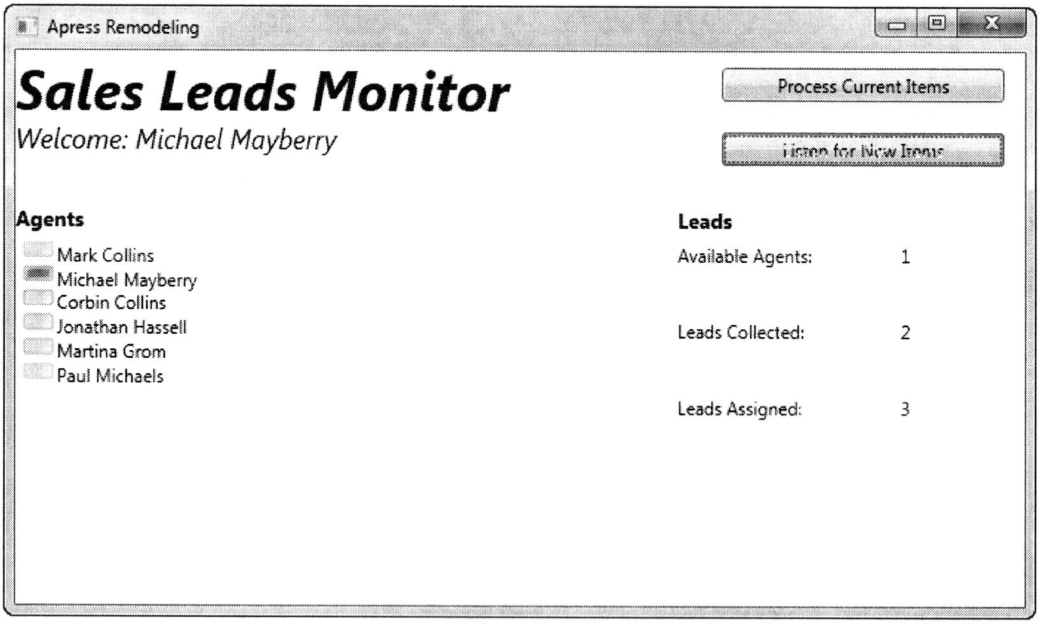

Figure 16-34. The Sales Lead Monitor application

Summary

This chapter demonstrated integration in Office365 by developing an application that incorporates three of the main technologies of the cloud-based service:

- Exchange Online

- SharePoint Online

- Lync

You developed a WPF application that uses Lync controls and integrates with Lync, but also communicates with SharePoint and Exchange in practical ways. Data flow is controlled and the business task of passing lead information to sales agents in real time is successfully accomplished.

This chapter incorporated many of the specific skills explained throughout this book. They have been brought together to customize the use of Office365 and present the result to an end user.

CHAPTER 17

Creating a Public Web Site

For the final step in this process, you'll create a public-facing web site. In Chapter 15 you created an Access 2010 web database that was published to Office 365. This database is used by internal staff to create and track customer jobs. In Chapter 16 you used Excel and Lync to facilitate the processing of incoming customer contacts. In this chapter, I'll demonstrate the other important feature of Office 365: it is a great platform for building an external, public-facing web site. This will be used as your online presence—the place where customers can find you, learn about your products and services, and contact you.

■ **Note** If you have a Small Business account, a public-facing web site was created for you. For Enterprise accounts, you'll need to create this yourself. I showed how to create a new site collection and public web site in Chapter 2.

Designing a Web Site

Your public web site is primarily content-based. The purpose of all the other sites you've worked on in this book has been to create, modify, and use data. This one, however, is focused on displaying static content to a relatively broad audience. The pages are almost all read-only, with the exception of a data entry form, which I'll describe later. Generally, the majority of your work in building a content-based web site is creating the content, which includes text, images, video, and other visual components.

With that in mind, you should start by deciding what the web site needs to communicate. This includes the technical details such as contact information and a description of the products or services that you provide. This also includes more intangible aspects such as what types of emotions your site should evoke. For example, the fictitious company for this project provides interior design services. So you'll want to include many pictures of pretty interiors. From the first look of the home page, you want your potential customers to say "Wow, I wish my home looked like that!"

Collecting the Content

The first step of the design process is to decide what information the web site needs to provide. Generally, this will include contact details like e-mail, phone number, and physical address as appropriate. This information will vary depending on the type of business and the way your organization operates. If you have one or more physical locations where you receive customers, including an interactive map is a nice touch.

Other key information that you'll need to provide is a description of the products and/or services that you want to advertise. What do you have to offer and why should a potential customer consider doing business with you? If you have many products, you should summarize the types of products that are available. You can highlight specific items that you want to promote or provide as examples. At this level, a lot of details will tend to send your audience elsewhere.

■ **Tip** If you have an e-commerce business where you sell products online, you will need a true shopping cart application. You won't be able to implement this on an Office 365 platform. The site I'm describing here will provide information about your company and then link to your shopping cart.

It's a good idea to provide some background information about your business. What is your vision, business culture, and mission? Perhaps a brief history of your organization would be helpful. Also consider including corporate highlights and accomplishments. Mission statements, corporate strategies, and core beliefs can be used as content as long as they are written from the customer's perspective.

■ **Note** I am using business terminology here but the same concepts also apply to non-profit organizations. What is the mission of your organization? What resources do you provide? What actions from potential constituents do you want to inspire? The content of your web site should answer these questions.

As you think through these topics, you should create a list of site pages. You don't have to finalize the content of each page but you should at least identify the pages that are needed. You can create pages from templates and fill in the details later. For this project, you will use the following pages:

- Home: A brief but compelling summary of your business; highlights current offers or events; provides links to key pages and/or sites.

- About Us: Provides company information including mission, values, and history.

- Design Services: This is where you'll get into more detail of the services that you provide.

- Contact Us: Provides all the appropriate ways to contact you (phone, fax, address, e-mail addresses). You will also implement a Contact Us form that will feed into the job tracking system you created in the previous two chapters.

If you have more than five or six pages, you should also consider how these should be organized. The navigation controls (explained in Chapter 4) provide several options for navigating to all of your site pages. Since you only have four pages, you'll use the default single-level control arranged vertically. However, if you have a lot of pages, you should think through how these can be grouped and then decide the best way to arrange the navigation controls.

In addition to the standard navigation controls, you should add custom links to key pages in your site. If the primary goal of your site is to drive potential customers to your shopping cart, then you should have easy-to-find buttons or links to take them there. In this site, you want them to use the Contact Us form, which will feed into the job tracking system.

Creating the Site Pages

If you are using an Enterprise plan, you'll need to create a site collection for the public-facing web site. Refer to Chapter 2 for instructions on how to do that. The default site contains the following pages:

- Home

- About Us

- Contact Us

- Site Map

This set of pages is not ideal, so let's work on it.

1. Go the Web Pages document library that contains the initial site pages. You can get there using the following URL:

`<Site URL>/Pages/Forms/allitems.aspx`

2. Put in your site's address for the Site URL place holder. For my site, the web pages are found at:

`http://www.apress365.com/Pages/Forms/allitems.aspx`

The list of site pages will look similar to Figure 17-1.

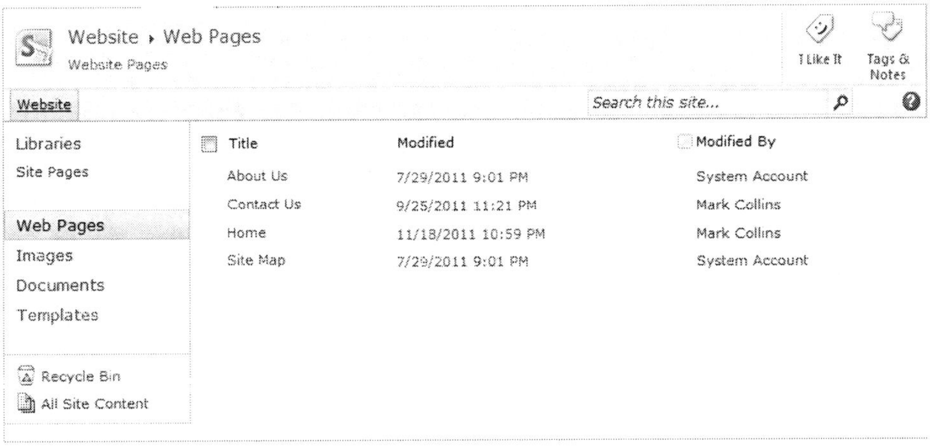

Figure 17-1. The initial default web pages

3. With this simple site, a site map is not necessary. Select the Site Map page and click the Delete button in the ribbon.

4. Next, add the Design Services page. Click the New Page button in the ribbon. In the first dialog box, select the Product or Service template, as shown in Figure 17-2.

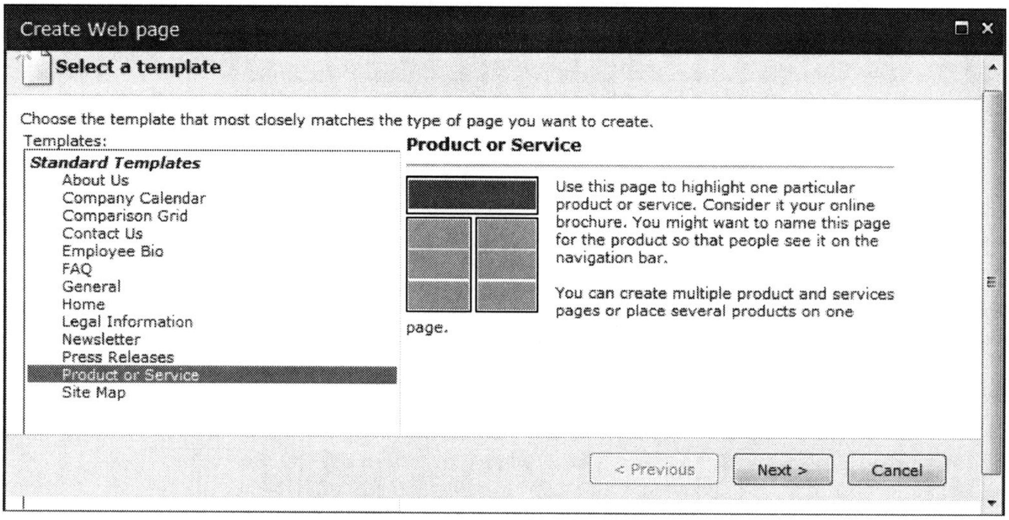

Figure 17-2. Selecting the Product or Service template

5. The second dialog box is where you will configure the new page. Enter **Design Services** for the page title and navigation title.

6. Enter **Design** for the web address. You can leave all the other fields with their default values. The dialog box will look like Figure 17-3.

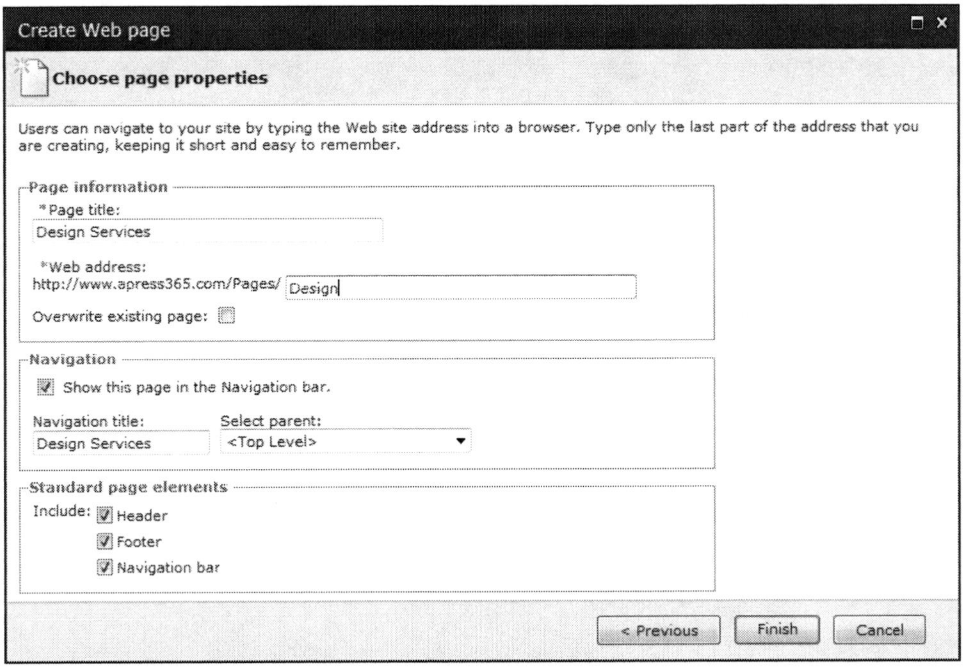

Figure 17-3. Configuring the Design Services page

■ **Caution** The web address can't contain spaces. Only letters and numbers are allowed.

Designing the Overall Site Properties

SharePoint Online provides a Website Design Tool that allows you to easily modify the visual aspects of the web site. This tool only works with public-facing web sites. I explained the details of the Website Design Tool in Chapter 4 and you can refer back to that chapter for reference. Rather than repeating this information, I will just describe the specific changes needed for this project.

1. Open any of the site pages to access the Design tab of the ribbon. The new Design Services page should already be open; if not, just select any of the pages.

2. Click the Color button and select the Mocha color block, as shown in Figure 17-4.

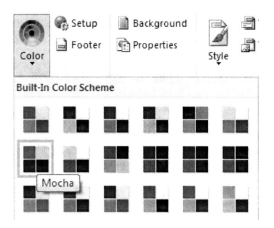

Figure 17-4. Selecting the Mocha color block

3. Click the Style button in the ribbon and then select the header style shown in Figure 17-5.

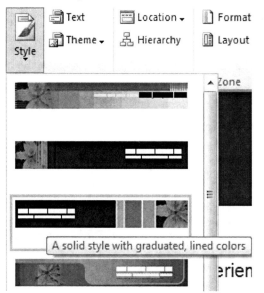

Figure 17-5. Selecting the header style

4. Click the Text button and enter **Apress Remodeling** for the title and **Specializing in fine interior spaces** for the slogan, as shown in Figure 17-6. The font color for both should be white.

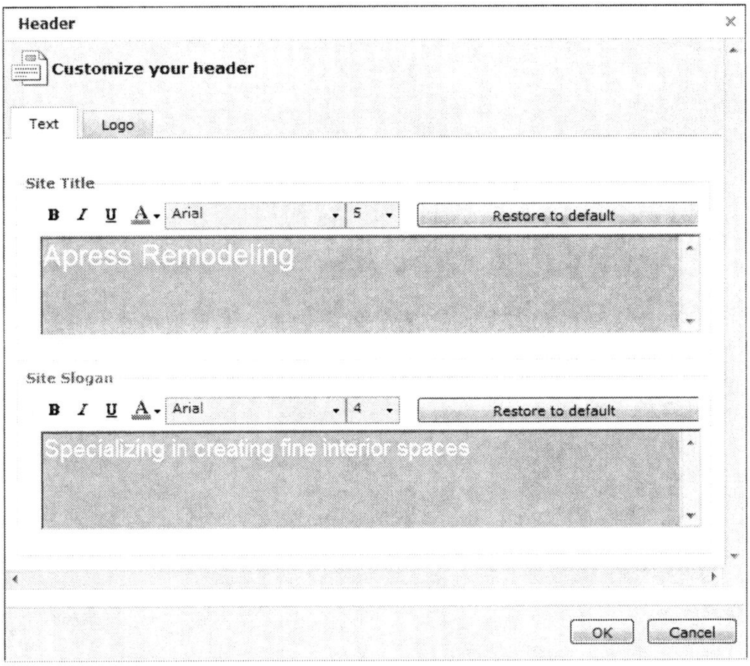

Figure 17-6. Entering the header text

5. You won't need to the Member Login link, which was created for you. Click the
    Setup button in the ribbon and unselect this check box, as shown in
    Figure 17-7.

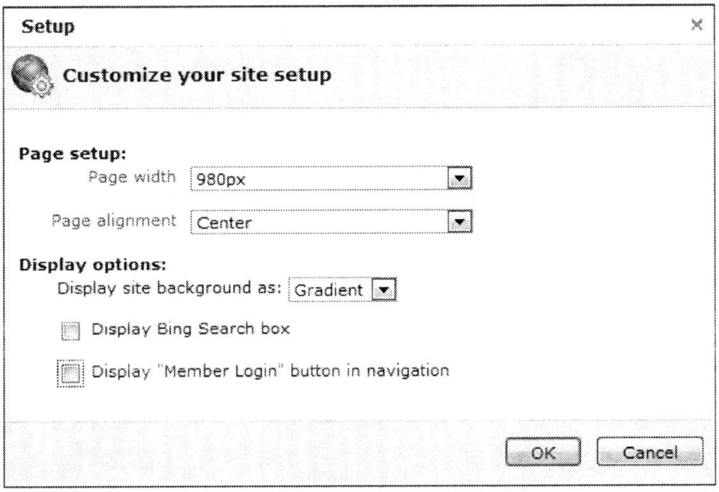

Figure 17-7. Removing the Member Login link

Adding Images

Images are an important part of a web site. When building your own site you'll need to find or create images to use throughout the site. This fictitious company provides interior design services so photographs of previous jobs are a great place to start. The home page will feature one of these images.

Uploading Images

The site was created with an Images library. You can load all of your images there and then draw from that library when designing each of the pages. You'll need to find some images; for this exercise, any images will do. Go to the Images library and the select the Upload Multiple Pictures link shown in Figure 17-8.

Figure 17-8. Uploading multiple images

You may see a pop-up dialog box warning you that the web site wants to access your computer. If you do, click the Allow button to continue. This will launch the Microsoft Picture Manager. Browse to the location of your image files and select some sample images, as shown in Figure 17-9.

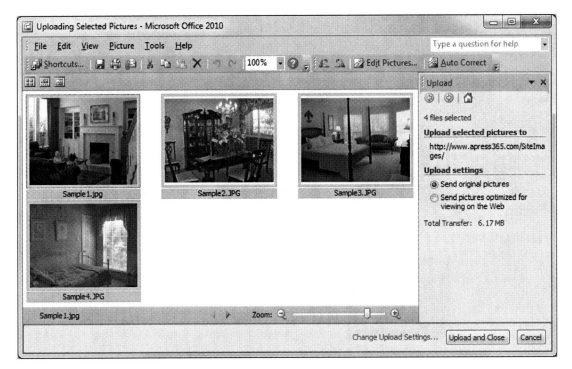

Figure 17-9. Selecting the desired files to upload

The Images library should look like Figure 17-10.

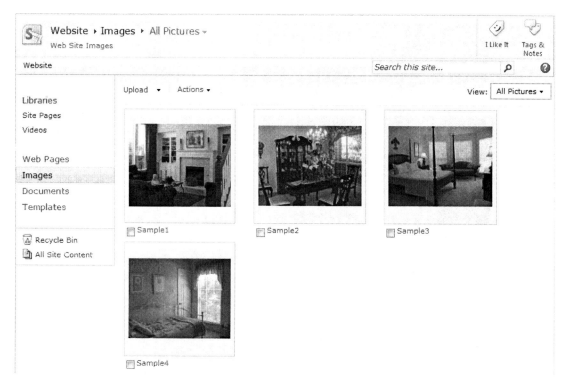

Figure 17-10. The contents of the Images library

Modifying the Header Image

The default page header includes an image. In Chapter 4, I showed you how to change this using a stock image included with Office 365. For this site you'll use one of the custom images that you just uploaded.

1.   Open any of the site pages and go to the Design tab of the ribbon.

2.   Click the Theme button in the ribbon and select the Upload image link, as shown in Figure 17-11.

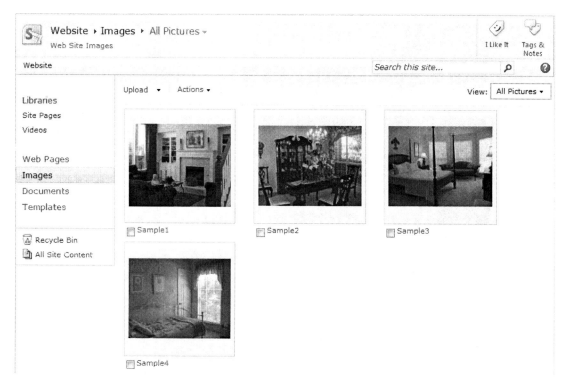

Figure 17-11. Selecting the Upload Image option

3. This will display the files in your Images library. You could also select a file from your local computer. Select one of the images, as shown in Figure 17-12.

4. Click the Insert Image button to use the selected image.

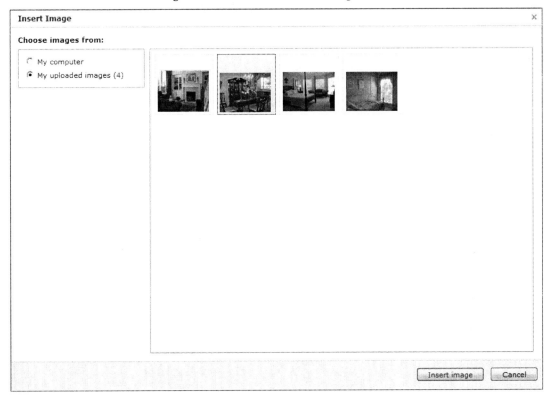

Figure 17-12. Selecting the image to use in the page header

Adding an Image to the Home Page

The image in the page header is just a thumbnail. To really make an impact, the home page should have a large image of a newly remodeled room. You'll now use one of the uploaded images as the focal point for the home page. You'll start by replacing the default image and then update the text with some appropriate content.

Open the home page for editing. You may need to go to the Web Pages library using the `<Site URL>/Pages/Forms/allitems.aspx` URL and then select the home page. The default content of the home page will look similar to Figure 17-13.

Figure 17-13. The initial content of the home page

Right-click the image in this first zone and select the Replace Image link shown in Figure 17-14.

Float Left
Float Right
No Text Wrapping

Cut
Copy
Paste
Replace Image
Delete

Create/edit hyperlink
Remove hyperlink

Figure 17-14. Replacing the default image

This will display the same dialog box that you used to change the header image (see Figure 17-12). Select one of the uploaded files.

Modifying the Text

Now you'll replace the text on this page.

1. Clear out the text that says "Put your home page content here." You'll leave a blank line in its place.

2. Replace the "Home Page" text with "Simply some of the finest interiors you'll ever experience".

3. Underneath the image, change the first line to read "Let us design your dream home."

4. Replace the body of the page with some appropriate text.

The final layout will look like Figure 17-15.

Figure 17-15. The updated home page content

Adding a Hyperlink

It is generally a good idea to add a hyperlink to images, especially on the home page. In this case, you'll create a link that will navigate to the Design Services page. When someone goes to the home page and clicks on this image, they'll be taken to the Design Services page where you can give them more information. They liked the picture; now you'll take them to the next step to see how you can provide services for them.

1. Right-click the image and select the "Create/edit hyperlink" link. This will display the "Insert a link" dialog box.

2. Select the "Page on my site" radio button and the select the Design Services page, as shown in Figure 17-16.

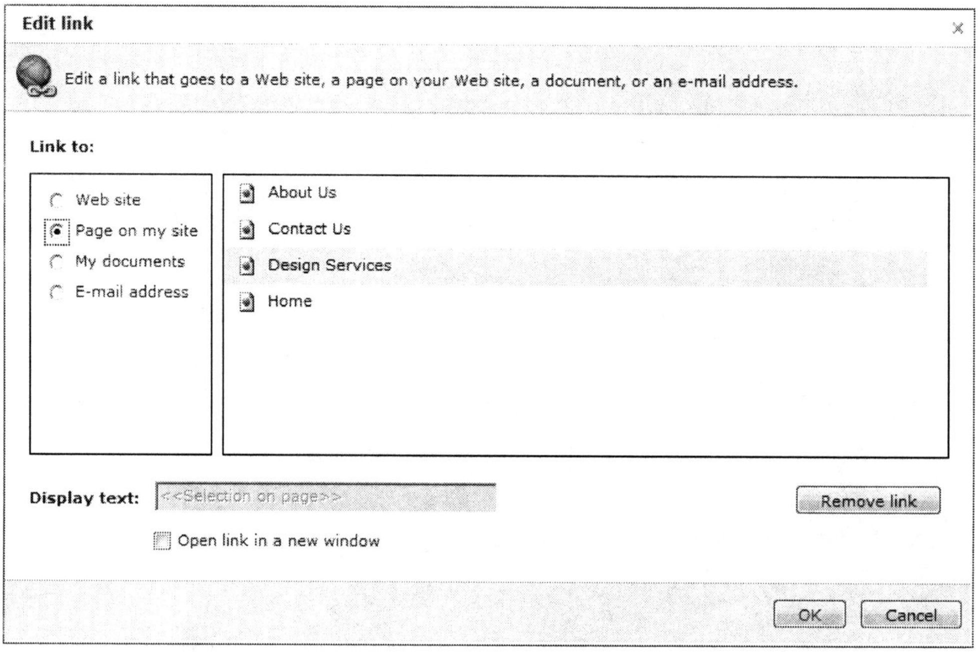

Figure 17-16. Adding a link to the image

3. Save your changes and view the home page using the View button in the Home tab of the ribbon. The final home page will look like Figure 17-17.

Let us design your dream home.

At Apress Remodeling, we believe that your home should inspire you. Sure it needs to be functional and practical. But there is something to be said for living in beautiful places. It's good for the soul.

Of course, beauty is in the eye of the beholder. No two people are alike so why should their homes be. That's why each job is a custom creation. We first seek to understand your needs and desires and combine them with state-of-the-art craftsmanship and timeless design principles.

Figure 17-17. The final home page design

Creating a Contact Us Form

In Chapter 4, I showed you how to add a form to the Contact Us page. You'll need to follow those same instructions to add one to this site. The default Contact Us page is shown in Figure 17-18.

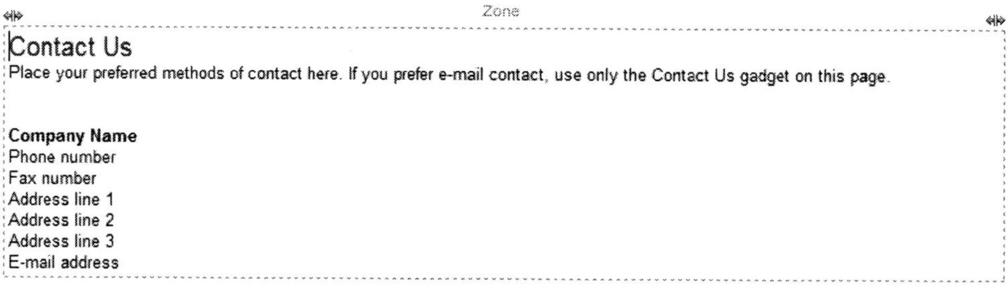

```
◄╫►                                    Zone                                    ◄╫►
Contact Us
Place your preferred methods of contact here. If you prefer e-mail contact, use only the Contact Us gadget on this page.


Company Name
Phone number
Fax number
Address line 1
Address line 2
Address line 3
E-mail address
```

Figure 17-18. The default Contact Us page

1. Open the Contact Us page and put the cursor after the existing text.

2. From the Insert tab of the ribbon, click the Contact Us button to add this gadget to the page.

3. In the Contact Us dialog box, enter the address of the inbox used in the previous chapter: websales@apress365.com (see Figure 17-19). This is the inbox that is being monitored by the Exchange/Lync application you created in Chapter 16.

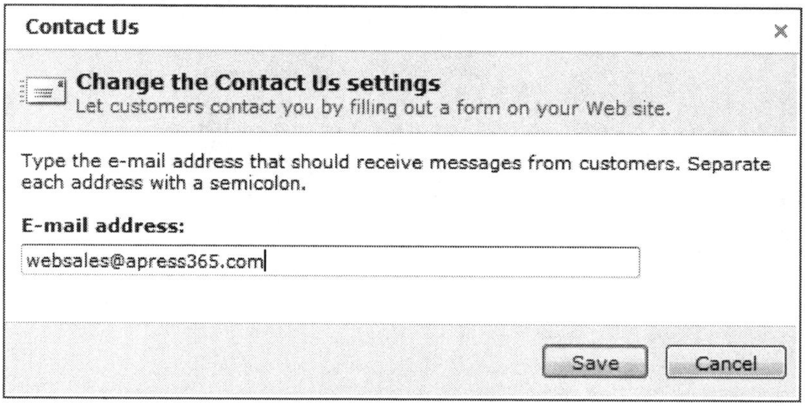

Figure 17-19. Specifying the destination e-mail address

4. After you have added the gadget, edit the text (see Figure 17-20).

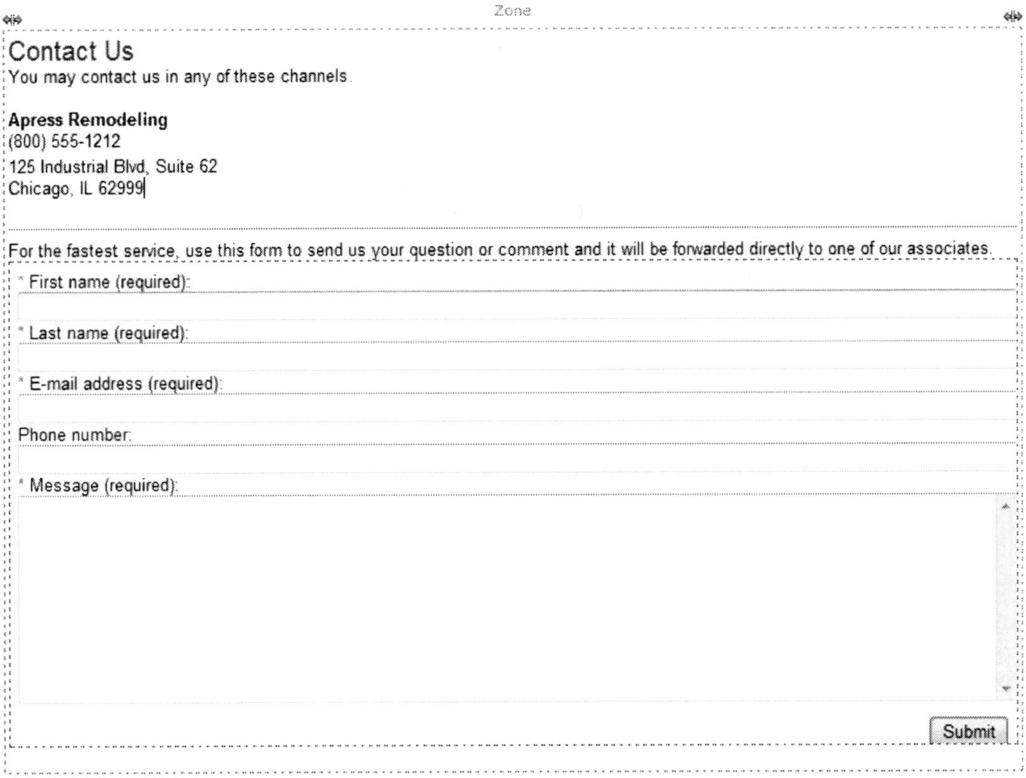

Figure 17-20. The final Contact Us page

Note that in order to encourage customers to use the form, you're not including the company's e-mail address.

Adding Videos

As more people have access to broadband, video is becoming an increasingly important aspect of a web site. I'll show you two ways to add video to your site. You will embed the videos on the new Design Services page. The easiest way to incorporate video is to take advantage of existing hosting services such as youtube.com. The video is uploaded to their site and streamed from there; you simply embed the video viewer in your web page. You can also host the video on your Office 365 site. I'll show you both techniques.

Linking to a Hosting Service

The easiest way to show a video is by simply adding a hyperlink to the URL of the hosting service. For example, you could add a hyperlink to this video:

```
http://www.youtube.com/watch?feature=player_embedded&v=OYiV1EwfLrY
```

However, you would have then navigated your potential customer away from your site and onto the YouTube site. There is a better way; instead of linking to the YouTube site, you can embed the video inside your page using an `iframe`. When you view a video on one of these hosting sites, there are some controls underneath it similar to those shown in Figure 17-21.

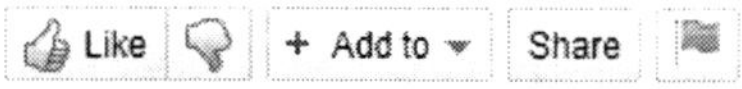

Figure 17-21. The video controls on YouTube

When you click the Share button, the window will open and show the URL for this video. Clicking on the Embed button reveals more options, as shown in Figure 17-22.

Figure 17-22. Generating the HTML for embedding this video

You can select the options you want, such as the window size, and the embed HTML will be generated for you. The generated HTML for embedding this video is

```
<iframe width="640"
        height="360"
        src="http://www.youtube.com/embed/0YiV1EwfLrY?rel=0"
        frameborder="0"
```

```
        allowfullscreen>
</iframe>
```

■ **Caution** I formatted the HTML code on multiple lines so it's easier to read. However, you'll need to concatenate it onto a single line before loading into the Video gadget. Also, note that each site works differently and these options may not be available on every site.

Open the Design Services page and delete the default image. In its place, insert a Video gadget from the Insert tab of the ribbon, as shown in Figure 17-23.

Figure 17-23. Inserting a Video gadget

In the Video dialog box, paste in the embed HTML, as shown in Figure 17-24, and click the OK button.

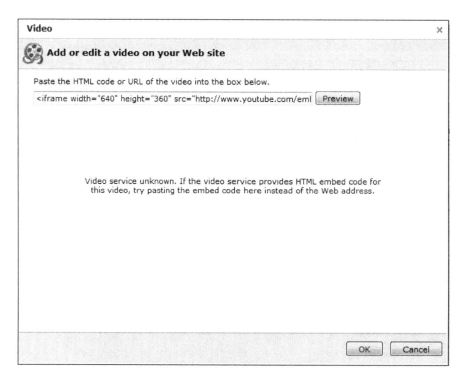

Figure 17-24. Pasting in the embed HTML

■ **Note** I have not found the preview function to work consistently. If you get an error such as the one shown in Figure 17-24, just ignore it.

I added some text to introduce the video, so the Design Services page looks like Figure 17-25.

Figure 17-25. Displaying an embedded video

Hosting Your Own Flash Videos

There are some advantages to using a third party hosting system for your videos.

- It's easy to implement.

- The streaming bandwidth is on their site, not yours.

However, for most professional applications you will want to host the videos yourself. This will avoid any issues if the hosting service decides to block, move, or delete your videos. This is also fairly easy to do, as I will now demonstrate.

Installing Flowplayer

Flowplayer is a free application that will enable you to stream Flash videos from your SharePoint site. The free version will display their logon on your site, however. You can purchase a commercial license if you want to remove this.

To download Flowplayer, go to `http://flowplayer.org`. From this site you can download a `flowplayer-3.2.7.zip` file. Unzip this file and upload the following files to the Documents library on your SharePoint site:

- `flowplayer.controls-3.2.5.swf`

- `flowplayer-3.2.6.min.js`

- `flowplayer-3.2.7.swf`

- `style.css`

■ **Note** These file names are based on the current version when this was written. You may see different versions of these files; just use the most recent files.

Your Documents library should look like Figure 17-26.

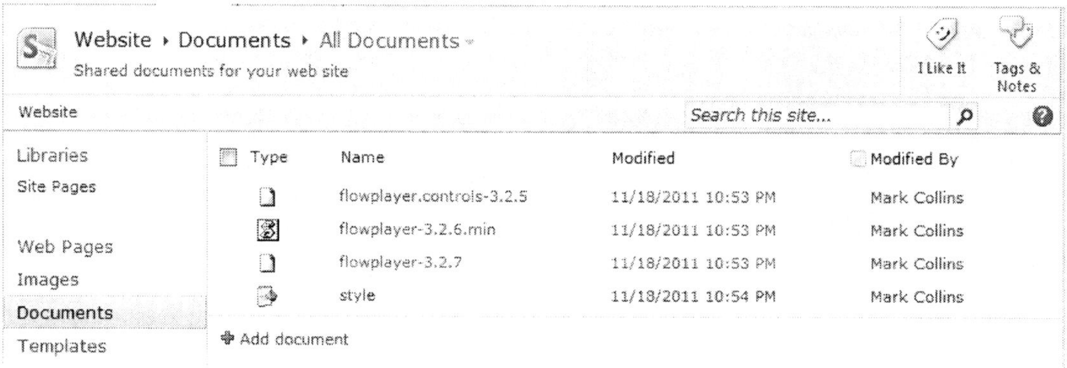
Website ▸ Documents ▸ All Documents
Shared documents for your web site
I Like It
Tags & Notes
Website
Search this site...
Libraries
Site Pages
Web Pages
Images
Documents
Templates
Type
Name
Modified
Modified By
flowplayer.controls-3.2.5
11/18/2011 10:53 PM
Mark Collins
flowplayer-3.2.6.min
11/18/2011 10:53 PM
Mark Collins
flowplayer-3.2.7
11/18/2011 10:53 PM
Mark Collins
style
11/18/2011 10:54 PM
Mark Collins
Add document

***Figure 17-26.** The Documents library with the Flowplayer files installed*

Creating a Videos Library

It's not a requirement but I recommend that you create a new document library to store the videos that you will be hosting from your site. From the All Site Content page, click the Create button to create a Videos library, as shown in Figure 17-27.

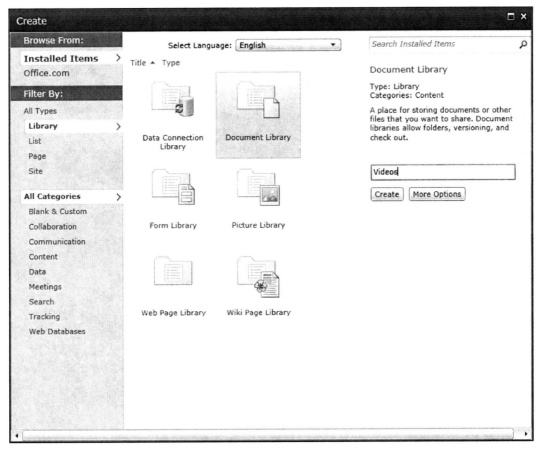

Figure 17-27. Creating the Videos library

There is nothing special about the Videos library; it's just a standard document library. If you only have a few videos, you could store them in the existing Documents library.

Converting Existing Videos into Flash Videos

As I mentioned, Flowplayer will host Flash videos. If you have videos in other formats such as `.wmv` or `.avi`, you'll need to first convert them to Flash video files (`.flv`). For this demonstration I will use the sample `Wildlife.wmv` file that is provided with Windows. I will need to first convert it, however.

Fortunately, there is free software available that will convert these files for you. I used an application called Free Video to Flash Converter that you can download and install from this site:

`http://www.dvdvideosoft.com/products/dvd/Free-Video-to-Flash-Converter.htm`

After installing this application, you select the file(s) that you want to convert and it will create an .flv version for you in the specified output folder (see Figure 17-28).

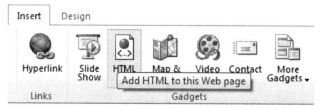

Figure 17-28. Converting the Wildlife.wmv file

After the Flash file has been created, upload the .flv file to your Videos library.

Displaying the Hosted Video

Now you're ready to display this video on the web page. Go back to the Design Services page and put the cursor where you want the video to be displayed. Insert an HTML gadget, as shown in Figure 17-29.

Figure 17-29. Inserting an HTML gadget

In the HTML dialog box, enter the following code (also shown in Figure 17-30):

```
<SCRIPT type=text/javascript defer
    src="/Documents/flowplayer-3.2.6.min.js">
</SCRIPT>
<LINK rel=stylesheet type=text/css href="/Documents/style.css">
<A style="WIDTH: 640px; DISPLAY: block; HEIGHT: 400px"
    id=player
    href="/Videos/Wildlife.flv"></A>
<SCRIPT defer> flowplayer("player", "/Documents/flowplayer-3.2.7.swf"); </SCRIPT>
```

Figure 17-30. Inserting the HTML code to display the video

Save the page and view it from your public web site. The page should look like Figure 17-31.

Figure 17-31. Displaying the hosted video file

Summary

In this chapter you created a web site that looks very clean and professional. This is the last piece of the final review project that you have been implementing over the previous few chapters. The site uses color, images, and videos to make a great impression. It also drives the potential customer to your job tracking system through the Contact Us form.

A public-facing web site is very different from the typical SharePoint site. It is more content-based and less functional than most internal sites. The Website Design Tool provides some great features for designing public web sites. And with the ability to include custom images and videos you can implement a full-featured web site on your Office 365 platform.

The techniques used in this chapter include:

- Uploading and using custom images.

- Implementing a Contact Us form.

- Embedding video from other hosting services.

- Hosting your own Flash videos using Flowplayer.

- Converting videos to Flash.

I also provided some advice for planning and organizing content for a public-facing web site.

SharePoint Primer

This appendix is intended for anyone who is fairly new to the SharePoint technology. I'll give you a brief description of the various types of objects that are used to implement a SharePoint solution. In a very loose sense, SharePoint can be thought of as a database where the "tables" are the lists and the "rows" are the items you put in the lists. Because SharePoint also provides the visualization of this data, presentation aspects are considered at every level in the "database" design.

Note Most of the figures included here were taken from the SharePoint Designer, a client application that is used to customize a SharePoint site. You can also modify these same objects using web pages within SharePoint itself. The user interface is a little different but the concepts are the same.

Columns

The basic building block is the column, which holds a single piece of information.

Note Columns are also referred to as *fields*. In the SharePoint object model, columns are accessed through the `SPField` class. The SharePoint Designer calls them columns. So you will see the terms *column* and *field* used interchangeably.

Each column definition must include the column type, which specifies both storage and presentation details. Figure A-1 lists the available column types.

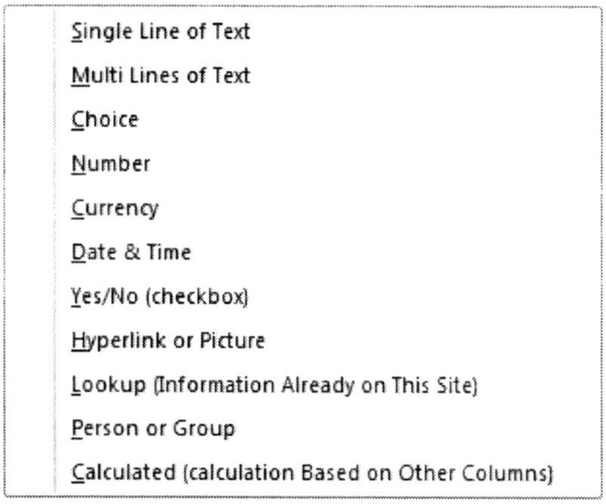

Single Line of Text

Multi Lines of Text

Choice

Number

Currency

Date & Time

Yes/No (checkbox)

Hyperlink or Picture

Lookup (Information Already on This Site)

Person or Group

Calculated (calculation Based on Other Columns)

Figure A-1. Column types

Text Columns

Notice that there are two text types: one for a Single Line of Text and another for Multi Lines of Text. While the storage requirements of these two are identical, the display details are not. A multi-line text field will take up more space on the form (you can specify the default size) and has additional display options. Figure A-2 shows the column editor for a Multi Line of Text column.

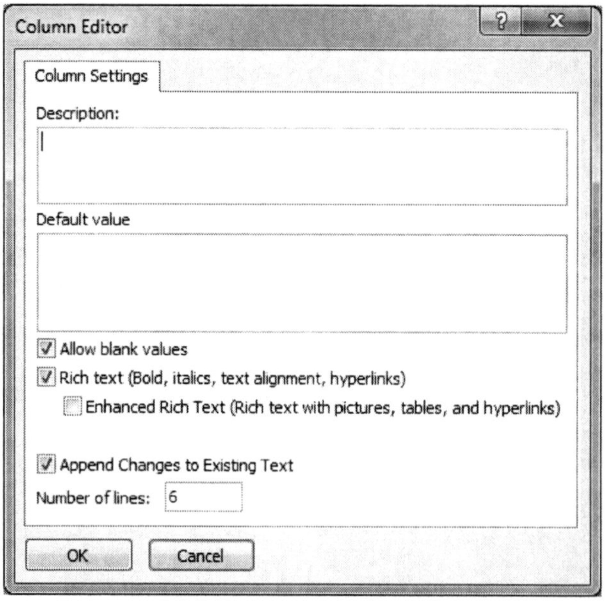

Column Editor

Column Settings

Description:

Default value

☑ Allow blank values
☑ Rich text (Bold, italics, text alignment, hyperlinks)
  ☐ Enhanced Rich Text (Rich text with pictures, tables, and hyperlinks)

☑ Append Changes to Existing Text
Number of lines: 6

OK   Cancel

Figure A-2. Multi-line text field settings

One of the particularly interesting features of the multi-line column is the append option. If you select the "Append Changes to Existing Text" checkbox, the text entered in that field is appended to the existing contents. This is often used on a comments field. If the item is edited multiple times, the comments are appended at the end of the previous comment, giving you a running history of all the comments. A multi-line column can also support rich text formatting and even pictures. Contrast this to the settings for a Single Line Text column shown in Figure A-3.

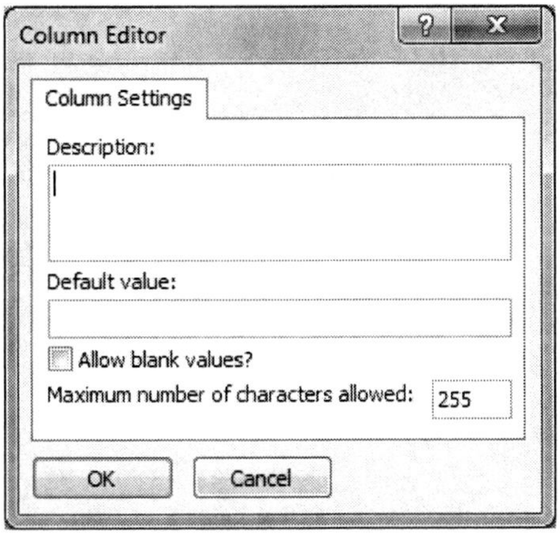

Figure A-3. Single-line text field settings

Date & Time Columns

When defining a column you can also specify a default value. For example, when creating a Date & Time column you have an option to default to the current date and time or a fixed date, as shown in Figure A-4.

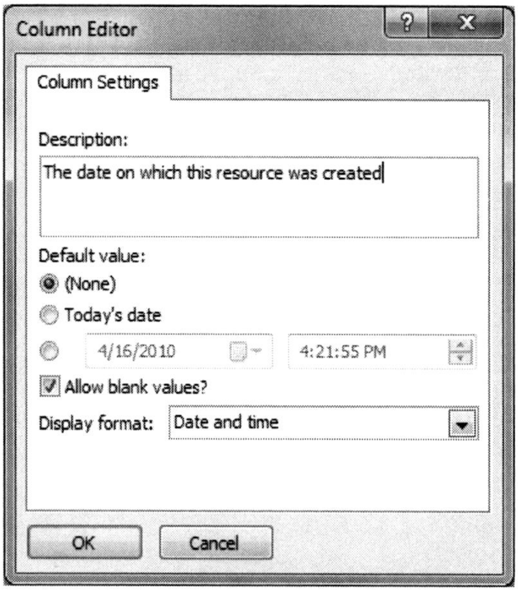

Figure A-4. The date & time column settings

Notice also that you can choose to display the value as a date only or as both date and time.

Person or Group Columns

If you use a column type of Person or Group, the edit form will use a PeoplePicker control. You'll use this control a lot and it's a very useful way to select users, ensuring only valid choices are allowed. The column editor shown in Figure A-5 illustrates the settings you can use to configure how this control works.

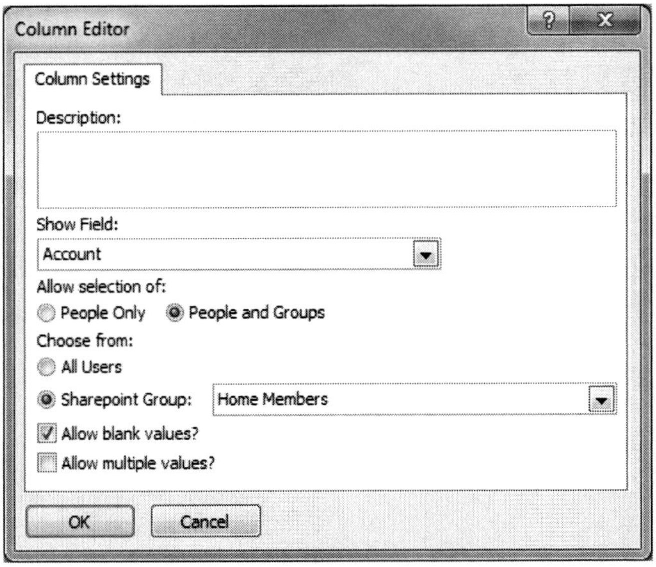

Figure A-5. Person or Group column editor

You will use these settings to determine what attribute of the user to display. By default this is the account or login name. However, you could display the name, e-mail address, phone number, or whatever is appropriate for your application. You can also control which users or groups are allowed and if multiple people or groups can be selected.

Choice Columns

The Choice type is another interesting column type. You'll use this when you want to provide fixed values for the allowable options. The column editor for a Choice field is shown in Figure A-6.

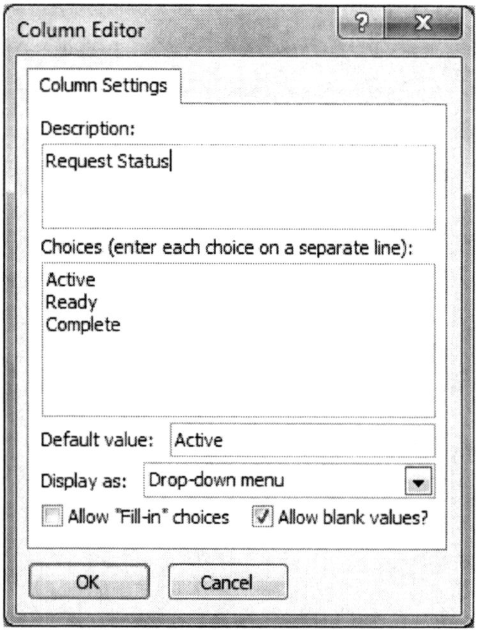

Figure A-6. Choice column type editor

When defining the column, you'll specify the available options in the Choices list. You can decide how the choices are presented. There are three options.

- Drop-down list
- Radio button
- Check boxes

Lookup Columns

The Choice type should not be confused with the Lookup type. A Choice column has a fixed set of allowable values. Often, however, you'll want to restrict values to a dynamic list. The Lookup type allows you to do this by specifying another list as the source of the allowable values. For example, if you have an Order list and you want to select the customer for this order, you can create a list of customers and then use that list to look up customers on an Order list. The column editor for the Lookup column type is shown in Figure A-7.

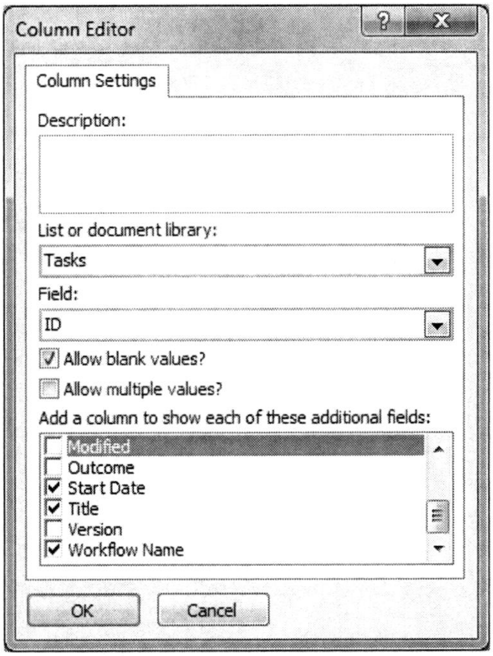

Figure A-7. Lookup column type settings

You must first choose the list to be used for the lookup. You'll then select the field that will be stored in the new column. This is typically an ID field or some other unique identifier. You can also select additional fields that will be displayed on the form.

Lookup columns are the mechanism that you'll use to ensure referential integrity. In database terms, this is equivalent to a foreign key relationship. By defining a Lookup column, you ensure that selected values are valid. This also improves the user interface. The user can search for the customer using any of the additional fields that you specify.

Calculated Columns

A Calculated column allows you to define a column with a formula that includes the values of other columns. A sample is shown in Figure A-8.

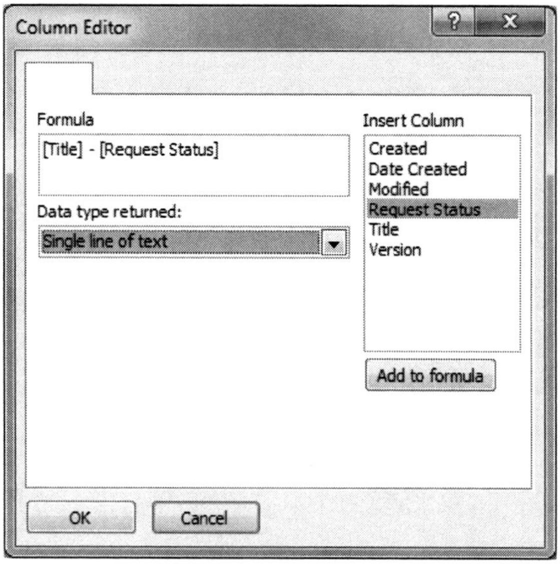

Figure A-8. A calculated column

In this example, the Title and Request Status columns are concatenated to form a new column.

Site Columns Collection

SharePoint provides a set of column definitions referred to as Site Columns. These are defined as independent pieces of information that you can assemble into your own custom lists. You can use any of these existing columns when creating a list. Site columns are organized into groups. You can also define new site columns and new groups to help organize them.

When creating a list you also have the option of creating a new column that is only used by that list. The difference is in how the column is created. In the first case, the column is created, added to the Site Columns collection, and then added to the list. In the second case, the column is created and added to the list. It requires an extra step to create reusable column definitions.

In SharePoint, the mantra is "Build once, use often." A column definition should be reused wherever appropriate. This means taking the extra step to define the column first and then add it to the list. But it also means carefully considering the design of the column and how you expect it to be used. Keep in mind that if you change an existing site column, everyplace that it is used will change. This can be a good thing if used properly. Give your columns meaningful names and descriptions that explain the intended use. When choosing an existing column, don't just look for one with the correct column type. Make sure the description matches how you're planning to use it.

Content Types

Content types define a reusable collection of properties and are used throughout SharePoint. One use of content types is to define the items (rows) that are contained in a list or document library. A content type specifies a collection of columns. For example, the columns included in the Task content type are shown in Figure A-9.

Column Name	▾	Type	▾	Property
Title		Single line of text		Required
Predecessors		Lookup (information already on this site)		Optional
Priority		Choice (menu to choose from)		Optional
Task Status		Choice (menu to choose from)		Optional
% Complete		Number (1, 1.0, 100)		Optional
Assigned To		Person or Group		Optional
Body		Multiple lines of text		Optional
Start Date		Date and Time		Optional
Due Date		Date and Time		Optional

Figure A-9. The columns included in the Task content type

To control how the field is displayed in the form, columns can be specified as either Required, Optional, or Hidden. For each content type, you can specify a custom form to be used. SharePoint uses the following three forms for each content type:

- New: Used when creating a new item.

- Display: View-only form used to display an item.

- Edit: Used to modify an item.

Content types support inheritance, which means you can derive a new content type from an existing one. The new content type will inherit the columns and properties of its parent content type. The base content type is Item and all other contents are derived (directly or indirectly) from Item. The Document content type, which is derived from Item, is the root type for all document libraries.

Lists and Libraries

If content types represent the *things* in a SharePoint site, lists are the *containers* they are stored in.

▓ **Tip** A document library is just a special type of list, so I will often use the term *list* to refer to both.

Supporting Content Types

One thing that is somewhat unique about SharePoint and different from traditional databases is that a list can contain items of different types. For example, the standard Tasks list created by the Team Site template allows the content types shown in Figure A-10.

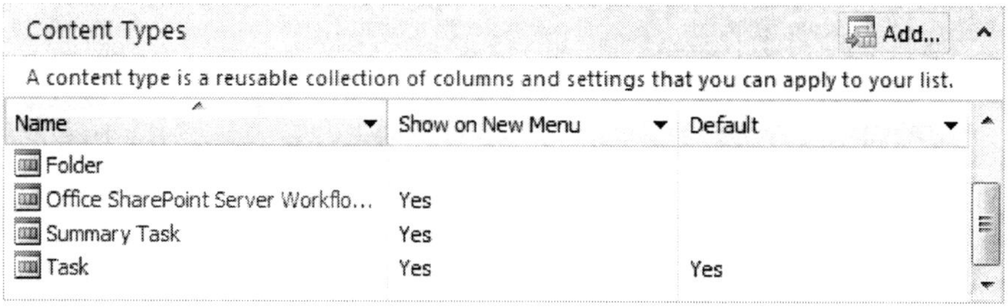

Content Types		Add...	^
A content type is a reusable collection of columns and settings that you can apply to your list.			

Name ▼	Show on New Menu ▼	Default ▼	^
Folder			
Office SharePoint Server Workflo...	Yes		
Summary Task	Yes		
Task	Yes	Yes	

Figure A-10. Content types supported by the Tasks list

This is a really handy feature. For instance, a document library can contain different types of documents. The Tasks list is another good example. This allows you to have a single Tasks list that contains different types of tasks. This is demonstrated in Chapter 5.

You can also create a new list and add columns to it without using content types. In this case, a content type definition is inferred from the list definition. This is a quick way to create a custom list.

Views

You can define any number of views for each list. A view usually includes a filter to define a subset of the items in the list. The Tasks list, for example, provides views to show only active tasks or only tasks assigned to the current user. Views can also define a subset of columns that are to be displayed. A collapsed version of a view definition page is shown in Figure A-11.

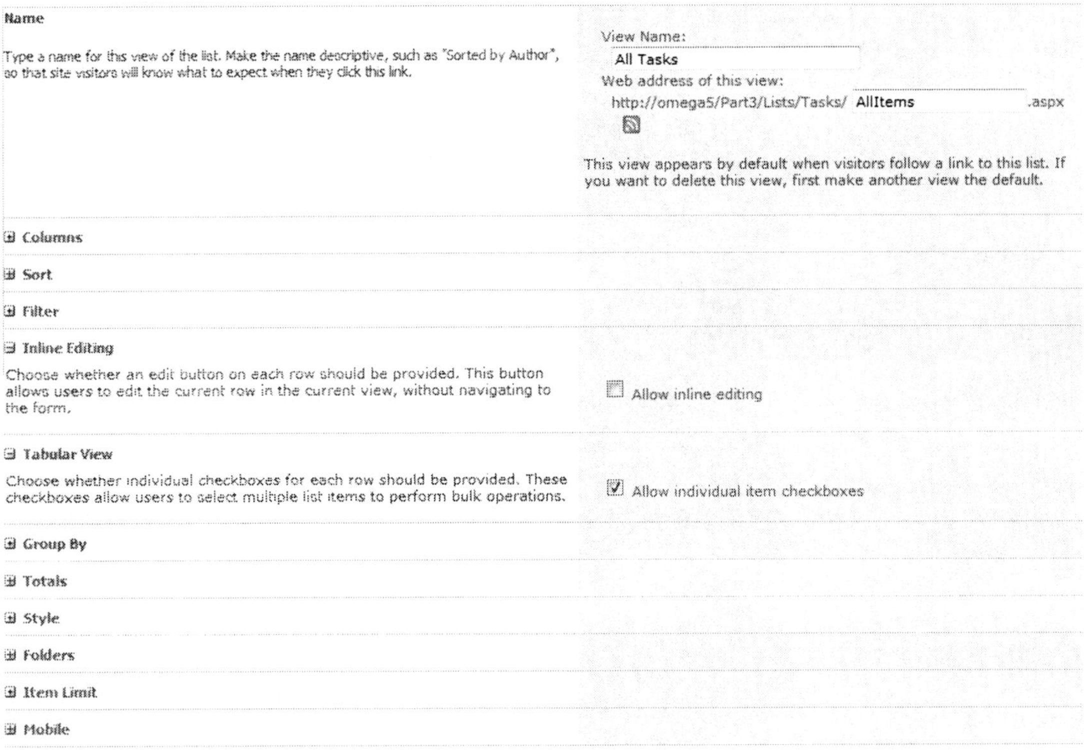

Name

Type a name for this view of the list. Make the name descriptive, such as "Sorted by Author", so that site visitors will know what to expect when they click this link.

View Name:

All Tasks

Web address of this view:

http://omega5/Part3/Lists/Tasks/ AllItems .aspx

This view appears by default when visitors follow a link to this list. If you want to delete this view, first make another view the default.

⊞ **Columns**

⊞ **Sort**

⊞ **Filter**

⊟ **Inline Editing**

Choose whether an edit button on each row should be provided. This button allows users to edit the current row in the current view, without navigating to the form.

☐ Allow inline editing

⊟ **Tabular View**

Choose whether individual checkboxes for each row should be provided. These checkboxes allow users to select multiple list items to perform bulk operations.

☑ Allow individual item checkboxes

⊞ **Group By**

⊞ **Totals**

⊞ **Style**

⊞ **Folders**

⊞ **Item Limit**

⊞ **Mobile**

Figure A-11. Edit View page

As you can see from the Edit View page, there are a lot of options that you can configure using a view, including sorting, grouping, and subtotals.

Subsites

You can create subsites on a SharePoint server. Site columns and content types are inherited by all subsites. All the columns and content types that are defined by the home site are also available to any subsite. However, any custom column or content type defined on a subsite is not available on the home site. For this reason, it is best to define site columns and content types at the home (or root) site. Subsites can have their own subsites, creating a hierarchy of sites. Lists are not inherited, however. A Tasks list on one site, for example, is not available to child (or sibling) sites.

■ **Note** Columns, content types, forms, and permissions are inherited from the parent site. Lists and content are not inherited. Reusable workflows are also inherited.

When creating a SharePoint site for a large organization, each department will often have their own subsite so they can manage their own lists and libraries. Keep in mind that column and content type definitions are shared across all the subsites. This is why you should give some thought when defining them.

You can create columns and content types at each subsite as well. If a need is unique to a particular department, you may want to consider creating it at that level. If you do, it will not be available to other subsites. If you think other sites may want to use it, create it in the home site.

Templates

SharePoint provides templates for creating commonly used types of sites and lists. Templates are a convenient way of creating sites and adding site content.

Site Templates

When creating a new site (or subsite), you'll be presented with the dialog shown in Figure A-12 where you can choose an existing site template.

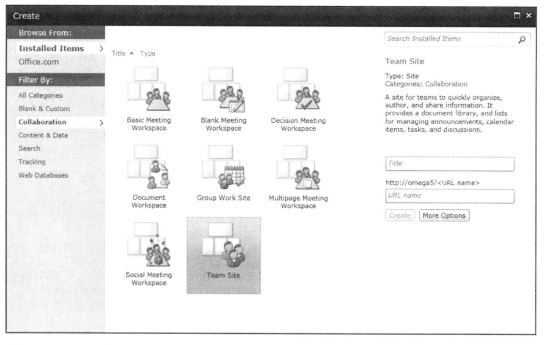

Figure A-12. Using the Team Site template

The template will create the lists and other content based on the template definition. One that you'll use in some of the projects in this book is the Team Site template. It will create a Tasks list, a Calendar, a Shared Documents library, and other lists. There are quite a few templates available, which should make it easy to get a basic site created quickly.

List Templates

You can also use templates to create commonly used lists. When creating a new list, you'll be presented with the dialog shown in Figure A-13 where you can choose an existing list template.

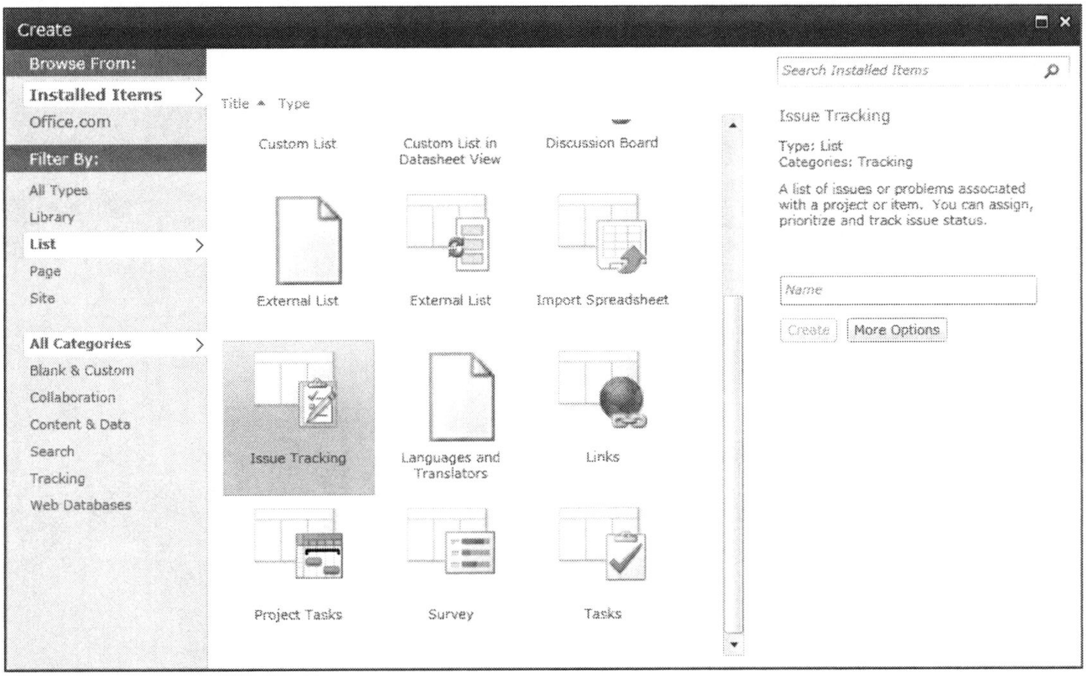

Figure A-13. *Using the Issue Tracking list template*

On the left side of this dialog you can filter the templates that are displayed. By selecting the type such as List or Library and choosing the category, you can narrow down the search to find an appropriate template. You can also browse the Internet to find other templates that may be available there. You can choose the Blank template if none of these suit your needs and create a custom list. In Chapter 5 you will create your own list template based on an existing list. You can then use it for creating the same list on multiple sites.

■ **Note** List templates reside at the home site and you can use them at any level in the site hierarchy.

Additional Resources

Office 365 Architecture

Office 365 Main Site	www.office365.com
Office 365 Services Overview	www.microsoft.com/en-us/office365/online-services.aspx#fbid=EgQ8k2nAtrX
Office 365 Tour for Users	http://office.microsoft.com/en-us/videos/office-365-a-tour-for-users-HA102657904.aspx
Office 365 YouTube	www.youtube.com/user/MicrosoftOffice365/featured
Office 365 Administration	http://onlinehelp.microsoft.com/office365-enterprises/gg524291.aspx
Single Sign-on Roadmap	http://onlinehelp.microsoft.com/en-us/office365-enterprises/hh125004.aspx
Comparing P and E Plans	http://blogs.technet.com/b/lystavlen/archive/2011/09/23/office-365-comparing-p-and-e-plans.aspx
Office 365 Service Descriptions (download)	www.microsoft.com/download/en/details.aspx?id=18128
Office 365 Community Site	http://community.office365.com
Office 365 on Facebook	http://www.facebook.com/office365
Office 365 on Twitter	@office365

Office 365 Development

One of the best overall resources for development against the Office 365 environment is a set of videos by Microsoft available in the Office 365 Developer Training Course. This site does a great job of introducing the features and explaining how they work through development examples and hands-on labs. Outside of this book, this is the next resource to check out.

Office 365 Developer Training Course	`http://msdn.microsoft.com/en-us/hh181605`
Office 365 Developer Hub	`http://msdn.microsoft.com/en-us/office/hh506337`
Office 365 Developer Training Kit Labs on Channel 9	`http://channel9.msdn.com/Series/Office-365-Developer-Training-Kit-Labs`

SharePoint Online Development

SharePoint Online Development Resource Center	`http://msdn.microsoft.com/en-us/sharepoint/gg153540`
SharePoint Online for Office 365: Developer Guide	`www.microsoft.com/download/en/details.aspx?id=17069`
MSDN: SharePoint Online: An Overview for Developers	http://msdn.microsoft.com/en-us/library/gg317460.aspx
Resource Usage Limits on Sandboxed Solutions in SharePoint 2010	http://msdn.microsoft.com/en-us/library/gg615462.aspx
MSDN: LINQ to SharePoint	http://msdn.microsoft.com/en-us/library/ee535491.aspx
MSDN: Client Object Model for SharePoint 2010	http://msdn.microsoft.com/en-us/gg620623
Using the SharePoint Foundation 2010 Managed Client Object Model	http://msdn.microsoft.com/en-us/library/ee857094.aspx
BCS Using Web Services	http://msdn.microsoft.com/en-us/library/gg318615.aspx
Managing BCS Applications: Configuring Permissions and Other Administrative Tasks	http://office.microsoft.com/en-us/sharepoint-online-enterprise-help/manage-business-connectivity-service-applications-HA102677933.aspx

Exchange Online Development

Exchange Server Development Center	http://msdn.microsoft.com/en-us/exchange/aa731543
Exchange Online Technical Articles	http://msdn.microsoft.com/en-us/library/gg193994(EXCHG.140).aspx

Lync Development

Lync Developer Center	http://msdn.microsoft.com/en-us/lync/gg132942
Lync Developer Downloads	http://msdn.microsoft.com/en-us/lync/gg394195

Index

Desktop application (*cont.*)
  Lync assemblies, 546
  Lync SDK location, 545
  MainWindow() method, 559
  MainWindow.xaml.cs, 565–570
  namespaces, 558
  OnNewItemEvent() method, 564
  ProcessMailItems() method, 561
  RedirectionUrlValidationCallback() method, 560
  SetStreamingNotifications() method, 564
  target framework, 547
  UpdateCollectCount() and
      UpdateLeadCount() methods, 560
  variables, 558
  in Visual Studio 2010, 545
  WPF XAML, user interface, 555–558
Domain name
  using Enterprise account
    adding a domain, 47–50
    adding a third-level domain, 53–54
    configuring the new domain, 50–51
    updating the DNS records, 51–52
  using Small Business account, 37
    adding a domain, 38–41
    changing the SharePoint address, 45–46
    moving the name servers, 41–43
    moving users to the new domain, 47
    viewing the domain, 43–45

■ E

Excel Representational State Transfer (REST)
    services, 271
  contents, 274
  Home page modification, 275–277
  Pivot chart extraction, 273
  spreadsheet, 271–273
Exchange Online server
  account availability
    Get Availability Button, 434–435
    retrieve results, 433–434
    testing, 435–436
  additional e-mail addresses, 62–64
  Autodiscover process, 421
    Code-Behind Class modification, 428–429
    ExchangeDataContextClass, 427–428
  distribution groups, 65
  external contacts, 67
  features, 421

folder contents
    displaying mailbox items, 430–431
    retrieving mailbox items, 429–430
    testing, 431–432
  mailboxes, 62
  migration plan, 68
  notifications, 421
  resources, 645
  room mailboxes, 64
  subscriptions
    pull notifications, 436–438
    push notifications, 437
    streaming notifications, 437–440
    testing, 440–441
  Visual Studio Project
    adding a reference, 425
    data class, 426
    EWS managed API, 424–425
    form design, 422–423
    full .NET client profile, 425–426
  WPF application, 421
Exchange Web Services (EWS), 94
External list, BCS
  configuration, 300–303
  external content type, 303–304
  Read operations
    Read Item operation, 310–312
    Read List operation, 307–310
  read-only list, 312–314
  specifying data source, 304–307
  Vehicles List testing, 314–315

■ F

Flowplayer
  Documents library, 620
  Flash video conversion, 621–622
  hosted video file, 622–624
  Videos library, 620–621

■ G, H

Gamma, Eric, 204
Gang of Four
  classic design patterns, list of, 139
  design patterns, essential features of, 138
GDB debugger, 188
generalization, 88, 112
getInstance(), 142
getMessage(), 177

CPSIA information can be obtained at www.ICGtesting.com
Printed in the USA
LVOW120213290212

270913LV00004B/1/P

9 781430 240747